Humans in Shackles

Humans in Shackles

An Atlantic History of Slavery

ANA LUCIA ARAUJO

The University of Chicago Press
Chicago and London

The University of Chicago Press, Chicago 60637
The University of Chicago Press, Ltd., London

Published 2024
Printed in the United States of America

33 32 31 30 29 28 27 26 25 24   1 2 3 4 5

ISBN-13: 978-0-226-77158-8 (cloth)
ISBN-13: 978-0-226-83282-1 (e-book)
DOI: https://doi.org/10.7208/chicago/9780226832821.001.0001

Library of Congress Cataloging-in-Publication Data

Names: Araujo, Ana Lucia, author.
Title: Humans in shackles : an Atlantic history of slavery / Ana Lucia Araujo.
Other titles: Atlantic history of slavery
Description: Chicago ; London : The University of Chicago Press, 2024. | Includes bibliographical references and index.
Identifiers: LCCN 2024005202 | ISBN 9780226771588 (cloth) | ISBN 9780226832821 (ebook)
Subjects: LCSH: Slavery—Atlantic Ocean Region—History.
Classification: LCC HT867 .A72 2024 | DDC 306.3/6201821—dc23/eng/20240214
LC record available at https://lccn.loc.gov/2024005202

♾ This paper meets the requirements of ANSI/NISO Z39.48-1992 (Permanence of Paper).

Contents

Maps and Figures

Maps

Figures

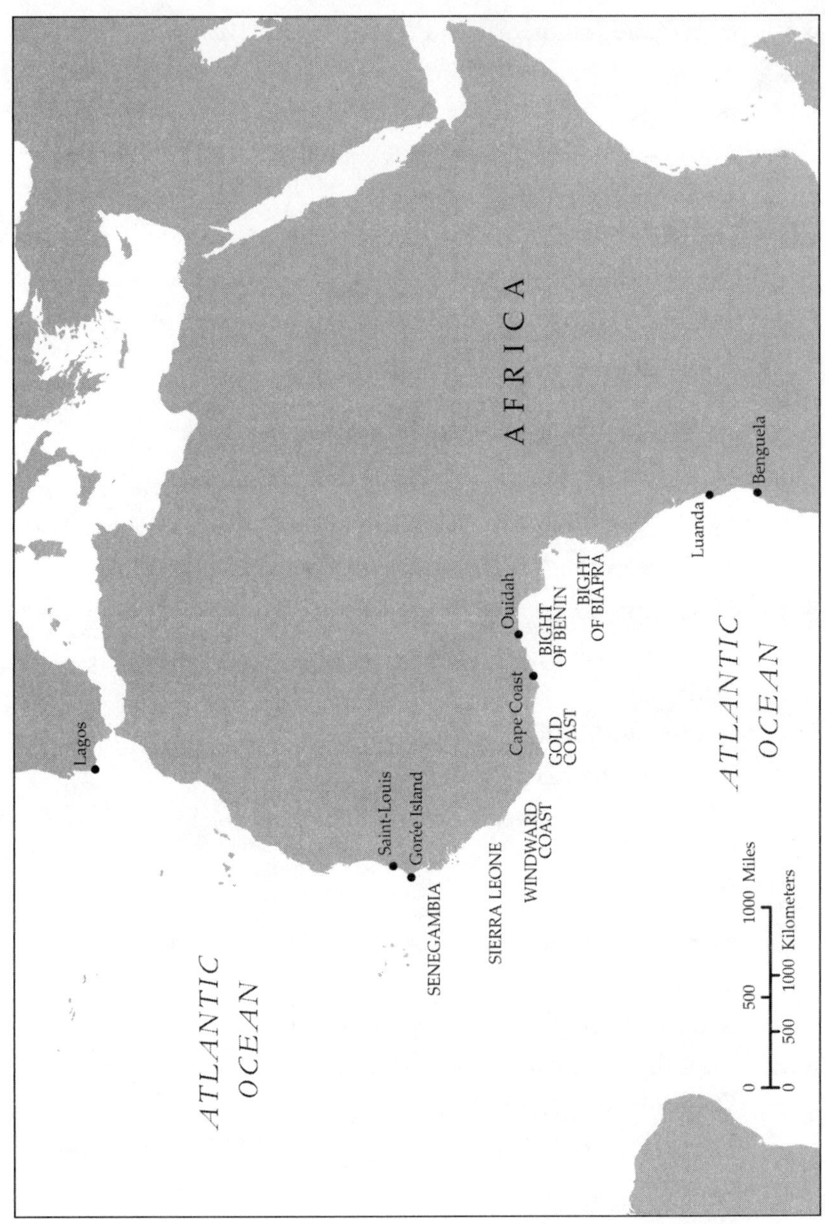

MAP 1. Main Atlantic regions and ports in West Africa and West Central Africa. Map by Tsering Wangyal Shawa, GIS and map librarian, Princeton University.

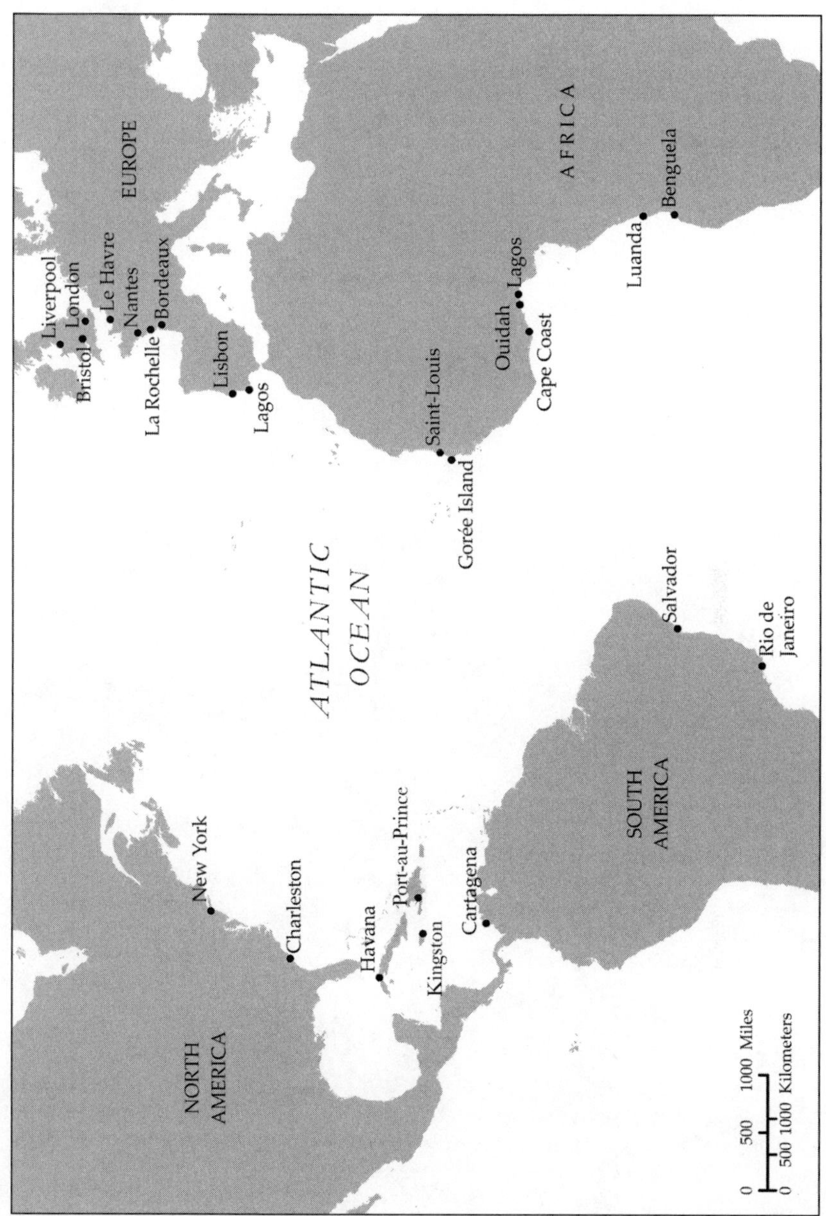

MAP 2. Main slave-trading ports in Europe, Africa, and the Americas. Map by Tsering Wangyal Shawa, GIS and map librarian, Princeton University.

INTRODUCTION

An Atlantic Cultural History

We are living in a moment in which slavery and its legacies are discussed more fiercely and publicly than ever before. How did we get here?

Since the late twentieth century, there has been growing attention to the history of slavery and the Atlantic slave trade. A series of commemorations since the 1990s led to the construction of monuments and memorials remembering the victims of the Atlantic slave trade in various countries across the Americas, Africa, and Europe. In 2007, the bicentennial of the British abolition of the slave trade propelled a huge wave of conferences, new books, and documentary films focusing on British participation in the trade of enslaved Africans, and motion pictures such as *Amazing Grace* (2006), which praised the role of William Wilberforce in fighting against the British Atlantic slave trade. In 2012, a few years before the commemoration of the sesquicentennial of the abolition of slavery in the United States, Steven Spielberg—who had already directed the 1997 film *Amistad* about the titular slave rebellion—released *Lincoln*, which, like *Amazing Grace*, featured a great emancipator in the figure of President Abraham Lincoln. Despite focusing on the history of slavery, however, these films emphasized the role of white saviors, thereby neglecting the many ways enslaved people fought for their *own* freedom.

During an era of ongoing violence against Black men and women, and following the emergence of Black Lives Matter as a global movement in 2013, new movies and television series began to focus on the lives of specific historical figures who were enslaved in the Americas. The film *12 Years a Slave* (2013), which told the story of Solomon Northup, a Black man born free in the state of New York but kidnapped in Washington, DC, and sold into slavery, won several Academy Awards in 2014, including for Best Picture. In 2016, *The Birth of a Nation* (which despite the title is not to be confused with the 1915 white supremacist movie by D. W. Griffith) brought to the big screen the bloody slave revolt led by Nat Turner in Southampton, Virginia, in 1831. Released in 2019, *Harriet* presented the story of Harriet Tubman, the enslaved woman who escaped slavery by the middle of the nineteenth century and helped emancipate many other bondspeople. The production of these movies responded to the demands of popular audiences tired of seeing the history of slavery presented through the lens of European and American men represented as heroes who abolished the Atlantic slave trade and slavery.

In Brazil, the painful memory of slavery since its abolition in 1888 has remained present through religious and public festivals such as Carnaval. But despite this visibility, it is only in recent years that federal, state, and municipal governments have begun to invest in permanent markers commemorating the country's history of slavery. Nonetheless, like the United States, Brazil also witnessed a growing number of cultural productions focusing on the country's history of slavery. Movies such as *Quilombo* (1984), directed by Cacá Diegues, tells the story of the Palmares *quilombo*, the largest and longest-lasting Brazilian runaway slave community. In recent years, several comic books have also told the story of the states created by enslaved, freed, and free Black individuals, born in Brazil and in Africa, to resist slavery in the seventeenth century.[1] Recently, African American novelist Gayl Jones published her epic novel *Palmares*, which also drew on the history of Brazil's most important *quilombo*.[2]

Cultural products addressing the history of slavery are also related to the growing number of academic studies exploring new dimensions of the lives of enslaved people in the Americas. Some of these works have focused on specific biographies and how bondspeople resisted against slavery.[3] Nonetheless, the impact of most work by historians of slavery has remained confined to the academy. But as slavery has become a topic of growing concern in public discussion, this landscape has dramatically altered.

The Enduring Significance of Atlantic Slavery

In the United States, 2019 became emblematic for Black history. That year marked the four hundredth anniversary of 1619, the arrival of the first documented enslaved Africans in the colony of Virginia.[4] The year 1619 has been associated with the birth of slavery in the United States, yet this date is also a construction. Indeed, as we will see in this book, since the sixteenth century, thousands of enslaved Africans had been brought to the Americas, not only to the West Indies, Brazil, and other regions of Latin America but also to the region encompassing today's United States. Nonetheless, the year 1619 became a landmark, a commemorative date that gained new visibility through a journalistic project of the same name led by Nikole Hannah-Jones and the *New York Times*, featuring essays by scholars, writers, and artists focusing on the present-day legacies of slavery in the United States.[5]

The emphasis on this specific year and the politicized reactions against the journalistic project triggered fierce public discussions in the media. Some academics questioned the project's accuracy, whereas politicians criticized it for making slavery central to the history of the United States.[6] But regardless of how political parties and individuals reacted, and despite the fact that 1619 did not mark the start of Africans being taken to the Americas, the year that for decades had already been a site of memory for many African Americans gained new meaning and began to be conceived as a reminder of how chattel slavery gave birth to anti-Black racism in a country that had failed to implement any national date of recognition to commemorate its tragic involvement in this human atrocity.

As the COVID-19 pandemic hit the world and following the murder of George Floyd in the summer of 2020, antiracist protests against police violence spread in the United States and in several countries in Europe and Latin America. Eventually, in June 2021, after many years of discussion, Juneteenth National Independence Day was officially instated as a federal holiday commemorating the emancipation from slavery in the United States.

The holiday is certainly an important achievement and a major step toward honoring formerly enslaved people and their descendants. But battles over the past have continued to evolve. Starting in 2020, several states in the United States introduced legislation banning books on the history of slavery and racism. These prohibitions are not related to the history of slavery itself; they are attempts to control how the history of slavery is taught, and they are expressions of how the past is politicized in the present, as I have discussed in previous works.[7]

Memory and Commemoration

Public, often contentious exchanges about slavery are not unique to the United States and did not happen in isolation. Caribbean countries have been commemorating slavery in public spaces since at least the 1960s through the construction of monuments honoring enslaved rebels such as Cuffy and Carlota. Mexico and Colombia have honored slave insurgents such as Bioho and Yanga for many years as well. Starting in 1888 and for nearly fifty years, Brazil had observed May 13, the date of the abolition of slavery, as a national holiday. Though this holiday was suppressed in the 1930s, since the end of the Cold War, dozens of cities around the country have adopted November 20, the date of the death of Zumbi, the leader of Palmares, as a national day to celebrate Black consciousness.

During most of the twenty-first century, Brazilian governments have passed legislation and promoted initiatives to recognize the history of slavery and the country's long-lasting connections with the

African continent. In recent years, however, fascist Brazilian president Jair Bolsonaro has claimed that the Portuguese never set foot in Africa and that therefore Brazil had no responsibility for the enslavement of Africans. Such positions show that, although the history of slavery and the role of the country in the Atlantic slave trade has long been documented and established, publicly elected authorities can at any time decide to make false claims about their country's history. These attacks confirm not only that historians *must* revisit and reilluminate this past but also that they need to engage in public debates taking place outside academic settings.

Since 2006, France has acknowledged its past involvement in the Atlantic slave trade and slavery on May 10, a national day commemorating the memories of the slave trade, slavery, and their abolition. In this climate, new debates about the need for reparations for slavery also reemerged, especially after 2014 when the Caribbean Community and Common Market (CARICOM), an organization comprising fifteen member states, released a ten-point plan demanding that European countries offer formal apologies and reparations for slavery, the Atlantic slave trade, and colonialism. CARICOM's call for redress was followed by heated discussions in the United States and European countries, showing slavery's continuing significance in today's world.[8]

In previous works, I have explored the reasons this new interest has surfaced in recent years, and I have especially sought to explain why and how the Atlantic slave trade and slavery are memorialized in Europe, Africa, and the Americas.[9] I have argued that this relevance has little to do with what happened in the past but is rather related to how racism and present-day social and racial inequalities perpetuate the exclusion of people labeled as Black in societies where chattel slavery existed. Because racism and white supremacy persist in Europe, Africa, and the Americas as legacies of Atlantic slavery, this long and painful past still matters. But the excessive focus on the present can also blur our ability to clearly address the study of chattel slavery and the Atlantic slave trade.

Brazil and Africa

Humans in Shackles is an Atlantic cultural history of slavery in the Americas that seeks to redress the distortions and imbalances of existing general histories of slavery, which have insisted on centering on the British North Atlantic world, especially the United States and the English-speaking Caribbean colonies. These histories have generally excluded the central role of Brazil in the Atlantic slave trade and slavery, while also ignoring the history of Africa and the role of enslaved women in the institution of slavery.

In addressing this unfair imbalance and approaching the long history of these human atrocities from a panoramic point of view, this book is in dialogue with the work of Marcus Rediker and Jennifer Morgan, who each have called for historians to write human histories of slavery and the Atlantic slave trade that emphasize the lived experience of enslaved men and women, not demographics and economics.[10] This book is also in conversation with the works of historians such as Michael Gomez, Herman Bennett, and Toby Green, who have similarly challenged historians of the Atlantic slave trade to embrace the long history of the African continent instead of engaging with Africa as a mere repository of enslaved labor.[11]

The persistent emphasis on the British colonies of North America, and later the United States as well as the British West Indies, tends to obscure the real dimensions of slavery and the slave trade in the Americas. Approximately 12 million Africans were brought to the Americas. During the entire period of the Atlantic slave trade, approximately 389,000 enslaved persons who had been forced into slave ships in African ports came ashore in mainland North America, and more than 3.4 million disembarked in the British and French West Indies.[12] Yet more than 4.8 million enslaved men, women, and children landed on Brazilian shores, the largest number in the Americas and nearly ten times more than the number of slaves forcibly brought from the African continent to the United States. Brazil was also the last nation in the Western Hemisphere to abolish slavery, in 1888. Today, in part as a reflection of this long slave-trading past, the country has the second largest population of African descent in the world, after Nigeria.

Challenging how the history of African bondage in the Americas is told and written, *Humans in Shackles* is a hemispheric and Atlantic history of slavery that puts side by side Brazil, the West Indies, the Spanish-speaking Americas, and North America.[13] To tell this long story, I place Brazil and the South Atlantic system at the center of the narrative, highlighting the realities of African societies during the era of the Atlantic slave trade and slavery. My main claim is that Brazil, the Luso-Brazilian slave trade, and its African contexts are central to fully understand the long and painful history of the Atlantic slave trade and slavery in the Americas.

Likewise, I argue that slavery in Latin America, including Brazil, was not a benign and more humane institution, as many people, including some scholars and students, still believe. I challenge the widespread and misleading idea that views slavery in Latin America and Brazil as milder compared with the harsh conditions of bondage in the British colonies of North America and the Caribbean. Instead, I contend, it was equally as violent, if not more so.

Enslaved Women and Resistance

Based on these premises, *Humans in Shackles* explores in especially great detail the social, cultural, and religious dimensions of the lives of bondspeople.[14] The book illuminates the crucial role of enslaved women in the Americas, even though in slave societies such as Brazil bondswomen were numerically inferior to men. This book offers a humanistic and narrative history that centers the experience of bondswomen who resisted slavery in multiple ways and emphasizes the important economic, social, and especially cultural roles of enslaved Africans and their descendants in the construction of the Americas. By taking an approach that relies on the importance of memory, I argue that the lived experiences of enslaved women are crucial to understanding slavery as well as its aftermath in the Americas.

This book focuses on all forms of resistance, individual and collective, including cultural as well as violent resistance. Ultimately, I show that, through the process of affirming their humanity by preserving their languages, deities, and festivities; fighting back against their owners; and maintaining a constant dialogue with the African continent, Africans (especially African women) and their descendants played a central role in the construction of the Western Hemisphere's social and cultural fabric.

Although most primary sources explored in this book were mediated or produced by male historical actors, I try to highlight the stories of enslaved persons to show them as protagonists and not as mere supporting figures. I show that despite having been relegated to the background of historical narratives, enslaved women were central pillars of Atlantic slavery, even if they were outnumbered by men among enslaved Africans transported to the Americas by a ratio of two to one. Enslaved women gave birth to children who were born in slavery. They nursed the offspring of their owners. They took care of the children of other bondswomen. On the cotton plantations of Louisiana in the United States or on the coffee plantations of São Paulo in Brazil, women performed strenuous physical work. In cities of Latin America and the Caribbean, such as Lima, Rio de Janeiro, Mexico City, and Havana, bondswomen toiled all day in the streets selling food, often in order to be able to buy the freedom of their loved ones. Enslaved women worked by cooking, cleaning, sewing, seeding, and harvesting. Slave owners sexually abused enslaved women, for whom refusing their advances could result in severe punishment. Even then, enslaved women resisted by running away, by killing their owners, or by accumulating meager sums to purchase their own freedom.

A Transnational History

A historian can follow diverse threads to write the painful history of slavery and the Atlantic slave trade. Most general history books about slavery in the Americas have focused on the United States.

Since the mid-twentieth century, books examining the economy of slavery have also privileged a national perspective, even though slavery and the Atlantic slave trade relied on transnational economic systems of human exploitation, exchange, and competition.[15] With few exceptions, none of these national histories of slavery in the United States evinces a substantial attempt to examine the lives and work of enslaved people by considering the African continent as an important component of Black life in the Americas.[16] In many respects, even today, cultural approaches are considered to be the work of sociologists and anthropologists.[17] Several monographs and books intended for large audiences have especially focused on slavery as part of the context of the Civil War in the United States.[18] Written by men, most of these general books about slavery in the Americas have also tended to ignore the work, lives, and experiences of enslaved women, leaving African American women historians to examine these histories in separate books.[19]

Humans in Shackles stands apart from existing general books studying slavery by providing a wide overview of Atlantic slavery in the Americas. While engaging with the history of slavery in the United States, the Caribbean, and Latin America, the book argues that Brazil was a crucial player in the continental and transoceanic history of slavery and the Atlantic slave trade. I also insist that Brazil is inseparable from the African continent until at least the middle of the nineteenth century, which is also why Brazil, Africa, and Africans occupy a prominent position in the book.

Slavery existed in many societies around the world, even before antiquity. In all these societies, slavery had both similar and contrasting elements. Still, because slavery was a mode of production and also an institution regulated by customary and statutory law, it is hard to make generalizations regarding what slavery is or is not. But despite changing over time and space, human bondage persisted in bearing a set of features that make it identifiable as slavery. I insist on the set of features because if taken individually, each of these elements is not sufficient to define a labor regime or mode of production as slavery, which is also why sociologists and anthropologists examining various societies have disagreed about a definition of slavery.

French anthropologist Claude Meillassoux relied on his fieldwork in West Africa to explain what slavery is and how a person becomes a *slave*. According to him, "desocialization and depersonalization are at the origin of the slave state."[20] Classical scholar Moses I. Finley also emphasized the alien condition of enslaved persons by insisting on three features: "the slave's property status, the totality of the power over him, and his kinlessness."[21] During the same period, sociologist Orlando Patterson defined *slavery* as "the permanent, violent domination of natally alienated and generally dishonored persons," suggesting that slave status was associated with individuals alienated from their society of origin.[22] Meanwhile, historian Paul E. Lovejoy also underscores alienness as a central feature of a *slave*. As he observes, "outsiders were perceived as ethnically different . . . [and t]he absence of kinship was a particularly common distinction."[23] In a later book, Meillassoux again stressed that "through capture and trafficking the captive is engaged in a process of extraneity which prepares him for his state of absolute stranger in the society to which he will be delivered."[24] Despite these definitions, only the first generation of enslaved individuals were foreigners to the society in which they were enslaved. Moreover, in various communities, locals could be enslaved as a result of judicial punishment—for example, if they committed a crime, or if they contracted a debt they could not pay—even though once enslaved, these individuals would be sold elsewhere.

Historians must take these distinctions into account when examining slavery in the Americas, as it was only with the rise of the Atlantic slave trade that the institution of slavery started specifically targeting Black persons from the regions encompassing West, West Central, and Southeastern Africa. Transplanted to the Americas by European colonizers starting in the late fifteenth century, the institution of slavery was an economic system of dependence. Slavery sanctioned the possession of human beings as movable property and could only exist through violence and coercion, even though customs and laws regulated its existence. Regarded as commodities, enslaved persons could be bought, sold, displaced, overworked, tortured, beaten, violated, and murdered. But more than providing forced labor to an owner, bondspeople were subjected to relations of power.

In societies around the world where slavery existed prior to the late fifteenth century, including the Greco-Roman world, Black Africans were never the majority of the enslaved population. The institution of slavery also existed in ancient Egypt, albeit slaves never existed in large numbers. Moreover, Black Africans represented only a fraction of those living in bondage. Historians pay attention to the number of enslaved people in each society to determine the nature of these societies in terms of the relative importance of slavery as an institution within them. Simply put, *slave societies* were those with great numbers of slaves and in which slavery played a central role in production, whereas in other *societies with slaves*, the institution of slavery played only a secondary role in the economy. According to this view, introduced by Finley, the five slave societies were ancient Greece and Rome, Brazil, the US South, and the West Indies, whereas other parts of the Americas were "societies with slaves," or societies in which slavery existed.[25] In recent years, scholars have called for a reappraisal of Finley's categories by pointing out that his definitions of *slave societies* and *societies with slaves* were far too broad, vague, and ethnocentric.[26] But at least regarding the Americas, my focus in this book, Finley's proposed framework remains valuable, even though, as with any other concepts, it can benefit from further nuance.

Slavery as well as internal slave trades were already in place on the African continent long before Europeans reached the shores of West Africa in the fifteenth century. By this time, the African continent had already been supplying captives to the Eastern slave trade (also known as the Muslim slave trade) for at least six centuries. Slave traders transported enslaved people from West Africa, West Central Africa, and Southeast Africa to northern Africa and the Mediterranean, as well as to the Middle East and as far as western India and China.[27] Estimates for the internal slave trade remain unclear, but historians have calculated that as many as seventeen million Africans were displaced in the context of the Eastern slave trade. But despite the scale of these slave trades, the Atlantic slave trade remains the largest transoceanic forced migration of enslaved Africans. More important, only with the rise of the Atlantic slave trade in the late fifteenth century did slavery became a racialized institution that specifically targeted Black populations in West Africa, West Central Africa, and Southeast Africa.

Africans and their descendants were not the first populations to be enslaved in the Americas. Slavery existed in Native American societies prior to the arrival of Europeans in the Western Hemisphere and persisted after European conquest.[28] Moreover, even though this book does not examine the trade and the enslavement of Indigenous populations in the Americas, I emphasize that as Europeans invaded and occupied the territories of these First Nations, they enslaved these men, women, and children and also created other slavery-like institutions to exploit their workforce. Although often illegal and concealed from public view, the trade in Indigenous peoples continued to exist in Brazil in the eighteenth century and in the United States throughout the nineteenth century during the occupation of the West.[29]

Centering Culture

This book also differs from studies that privilege the analysis of economic structures of chattel slavery as well as demographics and statistics.[30] It is a cultural history crafted to show the human perspective of enslaved Africans and their descendants. Following a chronological and thematic approach, *Humans in Shackles* surveys the trajectories of men, women, and children from Africa to the Americas by examining how European powers reached Africa and traded with African societies, and how Africans were captured, were transported to the coast, and crossed the Atlantic Ocean in the holds of slave ships. The book explores how African captives were sold in slave markets and other settings in the Americas. I look at their living and working conditions on plantations and in urban areas, paying particular attention to the work of enslaved women who often fed the cities by selling food in the streets and urban markets.

Humans in Shackles shows how, despite the violence they had to endure, bondspeople created families. The book also examines the ways enslaved women and men were sexually abused by their male and female owners. Several chapters explore how enslaved people daily resisted slavery by joining runaway slave communities, congregating and re-creating their cultures and religions, and organizing rebellions. In all these instances I show how enslaved people's past and ongoing connections with the African continent mattered. Finally, the book discusses how bondsmen and bondswomen sought ways to be freed or to purchase their freedom, up until the legal end of slavery. I explain how thousands of freedpeople organized themselves to leave the Americas to settle on the African continent, and I also highlight the challenges faced by most former bondspeople who remained in the Americas after emancipation.

Over more than three hundred years, slavery was shaped by economic, social, political, and cultural changes in the Americas. These changes varied according to regional specificities. I contend here that slave systems were interconnected. Therefore, I seek to show that, whether in Brazil, the United States, Cuba, Saint-Domingue, or Jamaica, the institution of slavery and the individual and collective experiences of enslaved people had many parallels. Addressing the significance of the role of enslaved women in the Americas, *Humans in Shackles* underscores the importance of urban slavery in which bondswomen played important roles, especially as street vendors, marketeers, and domestic workers. To provide this broad panorama, highlighted by specific examples, I draw on a large array of printed and manuscript primary sources such as travel accounts, pamphlets, newspapers articles, slave ship logs, ship captains' journals, fugitive slave advertisements, slave narratives, wills, speeches, laws, and correspondence in English, Portuguese, French, and Spanish, and I also incorporate visual sources including oil paintings, watercolors, engravings, photographs, artifacts, novels, motion pictures, monuments, and heritage sites, materials that are often overlooked by historians.

Humans in Shackles is comprehensive in its scope. I rely and expand on the existing scholarship on the Atlantic slave trade and slavery in the Americas with the goal of contributing to a better understanding of the global legacies of the Atlantic slave trade and human bondage. By doing so, I underscore that the Atlantic slave trade in the South Atlantic world and the history of slavery in Brazil are central to comprehending the full dimensions and multiple complexities of the inhuman institution in the Western Hemisphere. I also argue that the internal contexts of West Africa and especially of West Central Africa not only shaped the rise of the slave trade to the Americas but also continued to affect the patterns of the trade in enslaved Africans until its abolition in the second half of the nineteenth century. Here, I remind the reader that Brazil, since its early colonization, developed privileged links with West Central Africa, especially the region of present-day Angola. These specific ties, favored by the predominance of a bilateral trade between Angola and Brazil and between Brazil and the Bight of Benin, gave birth to the South Atlantic system. In this space, these continuous exchanges were so important that they persisted even after the end of the Atlantic slave trade.[31]

Because of its large annual imports of African-born individuals, Brazil became a crucial spot where African cultures and religions survived, evolved, adapted, mixed, and more than anything else developed a dialogue with European and Native American cultures. Although this process carried features similar to other parts of Latin America and the Caribbean, these cross-cultural exchanges often contrasted with the British colonies of North America and what later became the United States, where the imports of enslaved Africans were more than ten times smaller than in Brazil. Yet, to juxtapose the South Atlantic and the North Atlantic systems, I also underline that a significant proportion of African-born bondspeople were introduced in mainland North America through the intra-American slave trade, especially through the Caribbean. I highlight the dramatic growth of US enslaved population between 1790 and the years preceding the Civil War (1861–65). This new phase, greatly provoked by the rise of the cotton industry and the invention of cotton gin, marked a new expansion of slavery in the United States. The Saint-Domingue Revolution and its aftermath also contributed to the expansion of the sugar and coffee industries in Cuba and Brazil. This new increase, I explain, propelled a new development of the institution of slavery entangled with the rise of industrial capitalism, a phase that historians have designated as the "second slavery."[32]

Challenges of Generalization and My Position as a Historian

Writing this hemispheric history also carries challenges. There are very few syntheses of the history of slavery in the Americas. Male scholars identified as white have authored ones that largely focus on the English-speaking Americas.[33] My position is very different from that of these historians. I was born in the former Third World, now known as the Global South, and English is my third language (after Portuguese and French). I was raised in a peripheric region of southern Brazil known as Rio Grande do Sul, where I spent most of my youth. As far as I know, my ancestors have links with the early Portuguese and Spanish colonizers who settled in the region in the eighteenth century, even though there is no formal recognition that these ancestors ever had children with Indigenous and Black persons—though, as with any of these early settlers, in a region where there were very few women, this hypothesis is likely. Despite this configuration, typical of many regions in Latin America, I was raised as a white person. This insider position changed in my late twenties, when for nearly a decade I migrated, lived, and studied in the Canadian province of Quebec. In this new context, in a province historically separated from English-speaking Canada, because of my origin, black hair, darker skin, and strong accent, I was identified as a Latina, and therefore labeled as visible minority.

My then-new minority position as a South American woman who had to become fluent in French allowed me to conduct archival research and fieldwork in French-speaking West Africa. My new complex position not only transformed my perspective of the history of slavery and the Atlantic slave trade but also of the history of Brazil, the country that imported the largest number of enslaved Africans during the era of the Atlantic slave trade. Eventually, I made my academic career as a professor of history in the United States, where I continue to be a Latina. Still, depending on the political context and the social actors involved, I can be perceived as being white, nonwhite, or a woman of color. But more important, since 2008 I have had the privilege of teaching at a historically Black university, where most of my students and colleagues are racialized as Black persons with roots all over the African diaspora. At Howard University, all students in the humanities and sciences must take courses on the history of the African diaspora. This rich context allowed me to develop multiple courses focusing on the history of slavery, the slave trade, and the African diaspora. Certainly, I benefited from the advantages of being racialized as a white person during my youth in my home country. But after having spent more than twenty years, and basically two-thirds of my adult life, studying and working in North America and Europe, where I am perceived as an outsider in academic circles, I also acquired a different and more distanced perspective of Brazilian history. Through my personal and academic journey as an immigrant, I soon realized how the existence of slavery and the central role of Africans in the construction of the country have been annihilated in Brazilian history and public memory. Once in North America, I also understood how Brazil and the African continent were continually excluded from the historiography of slavery that insisted on focusing on the North Atlantic system, the United States, and the Anglophone world. Hence, in many ways, this book is part of a collective and individual continued effort to recenter Brazil and Africa in this large tragic history of the Atlantic slave trade and slavery, and to give enslaved women their rightful place in this story. The book is also a testament of more than twenty years studying the history of slavery and the Atlantic slave trade through archival research and fieldwork in English, Portuguese, French, and Spanish on three continents.

Just as any other work of synthesis, this book is not an encyclopedia and obviously remains incomplete. Not all regions, themes, and periods receive the same attention. These choices were guided by the availability of primary and secondary sources and by my own experience and interests researching and teaching the history of slavery and the Atlantic slave trade and African diaspora history. While providing a comparative and transnational perspective of the history of these human atrocities, the book follows the approach of African diaspora history, which treats the history of enslaved Africans and their descendants in the Americas as the continuation of their experiences on the African continent.[34] The various chapters draw from fieldwork and primary sources in archives, libraries, and museums in Brazil, the Republic of Benin, the United Kingdom, Canada, the United States, France, and Portugal conducted between 1999 and 2023. I also rely on the work of historians, anthropologists, sociologists, and art historians who excavated archives and uncovered objects, songs, dances, martial arts, and testimonies in order to study in detail the history of slavery and the Atlantic slave trade in various regions and periods.

My point of departure to write an Atlantic history of slavery was the idea that, despite specific national and regional contexts and the trends that oriented the Atlantic slave trade from disparate regions in West Africa and West Central Africa to each part of the Americas, there were also many similarities between the institutions of slavery all over the Americas. As I conducted research and wrote this book, these similarities became even clearer. In all the regions of the Americas where slavery existed to a greater or lesser extent, enslaved Africans and their descendants left deep imprints in urban and rural landscapes, shaping foodways, religions, and cultures. In these various areas, white settlers created mechanisms to prevent the emancipation of enslaved populations and to control freed populations even after the end of slavery. Although the long history associated with slavery and the importance of populations of African descent has been acknowledged in some parts of the Americas more than in others, full recognition of the harms caused by slavery and the Atlantic slave trade remains unachieved, which is why the past of Atlantic slavery remains such an important topic of debate in the public sphere. And this is also why my work, shaped by the approach of memory studies, gives me a unique point of view when writing an Atlantic history of these human atrocities.

Ultimately, the reverberations of this past have remained alive in the present. But because this past still matters, this book proposes to cross this memory's foggy zone and attempt to better understand the long era in which humans racialized as Black were placed in shackles to construct the hemisphere we know today as the Americas.

CHAPTER I

Violent Encounters

In his sixteenth-century bestseller *The Cosmography and Geography of Africa*, North African diplomat al-Hasan ibn Muhammad al-Wazzan, known as Johannes Leo Africanus, described Jenne, a town in present-day Mali, as being a rich land, "lush with wheat, barley, livestock and cotton, and its inhabitants are very wealthy because they do a good trade in cotton fabrics." He also mentioned that North African merchants sold "many wares in this kingdom, especially European textiles, copper, brass and weapons such as swords and lances. They pay with gold that has not been struck into coin, though for small things they pay in iron pieces."[1] As this scholar explained, West African and West Central African societies have been part of economic and cultural exchanges with other parts of the globe for centuries, long before the Portuguese began exploring the coastal regions of West and West Central Africa in the fifteenth century.[2]

Purchasing and transporting enslaved Africans across the Atlantic Ocean from these two regions became more affordable in comparison with purchasing the increasingly expensive slaves from the Ottoman Empire and the Moroccan state, regions that previously provided captives to European markets through the Saharan routes. To better understand the complex mechanisms of the Atlantic slave trade, the best place to start is the history of the contact between the inhabitants of the African and the European continents that started centuries before, reaching back to antiquity.

It is undeniable that the first Portuguese expeditions to West Africa had economic and religious motivations. The Portuguese waged "just war" against non-Christians, especially against the Muslims and other non-Christian populations, and this religious excuse at least initially justified their enslavement. I emphasize here the extreme violence that characterized the first incursions of Portuguese explorers in the coastal areas of West Africa and West Central Africa, which were modeled on their early experiences fighting Muslim invaders in the Iberian Peninsula. I especially stress that the first exchanges between the Portuguese and West African societies during the first century of the Atlantic slave trade did not truly rely, as others have claimed, on the willingness of local rulers to sell prisoners or outliers into slavery. Though Portuguese and African authorities established trade agreements in the late fifteenth century, earlier raids set the tone for future exchanges. In these initial contacts as well as in later ones, rulers and commoners of African polities were not forced to enter the business of selling human beings to European traders, but they also did not do so entirely voluntarily. The reality is that, very often, they were left with few (if any) alternatives.

Africa before the Rise of the Atlantic System

Africa and Europe were already connected before the emergence of the Atlantic slave trade. For many centuries, trading routes linked the two continents, whose peoples and goods traveled across the Sahara Desert through the Mediterranean Sea and the Red Sea. The ancient Greek historian Herodotus not only wrote about "Ethiopians" (Black Africans) in his works; he also traveled to and described the African continent.[3] During the expansion of the Roman Empire, in the context of warfare between Greeks and Romans, Africans—representing a small minority of enslaved persons in the Greco-Roman world—reached southern Europe, and they also entered the Mediterranean world by way of Egypt, Nubia, North Africa, the region south of the Nile River, the Sahara borders, and West Africa.[4]

African and European exchanges continued in the next centuries. Romans conquered the Iberian Peninsula (known as Hispania) in 220 BCE, and following several Germanic invasions in the fifth century CE, the region was dominated by the Kingdom of the Visigoths. In addition, as early as the sixth century, the trans-Saharan trade that transported gold from West Africa to the Byzantine Empire connected African and Mediterranean populations.[5] Then, taking advantage of internal divisions among Christian groups, Muslims coming through North Africa invaded the Iberian Peninsula in 711 CE. Referred to as Al-Andalus by the Muslim occupiers, the region was inhabited by Muslims, Christians, and Jews. During the many decades following Muslim occupation, Muslims and Christians fought to control the region. Gradually, Christian kingdoms emerged in the north. Between 850 and 1250, Christians expanded their influence southward to secure land. Through this long process known as the Reconquest, Christians led military campaigns plundering property and enslaving Muslim occupants, a strategy employed by the Portuguese two centuries later when they reached West Africa. Eventually, in 1147, Christians controlled Lisbon. In 1179, Afonso I of the House of Burgundy became the first monarch of independent Portugal. Muslim occupation of the Iberian Peninsula lasted until 1492, when Christians eventually took possession of Granada.

Ethiopia, which had fought against the Muslims since the thirteenth century, was also in contact with the Mediterranean world through Italy and Egypt. Although several historians have mentioned an embassy from Ethiopia sent to the court of Pope Clement V in Avignon in 1306, recent scholarship has questioned the existence of this early mission.[6] Yet, one century later, in 1427, a diplomatic mission from Ethiopia traveled to Valencia., in present-day Spain. The group of emissaries met King Juan V of Aragón, who also sent a diplomatic mission back to Ethiopia, although his ambassadors never made it to their destination.[7] Aragón also attempted to build an alliance through a dynastic marriage between Emperor Ishaq of Ethiopia and Joana d'Urgell, the sister of King Alfonso V, as well as an alliance between the infant Dom Pedro and an unknown Ethiopian princess. However, none of these attempts were successful.[8]

When Portuguese sailors began exploring the coasts of West Africa in the early fifteenth century, the populations of Western Europe, West Africa, North Africa, and Northeast Africa had already been trading for several centuries. Unified since 1128, Portugal was a small kingdom located in the Iberian Peninsula between the Atlantic Ocean and the Kingdom of Castile in present-day Spain, which by that time was divided into four other polities, the kingdoms of Aragón, Navarre, Granada, and Majorca. This geographical position left the Portuguese no choice other than to consider territorial and commercial expansion by using the pathways offered by the Atlantic Ocean.

Drawing from the long-standing connections established during the Muslim occupation of the Iberian Peninsula initiated in 711, trade and cultural links between the Kingdom of Granada and the cities of Gao and Timbuktu in the West African empire of Mali flourished by the fourteenth century. In 1341, the Portuguese sponsored an Italian expedition in the region of Mar Pequeña, the part of the Atlantic Ocean encompassing today's islands of Madeira and Azores, as well as the Canary Islands, first explored by a Genoese navigator in 1312. Ultimately, navigating the Atlantic Ocean would allow the Portuguese to reach Asia's spice route and to access West Africa's coveted gold production.[9]

Following their pro-Christian orientation of a holy war against the Muslims, the Portuguese conquered Ceuta in North Africa in 1415 and then moved along Maghreb's Atlantic coast. By 1418, these navigators explored the island of Madeira. In the following fifteen years, they also made attempts to colonize the Canary Islands and visited the Azores. Portuguese explorers were a heterogenous group composed of sailors, lesser members of the nobility, and merchants. Searching for wealth, these navigators benefited from growing knowledge of South Atlantic sea currents and winds and the creation of a new small three-masted vessel called the *caravela* (caravel). The innovative ship allowed travelers to sail against the wind much faster than previously existing boats. Once limited to sailing along coastal areas, these first navigators employed this technological innovation to successfully travel long distances, eventually establishing connections with the gold-producing region of West Africa.[10] After passing Cape Bojador in 1434, Portuguese seamen explored the Northern African coastal region of present-day Morocco, reaching the Bay of Arguin in 1443, and in 1445 the mouth of the River Senegal and the Cape Verde islands.[11] In 1445, the Portuguese began settling in Madeira and the Azores, which, like Cape Verde, were previously uninhabited.

Portugal and West Africa: The Rise of the Atlantic System

Extreme violence dominated the first twenty years of contact between Portuguese explorers and West African populations. The Portuguese drew from their earlier warfare practices in North Africa by attacking, raiding, and capturing men, women, and children on the Atlantic islands and the Saharan coastal areas.[12] Despite recognizing this early context in which raids predominated, several historians have tended to emphasize that African polities controlled the trade in West African ports during the era of the Atlantic slave trade, arguing on this basis that they must have agreed to selling enslaved people to European traders.[13] Against this view, a closer examination of the initial incursions by the Portuguese in the West African littoral show that brutal raids marked their first engagement in the Atlantic slave trade.

During this significant period, West Africans repelled Portuguese invasions. They used naval power to fight back, resisted inland, and also opted to escape to the interior. In these early years of the Atlantic slave trade, Portuguese chronicler Gomes Eanes de Zurara authored one of the first detailed narratives of the enslavement of Africans and their arrival on European soil. Zurara explains that in 1444, Lançarote de Freitas, an assistant of Prince Henry (Henrique), also known as Prince Henry the Navigator, launched an expedition of six caravels with soldiers and sailors that departed from the southern Portuguese port of Lagos to the Bay of Arguin, in the coastal area of today's Mauritania. Once in Arguin, they raided the coastal area, capturing more than two hundred people.[14]

After the raids were completed, the Portuguese boarded nearly 240 enslaved persons in packed caravels that took almost three months to sail from Cape Blanco to the port of Lagos. After this long sea journey, African captives arrived extremely sick and weak on Portuguese shores, where they had never set foot before.[15] Zurara's chronicle includes observations of the various skin tones of the African captives, confirming that, as early as the fifteenth century, European observers were paying close attention to skin color. According to Zurara, among the captives, "there were some reasonably white, beautiful and elegant; others were less white like brown; others were as black as Ethiopians, whose faces and bodies were so disfigured."[16] Framing Black Africans according to their physical traits, his observations reveal his perceptions of individuals with lighter skin as beautiful, in contrast to those with darker skin, whom he refers to as ugly.

The group of captives disembarking in such horrible conditions provoked reactions of sadness and pity among the inhabitants of Lagos who attended their arrival. Zurara portrays in vivid detail the dramatic conditions of newly arrived African captives who "kept their heads low and their faces washed in tears looking at each other, others were moaning very painfully, looking up at the heavens, shouting loudly as if asking for help from the father of nature. Others wounded their faces with the palms of their hands, hurling themselves to the ground. Others made their lamentations with songs, as was the custom in their homeland, and although the words could not be understood by us, they well corresponded to the degree of their sadness."[17]

As the Portuguese consolidated their presence in West Africa, they continued navigating along its Atlantic coastline. In 1445, Portuguese explorer Dinis Fernandes arrived in Cape Verde, an uninhabited archipelago of ten islands and five islets divided into two groups, Barlavento (Santo Antão, São Vicente, Santa Luzia, São Nicolau, Sal, and Boa Vista) and Sotavento (Maio, Santiago, Fogo, and Brava).[18]

In the years that followed, Portuguese settlers brought enslaved Africans to Cape Verde, and migrants from the Kingdom of Jolof who were escaping enslavement also settled on the islands. Together, these groups gave origin to most of the archipelago's population.[19] Beginning in the middle of the fifteenth century, in all the Atlantic islands of West Africa such as the Azores, Cape Verde, Madeira, and São Tomé in the Bight of Bonny, the Portuguese developed sugarcane plantations. They also established sugarcane plantations on the Canary Islands, but the Kingdom of Castile took over the archipelago in 1479. As early as the first half of the sixteenth century, the sugar produced in São Tomé was exported to Antwerp and then redistributed to England, France, Flanders, and Germany.

In 1455, Pope Nicholas V issued the bull *Romanus Pontifex* that gave the Portuguese not only the exclusive right to explore the Atlantic coast of West Africa but also to convert its populations to Roman Catholicism. As the trade in enslaved Africans to the Iberian Peninsula and to the islands increased, the raid strategy that predominated in the first years of the Portuguese's pioneering engagement in the Atlantic slave trade was eventually reconsidered. This wasn't, however, out of any kind of humanitarian concern. Rather, one historian explains, it was only a result of the Portuguese realizing that risky raids such as those they had previously undertaken would get in the way of satisfying the new growing demand for an enslaved workforce.[20]

In the 1460s, Portugal started developing diplomatic relations with West African societies, a process that led the kingdom to seal peace treaties and trade agreements with local rulers.[21] Gradually, Portuguese agents established trading posts in Senegambia, the zone between the Senegal River in the north and the Gambia River in the south, encompassing today's Senegal, the Republic of the Gambia, Guinea-Bissau, and parts of Mauritania, Mali, and Guinea. This sustained presence allowed Portugal to develop trade relations in other parts of West Africa as well. In the late fifteenth century, Portuguese traders acquired African captives by way of the existing trading routes that crossed the Sahara. However, African polities also hired Portuguese soldiers as mercenaries, and therefore during the early years of the Atlantic slave trade in West Africa, they captured and enslaved people directly.[22]

Though the Portuguese were initially alone in their oceanic expansion, other European kingdoms gradually developed interests in the West African trade as well. Until the second half of the fifteenth century, the Portuguese fought over control of the Atlantic islands along the West African coast with the now unified Kingdoms of Castile and Aragón, whose respective monarchs Isabella and Ferdinand married in 1469. Because the king of Portugal was married to Joanna "la Beltraneja," who was a candidate to the throne of Castile, the War of the Castilian Succession emerged between Portugal and Castile. This conflict spread through the Atlantic world and was transformed into a battle to dominate trade in Upper Guinea, where the kingdoms of Portugal and Castile competed to control access to trade in gold and enslaved Africans.

Eventually, the Portuguese won the maritime war. In 1479, the Treaty of Alcáçovas sealed the peace between the two kingdoms. Portugal gained control of the islands of Madeira, the Azores, and the north of Morocco (Kingdom of Fez), Cape Verde, and the explored or yet-to-be-explored lands of West Africa and West Central Africa, whereas the Kingdom of Castile took possession of the Canary Islands.[23] Gradually, the Portuguese expanded and consolidated their influence in Atlantic Africa. Known as *lançados*, Portuguese sailors and Jewish Portuguese traders, who left Portugal to avoid religious persecution, settled in the region stretching from the Petite Côte in Senegal (between the Cape Verde peninsula and the border of present-day Gambia) to Sierra Leone.[24] These settlers did not seek to establish colonies in West Africa; instead, they solidified their presence in the region through trade. By marrying local women, they developed ties that attached them to the local communities, a strategy that Portuguese settlers replicated in other spaces they colonized in Africa and later in Brazil.

War and Diplomacy

Starting in the thirteenth century, the populations of the Upper Guinea region in present-day Senegal, Republic of the Gambia, Guinea, Guinea-Bissau, Sierra Leone, Liberia, and the western part of the Republic of Côte d'Ivoire (also known as Ivory Coast) were impacted by the westward migration of Mandinka groups from the Mali Empire. Despite the scarcity of written sources documenting the history of this region, European reports, travelogues, visual images, oral histories, and archaeological research allow us to draw a broad, albeit imperfect and biased, picture of West African societies during the fifteenth century.

The Mandinka established themselves along the Gambia River and gradually became hegemonic over other smaller polities in the region. The rise of the Mandinka was connected to the expansion of the trade in gold and enslaved persons across the Sahara and was also linked to the ascension of Islam in the Sahel region.[25] The region of Senegambia was also undergoing transformation. By the middle of the fourteenth century, the Wolof broke with the Mali Empire, located in the hinterland, and formed the Kingdom of Jolof along the basin of the Senegal River. As in Mali, Islam predominated in the new Wolof state, which controlled five vassal kingdoms: Waalo, Kajooor, Bawol, Sine, and Saloum.[26]

Portuguese traders and mariners not only promoted their commercial interests in Senegambia; they also made efforts to convert Muslim local rulers to Catholicism. In many ways this approach extended to West Africa their earlier conception of "just war." According to a contemporary report by João de Barros, the Portuguese king "always ordered the captains who went to trade in those ports to have a conversation about the things of faith."[27] For example, Portuguese sailors offered gifts to the Wolof prince Bor Biram with the intent to convert him to the Catholic faith through baptism, but the prince always rejected these offers. Later, however, one of his half brothers killed him and waged war against his other half brother Buumi Jeleen, who was also a competitor for the throne. To defeat his opponents and recover the throne, by 1487, Buumi Jeleen sent his nephew to Lisbon to request that King João II provide him with horses, weapons, and people. The Portuguese king granted the request under the condition that the Wolof prince agree to convert to Catholicism. To encourage this conversion, the king sent Buumi Jeleen a few horses. Portuguese traders and clergymen escorted the prince's nephew back to Senegambia. The prince's willingness to open the kingdom to maritime trade went so far that he moved its capital to Waalo on the coast.[28] But months later, as the local trade proved to be unprofitable and the prince did not convert, King João II called the party back to Portugal.

To avoid losing Portuguese support, Buumi Jeleen sent his nephew with the group to Portugal once again, this time bringing as gifts one hundred enslaved persons and a huge gold *manilla* (bracelet), used as a diplomatic credential. In the meantime, however, local opposition against Buumi Jeleen continued to increase. In 1488, the prince and twenty-four remaining followers had to escape by sea and went take shelter at the Portuguese fortress at the port of Arguim, nearly 250 miles north. From there, Buumi Jeleen and two dozen supporters went to Portugal to meet King João II.[29]

In Lisbon, the Wolof prince and his followers were treated with pomp and ceremony. The delegation was provided with fine clothes to attend court activities. In preparation for their conversion to Catholicism, the group attended a Catholic mass, and on November 3, 1488, Buumi Jeleen was baptized Dom João Bemoim, having as godparents King João II, Queen Leonor, Prince Afonso, a duke, an emissary from the pope who was at the court, and a bishop. A few days later, Buumi Jeleen was awarded with the title of Christian knight and given a coat of arms, and his companions were baptized as well. The Wolof prince was then sent back to West Africa along with a fleet of twenty caravels and hundreds of sailors who would continue the construction of a Portuguese fort at the mouth of the Senegal River.[30] Yet, upon his arrival on the coast of Senegal, the fleet's captain, Pero Vaz da Cunha, stabbed the Wolof prince to death and then abandoned his companions on the island of Santiago, in Cape Verde. According to one Portuguese report, the murder occurred because of the prince's alleged treason and also because the captain may have feared disease and wanted to return to Portugal.[31] Although disgusted by Bemoim's tragic fate, King João II did not punish Cunha.[32]

Bemoim's story suggests that, even if in these early diplomatic contacts Portuguese rulers may have considered African rulers as equals, the exchanges between the Portuguese and the inhabitants of the Upper Guinea coast were ultimately uneven. The Portuguese procured enslaved people in Senegambia in exchange for goods such as cloth, gold, and guns that supported internal conflicts, while also demanding that African rulers convert to Catholicism. This practice, like the early raids, derived from the period of Reconquest of the Iberian Peninsula, when the enslavement of non-Christians was justified as part of the principle of "just war."[33]

Although the Portuguese understood they were dealing with African noblemen, there is ample reason to believe that Black Africans were already stigmatized. By the end of the fifteenth century, the Portuguese were already transporting enslaved people from West Africa to the Iberian Peninsula. It is then plausible to think that, already in this early period, there was an increasing association between Black Africans and the legal status of being enslaved. Therefore, as Herman Bennett suggests, when examining these early encounters between Africans and Portuguese, scholars should consider not only the economic but also the political dimensions of these interactions.[34] In this context, Bemoim's assassination is perhaps the most powerful early depiction of how power imbalance marked the first exchanges between Europeans and Africans, signaling fundamental disparities that would only intensify as the Atlantic slave trade evolved.

Purchasing Enslaved Africans with Gold

In 1471, as the Portuguese moved along the coast of West Africa, they arrived on the Costa da Mina (Mina Coast), a namesake related to the important gold deposits of the basins of the rivers Pra, Ofin, and Volta.[35] The Mina Coast corresponded to the zone between the Comoé River in the west and the Volta River in the east, covering parts of the littoral of present-day Côte d'Ivoire, Ghana, and Togo.[36] In this early period of the Atlantic slave trade, most of the Mina Coast was referred to as the Gold Coast, the area corresponding to the coast of modern-day Ghana.[37] Later on, however, references to the Mina Coast instead referred to the region east of the Volta River, known as the Bight of Benin. Moreover, the French also used the term "Côte d'or" (Gold Coast) when referring to the Bight of Benin. Since the early years of 1000 CE, caravans of gold traders expanded south of the Sahara by traveling through the rainforests of the Gold Coast (see map 1). During the fifteenth century, Portugal's interest in exploring the region was not yet connected to the trade of enslaved Africans but rather pertained to obtaining access to these gold sources in the hinterland.

The Gold Coast encompassed several polities and peoples who spoke a variety of languages such as Ga, Adanme, Ewe, and Akan.[38] Whereas Akan-speaking populations may have migrated from the Sahara or from the regions of Sahel and the Atlantic Africa savanna to the Gold Coast, peoples speaking other languages such as Ga, Adanme, and Ewe may have reached the region coming from the east.[39] Despite being erroneously represented as one single people, Akan speakers were not unified and were in constant interaction with communities whose languages belonged to other clusters.[40] As early as 800 CE, Akan peoples developed sophisticated agricultural practices. Using iron tools, they opened inland forests and created earthwork settlements, where they produced palm oil and grew yams. But an epidemic is thought to have caused the dramatic decline of the population, which led to a sharp decrease in farming. When the Portuguese arrived on the Gold Coast in the second half of the fifteenth century, agrarian activity was resurging, but population growth and farming communities took more than one hundred years to fully recover.[41]

In 1481, Portugal sent the nobleman Diogo de Azambuja to the Gold Coast with ten caravels and two additional ships loaded with building supplies such as lime and stones as well as weaponry. The expedition was intended to construct a castle in a village then called Aldeia das Duas Partes (village of two parts), present-day Elmina, a coastal town controlled by Eguafo, one of the several kingdoms of Akan speakers on the Gold Coast. After their arrival in the region, the Portuguese obtained permission to disembark. Dressed in ceremonial outfits, the group of hosts included men playing trumpets, tambourines, and drums, who were prepared to introduce Kwamena Ansa, the local ruler. Likewise, the West African ruler came to welcome the newcomers accompanied by a large procession of men playing drums and cowrie shell shakers. They were also blowing horns and carrying arrows, bows, spears, and shields. Each man of noble rank was followed by two naked pages, one bringing a wooden stool for him to sit on and the other holding a shield. In a performance intended to display his wealth in gold to the Portuguese explorers, Ansa was sitting on a high chair. Wearing just a brocade cape, his arms, legs, and neck were totally covered with a variety of gold jewelry, chains, beads, and bells dangling from his hair, beard, and head.[42]

An interpreter translated the exchanges between Ansa and Azambuja, who told the West African ruler that his king sent him there to "trade, secure peace and friendship forever" and to make that territory the "perpetual site of many and very rich goods, so that by their good treatment, they, and those who descended from him, would always be richer and more ennobled."[43] But to achieve this goal, the Portuguese needed permission to obtain a place to store their merchandise and accommodate their men. Ansa responded to the captain that up to that day very few, dirty and vile, Christians arrived in the region. But the current Portuguese expedition was different. According to Ansa, Azambuja was exceptionally well dressed and looked like the son or the brother of the king of Portugal.

Following this first meeting, Ansa gave the Portuguese permission to build a castle, the first European building on the African coast. The Portuguese rapidly selected the construction site on top of a high cliff. Sea captain and explorer Duarte Pacheco Pereira, who recorded the Portuguese expedition to the Gold Coast in writing, noted that the communities living in the surroundings of the castle consisted mostly of fishermen. The next day, as the Portuguese started breaking ground to launch the construction of the castle, they disrespected local religious practices by destroying sacred rocks used as shrines by the town's inhabitants.[44] Not surprisingly, the residents responded by violently attacking the newcomers. But Azambuja quickly understood that their reaction was rather related to the delay in delivering the gifts promised to Ansa, which in this context can be understood as tributes. Eventually, as the gifts such as cloth, basins, and *manillas* were provided as previously agreed, the Portuguese were able to dispel the animosity of the local population, and the construction of the castle proceeded.[45]

Chroniclers at that time narrated this early conflict as a minor incident. However, they also pointed out how, after the confrontation, the Portuguese proceeded with caution as the castle's construction progressed. In other words, this attack scared the Portuguese newcomers, who were certainly impressed by the villagers' locally made iron weaponry.[46] In 1482, the Portuguese completed the construction of the imposing castle São Jorge da Mina (known as Elmina castle), intended to protect gold and other commodities from attacks by other European powers. The gold trade was an extremely lucrative business. According to Captain Pereira, the Gold Coast merchants provided the Portuguese the equivalent of 170,000 *dobras* (coins) of "good fine gold" on an annual basis. In exchange, the Portuguese paid them with *lambéls* (a blue-and-red striped cloth), brass *manillas*, scarves, corals, red shells, white wine, and blue glass beads.[47]

Gradually, the trade in gold became intertwined with the trade in enslaved Africans. In 1486, as the Portuguese continued navigating eastward, they reached the Kingdom of Benin, whose territory encompassed part of present-day southern Nigeria. Inhabited by the Edo-speaking people, this kingdom already maintained exchanges with the Gold Coast by purchasing gold and selling beads, cloth, and also slaves. In 1486, the Portuguese founded a trading post in the port of Gwato (or Ughoton), not far from Benin City, the kingdom's capital. As it had done in Senegambia, Portugal developed diplomatic relations with Benin, and the two kingdoms exchanged reciprocal diplomatic missions. The encounter with the Portuguese coincided with a period of territorial expansion, in which Benin's ruler (called an *oba*) waged war against his neighbors and sold his prisoners into slavery. Once in Benin, the Portuguese purchased ivory, timber, cloth, and pepper. They also acquired enslaved individuals whom they sold in exchange for gold to local traders on the Gold Coast.[48] These same enslaved persons would then extract the gold from inland riverbeds and transport it by land or through the waterways to the coast. Enslaved people also helped clear the forests for farming, one of the main economic activities in the region, along with the production of salt and fishing.[49]

During the early period of the trade, Gold Coast polities maintained their political power. Yet, once the Elmina castle was established, competition among local societies to participate in the gold trade dramatically increased. Occasionally, the Portuguese intervened in the wars in the region to prevent the disruption of the gold trade. They also created alliances with local states to attempt to control the trade and eliminate European competitors. This approach helped generate more wars in which the Portuguese and their local allies on the Gold Coast actively opposed other states, which sometimes received support from competing European traders.[50]

West Central Africa

Portuguese expansion continued along the coast of West Africa. In 1483, Diogo Cão arrived at the mouth of the Congo River in West Central Africa. Here, the Portuguese again developed relations with various local states, the largest states being the Kingdom of Kongo and the Kingdom of Ndongo. The exchanges with these kingdoms were crucial for the future development of the Atlantic slave trade because the largest number of enslaved Africans transported to the Americas were embarked in the ports of West Central Africa.

The formation of the Kingdom of Kongo dates back to the thirteenth century. Located south of the Congo River, its territory roughly corresponds to today's northern Angola and western Democratic Republic of the Congo. At the time of the Portuguese arrival, the Kingdom of Kongo's population was more than half a million inhabitants, most of whom were speakers of Kikongo, a language of the Bantu family. Like the societies of the Gold Coast, the Kingdom of Kongo was rich in mineral resources such as iron ore and copper. A centralized state like other African polities, Kongo was a stratified society, divided into nobility, commoners, and enslaved people.[51] In the territories of the kingdom's various provinces, its rulers appointed various agents who were in charge of collecting taxes. Also like other African societies, the kingdom had various currencies, including cowrie shells, or *nzimbu*. Its population was spread out to take advantage of the land's multiple resources that could generate income to pay tributes. As a result, the generation of wealth was often, although not exclusively, associated with what historians and anthropologists have defined as "wealth-in-people," meaning the ability to organize and control people, therefore transforming them into dependents through which to secure access to resources and increase production.[52] To achieve this goal, Kongo engaged in wars against neighboring polities as a means not only to expand its territory but also and especially to acquire prisoners. These conquered populations were displaced to densely populated areas near the capital Mbanza Kongo, located about 120 miles inland, where the *manikongo* (ruler) resided.

The encounter between Portugal and Kongo impacted both kingdoms.[53] After his arrival, Cão took several individuals as hostages to force them to learn Portuguese. As in previous encounters with African rulers, the two kingdoms exchanged embassies, with Kongo emissaries sent to Lisbon and Portuguese diplomats directed to the Kingdom of Kongo. As Portuguese priests hosted the emissaries, they learned the Kikongo language, and Kongo's ambassadors learned to speak, read, and write in Portuguese. Literacy in Portuguese contributed to facilitating the potential conversion of the *manikongo* and other members of the noble class to Catholicism. Therefore, by 1490, as they did in other parts of Africa, the Portuguese engaged in imperial expansion by relying on the dictates bestowed on them by the papacy. Portuguese agents made an alliance with the Kingdom of Kongo, relying on the idea that West Central Africans were pagans and needed to be evangelized. The *manikongo* Nzinga a Nkuwu, along with his family and members of his court, embraced Catholicism. The ruler was baptized according to the Catholic doctrine by taking the name João I. Christian conversion provoked initial opposition from rival factions who supported other candidates to the throne, but eventually his son, Mvemba a Nzinga (baptized with the Portuguese Catholic name Afonso), was enthroned as his successor. During Afonso's reign, the Portuguese armed him with weapons to wage war against neighboring states. Some of the Portuguese men, along with their mixed-race children, also integrated the kingdom's army, capturing prisoners of war who were then sold into slavery.[54]

We will never know the true motivations that led to the conversion of Kongo's rulers to Catholicism, as most of the surviving written sources about these early exchanges were produced by the Portuguese. However, the kingdom's incorporation of Christian symbols was not only the result of Portuguese influence, given that motifs including the cross were already present in West Central African visual culture prior to the kingdom's contact with Portuguese outsiders.[55] What we do know from other similar attempts to convert African rulers during this and later periods is that conversion to Christianity served as a strategy to allow access to European commodities. At the same time, adherence to Catholicism never fully supplanted African cosmologies, rituals, and practices; Catholicism and African religions often operated side by side.[56] Yet, during his reign, Afonso sent members of his court to study in Portugal. Back in Kongo, these returned nobles not only created schools to train the local population in the Catholic doctrine but also engaged in destroying local shrines and objects of devotion.[57] These early religious and diplomatic exchanges prepared the way for the Portuguese colonization of the region south of the Congo

River, where two of the three largest slave-trading ports, Luanda and Benguela, would be located.

As in other regions of West Africa and West Central Africa, the institution of slavery had existed in the Kingdom of Kongo at least since the fourteenth century, prior to the arrival of the Portuguese. Already in the fifteenth century in West Central Africa, resources and people that generated wealth were treated as capital.[58] By this same period, the Portuguese were already exporting enslaved Africans from the Kingdom of Kongo to labor on plantations on their islands off the African Atlantic coast. Portuguese traders also transported enslaved people to ports on the Iberian Peninsula. Although conversion to Christianity was part of the Portuguese colonial project, by the end of the fifteenth century the trade in enslaved Africans became a central element of the exchanges established with African polities along the Atlantic coast.

Kongo's rulers increased their number of dependents by displacing residents from less populated regions and relocating them to densely occupied areas such as those surrounding the kingdom's capital, where they engaged in agricultural activities.[59] In this early period, people were enslaved in a variety of ways, as we will see in greater detail in chapter 2. Overall, the gradual contact with the Portuguese led West Central African rulers to accumulate more dependents while acquiring foreign goods such as weapons, alcohol, and textiles. These products contributed to the power of the African potentates. However, as these sovereigns gradually became important players in Atlantic networks, they had to sell into slavery the newly acquired dependents to the same European traders from whom they imported commodities.[60] As the slave trade intensified, similar dynamics emerged in other parts of the coast of West Africa and West Central Africa, and new European players entered the competition for trade with African polities.

The Atlantic Slave Trade in Motion

The development of commercial, cultural, and religious exchanges between Portuguese and African agents is entangled with European oceanic expansion, which started in Africa and reached the Americas and Asia. As early as the fifteenth century in Senegambia, Portuguese agents raided local populations, transporting them as slaves to the Iberian Peninsula and the islands on the Atlantic African coasts. As the need for an enslaved workforce increased, the Portuguese developed diplomatic relations with African potentates. Through their sustained access to African markets, the Portuguese became central actors in the development of the slave trade with Europe. With the arrival of Christopher Columbus in the Americas, the Portuguese also became crucial players in the Atlantic slave trade with the newly conquered continent. Likewise, as Portuguese navigators reached Brazil in 1500, their presence and the future arrival of Brazilian-born traders in West Central African ports accelerated existing divisions among states and chiefdoms that competed to gain territorial expansion and control larger numbers of subjects.[61] As we will explore in subsequent chapters, the impact of the presence of the Portuguese (and later of other European powers on the coasts of West Africa and West Central Africa) differed from region to region and varied over time. But understanding these early interactions allows us to explore in chapters 2 and 3 the development of the trade in enslaved Africans to the Americas between the sixteenth and the nineteenth centuries.

CHAPTER 2

Catching People

Akeiso, or Florence Hall, as she was renamed in Jamaica, was born in Igboland, in today's southeastern Nigeria. Her memories of West Africa were scant, after many years of captivity in the Americas: "I can scarcely remember beyond that I was still unclothed, sometimes employed in attending our people, while engaged in Fishing, at other times guarding the fowls and chickens from Hawks, or more frequently at play with other children." Still, she had a few recollections of that tragic evening of her childhood: "While at a distance from our houses a party of the enemy came around and drove us, into an enclosed place, and immediately secured us—our hands were tied—while in vain our cries and screams were raised, but unheard, if heard, unattended."[1] She and other members of her community were transported to the coast to be sold into slavery.

Documentary films, motion pictures, and television series have misleadingly portrayed the horrors of the Atlantic slave trade by featuring Europeans randomly catching men, women, and children along the coasts of Africa.[2] What these popular narratives omit is how these Africans were *actually* captured in the coastal areas and the hinterlands of West Africa, West Central Africa, and Southeast Africa. In this chapter, I examine the forms such enslavement took in reality, and I show how they evolved over time and varied across regions during the era of the Atlantic slave trade. Exploring how free men, women, and children were captured on the African continent to be sold in the

Americas, I argue that in all its forms, enslavement always involved violence. Though warfare was the most common method to capture large numbers of people, other actions such as raids, banditry, and kidnapping were also widespread. Enslavement could also occur as a result of religious punishments and sentences associated with crimes such as theft, adultery, robbery, and homicide.

In correspondence and other written and visual accounts, formerly enslaved individuals described how they were captured on the coast or in the hinterland of Atlantic Africa. African rulers also narrated how they led military campaigns against neighboring states and how they enslaved prisoners of war. The enslavement of Africans is also reported in European travelogues and other accounts. These sources shed light on the circumstances that made free persons "eligible" to become enslaved individuals. Whereas in West Africa, African middlemen most of the time captured men, women, and children to be sold to European slave traders, in West Central Africa, Portuguese agents actively participated in the process of seizing people for the Atlantic slave trade. While considering the social, economic, and political dynamics that intensified the enslavement of Africans, this chapter explores published and unpublished firsthand narratives by enslaved persons to reveal the problems that still affect our understanding of enslavement in Africa. Even though the vast majority of enslaved persons were captured during wars, most published slave narratives emphasize kidnapping as the main method of enslavement. Accounts from various regions and periods show that the growth of the Atlantic slave trade caused increased war and conflict, which propelled other forms of obtaining captives to be sold into slavery.

Seeking to emphasize the lived experiences of men, women, and children who were captured and enslaved is not without its challenges. Most existing published narratives were produced by freedmen who were enslaved in West Africa and transported to British North America and the West Indies. Hence, such accounts may not represent the experiences of the majority of enslaved Africans who were captured in West Central Africa and transported to South America, especially

Brazil. Compared with the various enslaved men transported to the British colonies in the Americas who authored slave narratives, just one enslaved African brought to Brazil published a slave narrative, and in it he dedicates only a few pages to his ordeal in Brazilian territory.[3] Similarly, although enslaved women born in the West Indies and North America left published slave narratives, no African-born enslaved woman published an autobiography narrating her experience of enslavement on the African continent. In the pages that follow, then, I seek to fill these gaps by considering the experiences of these neglected figures by combining fragments of their voices from existing written archival documents of the eighteenth and nineteenth centuries.

How People Were Enslaved

Slavery existed before the arrival of the Europeans in West Central Africa and Africa, even though it is hard to determine how widespread the institution was because of the scarcity of information, which is often not available for all regions of the continent. As in many world societies where slavery had existed since antiquity, most enslaved people were outsiders captured during wars.[4] Before and during the Atlantic slave trade, prisoners of war could remain locally enslaved to provide a variety of services, including agricultural work. In West Africa, war captives could be sold to Muslim traders, who transported them across the Sahara to the Maghreb and North Africa, and throughout the Arabian Peninsula to the Middle East.

Painting the complex panorama of enslavement in West Africa and West Central Africa during the four centuries of the Atlantic slave trade is a difficult task. Most of the nearly 12.5 million enslaved Africans who boarded slave ships on the shores of the African continent from the fifteenth century until the middle of the nineteenth century were captured through warfare. Africans recounted how these wars affected their home countries in correspondence, oral and written slave narratives, and visual records. These accounts, as with any source, carry biases. Because in some cases they drew from childhood recollections and were shaped by the context of the abolitionist movement, they frequently provided an idealized image of Africa. Also, most narratives by African-born individuals were neither written by the narrator nor produced in an African language.[5] None of the published narratives of enslaved persons born in Africa were written by women. Also rare are the published accounts by prisoners of war who were subsequently sold into slavery, even though their testimonies survived through archival sources, especially in the nineteenth century, offering a wealth of information to help us understand the processes of enslavement in West Africa. Moreover, even though the majority of enslaved individuals transported to the Americas were boarded on slave ships departing from West Central African ports, including the ports of Luanda, Benguela, Loango, Cabinda, Ambriz, and Malembo, nearly all published slave narratives were written by Africans enslaved in the coastal areas or hinterland of West Africa. Still, existing written sources provide historians with a small window through which they have access to those experiences of enslavement.

During the period of the Atlantic slave trade, through the rise of European rule in Africa at the end of the nineteenth century, until African independences were achieved in the middle of the twentieth century, the current borders of African states did not exist yet. Therefore, like today, African societies and peoples were diverse. In this context, most of the time, persons eligible to be captured, kept locally enslaved, or sold away into slavery were foreign individuals. However, there were exceptions to this rule. Enslaved people taken to the Americas all came from the regions of West Africa, West Central Africa, and Southeast Africa. But on a regional level, men, women, and children captured and sold to European and American merchants were aliens in the societies that traded them into slavery.

In various regions, African populations could be organized in chiefdoms whose structures were based on kinship. Until the nineteenth century, most West African and West Central African populations lived in decentralized societies. But some states were bigger, more complex, and clearly centralized. For example, in regions surrounding the port of Benguela in West Central Africa, this diversity explains why groups that carried distinct cultural affiliations and spoke varied languages raided each other during the era of the Atlantic slave trade.[6] Hence, until at least the middle of the nineteenth century, men and women living on the African continent built their identities along the ethnic lines that shaped their lineages and clans, which is why it would be inaccurate to refer to the existence of a common African identity, an idea that only emerged later in the Americas, as one of the consequences of the Atlantic slave trade, and in Africa, as a response to European colonial rule.

As the Atlantic slave trade evolved, the fate of war prisoners gradually changed. During the sixteenth century, thanks to the support of Portuguese allies, most bondspeople in the Kingdom of Kongo were prisoners captured during wars waged against the Kingdom of Ndongo (a state inhabited by the Kimbundu-speaking Mbundu people, also identified as Ambundu, plural of Mbundu). Kongo also made captives north of its territory, across the Congo River in the Tio Kingdom (also known as the Kingdom of Anziku), a polity that covered the area surrounding the Malebo Pool, in the lower Congo River, which marks the border between today's Democratic Republic of the Congo (south) and the Republic of Congo (north). As shown by one historian, these external sources initially satisfied Kongo's demand for slaves, while protecting freeborn individuals from enslavement.[7] Nevertheless, starting in the last decade of the sixteenth century, freeborn Kongo subjects could also be sold to the Atlantic slave trade for a variety of reasons, including participation in rebellious activities.

Most persons captured in West Central Africa and West Africa who were sent to Europe and the Americas between the fifteenth century and the late nineteenth century were originally outsiders. But the intensification of the commerce in human beings led also to the enslavement of locally born individuals. In the sixteenth century, Portuguese agents obtained slaves from Kongo by participating in local wars as mercenaries.[8] Kongo rulers blamed Portuguese subjects who enslaved freeborn people (including nobles) and sent them to Portugal, São Tomé, and Brazil. As evidence shows, occasionally, the king of Kongo tried, with some success, to ransom these illegally enslaved individuals and bring them back to the kingdom.[9] In 1575, the Portuguese founded Luanda, south of the Congo River, which gradually became a colonial settlement and the largest slave-trading port in West Central Africa. In 1617, the Portuguese established the colony of Benguela. South of Luanda, the colony later became the second busiest slave-trading port in West Central Africa. By the time, the Portuguese engaged in practices like those they had already utilized in Senegambia (as explored in chapter 1), first raiding villages, then kidnapping and enslaving their inhabitants.[10]

European and American Players

The establishment of commercial, cultural, and religious exchanges between Portugal and Africa coincided with European expansion in the Americas. West Central African and West African rulers purchased firearms and gunpowder from the Portuguese. Through their growing contact with African markets, the Portuguese became central actors in the development of the slave trade. As the Atlantic slave trade expanded in the seventeenth century, Portugal was joined by other European competitors such as England, the Dutch Republic, France, Spain, and Denmark. In 1612 the Dutch had already established a fort in Mouri (also spelled Moree or Moure), between Cape Coast and Anomabu. At the end of the sixteenth century, the Dutch attempted to take control of the Elmina castle on the Gold Coast, but it was not until 1637 that they succeeded in defeating the Portuguese and seizing the imponent trading post. Likewise, in the seventeenth century, other European powers began competing to gain access to the gold trade in the region. Brandenburg, Denmark, England, France, and Sweden built fortresses along the Gold Coast, leading the Portuguese to lose their grip on the region. In this period, this new cosmopolitan context increased local elites' growing dependency on European commodities, ultimately negatively altering the balance of power in the region.

Slave merchants from Europe and the Americas also joined the lucrative venture as the slave trade reached a peak in the eighteenth century. Meanwhile, West Central African and West African societies were marked by increasing insecurity, as more and more locally born men, women, and children feared being captured. As in Kongo, existing customary law and legal mechanisms in other parts of West Central Africa protected certain individuals from enslavement, but starting in the eighteenth century, what often prevailed for the Portuguese and local agents was the opportunity to make profits.[11] In this context, local rulers were often unable to protect their own subjects. Outsiders, women, and children were especially vulnerable to enslavement, but they were not the only ones, since male and female slave traders could also be captured and sold themselves. In other words, on the coast and in the hinterland, virtually anybody could be captured and sold into slavery, including fully integrated members of local societies, such as members of the royal elites, mixed-race individuals who spoke European languages, and even caravan workers who worked transporting enslaved persons from the hinterland to the coast.[12]

During the second half of the sixteenth century, the Portuguese explored and waged war against the states and populations located south of the Kingdom of Kongo. They conquered and claimed the Kingdom of Ndongo, north of the Kwanza River, by renaming it the Kingdom of Angola and founding the island of Luanda in 1575. In the first two decades of the seventeenth century the Portuguese claimed the region south of the Kwanza River, named it the Kingdom of Benguela, and found the coastal town of Benguela in 1617. As the Portuguese established these colonies, they imposed treaties of vassalage with existing states in this West Central African region.[13] In general, vassal states agreed to provide the Portuguese administration with soldiers to fight nonvassal African polities, porters for the internal trade, and free passage for itinerant traders crossing their territories. In theory, holding a vassal status protected the state's subjects from being raided. But these agreements were constantly infringed upon. In 1725, as shown by historian Mariana P. Candido, the ruler (*soba*) of Kiambela, a polity located near the Portuguese fortress of Caconda (on the highlands southwest of Benguela, near the source of the Catumbela River) refused to pay taxes to the Portuguese crown, with whom three years earlier he had signed a vassalage treaty. In retaliation, the Portuguese officer in charge led the raid of Kiambela. The operation captured nearly 600 individuals, including the *soba* and members of the royal family. Yet, he sent only 130 prisoners as payment of royal duties to the port of Benguela, which means that most of these captives were for his personal benefit.[14] Local sovereigns whose subjects were seized complained to Portuguese governors, and sometimes they were successful in their demands to release men, women, and children captured in these incursions. Nonetheless, the Atlantic slave trade established an endless cycle of violence. Eventually, in their own turn, the same rulers raided by the Portuguese attacked other polities in order to pay royal duties to obtain commodities such as alcohol and weapons.[15]

Likewise, as examined by historian Roquinaldo Ferreira, a white former slave ship captain named Francisco Roque Souto (who served in Brazil but who may have been Portuguese) led an expedition to conduct free trade with the inland Kingdom of Holo in 1739. But the neighboring Mbundo kingdoms of Kasanje and Matamba (two past Portuguese allies) violently reacted against such interference, which would eliminate their roles as intermediaries in the commerce between Holo and Luanda, by killing traders and seizing enslaved people and goods. In retaliation for this attack, Luanda sent against Matamba an armed expedition composed of thousands of soldiers, including African men, who occupied its capital for more than two weeks and enslaved 1,500 individuals. This military attack increased the flux of enslaved captives to Luanda and forced the queen of Matamba to sign an agreement allowing the Portuguese free access to her territory.[16] Events such as these debunk the notion that Europeans had no participation in the enslavement of individuals sold in the coastal areas.[17]

In the West African coastal area of today's Guinea-Bissau, where decentralized societies prevailed, European traders acquired enslaved Africans from local communities who waged wars or raided each other along the littoral areas of the ports of Cacheu and Bissau. As already discussed, local traders sold captives captured during these operations in exchange for a variety of goods (or rather currencies), such as cloth, gunpowder, and alcohol. But the most coveted commodity in the region of Guinea-Bissau was iron, usually obtained from Mandinka traders. Starting in the sixteenth century, the development of contacts with European traders altered this context. Over the seventeenth and eighteenth centuries, the external trade in the region gave rise to an economic cycle of selling enslaved captives in exchange for iron bars used to fabricate agricultural tools as well as hunting and warfare weapons.[18]

By 1680, the coastal polities of the Gold Coast, Eguafo, Fetu, Asebu, Fantyn, and Agona sought to acquire control of the gold trade routes and markets, and therefore waged wars against each other. Again here, European traders were not mere spectators of these developments. They provoked some of these conflicts by offering particular states money and commodities such as firearms and gunpowder. They also occasionally hired African mercenaries to attack coastal polities and rival European powers.[19] Consequently, between 1690 and 1730, the largest number of captives placed on ships on the Gold Coast to be sold into slavery in the Americas originated from these armed conflicts. But this context changed at the height of the Atlantic slave trade in the last three decades of the eighteenth century. The gold trade, and then the trade in enslaved Africans, created competition and therefore wealth inequalities among local states and also among individuals and groups within communities.[20] Such rivalries fueled warfare and raids among Gold Coast societies, generating more captives for the Atlantic trade.

Starting in the seventeenth century, centralized Akan states emerged on inland Gold Coast's south and central regions. The Kingdom of Akwamu covered part of modern-day eastern Ghana, from today's Akwapim and the region stretching between the Volta River (modern-day Lake Volta) and today's border of Ghana and Togo. The Kingdom of Denkyira developed on the western region of today's Ghana, expanding north toward the modern-day border of Ghana and Côte d'Ivoire, and also along the region's western coastline. But their expansion stopped in the eighteenth century. Akan speakers created the Asante Kingdom, a centralized state whose capital Kumasi was nearly 125 miles from the coast. The Asante conquered Denkyira in 1701 and Akwamu in 1742, thereby becoming the strongest empire on the Gold Coast. The Fante was another heterogenous group of Akan speakers established along the coast during the fifteenth century.[21] This group encompassed migrants from inland and other parts of West Africa who gradually adopted a common identity.[22] As cosmopolitan agents, accustomed to contact with European outsiders, they became the most prominent group in the coastal area of the Gold Coast during the era of the Atlantic slave trade, until the early nineteenth century.

Gold Coast and Dahomey

In the first two decades of the eighteenth century, the Atlantic slave trade from the Gold Coast to the Americas dramatically increased. This growth coincided with the expanding political, economic, and military influence of the Asante Kingdom. Through its military campaigns, the kingdom could exert control on the inland reserves of gold and ivory. War generated prisoners, and conquered polities paid tributes to the Asante in the form of slaves as well.[23] Captured dozens of miles inland, these persons were sold to West African agents who transported them to the coast, where they were sold to Fante intermediaries, who in turn traded them to European merchants.[24] The Asante Kingdom waged wars in the north, west, and southeast regions of the Gold Coast but sometimes also challenged Fante's dominance along the coast. To ensure their role as intermediaries of the Atlantic slave trade, the Fante also built alliances with other states to prevent the Asante from gaining access to the coast. During occasional direct conflicts, the Fante captured Asante prisoners, whom they sold into slavery as well. While the sale of African captives financed further Asante military campaigns, warfare propelled raids and banditry, which also became additional methods to acquire slaves. As in other West African regions, the growing volume of the Atlantic slave trade during this period impacted local communities, who experienced growing insecurity and exposure to violence.

The Fon Kingdom of Dahomey (in today's southern Republic of Benin) emerged in the seventeenth century. As the kingdom expanded, warfare also became its main form of acquiring enslaved individuals. As in the Kingdom of Kongo, the tradition established during the reign of King Wegbaja, who ruled the kingdom from approximately 1645 to 1685, prevented selling Dahomean residents. Rulers enforced this norm so strictly that they even prohibited the sale of female captives who became pregnant during their transit through the kingdom's territory.[25] But despite these restrictions, there are several examples of Dahomean subjects sold into slavery, especially during the tumultuous periods of succession to the throne.[26]

During the reign of King Agaja, Dahomey conquered the Kingdom of Allada in 1724 and the Kingdom of Hueda in 1727. These kingdoms were two epicenters of the external slave trade from the Bight of Benin. These conquests led to an expansion of Dahomey's territory that gave the kingdom access to the Atlantic seaport of Ouidah, once part of the Kingdom of Hueda. In the following years, Dahomey became a central player in the Atlantic slave trade and constantly led military campaigns against its neighbors, including the Mahi in the north, the Ewe in the west, and Yoruba-speaking polities from the northeast (including the Yoruba town of Ketu) to farther east in the Egba region, corresponding to today's region of Abeokuta in Nigeria. Dahomey could keep prisoners of war enslaved locally to perform a variety of tasks such as agricultural work, as well as in professions such as soldiers, healers, diviners, and artisans. Other captives were sacrificed during the Annual Customs. These religious ceremonies (figure 2.1) attended by European agents such as Archibald Dalzel,

FIGURE 2.1. *Last Day of the Annual Customs for Watering the Graves of the King's Ancestors*. Archibald Dalzel, *The History of Dahomey: An Inland Kingdom of Africa* (London: T. Spilsbury and Son, 1793), facing p. 55.

the director of the English fort in Ouidah between 1767 and 1770, were designed to honor royal ancestors and deities of Vodun, a religion characterized by trance, spirit possession, and the worship of numerous gods.[27] The festivities were also occasions for the king to display and distribute material wealth.[28] However, as the Atlantic slave trade evolved during the eighteenth century, most of these captives were sold to European and American merchants established on the coast.[29]

Despite its power, Dahomey domination in the region was constantly challenged. Since the seventeenth century, the Yoruba Kingdom of Oyo had expanded its territory to become the largest and richest West African empire in the eighteenth century. After several incursions in the 1720s and 1730s, Oyo made Dahomey a tributary state in 1748, a position that lasted until 1823, even though Dahomey frequently refused to pay tributes.[30] Royal artisans narrated these conflicts and other wars in appliqué hangings, a technique still employed by Abomey artisans who sell their works to tourists at the palace's courtyards. These military campaigns are also depicted in bas-reliefs displayed on the walls of the eighteenth-century earthen royal palaces of Abomey, the kingdom's former capital city. Produced by artisans in the service of the kings, the rich bas-reliefs depict the emblems of the various rulers as well as warriors fighting and beheading their opponents. For example, one bas-relief on the facade of King Glele's palace shows a Dahomean warrior pointing a shooting gun at another warrior holding a bow. Other bas-reliefs show Daghessou, a mythical personage with an animal head and horns and a human body, holding a firearm and other kinds of weapons. The facade of King Gezo's palace displays bas-reliefs depicting Dahomean women warriors (labeled by European chroniclers as "amazons") carrying prisoners of war on their backs. Another represents horses transporting the head of a neighboring polity's chief. Ultimately, these poignant visual accounts of the wars Dahomey waged against other polities illustrate how warfare was used as a method to acquire slaves in the area during the period of the Atlantic slave trade.[31]

Like any kind of art produced in a royal court, the bas-reliefs were instruments of royal propaganda intended to memorialize the feats of the various Dahomean rulers. Still, these depictions are not just creative renderings. Many existing accounts from the period support these visual representations of violence. European travelogues along with the extensive correspondence between Dahomean and Portuguese rulers from the middle of the eighteenth to the early nineteenth centuries narrated in detail the wars waged by the Kingdom of Dahomey against its neighbors.[32] Sieur Pierre Raingeard, the captain of the French slave ship *Mars* from Nantes, left an account describing the invasion of the Kingdom of Hueda by the Dahomean army.[33] According to what locals reported to him, the Dahomean army captured their people, sold the best individuals, and left the others to die.[34] In addition, after a visit to Savi, the ancient capital of the Kingdom of Hueda situated near Ouidah, Raingeard was led to the beach, where he met the merchants and captains of the French Compagnie des Indes, who told him that in the last fifteen days very few captives were available, leading him to conclude that the war was hindering the slave trade in the region.

Many men and women were captured in the hinterland of the Bight of Benin during the wars that ravaged the region in the eighteenth and nineteenth centuries, even though sometimes the firsthand accounts left by the victims of the Atlantic slave trade are unclear on whether they were captured during a specific war or kidnapped as byproducts of these conflicts. Between 1728 and 1732, the Dahomean army captured the healer Domingos Álvares in the Mahi country at the north. From there he was brought to Jakin (a port near present-day Godomey between Porto-Novo and Ouidah, in the Republic of Benin) and sold into slavery in Brazil.[35] In 1782, a freedwoman named Belinda petitioned the Massachusetts legislature in the newly independent United States to obtain a pension from the estate of her deceased owner, the wealthy loyalist Isaac Royall Jr.[36] Likely written by her attorney, the petition is a third-person narrative recounting Belinda's enslavement in West Africa and her ordeals as an enslaved woman in Antigua and colonial Massachusetts.[37] According to the narrative, she was captured before the age of twelve, placing her enslavement in the 1720s. The petition also described her captors as white men, armed with bows and arrows, who transported her and other people from her country in chains to be sold into slavery on the coast. As we have already discussed, the presence of European raiders in the interior of West African coasts was unlikely in the eighteenth century, as in this region they were usually limited to the coastal areas. The account referring to an idyllic West Africa of "mountains Covered with spicy forests, the valleys loaded with the richest fruits" provided in the petition places Belinda in a location at the banks of the Volta River on the Gold Coast.[38] But the account also mentioned the Orisha, a religion practiced by Yoruba speakers, therefore suggesting that she could have been captured in Yorubaland (where several polities of Yoruba speakers were located) and that her homeland could be near the coast or the hinterland of the Bight of Benin. Therefore, despite the petition's embellished and vague narrative, Belinda, like other young men, women, and children captured in this region to be sold to the Americas, may well have been a victim of a raid or a prisoner of war.

Captured and Sold through Warfare

At the turn of the nineteenth century, the Oyo Empire started to decline as a result of Muslim states that had begun to expand their influence north of its territory over the course of the previous century.[39] Islam gradually penetrated northern Hausa states and Oyo-controlled Yoruba polities. Oyo itself relied on slave labor, and most of its slave workforce was composed of Hausa Muslims who came from the northern areas. As one of the main slave-trading states in the Bight of Benin, Oyo was also facing growing external competition from neighboring polities seeking to sell their captives on the coast. These growing conflicts led the polities and peoples under Oyo's domination, such as Dahomey in the west and the Nupe people in the northeast, to seek their independence and get rid of the heavy tributes imposed on them.

In addition, other conflicts complicated this context. From 1812 to 1822, the Owu War opposed Oyo against Yoruba polities such as Owu, Ife, Ijesa, and Ijebu.[40] In 1817, a major Muslim slave rebellion erupted in Ilorin, by then the capital of a polity subordinated to Oyo. This context contributed to the spread of more unrest across other neighboring city-states. Exerting their authority over the Hausa at the north, the Muslim Fulani created the Sokoto Caliphate and incorporated Ilorin as an emirate in 1823. As a result, Ilorin expanded its influence over other Yoruba polities in the region. Eventually, Ilorin forces invaded and destroyed Oyo-Ile, Oyo's capital city. This convergence of internal and external conflicts in Oyo and its environments eventually led to the collapse of the empire in 1837. As a consequence of these wars, which include other conflicts such as the Nupe Wars (1822–56) and an unsuccessful Muslim insurgence in Borgu in 1835, a huge number of prisoners were sold into the Atlantic slave trade.[41] These men, women, and children were sent to the Americas, mainly to Brazil and Cuba, where the international slave trade remained in operation until the 1860s. Already converted to Islam, most of these war captives were Yoruba and Hausa speakers. None of these men and women published autobiographies as Olaudah Equiano and Ottobah Cugoano did. Still, historians have uncovered their stories since the 1960s.

In the early 1820s, a Muslim man named Abuncare was captured near Oyo-Ile, the capital of Oyo. Sold to slave traders, he was probably forced onto a ship in the West African port of Lagos (also referred to as Onim) and sent into slavery in Salvador, in the Brazilian province of Bahia, where he was renamed Rufino José Maria.[42] Also in Bahia, French naturalist Francis Castelnau interviewed a man named Mohamah (renamed Manuel), who had suffered a similar fate. A Hausa speaker, born in Kano (north of modern Nigeria), he claimed to be a member of the ruler's military forces. In 1842 or 1843, during a military expedition into Borgu, his regiment was attacked. As he tried to escape, his horse was killed by an arrow, and he was captured. With his arms bound, he was walked to Ilorin, sold into slavery, and then transported to Lagos, where he was placed on a ship to Salvador, Bahia.[43]

Like Mohamah and Abuncare, many West Africans were captured in wars and sent to Brazil during the first half of the nineteenth century. These Africans and their descendants kept alive the memories of these wars and their subsequent enslavement. In the 1930s, Martiniano Eliseu do Bonfim, a Candomblé priest born in Bahia, gave an extensive interview to American sociologist Donald Pierson, in which he told the story of Majéngbásán, his African-born enslaved mother, whose Brazilian name was Felicidade Silva Paranhos. In his testimony, he identified her as a Yoruba speaker from Ijesa, a polity west of Oyo in present-day southwest Nigeria. According to him, she was captured by Dahomean warriors, sometime between 1814 and 1823, when she was between ten and fifteen years of age, placing her enslavement during the turbulent decade of wars that led to Oyo's fall. Where she was captured and later sold is unclear, but in another interview with African American linguist Lorenzo Dow Turner, Bonfim mentioned that his mother was first brought to Lagos, and then to the port of Badagry, from which she was transported to Brazil.[44]

Other accounts of enslavement in the same region during the wars fought on the eve of Oyo's collapse were also well documented. Historian Kristin Mann uncovered the stories of three members of the same family captured during the period of the Owu War, between 1817 and 1822. The younger girl, Ayebomi, was sold to a woman in Ijebu, where she lived in slavery for several years and then was redeemed and reunited with her mother in Abeokuta. The other two children, a boy and a girl, were sold into slavery and sent to Brazil. Despite their long Atlantic ordeal, both were able to buy their freedom in Brazil. Shetelu (whose Brazilian name was Francisco Gomes) returned to Lagos in 1844 and Ajatu (whose Brazilian name is recorded as Luisa Ajatu) in 1854.[45] Oral tradition also refers to episodes of enslavement during military expeditions led by Dahomey. According to the oral tradition of the Alaketu Candomblé temple in Bahia, one of its putative founders Otampê Ojaró was a member of the royal family of Ketu, captured by Dahomey soldiers when she was a girl.[46] Other similar stories also remained alive in collective memory of the descendants of enslaved people in Brazil.

Kidnapped and Sold into Slavery

Although most Africans were enslaved through warfare, other men, women, and children were kidnapped and sold into slavery. As early as the sixteenth century, European agents described the growing insecurity associated with the rise of the Atlantic slave trade in the Gambia region. In the *Tratado Breve dos Rios de Guiné do Cabo-Verde*, the Cape Verdean merchant André Alvares d'Almada narrated the intensive slave trade activity in the Gambia River and how the local population took protective measures against slave raids.[47] In this early period, the populations established along the coast often complied with Portuguese enslavers to avoid their own enslavement.[48]

Descriptions of the general atmosphere of insecurity persisted and even increased in the following centuries. Europeans who sailed along the coasts of West Africa during the eighteenth century witnessed how local chiefs and ruling men experienced the vulnerability associated with the Atlantic slave trade. According to British naval surgeon John Atkins, who sailed from Sierra Leone to Cape Lopez (a headland marking the westernmost point of present-day Gabon), robbery and kidnapping were widespread in the region, forcing local chiefs to carry firearms on a regular basis. As in the Upper Guinea, engaging in slave-trading activities was a means to prevent being enslaved: "Each knows it is their Villanies and Robberies upon one another that enables them to carry on a Slave-trade with Europeans; and as Strength fluctuates, it is not unfrequent for him who sells you Slaves today, to be a few days hence sold himself at some neighbouring Town."[49]

Oftentimes, kidnapping, raids, and warfare were intertwined. In their accounts published in the eighteenth and nineteenth centuries, enslaved Africans explained how they were abducted by outsiders when they were children, and therefore more exposed to enslavement. For example, Broteer Furro (later Venture Smith) was victim of a slave raid in 1739, when he was about twelve years old, then was sold into slavery and sent to Rhode Island in colonial North America.[50] In an account published in the late eighteenth century, he described how captors "came to us in the reeds, and the very first salute I had from them was a violent blow on the head with the fore part of a gun, and at the same time a grasp round the neck. I then had a rope put about my neck, as had all the women in the thicket with me. . . . In this condition we were all led to the camp."[51] Although Smith can hardly be identified as a prisoner of war, his enslavement in the hinterland of the Gold Coast has been connected to several disputes, including a Fante assault on Elmina in 1738, an invasion of Little Popo and Ketu by the Kingdom of Dahomey around the same period, and, more likely, a series of conflicts involving the Fante and the Akyem, who ended up occupying the coast of Accra.[52] Like many captive Africans, he was brought to the Gold Coast, but when the coffle (a line of enslaved persons tied together) arrived at the port of Anomabu, the captives were attacked and seized, an episode that evokes the practice described as "panyarring," which "involved the seizure of goods that were considered to be legitimate compensation for a debt."[53]

Likewise, African-born Olaudah Equiano wrote the most famous narrative authored by a formerly enslaved man, describing the social unrest caused by warfare in his homeland of Igboland, in contemporary southeastern Nigeria.[54] Equiano explained the growing insecurity that predominated in his homeland. When adults were absent and children remained outside to play, one child was typically assigned "to get up a tree to look out for any assailant, or kidnapper."[55] Equiano reported in detail his abduction, which took place despite constant surveillance by the members of his community. According to him, he was captured in 1753, when he was still a young boy of possibly seven or eight years old: "One day, when all our people were gone out to their works as usual, and only I and my dear sister were left to mind the house, two men and a woman got over our walls, and in a moment seized us both; and, without giving us time to cry out, or make resistance, they stopped our mouths, tied our hands, and ran off with us into the nearest wood."[56]

Another abolitionist, Quobna Ottobah Cugoano, was also kidnapped during his childhood. Born by 1757 in Agimaque (today's Ajumako), a Fante village of the Gold Coast, Cugoano was captured in 1770, when he was about thirteen years old. In his *Thoughts and Sentiments on the Evil and Wicked Traffic of the Slavery and Commerce of the Human Species*, published in 1787, he explained that despite being aware of the dangers of being captured, he was abducted in the woods, in what seems to have been a raid, as he reported that nearly twenty other children were also taken: "We went into the woods as usual; but we had not been above two hours before our troubles began, when several great ruffians came upon us suddenly. . . . Some of us attempted in vain to run away, but pistols and cutlasses were soon introduced, threatening, that if we offered to stir we should lie dead on the spot."[57] Like others, Cugoano was transported to the coast and sold into slavery in the British West Indies.

Osifekunde was a native of Makun in the Yoruba Kingdom of Ijebu, south of Ile-Ife, in a region encompassed by present-day Nigeria, northeast of Lagos. Born into a family of merchants of royal lineage, Osifekunde used to travel by water, buying and selling European goods. In 1820, when he was in his early twenties, the young man was returning in his boat from Lagos, where he had been purchasing European merchandise. A group of Ijaw (a people established in the mangrove swamps of the delta of the Niger River) pirates stopped his boat and abducted him.[58] Transported to multiple locations along the coast eastern of Lagos, he was eventually sold into slavery and sent to Brazil, where he was purchased by a French merchant. Renamed Joaquim, Osifekunde lived seventeen years in Rio de Janeiro before going with his owner to Paris, where he benefited from the free soil legislation that made him a freedman.[59] Although this case suggests kidnapping as a form of enslavement, the enslavement of Osifekunde is closely associated with the context of the Owu War that disrupted the Yorubaland during the second decade of the nineteenth century, creating opportunities for raids and boosting the slave trade in the region.[60]

Betrayed and Sold

Treachery is also described as one of the ways of capturing people to be sold into slavery. Ukawsaw Gronniosaw narrates how he was enslaved in Borno (modern Nigeria) in the 1720s, when he was about fifteen years old. His narrative is unclear on whether he was a victim of slave traders' treacherous conduct or whether his family handed him over as a pawn to pay a debt. According to Gronniosaw, when he became a young man and started experiencing physical and emotional disturbances, his parents agreed to send him to the Gold Coast with a merchant of ivory who, in his own words, "expressed vast concern for me, and said, if my parents would part with me for a little while, and let him take me home with him, it would be of more service to me than any thing they could do for me."[61] Omitting any references to slave ships, the merchant attracted Gronniosaw by telling him he would "see houses with wings to them walk upon the water, and should also see the white folks."[62] After a long trip by land, once the young captive reached the Gold Coast, he was sold into slavery to a captain of a Dutch slave ship.

The enslavement of Mahommah Gardo Baquaqua, the only known enslaved African brought to Brazil whose written narrative was published, is also associated with treachery. Baquaqua was born in Djougou (northwest of Ouidah in the modern-day Republic of Benin) between 1820 and 1830, and in approximately 1844, he was captured, sold, and sent into slavery to Recife, Pernambuco, in northeast Brazil, where he may have landed in 1845.[63] In his biography, published in 1854, he described the internal conflicts that provoked wars in his homeland and how captives were sold to the Atlantic slave trade: "The kings are continually quarreling, which quarrels lead to war. . . . When a king dies, there is no regular successor, but a great many rivals for the kingdom spring up, and he who can achieve his object by power and strength, becomes the succeeding king, thus war settles the question. . . . Slavery is also another fruitful source of war, the prisoners being sold for slaves."[64]

Baquaqua's account confirms that among royal families, during the period of succession, it was not uncommon to sell members of opposing factions into slavery. Similar to Equiano's narrative, Baquaqua narrated his enslavement as the result of the deceitful behavior of a group of fake admirers, who encouraged him to drink a copious amount of an alcoholic beverage and managed to lead him to a house in a neighboring village where they said a king lived. The following morning, he realized he had been betrayed and sold into slavery. However, in an earlier account of 1847, Baquaqua told that he was "taken captive when a child, while playing at some distance from his mother's door." Then later, in another version, he stated he was kidnapped "while playing truant from school."[65] As Baquaqua's story indicates, enslavement as the result of betrayal is common in slave narratives, travelogues, oral tradition, and historical records, and usually involves alcohol, which was a major commodity with which European traders purchased enslaved Africans.[66]

In West Africa, oral traditions also evoke the use of treachery to enslave men, women, and children. Traditions passed down through various generations and recorded by historians Sandra Greene and Anne C. Bailey each report a horrifying episode that occurred at the Anlo village of Atorkor in southeast Gold Coast in 1856. According to the story, the crews of a group of European slave ships anchored at the shore, supposedly attracted by the local music, and invited a group of drummers to come aboard one of the ships to play for them. The musicians accepted the invitation and boarded the vessel, followed by women and children. To award and celebrate the performance, the European crew gave their African musicians a great amount of alcohol, and the guests were so intoxicated that they failed to notice that the ship was sailing away.[67] Other informants provided Bailey different versions of the same story. In one version, a local chief suggests that the conflict was caused because Atorkor's agents were indebted to Europeans from whom they bought tobacco.[68] Even though Europeans leading a large group of Africans to inadvertently embark on a slave ship and taking them away is rather implausible, Atorkor's story is an expression of the collective memory of the Atlantic slave trade. More probably this story is an amalgamation of several episodes. As we have seen, historical records clearly show that as the Atlantic slave trade increased over the eighteenth century, individuals and entire communities living along the coast feared being captured and sold to slave traders. Although the account suggests that Atorkor's residents were unaware of the dangers of being captured by European enslavers, evidence clearly shows previous cases of Anlo individuals being kidnapped and sold into slavery.[69] Hence, by the mid-nineteenth century, in the final years of the Atlantic slave trade, it would be rather unlikely to find a coastal community on the Gold Coast unaware of these risks. More probably what happened in Atorkor was an episode of *panyarring*, an organized action targeting "a family, kin group, or community, which was held collectively responsible for the debt, crime, or violation."[70] In some cases, individuals seized through panyarring could also end being sold in the Atlantic slave trade market, which may explain why Anlo inhabitants remembered this traumatic story probably as a cautionary tale evoking episodes in which local people were deceived and sold into slavery.

Pawns and Family Members

The custom of keeping free individuals as pawns in slave ships and European forts for the duration of slave-trading transactions was a common practice during the era of the Atlantic slave trade. In certain slave-trading ports in West Africa, such as Anomabu on the Gold Coast, European merchants provided Fante traders with "cloth, liquors, metal wares, beads, weapons, and other goods," which they used to procure enslaved people in the interior. Meanwhile, these Fante agents also offered their own children to European traders, who kept these pawns as collateral either in the forts or aboard their ships, sometimes for several weeks or even months.[71] Still, records of the Royal African Company, the English mercantile company that engaged in the trade of human beings in West Africa starting in 1660, reveal that in the late seventeenth century ship captains also provided European crew members as collateral to African traders.[72] Likewise, as noted by the French officer Robert Durand during the voyage of the slave vessel *Le Diligent*, French slave merchants also offered hostages to local agents east of the Gold Coast.[73] In West Central African ports, European agents also took African men, women, and children as pawns to secure the delivery of human cargo.[74] On the ports of the Loango coast, north of the Congo River, observers at that time reported that local agents provided relatives as collateral to ship captains.[75] When African agents failed to respect the terms of these commercial agreements, these pawns could be sold into bondage. To different extents, Atorkor's story evokes several forms of enslavement, including pawnship and panyarring.

Selling members of the same family was not a significant way to provide captives for the Atlantic slave trade. But there were exceptions. In Dahomey, because there was no consensus on who had the authority to choose the new king, periods of succession to the royal throne were marked by political instability, giving rise to plots involving the mothers and brothers of the aspirant successors. When the new ruler was eventually selected, it was not uncommon that he punished the defeated competitors for the throne, as well as their supporters, by selling into slavery the members of the opposing factions to other neighboring regions or to the Americas.[76] This was the fate of Na Agontimé. She was one of the several wives of King Agonglo and putative mother of the future King Gezo, who reigned Dahomey between 1818 and 1858. Agontimé may have participated in the conspiracy that led to the assassination of her husband, King Agonglo. After a long period of disputes, one of Agonglo's sons, Adandozan, was enthroned. According to oral tradition, once made king, he avenged his father by selling into slavery all Dahomean subjects who allegedly took part in the plot that led to his father's death. Among these individuals was Na Agontimé, who was sold into slavery and sent to Brazil. Despite the lack of archival evidence, Agontimé became a legendary figure in Brazil as the woman who probably introduced into the country the Vodun of Dahomey and founded the Candomblé temple Casa das Minas in Maranhão.[77]

Families also sold their own kin to pay debts and to get rid of undesired family members. These stories not only appear in written archival records but also remained alive in oral tradition. In the early nineteenth century, a Nupe man named Gouye, from Bida (present-day west-central Nigeria), a region also affected by the wars that led to the collapse of the Oyo Empire, was sold by his family and sent into slavery in Rio de Janeiro, Brazil, where he was baptized as Sabino. After purchasing his freedom, Sabino took the last name of his owner, Vieyra, and returned to the Bight of Benin, settling in Ouidah with other former slave returnees. In the early 1990s, one of his descendants explained that Sabino's brothers sold him to the slave merchants, probably because of a dispute related to the family's inheritance.[78] However, in 2005, a younger female member of the family told a slightly different story about her ancestor's enslavement, which was quite comparable to Baquaqua's biographical account. According to her, Gouye was not an ordinary person but the son of a Nupe chief. By omitting any family dispute, she also explained how her ancestor was deceived by his Brazilian friends: "He came with his white horse to see the Brazilian ships that arrived at the coast, they became friends with him, and very gently they made him enter in the ship and the ship departed very gently and he left."[79] Although keeping the idea of treachery, and perhaps because she ignored the full story, this member of the Vieyra family embellished her ancestor's enslavement story by suppressing all traces of violence.[80] At the private level, these embellished accounts allow the descendants of enslaved individuals to cope with the inherited trauma of enslavement. But because these descendants of bondspeople very often still occupy positions of political and economic power in West African societies, when these accounts are disseminated in the public sphere, they are rather intended to conceal the embarrassment associated with the sale of family members into slavery, and also to diminish the role of those who benefited from the Atlantic slave trade. Still, selling relatives into slavery was also the result of the general disorder caused by the Atlantic slave trade. For example, the death of the head of the family usually provoked rivalries. On these occasions, as in the disputes for the throne in the royal families, disagreements related to the division of assets or quarrels regarding who would become the next chief of the family could easily result in selling to slave merchants kinfolk considered to be undesirable or perceived as competitors, even though most enslaved Africans were sold into slavery as the result of warfare and raids.

Existing estimates show that nearly 5.7 million enslaved Africans boarded slave ships from the ports along the coast of West Central

Africa, including the Loango coast.[81] Of all regions of Atlantic Africa, this is the area that provided the largest number of captives to the Atlantic slave trade. Most of them were transported to Brazil. But despite the centrality of West Central Africa, there is no published firsthand account by Africans who boarded in West Central African ports such as Luanda and Benguela.

European agents rarely directly abducted men, women, and children. Yet, some isolated episodes are worth exploring. In 1767, British slavers captured Little Ephraim Robin John and Ancona Robin John, two members of one of the slave-trading ruling families of the Efik city-state Old Calabar (present-day Calabar), a major port on the Bight of Biafra (the coastal area from the Niger Delta to Cape Lopez) during the era of the Atlantic slave trade. Historian Randy Sparks, who studied this case in great detail, has showed that the incident occurred in the context of persisting conflicts between British slave ship captains and opposing African agents in the neighboring ports of Old Town and New Town. The two princes who acted themselves as slave traders were invited to board the slave ship *Duke of York*, one of the seven vessels anchored in the river at Old Calabar, to mediate the conflict between the two parties. As a bloody battle emerged between the British slave traders and the agents of Old Town and New Town, the Robin Johns were made captives. Dragged to the hold of the *Duke of York*, they were sent into slavery in the British colony of Dominica along with other enslaved individuals who survived the massacre.[82] Once in the West Indies, they were sold again to the North American British colony of Virginia, whence they eventually escaped to Britain and finally returned to West Africa.

Since their arrival in West Central Africa, Portuguese agents kept meddling in regional affairs. As late as the early nineteenth century in the hinterland of Benguela, Portuguese and Brazilian officers continued to organize wars, conduct raids, and kidnap people to meet the external demand for African captives. Despite the gradual prohibition of the Atlantic slave trade by various European and American nations starting in the early nineteenth century, the trade to Brazil, Cuba, and even the United States increased on the coasts of West Africa and West Central Africa, consequently amplifying the demand for enslaved people. Between 1808 and 1862, following the abolition of the British slave trade, ships illegally transporting enslaved Africans to the Americas or other African destinations were intercepted mainly by the British Royal Navy. These apprehensions led to the emancipation of approximately 175,000 enslaved Africans of the total of 2.8 million transported during this period. These men and women went before courts that recorded their testimonies, creating registers providing information about how they were captured and enslaved.[83] By 1850, in Sierra Leone, German missionary Sigismund Wilhelm Koelle, who worked for the Church of Missionary Society, interviewed 179 formerly enslaved persons, who according to estimates were captured in their homelands between 1795 and 1847, then sold into slavery in Africa or the Americas.[84] As in the previous century, most of these "liberated" Africans and also Koelle's interviewees were enslaved through warfare. Still, several testimonies highlight stories of individuals who were kidnapped, traded by their relatives or superiors, or sold to pay debts contracted by family members, or who were enslaved through judicial process because of robbery or adultery. These cases illustrate that members of various African societies could temporarily give away relatives as collateral for a loan or credit, a practice known as *pawnship*. Although these arrangements were intended to be temporary, as the slave trade increased, a growing number of pawned persons could be simply sold into slavery, therefore breaking customary law.[85]

No One Was Safe

Most enslaved Africans brought to the Americas during the era of the Atlantic slave trade were captured through warfare. Although mechanisms of enslavement varied from region to region and evolved over the four centuries during which the Atlantic slave trade remained active on the coasts of West Africa and West Central Africa, existing published and unpublished narratives reveal several similarities.

Enslavement always involved violence. With the expansion of the Atlantic slave trade and as African societies increasingly depended on selling enslaved persons, warfare also intensified and pushed the growth of other forms of acquisition of slaves, such as raids, kidnappings, pawnship, and panyarring. Stories of enslavement in slave narratives, accounts recovered from archival documents, interviews, and oral traditions are often embellished and recurrently omit detailed descriptions of violence. But whether in the Upper Gambia, the Bight of Benin, the Gold Coast, the Bight of Biafra, or West Central Africa, these stories carry many elements in common. They show how insecurity became widespread and how men, women, and children of diverse social positions and ages could become the target of African and European enslavers seeking to harvest the profits of the lucrative slave trade.

CHAPTER 3

Trading in Humans

The loud noise of Dahomean soldiers breaking the gate of his town woke up Oluale Kossola. He could hear the attackers yelling and running fast to invade his compound. In a matter of minutes, they killed the king and captured the men, women, and children who were not able to reach the forest and escape. Banté, the town where he spent his childhood, was destroyed. Taken by Dahomean soldiers, nineteen-year-old Kossola was lined up and bound into a coffle with other townspeople.[1] As the sun rose that morning, the new captives marched southward tied together under the hot sun of the dry season. After a harrowing journey on foot that lasted nearly three weeks, Kossola was brought to the port of Ouidah, where, along with 109 other captives, he was put on the slave ship *Clotilda* that sailed to Alabama in the United States on May 11, 1860.[2] When Kossola (alias Cudjo Kazoola Lewis) was captured, transported to the coast, and eventually sold into slavery to the United States, the Atlantic trade in captive Africans to the Americas had been in motion for more than three centuries.

We only know Kossola's story because he survived this ordeal. In 1927, when he was eighty-six years old, he provided an account of his enslavement to African American author and anthropologist Zora Neale Hurston. Kossola is among the last men enslaved in West Africa and brought to the United States. His enslavement occurred late in the nineteenth century, when the Atlantic slave trade from

Africa to the Americas had already been made illegal by most nations. Nevertheless, his late experience has certainly much in common with that of thousands of Africans, making it a useful point of departure to understand how African agents controlled the slave trade in ports such as Anomabu on the Gold Coast, Ouidah in the Bight of Benin, and Cabinda, Loango, and Malembo in West Central Africa. In all these coastal regions, European merchants often competed to obtain a monopoly on the trade. By contrast, in West Central Africa, the Portuguese alone dominated Luanda and Benguela, the first and the third busiest African ports, respectively, during the period of the Atlantic slave trade. Based on travelogues by European officers, journals of ship captains (or shipmasters), correspondences, and slave narratives, this chapter explores the social, economic, and cultural dimensions of the interactions between African rulers, middlemen, and local women, and a variety of European and American agents who visited or were permanently established in trading posts, forts, and castles along the coasts of West Africa and West Central Africa.

Drawing on examples from these two broad regions, in this chapter I explore the human dimension of the long journey endured by the captives transported from the hinterland to the coast. While men, women, and children waited to be loaded onto slave ships traveling to ports in the Americas, they were kept for several months in a variety of temporary and permanent coastal structures such as forts, barracoons, and other provisional constructions used to detain enslaved individuals. In some regions, as caravans transporting enslaved people reached the coast, ship captains gradually purchased men, women, and children and transferred these captive Africans to the holds of slave ships, where once again they could wait for several weeks.

I also highlight that the economic engines of the trade in human beings extended from the coast to the hinterlands. Currencies such as iron bars, textiles, tobacco, alcohol, firearms, and gunpowder, as well as luxury products such as some European and Asian cloth, hats, and a variety of objects, shaped the commercial transactions between European, American, and African traders and local agents. These exchanges oriented the dynamics of the Atlantic slave trade between the various ports of Upper Guinea, the Gold Coast, the Bight of Benin, the Bight of Biafra, the Loango coast, the vast region labeled as Angola in West Central Africa, and the various parts of the Americas (see map 1 at the beginning of the book).

Harrowing Journeys to the Coast

For the men, women, and children taken captive in the hinterland of West Africa and West Central Africa, the ordeal was just starting. Kidnappers, raiders, and soldiers immediately started transporting these captives through land and water pathways of preexisting trading routes, traversing many regions until they reached the coast. Once captured, enslaved people could stay confined in permanent structures such as coastal forts or barracoons between six and twelve months, with an average waiting period of three months, before being boarded on slave ships.[3] During this long process, these men, women, and children were gradually transformed into living commodities. Unfortunately, up until the late eighteenth century, only a handful of firsthand accounts about these harrowing journeys from the interior to the coast have survived.

The two individuals who captured Olaudah Equiano and his sister in the interior of the Bight of Biafra in approximately 1753 knew in detail the path they needed to take to get to the coast.[4] For several days, the two young captives and their West African kidnappers walked all day and stopped only during the night to eat and sleep. Despite his scattered memories, Equiano explains how during his journey to the coast, they crossed through many villages and towns, and they saw other people but only from a distance.[5] Such journeys, however, were not totally unknown to him, as in his own narrative he mentions neighboring traders who traded European items such as firearms, gunpowder, hats, and beads in exchange for "odoriferous woods and earth" as well as "salt of wood-ashes."[6] According to him, these traders

> always carry slaves through our land. . . . Sometimes indeed we sold slaves to them, but they were only prisoners of war, or such among us as had been convicted of kidnapping, or adultery, and some other crimes which we esteemed to be heinous. This practice of kidnapping induces me to think, that, notwithstanding all our strictness, their principal business among us was to trepan [trick] our people. I remember too they carried great sacks along with them, which, not long after, I had an opportunity of fatally seeing applied to that infamous purpose.[7]

The slave trade on the coast and in the region of present-day Angola in West Central Africa operated in similar ways. Yet, unlike West African ports of the Bight of Biafra, the Bight of Benin, and the Gold Coast that were controlled by African polities, starting in the late sixteenth century the Portuguese founded Luanda and Benguela, whose harbors became the two largest West Central African ports. In these areas, there was a web of decentralized networks of itinerant traders who traveled between the coast and the hinterland. Agents based in the ports of Luanda and Benguela, and sometimes also in Portugal and Brazil, provided these traders with imported items such as Indian and European textiles, firearms, and gunpowder, as well as *cachaça* or *aguardente* (a Brazilian distilled spirit made of sugarcane, locally known as *gerebita* or *jeribita*). Sometimes these itinerant traders were based in markets controlled by the Portuguese administration in Luanda. But very often they entered the backlands, where they sold these commodities on credit.[8] And from these same communities, caravan traders obtained captives, enslaved through various means, as discussed in chapter 2. Yet, as the caravans moved from inland to the coast, captured Africans resisted enslavement by attempting to escape, fighting, and even killing their abductors.[9]

Equiano was separated twice from his sister during the long journey to the coast. He passed through the hands of various traders as well. Aware he was moving west, he gradually understood how far he was from his hometown. During this voyage toward the coast, he remained several days with a family of Igbo speakers like himself. At one of these multiple stops, he was sold again for 172 "little white shells."[10] These cowrie shells (originated in the Maldives Islands in South Asia) were introduced on the African continent by Muslim traders through the Near East or the Indian Ocean via caravan trades that crossed the Sahara as early as the eleventh century. First recorded in Arabic sources in the fourteenth century, in the sixteenth century, the Portuguese started transporting cowries by sea around the Cape of Good Hope.[11] Between the sixteenth and the nineteenth centuries, cowries became the major form of currency used in West Africa and West Central Africa (where they were known as *nzimbu*). During the eighteenth century, observers who visited Ouidah reported the use of cowries as currency.[12] Likewise, French slave ships that sailed to Ouidah in the eighteenth century purchased captives using cowrie shells.[13] Cowries were imported in Upper Guinea, the Gold Coast, the Bight of Benin, the Bight of Biafra, and Angola, even though in some of these regions cowrie shells were not domestically used as currency but rather transported to the interior, where traders used them to purchase enslaved people and other commodities.[14]

Captured on the Gold Coast in 1770, Cugoano was led to the coast along with other children. As they did with Equiano, the kidnappers stopped at many places during the long walking journey. As days passed and Cugoano gradually lost hope of being able to ever return home, the traces of the eighteenth-century trade with Europeans appeared as they approached the coastal area: "When next morning came, I asked for the men that brought me there, and for the rest of my companions; and I was told that they were gone to the sea side to bring home some rum, guns and powder."[15] Like in Equiano's experience, as Cugoano approached the coast, he reports the presence of white individuals: "Next day we travelled on, and in the evening came to a town, where I saw several white people, which made me afraid that they would eat me, according to our notion as children in the inland parts of this country."[16] His fear of being eaten reveals how the Atlantic slave trade gave rise to the circulation of legends about cannibal white men.[17] In these stories, slave merchants who took away African people metaphorically ate them. The blood of their bodies was transformed into wine, their brains converted into cheese, the ashes of their burned bones transmuted into gunpowder. In this allegory, white men would purchase newly enslaved Africans with the very commodities extracted from enslaved bodies.[18] Cugoano's account of his reaction to the presence of these outsiders also confirms that on the Gold Coast, West African agents controlled the inland slave-trading routes and slave-trading posts. As discussed in chapter 1, Europeans were restricted to the coastal areas in this region of West Africa, where they had been established since the second half of the fifteenth century.

In the Gambia River region, Europeans had to regularly negotiate permission with local rulers to build fortresses to conduct their affairs on their land.[19] On the Gold Coast, European powers were allowed to construct permanent trading posts, including castles and fortresses, as the Portuguese did when they built the Elmina castle in 1481 and then a wooden trading station in Cape Coast in 1555. Gold continued to dominate in the Gold Coast external trade during the entire seventeenth century. In 1652, the Swedish African Company built in Osu (today's Accra), the Fort Christiansborg, which the Danish purchased one decade later. In 1653, the Swedes also built a timber fort in Cape Coast. Reconstructed by the English in 1663, this building became known as the Cape Coast Castle, one of the most important European trading posts on the Gold Coast during the period of the Atlantic slave trade. (The castle still stands today and has been visited by tourists and many international authorities such as the former US president Barack Obama.) As the trade in enslaved Africans to the Americas became the dominant commercial activity in the region, these castles (originally conceived for the gold trade) became the European headquarters of the Atlantic slave trade. Upon his arrival on the coast, Cugoano was first kept in an unidentified fort and then was imprisoned at the Cape Coast Castle, where he described his experience of confinement with other captives in one of the dungeons: "I was soon conducted to a prison, for three days, where I heard the groans and cries of many, and saw some of my fellow-captives."[20] Like him, many other West Africans transported by the British, the Dutch, and the Danish to the West Indies were imprisoned in the castle's dungeons during the eighteenth century.

No Way Back

During these long journeys between the hinterland and the coast, captive Africans resisted their enslavement. Occasionally they attempted to escape from coffles, but most often they were unsuccessful. Fulani Muslim warriors enslaved Samuel Ajayi Crowther in Osogun, a town located northwest of Lagos (in present-day Nigeria) in 1821, when he was about thirteen years old. Reaching the coast took nearly fourteen months, as Crowther changed owners several times, traded first for a horse and later for currencies such as rum and tobacco.[21] During this long journey, he saw many "grandmothers, mothers, children, and cousins, [who] were all led captives. . . . The aged women were to be greatly pitied, not being able to walk so fast as their children and grandchildren."[22] It was when he arrived on the coast that he "received, for the first time, the touch of a White Man, who examined me whether I was sound or not." Describing how men and boys were bound together "with a chain of about six fathoms [12 yards or about 11 meters] in length, thrust through an iron fetter on the neck . . . and fastened at both ends with padlocks." Crowther underscores the sentiment of anger among these captives who in vain resisted the horrible conditions of their imprisonment that lasted about four months before being embarked: "The men sometimes, getting angry, would draw the chain so violently, as seldom went without bruises on their poor little necks; especially the time to sleep, when they drew the chain so close to ease themselves of its weight, in order to be able to lie more conveniently, that we were almost suffocated, or bruised to death, in a room with one door, which was fastened as soon as we entered in, with no other passage for communicating the air than the openings under the eaves-drop."[23] Crowther's experience of confinement anticipated what he would experience in the hold of a slave ship heading to the Americas.

Joseph Wright was captured in approximately 1826. In his short autobiography, he identifies himself as Egba Alake, member of a people occupying the Egba region of southern Yorubaland, north of Lagos, in today's Nigeria. Like many Africans captured in this region during the two first decades of the nineteenth century, his enslavement was part of the conflicts associated with the fall of the Yoruba Oyo Empire, including the Owu War that led to the invasion of Egba towns, as discussed in chapter 2. A coalition of Ife and Ijebu forces besieged Wright's hometown. Hunger came next, and eventually the attackers took control of the city, destroying it and violating, enslaving, and killing his people: "The enemies satisfied themselves with little children, little girls, young men, and young women; and so they did not care about the aged and old people. They killed them without mercy. . . . Abundant heaps of dead bodies were in the streets, and there were none to bury them."[24]

Wright was sold and moved to other cities several times. During this long journey, he witnessed the state of destruction of the neighboring areas. The invaders dug dead bodies from their graves to take their clothes and other valuable belongings. Many prisoners of these multiple attacks were sold into slavery. There were also slave markets along the way, where "many hundreds of slaves, we were put in rows, so that we all could be seen at one view by the buyers; and in about five hours another trade man came and bought me." At some point, Wright was boarded on a canoe. After sailing all night, they stopped at another market, where the trader purchased more people: "At the time of evening, the canoe was loaded with slaves and we sailed for his home directly. We arrived about twelve o'clock in the night. The town where we had just arrived, by name of Ikko [Lagos], is the place where the Portuguese traded." Eventually, the human cargo was brought to a Portuguese man who, after examining their bodies, sent selected captives to a slave pen: "When we entered into the slave fold, the slaves shouted for joy for having seen another of their countrymen in the fold."[25] Eventually, Wright was sold to the Portuguese, who paid for him with "tobacco, rum, clothes, powder, gun, cutlasses, brass, iron rods, and jackey [*jaki*], which is our country money."[26]

Many other men, women, and children experienced similar fates. Mahommah Gardo Baquaqua, as discussed in chapter 2, was captured in Djougou, in the Bight of Benin in 1844. Like other captives who left accounts telling how they were enslaved and gradually moved to slave ports in the coastal areas until reaching the port of Lagos, Baquaqua was sold several times. In the long route to reach the coast, he passed through villages and inhabited forest regions, sometimes with "no regular road," and "crossed several large streams of water."[27] Although reporting that his captors treated him well during the day, they "tightly kept" him during the night to prevent him from escaping.[28]

After stopping for several days in various places, traveling during the day and resting in the woods at night, Baquaqua eventually arrived in Abomey, the capital of the Kingdom of Dahomey. According to him, gates surrounded the city, and a "toll was demanded on passing through." Although he did not see the royal palaces, he was told that "the king's house was ornamented on the outside with the human skulls."[29] Finally, Baquaqua was led to Ouidah, where he saw a white man for the first time. Along with other captives, he was transported by canoe through the lagoon to be embarked at a nearby port, probably Little Popo. Because during this period the slave trade from the Bight of Benin to the Americas had been banned, this measure was aimed to avoid attracting attention from the British squadron patrolling the coast.[30] Before being embarked, the group was put into a slave pen. A man holding a whip oversaw them, while another one branded them with a hot iron. Sold and branded, Baquaqua and his companions of misfortune were then "chained together, and tied with ropes round about our necks, and were thus drawn down to the sea shore."[31]

After being captured in Banté, north of Kingdom of Dahomey, Oluale Kossola (alias Cudjo Kazoola Lewis) was moved to the coast, even though his account suggests that the Dahomean army first headed east.[32] On his way to Ouidah, he passed through Abomey, which, like Baquaqua, he described as a city surrounded by gates. Kossola also reported on the "house of the king" and mentioned that "de house de king live in hisself, you understand me, it made out of skull bones. . . . Dey got de white skull bone on de stick when dey come meet us, and de men whut march in front of us, dey got de fresh head high on de stick."[33]

In Dahomey, vanquished enemies were decapitated during wars and their heads carried as trophies. As early as in 1727, the British ship captain and slave merchant William Snelgrave witnessed the Dahomean army returning from a battle and carrying heads of dead prisoners as trophies of war.[34] This was not a fabulation by European observers. King Adandozan, who ruled Dahomey between 1797 and 1818, sent a letter to Prince Regent Dom João Carlos de Bragança of Portugal in 1810, in which he described a campaign against the Mahi country, when his army killed people and took off the jaws of his enemies "to display at the doors of my house, and nailed them to wood sticks."[35] Skulls of defeated enemies were symbols of power intended to intimidate not only Dahomey subjects and neighboring polities willing to challenge Dahomey supremacy but also external agents from Europe and the Americas. Bulfinch Lambe, Robert Norris, Richard Burton, and Frederick E. Forbes, who sojourned in Abomey between the eighteenth and nineteenth centuries, reported that kings purchased heads and that human skulls not only were employed to mount the thrones of Dahomey's rulers but also tiled some rooms of the Abomey palaces.[36] The display of human skulls certainly shocked British visitors. But the practice of displaying trophy heads on spikes was far from exclusive to Abomey and existed in European cities such as London and Paris during the seventeenth and eighteenth centuries.

After staying three days in Abomey, Kossola and the other captives were led to Ouidah, the main port of embarkation of the Bight of Benin, controlled by the Kingdom of Dahomey and its agents. In Ouidah, they were placed in a barracoon "behind a big house," which by then was probably the building of the Portuguese fort São João Batista da Ajuda as by the time of Kossola's enslavement the other

European forts were abandoned. With its construction concluded in 1727, the fort was located approximately two miles from the beach. The three-week period of Kossola's confinement in the barracoon was not very long. Although enslaved in 1860, when the slave trade for the Americas had been made illegal and dramatically declined, Kossola also reported the existence of other slave pens: "Dey got plenty of dem but we doan know who de people in de other pens." Like Cugoano, Crowther, and Baquaqua, it was during his waiting period at this coastal barracoon that Kossola saw white men for the first time "and dass somethin' he ain' never seen befo'." In this last period of confinement before boarding the slave ship, the slave traders and other agents scrutinized the bodies of enslaved men, women, and children: "Dey make everybody stand in a ring—'bout ten folkses in each ring. De men by dey self, de women by dey self. Den de white man lookee and lookee. He looke hard at de skin and de feet and de legs and in the mouth. Den he choose."[37]

Left Behind

Dahomean soldiers killed on the spot captives considered unfit to be sold. But the crowded coastal barracoons with horrible hygiene conditions also exposed the weak and poorly fed men, women, and children to diseases. Many died prior to embarkation. This is why the inspection of captive Africans, as Kossola's description shows us, was a crucial stage of the various operations performed before their sale to European and American merchants. African traders attempted to conceal any illnesses and physical problems by carefully preparing enslaved Africans for sale. They shaved the heads of male captives to conceal gray hair, anointed their bodies with palm oil to disguise any wounds, and dressed enslaved women with several layers of cloth to make them attractive. In Ouidah, surgeons of slave ships violated the bodies of captive Africans by scrutinizing their external genital organs in search of signs of sexually transmitted disease. In Anomabu, on the Gold Coast, African captives were also inspected in detail. Ultimately, ship captains decided which captives were loaded onto the ship and which captives were left behind.[38]

British slave ship captain John Newton, the author of the popular hymn *Amazing Grace* who in his later years became an important voice in the abolitionist movement, wrote a detailed journal of his voyages as a ship captain to the Windward Coast (namely, the western coast of Africa stretching from Cape Mount in modern-day Liberia's northern corner to Assinie on present-day Côte d'Ivoire's eastern border). During his first voyage (1750–51), aboard the vessel *Duke of Argyle*, he was offered an enslaved woman while anchored in Sierra Leone by Portuguese traders stationed there. But because she was "long breasted," he refused to purchase her as well as several other enslaved women who were later offered to him, showing how "attractiveness" was an important criterion in the selection of enslaved women to be sold to the Americas.[39] Still, the fate of captives who were rejected for sale remains unclear. In Ouidah, like in Cape Coast, unsold Africans may have been killed or locally traded.[40]

Although Kossola refers to men and women in his late account of enslavement and transportation to the coast, the proportion of enslaved men and women who boarded slave ships on African shores and those who disembarked in the Americas to toil on plantations and in urban areas varied according to regions and during specific periods. But despite these variations, an average of two enslaved men to one enslaved woman forcibly crossed the Atlantic Ocean in the hold of slave ships during the era of the inhumane trade. This imbalance was caused by two main factors. Although it is true that slave merchants from Europe and the Americas procured men because they believed they were better fit to perform agricultural labor, African agents valued women, who tended to be kept locally to perform agricultural activities or sold in the trans-Saharan slave trade that prized women to serve as enslaved concubines.[41] Nonetheless, existing data suggest that in the last twenty-five years of the seventeenth century, 50 percent of the enslaved Africans who were forced to board slave ships in West Central Africa were women. After 1807, when the British slave trade was abolished, children younger than fourteen years old corresponded to nearly 40 percent of the enslaved Africans transported to the Americas.[42]

Competing European Powers

Slave merchants remained stationed on the coast, waiting to embark enslaved Africans into slave vessels heading to ports all over the Americas. But a variety of factors such as internal conflicts and the fact that local slave traders wanted to increase the price of captives could directly impact the offer of African captives. For example, the British slave ship *Sandown* remained anchored in Rio Nunez (present-day Guinea) for several weeks, but very few captives were available. Its captain, Samuel Gamble, assiduously reported this scarcity in the ship log entries. On November 18, 1793, he deplored that there was "no Prospect of any Slaves coming down."[43] As ship captains waited for weeks for the gradual arrival of enslaved persons on the coast, the crew and African captives were exposed to disease. Therefore, it was not uncommon for various crew members, including carpenters and ship mates, to succumb to illnesses during the trading period on the African coasts before the beginning of the Atlantic crossing to the Americas. In the many weeks during which his vessel remained on the coast purchasing African captives in the early 1750s, Newton reported in his journal the death of carpenter Andrew Corrigal and chief mate John Bridson.[44] Insurrections and escapes could also occur during this long waiting time.[45]

The terms of the European presence along the coast varied depending on the period, the region, and specific ports. As explored in chapters 1 and 2, although the Portuguese launched the transportation of enslaved Africans to the Iberian Peninsula and then to the Americas in the fifteenth and sixteenth centuries, their presence in the Atlantic coastal areas of West Africa and West Central Africa was followed by other European powers. In the early seventeenth century, Dutch merchants started trading on the Loango coast, the coastline north of the Congo River, in West Central Africa. This region, unlike the colonies of Luanda and Benguela, was never controlled by the Portuguese. Yet, in these early exchanges the Dutch basically sold a rich array of cloth to the polities of the Loango coast, in exchange for ivory and a red wood (locally known as *takula*) used to produce red hues in the textile industry.[46]

The Dutch Republic and England also secured their presence on the Gold Coast. During the seventeenth and eighteenth centuries, the Dutch and the English, respectively, built one lodge and two forts in Anomabu, making it the busiest slave-trading port of the Gold Coast. In this region, most captives were acquired through warfare led by the Asante during the eighteenth century. But the trade in enslaved people at the Gold Coast seaports such as Elmina, Cape Coast, Accra, and Anomabu remained controlled by a coalition of several Fante polities until the early nineteenth century. Only in 1807 did the armies of the Asante Kingdom conquer the Fante-speaking coastal area, in the same year of the British abolition of the slave trade, which also marked the launching of several anti-slave trade policies in the region.[47]

England, Sweden, and Denmark initially engaged in the gold trade on the Gold Coast. But as the colonization of the Americas evolved, European powers increasingly turned to Atlantic Africa to purchase enslaved people to work in the booming sugar industry of Brazil and the West Indies. In the eighteenth century, Portuguese, British, and French slave traders marked their presence in the Bight of Benin, where they erected fortresses. Along with the Dutch, these same European powers were also active in the trade of enslaved Africans at the ports of the Loango coast such as Cabinda, Malembo, and Loango. Here, during the eighteenth century, rivalry among European merchants was so pronounced that none of them were ever successful in obtaining the monopoly on the trade in enslaved Africans. European merchants were not allowed to build permanent buildings to conduct their trade on the Loango coast, as they were on the Gold Coast and the Bight of Benin.[48] Therefore, ship captains and their crews erected provisional structures that mainly served as warehouses. Ship captains and their crews avoided sleeping offshore by often spending the night in their own vessels. Basically, slave vessels were transformed into floating barracoons.[49] These precautions were in part motivated by fear of catching diseases, but also because these seamen were scared of being attacked by local agents and other European merchants. Still, following the rise of the Saint-Domingue Revolution in 1791 and the British abolition of the slave trade in 1807, French and British slave traders stopped their activities in the region. For most of the nineteenth century, the trade in enslaved Africans on the Loango coast remained in the hands of Portuguese and Brazilian slave merchants.[50]

As the Dutch Republic, England, France, Denmark, and Sweden entered the Atlantic slave trade starting in the seventeenth century, they formed chartered maritime companies to regulate and centralize their commercial exchanges with Africa and the Americas. Portugal also developed similar ventures, but unlike those of its European counterparts, Portugal's attempts to create chartered companies were short-lived. Thus, private merchants, many of whom were Brazilian-born individuals, kept the control of the slave trade between Atlantic Africa and Brazil. Although changing over time and varying from region to region, the Atlantic slave trade followed two systems shaped by the winds and sea currents that moved clockwise in the North Atlantic and counterclockwise in the South Atlantic.[51]

In the North Atlantic system, encompassing North America, the West Indies, Western Europe, and West Africa, the so-called triangular trade prevailed. In this model, shaped by clockwise winds and currents, slave ships outfitted in European and American ports sailed to Africa. They carried a variety of goods used as currencies to purchase enslaved Africans, who were then transported to the Americas, whence these same ships then transported raw products back to European ports.[52] A slave voyage in the North Atlantic could start in any of the several many major European slave ports such as London, Liverpool, Bristol, Lancaster, Nantes, Bordeaux, La Rochelle, or Le Havre. During the seventeenth century, but especially in the eighteenth century, slave ships outfitted in European ports with cloth, iron bars, copper, alcohol, gunpowder, firearms, and manufactured goods sailed to the African ports of Gorée Island, Saint-Louis, Anomabu, Cape Coast, Ouidah, Loango, Malembo, and Cabinda, where they purchased captives. This human cargo was then transported to British North America, and later to the independent United States, as well as to the various British and French colonies in the West Indies.

In the South Atlantic, slave voyages were shorter not only because the distance between South America and Atlantic Africa was shorter but also because of the favorable counterclockwise winds and ocean currents. Here, for the most part, slave voyages did not follow thc traditional triangular model. Instead, slave merchants sailing to West and West Central Africa often departed from Brazil and not from Portugal. Portuguese and Brazilian slave merchants navigated from the Brazilian cities of Rio de Janeiro, Salvador, and Recife, the three largest slave ports in the Americas, mainly to African ports such as Ouidah, Benguela, and Luanda.

The rise of these two Atlantic systems and the development of the Atlantic slave trade were deeply associated with imperial expansion. European rivalries in Atlantic Africa mirrored the balance of power in the Americas. Over the course of the seventeenth century, the North Atlantic and South Atlantic systems became the battleground of conflicts among European empires that sought to control the slave trade from Africa to the Americas and to monopolize the burgeoning and profitable sugar industry. Spain entered the Atlantic slave trade in the sixteenth century as well. Initially, the crown sold licenses (*asientos*) to private foreign individuals or compagnies who transported enslaved Africans to its colonies in the Americas. But this dynamic changed by the end of the century.[53] In 1578, the Portuguese ruler died in the battle of Alcácer-Quibir against the Muslims of North Africa. His uncle, who succeeded him on the throne, died two years later, without leaving any successor. This crisis eventually led to the victory of one of the candidates to the Portuguese throne, the Spanish king Philip II. As a result, between 1580 and 1640, the Portuguese and the Spanish crowns were unified and Portugal obtained the Spanish *asiento*. During this period Portugal carried approximately 289,000 enslaved Africans to the Spanish Americas, whereas nearly 188,000 Spaniards migrated to the region.[54] When the crowns were separated in 1640, the slave trade to New Spain decreased and continued to decline during the eighteenth century when, after massive extermination, a larger Indigenous workforce became gradually available.

The union of the Iberian crowns negatively impacted the relations between Portugal and the Dutch Republic. Although the Dutch were the major commercial partner of the Portuguese in Brazil, they were enemies of Spain, against whom they rebelled by declaring independence in 1588 during the Eighty Years' War (1568–1648). These conflicts led the Dutch to start a series of actions to take control of Portuguese domains in the Americas and Africa. In 1624 the Dutch occupied Salvador, then the Brazilian capital, which by that time was the second largest sugar-producing captaincy of the Portuguese colony. In 1625 the Portuguese expelled the Dutch, but in 1630 the Dutch successfully seized Recife, the capital of the captaincy of Pernambuco and Brazil's first sugar producer. These conflicts reverberated in Africa as well. In 1637 the Dutch took control of the Elmina castle on the Gold Coast. In 1641 they also invaded Luanda and eventually controlled the coast of the Portuguese colony of Angola in West Central Africa.[55] Eventually, in 1654, the Portuguese expelled the Dutch from Brazil. As a result, the Dutch migrated on a massive scale to the West Indies, where their colonies expanded.

European rivalries transformed commercial exchanges during the seventeenth century. This increasing competition among European colonizers in the Americas coincided with the rise of the tobacco industry in Virginia, where by the middle of the seventeenth century, being a Black person already meant carrying the legal status of slave. During this same period, European powers secured their position in the West Indies. In 1655 England seized Jamaica, and by 1659 France occupied the western part of Hispaniola that became the colony of Saint-Domingue. Spain kept the eastern part of Hispaniola (Santo

Domingo, present-day Dominican Republic), Cuba, and Puerto Rico. France and England seized a big part of the West African slave trade. Meanwhile, the Luso-Brazilian slave traders continued to control the slave trade south of the Congo River in the West Central African ports of Luanda and Benguela. As European empires fought to take over the new colonies in the Americas as well as the slave markets in Africa, the Atlantic slave trade intensified. In the seventeenth century, an estimated number of 1,875,600 enslaved Africans were transported to the Americas, and in the eighteenth century, nearly 6.5 million African captives boarded slave ships heading to the various regions of the Americas.[56] In these two centuries, more than 3 million enslaved Africans were exported to the Portuguese colony of Brazil alone.

The competition among European traders in West African and West Central African ports continued to impact the operations of the Atlantic slave trade until the early nineteenth century, when Britain and France banned their respective slave trades. Although in most regions of West Central Africa and West Africa, local rulers remained in control of the territory and the trade, their relations with European traders often remained asymmetrical. West Central African and West African rulers purchased guns and a variety of goods from the British, French, Dutch, and Portuguese. The access to these weapons allowed them to wage war against neighboring states, which, in part, accelerated the cycle of acquisition of war captives to be sold into slavery.

Currencies and Goods to Purchase Enslaved People

European and American slave ships headed to Africa, carrying a great variety of commodities from Europe, Asia, and the Americas that were used as currencies, including gold, sugarcane brandies, wines, tobacco, textiles, firearms, and gunpowder. Slave ship cargoes also included foodstuffs such as manioc flour and beef; manufactured items such as glassware, metalware, apparel, hats, pipes, knives, and spears; and luxury articles such as fine textiles, swords and other insignias of power made of silver and gold, as well as clothing items. Some of these items were intended to be given as gifts to African rulers, traders, and other intermediaries to obtain particular favors during their transactions. These presents, which in many cases operated as a customs fee, were an important element of the commercial exchanges between Europeans and Africans during the era of the Atlantic slave trade.[57] Vessels heading to Africa also transported food and water for the crew members and an assortment of shackles and chains to restrain the human cargo to be transported to the Americas. Although the bilateral trade predominated in the South Atlantic system, some voyages followed the classic triangular model. Vessels carrying goods also departed from Portugal and sailed to Africa to trade in enslaved Africans and then crossed the Atlantic Ocean again to reach Brazil.[58]

By the seventeenth century, Portuguese and French merchants purchased enslaved Africans from West African and West Central African traders by paying them with bundles containing various goods, conceived as a unit. In these regions, each set comprising specific products in predetermined sizes was referred to as a "piece" and later as a "head," a clear reference to the enslaved person to be acquired with the bundle of merchandise.[59] In each port controlled by a given polity, there was also a particular protocol before initiating the trade, which included exchanging messages, providing gifts, and scheduling meetings. On the coast and inland, the Atlantic trade in enslaved Africans relied on intermediaries who acted as domestic traders and brokers. African agents, stationed on the coast to regulate the trade, occupied particular offices and were at the service of their rulers. These middlemen were in charge of giving permission to Europeans to start the trade. They also collected taxes, received gifts, and provided other agents with goods allowing them to procure enslaved individuals to be sold on the coast.

Some observers from Europe saw Africa as having no currencies. Their accounts often described the commercial exchanges during the era of the Atlantic slave trade as barter, in which Europeans acquired enslaved Africans with baubles. For example, Samuel Robinson, a young British sailor whose correspondence was published in the nineteenth century, stated in a letter of April 1800, that "there is no money circulating in Africa, all business is transacted by way of exchanging one commodity for another."[60] This idea is obviously inaccurate. As historian Toby Green has explained, even before the rise of the Atlantic exchanges, Africans had been using a variety of currencies in the trans-Saharan trade.[61] Therefore, the trade between African and European agents consisted of complex and monetized operations. In other words, European traders never purchased enslaved Africans with random items. They procured African captives by paying local agents with commodities such as iron bars, cowrie shells, and various types of cloth in colors and patterns that were appreciated and widely employed as currencies in the ports of West Africa and West Central Africa, regions that also produced their own textiles used as currencies earlier before the rise of the Atlantic slave trade.[62] Textiles in specific sizes transported in European ships were initially imported from China and India, but by the late eighteenth century, Portugal, France, the Dutch Republic, and Britain had developed their own imitations.[63] Either textiles or iron bars had also a use value. Blacksmiths could transform iron bars into a variety of weapons and agricultural tools. Tailors could also convert cloth strips into pieces of clothing.[64]

Other forms of currency included lengths of copper (called "Guinea rods") and *manillas* made of brass and copper-lead amalgam in various sizes, shapes, and weights.[65] Each region had its preferred currencies, which changed over time as the Atlantic slave trade developed.[66] Coral, amber, crystal, and especially glass beads were also used as currencies. Although there is no consensus about where these beads originated in Africa, a huge number of varying trade beads from West Africa, Asia, and the Mediterranean were uncovered in two West African archaeological sites dated between the ninth and tenth centuries in Mali and southeastern Nigeria earlier, before the rise of the Atlantic slave trade.[67] Sixteenth-century written records also refer to the use of beads in commercial exchanges between Europeans and Africans. As they were greatly appreciated, Europeans also started manufacturing them in a variety of colors and designs. In Dahomey, oral tradition that still survives today refers to glass beads as symbols of wealth. They were believed to derive from the excrement of the snake (*dan*), a sacred animal (and deity) symbolizing the kingdom.[68]

The tastes and specific preferences for particular commodities and luxury products by African rulers and their subjects shaped the Atlantic slave trade. Both in the North Atlantic and the South Atlantic systems, slave merchants from Europe and the Americas transported valuable goods that responded to the demands of African traders and inland communities. For African rulers, the display of refined imported objects was a powerful statement of their economic, political, and symbolic power. Take the example of the rulers of the Kingdom of Dahomey who during the eighteenth century developed a preference for a Brazilian third-rate tobacco cultivated in Bahia.[69] This predilection propelled Portuguese and Brazilian traders to settle in the ports of the Bight of Benin such as Ouidah, where they purchased enslaved Africans with Bahian tobacco. In the region of Luanda and Benguela, local rulers and their dependents also appreciated Brazilian *aguardente* introduced in the region in the seventeenth century, with which slave merchants acquired enslaved Africans.[70] Local agents and their subjects knew in detail the goods they were obtaining and protested when they were cheated. African agents complained when merchants sold substandard merchandise such as firearms, for example. In 1777, Jacques Guestard, then the director of the French fort in Ouidah, refused to pay compensation to King Kpengla for defective muskets that allegedly "punctured, killed, and injured" his subjects. By refusing to pay an indemnity, Guestard claimed to protect the interests of the French nation and slave merchants because such claims could become the norm.[71] In the early nineteenth century, the king of Dahomey also complained that the storekeeper of the Portuguese fort was watering down the barrels of *aguardente*.[72]

On the Gold Coast, the intensification of the Atlantic slave trade in Cape Coast and Anomabu during the eighteenth century gave more power to Fante intermediaries who increasingly demanded that British slave merchants provide them with luxury items.[73] Likewise, in the ports of the Loango coast as well as in Luanda, these local agents accumulated more wealth. In some cases, their growing affluence threatened the political power of members of the local nobility, creating divisions in their home societies.[74] Similar offices also existed in Dahomey. In Ouidah, its main slave port, the king of Dahomey appointed middlemen holding the title of *tegan* and later that of *yovogan*, meaning "chief of the white men."[75] These individuals were "governors" of sorts, who negotiated the terms of the slave trade with the Portuguese, the French, and the English, who, starting in the eighteenth century, established fortresses in Ouidah. Occasionally, these local agents could enter into conflict not only with the king of Dahomey but also with Brazilian merchants and European governors posted in these forts.[76]

In the ports of Senegambia, such as Gorée Island and Saint-Louis, slave traders also included the offspring of enslaved and free African women of various ethnicities with Portuguese, French, British, Irish, Alsatian, and American men, as well as other locally born African men and women.[77] In Accra, on the Gold Coast, locally born free African women married Danish traders stationed at the Fort Christiansborg.[78] Likewise, in Cape Coast, local women who engaged in unions with British men also became crucial agents in the Atlantic slave trade.[79] In Luanda and Benguela, the two Portuguese colonies and main slave ports of West Central Africa, many intermediaries who settled on the coast were Portuguese and Brazilian individuals and their descendants.[80] Itinerant traders who went inland to procure slaves in caravans composed of hundreds of individuals also included Africans and Luso-Africans.[81] In these ports as in the various parts of Atlantic Africa where these unions occurred, African women became trade partners of their European spouses. Their African-European children also became important players in the Atlantic slave trade, especially during the eighteenth and nineteenth centuries. Yet, these alliances were not always based on harmonious exchanges. As already discussed in chapter 2, despite being traders, as the slave trade intensified during the eighteenth century, local agents and even royals were never totally protected against being captured by raiders and sold into slavery themselves by their opponents, especially in periods of greater instability.

A Complex Trade Shaped by Both Sides of the Atlantic Ocean

Captive Africans were submitted to harrowing journeys before boarding slave ships. Their rare surviving accounts provide details of how they were sold multiple times along the path between their homelands and the Atlantic coast. Their narratives highlight the horrible time they spent confined in forts and barracoons while waiting to be sold. Although most of these stories are based on childhood recollections, the information they provide coincides with existing written records that show the organization of the trade as based on preexisting routes. A variety of African representatives dominated these inland networks and the trade on the coast. Moreover, except for the ports of Luanda and Benguela, controlled by the Portuguese during the entire period of the Atlantic slave trade, other ports in Atlantic Africa were not controlled by Europeans but remained under the control of local African rulers and agents. Hence, European merchants not only needed to obtain their permission to establish forts and conduct the trade but also had to pay customs fees and provide gratuities in the form of gifts to get preferred treatment from African traders. These transactions were shaped by these human exchanges and by the goods traded by these agents. Depending on periods and regions, African rulers and traders demanded specific commodities as well as manufactured and luxury goods. These items responded to their own specific needs and tastes as well as those of the populations living inland who also developed preferences over the many decades of the Atlantic slave trade.

Exchanges between both sides of the Atlantic Ocean favored the creation of connections between regions producing specific goods in the Americas and African consumers in specific zones of the Atlantic coast. As a result, enslaved people from these regions were exported to the same areas of the Americas where the goods sent to these African regions originated. This is the case of Bahian tobacco, greatly appreciated by African rulers in the Bight of Benin, that led to the transportation of great numbers of African captives from the Bight of Benin to Bahia. As enslaved Africans reported in their own accounts, African traders transported far into the interior of West Africa and West Central Africa gunpowder, firearms, and other manufactured products introduced in the region by European merchants, fueling the cycle of violence introduced with the Atlantic slave trade. In most African regions, European merchants remained restricted to the coast. African rulers and their representatives relied on wide networks of traders and caravans that went far into the interior to acquire captives with a large array of products to be sold on Atlantic Africa seaports. Many of these traders were African-born men and women. But among them there were also the descendants of European men and African women, who nurtured alliances that persisted since the arrival of the first Europeans in the continent. Competition often marked the interactions among European merchants in Atlantic Africa. The exchanges between these same merchants with African men and women also oriented the development of the slave trade to the Americas.

CHAPTER 4

Atlantic Crossings

Mahommah Gardo Baquaqua could see the slave ship from the beach. Around him were many other men, women, and children. How long they had been there it was hard to say, but they were brought from various regions of the hinterland of the Bight of Benin. Naked, weak, and desperate, they waited to be boarded on canoes that would lead them to the slave ship. West of Ouidah, probably in the port of Little Popo (today's Aného), where these events were unfolding in approximately 1845, the surf was dangerous, as many observers at that time noted. Baquaqua witnessed it with his own eyes, when the powerful surf overturned one of the canoes carrying thirty-one captives. Just one person survived.[1] After several weeks confined in coastal warehouses, it was now time for Baquaqua and his fellow captives to board the floating tomb, or *tumbeiro*, as Portuguese and Brazilian slave traders had referred to slave ships since the seventeenth century.[2] They were scared, although neither Baquaqua nor his captive companions knew exactly what was waiting for them. But now they realized that there was no way back. If they survived the lengthy voyage across the Atlantic Ocean, a new long ordeal would start.

Many historians have tried to explain the Middle Passage, the term referring to the voyage of slave ships carrying enslaved persons across the Atlantic Ocean from Africa to the Americas. Their descriptions account for the number of enslaved people who were forcibly boarded onto slave ships, the tonnage of the vessels, their various compartments, the goods they transported, the winds and sea currents that drove the ships during the Atlantic crossing. Ship manifests and journals of slave ship captains (or shipmasters) and surgeons (or ship doctors) provide other scarce information about these deadly voyages marked by death, disease, sexual violence, and also slave uprisings. But neither the descriptions of the physical features of slave ships nor the crew members' accounts capture the experience of physical and emotional pain lived by enslaved Africans during these crossings. No firsthand account, document, memoir, novel, poem, motion picture, or painting will ever be able to fully capture the horrors of the Middle Passage. But along with the narratives left by enslaved Africans such as Baquaqua, Olaudah Equiano, Quobna Ottobah Cugoano, Samuel Ajayi Crowther, and Joseph Wright, existing traces of this tragic experience provide us with a window through which we can glimpse what enslaved men, women, and children went through during these Atlantic crossings.

Although the Portuguese led the first slave voyages to the Iberian Peninsula in the fifteenth century, it was after the arrival of Christopher Columbus in the Americas in 1492 that the trade in enslaved Africans intensified. Overall, though, more than 80 percent of enslaved Africans were transported to the Americas in the holds of slave ships between 1700 and 1850. Therefore, most existing accounts of slave voyages cover the eighteenth and nineteenth centuries. Drawing from multiple accounts documenting the Atlantic crossing aboard slave vessels, this chapter discusses this dreadful segment of the slave trade from Africa to the Americas. I explore the Middle Passage in the North Atlantic system, in which slave ships sailed from Africa to North America and the West Indies. Because nearly 50 percent of enslaved Africans who were forcibly transported to the Americas during the Atlantic slave trade were brought to Brazil and not to the United States, I also focus on the experiences of crew members and captives who crossed the South Atlantic region. Although the conditions of transportation of enslaved men, women, and children varied in the North Atlantic and the South Atlantic systems, and changed over time, the systems also bore many similarities.

Unlike their French and British counterparts, Portuguese and Brazilian slave merchants left scarce records of their slave-trading journeys. Most of what we know about their voyages dates to the first half of the nineteenth century and results from the British anti-slave-trading activities starting in 1807. As a result, it is hard to examine these journeys without bias because even though most enslaved Africans were captured in West Central Africa and transported to Brazil, the majority of the surviving records that tell us the horrors of these Atlantic crossings belong to slave vessels that sailed from West Africa (and sometimes from the Loango coast in West Central Africa) to the British and French colonies in the West Indies and North America. The slave vessel that carried African human cargo across the Atlantic Ocean is the quintessential link in a long chain of violent actions that attempted to transform human beings into things. Despite being regarded as assets, African men, women, and children were deliberately killed during the dreadful journeys on board slave vessels. Contradictorily, they were treated as both economically valuable and yet, at a human level, utterly, brutally dispensable.

The Slave Ship

Africans captured in the interior of West Africa and West Central Africa were transported through land and water pathways until they reached the coast. After arriving in slave ports such as Cape Coast, Ouidah, and Luanda, they were kept confined in castles, barracoons, warehouses of all sizes, fortresses, and other provisional structures for weeks or months, waiting to board slave ships that crossed the Atlantic Ocean to reach the Americas. The oceanic stage of this ordeal that started with enslavement in Africa could last between thirty-five days in the South Atlantic system to as long as ninety days if the vessel crossed the North Atlantic Ocean.[3] Not even those Africans who experienced this tragedy could ever fully describe in written words, oral narratives, or visual images the experience they went through in the hold of slave ships.

Crewmen who sailed from Europe and the Americas to the Atlantic coasts of Africa were quite familiar with the vessels that transported African captives across the ocean. Many of them made the same trip several times, even on board the same slave ships. But to the victims of the Atlantic slave trade, slave vessels were monstruous structures. When captive Africans boarded the slave ship, they entered an unknown stage of their forced migration.

Some men, women, and children, captured not far from the coast, may have heard accounts about big ships that came through the sea. And perhaps they had even seen slave vessels, as stories such as the ones collected at the Anlo village of Atorkor in the Gold Coast, explored in chapter 2, suggest. But for those captured in the interior of Atlantic Africa, the first view of the ship was imprinted in their memory for many years.

In his recollections, Equiano wrote that "the first object which saluted my eyes when I arrived on the coast was the sea, and a slave-ship, which was then riding at anchor, and waiting for its cargo." This image was followed by fear and terror: "This filled me with astonishment, which was soon converted into terror, which I am yet at a loss to describe."[4] Quite often, the first time enslaved African captives saw the ships that would carry them to the Americas was on the eve of being forcibly embarked.

Like Equiano, Cugoano reported how terrified he was when he first caught sight of a slave ship, and how the vessel's image was intertwined with the view of fellow naked men, women, and children chained together. Their movements were followed by the distressing sound of "rattling of chains, smacking of whips, and the groans and cries of our fellowmen."[5] Decades later, Baquaqua and other enslaved men, women, and children from many parts of the Bight of Benin, "chained together, and tied with ropes round about our necks," were brought to Ouidah and then transported through the lagoon to a neighboring port to be boarded on the vessel.[6] Then, from the beach, he saw for the first time the slave ship that would transport him to the Americas. Similar to Equiano and Cugoano, he was frightened and distressed: "I had never seen a ship before, and my idea of it was, that it was some object of worship of the white man. I imagined that we were all to be slaughtered, and were being led there for that purpose. I felt alarmed for my safety, and despondency had almost taken sole possession of me."[7]

In several African ports, enslaved people were transported by canoe to be forcibly embarked onto slave vessels. In Ouidah and other ports of the Bight of Benin, slave ships remained anchored nearly one mile away in the sea. Still, as depicted in written narratives and visual images of the period, the surf was so strong that canoes carrying enslaved individuals to the slave vessel commonly were overturned, drowning enslaved men, women, and children.[8] Like Baquaqua's, the harrowing journey across the Atlantic Ocean for Oluale Kossola (alias Cudjo Kazoola Lewis) started in the Bight of Benin. Upon arriving at their destination, he and the other captive Africans were unchained and stripped of their clothes before being taken in several smaller boats to the beach nearest where the slave ship was anchored.

Historian Marcus Rediker defined the slave ship as a "combination of war machine, mobile prison, and factory."[9] These vessels were loaded with cannons that could be used especially against other competitors active in the slave trade business. Divided to confine and separate enslaved men, women, and children from crewmen, the floating prison transported a variety of chains, handcuffs, shackles, iron collars, and branding irons.[10] Armed with weapons and instruments of restraint, crewmen guarded African captives, punishing those who refused to comply. Continuing the process that started with their capture, transportation to the coast, and imprisonment in filthy depots along the shores of West Africa and West Central Africa, during the long crossing of the Atlantic Ocean in these prison vessels these men, women, boys, and girls were gradually transformed from human beings into property.

Multiple kinds of ships were used to transport enslaved Africans to the Americas. The ships operating both in the North Atlantic and the South Atlantic systems could be as small as eleven tons and as big as several hundred tons, even though the average tonnage was approximately two hundred.[11] Various models of vessels were used in the Atlantic slave trade, such as the yacht, brig, brigantine, snow (or snauw), bark, frigate, and sloop, as well as "the ship," which was the generic term referring to any vessel but also corresponded to the three-masted and largest model of vessel used in the inhumane trade. Bigger vessels could also carry smaller boats that would trade along the coasts of the West Africa and West Central Africa, gradually transporting captives to the slave ship. Ultimately, any vessel could be adapted and transformed into a slave ship.

During the entire period of the Atlantic slave trade, the number of captives carried in slave ships varied according to several factors, including the size of the vessels and the voyages' distance. Vessels sailing from West Central Africa to Brazil and the West Indies were usually larger, whereas ships sailing from West Africa to North America tended to be smaller. But these patterns changed over time and according to the specific developments of the trade. In many cases, the small size of the vessels was also adapted to enter shallow African harbors.

Slave vessels could transport between a few dozen up to more than one thousand enslaved people in a single voyage. In 1664, slave traders identified as residents of the Kingdom of Angola petitioned the Portuguese king to request the nomination of two agents to inspect vessels departing from Luanda. According to the petitioners, transporting many more captives than the vessels could carry with low supplies of water was provoking the "death of so many souls."[12] Although these demands were not immediately heard, by the late seventeenth century, Portugal and other European nations started enacting legislation limiting the number of enslaved Africans to be transported in slave vessels according to their size.[13] In 1684, Portugal issued a decree regulating the transportation of enslaved Africans from Angola, as well as São Tomé and Cape Verde, to Brazil.[14] In the law's preamble, the king recognized that African captives were packed together so tightly in the slave vessels that not only did they die during the voyage, but those who arrived alive disembarked in "wickedly pitiful" condition. Organized in twenty-one chapters, the Portuguese decree stated the responsibilities of the captain and other officers in charge of the slave vessel. One chapter of the decree determined that the space of each vessel should be measured, and the number of captives transported in each section of the ship should allow enough space to accommodate each captive. Another chapter established that each ship should carry enough water and food to feed the captives three times a day and provide forty-seven ounces of water to each captive daily.[15] These measures were intended to avoid dissemination of disease and preserve the human cargo doomed to be sold in the Americas. But these restrictions were never fully respected. Water was nearly always in short supply and captives ate only two times a day. Shipowners and captains constantly overloaded slave vessels any way they could, by cheating the inspection process and even by boarding more enslaved children to fill out remaining spaces.[16] For example, annual statistics of slave exports from Luanda to Rio de Janeiro from 1723 to 1771 show that slave vessels transported on average 396 enslaved persons, including children.[17]

In Europe, slave-trading vessels were built in the regions surrounding slave ports such as Liverpool, Bristol, London, Nantes, Bordeaux, La Rochelle, Le Havre, Amsterdam, Copenhagen, and Lisbon. European nations occasionally imported vessels built by their European competitors. In North America, most slave ships were built in Rhode Island, Massachusetts, Connecticut, New York, and Maine.[18] Shipbuilding activity also existed in Maryland, Virginia, and South Carolina, as well as in Cuba and Bermuda in the West Indies.[19]

In Brazil, shipbuilding activity had existed in Salvador since the sixteenth century and expanded during the eighteenth and nineteenth centuries. Yet, in the second half of the eighteenth century, Brazil's capital moved from Salvador to Rio de Janeiro. Hence, the new capital became the first Brazilian slave-trading port and a hub of shipbuilding activity.[20] But until 1808, when the Portuguese royal court moved to Rio de Janeiro to escape the invasion of Napoléon Bonaparte's army, most ships active in the Luso-Brazilian slave trade were built in

Portugal. During the first three decades of the nineteenth century, the high demand for ships to operate in the Atlantic slave trade also led Brazilian traders to charter and purchase ships from other nations such as Britain and the United States.[21] Whether in North America or in Brazil, enslaved Africans as well as freemen and bondsmen born in the Americas composed a considerable part of the shipbuilding workforce.

Crew Members on Slave Ships

The profiles of crew members of slave ships operating in the North and South Atlantic systems bear a few similarities. The typical age of crew members of eighteenth-century British slave ships could vary between fifteen and forty-two, but the average age was midtwenties. For example, the crew of *Peggy*, which sailed from London to an unspecified port in Africa in August 1748, was composed of thirty-nine men coming mainly from port cities. But the crew list also included men from various parts of Britain such as England, Wales, and Scotland as well as from Ireland, Sweden, the Netherlands, Genoa, and West Africa, who sailed between Europe, Africa, the West Indies, North America, Asia, and the Mediterranean.[22] Aboard French ships sailing from La Rochelle, most mariners came from the surrounding regions. But after 1783, following the end of the American War of Independence, as noted by Jean-Michel Deveau, a significant and growing number of crew members on La Rochelle's slave vessels came from Spain, Britain, Italy, Prussia, Savoy, Ireland, the Netherlands, and even the United States, as well as many more French regions. As in British slave vessels, few French mariners identified as Black.[23]

The average age of crew members aboard vessels transporting African captives to Brazil between the two last decades of the eighteenth century until the end of the slave trade was similar to that of eighteenth-century British slave vessels.[24] Only a few crew members on these ships came from other parts of the world, such as India, Macao, Cambodia, Chile, Uruguay, and Cuba. According to Jaime Rodrigues, based on a limited sample of 179 crews of vessels transporting enslaved

Africans to Brazil between 1780 and 1863, 70 percent of the crew members were born in Portugal, especially in Lisbon. This same study suggests that during this period, sailors born in Brazil, who were either Black or white, enslaved or free, made up approximately 12 percent of the crews. Meanwhile, approximately 17 percent of these seafarers were born in West Central Africa and West Africa in the regions of the Bight of Benin, as well as Angola and Benguela, where the Portuguese had a monopoly on the slave trade.[25] Drawing on a different set of documents, one historian showed that most sailors aboard slave ships heading to Rio de Janeiro were enslaved men.[26] Based on these two sets of data, it is possible to conclude that in contrast with British and French slave ships, in most Brazilian and Portuguese slave vessels, crew members were Black individuals.

Likewise, enslaved Black seamen outnumbered free white seamen on Portuguese slave vessels.[27] For instance, another sample of 230 enslaved sailors in Portuguese slave ships between 1760 and 1825 shows that approximately 80 percent of the crew members were born in Africa, mostly in Angola, followed by the Bight of Benin and Benguela. Overall, the regions of origin of these mariners suggest that, most of the time, ship captains hired African-born mariners from the regions where they conducted their slave-trading activities.[28] In the case of Portugal, and consequently its colony Brazil, this trend shows the two regions' deep connections with African slave-trading ports such as Luanda, Ouidah, and Benguela, whence the vast majority of enslaved Africans sent to the Americas were boarded. As Portuguese and Brazilian vessels transported the largest number of enslaved Africans to the Americas, they needed more crew members to conduct a greater number of slaving voyages. African-born crew members knew the regions where these slave ships were trading. They also knew the local agents, their languages, and their customs, and consequently they were also familiar with the languages and cultures of enslaved Africans they transported in these ships.

Jorge, a man born in Ouidah in the late eighteenth century, was one of these sailors. When he was a young man, he was captured, transported, and sold into slavery in Bahia, Brazil. His owner, Joaquim Carneiro de Campos, rented him to work as a sailor in the schooner *Emilia*.[29] Jorge's case was not unique. For example, enslaved sailors José Majojo and Francisco Moçambique were owned by the slave merchant Antônio Gonçalves da Luz. Brought to Rio de Janeiro from Mozambique in the early decades of the nineteenth century, both men were crew members of the Brazilian slave ship *Dois de Fevereiro* that was captured by the British Royal Navy in 1841 while illegally transporting human cargo from Benguela to Rio de Janeiro.[30]

On the slave-trading route connecting Salvador (Bahia) to West Africa, most mariners were enslaved and freedmen, born either in Africa or in Brazil.[31] Ads in one early nineteenth-century newspaper of Salvador show announcements selling enslaved sailors both locally born and born in West Central Africa and West Africa.[32] An even larger number of ads announce enslaved sailors for sale in Rio de Janeiro's newspapers during the first three decades of the nineteenth century. For example, an ad announced the sale of an enslaved sailor born in West Central Africa, identified as Benguela, who wanted to be sold to be employed in the slave trade.[33] Moreover, several other announcements searched for enslaved mariners who ran away. Therefore, crews of slave ships of all nations transporting enslaved Africans to the Americas included African-born and American-born Black sailors, either enslaved or free, even in small numbers.[34]

Freedmen also worked aboard slave ships. Consider the case of Antônio Narciso Martins da Costa. He was born in the Bight of Benin and sent into slavery in Salvador (Bahia). Once emancipated, he became a slave ship captain. At least one of his voyages is well documented. In 1813, he traveled from the Bight of Benin as a captain of the vessel *Pistola* that transported 366 enslaved Africans to Bahia.[35] Likewise, João de Oliveira, an enslaved sailor and Yoruba speaker, was captured when he was a boy in the early eighteenth century and sold into slavery to a slave merchant in Recife, Brazil. After making the voyage between Brazil and Atlantic Africa several times, Oliveira eventually was able to purchase his own freedom. But once emancipated, he settled at the

Bight of Benin and became a slave merchant as well.[36] Still, unlike enslaved Africans such as Equiano and Cugoano, existing documents give us little information about how these enslaved and freedmen, who were captives during the Middle Passage, experienced their journeys across the Atlantic Ocean multiple times transporting African captives.

In the North Atlantic and the South Atlantic system, freeborn and freed Africans also boarded slave ships as free travelers, sometimes alone and sometimes with their former owners. Their voyages as free passengers in slave vessels show that the connections between Africa, Europe, and the Americas during the era of the Atlantic slave trade also made possible the circulation of free African-born individuals who kept personal and commercial ties with both sides of the Atlantic Ocean.[37] For example, Marie Baude, an African woman, boarded the French frigate *Galathée* as a passenger to meet her husband in Louisiana. The vessel departed from Gorée Island in Senegambia carrying 400 enslaved men, women, and children, but as disease hit during the voyage, only 260 arrived alive in New Orleans in 1728.[38]

Most slave merchants were men born in Europe and the Americas. However, there were white women deeply involved in the trade of enslaved Africans. In the French port of La Rochelle, Marguerite Bouat, Marguerite Boucher, Anne Busquet, and Marie-Madeleine Denis represented slave-trading companies during the eighteenth century.[39] In the early nineteenth century Margaret Schutt in Charleston, South Carolina, and a woman known as "Mrs. Johnson" from Philadelphia both organized slaving voyages to the coasts of Africa.[40] There were a few cases of African-born women among slave merchants and shipowners, especially in Luanda and Benguela. These mixed-race women had privileged ties with European merchants and were often the daughters of Portuguese and Brazilian men, by local African women. Their existence and activities attest to the long-lasting presence of Luso-Brazilian traders in the slave-trading ports south of the Congo River. The trade in human beings led by their forebears made them wealthy and provided them with social mobility. Among these women was Florinda Joanes Gaspar, an African female merchant who lived in Benguela and kept businesses on both sides of the South Atlantic world, and who boarded the brigantine *Maria*, which arrived in Rio de Janeiro in 1836, transporting 444 enslaved persons.[41] African women also owned slave ships. Among the most notorious slave ship owners was Dona Ana Joaquina dos Santos Silva. Born in the West Central African port of Luanda in 1789, she became a powerful businesswoman. Between 1824 and 1832, she acquired no fewer than four ships to transport enslaved Africans to the Americas. In 1827, one of her vessels, the brigantine *Boa União*, sailed from Luanda to Pernambuco in Brazil, transporting 449 enslaved persons.[42]

The number of crew members, including ranked officers, petty officers, and sailors, in a slave ship varied according to its size. Each officer usually had one or two mates to replace him in case of death and disease. Typical slave ships had a captain. Other members included a first and second mate, a surgeon (or ship doctor), a carpenter, a boatswain, a gunner or armorer, a cooper (barrel maker), a cook, ten to twelve seamen, a few landsmen, and two shipboys. Larger ships would have additional mates, mates for the doctor and various skilled workers (especially carpenter and gunner), and additional seamen and landsmen. The carpenters oversaw the ship's structure and transformed ordinary merchant vessels into vessels to transport human cargo. During the voyage from American or European ports to the coasts of Africa and while anchored in African ports, carpenters built the main deck's barricade, along with the bulkheads and wooden platforms of the lower deck, where enslaved men, women, and children spent the night.[43] Carpenters also built temporary structures ashore, in regions such as the Loango coast, where Europeans were not allowed to establish permanent trading buildings.

Ship Captains and Surgeons

There was a hierarchy, and wages corresponded to these various ranks of crew members. The captain represented the merchant, and he hired the crew, procured provisions, attended the loading of the cargo, and conducted all business of the voyage, including purchasing the captives in Africa. He controlled the navigation, tended the compass, ran one of two watches, and gave the working orders. Many ship captains made more than one voyage to the coasts of Africa. A sample of 932 captains who traveled from Bahia to Africa from 1690 to 1760 shows that nearly 8 percent made five or more voyages. Still, 66 percent of these seamen traveled from Bahia to Africa only one time, suggesting that during this period mortality and morbidity rates among captains may have been significant.[44] Unfortunately, unlike their British and French counterparts, captains of Portuguese and Brazilian slave vessels left few journals and logbooks that could provide more details about their journeys across the Atlantic Ocean.

In the eighteenth-century British slave ships, few captains seemed to have owned shares of their vessels or the human cargos they transported.[45] When the French slave vessel *Le Diligent* left the Bight of Benin in 1731, its captain Pierre Mary personally owned twenty-six captives on board.[46] In the South Atlantic system, ship captains were often also slave merchants, who outfitted their ships and also owned most of the African captives they transported.[47] In the first half of the nineteenth century, experienced Brazilian and Portuguese ship captains sailing between Bahia and the Bight of Benin became the owners of slave vessels. Inocêncio Marques de Santa Anna, for example, owned the vessels *Juliana*, *Santa Anna*, *Flor d'África*, and *Flor d'América*. João Cardozo dos Santos, also based in Bahia, was the captain of the brigantine *Henriqueta* in six voyages to the African coasts and also of the schooner *Terceira Rozália*, and he later became the owner of the schooner *Umbelina*. The Portuguese-born captain Manoel Cardozo dos Santos served as captain on board the slave vessels *Victoria* and *Cerqueira*, and he later became the owner of the brigantines *Heroína* and *Tibério* and of the schooner *Maria Thereza*.[48]

In general, ship captains had one or two mates. In Portuguese and Brazilian vessels, these officers were called *pilotos* (pilots), whereas in French slave vessels, the mate of the ship captain was referred to as *seconde capitain* (second captain). Ranked just below the captain, they assisted and replaced him in case of death. One of the mates commanded a watch. Mates were also in charge of the security, making sure that the enslaved persons were under control, that they were fed, and that they stayed healthy. In Britain, sailors boarded slave ships for a variety of reasons, and several mariners reported having been recruited by crimps, deceitful labor agents.[49] Forced or not to work on board these vessels, they were submitted to mistreatment, physical punishment, and exposure to fatal illnesses. Being a relative of a slave merchant or having served as a surgeon aboard a ship offered the best chances to become a slave ship captain in British vessels.[50] For example, John Newton started his career when he was still a boy, accompanying his father, who was a shipmaster in the Mediterranean trade. He later became a foremast man and then a ship captain when he was twenty-five years old.[51] Most captains of French slave ships from La Rochelle, for example, belonged to the middle bourgeoisie, including sons of ship captains and master artisans.[52] After completing a few voyages, several French slave ship captains became very prosperous individuals, who acquired opulent townhouses, plantations, and enslaved people in the French West Indies during the eighteenth century.[53]

During the eighteenth century, smaller and faster slave ships did not carry a surgeon or ship doctor, who in European slave ships were usually men born in Europe. Only after 1788, all British ships were required to have a doctor on board.[54] In addition to assisting in the purchase of captives, the surgeon oversaw the enslaved captives daily to identify any illnesses. He also took care of the crew.[55]

Some of these health professionals left accounts of their journeys on slave ships. For example, in 1693, Johann Peter Oettinger, a twenty-seven-year-old German barber-surgeon arrived at the seaport of Ouidah in the Bight of Benin aboard the *Friedrich Wilhelm*. The slave ship was owned by the Brandenburg African Company (which was also known by other names), the short-lived Brandenburg-Prussia charter company created in 1682. From there he was brought inland to the town of Savi, the capital of the Kingdom of Hueda, where European slave merchants conducted business before the kingdom was conquered by the Dahomey.[56]

In seventeenth-century Europe, in contrast with physicians, barber-surgeons were craftsmen. Whereas physicians received university training and performed internal interventions, barber-surgeons were only allowed to perform external interventions, including bloodletting, dressing wounds, and stitching cuts, as well as treating fractures, ulcers, and burns. Barber-surgeons also removed teeth and provided the regular services that barbers did, such as shaving and giving haircuts.[57] Similar to other manual workers such as tailors, butchers, shoemakers, and smiths, barber-surgeons were organized in guilds, associations of artisans that were awarded special advantages by cities and monarchs. Starting in the eighteenth century, surgeons, barbers, and bleeders could appear as separate categories in muster rolls of British slave ships. Yet, in dozens of eighteenth-century French crew lists, there was usually one surgeon, and sometimes a second surgeon.[58]

Brazilian and Portuguese vessels rarely carried health professionals and practitioners, but when they did, enslaved and free African-born and Brazilian-born individuals often appear performing the roles of surgeons, barbers, and bleeders.[59] Vessels that sailed from Europe and the Americas to the coasts of Africa to purchase enslaved captives were adapted to transport the human cargo. There were variations across time and, depending on the ships' sizes and nationalities, there were various spatial arrangements. In general, each vessel had a main upper deck; a lower deck, where the human cargo was transported; and the hold, occupied by barrels of water, foodstuffs, and all goods used to purchase enslaved people. One of the distinguishing features of a slave vessel was the barricade. This wooden barrier, which measured ten to twelve feet high, was "fixed across the deck, just before the mainmast, projecting over the sides," dividing the main deck in two parts.[60] This device, which could be added to virtually any kind of vessel used in Atlantic voyages, was designed to restrict the movement of male captives and protect the crew from possible insurrections. The upper deck was also where sailors slept in hammocks. When enslaved persons were sick during the Atlantic crossing, they were also brought to the main deck to remain apart from the other African captives.

Diseases and Mutinies

A grating separated the upper deck from the lower deck of slave ships. These grids not only allowed the air to circulate but also facilitated moving the captives to the main deck and back to the lower deck, where enslaved men, women, and children were packed in separate compartments. The lower deck also had a distinctive feature consisting of removable wooden platforms on top of or under which male captives lay during the voyage.[61]

A bulkhead at the back of the men's compartment and additional holes in each side of the vessel provided extra ventilation. Enslaved men were usually shackled in pairs during the entire voyage. In contrast with their male counterparts, as noticed by Cugoano in his narrative, enslaved women along with enslaved children were often unchained during the Atlantic crossing.[62] Together they occupied a compartment adjacent to the men's section from which it was often separated by a space that allowed the crew to circulate and also to reach to the hold of the slave ship.

In British slave ships, children could often circulate between the two sections of the lower deck. Therefore, to prevent possible uprising attempts, the barricade was mounted with spikes and guns pointing down to the main upper deck. Another feature in several slave ships was a net stretching from the hull to prevent African captives from jumping overboard.[63] When enslaved men were brought to the main deck, they remained shackled, often in pairs, and attached to a long chain that restricted their movements. The barricade separated them from women and children. Heavily armed, most of the crew spent the day on the deck while overseeing the human cargo. The ship captain, as well as the surgeon and the first mate, occupied two other rooms above the women's compartment, beneath the quarterdeck, which was located at the rear of the vessels. This spatial distribution allowed crew members to freely violate unchained enslaved women during the Atlantic crossing.

Despite any written regulations stating otherwise, in the North Atlantic and the South Atlantic systems, food rations on board slave vessels were limited to no more than two meals a day that could include rice, yams, beans, corn, and palm oil. Captains depended on enslaved African women, who most of the time were in charge of preparing food on board slave ships.[64] If weather allowed, every morning, enslaved individuals were brought in groups to the main deck, where they could breathe fresh air, be fed, and wash. They were also forced to exercise, a procedure intended to keep the captives minimally healthy to arrive alive to be sold in the Americas.

But these measures were far insufficient to prevent disease and death. In his journal narrating his voyage from Ouidah to the Danish West Indies at the end of the seventeenth century, barber-surgeon Oettinger mentioned that enslaved men were transported in the hold of the slave ship chained by their legs two by two. The Danish vessel *Friedrich Wilhelm* left the Bight of Benin transporting 738 men, women, and children. Already in the beginning of the voyage, 10 captives died of dysentery, and several became sick. As established since the end of the fifteenth century, the ship stopped at São Tomé to fetch provisions, including water and food such as beef, veggies, maize, yams.[65] But as the passage continued, the journal shows that many other enslaved people died during the crossing. Thrown in the sea, their dead bodies were attacked and eaten by sharks that usually followed the slave ships across the Atlantic Ocean. The atrocious Atlantic crossing also favored the spread of disease that killed many captives and members of the crew. When the ship eventually arrived at Saint Thomas, by then a Danish island in the West Indies, only 659 enslaved men, women, and children were alive.[66]

Bacterial and viral infections such as dysentery, smallpox, and yellow fever infested slave vessels. As historian Stephanie Smallwood notes, the lack of sanitation, added to "exhaustion, malnutrition, fear, and seasickness resulted in depressed immune systems and increased vulnerability to disease."[67] This context evidently favored slave insurrections during the Atlantic crossing. The eighteenth century, the period during which the largest number of African captives were transported to the Americas, reveals also the highest number of episodes of slave resistance on board slave ships. Small and large uprisings could often occur near the coasts of Africa. On September 6, 1721, unchained enslaved men and boys on board the sloop *Cape Coast* that was trading at Winneba on the Gold Coast attacked the crew and seized the vessel. Liberated, they went ashore where they escaped before the sloop's departure to the Americas.[68] Members of the crew also risked being killed by a variety of diseases or if a slave rebellion broke out during the voyage.[69] Given these horrible conditions, crew members also organized mutinies.[70]

Because they were kept unchained during the Atlantic crossing, enslaved women and children often played important roles in slave ship insurrections.[71] On May 26, 1751, a revolt broke out on board the Liverpool snow *Duke of Argyle* just a few days after it sailed off the western coast of Africa to Antigua. In his journal, Captain John Newton recognized the imminent threat: "Their plot was excedingly [*sic*] well laid, and had they been let alone an hour longer, must have occasioned us a good deal of trouble and damage."[72] On December 11, 1752, during another voyage to the Windward Coast, Newton discovered another conspiracy. He surprised two enslaved Africans trying to free themselves from their irons. After searching their quarters, he found weapons such as knives, stones, and a cold chisel supplied to the African captives by the enslaved boys, who were kept unchained in the vessel. To punish the rebels, Newton gave orders to restrain the enslaved men in collars and put the boys in irons.[73]

Insurrections on board slave ships are still today memorialized in small and larger museums. Adjacent to the campus of Brown University in Providence, Rhode Island, is a three-story eighteenth-century brick mansion. The luxurious house was owned by John Brown, a stateman and slave merchant who made his fortune in a variety of ventures such as candle works, a chocolate mill, rum distilleries, and

FIGURE 4.1. Exhibition on *Sally* slave ship, John Brown House Museum, Providence, RI, United States. Photograph by Ana Lucia Araujo, 2018.

ironwork. These businesses complemented the profits made by the Brown family in the notorious Atlantic slave trade. Brown's sons, known as the Brown brothers (Nicholas, John, Joseph, and Moses) contributed to the creation of the College of Rhode Island, renamed Brown University in 1804 to pay homage to Nicholas Brown Jr., son of the oldest of the four brothers, who made a significant gift to the institution. Today the Brown family mansion houses the John Brown House Museum.

One of the museum rooms tells the story of the catastrophic voyage of the brigantine *Sally*, owned by Nicholas Brown and Company, the merchant firm of the Brown brothers (figure 4.1). In August 1764, *Sally* was outfitted. Slave vessels leaving from Rhode Island in those years were instructed to "purchase young, male captives; feed them well so they will survive the journey; complete the voyage as quickly as possible to minimize the number of deaths from disease; keep the peace between officers and men."[74] Obviously the guidelines were not always followed. Captains made bad decisions, and all kinds of accidents happened. Water and food shortages as well as outbreaks of disease and insurrections were common during the Middle Passage, and when these problems occurred, another terrible layer was added to the already horrible conditions of these tragic voyages.

The *Sally* sailed to West Africa in September 1764, transporting bunches of onions, barrels of beef and pork, dozens of sugar loaves, and boxes of whale candles produced in the Providence Candleworks, owned by the Brown brothers. Yet, the most valuable items of the cargo were the hundreds of barrels containing 17,274 gallons of rum produced in New England. After ninety days sailing the Atlantic Ocean, in December 1764 the *Sally* arrived on the Windward Coast. The brig remained anchored near today's Guinea-Bissau most of the time. During the stay on the coast, the ship captain purchased 196 enslaved Africans. But before leaving the coast, nearly 20 enslaved persons had died on board the ship, then 20 other captives were sold on the coast. In August 1765, the *Sally* finally sailed to the West Indies, transporting 155 enslaved Africans. After one week at the sea, an African woman, two boys, and a girl perished. At the end of that same week, the human cargo led a rebellion.

Following the *Sally*'s insurrection, the death toll increased. Several captives died by suicide by jumping overboard, and others died of disease. After seven weeks at the sea, the brigantine eventually arrived on the island of Antigua in the British West Indies. Sixty-eight African captives perished during the Middle Passage, in addition to twenty who perished upon arrival. Nearly sixty surviving captives, sick and weak, were sold in Antigua for very low prices.[75] As the ship sailed back to Rhode Island transporting four or five young enslaved persons to be employed as domestic servants, one additional captive died. Ultimately, more than half the African captives boarded on the *Sally* died—on the coasts of Africa, during the Middle Passage, upon arrival in Antigua, or sailing back to Rhode Island.[76] David Eltis and David Richardson underscore that acts of resistance must have occurred in nearly all slaving voyages, even though they are documented in less than 2 percent of the 36,110 voyages listed in the *SlaveVoyages* database. However, in their estimates, 10 percent of slave ships that departed from Africa to the Americas either experienced a slave rebellion or were attacked from the African coast.[77]

Murdered and Raped

African men, women, and children forcibly transported aboard the Liverpool slave ship *Zong* experienced one of the most horrible atrocities committed during the era of the Atlantic slave trade. In September 1781, the *Zong* sailed from the Gold Coast to Jamaica. Overloaded, it carried 440 enslaved Africans when its size could accommodate only half of this number. When the ship approached Jamaica, a few crew members were ill, and 60 African captives had already died. But a navigation error led the ship to pass Jamaica, therefore dramatically increasing the voyage's length. At this point, crew members already realized that water reserves were insufficient. Under the conditions of poor hygiene in an overcrowded ship in which captives and crew members were ill and needed to remain hydrated, a great disaster was imminent. Disease also started spreading. Thus, Captain Luke Collingwood, who was reportedly very ill, or whoever was replacing him, ordered crew members to throw the sick captives overboard in order to keep the salable ones alive, knowing that insurers would not pay claims for captives deceased after disembarkation. Once the decision was made, the crew threw 54 women and children into the sea. Two days later, 42 men were pushed overboard. Sometime after that, 38 more Africans were thrown into the sea. Ten other captives who realized what their fate would be preemptively jumped into the sea. Upon the *Zong*'s arrival in Jamaica, the shipowners requested that their insurers pay for the loss of these enslaved Africans. The total number of African captives killed aboard the *Zong* remains unclear, even though the legal hearings estimated that 122 enslaved persons were murdered.[78]

Depicted in novels, paintings, poems, artistic performances, and plays, the tragedy of the *Zong* inspired the abolitionist movement to denounce the horrors of the slave trade. Nineteenth-century British artist Joseph Mallord William Turner took inspiration from the tragic fate of the *Zong* to produce his famous painting *Slave Ship* (originally titled *Slavers Throwing Overboard the Dead and Dying, Typhoon Coming On*).[79] Displayed today in the United States at the Museum of Fine Arts in Boston, the painting shows a slave vessel lost in a dramatic background of clouds and waves. In the foreground, a rough sea, along with sharks, swallows the bodies of the enslaved Africans who were thrown overboard.[80] Turner's *Slave Ship*, symbolizing the *Zong*'s case, became a quintessential representation of the atrocities committed against enslaved Africans during the Middle Passage.

Ship captains selected, punished, and discarded the bodies of African captives. No one was spared, not even the babies. In the early sixteenth century, Gonçalo Roíz, the captain of the Portuguese slave ships *Feco* and *Galocha*, ordered that living enslaved babies be thrown overboard to allegedly spare the lives of enslaved African mothers.[81] Captains and members of the crew also raped and murdered enslaved women and girls during the Atlantic crossing. In May 1791, ship captain John Kimber sailed from Bristol on board the ship *Recovery* to the port of New Calabar in West Africa. After a few weeks trading on the coast, about three hundred enslaved African men, women, and children were embarked on the vessel, headed to Jamaica.[82] Before the *Recovery*'s departure, the ship surgeon Thomas Dowling was treating one enslaved girl nearly fifteen years of age "who had been afflicted with a virulent gonorhea [*sic*], and lethargy, or drowsy complain, of which latter ailment he could never learn the cause."[83] Feeling so ill, the girl stopped eating and could not join the other captives who were forced to exercise on the deck. The captain "was so irritated" that he "flogged her himself with a whip, the handle of which, was one foot long, and the lash, two." Three weeks after sailing from Africa, "he beat her in this manner with uncommon severity." Then on December 22, when the ship was about seven hundred miles from Grenada,

Kimber perceived she was not dancing with the other enslaved women on the deck, and ordered a cabin boy to bring a rope to torture the girl. The body of the sick enslaved girl was lifted from the deck, and held suspended for several minutes, as the captain flogged her. Letting down her weak and wounded body, he slapped her on the face, saying "the bitch is sulky," then repeated the operation several times for nearly thirty minutes. Seriously injured, the unnamed girl was dead three days later.[84] Kimber was also accused of killing another girl named Venus during the same dreadful voyage of the *Recovery*. After the murders, disease continued to attack the *Recovery*'s human cargo. Nearly 30 percent of the African captives transported from West Africa to Jamaica perished during the Middle Passage.

The murders of two enslaved girls on board the *Recovery* exposed the sadistic nature of physical punishment and sexual violence inflicted on enslaved women in the context of the Atlantic slave trade.[85] Sexually abused African women and girls regularly contracted gonorrhea and other sexually transmitted diseases during the long waiting period in a barracoon and aboard the slave ship.[86] Ship captains and crewmen frequently sexually assaulted enslaved women. This continuous violence cannot be dissociated from the exemplary punishment inflicted by Kimber on the enslaved girl. As in the *Zong* case, the torture and the two murders on board the *Recovery* fueled the abolitionist campaign and were denounced by William Wilberforce during a historic parliamentary speech on April 2, 1792, in which he called for the end of the slave trade.[87] The brutal homicide of the unnamed girl also inspired visual renderings such as the colored satirical engraving *The Abolition of the Slave Trade* by Scottish cartoonist Isaac Cruikshank. He depicts her naked body suspended by her ankle from a rope over a pulley, while the ship captain whips her. Not surprisingly, in both cases, Kimber was acquitted.

Mortality of African captives on board slave ships varied over time and depended on transportation conditions. Although the average mortality rate during the Middle Passage in the North and South Atlantic systems was 20 percent, the death toll decreased in the second half of the eighteenth century. But this context kept changing. After the abolition of the British slave trade in 1807 and its prohibition in various nations, slave merchants persistently overloaded the vessels with many more captives than they could accommodate in order to make as much profit as possible. Conditions of transportation dramatically worsened in the period of the illegal slave trade to Brazil and Cuba between 1831 and 1867. During this time, overcrowded slave vessels led mortality rates to jump to nearly 30 percent. Following continued British pressures to end its slave trade, Brazil enacted the Feijó Law of November 7, 1831, which banned the importation of enslaved Africans. In the two decades after this prohibition, slave traders illegally transported to Brazil more than one million enslaved Africans in overcrowded vessels.[88] In 1838, the 96-ton schooner *Providência* transported from Mozambique to Brazil 472 men, women, and children. Only 422 arrived alive in Rio de Janeiro. The 45-ton yacht *Mariquinhas* disembarked 201 enslaved Africans on a Brazilian beach in Pernambuco in 1843.[89] Slave merchants preferred these smaller two-masted vessels such as the yacht and the schooner because they were faster and decreased the chances of being intercepted by the British squadrons.[90] But slave traders also used large slave ships to engage in similar atrocious practices. On February 1859, the US vessel *Memphis* (a 798-ton ship constructed in New York) left New Bedford, Massachusetts, to trade in Ambriz in West Central Africa, transporting 1,970 enslaved Africans. Of the original human cargo, 1,700 enslaved persons disembarked alive in the Cuban slave port of Cárdenas.[91] This horrible context added more terror to the already gruesome journey experienced by enslaved Africans carried by force to the Americas.

Floating Tombs

For enslaved Africans, the Atlantic crossing from Africa to the Americas meant confinement, physical violence, and sexual violation. Slave merchants packed their vessels with hundreds of naked, weak, and distressed men, women, and children. Restrained in chains, many of them did not know where they were going. The dark and suffocating hold of the slave ships was frightening. African captives were exposed to extreme heat, humidity, and cold. They shared sweat, saliva, urine, feces, blood, tears, and all kinds of secretions. But even facing trauma, human beings are resilient. African captives were husbands, wives, fathers, sons, daughters, sisters, warriors, farmers, healers, and traders, who spoke a variety of languages, belonged to various lineages, lived in several villages, and worshipped distinct deities. Even if the experience of confinement in the floating tomb was designed to erase their individual stories and transform these men, women, and children into numbers, the slave trade machine was never successful in smashing these individual stories. During the dreadful voyage, enslaved people created bonds of affection and solidarity. Many resisted, revolted, and survived. Still, the number of African captives who perished during the Middle Passage is staggering, and even more men, women, and children died after arriving in the Americas, before being sold. Chapter 5 tells their story.

CHAPTER 5

Discarded Lives

Death is a crucial dimension of life itself in many West African and West Central African societies. In West African societies of the Loango coast, a region stretching north of the Congo River, funeral ceremonies could last months, especially if the deceased person was a prominent individual in the community.[1] But funeral rites varied over time, according to regions and the religious practices of each African community. As a Muslim born in the Bight of Benin, Mahommah Gardo Baquaqua described in his narrative the funeral ceremonies in his homeland by stating that "when a person dies, they wrap the body in a white cloth, and bury it as soon as possible. After the body is laid out facing the east, the priest is sent for, and a religious ceremony performed, which consists of prayers to Allah for the soul of the departed." Funerals lasted for six days and included "great lamentations . . . loud and bitter cries and wailings" and at the "seventh day, a great feast is held and the term of mourning ends."[2]

In West African Vodun and Orisha religions, as well as in African-based religions in the Americas such as Candomblé and Santería, deceased ancestors continue to play important and ongoing roles in the world of the living. They become deities to whom living persons must pay homage by performing rituals that often involve the sacrifice of animals and offerings of food and drinks. As a result, funeral rites and burial grounds were and are still central to the survival and cohesion of African societies and groups. Throughout the era of the

Atlantic slave trade, this was well known to slave merchants, ship captains, and other crew members who traded on the coasts of Africa. In their journals and travelogues, they describe long, sophisticated funeral ceremonies, which they witnessed during the time they were trading in African ports.

Death was a constant threat for African captives who were taken from their homelands and confined in slave ships. Those who died in transit left no tangible traces of their existence. Although African men, women, and children were purchased as precious commodities, ship captains and crew members relentlessly devalued their lives. The thirst for profit led ship owners and slave merchants to overcrowd their vessels in sea voyages marked by water and food shortages, deeply unsanitary conditions, and disease. In the first two centuries of the Atlantic slave trade, many African captives died during the Atlantic crossing. Therefore, enslaved persons who perished at sea also passed from this world unnoticed, as their names were rarely recorded. As they remained nameless during these slave voyages, their demise would be documented by no more than a line in the journals of ship captains, where they were usually identified only by a number.[3]

Until the nineteenth century, especially in Brazil and the West Indies, enslaved persons often had no access to a proper burial. Africans who endured the Atlantic crossing as captives knew that their time at sea was only one of the several tragic stages of their journey. Although the exact numbers are impossible to determine, many enslaved men, women, and children perished soon after disembarking on American shores. Others survived for a few weeks but died before being sold; their bodies were often discarded in common graves and waste dumps.

Even after the inhumane trade and slavery were abolished during the nineteenth century, this erasure continued. Public buildings, parking lots, squares, paved avenues, and highways gradually covered the old burial sites, condemning those interred there to oblivion. Probably the most well-known among these forgotten burial sites is the African Burial Ground in New York City, where the remains of enslaved

Africans and their descendants were put to rest starting in the seventeenth century. In slave societies and societies in which slavery existed, such as colonial British North America, and later the United States, in addition to Brazil, Portugal, Mexico, Guadeloupe, and Barbados, enslaved people were buried in a variety of sites, including churches, churchyards, and plantations, quite often in unmarked tombs. Drawing from travel accounts, newspaper articles, parish records, and recent archaeological reports, as well as research on plantation and urban heritage sites and churches in Brazil and the United States, this chapter brings attention to the history of these burial grounds. I argue that, even in death, the humanity of enslaved Africans (and their descendants) persisted in being systematically devalued.

Death on the Coasts of Africa

Detailed information about what happened to the cadavers of enslaved Africans who died before being boarded on slave ships on African shores and upon arrival in the Americas remains scarce. Consider the example of the West Central African ports of Luanda and Benguela, two Portuguese colonies, which were, respectively, the largest and the third-largest ports from which African captives were transported to the Americas. In Benguela, cadavers of enslaved Africans were deposited on the beach until the end of the eighteenth century. Despite the creation of a cemetery for slaves who remained unbaptized or who died before boarding slave ships, the number of dead was so huge that cadavers of captive Africans kept accumulating, serving as food for the local fauna, forcing gravediggers to burn the corpses.[4] On the coast of West Central Africa, as late as in the first two decades of the nineteenth century, slave merchants "expressed the valuelessness of dead slaves . . . by dumping the bodies in a heap in a small cemetery adjacent to the Nazareth chapel near Luanda's commercial district, or depositing them in shallow graves in numbers far greater than the ground could cover decently."[5] Greedy and careless, traders left the remains to be eaten by hyenas and other animals in order to avoid paying fees to have the bodies taken into the charge of the Roman Catholic Church.

Death also occurred when European and American slave ships were trading on the African coasts. Crew members obviously treated their own dead differently from the enslaved people on board their vessels. Seamen from Europe and the Americas had no burial rights on most African coasts. When possible, ship captains made efforts to bury them ashore in shallow graves. In the logbook of the British slave ship *Sandown*, which traded on the coast of present-day Guinea, West Africa, ship captain Samuel Gamble recorded the interment of seamen ashore in several instances. An entry of August 5, 1793, reports that two crewmen were deceased. To bury them aground, he had "to pay the King a duty of 15 Barrs a[nd] ¾ for every Whiteman that died in the River."[6] Later, on September 23, 1793, another young crewman died. As no white individuals were available to help Gamble bury the seaman, he paid *grometas* (African employees of local traders) with brandy in addition to the duties requested by the local ruler to perform the interment.[7]

In Bonny, one of the main slave ports of the Bight of Biafra, on the coastal region of present-day Nigeria, seamen were buried ashore, probably because, as put by one ship captain, Bonny River had so many sharks that even washing one's hand over the boat's side was dangerous.[8] In the late eighteenth century, British surgeon Alexander Falconbridge even reported that because the bodies were buried just "below the surface of the land, the stench arising from them is sometimes noxious."[9] Not surprisingly, most dead crew members were "buried at sea."[10] Thrown overboard, their corpses were immediately attacked by sharks who took advantage of the abundant human flesh offered by slave vessels. To avoid this carnage, when navigating in high seas, seamen attempted to prevent sharks from eating corpses by wrapping the dead bodies of their fellow crew members in their own hammocks. As previously emphasized in chapter 4, however, enslaved people had none of these privileges. Sailors usually waited until nighttime to throw the dead bodies of enslaved Africans overboard, mainly to prevent commotion among the human cargo.[11] In countless cases, sharks ate the corpses.

Eighteenth-century British slave ship captain Hugh Crow, who completed several voyages to purchase enslaved people in West Africa, noted in his memoirs that during funeral rites in the Bight of Biafra, African men and women gathered around the body "crying, leaping, clapping their hands, and making a terrible noise." In these ceremonies, an "animal is killed, and the fetish of the deceased is sprinkled with the blood as propitiatory offering to the priest." Crow also observed that "it is customary to put into the coffins of great men some articles of value . . . which are buried, after two or three days, under the ground of their houses."[12] Danish merchant Ludewig Ferdinand Rømer, who worked for the Danish West India and Guinea Company through the first half of the eighteenth century, reported on the funeral practices of the Gold Coast. In his account, he explains that people "weep during the first day, but then play and dance for eight days."[13]

Music and musical instruments such as drums, horns, hollow irons (called "klink klink") and a sort of flute (called a "kitt") also played a crucial role during the funerals, even those of ordinary people.[14] The grandness of these ceremonies is just one indication of how seriously West Africans took the transition from life to death. Burial grounds were and still are sacred sites connecting the dead to the world of the living. Graves memorialize the ancestors by creating an ancestral connection to the land. Marked with a tree, a stone, and even carved figurines representing deities and ancestral persons, they physically and spiritually connect African communities and individuals to their lineages. Therefore, discarding dead bodies in the sea had profound social, cultural, and spiritual consequences for African men, women, and children, who had already been violently separated from their communities of origin.

Christian Burial Denied

As death pursued enslaved Africans beyond their Atlantic crossing, on several occasions slave merchants and slave owners continued to deny bondspeople a proper funeral and a peaceful place to lay their bodies to rest. Africans transported to both the Iberian Peninsula and Latin America, where Catholicism predominated, were baptized either before their departure from the continent or upon their arrival at their destination. Hence, at least in theory, when enslaved Africans died, they had the right to funerals and the Catholic rites that usually included the final anointing (*Extreme Unction*), a mass, a procession, and a proper burial site.

In the Portuguese colonies of Angola and Brazil, until the early nineteenth century, before the existence of modern cemeteries, baptized Africans were supposed to be buried within the walls of church buildings. For example, in 1665 the Portuguese won the battle of Mbwila (or Ambuíla) against António I (Nvita a Nkanga), the Catholic ruler of the Kingdom of Kongo, who had challenged their domination. During the battle, Portuguese-led troops shot and decapitated Nvita a Nkanga. Still, the Portuguese organized his funeral "with all the pomp and ostentation." The Catholic brotherhood of Our Lady of Mercy led the funeral ceremonies, including a procession by its members. This brotherhood was one of the many fraternal organizations that existed in Portugal and Spain and their overseas colonies during the era of the Atlantic slave trade. Following the model established by brotherhoods gathering white individuals, these mutual aid assistance associations congregated free, freed, and enslaved Africans and their descendants to honor a patron saint, and they provided their members with welfare assistance, including proper burial services and the opportunity for participation in religious festivals. Nvita a Nkanga's head was then buried in the main chapel of Luanda's Church of Our Lady of Nazareth (Nossa Senhora de Nazaré), a temple devoted to the saint venerated by André Vidal de Negreiros, the governor of Luanda, and to whom he attributed the Portuguese victory.[15]

Other Africans were buried in Catholic churches in Portugal as well. More than one century after the funeral of António I, a West African emissary from Dahomey was buried in a Catholic church in Lisbon. Two ambassadors representing King Agonglo of Dahomey went to Salvador in Bahia, and then to Lisbon in Portugal, to negotiate with the Portuguese rulers the terms of the Atlantic slave trade. Once in Lisbon the two Dahomean representatives were baptized as João Carlos de Bragança and Manoel Constantino Carlos Luiz. But as explained in a letter from Queen Maria to King Agonglo, Manoel became sick and died on February 19, 1796. Therefore, as a Christian who had been baptized, he was buried in the Convent of Francesinhas in Lisbon, with all expenses related to his funeral covered by the Portuguese crown.[16] Unfortunately, unlike the Church of Our Lady of Nazareth that is still standing in Luanda, the convent was deactivated in 1890 and then demolished, leaving unknown what happened to the remains of the ambassador and other possible African notables interred there.

Unlike African officials who were buried in the buildings of Catholic churches in their homelands or while they were sojourning in the Iberian Peninsula, many enslaved Africans who died in slave-trading ports in Europe, Africa, and the Americas were laid to rest without any funeral ceremonies. In Catholic societies of Latin America, including Brazil, until the nineteenth century, in urban areas, the bodies of enslaved men, women, and children could be discarded in waste dumps, as there was obviously not enough available space to accommodate the large number of remains of bondspeople inside the walls of church buildings, especially in contexts where the enslaved population was huge, even outnumbering the free Black and white populations. Ultimately, although forced to convert to Christianity, enslaved Africans in Lisbon or in the port cities colonized by the Portuguese, such as Rio de Janeiro in Brazil or Luanda and Benguela in West Central Africa, especially those who died before being sold, never fully received the Christian privileges of proper funeral ceremonies and burial services.[17]

As discussed in chapter 1, enslaved Africans disembarked in the Portuguese port of Lagos as early as 1444. Situated nearly 190 miles south of Lisbon, Lagos received some international attention in 2009, when during the construction of the Anel Verde Parking Lot in the Gafaria Valley, archaeologists uncovered the remains of 155 enslaved Africans in an urban waste dump that functioned as a "Blacks' pit" dating back to the period between the fifteenth and the seventeenth centuries.[18] The site is among the oldest and rarest burial grounds of enslaved Africans uncovered in the Iberian Peninsula. The common grave confirms existing archival documents showing that between the 1570s and the 1580s, nearly 10 percent of the deceased individuals in Lagos were enslaved.[19] Most of the recovered remains belonged to adult men and women, but there were also remains of children. The lateral, dorsal, and ventral positions of the skeletons, sometimes even with the arms and legs attached, indicate that most corpses were not inhumed but rather thrown in the urban waste dump without following any Christian burial rites. But 7 percent of the skeletons were interred with belongings such as rings, necklaces, and coins, suggesting they were treated with some care. The presence of this small number of skeletons that appeared to have been sensibly interred suggests that those who performed these burials may have had emotional ties with the deceased.[20] Such an explanation is plausible, and this practice certainly persisted in the Americas, where enslaved people were buried by their own relatives and other fellow bondspeople.

In a decree of November 13, 1515, King Dom Manuel I ordered Lisbon's municipal chamber to construct a whitewashed stone pit to serve as a common grave to inter the city's enslaved population, with the goal of preventing slave owners from discharging their remains in the city's outskirts where the corpses were eaten by animals.[21] Some scholars debate about whether or not the pit to discard the remains of enslaved persons was ever constructed.[22] Other scholars insist that the pit effectively existed and was located outside the walls of the city, in the vicinity of the Street of the Blacks' Pit (Rua do Poço dos Negros), even though this street name (figure 5.1) only appeared in existing sources for the first time in 1681, more than a century later.[23] Despite these disagreements, similar pits were constructed in Lisbon and other Portuguese cities such as Elvas in the following years. Regardless of the existence of these common graves, records dating back to the early sixteenth century show that most baptized enslaved Black people in

FIGURE 5.1. Rua do Poço dos Negros (Street of the Blacks' Pit), Lisbon, Portugal. Photograph by Ana Lucia Araujo, 2022.

the Iberian Peninsula received full Christian burials. Still, most who were interred in churchyards or inside church buildings were members of Catholic lay Black brotherhoods, comprised of enslaved people owned by affluent families. Challenging the dehumanization imposed on bondspeople, these organizations provided a variety of services to support their members, including access to a dignified interment.[24]

As these brotherhoods made their way to the Catholic colonies of the Americas, they could offer their enslaved members spiritual and material comfort in a context in which their human dignity was denied.

Death on American Shores

As the Atlantic slave trade to the Americas evolved between the seventeenth and nineteenth centuries, slave merchants and slave owners continued to discard the remains of deceased enslaved persons, especially newly arrived enslaved Africans, into the ocean. In Cuba, as late as the nineteenth century, greedy slave traders threw the dead bodies of recently disembarked enslaved Africans into the sea to avoid paying burial fees. Not surprisingly, the tide often carried the bodies back to the beach. As in the West Central African port of Benguela, animals ate the corpses of enslaved persons buried in shallow graves.[25] The cadavers of enslaved men, women, and children were also discarded in lakes and interred in courtyards of jails, hospitals, and private residences. Similar to what happened in Portugal and Spain, in South America and North America, bondspeople were also interred in churchyards and inside church buildings. But although enslaved Africans were forced to convert to Christianity in the Spanish, French, Dutch, and the British West Indies, they continued to mourn their dead according to the rites of their homelands. Funeral ceremonies, like processions, included singing, dancing, and drinking alcoholic beverages.[26]

A few enslaved people owned by rich slave owners in New England urban areas were also buried in churchyards with tombs bearing their names. The enslaved girl Cicely, owned by the Reverend William Brattle, for example, died in 1714 during a measles epidemic. Her tombstone (figure 5.2) is still visible today at the Old Burial Ground in Cambridge, Massachusetts. But despite this case and a few other exceptions, most graves of enslaved people in colonial North America had no tombstones, especially in the South. Even in the cemeteries for enslaved people in Virginia plantations such as Mount Vernon, Mon-

FIGURE 5.2. Cicely's tomb, Old Burial Ground, Cambridge, MA, United States. Photograph by Ana Lucia Araujo, 2022.

ticello, and Montpelier owned by the US founding fathers George Washington, Thomas Jefferson, and James Madison, respectively, there were no gravestones.

In colonial North America and the independent United States, mourning the dead was a central element of the spirituality of enslaved people, as it was for their African ancestors. Black priests or other assigned members of the enslaved communities oversaw these services. Funerals were also opportunities to congregate, sing, dance, and drink. But since reunions of this kind also offered opportunities to plan insurrections, slave owners kept a watchful eye on these gatherings. Mirroring the hierarchy among enslaved people, those who were closer to their owners, such as overseers and old enslaved women who performed their duties in the big houses, received more elaborate funeral ceremonies. During the burial service, enslaved family members and other attendants placed wooden crosses and other adornments on the graves of the deceased persons, even though these markers did not resist the passage of time.[27]

Archaeological excavations in various burial sites in the Americas have revealed the presence of personal items interred with enslaved persons. In graves of Montserrat, a Caribbean island and British overseas territory, archaeologists retrieved artifacts such as an eighteenth-century glass bottle of Turlington Balsam of Life that may have contained alcohol for the deceased or perhaps was employed to pour medicine in the grave, as well as metal disks used as tokens to open the path for the dead person to return to the homeland. In the cemetery of Anse Sainte-Marguerite in the littoral of Guadeloupe, a Caribbean archipelago and French overseas department, one grave contained religious objects such as a Catholic rosary.[28] In Barbados, a grave of an enslaved healer, who may have been born in Africa, dating back to the seventeenth century or early eighteenth century, contained a variety of personal objects such as an iron knife, metal bracelets and finger rings, a clay pipe, and an elaborate necklace, all of which attested to the important position of the deceased among the local slave community.[29]

In Latin America, enslaved people could also be buried inside church buildings. British traveler Maria Graham arrived in Brazil in September 1821. During her stay, she observed and documented in detail the living and working conditions of enslaved people. After spending three years in the country, she published a travel account documenting the various dimensions of Brazilian life in the years that led to the country's independence. Graham was among the very few women who published travel accounts recounting the period spent in Brazil and other parts of the world during the nineteenth century. In Salvador, Bahia, Graham visited the Church of Our Lady of the Conception of the Beach (Nossa Senhora da Conceição da Praia), the city's oldest church. In an entry of October 20, 1821, she explains how the dead were put to rest in the building's ground: "The flooring is laid in squares with stone, and within each square there is a panelling of wood of about nine feet by six; under each panel is a vault, into which the dead are thrown naked, until they reach a certain number, when with a little quick-lime thrown in, the wood is fastened down, and then another square is opened, and so on in rotation."[30] Despite not providing any details about who was buried in the church, existing records show that until the middle of the nineteenth century, slave owners, slave traders, and enslaved people (even those who were born in Africa) could be buried inside Brazilian churches as they were in Portugal and Spain. For example, by 1750 Ignácio de Sampaio was captured in West Africa, in the Bight of Benin, and sent into slavery to Bahia at a young age. He then became a member of the Catholic brotherhood Good Jesus of Necessities and Redemption, and in less than twenty-five years, he was able to purchase his freedom. He married another African-born woman, had a daughter, and became the owner of several enslaved persons, three of which he buried at the Church of Our Lady of the Conception of the Beach between 1788 and 1800.[31] Like him, many others were interred in this church and other church buildings in Salvador.

But the hierarchy of Brazilian colonial society was reproduced even inside the churches. Richer donors such as white slave owners and slave merchants occupied the best niches, where their names and dates of birth and death were also included. Enslaved people were obviously not awarded the same honor. Yet, this context was different in the church buildings maintained by Catholic lay Black brotherhoods. Consider the example of the brotherhood of Our Lady of the Rosary of the Black Men in Salvador, Bahia, whose church was erected during the eighteenth century. Unlike in the rich white churches, the building's floors feature the surviving tombstones displaying the names of free Black individuals and formerly enslaved people who were members of the Rosary brotherhood. But even in a Black church, burial spaces followed a hierarchy, with the best spaces occupied by wealthier members. During the nineteenth century, when building space was dramatically reduced, several tombstones of prominent brotherhood

FIGURE 5.3. Burial ground, once unmarked, of the enslaved members of the Black brotherhood of Our Lady of the Rosary of the Black Men, Salvador, Bahia, Brazil. Photograph by Ana Lucia Araujo, 2009.

members were placed in the sacristy instead of the central nave. Still, as elsewhere, people who remained enslaved had fewer privileges. Although the brotherhood took charge of the burial services of enslaved members, many of them were buried outside the building in a common unmarked grave, recovered only in the twenty-first century (figure 5.3). Overall, the majority of Salvador's enslaved men, women, and children, as well as the city's free Black and white unprivileged population, were deprived of Catholic rites upon their death. Most of them were buried outside church buildings, especially in the large burial ground of Campo da Pólvora (Gunpowder Field).[32] In Salvador, as in other cities and rural areas of the Americas, enslaved Africans, especially those who had recently disembarked from slave ships, along with their descendants, rarely had access to a respectable funeral.

Death before Being Sold

In the days following the arrival of slave ships sailing from African ports to the Americas, death was still a great threat to enslaved Africans, who came ashore weak, malnourished, dehydrated, and ill. Journals kept by slave ship captains and other officers who described their Atlantic journeys do not always provide precise information about what happened to enslaved persons who died before being sold to a slave owner. Only a small number of Africans who left narratives of their Atlantic crossing described the moment of their disembarkation in the Americas.

Consider the case of Venture Smith, whose African name was Broteer Furro. Like other Africans who published narratives about their enslavement in Africa and transportation to the Americas, such as Olaudah Equiano and Quobna Ottobah Cugoano, Smith was captured when he was still a boy of between six and twelve years of age. Although his exact place of birth on the Gold Coast is unclear, he was captured during an episode of warfare and transported to the coast. At Anomabu on the Gold Coast, he boarded the ship *Charming Susanna* that sailed to Barbados (and subsequently to Rhode Island) in 1739.[33] Smith reported that 260 captives were boarded on the vessel, but during the voyage a smallpox outbreak killed nearly sixty enslaved Africans. The other 200 enslaved persons who arrived alive in Barbados were all sold, except for Smith and two other captives who were brought to Rhode Island.[34] Based on old personal memories and dictated to a literate individual who made possible its publication many years after his arrival in the Americas, Smith's account does not provide any details about what happened to the men and women who died during the Middle Passage, even though it is possible to imagine that most bodies were either thrown overboard or removed from the ship and buried in a common grave not far from the place of disembarkation.

A few years later, in 1754, Equiano also landed in Barbados. He omitted slave mortality during the Middle Passage but explained that when the merchants came to examine the captives, they were terrified of being eaten: "We thought by this we should be eaten by these ugly men, as they appeared to us; and, when soon after we were all put down under the deck again, there was much dread and trembling among us and nothing but bitter cries to be heard all the night from these apprehensions."[35] African fears of white cannibalism were probably unfounded. But at least one documented case, that of the Portuguese schooner *Arrogante*, apprehended by the British Royal Navy nearly one century later in 1837, suggests an instance in which crew members literally ate an enslaved African on board a slave ship.[36]

Maria Graham spent the first weeks of her stay in Recife, the third-largest Brazilian slave port in the nineteenth century. In an entry from September 28, 1821, she narrated a promenade in the adjacent city of Olinda. While walking along the beach, she witnessed a dog dragging "the arm of a negro from beneath the few inches of sand, which his master had caused to be thrown over his remains."[37] Such incidents were very similar to what other observers from that time reported in Luanda and Benguela, where the bodies of enslaved Africans, simply discarded along the beach and barely covered with sand, were left exposed to the elements and eaten by hungry animals. Graham also reported the lack of any funeral ceremonies: "When the negro dies, his fellow-slaves lay him on a plank, carry him to the beach, where beneath high-water mark they hoe a little sand over him." But Graham also noted that the fate of newly arrived Africans was even worse: "To the new negro even this mark of humanity is denied. He is tied to a pole, carried out in the evening and dropped upon the beach, where it is just possible the surf may bear him away."[38] A few days later, also in Olinda, after observing the sumptuous burial procession of a monk, she could not help comparing the ceremony that followed all rites prescribed by the Catholic Church with the way the bodies of enslaved persons were carelessly abandoned on the beach.[39] Even in death, enslaved Africans and their descendants were destined to be discarded, attacked by animals, and swallowed by the sea, their memory consigned to oblivion.

Not surprisingly, bondspeople in Rio de Janeiro were submitted to comparable mortuary practices. The Catholic Church with its various religious orders and brotherhoods took charge of the interment of enslaved persons, but as the city's population increased along with its enslaved population, burial space became scarce. The Rocio Cemetery (known as Mulatos Cemetery) opened in 1613.[40] The Holy House of Mercy (Santa Casa da Misericórdia) was another institution in charge of burying enslaved people and other underprivileged individuals. This lay Catholic brotherhood and philanthropic institution, created in Portugal in the late fifteenth century, had chapters in various parts of the Portuguese empire, including Rio de Janeiro, where its headquarters were established in 1582. As part of its mission to support the sick, disabled people, and abandoned newborns, it maintained a hospital and also created a mass grave for enslaved people in 1623. The Franciscans also opened a cemetery to bury enslaved people near present-day Carioca Square (Largo da Carioca) in 1709.[41]

British Army officer Henry Chamberlain described how bondspeople were buried in the Field of Mercy (Campo da Misericórdia), in early nineteenth-century Rio de Janeiro. This burial ground, comparable to Campo da Pólvora in Salvador, was maintained by the Holy House of Mercy Catholic brotherhood. In 1821, the city's population reached 333,000 persons, of which nearly half were enslaved.[42] Chamberlain explained that the cadaver was "sewn up in a coarse Bag, put into a Hammock slung to a Pole, and an old Blanket flung over all," then transported to the grave by two enslaved men. With no "ceremony or Mourners; a short Prayer is then muttered over the Body, and the Earth is thrown in by one of the Polebearers, whilst the other with his Feet and a heavy wooden Stake, beats it down compactly over the Body."[43] The watercolor portraying the funeral that accompanies the text reveals the city's scenic mountains and seashore where the cemetery was situated, in an area not far from today's Santos Dumont Airport.

Irish clergyman and physician Robert Walsh, who spent almost one year in Rio de Janeiro between 1828 and 1829, published a travelogue reporting his sojourn in Brazil. He also explained how enslaved people and poor persons were interred in common graves in the Field of Mercy's burial ground, where according to him there were also four or five bodies waiting to be buried. The burial process consisted of depositing the corpses in a "trench without coffins; sometimes naked, but more usually sewed up in coarse canvass, or the fragment of a mat, and their bodies are laid across, generally the head of one to the feet of the other."[44] According to French physician Joseph François Xavier Sigaud, the founder of the Society of Medicine of Rio de Janeiro, in 1830, just one year before the ban of the introduction of Africans to Brazil, the Holy House of Mercy buried between seven hundred and eight hundred enslaved persons every month in Rio de Janeiro.[45] But because the shallow graves generated increasing hygiene concerns, in 1839 the burial ground was transferred to a surrounding area that later accommodated the Caju Cemetery (São Francisco Xavier Cemetery), one of the largest cemeteries of today's Rio de Janeiro.[46]

Emerging Burial Grounds

Until the middle of the eighteenth century, enslaved Africans transported to Rio de Janeiro were disembarked at Fish's Beach (Praia do Peixe), the waterfront across the Carmo Square, at present-day XV Square (Praça XV), the former Imperial Palace Square (Largo do Paço), where several public buildings such as the Customs House and the Royal Palace were established during the first decades of the eighteenth century. From there, naked and enchained, African captives walked into the city, to be sold from the dozens of slave pens located at Direita Street, present-day Primeiro de Março Street, stopping along the way to urinate and defecate in the streets. By the middle of the eighteenth century, colonial authorities had ordered the transfer of the slave market to the Valongo neighborhood, a more remote region located about three miles away, not far from the waterfront of present-day Avenue Barão de Tefé.[47]

Portuguese officials willfully ignored the atrocious transportation conditions in overcrowded slave ships, which were floating incubators for all kinds of diseases. But they still feared that disembarking enslaved Africans near Rio de Janeiro's main public buildings would contribute to the spread of disease on the mainland. Displeased by the sight of long lines of naked slaves entering the city, they determined that enslaved Africans should be disembarked in the Valongo region, where the market was gradually established between 1769 and 1779, and where a wharf was also constructed. Between 1780 and 1831, when the trade of enslaved Africans to Brazil was made illegal, the Valongo region and its wharf became the main site of disembarkation of enslaved Africans in Rio de Janeiro, where scholars estimate that nearly 800,000 enslaved men, women, and children came ashore.[48] After 1831, the traces of the wharf were gradually concealed by successive public works. Only recently, in 2011, its original structure was uncovered, when the city of Rio de Janeiro conducted works in the area to prepare for the Olympic Games in 2016. Recognizing its importance, UNESCO included Valongo in its World Heritage List in 2017.[49]

During the eighteenth century and especially in the three first decades of the nineteenth century, when slave ships anchored on Rio de Janeiro's shores, health authorities were supposed to inspect the bodies of enslaved Africans. When they judged it necessary, they would put the human cargo in quarantine for eight days to avoid spreading any kind of contagious diseases.[50] Dehydrated, undernourished, and often ill, a number of newly arrived enslaved individuals died before being sold. These men, women, and children had to be buried ashore. As early as in 1722, because of the growing number of deceased enslaved persons, especially those recently disembarked from Africa, the clergymen chapter of Rio de Janeiro's cathedral requested permission from the Portuguese Overseas Council to construct a cemetery to bury them, an initiative that led to the creation of the Santa Rita Cemetery at Santa Rita Square (Largo de Santa Rita).[51]

Starting in 1722, enslaved Africans who perished prior to sale were interred in the burial ground at Santa Rita Square, also located in the area surrounding the Valongo region. But residents and local authorities continuously complained about the hygiene problems created by the presence of these cemeteries in the middle of urban areas. In 1769, the burial ground for newly arrived enslaved Africans moved to another site, also in the Valongo area, known as the Cemetery of New Blacks (Cemitério dos Pretos Novos), in present-day Gamboa neighborhood. When German naturalist Georg Wilhelm Freyreiss visited the cemetery in 1814, he noticed the piles of bodies waiting to be buried in shallow graves: "Probably burial is carried out only once a week and as the cadavers have already decomposed, the stink is unbearable. Eventually, the best solution was to occasionally burn a pile of semi-decomposed corpses."[52] Mortality among newly arrived enslaved Africans persisted during the nineteenth century. Although death rates during the Middle Passage from Africa to Brazil varied between 4.5 percent and 16.4 percent, there are no exact numbers for those who perished after disembarking. Existing records suggest that nearly 15 percent of the enslaved Africans who disembarked in Rio de Janeiro perished between their arrival and the conclusion of sales.[53]

More than six thousand newly arrived Africans were buried in the Cemetery of New Blacks. Among them, however, were a very small number of African-born people who had been enslaved in Brazil for several years and some Brazilian-born persons. As in other urban burial grounds, residents complained about the horrible smell of decomposing bodies. Many people reported having to keep the windows closed all day. The number of corpses interred in the site was evidently far too high for the size of the cemetery, estimated at approximately 115 by 120 yards (about 105 by 110 meters).[54]

Eventually, following the official ban of the slave trade from Africa to Brazil in 1831, the burial ground was permanently closed.[55] Given this closure, during the next two decades of illegal slave trade, we can assume that Africans who died before being sold were buried in clandestine burial grounds. Over more than a century, the urbanization process concealed the Cemetery of New Blacks. But in 1996, an archaeological excavation in a private property at 36 Pedro Ernesto Street (formerly Cemetery Street) in the Gamboa neighborhood exposed a burial ground containing bones of dozens of African enslaved men, women, and children. The site was identified as being the Cemetery of New Blacks. This new discovery allowed for an examination of the remains that revealed details about burial practices and the enslaved persons interred in the site. Although many of these recently disembarked Africans had already been baptized, their cadavers were literally thrown in the common grave, as had been done in Lagos's sixteenth-century burial ground in Portugal. On top of one another, naked or wrapped in mats, most corpses were likely buried without the performance of any Catholic rituals.

Similar grounds where cadavers of enslaved persons were discarded existed all over the Americas, especially in slave-trading ports. Unlike other graveyards that were intended to preserve the memory of the dead, the continuous existence of unmarked places where the dead bodies of enslaved Africans were discarded reinforced the dehumanization imposed on enslaved people. As historian Vincent Brown observed when exploring the burial landscape in nineteenth-century Jamaica, the battles for "memorials to the dead and over burial grounds were, in turn, important elements in those claims and a critical dimension of the politics of the enslaved."[56] Whether in Jamaica, Brazil, or the United States, these claims were denied to most enslaved people. Therefore, when bondspeople were deprived of dignified burials, not only were their connections with their ancestors disrupted, their links with the land and their descendants were brutally broken, too.

As major gatherings that involved drinking, dancing, and singing, funerals of enslaved people could be also an occasion for insurrection, which is also why in New York City, when ceremonies occurred, they had to take place during daylight and the number of attendants was restricted to twelve people.[57] During the colonial period in New York City, Africans and their descendants were not allowed to be buried in churchyards, but they had their own cemetery, the Negroes Burial Ground, which was active during the eighteenth century. The burial ground was rediscovered during an excavation to construct a new federal building at 290 Broadway, when construction workers uncovered more than 400 skeletons of persons who were either African-born or of African descent. Scholars estimate that between ten thousand and fifteen thousand persons were interred in the graveyard. As in Rio de Janeiro, even if historians knew about the existence of a cemetery where enslaved, freed, and free Black persons were interred, most New Yorkers were not even aware that slavery existed in the city. However, unlike Rio de Janeiro's Cemetery of the New Blacks, the Manhattan Black cemetery, today known as the African Burial Ground, was not a landfill for recently arrived enslaved Africans but rather a graveyard where enslaved and freed Africans and their descendants were carefully interred, "wrapped in linen shrouds with care and methodically positioned in well-built cedar or pine coffins."[58] Likewise, the presence of grave goods such as beads, shells, knives, and tobacco pipes suggest that dignified burial practices prevailed in the site.[59] Various Black individuals and groups of residents of New York City claimed the site as a place that represented the long history of the African American community in the city and fought to commemorate it as the African Burial Ground through the construction of a memorial.

Enslaved people were doomed to be forgotten even in death. But as in the period of slavery, when dumped bodies thrown into the sea came back ashore or reemerged from shallow graves, during the twenty-first century, news outlets have shown that slave burial grounds have been recovered almost on a monthly basis in the Americas.[60] In 2013, during the renovation of Gaillard Center, construction workers uncovered graves of thirty-six persons in downtown Charleston, South Carolina, the largest US former slave-trading port where nearly 150,000 enslaved Africans disembarked during the era of the Atlantic slave trade. After the excavations, scholars concluded that the remains belonged to eighteenth-century men and women who were likely either born in Africa or were descendants of African individuals. As in the African Burial Ground in New York City, archaeological analysis found pins used with burial shrouds as well as a variety of grave goods, such as mother-of-pearl buttons, glass beads, and clay pipe bowls. The Gullah Society engaged the Charleston Black community in actively reclaiming the site. The organization also led the scientific study of the archaeological site, referred to as the Anson Street burial ground.[61] For the populations of African descent, reclaiming the remains of their ancestors found in these forgotten graves became an instrument to reappropriate the humanity stripped from enslaved Africans and their descendants during the era of the Atlantic slave trade and slavery.

Dignity in Death

For African peoples, death and the end-of-life rites that accompanied this transition have always been a crucial dimension of their local cultures. During the era of the Atlantic slave trade, people in diverse West African and West Central African societies cared for the dead and paid homage to them at their departure just as they do today. Families and communities assigned a dignified burial site to their dead ones, thus connecting them to the land of their ancestors. By doing so, they would be always remembered. The Atlantic slave trade disrupted these critical components of the transition from life to death. The remains of most enslaved persons who died during the Atlantic crossing were thrown into the sea. The bodies of many deceased slaves were abandoned along African and American shores. Despite being baptized as Catholics, the cadavers of many enslaved persons were also discarded in waste dumps and buried in shallow, unmarked graves. Only a small number of bondspeople received a dignified burial in graveyards, churchyards, and even inside church buildings. With the end of slavery and the growing process of urbanization of cities that had formerly served as slave-trading ports in Europe, Africa, and the Americas, these burial grounds were gradually forgotten and erased from the urban space. But as cities such as Rio de Janeiro, Lagos, Charleston, and New York City underwent transformation, construction projects have led to the rediscovery of forgotten burial grounds where enslaved people were put to rest. Local and international Black communities reclaimed these sites, which were transformed into vital reminders of the importance of slavery in these cities. By recovering these sites, Black communities reassigned their Black ancestors the humanity they lost by also reaffirming their own dignity.

CHAPTER 6

Markets of Human Flesh

"The sons seeing their fathers on the other side, rose up with great energy and went towards them; the mothers hold their other children in their arms and threw themselves with them on the ground, wounding their own flesh mercilessly, to prevent them from being taken away."[1] This is how the Portuguese explorer Zurara described the dramatic moment of the sale of newly arrived enslaved Africans in the Portuguese seaport of Lagos in the 1440s. Already in these first sales in the early days of the Atlantic slave trade, family separation haunted captive Africans transported from West Africa to the Iberian Peninsula and the Americas. At the site of this sale, there stands today the seventeenth-century two-story building called Slave Market (figure 6.1), now transformed into a museum. The name of the building evokes this early sale and Lagos's role in the Atlantic slave trade. Although enslaved people were not sold inside this later building, its name shows how this tragic past has remained alive in the city's collective memory. Auctions of African captives added a further layer to the commodification of human life that began on African shores and continued through the Middle Passage.

As the trade in enslaved Africans expanded to the Americas during the sixteenth and seventeenth centuries, and especially throughout the eighteenth and nineteenth centuries, slave sales took multiple forms. In this painful context, the experiences of enslaved Africans and their descendants in the slave market changed as well. Enslaved Africans

FIGURE 6.1. Slave Market, Lagos, Portugal, 2020. Courtesy of Roundtheworld, via Creative Commons Attribution-Share Alike 4.0 International license, https://en.wikipedia.org/wiki/File:LagosSlaveMarket1.jpg.

who survived the Atlantic crossing and the first days ashore were inevitably sold and became the property of slave owners in cities, mines, and plantations across the Americas. Although all were enslaved, their experiences of being sold in private and public spaces varied depending on the period of their arrival on American shores, the region where they landed, the activities they performed, and their age and sex. The human cargo of a slave ship had often already been consigned to specific buyers, including ship captains and other officers, as discussed in chapter 4. Still, many men, women, and children were kept in slave markets and slave pens. In these specific sites located at seaport cities such as Salvador, Recife, Rio de Janeiro, Cartagena, Havana, New York City, New Orleans, and Charleston, enslaved people waited to be sold and sometimes transported to other regions in the interior where they would work on plantations, in mines, and in various other settings in urban and rural areas. Other enslaved persons ended up in the slave market for a variety of reasons. The death of a slave owner, financial hardship, and even revenge against insubordinate behavior of bondspeople could provoke the sale of enslaved property.

Slave sales were held in many kinds of sites. Newspaper ads show how, especially in urban areas, slave owners sold bondspeople directly to individual buyers. But on several occasions, enslaved people were sold in shops and spaces designated as slave markets. Some of these markets were closed when the slave trade from Africa was banned in various regions of the Americas starting in the early nineteenth century, but as slave owners continued to sell and purchase people in the national domestic trades, other sale spaces emerged. Some of these sites remained active until the legal abolition of slavery in each country. Descriptions of slave markets of the United States, Brazil, and Cuba, particularly in travel accounts, are more abundant as these three countries were the largest slave societies in the Americas. But other records, including slave narratives, visual images, and newspaper ads, provide descriptions of similar markets in other parts of the Western Hemisphere such as the French colony of Saint-Domingue. This chapter explores the experiences of enslaved African men, women, and children who, after crossing the Atlantic Ocean, were sold in the Americas. I also examine cases of individuals and groups put on sale by their owners in the domestic market, by looking at the activities of sellers and buyers and the roles they played in these inhumane commercial transactions. Considering these various contexts across the Americas, especially during the eighteenth and nineteenth centuries, this chapter argues that these sales were a pivotal stage of the commodification of enslaved Africans and their descendants. But even then, enslaved people resisted to be treated as things, by continuously affirming their humanity.

New Africans

Markets were places of despair. Like the depots on African coasts and slave vessels, slave markets were sites of violence, dehumanization, and commodification where enslaved people were chastised, disciplined, and sexually violated. Markets were also places of transition. At least for African-born individuals, these spaces were where they had the first contacts with enslaved people who, unlike them, were born in the Americas. As a microcosm of slave societies, the slave market provides a glimpse of the conditions of life under slavery in the Western Hemisphere.

Newly arrived Africans left few testimonies of the period they spent in slave pens and slave market buildings waiting to be sold. But in the middle of the eighteenth century, more than three hundred years after the sale of African captives in Lagos, and during the summit of the Atlantic slave trade, similar scenes of despair continued to occur in the Americas. Take the example of Olaudah Equiano. After a long Atlantic crossing, Equiano and his fellow captives finally arrived in Bridgetown, Barbados, in 1754. Planters and merchants, probably accompanied by a health professional, came on board to inspect the human cargo. Still terrified after the dreadful journey on the sea, men, women, and children feared they would be eaten by the white men. But after this scary first contact with future buyers, other enslaved workers in the port area came on board to calm them down by reassuring them that they were not going to be eaten but were instead there to "work, and were soon to go on land" to meet other Africans.[2]

Sadness and fear marked the landing of enslaved Africans in the Americas, even though for some enslaved persons, coming ashore may also have been a short-lived moment of relief, albeit as a result of false pretenses. Equiano reports that as soon as they landed, they were led to the merchant's yard, the market where recently arrived slaves were sold.[3] On their way, Africans speaking all languages came to him and his shipmates. These were precious moments, as during these first contacts, enslaved Africans working in the port area could ask newly arrived captives, who spoke their native languages, if they had news from their villages and towns and if they had any word from their relatives left behind on the African continent. In these first interactions, local enslaved men and women certainly provided newly arrived enslaved Africans with information about the new land.[4]

Equiano did not spend many days in the slave market waiting to be sold, but he briefly described the slave auction, in which one could observe how starkly the attitude of buyers who selected human commodities contrasted with the horror of the Africans on sale: "On a signal given, (as the beat of a drum) the buyers rush at once into the yard where the slaves are confined, and make choice of that parcel they like best. The noise and clamour with which this is attended, and the eagerness visible in the countenances of the buyers, serve not a little to increase the apprehensions of the terrified Africans."[5] Whereas to merchants and buyers, purchasing and selling human flesh was a common activity, to enslaved Africans the auction meant separation from relatives, countrymen, and shipmates. Equiano remembered enslaved men who shared the same men's compartment in the slave ship and who were separated during the sale: "It was very moving on this occasion to see and hear their cries at parting."[6]

Equiano knew that this tragedy was just beginning. Repeated separations from kinfolk and comrades haunted enslaved men, women, and children during the entire period they remained enslaved in the Americas. Like Equiano, but more than one century later, Oluale Kossola (alias Cudjo Kazoola Lewis) also remembered his landing in the United States in similar ways. In 1860, when the international slave trade had been illegal in the country for more than five decades, the slave ship *Clotilda* entered the Mobile River in Alabama. Crew members discreetly disembarked African captives on Twelvemile Island, where they were given clothes for the first time. Kossola clearly recalled when the shipowner Timothy Meaher took thirty-two captives to sell them separately. This new separation led him to relive the trauma experienced on the African continent when he was torn apart from his family and community: "We were very sorry to be parted from one 'nother. We cry from home from our people. We seventy days cross de water from de Affica soil, and now dey part us from one 'nother. Derefore we cry."[7]

Similar scenes of despair occurred in other parts of the Americas as well. Portuguese and British chartered companies such as the Cacheu and Cape Verde Company (Companhia de Cacheu e Cabo Verde) and the South Sea Company (created respectively in the seventeenth and eighteenth centuries) were represented by a variety of slave merchants in the port of Cartagena, in present-day Colombia. Larger traders could purchase groups of dozens more enslaved persons to be distributed in the interior, whereas smaller-scale merchants could purchase a few slaves to resell along with various goods. Upon anchoring in the bay of Cartagena, the slave ships were inspected by port authorities, and as in other ports, slave merchants came on board. After examining the human cargo in search of any signs of illnesses, slave traders paid the duties for each enslaved person according to calculations that varied over time but considered age, sex, and physical condition. Sometimes, slave traders branded the bodies of African captives while yet on the coasts of Africa. In the port of Cartagena, during the colonial period, slave traders employed a hot iron or silver device to first brand newly arrived captives with a Spanish crown emblem, in order to avoid illegal imports of enslaved persons. A second mark was then added to identify the holder of the *asiento*, an agreement established between the Spanish crown and an individual or company representative who engaged to provide the Spanish colonies with enslaved Africans. Finally, a third brand identified the owner of the enslaved persons purchased in the markets of Cartagena. The repetition of this excruciating procedure that left permanent scars on the bodies of enslaved people was not only designed to distinguish them as human property but was also intended to extend the broader process of managing and controlling African bodies.

As early as the sixteenth century, enslaved Africans who disembarked in Cartagena were confined in several warehouses located close to the harbor and the city walls. Enslaved Africans were sold in plain sight near Cartagena's elite family residences and churches.[8] Slave merchants also gathered new Africans in yards and buildings adjacent to their residences. Many others were lodged in barracoons spread around the city or in surrounding neighborhoods. Enslaved Africans came ashore ill and weak with scurvy, yaws, and dysentery, and often infected with diseases such as typhus, smallpox, typhoid fever, measles, and yellow fever.[9]

Spanish Jesuit priest Alonso de Sandoval, who was a missionary in Cartagena in the early seventeenth century, described the dreadful conditions he witnessed at these slave depots in his *De instauranda Aethiopum salute*, published in 1627. According to him, on one occasion he saw "two slaves already dead, naked on the floor, as if they were beasts, facing upward with their mouths open and full of flies." In another house, he discovered a recently arrived enslaved man who had died "in the middle of a patio where many people were living. He was naked, face down with his mouth open to the floor, covered in flies that seemed to want to eat him. There he was left as if he were less important than a dog."[10] In these new spaces of confinement, other slaves were in charge of overseeing, cooking, and feeding the newly arrived slaves, who remained naked and poorly fed, a context that barely differed from African coastal barracoons or the holds of slave ships.[11]

Captive Africans could remain in these insalubrious slave pens for more than one year waiting to be sold. In Cartagena, slaves who were not consigned to specific owners and traders were brought to be auctioned at the public square, a site that attracted dozens of buyers from various regions, who were invited to make their bids. A similar context was also visible in Jamaica's slave-trading port of Kingston, which imported nearly one million enslaved Africans in the era of the Atlantic slave trade and was also the entry port for captives who would be transported to Spanish colonies in the Caribbean region. In the eighteenth century, Kingston was one the five largest British cities in the Americas, along with Boston, New York, Philadelphia, and Charleston. During this period, most enslaved Africans who disembarked in Kingston were acquired by traders on consignment from British merchants and their agents based in Britain, or other representatives based in Kingston. In this system, the human property was loaned to the merchants. If the captives were sold, the traders received a percentage of the selling price. Still, other slaves were sold wholesale. In other words, local merchants directly purchased the captives at a reduced price, placed them in urban yards and pens, and only then made profits by reselling them retail in the local market to local buyers. Even though they rarely spent a long time in these yards, as in Cartagena and Rio de Janeiro, many Africans who came ashore in Kingston spent their first days in the Americas confined in slave pens.[12] Starting in the early eighteenth century, in Kingston, British colonists, including women, also purchased enslaved persons directly from slave ships, especially enslaved African boys and girls to serve as companions for their own children.[13]

European travelers who visited Brazil during the eighteenth and nineteenth centuries described the slave markets of Brazil's main slave-trading ports, such as Salvador, Recife, and Rio de Janeiro. In the nineteenth century, British traveler Thomas Lindley, who sojourned in Bahia in 1802, described the slave market of Salvador similarly, again emphasizing the large numbers of recently arrived enslaved Africans: "The streets and squares of the city are thronged with groups of human beings, exposed for sale at the doors of the different merchants to whom they belong; five slave ships having arrived within the last three days."[14] Although acknowledging that the large numbers of enslaved Africans could increase the risk of slave rebellions, as had happened in the French colony of Saint-Domingue in 1791, Lindley expressed the view that enslaved Africans in Brazil were joyful and satisfied, "indulged to licentiousness, not over-worked, and enjoying their native vegetable food."[15] Emphasizing what he perceived to be the Portuguese's humanity toward their slaves, his take on the living conditions of enslaved people was probably derived from hearsay, and it was certainly not based on a close scrutiny of Salvador's slave markets.

Other European travelers who witnessed the disembarkation of Africans in the Americas reported scenes of deep sadness. On November 22, 1821, British traveler Martha Graham described in her journal the arrival of Africans in Salvador, Bahia: "This very moment, there is a slave ship discharging her cargo, and the slaves are singing as they go ashore. They have left the ship, and they see they will be on the dry land; and so, at the command of their keeper, they are singing one of their country songs, in a strange land."[16] In her visit to the port area of Salvador's lower city, Graham explained that the slave market was located in this part of the city: "Passing the arsenal gate, we went along the low street, and found it widen considerably at three quarters of a mile beyond: there are the markets, which seem to be admirably supplied, especially with fish. There also is the slave market, a sight I have not yet learned to see without shame and indignation."[17]

During her stay in Brazil, Graham also visited the slave market in Recife, the capital of the Brazilian province of Pernambuco and the third-largest Brazilian slave-trading port. This time, she also described the horrible conditions of men, women, and children on sale: "About fifty young creatures, boys and girls, with all the appearance of disease and famine consequent upon scanty food and long confinement in unwholesome places, were sitting and lying about among the filthiest animals in the streets."[18] Her description of emaciated enslaved Africans, which was also reproduced in an engraving illustrating her travel account, indicates that these men, women, and children had quite likely recently arrived from Africa and were still so weak as to be unfit to be sold to local slave owners. Although not detailed, Graham's descriptions clearly indicate the size and significance of these markets, in which thousands of enslaved Africans who crossed the Atlantic Ocean were sold every year.

Slave markets were not only the places where economic transactions took place; they also were sites of pain and sorrow. Amédée-François Frézier, an engineer working for the French Army Intelligence Corps, who had visited Chile, Peru, and Brazil between 1712 and 1714, seemed shocked by the presence of large numbers of enslaved people who were put on sale in horrible conditions in the slave market of Salvador: "There are shops full of these poor unfortunates, who are exposed all naked, and where they buy them like beasts and upon whom they acquire the same power, so that on minor discontent, they can kill them almost with impunity, or at least mistreat them as cruelly as they want."[19] Nude and debilitated, the conditions to which these enslaved Africans were submitted after landing in Brazil, differed little from what they experienced in the slave ships.

Sales of Bondspeople Born in the Americas

Bondspeople born in the Americas also made their way to slave pens, markets, squares, and auction blocks, where public sales were held. Many enslaved men, women, and children were also sold in larger or smaller sites such as squares, shops, and even private homes. In North America, river port cities such as Alexandria, Virginia, and Washington, DC, had active slave markets. Slave traders used riverways to transport enslaved persons from the coast to the interior, as well as from the North to the South. Nearly every town on the banks of the Mississippi River had a slave market. In 1808, when the prohibition of the international slave trade to the United States took effect, the cotton industry was growing and fueling the Southern plantation system. As slavery expanded to respond to the cotton production, the domestic slave trade intensified. Enslaved people were sold and moved to the growing Southern markets. Illegally enslaved free people also found themselves held captive, soon to be sold in these marketplaces.

In the West Indies and Latin America, especially in Cuba and Brazil, the slave trade from Africa continued through the middle of the nineteenth century. Cuba banned the international slave trade for the first time in 1820, but the illegal introduction of enslaved Africans continued until 1867, when legislation establishing a second prohibition was more effectively enforced. Brazil outlawed the import of enslaved Africans in 1831. Nonetheless, nearly 800,000 captives were introduced into the country until 1850, when new legislation barring the importation of enslaved people in the country passed and was eventually fully enforced. Therefore, between 1831 and 1850, the period of the international illegal slave trade to Brazil, auctions of recently disembarked enslaved Africans could no longer be announced in newspapers and held in public spaces. However, sales of Africans and Brazilian-born bondspeople who entered the country prior to 1831 were allowed during this period. Moreover, the domestic slave trade in Brazil remained active until 1888, when slavery itself was abolished in the country.

One of the major destructive consequences of slave auctions and sales was family separation. Enslaved men and women born in the Americas reported the horrible moment when they were sold and torn apart from their families. Their parents and relatives also told them how either they or their ancestors had been separated in these tragic sales, which often occurred after slave owners passed away. Take the example of Mary Prince, born in slavery in the British colony of Bermuda in 1788. Like many enslaved children, her early years were marked by family separation and grief. When she was a girl, her owner put her and her two sisters up for sale to raise money for his marriage, separating her from her mother. The day of the sale came, and her mother brought her and her sisters to the marketplace. In her narrative, published in Britain after she escaped slavery, Prince recounted the traumatic episode of her sale, when the market's organizer brought her to be auctioned: "He took me by the hand, and led me out into the middle of the street, and, turning me slowly round, exposed me to the view of those who attended the vendue. I was soon surrounded by strange men, who examined and handled me in the same manner that a butcher would a calf or a lamb he was about to purchase, and who talked about my shape and size in like words—as if I could no more understand their meaning than the dumb beasts."[20]

Harriet Jacobs, who was born into slavery in North Carolina in 1813, reported these appalling moments in her narrative, *Incidents in the Life of a Slave Girl*, telling how her grandmother, uncles, aunts, and parents were sold and separated several times. Jacobs lost her parents when she was a child. Along with her brother, she was raised by her grandmother, who was also enslaved. Her grandmother's owner always promised to free her, but she ended up dying before fulfilling her promise. When her estate was settled, Jacobs's grandmother was put up for sale: "When the day of sale came, she took her place among the chattels, and at the first call she sprang upon the auction-block. Many voices called out, 'Shame! Shame! Who is going to sell you, aunt Marthy? Don't stand there! That is no place for you.'" The seventy-year-old sister of Jacobs's grandmother's late mistress, who had known the bondswoman for several decades, made a bid and eventually purchased her for fifty dollars. As an adult, Jacobs recounted the day she witnessed an enslaved mother separated from her seven children on the auction block.[21] Both Jacobs and the bondswoman knew that the slave trader who purchased the children would sell them separately and that the mother would probably never see them again, though in some cases enslaved people were able to receive news from relatives who had been sold away.[22] In this tragic context of commercial transactions that ignored and willfully broke bondspeople's family ties, the most an enslaved person could hope for was that the owner to whom they were sold was not an overly abusive one.

Sales left deep scars on enslaved people who, decades after these traumatic events, still remembered being stripped from their loved ones. Enslaved families could be sold separately in the United States until the legal end of slavery in 1865. Only in 1871 did Brazil enact legislation prohibiting the separation of enslaved couples and children younger than twelve years of age from their parents. Enslaved men and women also passed down to their descendants memories of the horrible circumstances that led to their being sold, the time they spent confined in slave pens, and the traumatic experience of being shown, like livestock, in auction blocks. Although each individual experienced uniquely the process of being sold and separated from their dear ones, they also lived this trauma collectively.

On March 2 and 3, 1859, the second largest and most infamous of these sales held in the United States took place in Georgia.[23] Pierce Mease Butler, a planter from Georgia Sea Islands, sold his 436 enslaved men, women, and children, who had never been sold before, to pay his debts, mainly contracted in gambling. It was the largest slave sale in the history of the state of Georgia, and one of the largest in the United States.[24] The Weeping Time, as the massive sale became popularly known, did not take place at an ordinary auction block or slave market but rather at a racecourse in order to accommodate the massive number of enslaved persons on sale. Historian Anne C. Bailey examined the devastating sale, showing how this event imprinted long-lasting marks on dozens of separated enslaved families. After the end of the Civil War and the abolition of slavery in 1865 in the United States, as other freedpeople did, the descendants of the men, women, and children sold during the Weeping Time sought to find their relatives and recover their names.[25] The tragic sale remained alive in the collective memory of Georgia's Black population, and in 2008, the Georgia Historical Society and the City of Savannah dedicated a marker to pay homage to the men, women, and children sold during the dreadful event. Yet, many other enslaved people were sold in other sales across the United States. Although these stories rarely reached the public sphere, enslaved people passed down their memories of these painful episodes to their descendants.[26]

The Space of Slave Sales

Physical structures where slave markets operated ranged widely. Consider the example of Cartagena, a slave-trading port established by Spanish colonizers on the Caribbean coastal area of present-day Colombia, where nearly 150,000 enslaved Africans came ashore between 1501 and 1867. Although these captives were transported from various ports of Upper Guinea, the Bight of Benin, and the Bight of Biafra, most of them were embarked in West Central African ports. During the most intensive period of the trade to the region, during the seventeenth and eighteenth centuries, Cartagena became the major hub where enslaved Africans were gathered in slave depots to be transported to the Viceroyalty of Peru and other regions in the Spanish Americas.[27]

Seventeenth-century observers described Cartagena's open-air market as a site surrounded by barracoons separated by palisades.

Slave auctions were public spectacles and the most common way used to pay debts and liquidate estates. To hide scars and other wounds, slave dealers covered the naked bodies of enslaved men, women, and children with palm oil. Traders and buyers forced enslaved persons to walk, dance, sing, speak, and laugh. Women amounted to nearly 30 percent of customers in Cartagena's slave market during the eighteenth century. Although female buyers likely acquired one or two enslaved persons to perform domestic service, their significant presence in the market suggests that they engaged in reselling captives to other customers. Like the men, these buyers of human flesh manipulated, touched, and smelled the bodies of the Africans on display. In this arduous process, most enslaved persons, including men, women, children, and babies, were sold individually and in pairs, even though sales in groups also occurred, in numbers ranging from five to one hundred.[28] Although the slave trade to the region was legally banned in 1812, the internal trade persisted. Until the end of slavery in Colombia in 1851, sales of bondspeople were a common occurrence.[29]

Slave markets and auction blocks were major landmarks in most slave-trading port cities in the Americas. In important slave ports such as Cap Français (Le Cap) in the French colony of Saint-Domingue, through which one-third of the French imports of enslaved Africans arrived, most captives were sold on board the slave ships. As noted by David Geggus, African captives in poorer health were brought ashore and, as elsewhere in the Americas, they were gathered by the dozens in depots close to the shore, where they died in public view. In the late eighteenth century, French administrators ordered slave traders to transfer these barracoons to a new slave market in the south of the town, but the order apparently went unheeded, and mortality remained high. Depending on the year, as many as 18 percent of these newly disembarked enslaved Africans could die while waiting to be sold at Cap Français.[30]

Sites of slave sales also changed in Brazil, as the international slave trade was gradually banished. Starting in the early eighteenth century, when Portuguese colonizers uncovered mines of gold and diamonds in the interior of the colony, the coastal city of Rio de Janeiro gradually became the Brazil's largest slave-trading port and then the colony's capital in 1766. Slave merchants imported Africans, especially from the West Central African ports of Luanda and Benguela who, once disembarked in Rio de Janeiro, remained in the city and neighboring areas. During the period when most Africans were disembarked at Fish's Beach, the captives entered the city to be sold in the slave shops of Direita Street, but few descriptions of these early sites exist, as very few foreign travelers visiting Rio de Janeiro during that time published their accounts. During the last decades of the eighteenth century, most shops selling newly arrived enslaved Africans were located in Valongo, an area corresponding to today's neighborhoods of Gamboa and Saúde. But many Africans who had disembarked in Rio de Janeiro were also transported to plantations in other regions such as São Paulo, and especially the mining region of Minas Gerais. The Valongo complex included the Cemetery of the New Blacks, discussed in chapter 5, as well as a quarantine station and the shops where recently arrived enslaved Africans were sold.

Several travelers visited the Valongo slave market, the site with the largest concentration of recently arrived Africans available for sale. They often expressed shock at the horrible conditions of men, women, and children. British clergyman Robert Walsh described the infamous slave market in his travel account *Notices of Brazil in 1828 and 1829*. He explained that, after coming ashore, as in Cartagena, most slaves were sold by intermediaries in the slave market.[31] In Rio de Janeiro these intermediaries were Roma, a people originated in north India who had lived in Europe since the fifteenth century. Because of their nomadic lifestyle, language, and culture, they had been rejected since their arrival in Europe. In the eighteenth century, Portugal ordered that the Roma population be deported to its overseas colonies. In Brazil, the Roma initially integrated with the white lower classes. In Rio de Janeiro, the Roma not only became slave owners but also specialized in buying and reselling enslaved people, thereby making some of these Roma wealthy.[32] Eventually, their presence in Rio de Janeiro's slave market was so visible that several European travelers reported their activities in the text and images of their travelogues.[33]

Walsh explained that "almost every house in this place is a large ware-room, where the slaves are deposited, and customers go to purchase. These ware-rooms stand at each side of the street, and the poor creatures are exposed for sale like any other commodity."[34] He noted that the warerooms were spacious and could accommodate three hundred to four hundred enslaved men and women of various ages: "Round the room are benches on which the elder generally sit, and the middle is occupied by the younger, particularly females who squat on the ground stowed close together, with their hands and chins resting on their knees."[35] White Brazilian women also shopped in Valongo slave market. Well dressed, they arrived in groups, carefully inspecting the bodies of enslaved Africans before making their choice.

Walsh's description of Valongo perfectly corresponds to two lithographs published in the travel account *Voyage pittoresque et historique au Brésil* by French artist Jean-Baptiste Debret, who spent sixteen years in Rio de Janeiro and kept a studio in the Catumbi neighborhood, where the Roma slave dealers were based. For example, the lithograph *Shop of Valongo Street* (*Boutique de la Rue Val-Longo*) shows a large, neat depot where emaciated enslaved men, women, and children are sitting on benches or lying on the floor waiting to be sold under the supervision of a Roma dealer. The horrible scene represented in the lithograph is confirmed in the text accompanying the image, in which Debret explained that the "auction room, most often silent, is still infected of castor oil escaping from the pores of these wrinkled walking skeletons, whose look, curious, shy, or sad, reminds you of the interior of a menagerie."[36] Still, in spite of the horrible environment, he noted that sometimes the slaves waiting to be sold would sing and dance "turning on themselves and clapping their hands to mark the beat, a kind of dance quite similar to the savages in Brazil."[37] Music and dance were ways to cope with trauma, to collectively remember their homelands. Despite extreme despair, Africans were able to show resilience.

Bavarian painter Johann Moritz Rugendas, who sojourned in Brazil from 1822 to 1825, also observed the unhealthy and inhuman conditions of Africans kept in the various shops of the Valongo slave market, which in his travelogue is described as "a shocking and almost unbearable spectacle: all day these unfortunate, men, women, children, stand sit or lie close to the walls of these huge buildings, and mixed with each other; or, if the weather is good, we see them in the street."[38] His illustrated travelogue referred to the slave pens as "cowsheds" and described the horrible condition and odor of enslaved Africans who had been recently disembarked from slave ships. Captives were almost naked, wearing only a cloth around their hips. To recover and be sold, they were fed a diet consisting of cassava flour, beans, jerk beef, and fruits, much richer than it had been during the Atlantic crossing.[39] During nearly the same period, Maria Graham also described the Valongo slave market as the site where the slave trade "comes in all its horrors before one's eyes." Yet, she slightly differed from Rugendas by emphasizing that enslaved Africans were "subject to all the miseries of a new negro's life, scanty diet, brutal examination, and the lash."[40] But a few months later she visited Valongo again. This time, she provided a more detailed description of the desolate state of newly arrived Africans on sale in the various shops. With shaved heads and emaciated bodies, most of these men, women, and children were sitting on long benches placed along the walls. Other clearly weak captives were lying on mats. Graham, like other travelers, confirmed that the slave market was a site of transition between the brutality of the Middle Passage and the intrinsic violence of bondage in the Americas.

Selecting and Pricing Enslaved People

Over time, men and women who procured enslaved people in slave markets in the Americas developed their own preferences. Portuguese and Brazilian slave traders and slave owners identified Africans by "nation" (*nação*) such as "Nagô," "Jeje," "Congo," "Angola," "Benguela," "Mina," "Cabinda," and many others. Although these terms vaguely suggested some correspondence with alleged ethnic groups, in reality they only broadly referred to the large zones in which were situated the seaports from where these captives were boarded on slave ships. Still, over time, enslaved Africans themselves started embracing these denominations. Once in the Americas, Africans coming from neighboring regions shared similar religious systems and spoke languages of the same family. Therefore, they were able to communicate and understand each other. Especially in Latin America and the Caribbean, the commonalities of these so-called nations allowed Africans not only to physically and culturally survive the ordeals of slavery but also to rebuild an identity and create other forms of association, as I will discuss in chapter 14 with respect to how enslaved people congregated in pagan and religious festivals and holidays.[41]

In markets selling recently arrived enslaved Africans, enslaved men were available in higher numbers than women, usually in a ratio of two to one. As explained in chapter 3, this disparity was because slave merchants believed men were better suited for agricultural work, whereas African agents were more inclined to keep women to perform agricultural labor or to sell them to trans-Saharan traders to serve as concubines in Muslim societies. Buyers, in turn, also developed preferences allegedly based on ethnic origins, which in actuality relied on preconceptions associated with specific groups of enslaved individuals.

These stereotypes appeared early. In a treatise originally published in the eighteenth century, Italian Jesuit missionary and administrator Giovanni Antonio Andreoni (alias André João Antonil), who sojourned in Brazil in the seventeenth century, explained the alleged differences among these various nations. According to him, the "Ardas" (a denomination referencing the Kingdom of Allada on the Bight of Benin) and the "Minas" (also a generic reference to Africans of the Bight of Benin) were robust, whereas captives from Cape Verde and São Tomé were weaker. As stated by the Jesuit missionary, captives from Angola, especially those raised in Luanda, were more apt than the previous ones to learn mechanical trades. Moreover, the "Congos" (a broad label to refer to captives captured in regions of West

Central Africa under the authority of the King of Kongo and who spoke languages of the Kikongo cluster) were also quite industrious. They were effective at working not only in the sugarcane fields but also in workshops and domestic service.[42] These racist views persisted in the nineteenth century. The French physician Jean-Baptiste Alban Imbert, who came to Brazil in 1831, published an extensive treatise about the diseases affecting enslaved people. In this book, he reproduced pseudoscientific racial stereotypes by stating that Africans from the Gold Coast and the Bight of Benin were the best ones and advising planters to not purchase enslaved Africans from certain recognizably "bad" regions of provenance such as Benguela.[43]

Similar preferences based on long-lasting stereotypes also existed in colonial North America. Like Antonil, eighteenth-century British observers also praised the enslaved Africans transported from the Upper Guinea region, the Gold Coast, and the Bight of Benin as superior, robust, and hardy, and sometimes even as docile and obedient. In South Carolina, there was an apparent preference for African captives from Senegambia and the Gold Coast, whereas Africans from the Bight of Biafra were held in disdain.[44] Despite this, in his famous dictionary, Malachy Postlethwayt, who worked for the Royal African Company, also praised enslaved people coming from the region of Angola in West Central Africa as "more capable to undergo the labour and fatigue of cultivating and manufacturing sugar, tobacco, indigo, and the other hard work to which these poor wretches are commonly put."[45] During the eighteenth century, slave merchants and slave owners were suspicious of the insurgent and belligerent behavior of enslaved Africans who previously worked in British colonies of the West Indies. Preferring to acquire slaves who arrived directly from Africa, these agents also relied on preconceived ideas passed down via oral tradition and publications about particular qualities and abilities of enslaved people coming from specific African regions.[46]

As with the process of acquiring captives on the coast of Africa, purchasers sought individuals in good physical shape who would survive in horrible working conditions. Before transporting their slaves for sale in the New Orleans market, slave dealers shaved the beards and combed the hair of enslaved men. As age was a central factor in the selection process, they also dyed any existing gray hairs.[47] In various parts of the Americas, younger males were preferred to perform work on plantations, in mines, on cattle ranches, and in jerk meat factories, but buyers also procured enslaved women to work either on plantations or in urban settings as laundresses, cooks, and wet nurses who breastfed the offspring of slave owners. Enslaved women considered to be physically attractive were highly valued by male buyers.[48] Not only they could provide sexual services, but they were also possible good candidates to bear children who would become the property of their owners. In the United States, height was a prized element for locally born enslaved men who were sold in public auctions, and buyers paid more for tall males. They also paid the highest prices for young men between the ages of eighteen and twenty-five, and young women between fifteen and twenty—in other words, in the early years of reproductive age.[49]

Historians of slavery have conceived the value of an enslaved person as the "discounted sum of expected lifetime earnings net of consumption" that highly depended on "skills, life expectancy, and interest rates."[50] Prices of slaves varied over time and were determined by local and Atlantic markets. During the colonial period, the Spanish crown regulated the prices of enslaved Africans disembarked and sold in Cartagena. But as elsewhere, supply and demand often prevailed. A variety of factors impacted prices of enslaved people, including place of birth, region of provenance, age, and sex. Needless to say, physical and health conditions were also decisive elements, as they would determine how long and how much an enslaved person could produce.

In general, Africans who had recently disembarked in the Americas were priced lower than enslaved people who were either born in the Americas or who had lived there for many years. However, it seems that shorter life expectancy was a greater factor than language knowledge and skills in lowering the value of newly arrived enslaved Africans.[51] In Cartagena and Saint-Domingue, the prices of recently arrived enslaved

Africans were cheaper than locally born individuals. Buyers seemed to prefer enslaved men and women who spoke Creole as well as Spanish or French, and who were converted to Roman Catholicism, to perform work in the urban areas as artisans and domestic servants and to occupy higher positions in residences, on plantations, and in mines, as some of them also knew Portuguese and were adapted to local customs. In nineteenth-century Rio de Janeiro, the preferences were different, probably because of the great availability of African-born bondspeople. Newspapers featured numerous announcements selling African-born women who worked as domestic servants and African-born young men who were barbers and pages. Although purchasers sought African captives in good physical condition, in ports such as Cartagena, some buyers purchased enslaved persons who were considered physically and mentally ill because they could be acquired for very low prices. After a period of investment in their recovery, they could resell them for larger amounts and make great profits.[52]

It is not surprising that as the Atlantic slave trade grew and the demand for an African enslaved workforce to work especially on sugarcane plantations intensified, the prices of newly arrived slaves in the Americas gradually increased as well. For example, the average nominal price of male enslaved Africans disembarked in Jamaica between 1671 and 1675 was 25 pounds sterling. Nearly a century later, in the period from 1791 to 1795, the average price of a newly arrived enslaved African in Jamaica corresponded to 59.7 pounds sterling. The average price of a male African disembarked in the West Indies and the North American mainland between 1671 and 1675 was 21 pounds sterling, whereas the average price for the period between 1791 and 1795 for the same broad region was 59.2 pounds sterling.[53]

In seventeenth-century Cartagena, when the Portuguese held the *asiento*, the *asiento* representatives could not sell in credit newly arrived Africans directly to individual owners. Instead, they depended on intermediaries to purchase recently disembarked African-born captives in cash to resell them to individual customers. Most buyers were merchants who also traded other goods, but they might also be governors, public officials, clerks, artisans, and farmers.[54] During the slavery era as a whole, the Roman Catholic Church was the largest slave owner institution in the Americas. Thus, religious orders such as the Jesuits of the Society of Jesus were also important buyers of enslaved people who had recently arrived in Cartagena's market.

Slave owners could also sell their enslaved property individually or in small groups directly to interested customers. These sales were often intended to pay debts. In Brazil, owners of sugar plantations and mills obtained enslaved people from large slave merchants as advance payment for future sugarcane harvest. When they went into debt, their human property was seized and sold in public auctions.[55] Likewise, when slave owners were able to recover enslaved men and women who escaped, they also did not hesitate to sell them. In Latin America, local judges could also order a slave owner to sell a mistreated slave. In these various cases, enslaved people could be sold in public auctions where buyers made bids as well as private sales in which buyers and sellers engaged in direct negotiation.

In British North America, colonial eighteenth-century newspapers featured a considerable number of advertisements announcing slave auctions and sales, including sales of newly arrived enslaved Africans, many of whom came ashore in Charleston. The sales were announced on flyers distributed throughout the city and also advertised in the *South Carolina Gazette*.[56] On July 24, 1769, a poster (figure 6.2) announced the sale of ninety-four "prime, healthy negroes, consisting of thirty-nine men, fifteen boys, twenty-four women, and sixteen girls" "just arrived" in the Brigantine Dembia from Sierra Leone.[57] The poster is framed by two images representing an African man and an African woman. The man is holding a spear; both figures are bare-chested and only wearing a loincloth to cover the lower part of their bodies, and each one is accompanied by a child. Despite being depicted in an idealized fashion, similarly to the ways other Africans and even Indigenous populations were portrayed at the time, the presence of children in the image suggests that being healthy also meant having the ability to conceive healthy enslaved children.[58]

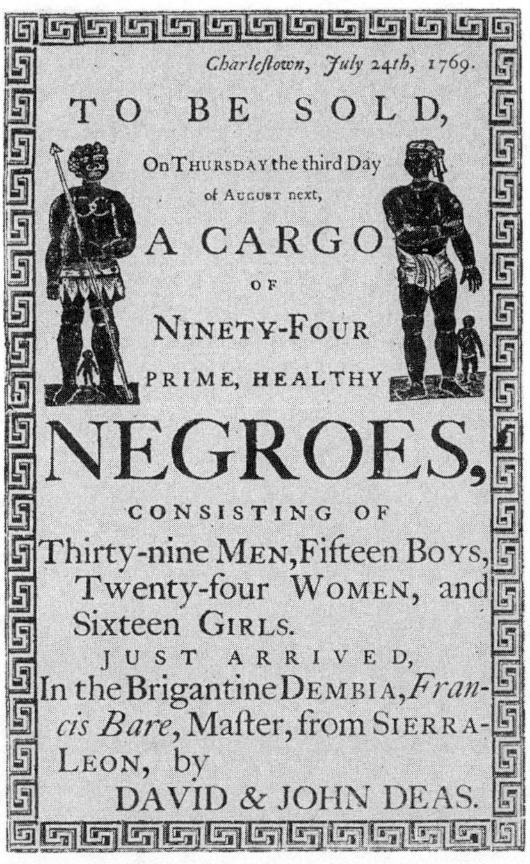

FIGURE 6.2. Advertisement for Sale of Newly Arrived Africans, Charleston, July 24, 1769. *Slavery Images: A Visual Record of the African Slave Trade and Slave Life in the Early African Diaspora*, accessed July 13, 2023, http://slaveryimages.org/s/slavery images/item/1971.

Private sales and public auctions also occurred after the death of the head of the family that required division of assets. An ad on December 26, 1770, published just after Christmas in the *Maryland Gazette* and the *Pennsylvania Journal*, announced that several enslaved men, women, and children were to be sold. The slaves were already the property of a local man, and although the ad did not reveal where they were born, it indicated that "amongst whom is a very good Blacksmith, and several good Forgemen, [and] Wood-cutters" who were part of the estate of the late Joseph Smith and would be auctioned in Baltimore, Maryland.[59]

The pages of nineteenth-century Brazilian newspapers showcased advertisements of slave owners offering enslaved people for sale in the middle of other announcements selling the most disparate things. One single page of the newspaper *Diário do Rio de Janeiro* from December 16, 1826, features a variety of ads selling a farm, a shop, a horse, a pestle, birds, all kinds of alcohol, and military uniforms, as well as several individual announcements marketing enslaved men, women, and children, including African-born slaves identified as Cabinda, Angola, and Mina. Directing buyers to private homes and to the shops of the Valongo slave market, the ads described in detail the skills of the human property on sale. While men were shoemakers, pages, gardeners, and barbers, enslaved women included street vendors and domestic workers who performed tasks such as cooking, running errands, and cleaning the house. Most ads conclude by emphasizing that the slaves on sale had no vices or ruses.[60]

Sales and auctions could also take place in private residences and on plantations. French naturalist Alcide Dessalines d'Orbigny, who traveled for eight years in several countries of the Americas in the first half of the nineteenth century, witnessed one of these sales in the French colony of Martinique, which took place after a planter went into bankruptcy. He seemed shocked to hear the merchant shouting, "Three hundred piastres the negro!" and then see buyers examining the bodies of enslaved persons as they were livestock: "The latter opened his mouth to count his teeth; this one bent down to inspect his feet, legs, thighs and chest, trying to make sure nothing was being concealed from him, neither varicose veins nor hernias."[61] The horrendous scene of a slave auction, so common throughout the Americas during the era of chattel slavery, is also depicted in one of the engravings illustrating Orbigny's account. The image also features women and children participating in the inspection of slaves on sale, showing readers how already at an early age all French free men and women were trained to treat the bodies of enslaved people as mere commodities. In Martinique, as in Rio de Janeiro, Cartagena, and even in New Orleans, white women attended slave auctions and went to the marketplaces where they sold and purchased enslaved people. Although historians such as Walter Johnson have stated that "it was only men who went to the slave market," recent magisterial works by Black women historians have proved that this statement is rather inaccurate.[62] In 1816, the creation of "Ladies Auctions" in several cities of the United States, such as Charleston, New Orleans, Nashville, Memphis, and Richmond, taught white female buyers how to bid on and purchase enslaved people like any other commodity.[63]

Starting in 1807 with the prohibition of the British Atlantic slave trade, Britain put growing pressure on other nations to stop the international trade. In addition, the rise of legislation gradually abolishing slavery in the US North and the successful revolution in Saint-Domingue that ended slavery in the French colony in 1804 made the enslaved African workforce even more limited. This scarcity impacted the prices not only of the newly arrived men, women, and children in the regions that still allowed imports of enslaved Africans, such as Brazil and Cuba, but also those of slaves born in the Americas.[64]

In the years of the cotton boom starting in the second decade of the nineteenth century, prices of enslaved people were practically determined by the price of cotton in the United States.[65] Although there were increases, there were also several oscillations. The growing cotton industry propelled the growth of the enslaved population as well as the intensification of the domestic legal and illegal slave trade. This new demand for enslaved workers also led to the rise in prices for them, especially in the two decades before the abolition of slavery. Take the example of New Orleans. Between 1824 and 1858, the average price of an enslaved man between twenty-one and thirty-eight years old varied from as low as $498 to as high as nearly $900.[66] New Orleans's French Quarter was crowded with slave pens, showrooms, and offices of various slave-trading companies, in addition to other prominent sites such as the rotunda of the St. Louis Hotel. Buyers visiting these sites scrutinized the bodies of enslaved men, women, and children the way they did in other parts of the Americas, looking for any defects that could affect the productivity of their future human property. They rubbed bondspeople's muscles, assessed the color of their skin and gums, counted fingers and teeth, touched bondswomen's breasts, palpated their abdomens, and searched for whipping scars, signs that revealed rebellious behavior.[67] They also forced men, women, and children to walk, jump, and talk to test their fitness. It was not uncommon for purchasers to request that the traders show them enslaved men and women naked.

Prices of bondspeople also increased in the Caribbean by the middle of the nineteenth century. On a Cuban plantation the average price of a locally born enslaved male was 668 pesos in 1856, whereas in 1863, it was 914 pesos.[68] In Brazil, prices of enslaved people tended to increase over time, even though there were variations according to region, period, and other features such as age, sex, and region of provenance. In this country where the slave trade from Africa was legally banned for the first time in 1831 and where slavery was only abolished in 1888, the prices of enslaved persons greatly increased in the last two decades before the final abolition.[69] A sample of nearly 800 enslaved persons sold between 1872 and 1874 in four districts of the Paraíba Valley, a coffee-producing region in Brazil, shows that enslaved men aged between fifteen and thirty-nine years old were sold for an average price of 1,758,118 *réis*, the Brazilian currency at the time, which in today's value very roughly corresponds to 44,000 *reais*.[70] However, these prices must be taken with caution. They are approximative and obviously not comprehensive, even though they can provide a general idea of the rising prices of bondspeople in regions where the demand for a slave workforce increased following the growth of cotton, sugar, and coffee production during the nineteenth century. Because these numbers varied according to each region and local currencies, they only make sense in comparison to the costs of other goods at the time. Therefore, the conversion of these prices to present-day currency can only provide an approximate idea of the high value of an enslaved person. Yet, based on the various figures discussed in this chapter, it is possible to suggest that the average starting price of an adult enslaved man in the United States and Brazil during the nineteenth century could be the equivalent of today's value of a midsize new car in either country.

Sites of Violence and Commodification

Separated by hundreds of miles, slave markets in North America, the Caribbean, and South America had many elements in common. For newly arrived enslaved Africans, slave markets were sites of transition, even though captives could remain unsold in these confined sites for several months. For captives who crossed the Atlantic Ocean and had recently come ashore, markets were sites of continuity. Since their enslavement on the African continent, these men, women, and children had been traded and displaced several times, then confined in slave depots, and eventually imprisoned in the hold of slave ships.

American seaports slave markets were another stage in a process that attempted to transform the bodies of Africans into commodities. The slave market was also a site of rupture, the final stage of a harrowing journey because many captives arrived so weak and ill that they perished before being sold. Those who survived were prepared to be sold by the traders and the various agents who worked for them. Traders and their agents provided them with more food and hid their scars and any other possible physical imperfections. Male and female buyers who attended these sales and auctions examined, scrutinized, touched, and abused enslaved men and women. Most Africans were stripped from their families when they were still on the African continent. Yet, when enslaved Africans crossed the Atlantic Ocean with family members, the slave market could be the last station of their torturous passage together.

In contrast, the experience of the slave market by enslaved people born in the Americas or who at least spent a long time in the Americas was different. These men, women, and children were put on sale for several reasons, but probably the most common were debt and the death of the slave owner. These private or public sales often meant separation from family members and other comrades. Ultimately, for most enslaved Africans and bondspeople born in the Americas, the slave market was the entryway to an entire life under slavery, unless they were able to find a path to emancipation. When sales and auctions were concluded, slaves were transported to the urban residences, farms, and mines of their new owners. All over the Americas, most bondspeople were directed to plantations of sugar, rice, indigo, wheat, tobacco, cotton, and coffee. But as at other junctures of the forced displacement of captive Africans to the American shores and throughout the Americas, even in this most horrible moment represented by slave sales in general and the iconic slave market in particular, enslaved people continued to affirm their humanity by seeking their compatriots, protesting the separation from their loved ones, fighting to keep their families together, creating new bonds of affection, and trying to survive, therefore challenging the attempts of slave owners and slave traders to control their bodies. Following this continuous fight for survival, chapter 7 explores the lives of enslaved persons in these plantation worlds.

CHAPTER 7

Plantation Worlds

"Slaves are the hands and feet of the owner of sugar plantations and mills; because without them, in Brazil, it is neither possible to create, maintain, and develop a plantation, nor to run a sugar mill," wrote Jesuit missionary André João Antonil in 1711.[1] More than one century later in the United States, Solomon Northup, who was kidnapped in Washington, DC, in 1841 and sold and sent into slavery to Louisiana, described "the dexterous fingers and quick motion of Patsey, who could fly along one side of a row of cotton, stripping it of its undefiled and fleecy whiteness miraculously fast."[2] According to Northup, Patsey was "the most remarkable cotton picker of Bayou Boeuf" and picking "five hundred pounds a day was not unusual for her."[3]

Between the sixteenth and nineteenth centuries, the rise of plantations of sugar, rice, tobacco, cotton, indigo, and coffee in the Americas drew upon the Atlantic slave trade and relied on the workforce of enslaved Africans. The work provided by bondspeople such as Patsey and Northup made possible the production of highly profitable crops on plantations that were vital for the formation of a wider mercantilist economic system sustained by European powers and their colonial empires. During the era of slavery and the Atlantic slave trade, these developments intensified international commercial exchanges and contributed to the rise of industrial capitalism as a new global economic and political order.[4]

Scholars have differentiated *slave societies* from *societies with slaves*, as briefly discussed in the introduction of this book.[5] Although greater nuance can be brought to this distinction, it is nonetheless helpful in allowing us to understand why plantations were so influential in the development of slavery in the Americas.[6] Put in a blunt way, in slave societies, the institution of slavery was a central element of social, political, and economic life, whereas in societies with slaves, slavery had a marginal role, and the number of slaves was normally small. Therefore, although slavery existed to a greater or to a lesser extent in all societies of the Americas, the regions where plantations dominated contained the largest concentration of enslaved laborers. The labor provided by bondspeople like Patsey and Northup remained the main force behind the development of sugar, indigo, wheat, tobacco, rice, cotton, and coffee plantations in the Americas until the late nineteenth century. Ultimately, as Antonil hinted, plantation slavery shaped the development of all American societies where slavery played a central role in the economy.

Plantation Slavery in the Americas

The establishment of plantation slavery in the Americas was one of the main outcomes of the fifteenth-century exchanges between Portugal and the societies located along the coasts of West Africa and West Central Africa. As explained in chapter 1, the Treaty of Alcáçovas, signed between the kingdoms of Portugal and Castile, put the mainland of West Africa and West Central Africa, as well as the islands of Madeira, Azores, and Cape Verde, under Portuguese power, making all these regions important to the development of the Atlantic slave trade. The Portuguese began by establishing sugarcane plantations on these Atlantic islands, and also on São Tomé, which along with the Cape Verde archipelago became a transitory zone for slave ships that would stop there to renew their water and food supplies before continuing the Atlantic crossing.

As global navigation expanded in the fifteenth century, other European players joined the race to find a maritime route to Asia.

King Ferdinand of Aragón and Queen Isabella of Castile married in 1469, unifying the kingdoms that would compose present-day Spain. Together, the powerful royal couple sponsored the first Spanish venture across the Atlantic Ocean led by Christopher Columbus. With his crewmen he sailed westward in search of Asia on board two caravels and one carrack in 1492. Weeks later, they landed in the Lesser Antilles for the first time. The voyage led to the iconic first encounter between Iberians and Native Americans, who had been established for thousands of years on the continents that would become known as the Americas. From North America to Patagonia, these first peoples organized their societies in a variety of ways. Taino inhabitants on the Caribbean islands and the Tupi-speaking peoples established along the coastal region of Brazil were both semisedentary groups, who relied on a shifting agriculture system. Sedentary populations occupied the central Andes in South America as well as Mesoamerica (central and southern Mexico and Guatemala), where they created large empires and complex civilizations.

In their first contacts with local populations and during their survey of the various Caribbean islands, Columbus and his crewmen quickly identified the presence of gold in the newly found territory. Further Spanish conquistadores explored Mexico and Central America, regions occupied by the Aztec Empire and the Mayan civilization, as well as the Inca Empire that stretched along western South America, where they, too, found gold and silver deposits. This search for riches drove the Spaniards to invade and conquer these territories, exterminating the populations who occupied these regions. The Spaniards fought and killed rulers and commoners alike during these wars of conquest, upon their initial arrival in the Caribbean and throughout their conquest of Mexico and South America. During this process, European conquerors spread diseases such as smallpox and measles, against which Indigenous peoples had no immunity. Most staggeringly, in just a few decades after their arrival, European conquerors killed millions of Indigenous men, women, and children through warfare and the imposition of forced labor regimes.[7]

When the Spanish took possession of the newly conquered land (as we have seen in chapters 1 and 5), the Portuguese had already been transporting enslaved Africans to the Iberian Peninsula. It is therefore not surprising that, during the sixteenth century, both enslaved as well as free Black men also participated as armed and unarmed auxiliaries in the conquest of Mexico, Florida, and the Greater Antilles, comprising the islands of Cuba, Puerto Rico, Jamaica, and Hispaniola (today's Haiti and Dominican Republic).[8] Among the most well-known of these Black conquistadors was Juan Garrido. Born in West Africa, he was transported as a slave to Portugal, where he was converted to Roman Catholicism and baptized, then moved to Seville, and reached Santo Domingo as a free servant of a Spaniard named Pedro Garrido. After participating in the expeditions that conquered Puerto Rico and Cuba, and possibly in the conquest of Guadalupe and Dominica, and even Florida, he joined the expedition that conquered Mexico between 1519 and 1521, and he eventually became a resident of Mexico City.[9] Once conquest was secured, Spanish colonizers transformed local servitude structures already in place to create new forced labor systems such as *encomienda* and *repartimiento* (or *mita*) to extract agricultural and mining work from Native American populations.[10]

As the Spanish conquest evolved, Portuguese nobleman and military leader Pedro Álvares Cabral commanded a fleet of thirteen caravels that landed in Brazil in 1500, unfolding the Portuguese conquest and colonization of this large territory in the Americas. The Portuguese, unlike their Spanish counterparts, did not find sedentary populations along the Brazilian coast. Instead, the various Tupi-speaking groups settled on the littoral were semisedentary peoples who spoke languages of the same family. Again unlike the Spanish, the Portuguese failed to find deposits of gold and silver in the first two centuries of their occupation of Brazil. Instead, they established trading posts along the Brazilian coast, which allowed them to barter with the coastal populations. With the support of Catholic religious orders such as the Jesuits of the Society of Jesus and the Franciscans, Portuguese settlers catechized and enslaved Brazil's Indigenous peoples, who in the first decades of colonization worked extracting *pau-brasil* (brazilwood) that produced a red dye utilized in the European textile industry.

The slave trade to the Spanish Americas emerged in the sixteenth century. In 1517 the first enslaved Africans came ashore in Hispaniola, and later in the mainland area controlled by the Spanish, including the Viceroyalty of New Spain (or Mexico), a large area encompassing today's Mexico, Central America, and several US states such as Florida, Louisiana, Texas, and California, as well as the Viceroyalty of Peru, which until the eighteenth century encompassed most of South America except for the region of today's Brazil. A few decades later, the New Spain's Black population was increasing so fast that local authorities demanded that the Spanish crown restrict the import of enslaved Africans to prevent the colony from becoming predominantly Black.[11] As the Indigenous population had decreased and the Iberian small population did not allow for a massive wave of migration to explore the natural resources of the new territory, the Spanish crown relied on the enslaved Africans to toil in its colonies in the Americas.

The presence of enslaved Africans in areas conquered and colonized by the Spanish varied over time and depended on the size of existing Amerindian populations. In general, African presence was more prominent in areas with smaller or more scattered Indigenous populations than in the regions where enslaved African and Indigenous workforces were combined. Overall, the enslavement of Africans and their descendants was important, but it had a secondary role in the mainland Spanish Americas. Meanwhile, Indigenous slavery persisted in varying degrees in the territory controlled by the Spanish, as well as in various parts of the Americas.

Sugar Rush

International competition among European powers seeking to seize and control the new land shaped the expansion of slavery in the Americas, as we have seen in chapter 3, and affected slave trade operations in the sixteenth and seventeenth centuries. As the major European nations and empires fought to take over the new colonies as well as the slave markets in Africa, the Atlantic slave trade intensified. The number of enslaved people transported to the various regions of the Americas in each century remains approximate, especially for the sixteenth and seventeenth centuries. Based on existing records, however, scholars have estimated that, in the seventeenth century, around 964,700 enslaved Africans were transported to Brazil, 327,000 to the British West Indies, 104,000 to the Spanish Americas, and 32,800 to the French and British colonies in North America.[12]

Although the enslaved African workforce was employed in all kinds of economic activities, including mining and pearl fishing, the majority of these imports were intended to provide workers for the sugar plantations in the West Indies and Brazil. Portuguese traders, who initially acquired wealth in South and Southeast Asia, provided capital, credit, and technology for the development of this emergent sugar industry, which somewhat followed the preexisting plantation models that existed in the Mediterranean and had already been tested by the Portuguese on the islands of Atlantic Africa.

In the West Indies, as most of the Indigenous populations were exterminated during the two decades following the arrival of the Spaniards in Hispaniola, gold mining activity declined by giving space to the development of sugar cultivation. In his second voyage to the Americas in 1493, Columbus likely brought the first sugarcanes from Madeira to Hispaniola. By the 1520s, dozens of sugar mills were in operation on the island. However, an economic crisis involving internal and external factors, such as the shortage of an African enslaved workforce and the competition with Brazilian sugar production, led to a steady decline of the sugar industry in the 1550s.[13] Sugar production did not fully reemerge until the seventeenth century when the French took control of the western part of the island, which became the colony of Saint-Domingue. Still, during this early period African slavery was not yet significant in the French portion of the island, as the number of enslaved people was smaller than the number of indentured servants transported from France.[14]

Enslaved men, women, and children who toiled on plantations faced working and living conditions shaped by the crops cultivated, as well as regions and time periods. In Brazil, Portuguese demand quickly exhausted brazilwood reserves, but sugar emerged as another promising source of wealth. The Brazilian Northeast offered good soil and plentiful rainfall for sugarcane cultivation. Relying on their previous knowledge of sugar production tested in Atlantic Africa, the Portuguese introduced sugarcane cultivation in Brazil starting in the 1530s.[15] Plantations established in the captaincies of Pernambuco and Bahia, in the northeast region of the colony, were the most successful. As in Atlantic Africa, the greatest challenge for the development of sugarcane plantations was the need for a sizable workforce, one capable of intensive and long work hours in a tropical environment, especially during the harvest period. With its small population, Portugal could not propel the migration of its peasants to toil in sugarcane fields that required a substantial number of workers; exploiting the enslaved Indigenous and African populations was the cheapest and fastest available alternative.[16]

Until the end of the sixteenth century, enslaved Indigenous workers outnumbered enslaved Africans in sugarcane plantations in Brazil.[17] As the Brazilian sugar industry expanded, however, relying only on the Indigenous workforce became unsustainable. Native Brazilian populations had been decimated, displaced, and enslaved. Although the Portuguese crown prohibited Indigenous slavery in 1570, enslavement of Indigenous people through "just war" was still permitted. Thus, insurgent groups who fought and resisted Portuguese colonization could still be captured and sold into slavery as late as in the middle of the seventeenth century.[18] Working conditions in sugarcane fields were atrocious, as we will see shortly, and the local populations, who had been unfamiliar with intensive agricultural labor, continued to resist enslavement. They attacked Portuguese settlements and fled to the interior of the territory, the terrain of which they knew better than anyone else.

Ultimately, the available Indigenous population became insufficient to provide the required number of hands for the growing Brazilian sugar industry.[19] The Portuguese realized that turning once more to Africa for its labor supply was the logical solution. They had already exploited the work of enslaved Africans on plantations established in the Atlantic islands along the African coast in the fifteenth century. They could also rely on sustained trade relations with West Africa and West Central Africa to provide them with the necessary number of slaves to toil in the sugar plantations of their only colony in the Americas. More important, to the Portuguese, the slave trade was a profitable business. Ultimately, purchasing slaves on the coasts of Africa (especially in the region of present-day Angola) and transporting them to Brazil was more viable and safer than insisting on the enslavement of insurgent local populations who resisted enslavement in their homeland.

Sugar Complexes

Sugar plantations and mills were called *engenhos* in Brazil and *ingenios* in the Spanish Americas.[20] Sugarcane estates were large complexes encompassing fields, stables, mills, furnaces, and workshops that supported their operations. These interconnected structures created a universe that could only exist through the work of enslaved Africans and their descendants, with men, women, and children performing a variety of tasks. Small numbers of Portuguese settlers as well as freed and freeborn workers of African descent were also employed in sugar estates, where they had more or less specialized professions.

In several parts of the Americas, sugar estates had various sizes and employed slightly differing techniques that improved over time. Yet, in Brazil and the West Indies, the process of sugar production carried many similarities. Sixteenth-century Brazilian *engenhos* were initially small. Most mills were powered by oxen or horses, with a few mills powered by water.[21] *Engenho* owners could be the state, companies, or private holders. Religious orders of the Roman Catholic Church such as the Carmelites and the Benedictines also owned *engenhos*, whose profits supported their activities. But in Brazil, the Jesuits of

FIGURE 7.1. Romeyn de Hooghe, *Braziliaanse suikerwerkers*, 1682–1733. Etching, 21.2 × 29.9 cm. Courtesy of Rijksmuseum, Amsterdam, Netherlands.

the Society of Jesus were the largest owners of sugar plantations. Jesuits were also slave owners in other parts of the Americas where they owned plantations.[22]

A few families controlled most existing *engenhos* in Brazil. These sugar production complexes included not only the cane fields, a mill, furnaces (figure 7.1), and workshops to produce tools (especially those required for sugar production) but also a big house, slave quarters, and the residences where free workers resided. In Brazil, large estates often included a chapel. Parts of the fields were used to raise cattle and other farm animals and to grow food crops such as corn, manioc, and beans for the subsistence of the planter, his family, and the plantation's free and enslaved workers.

Initially, enslaved Africans worked in the fields alongside Indigenous peoples in Brazil. But starting in the early decades of the seventeenth century, enslaved Africans progressively replaced the enslaved Indigenous workforce.[23] A painting by the Dutch artist Frans Post

FIGURE 7.2. Frans Post, *Brazilian Landscape with a House Under Construction*, c. 1655–60. Oil on panel, 70 × 46 cm. Courtesy of Mauritshuis, The Hague, Netherlands.

(figure 7.2) who sojourned in Brazil during the Dutch occupation of Pernambuco from 1630 to 1654 represents a sugar plantation setting. The depicted image evokes a scene that probably took place during a weekend, as Black and Indigenous characters featured in the painting are neither working nor under the watch of overseers. With dwellings suggesting slave quarters in the background, in the midground Black and Indigenous men, women, and children are standing or sitting along a path, interacting, gesticulating, playing drums, and displaying foodstuffs in what appears to be a weekend marketplace. Despite being a romanticized depiction of a plantation, represented as a harmonious space, the painting is a rich visual document attesting to the moment when enslaved Indigenous and Black workers coexisted in Brazil sugar estates.

Brazilian planters employed select wage workers as managers, foremen, overseers, and drivers, as well as other specialized positions such as sugar masters, who supervised the transformation of the sugarcane juice into processed sugar. Still, most of the workforce in sugar estates were enslaved African-born individuals and their descendants, who participated in all stages of sugar production, including planting, harvesting, milling, boiling, and curing sugar. As carpenters, potters, and blacksmiths, they also produced a large array of tools required to operate the plantation and the mill, including saws, hoes, sickles, hammers, and axes. Moreover, enslaved people, especially women, toiled in the big house performing domestic tasks such as cooking, cleaning, and taking care of the owners' children. They also worked as boatmen, caulkers, shepherds, and fishermen.[24]

In the seventeenth century, Pernambuco became the first sugar-producing captaincy in Brazil, followed by Bahia. In these two regions, sugar estates were large complexes, but most enslaved people toiled in the fields. Bondspeople performed heavy work during the harvest period, which lasted between six and seven months and occurred at the same time that sugarcanes were ground and transformed into sugar. When a new plantation was established, bondsmen cleared the land to plant the sugarcanes. After growing for twelve to eighteen months, according to the variety, the canes could get as high as twenty feet and be ready for harvest. When the harvest season arrived, mature sugarcanes had to be immediately cut and processed; otherwise, they were lost. Enslaved people harvested sugarcane from sunrise to sunset. In Bahia, most sugar plantations employed a task system, in which each enslaved person was assigned a certain amount of cane to cut on a daily basis. For example, each bondsperson was expected to cut 4,200 canes daily in the seventeenth and eighteenth centuries.[25]

Working in extremely hot temperatures and divided in groups, enslaved workers used cutlasses to chop the bottom of the stalks a few inches above the ground. This process allowed a new sprout to grow for the next harvest and could be repeated for several years before planting new canes. Overseers, who could be either enslaved or free, supervised the rhythm of the harvest to make sure each enslaved person was fulfilling the assigned quota. Overall, in Brazilian sugar plantations, enslaved people were constantly exposed to sun and rain, slept few hours, were barely clothed, and ate a meager diet for the kind of strenuous work they performed.

Because of these horrible conditions, it is not surprising that mortality rates among enslaved people were quite high in Brazil's sugar-producing areas, as they were in the West Indies.[26] Several Brazilian historians have asserted that after disembarking in Brazilian slave ports, enslaved Africans rarely survived more than seven or eight years toiling in sugarcane fields.[27] One demographic historian has challenged the life expectancy of seven to eight years by contending that overall mortality among enslaved people was not very different from what prevailed among the rest of the population for the nineteenth century.[28] Still, this general response is largely insufficient to disprove that enslaved Africans who were transported to Brazil to toil in sugarcane plantations during the sugar boom that started in the seventeenth century survived longer than eight years when it is clear that slave traders were introducing new enslaved Africans in Brazil to work in sugar estates more than in any other region of the Americas.

"Almost Purgatory, or Hell"

In seventeenth-century Bahia, the process of harvesting and processing sugarcanes was similar to what was done in the West Indies. Most bondspeople cut the canes while other slaves, including women, removed their leaves, bundled the stalks that were transported in oxcarts onto the backs of donkeys, and, depending on the plantation, carried them by canoe through existing pathways to the grinding mill and the adjacent structure where sugar was processed. Whereas work in the fields was conducted by day, the mills continued grinding overnight, operating between eighteen and twenty hours a day. In addition to performing arduous and repetitive work in the fields, especially in the West Indies, enslaved people also executed other heavy tasks and took additional shifts in the subsequent stages of sugar production.[29] About eight bondspeople, including enslaved women, operated the grinding mill under the supervision of a manager, either enslaved or free. Enslaved men and women introduced the canes into the roller that pressed the stalks and produced the juice. This stage of sugar production was risky. Accidents were common, especially in water-powered mills that turned faster.[30]

In Brazil, Saint-Domingue, Martinique, Jamaica, and Cuba, enslaved people, usually women, could easily lose a limb while feeding sugar mills. As noted by historian Richard S. Dunn, at the Mesopotamia plantation in Jamaica, two enslaved women lost an arm and a hand, respectively, in sugar mill accidents. Bella, a forty-two-year-old grass cutter, lost her hand in a mill accident in 1793. Still, she continued to cut grass and cook over the next twenty years. Rose was a fifty-year-old nurse who lost her arm in a mill accident in 1765, but who also continued to work, carrying water on her head for the next thirty years.[31] Similar accidents also occurred in Brazil. In his journal of the early 1800s, French traveler Louis-François de Tollenare described the tragic fate of Queen Teresa, an enslaved African woman who worked in Sibiró *engenho*, near Recife in Pernambuco. According to Tollenare, Teresa was a beautiful queen in her late twenties, identified as originating from Cabinda, the seaport of the Kingdom of Ngoyo in West Central Africa. Sold into slavery as judicial punishment for committing adultery, she was highly respected by her enslaved companions and often refused to work. But one day she had to replace another enslaved woman who worked feeding the sugarcane press, a task she was not used to doing. She got one hand caught in the press, and while trying to remove it with her other hand, both hands were smashed, and her two arms were amputated. Despite the horrible accident, she continued to work, overseeing the mill's activities.[32]

French Dominican missionary, planter, and slave owner Jean-Baptiste Labat explained in his multivolume seventeenth-century travel account that in Martinique, Guadeloupe, and Saint-Domingue, enslaved women were also the predominant workforce in sugar mills.[33] French planters assigned the weakest enslaved women to feed the mills. On various occasions, especially at night, enslaved women lost one or both of their arms or hands in the mill's rollers.[34] Attractive because it came with better food rations, the activity was conceived as punishment in the British West Indies, not because the work was hard but because the work was dangerous.

The juice extracted from the crushed sugarcanes flowed into the boiling house's tanks. In Brazil, bondspeople, usually born in the colony, stoked the furnaces with firewood that was methodically selected to process the liquid within thirty-six hours. Enslaved people stirred and skimmed the heated liquid in copper and iron cauldrons of various sizes, depending on the stage of the sugar-making process. The sugar master and his assistant were frequently freemen. They supervised the temperature of each cauldron and the appropriate moment to add lime, ash, and water to purify the liquid.[35] Using giant ladles, they ladled and skimmed the liquid to remove its impurities and then separated the crystals. In Brazil, the boiling house's dark atmosphere, with its heat, flames, and heavy clouds of vapors, led Jesuit priest Antônio Vieira to compare it to the hell during a sermon addressing enslaved people in Bahia in 1633.[36] In the early eighteenth century, Jesuit Antonil also provided the tragic same image of the furnaces as a "prison of fire and perpetual smoke and living image of the volcanoes Vesuvius, Etna, almost purgatory, or hell."[37] Enslaved workers toiling in these conditions were exposed to extremely high temperatures. Working day and night in these structures, they often faced the risk of falling into the furnaces when they were not protected by iron bars.

The final production phase took place at the curing or purging house. Bondspeople transferred the hot moistened crystals to earthenware conical pots with a hole at the bottom. Depending on the period, a cone could contain between twenty-five and sixty pounds of uncured sugar. Once the content cooled, the solid sugar stuck to the conical pot to create compact sugar cones, and the molasses that dripped out through the cone's hole could be fermented and distilled to produce *aguardente* or rum. Enslaved people were once again in charge of the final phase of sugar making. After the cones dried, bondspeople cut, separated, hit, crumbled, and packed the sugar in crates.

Expanding a Lucrative Business

Brazilian sugar production developed fast. By 1600, when sugar prices had increased, Brazil had two hundred sugar *engenhos* in operation and produced more than ten thousand tons of sugar annually.[38] As we saw in chapter 3, this period of peak production coincided with the Dutch occupation of Pernambuco between 1630 and 1654. Between 1630 and 1640, as imports of enslaved people intensified, Brazil dominated the international sugar industry. During this period, Brazilian sugar estates had an average of approximately 100 bondspeople, but 150 to 200 enslaved people toiled in each of the largest sugar estates. Moreover, some planters could own more than one plantation by accumulating the ownership of a large enslaved population.[39]

After Hispaniola's experiments with the sugar industry, sugar mills also emerged in Cuba at the end of the sixteenth century, but a robust sugar industry did not develop there until the early nineteenth century, after the revolution that abolished slavery in the French colony of Saint-Domingue.[40] Up until the early seventeenth century, the Spanish were the only European colonizers in the West Indies, but gradually, especially the English (as well as the Dutch, French, and Danish) established colonies in the Greater and Lesser Antilles.[41] In this context, Barbados became the first English colony in the region to develop an economy based on a plantation regime in the seventeenth century. Tobacco and cotton plantations initially prevailed, but they were mainly operated by English, Scottish, and Irish male and female indentured workers, including children as young as ten. These white servants were not slaves. Even though they could be bought and sold, and despite their working and living conditions being often as abysmal as those of enslaved people, adult indentured servants agreed to be transported to Barbados to work without compensation for a finite period, between four and five years, to pay for their transportation to the West Indies.[42]

In the 1640s, English planters obtained sugarcanes from a Dutch slave ship. The Dutch, by then settled in northeastern Brazil, also provided technological advice. As sugar emerged as the major crop cultivated in Barbados, the African enslaved population quickly outnumbered male European colonists and indentured servants. Barbados became the richest English colony in the West Indies, and the size of plantations and slaveholdings increased, varying from one hundred to two hundred enslaved persons.[43] Women made up an important part of the enslaved population on the island, and in some eighteenth-century estates, bondswomen represented half the slaveholdings.[44] Later, in the eighteenth and nineteenth centuries, enslaved women performed all kinds of physically demanding activities in Barbados's sugarcane fields. In addition to being exposed to sexual violence, bondswomen in these sugar estates were victims of brutal physical punishments inflicted by overseers and drivers.[45]

Also in the West Indies, and as in the English colonies, the plantations of the French colony of Saint-Domingue employed enslaved Africans and indentured servants during the seventeenth century. During this period Martinique also developed sugarcane plantations. By the 1650s, a plantation system emerged in Saint-Domingue and Jamaica, which became an English colony in 1659. Most of the planters of these two colonies, as well as other Caribbean islands colonized by the English and the French, actually resided in England and France. Based in their respective metropoles in Europe, these absentee slave owners operated their estates with the support of attorneys and managers, who administered various states and often were slave owners themselves.[46]

The rise of Jamaica and Saint-Domingue as the two main competitors of Brazilian sugar coincided with the expulsion of the Dutch from northeastern Brazil in 1654. After the Dutch were expelled from Pernambuco, they maintained their presence in Curaçao and Suriname, from where they continued to impact the development of sugar production in the West Indies, which eventually overturned Brazil's dominance in sugar production. Meanwhile, English colonies in North America did not become large sugar producers, but during the seventeenth century, tobacco plantations emerged in Maryland and Virginia. As in the early years of the colonization in Barbados, enslaved Africans performed agricultural activities alongside white indentured servants in these two North American colonies.[47] But as elsewhere, gradually the number of indentured workers decreased, and planters increasingly imported enslaved Africans to labor on the profitable plantations.

Saint-Domingue and Jamaica in the Eighteenth Century

The Atlantic slave trade and slavery dramatically increased in the eighteenth century. Relying on imports of enslaved Africans to respond to the growing consumption of sugar in Europe, Saint-Domingue and Jamaica became the two largest sugar producers in the Americas. Huge estates emerged in both colonies, replacing Barbados and Martinique as the leaders in this industry. Meanwhile, Brazil became the third sugar-producing colony in the Western Hemisphere. During the eighteenth and nineteenth centuries, as far as slavery persisted, plantation economies depended entirely on the workforce of enslaved Black men, women, and children.

As plantation slavery expanded and became a highly profitable business in the British, French, Dutch, and Spanish colonies in the West Indies during the eighteenth century, the sizes of plantations and slaveholdings increased. Estates of over two hundred acres and comprising at least 100 slaves became typical.[48] In the British West Indies, the enslaved population also increased exponentially. Replacing Barbados, Jamaica became the wealthiest British colony in the West Indies, with a population of 100,000 enslaved individuals in 1740.[49] Moreover, sugar production saw an impressive increase in the second half of the eighteenth century in Jamaica. The enslaved population growth followed suit. In 1788 the colony's population in bondage increased to approximately 255,000 slaves, who made up 90 percent of its total population.[50] Land ownership concentration also amplified during this period. Likewise, the average size of slaveholdings augmented to nearly 200 slaves per estate.[51]

In Jamaica, white planters had complete control over plantation and slave ownership, making the imbalance between the small white population (including slave owners, planters, managers, and overseers) and the huge number of enslaved persons, many of whom were African-born men and women, all the more stark. Unlike in Saint-Domingue, the free population of color was very small in Jamaica, where for each white individual, there were roughly ten enslaved persons.

As we will see in chapter 14, the disparity between the large number of enslaved Black workers, including many African-born bondspeople, and the small white population in colonies that mostly relied on a plantation economy, especially sugar production, was a matter of concern for slave owners, planters, and their agents, who feared slave revolts. But in times of relative peace, how did such a small population of white men, and few women, control the vast enslaved Black majority? There is no single answer to this question. Slave owners mastered a system designed to surveil, control, and punish enslaved people, leading bondspeople to constantly fear physical punishment. Planters and their agents also controlled weapons, tools, horses, and the circulation of information. Moreover, slave owners and managers used accounting to control enslaved populations.[52] Especially in large sugar plantations, accounting allowed planters to document all aspects of the daily life of bondspeople, including births, deaths, diseases, newly purchased enslaved individuals, insurgent behavior, distribution of food, supplies, and working tools, and also productivity. Planters understood that increasing efficiency led to bigger profits, therefore sugar estates were gradually transformed into early capitalist ventures. Still, physical brutality and efficient management were not the only available instruments of control. In Brazil, the Spanish Americas, and the US South, planters also used religion and small incentives such as amounts of money and food. These paternalistic attitudes encouraged enslaved people to submit and stay under control on sugar, tobacco, cotton, and coffee plantations.

As the production of sugar, coffee, and other crops increased, Saint-Domingue's enslaved population also grew. In 1700, the number of slaves was approximately 9,082 individuals. Just fifty years later, Saint-Domingue already had a population of 150,000 enslaved persons. As in Jamaica, this number greatly contrasted with the estimated white population of approximately 14,000 people. Four decades later, on the eve of the French Revolution, despite imprecise figures, historians estimate that in 1789, Saint-Domingue's population included approximately 465,000 enslaved men, women, and children, corresponding to nearly half the overall enslaved population of the West Indies. Many of these bondspeople were born on the African continent and transported to the colony. Again here, there was a great disparity between the large enslaved population and the small number of white people, then assessed at 31,000 individuals, and the population of free people of color was estimated at 28,000 individuals.[53] At the end of the eighteenth century, Saint-Domingue became the world's largest producer of sugar and coffee, while maintaining an important production of tobacco and indigo.

The size of slaveholdings increased with the expansion of plantation slavery in the West Indies as well. In the late eighteenth century, there was an average number of 185 enslaved workers in sugar plantations in Saint-Domingue. The use of an enslaved workforce also increased in Jamaica, even though estimates in terms of size of slaveholdings vary. Plantation inventories show that between 1725 and 1784, only 5 percent of Jamaica's sugar plantations had more than 150 enslaved workers. Yet most enslaved people toiled on plantations with large slaveholdings that ultimately dominated the island's economy.[54] Also in Jamaica, approximately 60 percent of the enslaved workers labored in the fields, while nearly 35 percent carried out specialized professions, and just 4 percent performed domestic activities. Both in Jamaica and in Martinique, enslaved women worked in significant numbers in the sugarcane fields. Although bondsmen exclusively performed land clearance tasks, such as removing trees and stones, all other activities were carried out by enslaved men and women of all ages.

Although hard to determine, morbidity is also an important indicator to evaluate the work and living conditions of enslaved populations in the Americas. But over the course of three centuries of plantation slavery, the mortality rate among enslaved people in Brazil and West Indies obviously varied. Certainly, in the plantations of Saint-Domingue, Jamaica, and Brazil, mortality was much higher than natural growth.[55] The highest mortality rate was among African-born bondspeople, as well as enslaved newborns and children, which explains in part why slave owners heavily relied on imports of new African captives to provide the required work on sugar plantations. A variety of factors such as poor diet and disease lowered the life expectancy of enslaved people, but working conditions were also a key factor. During the harvest period, bondspeople worked extremely hard for between twelve and sixteen hours a day on sugarcane plantations located in the hot and humid tropical Brazilian northeast region or in the French and British West Indies. As Vincent Brown reminds us, in Jamaica, where the working conditions on sugar estates were extremely hard, high mortality led slave owners to rely on vast imports of African captives as well, a choice considered cheaper than to "rear Negro children."[56] Likewise, in Saint-Domingue, an eighteenth-century observer emphasized that slaves were "always dying."[57] But on tobacco and cotton plantations in the United States and in coffee estates in Brazil, where the working conditions were less harsh, life expectancy was higher, and therefore natural growth existed without the overreliance on slave imports from Africa.

Rice and Tobacco in the Other South

Similar to Brazil, the thirteen colonies of North America encompassed many Indigenous nations settled along the coast, even though they were not comparable in size and development to the Indigenous empires and civilizations such as the Inca and the Aztec empires and the Maya civilization that occupied Mexico, Central America, and the Andean territory in South America—regions conquered by Spain. However, contrasting with Brazil and the Spanish Americas, the early colonization of North America relied on family farms.[58] Moreover,

European settlers had access to land ownership and political power through participation in elections and local institutions.[59] Despite regional differences, the use of an enslaved African workforce gradually emerged to respond to the early development of tobacco and rice plantations. Three main areas where plantations existed became slave societies between the seventeenth and the nineteenth centuries: first, the Chesapeake region including Virginia and Maryland; next, the coastal Lowcountry of South Carolina, Georgia, and Florida; and finally, the lower Mississippi Valley.[60]

In these three areas, slavery developed at different paces. But despite their particularities, they all shared plantation economies. Indigenous populations, including the Cherokee and Catawba nations, predominated in the area that later became known as South Carolina, where the first Africans set foot accompanying the Spanish explorers as early as in the 1520s. After unsuccessful attempts, starting in 1670, English colonists as well as their servants, mainly from Barbados, settled in South Carolina as well. According to reports from that period, 30 percent of the individuals accompanying these English settlers were Black persons, who were either indentured servants or enslaved people.[61] At the end of the seventeenth century, as Ira Berlin reminds us, two-thirds of the population of South Carolina was composed by "Europeans and European-Americans . . . including English, Dutch, French Huguenots, Scottish, and Scotch-Irish."[62]

While white indentured servants were also part of the workforce in South Carolina during the seventeenth century, English colonists began to increasingly introduce enslaved African workers in the colony during this period. Starting in 1695, rice production emerged in the region, and as the industry expanded in the next two decades, the enslaved Black population, including slaves born in Africa, gradually outnumbered white settlers.[63] As pointed out by historian Peter H. Wood, because enslaved Africans were outsiders, the use of their labor in South Carolina avoided the diplomatic problems of employing local Indigenous peoples. Nonetheless, there were initial obstacles. The price of enslaved Africans was higher than that of European indentured workers with limited-term contracts. Moreover, with the rise of other English colonies in the West Indies, including Jamaica, the demand for enslaved laborers increased. As a result, purchasing African captives became even more expensive. Despite these hindrances, the use of African labor also offered long-term advantages. Captive Africans transported through the West Indies and from West Africa were already familiar with the climate and the environment of the plantation. Moreover, their period of servitude was unlimited.[64]

During the eighteenth century, as rice cultivation expanded along the Lowcountry, the South Carolina coastal area, slavery became a central institution in the colony. Most of the enslaved Africans transported to South Carolina during the eighteenth century to work in rice plantations came from the Upper Guinea region (see map 1 at the front of the book), which corresponded to the region of present-day Senegal, The Gambia, Guinea-Bissau, Guinea, Sierra Leone, Liberia, and the western part of Côte d'Ivoire. These bondspeople brought to the Americas great knowledge of rice cultivation techniques. Therefore, this previous expertise was central for the success of rice cultivation in the region.[65]

As they did in West Africa, African women and their descendants played a crucial role in the Low Country rice culture. In large rice plantations, as historian Leslie A. Schwalm reminds us, enslaved Black women composed most of the workforce laboring the rice fields.[66] Slave owners also relied on bondswomen to give birth to enslaved children and increase their slaveholdings. Whereas gradual abolition of slavery emerged in the North of the United States following the American War of Independence, as examples of capitalist ventures, Southern rice plantations continued to generate profits on the backs of enslaved people until the eve of the American Civil War.[67]

The growth of the tobacco plantation economy led to a rising demand for an enslaved African workforce in the Chesapeake region in the early eighteenth century.[68] Virginia's enslaved population also increased, a tendency that continued in other southern colonies over the next decades. At the end of the eighteenth century, on the eve of the American War of Independence, both Virginia and Maryland had approximately one-third of the total population and half of the enslaved population of the thirteen British colonies in North America. Starting in the late eighteenth century, the gains of the tobacco industry started to decline, but the use of slave labor continued to be a lucrative choice and boosted other farming activities, including the cultivation of corn and grains.

The World of Cotton

The introduction of cotton cultivation in the Southern states in the 1780s transformed plantation slavery in the newly independent United States. Bondspeople sowed the soil between March and April. When the plants were mature, bolls containing the white cotton fibers and seeds hung from the extremities of the branches. Between July and November, enslaved men, women, and children spent long hours harvesting cotton by hand, plucking the fluffy white fibers from the bolls. Until the late eighteenth century, processing cotton was a time-consuming activity. After harvesting the bolls, enslaved workers separated the lint from the seeds attached to the fibers, again working by hand. But the invention of the cotton gin in 1795 mechanized this lengthy work, making separating the fibers from the seeds a much faster process.[69]

Cotton gins were initially powered by horses or mules, but by the 1830s the creation of steam engines and large presses for baling cotton dramatically increased plantations' productivity. Still, production relied entirely on enslaved workers. Bondspeople were required to handpick larger amounts of cotton to respond to the greater demand from Britain where cotton was transformed into yarn and textiles, feeding the flourishing Industrial Revolution.[70] In the US South, enslaved people also operated the new machinery.

Slave traders fed the cotton boom by selling enslaved people from states such as Virginia and Maryland to the Deep South; New Orleans became the largest slave market from which enslaved people were sold. The intensification of the domestic slave trade, as we will see in chapter 15, propelled the illegal enslavement of free Black men, women, and children, who were kidnapped and sold into slavery to the Southern cotton-producing regions. The story of Northup, mentioned earlier in this chapter and featured in the award-winning motion picture *12 Years a Slave*, is certainly the most well-known depiction of this tragic period. Born free in New York, he was kidnapped in Washington, DC, in 1841, then sold and sent into slavery in Louisiana, where he lived in bondage for twelve years. In his narrative published in 1853, Northup provided one of the most detailed descriptions of how cotton was produced during the last twenty years of slavery in the United States. He explained how an enslaved person was required to handpick as much as two hundred pounds of cotton on a daily basis: "An ordinary day's work is two hundred pounds. A slave who is accustomed to picking, is punished, if he or she brings in a less quantity than that."[71] Planters, managers, and overseers controlled the work of enslaved cotton pickers to make maximum profit. As put by Northup, "no matter how fatigued and weary he may be—no matter how much he longs for sleep and rest—a slave never approaches the gin-house with his basket of cotton but with fear. If it falls short in weight—if he has not performed the full task appointed him, he knows that he must suffer."[72] After picking all the cotton in a row of plants, bondspeople left unopened bolls for another picking. Because the bolls matured at different intervals, enslaved workers returned to the same plants several times during the harvest, which is why cotton plantations could be smaller in size than sugar and coffee plantations but still highly productive.

After the invention of the cotton gin and the screw press, cotton production witnessed an extraordinary growth. Slavery expanded to the interior of Georgia, South Carolina, Alabama, Mississippi, Louisiana, Arkansas, and even Texas.[73] Because of the prohibition of slave imports from Africa, enforced in 1808, more than ever the wombs of enslaved women became the site of production of new enslaved people. The number of slaves dramatically increased from 697,624 in

1790 to 3,953,760 in 1860, on the eve of the Civil War.[74] This growth, intended to sustain the expansion of cotton industry, relied on the institution of slavery. Simply put, bondspeople provided coerced labor to cotton planters who extracted their work through violence and control.

During the cotton era, which dominated the last fifty years of slavery in the United States, enslaved men, women, and children were expected to pick and process more cotton, working harder and faster than they ever did before, to make the project of Southern slave owners and cotton planters possible.[75] Thanks to the introduction of new machinery, nineteenth-century cotton production fueled Britain's industrialization, therefore marking a new phase of the capitalist world order. Just as the rise of sugar plantations in the Americas had propelled the development of merchant capitalism in the sixteenth century, the mechanized production of sugar and cotton in the early nineteenth century drove the Industrial Revolution.[76]

Capitalist Ventures in the Era of Second Slavery

Sugar and cotton contributed to the wealth of planters and their international associates, confirming the status of slavery as a profitable institution in both the West Indies and the United States. Between 1760 and 1820, sugar, cotton, and coffee industries benefited from technological innovations such as water and steam power, while relying on enslaved people to work the fields and operate new machinery. As we will see, the mechanization of cotton production in the US South, along with the rise of the Cuban sugar industry and the Brazilian coffee production in the nineteenth century, marked a turning point in plantation slavery. This period is often referred to as the "second slavery," a term coined by historian Dale Tomich to address the new stage that emerged especially in the United States, Cuba, and Brazil during the nineteenth century.[77] The "second slavery" was marked by the combination of technological innovations and the exploitation of an enslaved workforce that propelled a huge growth of the production of cotton, sugar, and coffee. This new explosion supported the rise of industrial capitalism in the Americas, Europe, and Africa, showing that capitalism and plantation slavery in the nineteenth century were not incompatible systems, but mutually reinforcing.[78]

How did Cuba contribute to the rise of the "second slavery"? The British occupation of the island during the Seven Years' War (1756–63) boosted agricultural slavery. During the eighteenth century, although Cuba was the only Spanish colony in the West Indies to produce and refine sugar, most *ingenios* were concentrated around the region of Havana. Not surprisingly, Cuban sugar production was not as robust as that of Saint-Domingue and Jamaica, its French and British competitors in the region.[79] But in the last years of the eighteenth century, the number of *ingenios* increased in the western portion of the island and in the region east of the Bay of Havana.[80] When a Spanish royal decree of 1789 limited enslaved people's working hours to between sunrise and sunset in the colonies of the West Indies, Cuban *ingenio* owners protested the order by arguing that enslaved people had to work by shifts day and night to keep the mills and boilers running during the harvest period.[81]

Cuba benefited from the disruption of Saint-Domingue's sugar production between 1791 and 1804. As the Saint-Domingue Revolution eventually ended slavery and made Haiti the first independent Black nation in the Americas, the international demand for sugar continued to fuel the island's sugar production.[82] In 1820s, Cuban sugar industry increased at extraordinary levels, making the island the world's largest sugar producer, a leading slave society, and a vital participant in the global capitalist economy. As with the cotton industry in the United States, Cuba greatly benefited from the introduction of new technology in the production of sugar.

In the 1830s, a growing number of Cuban *ingenios* adopted high-compression steam-powered grinding mills. As more sugar could be processed, sugarcane plantations could also increase in size. Mechanization made all the stages of sugar processing faster and more efficient.[83] Nonetheless, this was a period of uncertainty for Spanish

FIGURE 7.3. *Ingenio Flor de Cuba*, drawing by Eduardo Laplante, lithograph by Luis Marquier, in Justo G. Cantero, *Los ingenios: Colleción de vistas de los principals ingenios de azúcar de la isla de Cuba* (Havana: Litografía de Luis Marquier, 1857). Via Creative Commons CC0 1.0 Universal license.

authorities. Not only did they entirely rely on the island's fiscal contributions, they also feared external British or US invasion. In response, Cuba developed new local refining technologies to produce white sugar whose greater durability allowed the colony to increase exports. These developments were followed by the construction of a railroad system that facilitated the transportation of sugar from the *ingenios* to Havana's large new warehouses and modernized wharves.[84]

French-born artist Eduardo Laplante (Louis-Édouard de La Plante Dorson) documented Cuba's impressive technological transformation in twenty-eight colored lithographs (among them figures 7.3 and 7.4) depicting the most profitable *ingenios*, which were published in an illustrated album in 1857.[85] The workforce in these mills was still composed of a majority of enslaved people. Still, Laplante's images emphasize the giant buildings and the modernity of the machinery. As in an organized factory, enslaved workers appear as minute, insignificant

FIGURE 7.4. *Casa de calderas del Ingenio Asunción*, drawing by Eduardo Laplante, lithograph by Luis Marquier, in Justo G. Cantero, *Los ingenios: Colleción de vistas de los principals ingenios de azúcar de la isla de Cuba* (Havana: Litografía de Luis Marquier, 1857). Via Creative Commons CC0 1.0 Universal license

figures operating huge capitalist machinery. The reality was different. Despite the new machines, sugar production heavily relied on the work provided by enslaved people. Indeed, existing photographs of the time show deprived enslaved men, women, and children sitting on the dirt floor of a barracoon's kitchen (figure 7.5), therefore challenging Laplante's idealized images of plantation settings as modern and sanitized spaces during second slavery.

Independent from Portugal in 1822, Brazil also entered the second slavery. During the eighteenth century, the then Portuguese colony became the largest slave society of Latin America. Favored by the halt of Saint-Domingue's sugar and coffee production, like Cuba and the United States, Brazil participated in the new chapter of the development of plantation slavery in the Americas. Cotton production, although not comparable to the United States, developed in Brazilian captaincies of Maranhão and Pernambuco. Coffee cultivation started in the Paraíba Valley, in the country's southeastern region, at the end of the eighteenth century. Cattle ranching also emerged in the south-central region of the colony, along with old and new crops such as rice and coffee.[86]

Although behind Cuba, after the rise of the Saint-Domingue Revolution, Brazil's sugar industry resurfaced in Bahia, Pernambuco, and Rio de Janeiro, and continued to grow during the nineteenth century.[87] In 1823, British traveler and writer Maria Graham visited the Afonsos' *engenho* in the western region of present-day Rio de Janeiro, which by that time was operated by 180 enslaved persons and produced more than thirty-seven tons of sugar on an annual basis.[88] Likewise, French naturalist Auguste Saint-Hilaire reported his visit to several *engenhos* in the region of Campos de Goitacazes, north of the city of Rio de Janeiro. Among these large estates, there were several that once belonged to the Jesuits and another one owned by the Catholic order of Saint Benedict, which by that time relied on the workforce of hundreds of bondspeople. According to Saint-Hilaire, until 1769, there were fifty-six *engenhos* in the region, but in 1820 there were four hundred *engenhos* in operation.[89]

Brazil's coffee industry borrowed techniques from Saint-Domingue's and Cuba's planters. Benefiting from the increasing demand of North

FIGURE 7.5. *Plantation View: Kitchen of a Barracoon, with Group of Slaves*, [Cuba], c. 1860. Unknown maker, American, published by Edward Anthony (American, 1818–88). Albumen silver print, 84.XC.1158.55. Courtesy of Jean Paul Getty Museum, Los Angeles, CA, United States.

American and European markets that could no longer rely on Saint-Domingue's supply, Brazil quickly saw coffee become its most important export crop in the 1830s. The development of a profitable coffee industry made Brazil the world's largest coffee producer in the middle of the nineteenth century, surpassing the production of Cuba and Puerto Rico combined. Entire families of planters and slave owners made their fortunes with coffee production.[90] In the second half of the nineteenth century, Brazilian coffee estates comprised more than one hundred enslaved persons, a size comparable to that of the largest sugar estates once found in the country's northeast and in the West Indies.[91] At the height of the coffee industry during the era of slavery, large Brazilian estates could comprise between two hundred and five hundred enslaved workers. Yet, slaveholdings became more concentrated in coffee plantations. In other words, few slave owners owned a huge number of slaves and several plantations.

Coffee was grown on mountainsides of the Paraíba Valley, a region located on the border of the provinces of Rio de Janeiro, São Paulo, and Minas Gerais in southeast Brazil. Enslaved people cleared the forest and planted the trees. As the trees grew, bondspeople trimmed them to a height of six to eight feet to allow them to spread, facilitating the harvest process that occurred between April and September. Coffee trees started producing large red berries in four years and reached full maturity in six years. As emphasized by historian Rafael de Bivar Marquese, in the Paraíba Valley, Brazilian coffee planters adopted both the gang system, in which enslaved people worked all day picking coffee, and the task system, in which each enslaved person was assigned with a daily quota of berries to pick.[92]

A series of photographs taken by photographer Marc Ferrez in the 1880s, a few years before the abolition of slavery in Brazil, illustrate the various stages of coffee production on plantations of southeastern Brazil. Under the surveillance of overseers in a period when massive flights from Brazilian coffee plantations anticipated the legal abolition of slavery, enslaved people most likely posed for these photographs against their will. In some pictures, enslaved men, women,

FIGURE 7.6. Marc Ferrez, *Going to Work at a Coffee Plantation*, Rio de Janeiro, Brazil, c. 1888. Gilberto Ferrez collection of photographs of nineteenth-century Brazil, Series I. Marc Ferrez photographs. ID/Accession 92.R.14.-b15.13. Courtesy of Getty Research Institute Special Collections, Los Angeles, CA, United States.

and children display their working tools, such as straw baskets and trays, hoes, and wooden shovels, while defiantly looking directly at the camera (figure 7.6).[93] Although staged, these visual images provide a wealth of information not only about the coffee industry during the second slavery but also about the bondspeople who toiled in these plantations.

Organized in gangs (figure 7.7), enslaved people worked in shifts handpicking the coffee berries the entire day under the supervision of overseers and drivers. One photograph shows how young these enslaved workers were, among whom there were children and even pregnant girls (figure 7.8). Bondspeople transported the baskets filled with berries to terraces where the berries were washed and set out to dry in the sun. Once the drying process was complete, enslaved workers manually removed the shells to obtain the beans. The rhythm of this stage of

FIGURE 7.7. Marc Ferrez, *Picking Coffee*, São Paulo, Brazil, 1885. Gilberto Ferrez collection of photographs of nineteenth-century Brazil, Series I. Marc Ferrez photographs. ID/Accession 92.R.14.-b15.14. Courtesy of Getty Research Institute Special Collections, Los Angeles, CA, United States.

FIGURE 7.8. Marc Ferrez, *Coffee*, São Paulo, Brazil, 1885. Gilberto Ferrez collection of photographs of nineteenth-century Brazil, Series I. Marc Ferrez photographs. ID/Accession 92.R.14.-b15.16. Courtesy of Getty Research Institute Special Collections, Los Angeles, CA, United States.

FIGURE 7.9. Marc Ferrez, *Washing Coffee in a Plantation in the State of Rio*, Brazil, 1880–90. Gilberto Ferrez collection of photographs of nineteenth-century Brazil, Series I. Marc Ferrez photographs. ID/Accession 92.R.14-b19.33. Courtesy of Getty Research Institute Special Collections, Los Angeles, CA, United States.

coffee processing was obviously slow. But again, technology evolved. By the middle of the nineteenth century, coffee planters adopted water-powered shelling machines that sped up this stage of production. In 1866, US businessman William Van Vleek Lidgerwood, then based in Rio de Janeiro, patented a water-steamed coffee hulling and cleaning machine that allowed a dramatic acceleration in coffee processing. One photograph showcases the machine (figure 7.9) employed to wash the coffee beans. Yet, enslaved men and women worked spreading the coffee beans across large terraces to get them dried. After this process was concluded, bondspeople selected and weighed the beans, which were then ready to be brought to Rio de Janeiro for export. Ultimately, despite these technological innovations bondspeople provided essential the work to Brazil's coffee production, in part explaining why Brazil was the last country of the Americas to abolish slavery (in 1888).

CHAPTER 7

Plantation Profitable Worlds

More than twelve million enslaved Africans transported to the Americas made the rise of plantation systems possible. Tobacco, rice, indigo, and especially sugar plantations drove the development of merchant capitalism. Shaped by international exchanges and competitive markets, these estates did not exist in isolation. Cotton, sugarcane, and coffee fields, as well as mills, furnaces, terraces, and workshops, sustained the operations of estates of all sizes in the Americas. Particular crops cultivated and processed in these estates also shaped the development of slavery in the Americas. These interrelated configurations created a world in itself, a world that enslaved men, women, and children were forced to inhabit on a daily basis. Enslaved people had literally fed the plantation systems established in the Americas since the sixteenth century. In Brazil and the West Indies, plantation slavery, especially in sugar estates, was a brutal, often deadly, system. Mortality rates among enslaved men, women, and children were high in sugar plantations in the West Indies and remained higher than birth rates until the abolition of slavery.

Nineteenth-century technological innovations transformed plantation slavery as well. The invention of new machinery such as the cotton gin, the water-powered press, the steam-powered grinding mill, and the water-steamed coffee hulling and cleaning machine allowed the production of cotton, sugar, and coffee to increase at unprecedented levels. The capable and strong hands of enslaved men, women, and children planted, harvested, and processed crops by operating new machinery that transformed these crops into valued commodities.

Ultimately, the work of bondspeople not only sustained the rise and persistence of plantation economies in the Americas, but their labor also financed industrialization and pushed slave societies to enter a new era of global capitalism during the second half of the nineteenth century. Yet, as we will see in chapter 8, the work provided by enslaved people was also widespread in urban areas all over the Americas.

CHAPTER 8

Toiling in the City

Plantation systems were central to the development of slavery, but enslaved people all over the Americas also worked in cities and towns. This type of *urban* slavery was a critical element of slave societies as well as in societies where slavery existed but played a secondary economic role. Soon after his arrival in Brazil in 1845, African-born Mahommah Gardo Baquaqua was made to perform heavy work that included transporting stones to build a house for his owner. As he learned to speak Portuguese, however, he was sent to sell food in the streets, like many enslaved men and women working in urban areas. As he recounted, "One day when I was sent out to sell bread as usual, I only sold a small quantity, and the money I took and spent for whiskey, which I drank pretty freely, and went home well drunk, when my master went to count the days, taking in my basket and discovering the state of things, I was beaten very severely."[1] Baquaqua's account underscores the fact that enslaved people working in the streets had relatively greater autonomy and even opportunities to escape, making it a profoundly different context compared with plantation settings. Nevertheless, even when toiling in the cities, bondspeople performed arduous work and were often victims of the brutality of their owners.

Many observers during this period, including European travelers, commented extensively on the significant presence of enslaved, freed, and free Black men and women in the cities of Latin America, the West Indies, and the US South, especially in the nineteenth century.

Despite the racist views of their authors, European travelogues provide a wealth of information that helps us understand the living and working conditions of enslaved people in many cities of the Americas. Through text and images, these travelers described how slavery shaped the urban landscapes with its sites of physical violence and suffering, such as whipping posts and slave markets, and its refuge spaces, such as the churches housing Catholic Black brotherhoods.

Urban slavery emerged much earlier than the rise of slavery in the Americas. It existed in slave societies such as ancient Greece and Rome as well as in several cities of the Iberian Peninsula before and during the rise of the Atlantic slave trade. In Latin America, slavery in urban areas inherited features that had been well established in these otherwise distant times and places. For example, in Brazil's largest cities, such as Salvador, freed and free Black residents along with bondspeople made up more than half the population. For example, in 1849, when the city of Rio de Janeiro took the first census of its population, 41.2 percent were African-born enslaved people, and 13.2 percent were bondspeople born on Brazilian soil, making the total enslaved population 54.4 percent.[2] This huge number of urban slaves made Rio de Janeiro the city with probably the largest proportion of enslaved people in history, as even in cities such as ancient Rome at the summit of the empire, the proportion of bondspeople likely never reached even 40 percent of the total population. This context led nineteenth-century observers to describe Salvador and Rio de Janeiro as Black cities. The work provided by enslaved people supported the existence of several other inland and coastal cities throughout the Americas, such as Recife, Mariana, Baltimore, Bridgetown, New York City, Havana, Lima, Puebla de los Ángeles, Cartagena, Quito, Charleston, and New Orleans.

In these urban settings, enslaved men had a variety of jobs—coachmen, dockers, sellers, porters, barbers, wigmakers, gardeners, shoemakers, surgeons, healers, carpenters, tailors, craftsmen, blacksmiths, hatters, and silversmiths. Enslaved Black women could often outnumber men in urban areas, especially in Brazil but also in other cities of Latin America, where Indigenous women in the workforce became increasingly scarce. As we will see in more detail in chapter 9, this greater presence of Black bondswomen is associated especially with the demand for domestic workers in urban households, as in these patriarchal societies women were the ones who provided this kind of work. Other enslaved women worked in convents and shops and were also prostitutes, nannies, wet nurses, cooks, washerwomen, seamstresses, and street vendors.

The city was also a space for bondspeople moving through plantation and mining regions. Enslaved men and women from plantations on the outskirts of urban areas would regularly travel to cities looking for opportunities to sell products and offer their services. Urban spaces offered enslaved people a wide range of opportunities for acquiring skills, hiring their work, building networks, and eventually obtaining money to purchase their freedom. But as Baquaqua's story attests, cities were far from safe havens. They were also sites where bondspeople were confined and were closely controlled by public authorities and slave owners. Balancing these two aspects, this chapter underscores the importance of urban slavery in the Americas and shows how the institution of slavery shaped the urban landscape and the lives of Black populations in several important cities in the Western Hemisphere.

Slavery in European Cities

It is undeniable that plantation systems gave rise to a different form of racialized chattel slavery in the Americas. Most enslaved Africans transported to the Americas, in addition to descendants of theirs who remained in bondage, toiled on plantations. Despite this, however, slavery cannot be wholly equated with the plantation system.[3]

In the early years of European colonization, enslaved Africans and their offspring gradually became a significant part of urban area populations. In towns and cities of all regions of the Americas, bondsmen and bondswomen performed a variety of activities. The growing presence of African-born and Black bondspeople in emerging colonial cities of the Americas was neither a new nor an isolated trend but rather an extension of the wider Atlantic slave trade context. Put another way, as the notorious trade in captives from West Africa and West Central Africa emerged, the presence of enslaved persons categorized as "Black" became more visible in European cities such as Lisbon, Lagos, Seville, and Valencia.

Centuries before the rise of the Atlantic slave trade, urban slavery was central to ancient Greek and Roman societies. By the late first century BCE, slaves composed 20 to 30 percent of Rome's population. Nearly 40 percent of the Italian peninsula's population lived in urban areas, including Rome, at the height of the Roman Empire in the first century CE.[4] Since chattel slavery was not a racialized institution in Greece and Rome, Black Africans made up only a small fraction of the overall population of slaves in these two ancient societies. In Greece and Rome, slaves were property, but their humanity was recognized, especially in the existing legal codes. For example, Greek philosophers such as Aristotle conceived of slaves as part of the household. Given that communities, including urban areas, were formed by households, the acquisition of property was part of home management. In this context, a slave was not only considered a piece of property owned by a master, but also an animate instrument.[5]

Despite the existence of other forms of compulsory labor that are difficult to translate into modern-day terms, Roman and Greek laws clearly distinguished between free persons and slaves.[6] Whereas free persons were born free, freed persons were former slaves, emancipated by their owners. Freed persons could become citizens in Rome, depending on how they became slaves in the first place and their trajectories from slavery to freedom.[7] In Greece and Rome, slaves could obtain their freedom by purchasing it as well. In Greek and Roman urban areas, slaves were messengers, concubines, doorkeepers, chamberlains, and cooks. They also performed a variety of tasks in the household as attendants, nurses, playmates, managers, entertainers, shoemakers, street vendors, and even bankers. In cities such as Athens, slave owners hired out their slaves. They also owned wage-earner slaves, who worked independently and versed their incomes to their owners.[8] Despite the many nuances of the slave legal status in Greece and Rome, several dimensions of urban slavery in Europe and the Americas, especially in Latin America, during the era of the Atlantic slave trade, such as the ability of getting emancipated, were similar to these ancient societies.

With the rise of the Atlantic slave trade in the fifteenth century, European powers began to transport African captives from West Africa and West Central Africa to Iberian port cities. These bondspeople were identified as Black, but once in the Iberian Peninsula (the region corresponding to today's Portugal and Spain), they joined a slave workforce that included peoples of other backgrounds, including Muslim individuals, especially from North Africa, who had also been enslaved in the region for several decades.[9] Unfortunately, clear estimates regarding the size of the distinct enslaved populations living in Iberian cities during the sixteenth century remain elusive. That said, it is known that a significant part of the population in the region was identified as Black. But clearly determining their possible regional heritages and their legal statuses as free or slaves is a challenge for historians. Indeed, the use of the term *Black* (in Spanish *negro* and in Portuguese *negro* and *preto*) to refer to these enslaved persons in the fifteenth and sixteenth centuries can lead to unwelcome generalizations. For example, in the Kingdom of Castile (corresponding to a region in present-day Spain), the largest group of persons identified as *negro* came from African regions south of the Sahara. Most individuals in this group were enslaved, spoke African languages, and could be Muslims or Christians. Still, Arabic-speaking Muslims (freed or enslaved) from North Africa with origins in regions south of the Sahara, as well Christian Castilian speakers with African ancestors but who were born in the Kingdom of Castile, could also be identified as Black. In addition, *moriscos* (Muslims converted to Christianity) with African-born ancestors, as well as dark-skinned peoples from the Canary Islands, most of whom were enslaved, could be described as Black. Finally, Hindus or Tamils from India, and enslaved peoples brought to Castile by their owners during the period after the conquest of the Americas, could also be identified as Black.[10] As a result, the term *Black* had a broader use in the sixteenth-century Iberian Peninsula than it would later acquire in the Americas, because there were significant groups of people other than Black Africans who had the legal status of slave in Europe.

Historians estimate that the first enslaved West Africans officially disembarked in Lisbon in 1441. To respond to the growing influx of Black African captives, the Portuguese crown codified slavery in new legislation (*Ordenações manuelinas*) starting in 1512, which was supplemented with additional laws (*Leis Extravagantes*) over the course of the sixteenth century. The new code defined Black slaves as *escravos*, whereas Muslims were referred to as *mouros* (Moors).[11] The significant number of enslaved Black persons who lived and worked in Lisbon, then the largest city of the Kingdom of Portugal, is attested in King Dom Manuel I's 1515 decree requesting the construction of a pit in which to bury dead Black slaves, discussed in chapter 5. An assessment of 1551 determined that the total population of Lisbon was 100,000, and 9.95 percent of its residents were slaves.[12]

Other visitors also observed the large presence of individuals who they concluded were slaves in the streets of Portuguese cities during the same period. Flemish traveler Nicolas Cleynaerts, who visited Portugal in the early sixteenth century, not only stated that enslaved men and women seemed to outnumber free people in Lisbon, but he also compared Évora to a "city in hell" where "black people [were] everywhere."[13] These observations created confusion. Some historians assumed most of these bondspeople were Black, either born in Africa or locally, even though precise references to their origins are scattered, because the records were destroyed in the earthquake of 1755 and existing documents do not reveal specific information.[14] For example, one of the records of this presence is an eighteenth-century tile panel depicting a Black woman cleaning fish (figure 8.1), today displayed in the Museu da Cidade (City Museum) at Pimenta Palace in Lisbon. Yet, although she was likely enslaved, the image does not allow us to identify the cook as

FIGURE 8.1. Eighteenth-century tile panel representing a Black woman cleaning fish. Museu da Cidade (City Museum), Palácio Pimenta, Lisbon, Portugal. Photograph by Ana Lucia Araujo, 2022.

an African-born woman, either enslaved, freed, or free. Enslaved Black men, women, and children also lived in other cities such as Elvas, Braga, Minho, Lagos, and Porto. Still, it is probable that it was never the case in any of these localities that Black or enslaved persons generally ever outnumbered white Portuguese individuals.

After all, the presence of enslaved Black persons in urban areas in the Iberian Peninsula was visible before the emergence of urban slavery in the Americas. Late sixteenth-century observers often described cities such as Lisbon as "chess boards" because of the equal number of people regarded as Black and white visible in Iberian urban areas.[15] Similar trends were also observed in in Valencia and Barcelona in the Kingdom of Aragón, as well as Seville, in the Kingdom of Castile. In these cities, Black enslaved people may have been at least 10 percent of the total population at the end of the fifteenth century. Moreover, Black Africans and their descendants already made up the majority of the enslaved population in these cities during the sixteenth century.[16] Black bondspeople also lived and worked in several other cities, such as Madrid, Barcelona, Córdoba, Cádiz, and Granada.

In various cities of present-day Portugal and Spain, most enslaved Black women worked as domestic servants performing many tasks. They ran errands and cleaned their owners' houses. They were also seamstresses and cooks, and they could work as street vendors, selling food, supplies, and water.[17] Enslaved Black men were pages, gardeners, doormen, carpenters, and porters. In addition to all these tasks, slaves owned by noblemen could work as musicians and entertainers. Black bondsmen also toiled in the workshops of craftsmen—shoemakers, blacksmiths, bricklayers, and tailors. These enslaved men and women could hire themselves out and be hired out by their owners. Despite this significant presence of enslaved people in the region, by the middle of the sixteenth century, only wealthy individuals, such as nobles, members of the clergy, civil servants, businessmen, and owners of workshops could afford to own slaves.[18]

Although barely visible and in much smaller numbers than in the cities of the Iberian Peninsula, Africans and their descendants also toiled in other European cities such as London, Paris, Nantes, Bordeaux, and Amsterdam. Still, the status of enslaved persons who entered these European cities was often ambiguous because, in theory, the institution of slavery was not always codified in these European societies. In present-day Great Britain, the presence of free Black Africans dates back to the Roman occupation of Britannia, centuries before the development of the Atlantic slave trade. Africans and their descendants also lived and worked in England during the Tudor period, when the population greatly increased in urban areas, especially in London.[19] With the rise of English participation in the Atlantic trade of enslaved Africans in the late sixteenth century, a growing number of planters and merchants transported bondspeople to cities such as Bristol, Liverpool, and London, where these enslaved persons worked in several professions such as pages, domestic servants, and maritime workers. During the seventeenth and eighteenth centuries, several bondsmen traveled back and forth across the Atlantic Ocean to reach these port cities.

When the Dutch Republic joined the Atlantic slave trade during the seventeenth century, the populations of its cities were increasing. The number of residents of Amsterdam dramatically grew from 30,000 in 1585 to 200,000 in 1670.[20] Free and enslaved Africans gradually reached cities such as Utrecht, Rotterdam, and Leiden. Estimates of Amsterdam's very small Black enslaved population during the seventeenth and eighteenth centuries are unknown because, as in England, slavery had no legal grounds in the Dutch Republic. Still, European slave owners and slave merchants frequently brought their slaves to the city, where they remained in bondage.[21] Similar to England, most enslaved persons who settled in Amsterdam permanently or temporarily worked as domestic servants, but enslaved and free Africans also worked for the Dutch West India Company. These bondsmen came from the Iberian Peninsula and also from various regions of the African continent, including West Central African coastal areas, Cape Verde, and São Tomé, as well as the Gold Coast, where the Dutch established trading forts starting in the early seventeenth century. Enslaved people from the Americas, especially from the Dutch colonies in the West Indies as well as Brazil, where the Dutch were established between 1630 and 1654, also settled in the city.[22] The traces of the presence of an enslaved, freed, and free Black population in Dutch cities during this period are visible to this day in the Netherlands. From The Hague to Amsterdam, several museums display oil paintings depicting Dutch noblemen and members of the Dutch merchant elite accompanied by Black pages. Some seventeenth-century paintings by the celebrated Dutch painter Rembrandt also feature Black models. Tombs of enslaved and freed people also survive in Amsterdam's churches and cemeteries. Likewise, bondspeople from French and Danish colonies of the Americas followed their owners to European cities such as Bordeaux, Nantes, Paris, and Copenhagen starting in the eighteenth century.

Until the middle of the nineteenth century, when slavery was eventually abolished in most colonies in the Americas, slave owners continued to bring their enslaved servants to European cities. Take the example of James and Sally Hemings, who were owned by Thomas Jefferson. When Jefferson moved to Paris in 1784 as a minister of the new independent United States, the two enslaved siblings followed him into the French capital, where they lived for five years. In Paris, they were able to freely circulate in the city, learn new skills, and meet freedpeople and other enslaved men and women from the French West Indies who were sojourning in the city with their owners. Although French legislation in force at the time allowed enslaved people entering the metropole to petition for their freedom, none of the Hemingses took that path.[23] In 1783, John Pinney, a British merchant and planter, brought his enslaved property, Pero Jones, from the island of Nevis in the British West Indies to Bristol, then the second busiest British slave-trading port, where he lived and worked in his sumptuous house. Today, Pero's story is memorialized in Bristol, where a bridge is named after him. Likewise, many French slave owners brought their slaves from the French West Indies to spend long or short periods in metropolitan France.[24] The presence of bondspeople in port cities such as

FIGURE 8.2. Pierre-Bernard Morlot, *Marguerite Deurbroucq, born Sengstack, and an enslaved woman living in Nantes*, 1753. Oil on canvas, 64 × 51.6 inches. Photograph by Karine Garcia-Lebailly. Courtesy of Musée d'histoire de Nantes (Nantes History Museum), Nantes, France.

Nantes, Bordeaux, and La Rochelle is evident in archival records and also in many paintings displayed in the Museum of Aquitaine and the Nantes History Museum. One of these paintings (figure 8.2) features a female enslaved domestic servant and her mistress Marguerite Deurbroucq, the wife of one of Nantes's most prosperous slave merchants at the time. In the foreground, Deurbroucq is wearing a lavish floral white silk dress. Comfortably seated in an armchair, she is about to lift a coffee cup from its saucer that rests on a sophisticated marble side table next to her. The bondswoman, standing behind her and with head turned toward her mistress, is wearing a white dress and headscarf, as well as earrings. Around her neck is a delicate fabric and pearl choker reminiscent of a slave collar, perhaps intended to mark her slave legal status. The enslaved woman, whose position in the background confirms her adjuvant social status, holds a tray with a bowl of sugar cubes that she offers to her owner. Perched on Deurbroucq's armchair, an African grey parrot holding a sugar cube in its beak completes the scene, evoking the wealth generated by sugar plantations in the French West Indies that depended on a workforce of enslaved Africans and their descendants.

Latin America and the West Indies

In Latin America and the West Indies, enslaved Africans and their descendants made up a significant part of urban populations, especially in coastal areas and in regions in which mining activities prevailed. As early as the sixteenth century, the silver boom in the Andean region led to the rise of Potosí. Located in the Spanish Viceroyalty of Peru, in present-day Bolivia, Potosí became the largest city in the Americas, with a population of 140,000, even though the number dramatically declined in the seventeenth century. Enslaved Africans worked in Potosí, but most of its population was composed of Indigenous peoples, who were also enslaved and submitted to forced labor regimes.[25] Still, Potosí was an exception. Although estimated populations are not always accurate, until 1800, only Mexico City, the capital of the Viceroyalty of Mexico or New Spain, had more than 100,000 residents. Yet, until the nineteenth century, the populations of cities in the Spanish Americas and Brazil were, in general, larger than the populations of cities in the thirteen British colonies of North America.

Depending on the region, in the Spanish Americas and Brazil, in as early as the sixteenth century, slave ownership in urban areas was not limited to rich households. More modest families and individuals could own one or two enslaved persons, who hired themselves to perform a variety of services. European and locally born white settlers, including women (as we explored in chapter 6) owned enslaved people. But in cities such as Lima, the capital of the Viceroyalty of Peru, it was not uncommon to find men and women who owned Black enslaved persons, although rarely in great numbers.[26] A comparable context existed in Brazilian cities such as Salvador in Bahia, where studies suggest that during the nineteenth century, about 67 percent of slaveholders owned between one and ten slaves. Among the city's residents who registered postmortem inventories, only approximately 13 percent did not own any enslaved people.[27]

Black enslaved populations have been present in the Spanish Americas since the conquest and the early colonization period. But the use of an enslaved Black workforce in urban and rural areas often depended on the size of the available Indigenous population in the various Spanish colonies. Where the native populations became scarce after being decimated by military conquest, diseases, and excessive work, Spanish colonizers increasingly imported enslaved Africans. For example, as early as the sixteenth century, Spanish colonial cities such as Mexico City and Cartagena had significant populations of Black enslaved men and women who worked as domestic servants, laundresses, street vendors, tailors, blacksmiths, carpenters, gardeners, and shoemakers. By the seventeenth century, Indigenous, Black, and, to a lesser extent, enslaved workers from Asia (known as *chinos*) coexisted and often shared the same professions in this vast region.[28] In Lima and Puebla de los Ángeles, the second largest city of the Viceroyalty of New Spain (or Mexico), a significant number of enslaved Black workers labored in textile mills (*obrajes*) during the seventeenth century.[29] Enslaved people also worked in convents, hospitals, and colleges.

In Bridgetown in Barbados, enslaved women worked as prostitutes in brothels run by freedwomen at the end of the eighteenth century.[30] During this same period in Cuba, enslaved people made up approximately 28 percent of Havana's population.[31] As the city developed, many bondsmen worked in the city's defensive fortresses, construction sites, and shipyards. Havana's newspaper advertisements between 1791 and 1815 show enslaved men in a variety of professions such as blacksmiths, tailors, cooks, vendors, hairdressers, barbers, tobacconists, coachmen, helmsmen, and bakers. Enslaved women appear as cooks, laundresses, seamstresses, nurses, vendors, and nannies.[32] As with Bridgetown and other cities of the Americas, enslaved women also worked as prostitutes in Havana. Overall, in urban settings of the Spanish Americas and Brazil and the West Indies where the white population was small, Black bondspeople could improve their livelihoods and occasionally amass resources to purchase their own freedom, working in a variety of urban professions such as vendors, artisans, and apprentices.[33] Still, there were considerable obstacles that restricted the social mobility of Black and mixed-race individuals (known as *castas*).[34]

The eighteenth-century mining boom in the area of present-day Minas Gerais, Goiás, and Mato Grosso led to the increase of imports of enslaved Africans to Brazil. Many bondspeople lived and worked in gold and diamond mining towns such as Sabará, Ouro Preto, and Mariana in Minas Gerais. A number of men were *faisqueiros*. These enslaved men were itinerant miners who worked and lived away from their owners in exchange for providing them a fixed amount of their gains.[35] In the cities of this mining region, enslaved women worked as street vendors and prostitutes as well. These activities allowed them to save money to purchase their freedom, therefore contributing toward an increase in the region's freed population.[36]

The use of slave labor was widespread in all spheres of Brazilian society, and in urban areas, owning between one and five enslaved persons was common. In urban settings all over the Americas, even in the United States, but especially in Brazil and the rest of Latin America, enslaved Black men and women could work autonomously as wage earners. In this system, their owners allowed them to hire out their services. In exchange, they gave their owners a fixed daily or weekly amount of their income and kept part of it for themselves.[37] In Brazilian cities such as Rio de Janeiro, these enslaved workers were often in charge of their own housing and living expenses and resided outside their owners' households.[38]

In the Spanish Americas and Brazil, manumission (the practice of freeing enslaved persons) subsisted until the abolition of slavery and was much more widespread in the urban areas.[39] Because manumission, especially through self-purchase, was widely practiced in countries such as Brazil, and there was never any legislation preventing slave owners from freeing their enslaved property, many foreign observers concluded that social relations between slave owners and enslaved people were harmonious. As we will see in chapter 18, these views gave rise to the erroneous idea that slavery was more benevolent in Brazil and the Spanish Americas than in the United States.

However, this idea could not be further from the truth. Slave owners rarely granted unconditional emancipation. Most enslaved people purchased their own freedom in urban areas by accumulating over the years the necessary amounts. Once they amassed the resources, they usually purchased their freedom in several installments (*coartación* or *coartação*). In Cuba, for example, a royal order of 1778 determined that slave owners could not refuse to manumit enslaved persons who wanted to purchase their own freedom.[40] In other words, the fact that slave owners could free their slaves in Latin America was not an indication of the alleged benevolent nature of slavery in this region. As bondspeople paid the market price to purchase their own freedom, slave owners obtained financial gains with this practice, and they could use the money to purchase another enslaved person. In Rio de Janeiro, despite the large proportion of enslaved men, slave owners granted manumission especially to enslaved women and children and made it more difficult for African-born men. This lucrative strategy allowed them to reinvest profits in the slave market.[41]

Especially in the domestic space of urban areas, enslaved men, women, and children lived in close proximity with slave owners, as illustrated in European nineteenth-century travel accounts (figure 8.3).

FIGURE 8.3. *Une dame brésilienne dans son intérieur* (*A Brazilian Lady in Her Interior*), in Jean-Baptiste Debret, *Voyage pittoresque et historique au Brésil*, 3 vols. (Paris: Firmin Didot Frères, 1834–39), vol. 2, plate 6.

Yet, these illustrations showing households in which slave owners and enslaved people harmoniously interacted often conceal the horrors of slavery in domestic settings, where enslaved servants worked extremely hard and had to stay available day and night. Living so near to their owners also exposed many enslaved women to constant sexual abuse. Of course, bondspeople toiling in urban areas had much higher chances of purchasing their own freedom that eventually provided opportunities for social mobility. But despite many nuances, slave owners still regarded them as commodities, exactly as they were considered and treated on plantations.

North American Cities

Urban slavery existed in North America as well. Enslaved people labored in Montreal in present-day Canada during the French and

British rules.[42] Enslaved workers also toiled in New York City, where the Dutch West India Company introduced the first enslaved Africans in Manhattan in the early seventeenth century. The Dutch West India Company owned most enslaved laborers during the Dutch rule. But starting in 1665, when the English controlled the colony, slave ownership became widespread, with nearly 40 percent of European households owning enslaved people. The city continued to import enslaved people during the eighteenth century as well.[43] Like in other cities of the Americas, enslaved Africans and their descendants performed many activities alongside white workers, until the abolition of slavery in the state of New York in 1827. Bondsmen worked in markets, artisan workshops, and also in retail and trade businesses as tailors, shoemakers, bakers, butchers, carpenters, and dockers, whereas enslaved women worked as domestic servants cooking, cleaning, and providing childcare.[44] Urban slavery was prominent in New Orleans as well. As early as in the mid-eighteenth century, during French colonial rule in Louisiana, slave owners of New Orleans had benefited from a hiring system in which "craftsmen, such as carpenters, pastry-cooks, carters, domestics and wet nurses, could be rented out for a given task or for a certain period of time, ranging from a month to a year."[45]

After the thirteen British colonies gained their independence, slavery expanded in the urban centers of the United States. In 1790, Washington, DC, became the capital of the young independent country. In charge of planning the new city, French architect Pierre L'Enfant leased enslaved workers from their owners to construct the new United States Capitol and the White House.[46] Although the role of dozens of bondsmen played in the construction of these buildings has been recognized only recently (figure 8.4), without them these two major national landmarks would not exist. Enslaved people cleared the land, transported construction materials, and sawed lumber, while others worked as carpenters, masons, brickmakers, and bricklayers to erect the two new imposing buildings. Enslaved people, including bondswomen, worked in a variety of roles in the White House as well.[47]

FIGURE 8.4. Plaque on the construction of the White House, Lafayette Square, Washington, DC, United States. Photograph by Ana Lucia Araujo, 2021.

In Baltimore, Maryland, a growing number of bondspeople worked in various industries, including iron manufacturing and shipbuilding, as well as mining by the end of the eighteenth century. At the turn of the nineteenth century, as the city's enslaved population started to gradually decline, slave owners increasingly hired out their enslaved property. Therefore, enslaved laborers often worked side by side with white wage workers.[48] Nonetheless, the growing development of industrial capitalism in the North of the United States was not incompatible with the persistence and expansion of plantation and urban slavery. In the first six decades of the nineteenth century, with the rise of the "second slavery" propelled by the cotton production in the US South, the number of enslaved people increased in cities such as Richmond, Virginia. As it had in Baltimore, a system also emerged in Richmond wherein, to minimize costs, businesses (especially tobacco factories) rented enslaved workers from their actual owners for limited periods instead of purchasing them.[49]

Cities like those located near tobacco and cotton plantations offered opportunities for enslaved men who were trusted by their slave owners to venture into the city. For example, bondspeople who worked in Monticello, Thomas Jefferson's plantation in Virginia, could obtain passes to go sell vegetables and other produce in Charlottesville after completing their tasks during the weekend.[50] Occasionally, skilled enslaved workers such as blacksmiths sold the products of their specialized services to loyal urban customers who commissioned their work. Enslaved people knew the opportunities offered by the city. They could meet comrades, develop new skills, and encounter free Black workers and freedpeople. In their urban interactions, they built new networks that could eventually help them purchase their freedom or simply escape bondage by running away.

But in Virginia, unlike Bahia, enslaved and freed or free Black individuals were not the majority of the population. Hence, although to different degrees, slave owners and public authorities imposed huge restraints on enslaved people who lived, worked, and circulated in the cities. Such restrictions varied over time and, as we will discuss in chapter 14, could dramatically worsen in periods following slave insurrections. In Virginia, enslaved people venturing into the cities had to carry a written pass showing permission from their owners to travel to the city. As in Salvador and Rio de Janeiro, slave owners in cities such as New Orleans, Mobile, Savannah, and Charleston put their enslaved property to work in the streets in order to make profits from their income. Municipalities attempted to discourage this system by issuing codes that regulated this practice and forced slave owners to pay a registration fee to allow their human property to work in the city.

Already at the end of the eighteenth century, the city of Charleston, South Carolina, required freedpeople to wear identification badges to prove their free status.[51] Starting in 1808, enslaved people who hired out their services in the streets of New Orleans had to wear a brass badge with a registration number as well.[52] By 1818, similar municipal regulations required enslaved people hired out by their owners in Charleston to either carry a ticket or to visibly wear a metal badge to

FIGURE 8.5. Slave badge, copper, Charleston, 1818. Collection of the Smithsonian National Museum of African American History and Culture, Gift from the Liljenquist Family Collection, Object number 2016.166.27. Courtesy of the National Museum of African American History and Culture, Washington, DC, United States.

monitor their urban activities.[53] In a variety of sizes and shapes, but more usually in the format of squares, circles, and diamonds, Charleston's copper alloy badges are the only surviving items of this kind. Today these slave badges can be found in several museums in the United States, and dozens of them bearing words such as "porter," "mechanic," or "servant" that identified the professions of enslaved persons are housed in the collections of the National Museum of African American History and Culture in Washington, DC (e.g., figure 8.5).

Enslaved People in Brazilian Cities

The Brazilian cities of Salvador and Rio de Janeiro had substantial enslaved populations between the eighteenth and nineteenth centuries. Bondspeople, along with the freed and free Black urban residents, often outnumbered white residents. Still, bondspeople from nearby farms and plantations also temporarily circulated in the cities to sell their produce and run errands. As in other regions of the Americas, slaves were found in all professions that required manual labor. This huge presence led European observers during this period to describe Salvador and Rio de Janeiro as the two African cities of the Americas.

During the eighteenth century, enslaved workers were visible in the streets of Salvador, but starting in the first decade of the nineteenth century, African-born enslaved persons made up nearly two-thirds of the city's enslaved population.[54] The strong presence of enslaved workers in the streets of Salvador continued through the nineteenth century. The pages of *Idade d'ouro do Brazil*, the first newspaper of the province of Bahia, published biweekly in Salvador in the early nineteenth century, offered a lively picture of the activities performed by enslaved men, women, and children in the city. Between 1811 and 1823, the pages of the newspaper announced objects and real estate for sale side by side with ads selling one, two, or sometimes three enslaved persons. The ads contained the names of the male and female slave owners and also specified whether slaves on sale were born in Brazil (*crioulo* or *crioula*) or on the African continent. Ads selling African-born enslaved persons specified their nations or regions of provenance, covering three large areas corresponding to the Bight of Benin (Mina, Nagô, Jeje, Hausa, Benin, Borno, and Tapa), West Central Africa (Angola, Congo, and Cabinda), and Southeastern Africa (Inhambane and Mozambique).[55] Sometimes the ads indicated that captives for sale had arrived in Brazil as recently as six months prior. Providing some information on physical features, the announcements also underscore that the persons on sale were healthy, had "no vices," and did not "pull any shenanigans."

The ads show that enslaved women were in demand to work as washerwomen, ironers, embroiders, lacemakers, seamstresses, cooks, and shopkeepers. Street vendors were also in demand. These enslaved women sold a variety of goods, primarily food but also other commodities, giving their owners a fixed amount of their earnings on a daily, weekly, or monthly basis, as we will see in more detail in chapter 9. In several cases the ads specified that bondswomen could perform more than one of these tasks. Some advertisements announced the sale of enslaved women along with their newborns, underscoring that they had "milk of first womb," a term indicating they were lactating from their first pregnancy. Other ads sought enslaved wet nurses to breastfeed white newborns. A few advertisements specified a preference for young *mulatas*, mixed-race women assumedly born in Brazil. The ads also show that residents of Salvador sold and sought enslaved men to work as barbers, bleeders, butlers, bricklayers, carpenters, sedan chair porters, coachmen, painters, coopers, bakers, blacksmiths, shoemakers, tailors, rowers, fishers, sailors, and shipbuilders. Although domestic service was mainly performed by enslaved women in Brazilian cities, a few announcements advertised enslaved men who were cooks and who could perform domestic activities, and in rare occurrences enslaved men for sale knew how to read and write. A few buyers sought enslaved children, and some announcements advertised shoemaker boys for sale. Announcements selling bondspeople were as numerous as ads searching for fugitives, especially African-born men, women, and children. Describing in detail their physical characteristics and temperament, these ads suggest that because Salvador was a city with a large Black population, it offered a relatively favorable environment to escape bondage, as we will explore in more detail in chapter 12.

In Salvador, bondswomen often worked as street vendors, sometimes living outside the houses of their owners, and bringing a fixed amount of their incomes to their owners on a regular basis. Enslaved men also worked as street vendors in similar arrangements. Slave owners made their bondsmen hire out their services transporting goods of all kinds and sizes. The bondsmen then paid their owners a fixed amount of their income from this work, keeping the rest for themselves. Salvador's irregular street surfaces and the steepness separating the upper and the lower towns made it impossible to use carriages, thus making the work provided by enslaved male porters more crucial than in any other Brazilian urban center.[56]

When missionaries Daniel Kidder and James Fletcher visited Salvador in the 1830s and the 1850s, they noted the presence of enslaved, and possibly freed, porters whom they described as "tall, athletic negroes . . . moving in pairs or gangs of four, six, or eight, with their loads suspended between them on heavy poles."[57] In the anthill-like environment of the lower city, Black men shouted and sang while transporting heavy cargos. Others remained sitting weaving straw or lying in the alleys and corners while waiting to be called to work. According to Kidder and Fletcher, in every corner of Salvador's lower city there were lines of sedan chairs whose porters offered their services to passersby by asking, "Will you have a chair, sir?"[58] In the late 1850s, French artist François-Auguste Biard, who spent two years in Brazil, and briefly visited Salvador, also noticed the large number of enslaved men transporting sedan chairs "covered with a dark blue fabric" in the narrow streets of the city.[59]

In Salvador, African-born enslaved men and freedmen who hired out their services gathered themselves along ethnic lines associated with their African regions of provenance. They formed working groups named *cantos*, a Portuguese term referring both to the songs they sang while toiling in the streets and to the street corners they occupied while waiting to be hired.[60] Therefore, on June 1, 1857, the same year that Kidder and Fletcher published their travel account in the United States, nearly two thousand freedmen and enslaved men who hired out their services started a twelve-day strike that paralyzed the circulation of goods in Salvador. The movement was in protest of the city's decision not only to tax their services but also to impose on them a license requirement to toil in the streets and the need to wear a metal tag with their registration number, similar to the one worn by enslaved people in the streets of Charleston, South Carolina (see figure 8.5). The strike was successful in taking down the tax, but the metal tag was maintained. Overall, the movement illustrates the great extent to which Salvador relied on a Black workforce in the middle of the nineteenth century.[61]

Urban Slavery and Social Mobility

Working in the city offered enslaved men and women an array of opportunities to amass money. In Salvador, for example, there are curious cases of enslaved individuals who themselves owned slaves.[62] According to one historian, in a period between eight to ten years, enslaved men who hired out their services in Salvador could save enough to purchase their freedom.[63] Once emancipated, several freedmen and freedwomen became slave owners.[64] Take the example of Joaquim, whose original name was Gbego Sokpa. Born in Hoko, a town in the Mahi country in the Bight of Benin in present-day Republic of Benin, he was enslaved during the reign of King Adandozan and transported to Brazil, where in 1814 he became the property of the slave ship captain Manuel Joaquim de Almeida, with whom he sailed to the coasts of Africa. In 1830, Joaquim was emancipated and adopted the last name of his former owner.[65] As a freedman, Joaquim de Almeida became a prosperous slave trader himself and continued to travel back and forth between Bahia and the Bight of Benin. His will, drafted in 1844, fourteen years after obtaining his freedom, shows how wealthy he had become. His assets included large sums of money, 25 percent of the cargo of a slave ship, and real estate. Moreover, Almeida owned thirty-six slaves in Havana and twenty in Pernambuco. He was also the owner of nine enslaved Africans: Marcelino (Jeje), João (Nagô), David (Nagô), Feliciano (Mina), Maria (Jeje), Jezuinina (Nagô), Felismina (Mina), and Benedita (Nagô), all of them identified with nations of the Bight of Benin. As Almeida certainly did not need all these bondspeople working for him in his household, we can assume several of them worked as street vendors. Yet, as his will gave instructions to free Felismina and Benedita for the good services provided, it is also possible to conclude that at least these two enslaved women worked performing domestic service.[66]

As in Salvador, enslaved workers were found performing all kinds of activities that required manual labor in the streets of Rio de Janeiro as well. Their presence was noted by European visitors, such as the young Édouard Manet who, before becoming a famous painter, left France and spent several months in Rio de Janeiro between 1848 and 1849. Like several other travelers, Manet was not able to distinguish whether the Black workers he saw toiling in the streets of Rio de Janeiro were freeborn, freed, or enslaved, and therefore claims that all Black persons in the city were enslaved.[67] But in a letter to his mother he emphasized that the only residents visible in the streets were Black people.

Manet also observed clothing patterns among the enslaved population of Rio de Janeiro. According to him, enslaved men wore pants and sometimes fabric jackets. Yet, he emphasized that enslaved women were naked to the waist and that some wore neck scarves falling to the chest. Like other nineteenth-century European travelers, although describing enslaved women as ugly, he also underscored how other ones were beautiful and dressed "very gracefully. Some make turbans, others arrange their frizzy hair very skillfully, and almost all of them wear petticoats decorated with ugly flounces."[68] Despite these general remarks, Manet provided accurate observations about the ways bondspeople were dressed in the streets of Rio de Janeiro. As pointed out by one historian, most enslaved individuals in Rio de Janeiro "wore a plain loose-fitting shirt with short or long sleeves," but their outfits varied over time and according to the social positions of their owners.[69]

Still, a minority of enslaved persons wore richer outfits. In Rio de Janeiro, similarly to Salvador in Bahia and other Latin American cities such as Lima, Mexico City, and Santiago de Chile, wealthy slave owners provided enslaved women who performed domestic service with fine clothes, shoes, and even jewelry.[70] For example, French mariner Jacques Proa, who disembarked in Cap Français in the French colony of Saint-Domingue in 1777, observed in his journal that Black women were elegantly dressed and covered with jewelry, even though these travelers were rarely able to distinguish free, freed, and enslaved women.[71] Portuguese and Brazilian public authorities attempted to prevent Black women from wearing luxurious outfits, jewelry, and shoes.[72] At the middle of the eighteenth century, the Portuguese crown issued a decree to prevent enslaved women from wearing jewelry and fancy clothes in order to maintain the social distance between them and "respectable" white women.[73] But in practice, the law was never enforced. And the very existence of these ordinances confirm that enslaved women resisted and continued to wear refined clothing and jewelry in Brazil.

Eighteenth-century observers described enslaved women walking the streets of Salvador with their female owners, wearing rich satin skirts and embroidered blouses.[74] In the nineteenth century, British consul James Wetherell, who resided in Salvador between 1843 and 1857, described the elaborate outfits of Black women, enslaved and freed, who also had their arms "covered with bracelets of coral and gold, beads . . . the neck loaded with chains, and the hands with rings." He also noticed one particular garment; a shawl made of "coast cloth . . . thrown over the shoulder." As shown in nineteenth-century Bahia's newspapers, these cloths called *panos da costa* were imported from the Bight of Benin.[75] These textiles were "woven in small stripes of coloured cotton from two to four inches wide in striped or checked patterns, and the slips sewed together form a shawl," and were especially coveted by African-born women.[76]

A few eighteenth-century visual images featured Black women wearing beautiful dresses and jewelry as well. For example, one watercolor produced by Carlos Julião, a Luso-Italian military officer who spent time in Brazil in the second half of the eighteenth century, shows two Black women wearing necklaces and bracelets, presumably in gold and silver (figure 8.6).[77] An image alone is often not sufficient to determine whether these women were still enslaved or already freed. But both are bare-breasted and barefoot, and because Julião represented other Black women wearing shoes, it is not unreasonable to suppose that the artist represented two bondswomen in this image. Likewise, wills and postmortem inventories of freedwomen list a variety of clothes in sophisticated fabrics, jewelry, and objects in gold, silver, amber, coral, and pearls, which suggests that it is possible that these women may have started acquiring these items prior to their emancipation.[78]

Such a hypothesis can be corroborated by the case of Domingas Pereira, an eighteenth-century African-born woman who lived and worked in Mariana, a gold mining town in Minas Gerais. Before her emancipation, she already owned four slaves.[79] To purchase her freedom, she paid her owner with two pounds of gold and one additional slave, suggesting that at least in this region, enslaved women already had access to gold items. Nineteenth-century photographic portraits of freedwomen in Bahia, for example, show them wearing amazingly extravagant gold necklaces and bracelets (figure 8.7).[80] African-born women's taste for jewelry and luxury textiles may have emerged before the Middle Passage. In the late eighteenth century, West Central African women in the kingdoms of Ngoyo, Kakongo, and Loango, in the region north of the Congo River, greatly appreciated jewelry in silver and coral, items that were increasingly introduced into Atlantic Africa by European slave traders.[81] In nineteenth-century Portuguese-controlled Benguela in West Central Africa, dozens of wills of enslaved, freed, and free women showed a similar trend in which women purchased and wore fine clothes and jewelry to publicly display their social status.[82]

European observers who visited Brazilian cities during the period of slavery often repeated that enslaved people were forbidden to wear shoes. Take Debret, for example. The French artist commented that upon his arrival in Rio de Janeiro, he was surprised at the large number of shoemakers' shops spread all over the city. Soon he understood why. White Brazilian women wore silk shoes to walk the streets, but

FIGURE 8.6. Carlos Julião, "Noticia summaria do gentilismo da Asia com dez Riscos iluminados. Ditos de Figurinhos de Brancos e Negros dos Uzos do Rio de Janeiro e Serro do Frio. Ditos de Vazos e Tecidos Peruvianos" ("Summary news of Asian gentility with ten illuminated Risks. Sayings of Figurines of Whites and Blacks from the Uses of Rio de Janeiro and Serro do Frio. Sayings of Peruvian Vases and Fabrics"), c. 17—, plate XXVI. Courtesy of Biblioteca Nacional, Rio de Janeiro, Brazil.

FIGURE 8.7. Marc Ferrez, *Sister of the Sisterhood Boa Morte*, Cachoeira, Bahia, 1885. Photograph. Courtesy of Ethnologisches Museum der Staatlichen Museen zu Berlin, Stiftung Preußischer Kulturbesitz, Berlin, Germany.

the city's rough granite sidewalks quickly damaged the delicate shoes, which did not last for more than two day trips. As a result, women purchased new pairs and needed shops to repair the old ones. However, Debret noted that not only slave owners wore shoes. Because Latin American societies were driven by notions of honor and respectability, white women never ventured outside alone. This precaution was intended to ensure that if they were still single, they would remain virgins, and if they were married, they would not engage in extramarital sex. Hence, in their nearly daily visits to the church, the richest women were followed by their enslaved maids, who, like their owners, wore shoes. But despite being a luxury product, more modest women, including freed and freeborn Black women, also valued owning a pair of shoes, as Debret pointed out: "A well-appointed mulatto wants to put on a fresh pair of shoes every time she goes out, [and she does the same] for her children and her Negress. The wife of the poor craftsman almost deprives herself of necessities in order to wear new shoes to all parties; and finally, the free Negress ruins her lover to meet this expense repeated too often."[83]

Like fine clothes and jewelry, in Brazil and in other Portuguese colonies in the South Atlantic, wearing shoes was a symbol of social status that distinguished freed and freeborn Black individuals from their enslaved counterparts. At the end of the eighteenth century in Angola, Portuguese officials complained about the many individuals who were wearing shoes "to become nominally whites."[84] Therefore, urban bondspeople were not officially prohibited from wearing shoes, but it was customary for most enslaved people to go barefoot in Brazilian cities. Some historians have emphasized that enslaved men and women who were owned by rich individuals, especially enslaved workers who performed domestic service (including maids, cooks, nannies, pages, valets, butlers, and wet nurses), were well dressed and wore shoes.[85] Still, several of Rio de Janeiro's Black male and female street vendors whose legal status as enslaved, freed, or free is uncertain are portrayed barefoot in staged studio photographs (e.g., figure 8.8) in the middle of the nineteenth century.

FIGURE 8.8. Christiano Junior, Studio Portrait: *Female and Male Street Vendors with Baskets on Head, Brazil*, 1864–66. Albumen silver print, 3.4 × 2.1 inches. The Horace W. Goldsmith Foundation Fund, through Joyce and Robert Menschel, 2017. Courtesy of Metropolitan Museum of Art, New York, United States.

Slave Ownership as Social Prestige

In urban areas of Latin America, slave ownership was a way to assert prestige and high social and economic status. Illustrations in European travel accounts confirm this trend by often portraying scenes in which slave owners and their families are followed by a line of enslaved men, women, and children in the streets of Brazilian cities such as Rio de Janeiro.[86] Consider the example of Debret's well-known lithograph *Un employé du gouvernement sortant de chez lui avec sa famille* (*A Government Employee Leaving His Home with His Family*) in his travelogue *Voyage pittoresque et historique au Brésil*, published between 1834 and 1839.[87] The lithograph (figure 8.9) depicts a bureaucrat strolling with his family. The text explaining the illustration reminds readers that Black people predominated in the streets of Rio de Janeiro, a statement confirmed by the population estimates of

FIGURE 8.9. *Un employé du gouvernement sortant de chez lui avec sa famille* (*A Government Employee Leaving His Home with His Family*), in Jean-Baptiste Debret, *Voyage pittoresque et historique au Brésil*, 3 vols. (Paris: Firmin Didot Frères, 1834–39), vol. 2, plate 5.

the period. In 1821 the city's total population was 116,444, whereas the enslaved population consisted of 57,549 individuals.[88] Like many other European travelers, Debret also commented that it was uncommon to see white women in the streets, for they often remained secluded in the domestic sphere.[89] The artist explained that these respectable white families always walked in a line led by the male slave owner, in this case a government employee. The party respected the hierarchy of Brazilian slave society, from the higher to the lower rank. The man was followed by his children, the younger before the older, then by his pregnant wife. After the family comes the *mucama*, or housemaid, usually a Brazilian-born mixed-race woman who, according to Debret, was placed higher than the enslaved Black women domestic servants.[90] The other persons in the line were the Black wet nurse, then the slave of the wet nurse, the master's domestic slave, a young slave who was being trained in service, and, finally, a new enslaved boy, who according to Debret was the slave of all the others.[91]

The order of the characters in the line, their clothing, and their relative sizes show the sexual and hierarchical relations in the family and among the enslaved population. The white slave owner heading the line is visibly the most important and clearly distinct from the rest of the group. Whereas the domestic enslaved man seems to be somewhat integrated into the family, the new enslaved boy is clearly depicted as a commodity. The enslaved housemaid who usually had a close relationship with the mistress and often provided sexual services to the male slave owner occupies a prominent position in the family hierarchy, and her representation and clothing mirror that of her mistress. However, both the *mucama* and the wet nurse are represented barefoot, underscoring their slave legal status, even if in reality the ones working in richer households probably wore shoes. As we move farther down the line, the enslaved persons are younger and have darker skin. Their clothing and attitude are also more humble than those of the bondspeople who precede them in the line. Overall, Debret's lithograph exposes the complicated engines of Brazilian slave society and how racial hierarchies operated, especially in urban areas.

White slave owners occupied the highest positions, but there was also a hierarchy among enslaved people and freedpeople according to sex, color, and seniority. A freeborn mixed-race man had higher status than a freeborn mixed-race woman, and both occupied a better position than freed mixed-race individuals. Lower in the social and racial pyramid were mixed-race bondspeople, then enslaved Black men and women. African-born enslaved individuals had lesser status than their Brazilian-born counterparts. Even after purchasing their freedom, African-born men and women continued to be considered foreigners in Brazil.[92]

French artist Biard also documented the presence of enslaved men and women in Rio de Janeiro's streets, quickly realizing how slavery was vital to the existence of both Brazil's bigger cities and smaller towns.[93] Shortly after arriving in Rio de Janeiro, the artist expressed surprise that even white people of modest means were followed by bondspeople while walking in the streets, even when there was no need for them: "There was a very small embarrassment that has already arisen several times in Rio. In slave countries, it is customary to carry nothing; I have seen people both very well and not so well dressed being preceded by a Negro carrying packages so small that they could be put in one's pocket."[94] Like other visitors, Biard understood that as in other Latin American cities, owning enslaved property in Brazilian cities was also a matter of social prestige. As a result, whereas carrying objects and packages was perceived negatively in a society where only enslaved men and women performed manual work, displaying human property in public was a sign of wealth.

Social Mobility and Violence

Most enslaved people lived and worked in plantation areas in the Americas. Despite this concentration, many bondspeople labored in urban zones of the Americas, where they certainly experienced greater freedom of movement. Cities were sites where they could recreate previously broken connections with other men and women of

African descent and develop new networks. Working in the streets or in domestic spaces of inland and coastal cities provided bondspeople with opportunities to own and exchange things, including tools and clothes. Toiling in urban areas allowed enslaved men and women to earn wages and gradually accumulate resources to purchase their own freedom. But despite all these opportunities, the cities continued to be spaces of social control. Public authorities and white residents continually watched the steps of enslaved people. In cities with large enslaved, freed, and freeborn Black populations such as Salvador, Rio de Janeiro, and Charleston, bondspeople often lived under imposed movement restrictions. Yet, as we will see in chapter 9 and subsequent chapters, enslaved people, especially enslaved women, persisted in seeking multiple ways of circumventing such obstacles and carving out a better life for themselves and their descendants.

CHAPTER 9

Women Who Fed the City

When nineteenth-century French artist François-Auguste Biard first set foot in Bahia in 1858, he expected to see beautiful Black women in the city's streets: "I have heard that if you want to see beautiful Negresses you must go to Bahia. Indeed, I saw several who were not bad-looking, but all of them were swarming in the narrow streets of the low town, where French, English, Portuguese, Jewish, and Catholic merchants lived in an insalubrious atmosphere."[1] This passage of his illustrated travelogue, briefly mentioned in chapter 8, is one of the many references to the preponderance of Black women in Brazilian urban areas. Although nearly two-thirds of the enslaved Africans who had disembarked on the country's shores during the era of the Atlantic slave trade were young males, enslaved women were generally concentrated in higher proportions in cities. This concentration of bondswomen in urban areas, mentioned in chapter 8, can be explained by the overall sexual division of enslaved labor in Brazil and Latin America. Slave owners purchased enslaved men to toil on plantations, whereas they acquired enslaved women to perform domestic work. For example, in Rio de Janeiro, the city with the largest enslaved population in Brazil and the Americas as a whole, most bondspeople performed domestic tasks that were assigned to women. Therefore, among domestic laborers, bondswomen predominated.[2]

Enslaved women in the Americas incorporated social and cultural practices from West Africa and West Central Africa, regions where women were often in charge of cooking and also occupied relevant positions as traders, peddlers, and vendors in urban markets before and during the era of the Atlantic slave trade. Yet, in African ports and the hinterland, as well as in the urban areas of the Americas, marketing activities were not performed exclusively by enslaved Black women. In several cities of the Spanish Americas, Indigenous women dominated the marketplace. In cities such as Havana, Rio de Janeiro, and Charleston, Black women street vendors could be free, freed, or enslaved. Wills, travelogues, engravings, and photographs shed light on the activities of bondswomen street vendors and marketeers, including the products they sold, their customers, the areas of the cities where they were established, the material culture involved in their activities, and the specific arrangements they had with their owners and enslaved peers. These enslaved women greatly contributed to the economies of cities that could not have survived without their tireless activity. Whereas in urban areas, bondswomen prepared and cooked meals in the domestic space, both enslaved and freed Black women sold food in the markets and streets. Ultimately, in their various social, cultural, and economic roles, enslaved women had a visible, if not preponderant, presence in urban areas of the Americas. They literally fed the population of cities of the coastal and mining regions of the Americas, especially in the West Indies, in Brazil, and even in some cities of Latin America and the United States.

Gender and Labor in West Africa and West Central Africa

Gendered division of labor was present in African societies well before the rise of the Atlantic slave trade and the continued commercial exchanges with European traders. Men and women executed assigned tasks that could change over time, but in West Africa and West Central Africa certain women almost exclusively performed activities such as cooking and preparing food as well as rearing children. Women of lower social positions provided more grueling work than elite women in the Yorubaland, a West African region encompassing present-day Togo, the Republic of Benin, and Nigeria, where speakers of Yoruba languages and its variations were and still are established. They were also active participants in trade caravans, transporting loads of goods on their heads.[3] On the Atlantic coasts of Africa, women were also in charge of carrying water and wood, brewing beer, making palm oil, grinding corn, pounding millet, spinning, and weaving.[4] The amount of labor provided by women likely depended on their social position. Whereas women performed most of the subsistence agricultural work in many societies of West Central Africa and West Africa, men dominated agricultural activities in Yorubaland. Yet, women dominated commercial activities as traders, distributors, and sellers at the daily markets and other periodic markets in Yorubaland towns.[5] Likewise, travelers in all these regions of Atlantic Africa observed how women were also very active in the marketplaces where they sold fruits and vegetables, and where they also prepared foods during the early years of the Atlantic slave trade.[6] Because these West African women could own property independently from their husbands, fathers, and brothers, elite women were able to accumulate wealth.[7]

The presence of women vendors in African markets can be explained in part by the fact that selling food and other goods in marketplaces was an extension of women's agricultural activities. Their market activities also resulted from their participation in trade caravans that crisscrossed the hinterland of West Africa and West Central Africa. Olaudah Equiano, for example, remembered going to the market with his mother several times. He also had recollections of the various goods on sale. Even though his narrative does not mention women vendors, they were certainly active in the marketplace of his hometown in Igboland.[8] African women who were captured in the interior and along the coastal areas to be sold in the Americas may have not been marketeers, but they certainly witnessed the activity of fellow women vendors. As noted by one historian, the small-scale trade of foodstuffs in the Atlantic world between the seventeenth and the nineteenth centuries occurred in the shadow of the Atlantic slave trade.[9] But although in the shadow, this activity was crucial, and women were those executing these tasks.

In eighteenth-century Luanda, enslaved and free women of lower classes worked as traders, marketeers, and peddlers in the city's streets and outdoor markets. Hence, the term *outdoor market* (*kitanda* in Kimbundu) not only gave origin to the Portuguese terms *quitanda* (open market) and *quitandeira* (market vendor) but also traveled to Brazil, where enslaved women who worked as vendors in the streets or markets were called *quitandeiras* as well. In Luanda, enslaved and free street vendors sold fresh and cooked food, including dried fish, palm oil, fruits, vegetables, and pepper, as well as refined goods such as textiles and china.[10]

In West Central Africa, whereas free women worked autonomously, bondswomen who participated in retail trade were either employed or rented by their owners as street vendors. Asserting their independence, enslaved peddlers and marketeers, supported by their owners, often refused to observe increasing regulations and fees imposed by the local administration during the nineteenth century.[11] In 1850, when Luanda's population was estimated at approximately 12,000 individuals, including 1,240 white persons (820 men and 420 women) and nearly 6,020 enslaved persons, there were 200 women licensed street vendors, but many more operated without a license.[12] These women often gathered according to their native language and region of origin. They dressed in distinctive ways, wearing shawls and colorful clothes. Particular objects such as their baskets (*quindas*) were also emblematic of their activities in the city.[13]

As in Luanda, women street vendors were also central players in the urban sphere of Benguela, the third-largest slave-trading port in Africa, after Luanda and Ouidah. They circulated in the streets selling produce they cultivated. As early as 1760, the Portuguese colonial administration created a public market to regulate prices and control the work of women street vendors. But as in Luanda, the women resisted, and they continued to freely operate in the streets.[14] Documented by travelers, the presence of women street retailers remained prominent in Luanda and Benguela after the end of slavery throughout the nineteenth and twentieth centuries.[15] Not surprisingly, some enslaved women peddlers were able to accumulate resources and purchase their own freedom.[16] The stories and trajectories of African women who were captured and sent into slavery to the Americas are certainly connected to the activities of West Central African and West African women who were traders, marketeers, and peddlers for several centuries.

Spanish Americas and the West Indies

With the rise of the Atlantic slave trade, Black enslaved and freedwomen sold goods in the streets and markets of various urban areas in the Americas as well. Still, in cities of Mesoamerica such as Mexico City and in the Andean region, including Potosí, Santiago, Lima, and Quito, Indigenous women dominated marketplace activities as sellers.[17] In all these cities, Black women mingled with Indigenous women. They navigated streets and public markets looking for opportunities to improve their lives, increase their earnings, and obtain a path to freedom. As early as in 1656, the Spanish administration threatened to punish Black and Indigenous women who exchanged goods stolen from their owners, such as bacon, cheese, bananas, fruit, peanuts, and unrefined whole cane sugar, for valuable goods such as gold jewelry, as well as silver spoons and forks.[18] In the late eighteenth century, Black women marketeers were also visible in the Pacific Ocean port city of Lima in Peru. Czech naturalist Thaddeus Xaverius Peregrinus Haenke observed that although white, Black, Indigenous, and mixed-raced individuals all congregated in Lima's central square's public market, the women selling food at the marketplace were all Black.[19] Overall, enslaved, freed, and free Black women vendors predominated in the cities of regions with smaller Indigenous populations and where the presence of enslaved Africans and their descendants was huge, especially in Brazil and the West Indies.

In the British West Indies, enslaved women marketeers and peddlers were known by several terms, such as *hucksters*, *higglers*, and *hawkers*. In Barbados, as early as the middle seventeenth century, colonial authorities made efforts to regulate the activities of enslaved peddlers, most of whom were women.[20] Black female prevalence continued to be visible in later years. Bridgetown's Milk Market, located near Swan Street to the west, was controlled by enslaved and free women marketeers in the eighteenth century. Bondswomen toiled in great numbers at the great market in Cheapside as well. Found nearly everywhere in the city, they sold nonagricultural products, including cakes, drinks, and imported items.

In 1708, an act prohibited slave owners from employing enslaved men and women as street vendors in Barbados. As the measure was not successful, colonial authorities attempted to dissuade the activities of street vendors by adding a provision that required enslaved people selling milk, horsemeat, or firewood to wear a metal necklace attached to the neck or leg displaying, among other information, the owner's name and address. Despite increasing attempts to restrain and punish their activities, Bridgetown's enslaved women who fed the city kept selling food in the streets.[21] Official resolutions to limit the circulation of bondswomen street vendors continued and expanded during the eighteenth and nineteenth centuries, with British and French colonizers passing legislation to prohibit enslaved people from selling goods in towns of other British colonies and the French West Indies.[22] But as in Barbados, enslaved women always found ways to circumvent the restrictions. At the end of the day, colonial cities could not survive without the hard work provided by enslaved women marketeers and peddlers.

In the French West Indies, slave owners made profits from the work of enslaved women street vendors. In Saint-Domingue, bondswomen performing market activities in the city sought to make money and also found opportunities to escape. An ad from 1766 described a runaway African-born enslaved woman identified as Mina who worked selling bread at Cap Français. As discussed in chapter 6, the term "Mina," broadly used in Brazil and other parts of the Americas, identified African captives who had been embarked in ports situated along the Bight of Benin, and in several cases was a reference to Yoruba-speaking women. Another ad from 1775 sought Rose, an African-born enslaved woman who peddled in the streets selling bread. Although identified as "Congo," she was probably transported to the Americas from the Loango coast, and also escaped bondage in Cap Français.[23]

In other French colonies the activities of enslaved women street vendors continued to be visible during the nineteenth century. For example, on the eve of the French abolition of slavery in the 1840s, one observer reported the case of a female slave owner of Basse-Terre, in Martinique, who purchased bulk goods and put her enslaved women to work selling them in the city.[24] In addition, urban and rural bondswomen could also be found in the city selling their own products. In other words, these women could come to the marketplace on a regular basis not only to congregate with other enslaved and free persons but also to sell meats and the foodstuffs they grew in their own gardens such as herbs, melons, manioc, and sweet potatoes, as well as chickens and eggs.[25] Moreover, bondswomen visited the market to purchase and exchange goods for themselves and their owners. In some places, bondspeople bartered for food to improve the meager and monotonous diet offered to them at the plantations. Enslaved women who worked in the city or on neighboring farms and plantations went to urban markets not only to sell food surpluses but also to develop social connections that would possibly get them access to economic opportunities.[26]

Similar realities existed in the Spanish West Indies. The rising sugar economy of the Spanish colonies of Cuba and Puerto Rico propelled the development of the economies of the two islands and the growth of its main cities. In Havana, at the end of the eighteenth century, women composed 60 percent of the city's enslaved population. By 1871, women still represented more than 50 percent of Havana's enslaved population.[27] As in other cities of the West Indies, Black women peddlers (enslaved, freed, and free) sold food in the streets and markets of Cuba's biggest city. Likewise, in San Juan, on the island of Puerto Rico, women composed most of the city's population by the end of the eighteenth century. Black women, including those in bondage, worked in urban spaces selling food and drinks as small retailers and resellers. Some of them were also owners of small shops and businesses that prepared and sold cooked food. For example, in the streets of San Juan and other Spanish cities in the Americas, women who prepared and sold *mondongo* (a tripe stew) and were called *mondongueras* were mostly of African descent. But one must consider possible deeper links between these African-descended women street vendors and the *mondongo* they sold in San Juan's streets. Indeed, the term *mondongo* exists in Portuguese, where in the south of Brazil it still refers to the tripe stew. But more important, during the era of the Atlantic slave trade, especially in the eighteenth century, enslaved Africans of the Mondongue "nation" who had been embarked in the ports of the Loango coast appear in numerous records of the French slave trade to Saint-Domingue.[28] Today, it exists in the toponym Mondongo (a city in the present-day Democratic Republic of the Congo).[29] In San Juan, as in other cities of the Americas where Black women peddlers predominated, *mondongueras* were also persecuted. City officials perceived them as untrustworthy and often attempted to stop their activities by arguing that their establishments stayed opened until late at night and attracted other Black individuals, including fugitive slaves. Still, these frequent efforts to stop their activities were useless. San Juan's Black women persisted in selling *mondongo*, a dish still popular in many Latin American countries today. During the era of slavery, streets and public markets remained sites of resistance for bondswomen and freedwomen who tried to find ways to improve their dire conditions.[30]

South Carolina Meets Bahia

Enslaved street sellers also operated in North America and in the urban regions of today's United States. More than anywhere else in North America, enslaved, freed, and free Black women participated in the marketing economy of Charleston and New Orleans as street vendors. Since the colonial period, enslaved women marketeers were a dominant presence in the Lowcountry region. But as in the British colonies of the West Indies, colonial authorities soon recognized the potential of enslaved people's economic autonomy. Slave owners and planters feared that bondspeople were stealing goods to sell or exchange for other items in the marketplace. In 1686, legislators passed an act prohibiting free individuals, indentured servants, and slaves from bartering, purchasing, or selling any goods to or from servants and slaves.[31]

However, these legal measures did not prevent bondspeople from continuing to sell produce and whatever they could in Charleston's wharf and streets, where enslaved Africans and their descendants became increasingly visible during the eighteenth century. Except for butchers and fishermen, enslaved women predominated in the city's market house, which was unveiled in 1739.[32] But despite this visibility in the central market, it remains difficult to clearly distinguish the legal status of Black women marketeers as free, freed, or enslaved. It is also a hard task to identify the kind of arrangements these women had with their owners to secure their presence in the market. Certainly, some of them were sent by their owners to work in the streets because they brought most of their income back to their owners. Eighteenth-century observers noted that Black women worked all day selling fruit, eggs, rice, cakes, poultry, dry goods, and drinks. They also reported that enslaved women marketeers clearly privileged other Black and enslaved customers. Not surprisingly, after the 1739 Stono Rebellion, which took place nearly twenty miles south of Charleston (and which we will explore later, in chapter 16), there were growing official efforts to limit the movement of these enslaved peddlers. But enslaved women persisted in their market endeavors. Their presence obviously upset white residents, who complained about Black women's ability to purchase fine clothing.[33] Charleston's marketplace was not only a space where enslaved women sold food. As in many other cities of the Americas, where enslaved populations were significant, the market was a haven of sorts for enslaved people, including bondswomen, who escaped bondage by running away.[34] Ultimately, for Charleston's

Black population, the public market was a site of reunion, assertion, and resistance.

Despite their marketplace activities, and unlike in Brazil, enslaved people in South Carolina, including bondswomen who worked selling food in the streets, were rarely able to amass substantial amounts of money that allowed them to purchase their own freedom during the colonial era. This situation only changed after the United States became an independent country, when South Carolina's slave owners started relying much more on the income brought in by enslaved women and men they hired out. In 1783, as white residents increasingly protested the activities of enslaved peddlers, authorities once again passed additional legislation attempting to regulate enslaved street vendors in the city, including the introduction of a badge system (briefly discussed in chapter 8). But these provisions and other similar measures neither stopped nor decreased the activities of enslaved Black women sellers, even though growing surveillance certainly impacted their ability to freely circulate in the city.[35]

In other cities in the US South, enslaved people working as street vendors and marketeers were mostly women as well. In New Orleans, where women composed much of the enslaved population living and working in the city, peddling on the streets allowed them to seize the city's geography.[36] Despite the autonomy of enslaved women peddlers, however, slave owners paid close attention to the amount of money they agreed to receive on a regular basis from enslaved street vendors. If enslaved peddlers brought a smaller amount or were unable to sell the agreed-upon amount, they risked physical punishment. For example, according to the testimony of a New Orleans bondsman peddler in the middle of the eighteenth century, his owner's business partner forced a young enslaved woman who worked as peddler to swallow "the vegetables she had not managed to sell."[37] Although exposed to many dangers, including disease and physical violence, this great mobility offered bondswomen opportunities not only to make money but also to occasionally escape slavery.[38] Moreover, similar to other cities of the Americas, already in the eighteenth century, public authorities feared that the activities of enslaved street vendors disturbed the social order. In New Orleans, as in Charleston, officials attempted to impose regulations on slave owners who sent enslaved people to sell goods in the streets in the early nineteenth century. But as elsewhere, these cities' restrictions were never fully successful.

Enslaved women street vendors were ubiquitous in various cities of the Americas where slavery predominated, but nowhere else were bondswomen sellers more visible and important to the local economies than in Brazilian cities. Because Salvador had no central marketplace building structure until the 1850s, residents purchased food from peddlers and vendors established in three *quitandas* (open markets) where they sold fish, beef, bacon, whale meat, and vegetables.[39] In Salvador, most enslaved and freed women peddlers were born in West Africa, especially in the Bight of Benin, where women also worked performing marketing activities.[40] These Black women peddlers became iconic figures in the city's landscape. Still today, tourists who visit Salvador's historic center and other parts of the city are greeted by Black women called *baianas* (a term referring to Bahia's residents), whose existence became popular worldwide through the song "O que é que a Baiana tem?" ("What Does the Woman from Bahia Have?") composed by Dorival Caymmi in 1939 and immortalized by the voice of the popular Portuguese-born singer Carmen Miranda. Wearing long white skirts, colorful shawls (known as *pano da costa*), necklaces, and headscarves, most of today's *baianas* sell *acarajé*, a fritter made with black-eyed peas, traditionally fried in red palm oil.[41] Today's Bahia tourism industry embraced the activities performed by these Black women entrepreneurs. Perhaps many of them have no direct connections with the traditional Black women street vendors, but some have female ancestors who were also street vendors and who passed down their *acarajé* recipes to their descendants.

Written sources providing detailed information about the working and living conditions of enslaved and freedwomen street vendors in Salvador are scarce. Until 1821, peddlers had to obtain a license free of charge from the city to sell goods in the streets. Based on a sample of licenses provided to nearly one thousand peddlers between the end of the eighteenth century and the two first decades of the nineteenth century, one historian drew a broad profile of Salvador's street vendors and concluded that half of them were Black or of color, and most of them were women. More important, among the enslaved peddlers, nearly all were women.[42]

Arrangements between enslaved sellers and their owners were based on oral agreements.[43] Some paid their owners a daily or weekly amount from their sales. Other owners rented their slaves to other people who sent them out to sell goods. Enslaved women peddlers circulated in the streets of Salvador, carrying their merchandise on their heads. Some hawkers secured a place to display their items on mats and stalls, waiting for the customers to reach them. A smaller number of Black women marketeers also sold food in the three existing *quitandas* with permanent wooden structures that existed in the city by the end of the eighteenth century.[44]

Enslaved and freed street vendors offered a variety of food items and drinks, including milk, eggs, fresh meat, fish, manioc meal, salt, dried meat, dried shrimp, beans, and fruits such as bananas, oranges, tangerines, limes, mangoes, melons, grapes, guavas, papayas, and pineapples. Bondswomen street vendors also sold vegetables, including lettuce, greens, cabbage, okra, green beans, onions, cucumbers, corn, pumpkins, and yams. Some peddlers sold prepared foods such as sweets, corn cakes, and bread, as well as grilled fish, cooked pork, sausages, and beef. Portuguese bureaucrat Luís dos Santos Vilhena, who sojourned for more than a decade in Bahia in the late eighteenth century, described the various prepared dishes sold by Black street vendors, including famous Afro-Brazilian dishes such as *caruru* (a stew resembling gumbo with ingredients such as shrimp, coconut, okra, peanuts, cashews, and red palm oil), *vatapá* (a mashed creamy paste made of bread, shrimp, coconut milk, ground peanuts, and palm oil), *acaçá* (a paste made of white corn and coconut wrapped in a banana leaf), and the aforementioned *acarajé*, all of which are still today ritual foods in Afro-Brazilian religions.[45] More than one century later, British consul James Wetherell described the smells of "black cookeries" that assailed the noses of the lower city's passersby by the middle of the nineteenth century. In his account, he explained that Black people, assumedly women, cooked and sold "little fish, stewed and mixed with pepper," deep-fried sundry flour balls and plantains, little cakes made of flour or tapioca, and *caruru* they had prepared in large pots. They also sold "stewed salted codfish or grouper" as well as another dish that according to him consisted of boiled rice, corn kernels, roasted jerk beef, and pepper sauce that seems to be like present-day Hausa rice.[46]

To avoid waste and make profits, enslaved and freedwomen peddlers had to plan and bargain to sell their items until the end of the day. Working from sunrise to sunset under the sun, wind, and rain, and transporting food and stalls along the sinuous steep streets was exhausting. The work performed by enslaved women street peddlers and marketeers required great physical and mental strength. Like other slaves who hired themselves out, many women street vendors were responsible for their own living arrangements and shared with other enslaved persons rented rooms on the ground floors or basements of urban residences. Bondswomen who lived with their owners often occupied small windowless rooms on higher floors. Despite their arduous lives, depending on their health and other skills, several of Salvador's enslaved women food sellers were able to accumulate sufficient resources to purchase their own freedom. Once emancipated, several freedwomen purchased bondswomen to work for them as street vendors as well.

Historian Richard Graham explored the trajectories of some of these women. Take the example of Ana de São José da Trindade, a freedwoman, who obtained a license for herself and three of her slaves to sell food in the streets of Salvador in 1807. Working as a street vendor allowed Trindade to purchase her freedom and accumulate wealth. When she died in 1823, she owned a three-story house, land, several pieces of jewelry in gold and precious gems, silver objects, and nine bondspeople. Two of these enslaved persons worked for her selling food in Salvador's streets, including one young bondswoman whom she described in her will as being pregnant.[47] Owning bondspeople was the most efficient way for freedwomen to have access to social mobility in a society whose economy totally relied on slavery.

Sale advertisements of nineteenth-century Bahian newspapers also featured African origins of enslaved and freed women street vendors. Additional ads offered female cooks and confectioners as well.[48] Likewise, death announcements of enslaved and freed women street vendors give us an idea of their varied origins and ages. On July 17, 1877, the newspaper *Correio da Bahia* announced the death of a freed, single, sixty-year-old African woman street vendor, Eva Lisbôa Moreira, who died of cancer on July 5. On August 9, 1877, the same newspaper informed readers about the death of Felicidade dos Santos, an African-born woman, aged eighty years and a peddler, deceased of tuberculosis on July 20. On August 12, 1877, another announcement publicized that Felismina, a freed African woman, single, peddler, fifty years old, had died of beriberi on July 28. Brazilian-born enslaved young women also worked as street sellers. On May 10, 1878, the newspaper *O Guarany* informed readers that two days earlier Guilhermina, a twenty-two-year-old enslaved woman street vendor, identified as *parda* (mixed-race), had died of variola.[49] Until the abolition of slavery in 1888, these newspapers continued to feature announcements that confirmed the importance of bondswomen street vendors in Salvador.

Women Street Vendors in Rio de Janeiro

During the nineteenth century, European travelers spent much more time in Rio de Janeiro than in Salvador. This preference is partially explained because, beginning in 1763, Rio de Janeiro was Brazil's capital. Moreover, the Portuguese royal court fled Lisbon to avoid the invasion of Napoléon Bonaparte and settled in Rio de Janeiro in 1808. The Portuguese court promoted a series of public works to improve the city's infrastructure by opening it to foreign visitors, including

FIGURE 9.1. *Les rafraichissemens de l'après dîner sur la Place du Palais* (*After-Dinner Refreshments on the Palace Square*), in Jean-Baptiste Debret, *Voyage pittoresque et historique au Brésil*, 3 vols. (Paris: Firmin Didot Frères, 1834–39), vol. 2, plate 9.

travelers, artists, missionaries, and naturalists, who published a variety of illustrated travel accounts describing Rio de Janeiro's daily life, portraying the working and living conditions of its enslaved inhabitants.[50] Nearly all these travelogues described in words and images the activities of Black women street vendors who sold in the city's streets everything that could be carried in baskets and on wooden trays, especially food and drinks.[51]

When French artist Jean-Baptiste Debret published his travelogue *Voyage pittoresque et historique au Brésil* in 1834, nearly 40 percent of the enslaved population of Rio de Janeiro was composed of women. In the 1870s and 1880s, on the eve of the abolition of slavery in Brazil, women composed nearly 50 percent of the city's population who lived in bondage.[52] Not surprisingly, Debret's travel account features numerous lithographs representing bondswomen street vendors in Rio de Janeiro. One of these lithographs (figure 9.1) depicts enslaved women peddlers who sold sweets at the Palace Square (present-day XV November Square).[53] Since the seventeenth century, before the construction of the square, this large area facing the sea had been a traditional gathering point for enslaved street vendors.[54] Moreover, as discussed in chapter 5, until the construction of the Valongo wharf, enslaved Africans transported to Rio de Janeiro came ashore at this busy waterfront, where many ships were anchored, exactly as depicted in the lithograph's background.

Debret's lithograph offers an accurate portrait of the large square where the palace and other official buildings housing the royal government were located. Two enslaved women street vendors occupy the center of the image. Although barefoot, each woman is elegantly dressed, wearing a long skirt, a blouse, and a headscarf. The first bondswoman in the foreground is wearing large earrings. A typical Afro-Brazilian shawl (*pano da costa*) wraps one of her shoulders as well. Each enslaved woman holds a tray with sweets and a clay jar with water or other refreshments that they offer to white customers sitting on the pier parapet. The site where the busy square faced the wharf and where officers, sailors, and traders circulated all day long was an excellent spot for enslaved women to sell food and drinks.[55] Moreover, it was also an excellent spot to meet and gossip with other enslaved women street vendors and domestic servants. As depicted on the left side, in the background of the image, one of the main features of the square was its water fountain. As also represented on the lithograph, bondswomen visited the fountain, where they daily filled containers with water and carried them on top of their heads to their owners' households.

Visual and written descriptions of women street vendors and marketeers in Rio de Janeiro rarely indicate whether they were enslaved or freed, but in the early nineteenth century among freeborn and freed ones, most were Black women.[56] Likewise, the references to their birthplaces in Africa are often vague. Yet, travelogues and newspaper ads often identified African women as "Mina," a term referring to enslaved Africans originating from the ports of the Bight of

Benin, as already discussed in chapter 6. Like other enslaved, freed, and free Black women, Mina women worked as peddlers. Because they wore specific outfits, which often included elaborate headscarves, and their faces displayed specific scarifications, more seasoned travelers from Europe and the United States dared to identify them as being Mina, by reporting their visible presence as street vendors in Rio de Janeiro. For example, Thomas Ewbank, a British scientist based in the United States who visited Brazil in 1845 and 1846 and published a travel account in 1856, described in detail the activities of enslaved men and women peddlers in Rio de Janeiro, who transported and sold everything, including "fruits, edible roots, fowls, eggs, and every rural product; cakes, pies, rusks, *doces* [sweets], confectionery, [and] 'heavenly bacon' [toucinho do céu]," a moist Portuguese almond cake.[57] According to Ewbank, African women identified as Mina and Mozambique were the "most numerous, and reputed to be the smartest of *marchandes*."[58]

Although in smaller numbers, Black women also worked in permanent rented stalls of the Market Square, a public marketplace, next to the Palace Square in Rio de Janeiro in the nineteenth century. Here bondswomen were prevented from renting a stall, but they could work in the stands rented by their owners. Freedwomen, however, were able to rent a permanent place in this market, where they sold vegetables, legumes, eggs, and poultry. Existing records show that most of these freedwomen occupying permanent booths were born in the Bight of Benin in West Africa, and regardless of their actual specific ethnic origins, they were identified as Mina.[59] The presence of this specific group of African women marketeers who were able to purchase their own freedom and lease a permanent stand in the most important nineteenth-century public market in Rio de Janeiro reveals their great sense of resilience by also suggesting that their activities as sellers had deep connections with market traditions they brought to Brazil from their homelands.

Travelers who visited Rio de Janeiro in the nineteenth century noticed the presence of Mina women street vendors. Elizabeth Agassiz, the naturalist from the United States who accompanied her husband, the naturalist Louis Agassiz, in an expedition to Brazil between 1865 and 1866, visited Rio de Janeiro's Market Square in 1865. In an entry of her journal, later published as a travelogue, she commented how she loved to visit the market not only to see oranges, flowers, and vegetables but also to enjoy "watching the picturesque negro groups selling their wares or sitting about in knots to gossip." According to her, "the fine-looking athletic negroes of a nobler type, at least physically, than any we see in the States, are the so-called Mina negroes." Agassiz emphasized the "quite . . . dignified presence" of Mina enslaved women as marketeers and street sellers. The couple's pseudoscientific and racist views on the alleged racial superiority of women labeled as Mina reflected the racial hierarchies created by the slave market. Still, despite using the term "Mina," Agassiz also suggested that these women street vendors were Muslims, but more probably she was rather implying that in fact they were Yoruba speakers.

Agassiz's detailed description is accompanied by one wood engraving based on a studio portrait (figure 9.2) taken by French photographer Théophile Auguste Stahl (alias Augusto Stahl) who worked with him during his trip in Brazil. The photograph clearly shows the woman's facial scarifications, and identifies her as Ijesa, a term referring to a subgroup of Yoruba speakers in the region of today's southwest Nigeria. Similar to the women street vendors depicted in Debret's engraving (see figure 9.1), she wears a headscarf, and a huge shawl (*pano da costa*), a garment discussed in chapter 8. According to Agassiz, "the women always wear a high muslin turban, and a long, bright-colored shawl, either crossed on the breast and thrown carelessly over the shoulder, or, if the day be chilly, drawn closely around them, their arms hidden in its folds. The amount of expression they throw into the use of this shawl is quite amazing. . . . The Mina negress is almost invariably remarkable for her beautiful hand and arm. She seems to be conscious of this, and usually wears close-fitting bracelets at the wrist, made of some bright-colored beads, which set off the form of the hand and are exceedingly becoming on her dark, shining skin."[60]

FIGURE 9.2. Augusto Stahl, Studio Portrait: *Mina Igeichà*, Rio de Janeiro, 1865. Louis Agassiz Photographic Collection. Courtesy of the Peabody Museum of Archaeology and Ethnology, Harvard University, 2004.1.436.1.73, Cambridge, MA, United States.

As in Bahia, the ages of Black women street vendors in Rio de Janeiro varied. They could be as young as in their twenties or as old as in their sixties. Selling food allowed them to accumulate resources, opening paths for social mobility. Historian Juliana Barreto Farias explored two interesting cases. For example, the freedwoman Emília Soares do Patrocínio, who rented stalls in the Market Square, also owned several enslaved women, who probably worked for her in the market as well. Like their owner did, these bondswomen were able to purchase their own freedom by the middle of the nineteenth century.[61] Another freedwoman, Maria Rosa da Conceição, made good profits with two vegetable stalls that she rented at Rio de Janeiro's Market Square. After her death, her postmortem inventory, opened in 1868, included real estate, jewelry, and nine bondspeople, including five *quitandeiras* who certainly worked for her selling food.[62]

The examples of these two freedwomen are not isolated or unique. The wills of several West African–born freedwomen in Rio de Janeiro show that once they purchased their own freedom, they acquired enslaved African-born women to work for them. That freedpeople in Brazilian urban areas became slave owners is not a surprise; the fact that these formerly enslaved women decided to purchase women who, like them, were born in Africa, can be explained by various factors. First, in African cultures women were central figures in the marketplace, therefore by acquiring African-born bondswomen, freedwomen were sure of their investment. Second, this preference can also be associated with the fact that African-born freedwomen slave owners shared with their newly acquired African-born enslaved women a gendered tragic story of enslavement and forced migration, an experience they did not share with African enslaved males and Brazilian-born women street vendors.[63]

But what is certain is that either in Salvador, Rio de Janeiro, or other cities in Brazil, enslaved and freed African-born women often appear in existing visual and written records performing marketing activities. For example, Portuguese photographer Christiano Junior, who was active in Brazil in the 1860s, took studio photographs of Black women street vendors in Rio de Janeiro. Although staged, these pictures evoke their activities, including their way of dressing and their work tools. One photograph (figure 9.3) features a woman organizing the items on her wooden tray stand. Although wearing a shawl and earrings, she is modestly dressed. We do not know if her legal status is that of a free, freed, or enslaved woman, though the absence of facial scarifications can be an indication that she was born in Brazil. But another photograph (figure 9.4) featuring a boy and a barefoot woman street vendor clearly shows the woman's facial scarifications, allowing viewers to identify the sitter as a Yoruba speaker. Although her clothes are not elaborate, she is wearing silver or gold earrings as well as a voluminous headscarf similar to those worn by women labeled as "Mina."

Nevertheless, despite the visibility of West African women born in the Bight of Benin in travel accounts and existing licenses allowing them to operate in Rio de Janeiro rented stalls of the Market Square, nineteenth-century newspaper ads show that a huge number of enslaved street vendors were born in West Central Africa. This information is not surprising because this area provided the largest number of enslaved persons exported to Brazil in general and to the country's southeast region in particular. In addition, there were hundreds of runaway ads and daily announcements seeking to sell and rent enslaved African-born women street vendors identified by ethnonyms such as Congo, Benguela, Monjolo, Cabinda, Rebolo, Libola, Casange, and Moçambique, all of them evoking regions of provenance in West Central Africa and Southeast Africa. Sometimes indicating how much money these peddlers made on a daily basis, the ads reveal that enslaved women street vendors of all ages were active in Rio de Janeiro. Most ads underscore that bondswomen for sale were also good cooks and washerwomen. One advertisement, for example, announced the sale of an African-born woman aged between twenty-six and twenty-eight, identified as Benguela, who was being

FIGURE 9.3. Christiano Junior, Studio Portrait: *Woman Standing Wearing Shawl, Brazil*, 1864–66. Albumen silver print, 3.4 × 2.1 inches. The Horace W. Goldsmith Foundation Fund, through Joyce and Robert Menschel, 2017. Courtesy of the Metropolitan Museum of Art, New York, United States.

FIGURE 9.4. Christiano Junior, Studio Portrait: *Seated Woman and Standing Boy Street Vendors with Vegetable Baskets, Brazil*, 1864. Albumen silver print, 3.6 × 2.1 inches. The Horace W. Goldsmith Foundation Fund, through Joyce and Robert Menschel, 2017. Courtesy of the Metropolitan Museum of Art, New York, United States.

sold because her owner had died. Among her abilities described in the ad, she knew how to "well refine sugar, make sweets, and almonds" as well as to cook, take care of the house, and look after the children; she was also described as loyal and diligent.[64]

As in other cities of the Americas, public authorities constantly targeted Rio de Janeiro's enslaved women marketeers and hawkers. Their presence in the streets and the marketplace was often associated with disorder. Bondswomen street vendors were arrested for a variety of reasons during the nineteenth century, but especially because city officers suspected they had run away. Other enslaved women were also arrested with the accusation of failing to carry the appropriate permission to sell food or for vagrancy and alleged inappropriate public behavior.[65] Despite these hindrances, in a society where white women were prevented from going out unattended, enslaved women understood their ability to work as street vendors as a form of resistance against slavery and the Brazilian patriarchal system.

Surviving in the Streets

Enslaved African women and their female descendants continued and expanded their activities and roles in West Central African and West African markets in the Americas. Preparing and selling food allowed bondswomen to maintain and re-create their connections with the African continent. Enslaved women street vendors were tireless workers, and they had to be continuously vigilant because there was a constant risk of physical violence. Attempts to control and restrict the work of enslaved women marketeers and peddlers emerged as early as the seventeenth century in various cities of the Americas where slavery existed. Still, none of these repressive efforts were ever successful. Slaveholding cities needed the work of bondswomen street vendors to survive. For enslaved women peddlers and marketeers, the city was a site of resistance that they quickly learned to navigate. Despite constant threats of violence and periods of strict surveillance by public authorities and slave owners, the city environment with its dark corners, streets, and markets allowed bondswomen and freedwomen to circulate, develop networks, exchange goods, and make money with the hope of obtaining the bondswomen's freedom. As we will see in chapter 10, selling food and other goods in markets and streets also made it possible for enslaved people to create blood and spiritual families, sometimes even offering them hope of emancipation.

CHAPTER 10

Sex and Violence

On August 3, 1882, Honorata, a twelve-year-old enslaved girl, was purchased by Henriques Ferreira Pontes in Olinda, in the northeast state of Pernambuco in Brazil. Before bringing her to his house, Pontes took her to the place where Tiburcio, an enslaved man also owned by him, resided. Asking the bondsman to leave his residence, Pontes locked himself in his room and raped Honorata, who was a virgin.[1] Honorata's ordeal was not an exception, and her tragic story survived in the written record only because in 1882, slavery existed only in Cuba and Brazil. Therefore, publicity of the case was greatly influenced by the intensive abolitionist movement that was finally shaking Brazil.

In all societies where slavery existed in the Americas, slaveholders maintained coerced sexual relations with their human property. Not just slave owners but overseers as well subjected enslaved women and men to sexual abuse. In the domestic environment, enslaved maids and wet nurses lived under the continuous control of their owners. Sexual abuse often began in childhood, sometimes under the slave owner's promise of release from enslavement. Slave owners and overseers conceived the bodies of enslaved people as property and therefore available to them. In the beginning of the eighteenth century, Jesuit priests such as Antonil wrote about the abuses perpetrated by the overseers against enslaved women in Brazil. According to him, they inflicted physical punishments on bondswomen who refused to engage in sexual relations. These accounts of violence contrast sharply with the widespread image that until recently prevailed in Brazil and Latin American societies disseminated sometimes in European travel accounts but especially through the work of early scholars such as Gilberto Freyre, which advanced the misleading idea that enslaved women maintained harmonious and consensual sexual relations with slaveholders.[2]

People engage in sexual activities for many reasons, often in search of pleasure but also in response to social and religious demands from their communities. Bondspeople engaged in sexual exchanges with other bondspeople, freed persons, free people, and white individuals of various social positions. They also sometimes had sex with their owners. Needless to say, these relations were tainted by inherent imbalance of power, coercion, exploitation, and violence. For enslaved men, women, and children, the possibility of experiencing sexual abuse began when they were captured and gathered by force into coffles, then confined in coastal structures along Atlantic African shores. This potential for abuse continued in the holds of slave ships, and, once in the Americas, sexual violence haunted all activities involving enslaved people and their owners, overseers, and other free white individuals.

As this chapter will show, sex under slavery was shaped by relations of power and physical violence. Several slave narratives published in Britain and the United States reported that slave owners could claim the bodies of enslaved women to provide sexual services whenever they wanted. Indeed, in urban settings as well as on plantations located in remote rural areas, enslaved women were constantly exposed to sexual violence. Bondsmen were also victims of sexual abuse by their male and female owners. Regardless of racial ideologies that emerged during the era of slavery, bondswomen lived in constant threat of being raped by slave owners, other male members of the household, and overseers. By examining the problem of sex and slavery, this chapter argues that despite the existence of relations based on bondspeople's own choices documented in written documents such as wills, postmortem inventories, and marriage records, sexual violence against enslaved women and men was widespread throughout slave societies and societies with slavery in the Americas.

Sex in Atlantic West Central Africa and West Africa

Most of what we know about how people engaged in sexual activity in Africa was made available after the period of the early contact with European traders and colonizers. Biased by their Christian religious and moral values, these men produced accounts and travelogues that often described African sexual behaviors in derogatory ways. Their European views on what it means to be a man, a woman, or a child have predominated ever since, most often ignoring how African peoples assigned or associated particular roles and behaviors to people who were biologically identified as males and females.

Both today and in the era of the Atlantic slave trade, African sexualities are not homogeneous. Instead, they were as diverse as the numerous societies and groups whose members were sold into slavery. Cultural practices and traditions were not fixed and, in fact, continued to evolve during the more than three centuries during which the Atlantic slave trade devastated the African continent. Sexual preferences and activities varied across cultures and age. Religion and kinship framed the development of sexuality of African individuals, shaping gender roles at an early age.

As on other continents, sexuality was a crucial dimension of the lives of West African and West Central African men, women, and children who were enslaved and forcibly transported to the Americas. Yet, scholars have challenged the existence of cultural and social characteristics that distinguish what it was to be a man and to be a woman in Africa. In other words, gender appears to be a Western invention, an idea that may have been foreign to many African societies prior to the European arrival on the continent.[3] In Yoruba, a language spoken in several regions of present-day Nigeria and the Republic of Benin, the words *ọkọ* and *aya* (respectively translated in English as "husband" and "wife") are gender-free, and therefore can designate either a male or a female.[4] Likewise, in Yorubaland, the division of labor did not correspond to gender norms but was very often based on age. Young male bachelors had limited access to premarital sexual activity. Most marriages were monogamous, though polygamous practices existed as well. In Yorubaland and in other regions of West Africa, women abstained from sexual activity during pregnancy and until nearly three years after giving birth, as the tradition established that having sex during this period could put the child's life in danger.[5] Couples did not share the same room. Usually, the mother, her children, and sometimes several dependents occupied the same small room, making unlikely the idea of a husband sexually abusing a wife.[6]

In the decades that followed their first contact with African societies, Europeans described the sexual behaviors of African women as promiscuous, often referring to them as prostitutes and whores. But it was their own behavior that was predatory; Africanist scholars have highlighted how European men violated the bodies of African women during the period they remained stationed on the coasts of Africa. In 1588, the governor of the Portuguese fort São Jorge da Mina, in Elmina, on the Gold Coast, was denounced and sentenced by the Portuguese Inquisition for having had sexual intercourse not only with Christian women but also with young African women who were considered pagans by the Roman Catholic Church. As shown by historian Kwasi Konadu, the Inquisition trial revealed that Pessanha had his African agents bring young local African women to the fortress, where he raped them.[7]

Early European writers described African women as sexually available because their sexual practices and gender roles contrasted with Western and Christian views of European women, who were expected to marry as virgins and remain tied to the same man for their entire lives. Based on observations of European travelers, Olfert Dapper, a Dutch physician and amateur geographer who never visited the African continent, published an account in the seventeenth century that described the sexual practices of men and women in West Africa. According to him, in the Kingdom of Quodja (north of present-day

Sierra Leone), young people "make love like they do among us." Dapper supposed his readers would be surprised to learn that these young women slept with men before being married and that the men did not mind whether the women they were to marry were virgins as long as they pleased them.[8] When describing the populations living in the eastern part of modern-day Côte d'Ivoire up to the Gold Coast in today's Ghana, he observed that not only could men have several wives, but each village had two or three enslaved women who, after an initiation ceremony, were appointed as prostitutes (*abrakrees*) and would be paid to provide sexual services.[9] These "public women," as they were called, were enslaved women owned by Akan elite members who were recruited and "coerced into what was definitely a social institution designed to alleviate sexual pressures among unmarried men."[10] Despite these reports, however, it is possible that in this early period the European men from whom Dapper received his information were referring to polyandry, the practice in which a woman has more than one husband.[11]

Understanding these interpretations helps us measure the impact of enslavement on women who had previously held influential roles, who prior to their capture were not expected to submit to men's control but rather occupied complementary positions in their homelands. In the Kingdom of Dahomey, for example, the king's wives had important religious roles. They constantly influenced political decisions.[12] Dahomey also had a select group of royal women (*ahosi*) warriors (*agodjie*) referred to by Europeans as "amazons," a term evoking the mythological Greek female warriors. This group of women soldiers, whose story has been recently portrayed in the motion picture *The Woman King* (2022), may have emerged in Dahomey in the early eighteenth century as an armed royal guard that served Tassi Hangbé, the daughter of King Wegbadja (who reigned between 1645 and 1685), who ruled as a regent for a brief period following the death of Akaba, her brother and successor to the throne (who reigned between 1685 and 1708).[13] These Dahomean women warriors were legally considered as king's wives and regarded as his dependents. Drawing from European chroniclers, American anthropologist Melville J. Herskovits wrote that these women were unattractive and were expected to remain virgins.[14] Yet, as pointed out by Robin Law, they did not live in celibacy as they "were all legally married to the King."[15] For example, British officer Richard Francis Burton reported an incident when dozens of *agodjie* were imprisoned after becoming pregnant, in the second half of the nineteenth century.[16] More likely, their alleged virginity and unattractiveness were the products of male Europeans' prejudice and gaze. Although most "amazons" may have remained virgins while they were in active service, several of them were married before becoming warriors, whereas others had children, and their descendants still live in Abomey.

Depending on the period, women warriors could make up nearly one-third of the Dahomey army. They became central players in the military campaigns against neighboring polities that captured prisoners to be sold into slavery to the Americas.[17] In Dahomey and other West African societies, women married other women, even though these same-sex marriages did not always include sexual relations.[18] These features did not make West Africa a paradise where sexual freedom reigned absolute, however. Historian Nwando Achebe has noted that in Igboland, in today's north-central Nigeria, women were not "free to do as they wished with their bodies before marriage" but rather had several restrictions imposed on them to ensure their "sexual morality and chastity."[19] Olaudah Equiano reminds the readers of his narrative that in his native Igboland, women who committed adultery were sometimes sentenced to death or sold into slavery.[20] Overall, many Africans forced onto slave ships were captured at such a young age that they were prevented from experiencing the rites of passage into adulthood that would prepare them for sexual activity.[21]

In West Africa and West Central Africa, soldiers, traders, and middlemen raided villages, capturing men, women, and children. They also ventured into kidnapping vulnerable persons near the coast or in the regions far in the hinterland. These agents gathered the captives in coffles, tying them together in chains or restraining their bodies with bamboo or wooden collars and yokes to prevent them from escaping.

On foot or on board canoes, they transported these coffles of naked, sweaty, smelly, and soiled human bodies, moving them through narrow trails and, depending on the distance, crossing forests, rivers, and lagoons until they ultimately arrived at coastal trading posts.

European and African encounters generated more than derogatory representations of African peoples. As early as in the fifteenth century, European explorers and traders made implicit and explicit references to the sexual availability of African women and girls in their written accounts. In his first contact with the populations of Cape Verde islands in 1455, Venetian navigator and slave trader Alvise Cadamosto, by that time around twenty-five years old, reported that a local chief gave him as a gift "a girl twelve or thirteen years of age, Black and very beautiful [*una garzona de annj 12 in 13 negra e molto bella*]" to serve him in his room.[22]

We will never know how this West African girl faced the idea of having sex with a stranger who did not even speak her language. Was she a virgin? Was she an outsider who was locally enslaved? Or perhaps in her community being offered as a sexual partner to a foreigner placed her in an important position of intermediaries between European explorers and local African rulers? Admittedly, as briefly discussed on chapter 3, after Cadamosto's voyage, starting in the sixteenth century, European slave merchants, captains, and other lesser crew members who were established on African coastal regions engaged in sexual relations and even long-term relationships with free African women living in coastal areas such as Gorée Island and Saint-Louis, in today's Senegal, and Luanda and Benguela, in modern Angola, where their daughters, known as *signares* and *donas*, became prominent slave traders.[23] But in the context of the Atlantic slave trade, the bodies of African women also became sites that facilitated commercial transactions.[24]

Rape on African Shores and Slave Ships

European men and African male agents also introduced new forms of sexual exchanges, often shaped by violence.[25] In regions such as the Gold Coast, as early as the fifteenth century, either in their own homes or confined in forts, African women and girls provided sexual services to fulfill the demands of European traders established in the coastal areas. Flemish trader Eustache de la Fosse sailed to the Gold Coast in 1479. He walked the streets of Elmina, a coastal town in present-day Ghana, trying to sell two bowls. When he stopped at one of the houses, a young woman reportedly invited him to have sex with her while already taking off her loincloth, though apparently, he declined the offer.[26] During the eighteenth century, as the slave trade intensified on West African coastal areas, travelers and slave traders increasingly described the activities of African women who provided paid sex in other ports of the Gold Coast and the Bight of Benin.

West African rulers sent African women and girls onto slave ships anchored at their ports to provide sex to ship captains. Sometimes, although free, these women were sent into slavery to the Americas.[27] Men, women, and children remained vulnerable to sexual abuse during the entire time they remained confined in coastal trading structures waiting to board the slave ships. Amid hunger and exhaustion, sexual activity, once voluntary and private, was relocated in the shared spaces of dungeons, pens, and barracoons. As one historian has noted, the trading posts where slave merchants and ship captains resided during their long stays in the coastal area of Sierra Leone during the nineteenth century were "replete with food, wine, and sex slaves handpicked from the barracoons."[28] This forced and painful proximity exposed captives to continuous sexual abuse, even though the surviving records produced by European and American slavers obviously rarely provided explicit accounts of how they violated the bodies of enslaved women.

After the long waiting period in coastal enclosures ended, a new nightmare started. Enslaved men crossed the Atlantic Ocean attached in chains and shackles to prevent uprisings. Women of all ages and children traveled unchained, occupying a separate and more spacious compartment in the lower deck. In French slave ships, a rule prevented ordinary sailors, always in greater numbers, from having access to the women's quarters. Similar provisions were also applied in Dutch slave ships, confirming the dangers of enslaved women being raped by multiple men. Yet, in French slave ships, officers had "easy access to the women's compartment."[29] This context favored by the organization of various compartments surely allowed crewmen to sexually exploit enslaved women during the Middle Passage.[30] In Dutch slave ships, the women's quarters were referred to as the "whore hole" (*hoeregat*). Sailors and ship officers carefully selected not only women but also children and men as the most suitable sexual partners.[31] La Rochelle's mariner Jacques Proa, who sailed to Ouidah aboard the ship *Duc de Laval* in 1777, explains that as soon as the slave ship left the coasts of Africa transporting its human cargo, the ship captain and crew members selected their preferred African women to serve them "at the table and in bed."[32]

African men who published narratives of their harrowing lives under slavery in the eighteenth and nineteenth centuries reported episodes of sexual violence during the Middle Passage. For example, Quobna Ottobah Cugoano retained a vivid memory of the weeks he spent in the hold of the slave ship, which included a countrywoman "who slept with some of the headmen of the ship" as "it was common for the dirty filthy sailors to take the African women and lie upon their bodies."[33] In 1785, La Rochelle's slave ship *Caraïbe* returned from the Bight of Benin carrying 351 enslaved Africans. Upon anchoring in Port-au-Prince, a main port of the French colony of Saint-Domingue, the ship captain Etienne Dufaud brought to the hospital a sailor and the vessel's cook, who had both contracted a sexually transmitted infection, presumably either during their stay in West Africa or during the Middle Passage.[34]

Crew members did not spare pregnant women or young girls from their appetite for sex and violence. Although rape was rarely reported by captains until the rise of the movement to abolish the inhumane trade, a few written accounts denounce these violations. On May 11, 1776, the slave ship *L'Aimable Françoise* left from Nantes to Gorée Island and then to the Gambia. According to the report by ship captain Lazare-Antoine Peroty, the second captain Philippe Liot was arrested after mistreating the crew and the enslaved people on board the ship. Despite his detention, he managed to violently attack an African woman, described as "very beautiful." He broke two of her teeth and left her in such a bad condition that upon arrival in Saint-Domingue she was sold for a very low price and died fifteen days later. Liot also raped an African girl between the age of eight and ten for three consecutive nights, covering her mouth to prevent her from screaming, nearly killing her.[35]

A decade after Liot's crimes, abolitionist James Field Stanfield published a poem and a series of letters addressed to his friends, including the abolitionist Thomas Clarkson, in which he only alludes, without any details, to what might have been the rape of a young enslaved girl by a ship captain.[36] British surgeon Alexander Falconbridge, who participated in four slave voyages to Africa before becoming an abolitionist, noted in his account that "common sailors are allowed to have intercourse with such of the black women whose consent they can procure. And some of them have been known to take the inconstancy of their paramours so much to heart, as to leap overboard and drown themselves. The officers are permitted to indulge their passions among them at pleasure, and sometimes are guilty of such brutal excesses, as disgrace human nature."[37]

Although initially framing these encounters as consensual, and even suggesting that enslaved women died by suicide after falling in love with their rapists, the surgeon ended up admitting that British sailors raped captive African women. Likewise, British slave ship captain John Newton, who later became an evangelical priest and abolitionist, noted that women and girls were taken on board a ship "naked, trembling, terrified, perhaps almost exhausted with cold, fatigue, and hunger." Regarded by the crewmen as prey, the women were "divided, upon the spot, and only reserved till opportunity offers."[38] During the voyage of the British slave ship *African*, Newton also reported in his journal that William Cooney, a member of his crew, publicly raped a pregnant African captive, identified only as number 83, whom he forced "into the room and lay with her brutelike in view of the whole quarter deck."[39]

Bondswomen and children were victims of sexual violence in slave ships flying flags of all nations involved in the Atlantic slave trade. After the prohibition of the British slave trade in 1807 and the end of slavery in its colonies in the West Indies, Britain continued to pressure all countries that persisted in transporting enslaved Africans to the Americas, not only through the signature of treaties but also by patrolling Atlantic waters to search and apprehend vessels that violated these agreements. Consider the case of the Portuguese brigantine *Arrogante*. The vessel departed from Gallinas River in Sierra Leone to the port of Havana in Cuba in 1837 carrying 407 enslaved persons. The British Royal Navy intercepted the ship approaching the Cuban coast and brought the case to the Anglo-Spanish Court of Mixed Commission (a slave trade court based on British law) at Sierra Leone, where in 1838 the vessel was adjudicated and condemned for illegally practicing the trade in enslaved Africans.[40] During the voyage of the *Arrogante*, 75 slaves were killed. The 332 men, women, boys, and girls who survived the ordeal to the point of the British interception were disembarked in Jamaica and emancipated from slavery. Nearly 60 were reported to be very sick, having endured repeated beatings and rapes.[41] Abolitionist newspapers also reported the sexual violations against enslaved women on board slave ships during the nineteenth century. In January 1841, the British Royal Navy captured the overcrowded Spanish schooner *Jesus Maria*, which was carrying 252 enslaved Africans in deplorable conditions to Cuba. Upon rescuing the survivors, British officers found out that "instances both of rape and murder had taken place in the vessel and that the captain of the slave vessel had been guilty of those crimes."[42] With the rise of the abolitionist movement, sexual violence perpetrated by crew members on enslaved women, men, and children gained recognition for the first time.

Forced Reproduction

Sex continued to be linked to violence in the daily experiences of enslaved people in the Americas. Slave dealers sold women and men to perform a variety of tasks in cities, mines, and plantations. As discussed in chapter 6, buyers and sellers scrutinized, smelled, and touched the seminaked bodies of human commodities displayed in slave markets. This forced intimacy was a concrete form of violation. Slavers selected enslaved persons to perform a variety of activities, but physical strength and attractiveness were essential features that led them to purchase specific men and women and favor them over others. Slave traders knew the preferences of slave buyers who sought to purchase attractive enslaved women to become their sexual partners.[43] Regardless of age and sex, bondspeople were expected to provide sexual services to their owners and to whomever their owner chose for them.

For slave owners and slave dealers, the sexuality of their enslaved property was linked to their capacity for reproduction. Some slave owners also coerced enslaved people to engage in sexual activity as well. The practice of forced reproduction of bondspeople is documented in the Iberian Peninsula as early as in the sixteenth century and in colonial North America as early as the seventeenth century.[44] With the ban of the Atlantic slave trade to the United States in 1808 and the rise of cotton production in the United States in the early nineteenth century, some slave owners started forcing enslaved men and women to engage in sexual intercourse with the hope of increasing the size of the enslaved population.[45] Historian Daina Ramey Berry defined compulsory breeding among enslaved people as "third party rape." She reminds us not only that "rape and breeding are unified by the use of force—both physical and mental" but also that "slave breeding represented one form of sexual abuse that adopted the machinations and mannerisms of rape because it forced people to engage in unsolicited sexual activity."[46] Freedpeople and their descendants remembered forced reproduction with words associated with animal husbandry that compared bondspeople to mules and cows. As one historian reminds us, these analogies, largely employed in narratives by freedmen and freedwomen collected as part of the Works Progress

Administration's Federal Writers Project in the United States in the 1930s, underscored the "inhumanity of this practice."[47]

As the trade in enslaved Africans to Brazil continued until the 1850s, the country never witnessed the same birthrate levels as the United States. Surviving written records rarely document forced breeding in Brazil, but similarly to the United States during the twentieth century, journalists and historians collected testimonies by freedpeople and their descendants who reported the use of enslaved men as breeders in Brazilian plantations. For example, Roque José Florêncio (1827–1958), known as "Pata Seca," was an enslaved breeder in the coffee plantation Santa Eudóxia near São Carlos in the state of São Paulo in Brazil.[48] Oral tradition among Florêncio's descendants emphasizes his role as an enslaved breeder who fathered 249 children, though only nine of them were conceived by his wife.

Florêncio's story is not the only surviving account about enslaved breeders in southeast Brazil during the second half of the nineteenth century, when the trade in enslaved Africans was prohibited and the coffee industry blooming. Another former Brazilian enslaved man provided testimony that included telling details about his role as a breeder in a southeast coffee plantation in Brazil. In 1973, João Antônio de Guaraciaba, by that time reportedly 122 years old, told the journalist Jorge Andrade his mistress would bring him to the slave quarters and separate a "herd" of ten enslaved women. Some of them were as young as fifteen years old and were all in their fertile period. Guaraciaba told the journalist that to perform his work of breeder, he was well fed, with the same diet as his owner, which included beef, milk, and rice. Some bondswomen cried and resisted, but as he had one month to impregnate the women, he was able to convince them to have sex by offering them affection and sharing his food. According to him, "if a woman is at the 'moment' she becomes fiery, stepping on fire. Women are like sow, cow, mare. At her 'moment,' she delivers herself. Ugly or old, any male will do."[49] Guaraciaba's account, bragging about his manhood and evacuating the violence involved in forced breeding, is probably exaggerated, leading some historians to approach similar accounts with caution, very often labeling them as the product of collective memory passed down from generation to generation and not as reliable oral historical accounts.[50] But in the context of the second slavery and the final thirty years of slavery in Brazil, it is plausible that such a figure could have existed as recounted in Guaraciaba's telling.

Like the accounts of the Middle Passage, written records are often silent about sexual violence against enslaved men, women, and children. These gaps are not surprising, as these documents were written by white male officers who officially corroborated the views of elites who endorsed the Atlantic slave trade and slavery as legitimate, even after they became illegal. Indeed, almost everywhere in the Americas the silence of archival documents regarding sexual abuse and rape only confirms that usually slave owners and overseers who committed sexual violations against their human property were not breaking the law. In their roles as slaveholders, they could freely take possession of the bodies of their human property. Despite persisting gaps, a number of written accounts tell stories of sexual violence inflicted on enslaved persons in the West Indies, the United States, Latin America, and Brazil.

House bondswomen who performed domestic service in cities and plantations were especially exposed to sexual violence. More often than not, they could not escape the brutality of slave owners and overseers. In Jamaica, slaveholders systematically sexually abused enslaved women. Thomas Thistlewood, the notorious British overseer, planter, and slave owner who settled in Jamaica in 1750, maintained a detailed journal during more than three decades of residence on the island. His diaries report how white settlers, often heavily drunk, gang-raped bondswomen. This was the tragic fate of Eve, a young enslaved woman, who on the night of March 12, 1755, was raped by six drunk males.[51] In its multiple entries, Thistlewood's journals provide firsthand accounts of how he sexually assaulted enslaved women on a regular basis. On the first property where he worked as an overseer, he had sex with at least ten of the seventeen women he oversaw.[52] A self-confessed rapist and sadist, his diaries document with vivid details how he violated and tortured Sally, one of his bondswomen. But Sally was not his only victim. Thistlewood raped other slaves multiple times as well.[53]

Bondswomen endured sexual violence in other regions of the British West Indies. As explained in chapter 6, Mary Prince, who lived and worked as an enslaved woman in Bermuda, was sold multiple times to different owners who physically and mentally abused her. In her own words, one of her owners "has often stripped me naked, hung me up by the wrists, and beat me with the cow-skin, with his own hand, till my body was raw with gashes." According to her, this same man sexually molested her. He "often got drunk" and "had an ugly fashion of stripping himself quite naked, and ordering me then to wash him a tub of water. This was worse to me than all the licks. Sometimes when he called me to wash him I could not come, my eyes were so full of shame. . . . He was a very indecent man."[54]

Harriet Jacobs, the enslaved woman whose dramatic story was also briefly presented in chapter 6, went through similar experiences. Enslaved in North Carolina, she lost her mother at the age of six, and at twelve years old, her mistress died. Her early life was marked by family separation. As her owners either died or married, she and her relatives were separated. But when she became a teenager, she was constantly physically abused and sexually harassed by her owner James Norcom (whose pseudonym in the narrative is Flint). In her words, "He peopled my young mind with unclean images, such as only a vile monster could think of. I turned from him with disgust and hatred."[55] As Norcom continued his audacious advances, his wife became extremely jealous and confronted Jacobs. Meanwhile, Jacobs lived in fear, as she did not know for how long she would be able to repel a man who was notorious for raping other enslaved women and had already fathered eleven children on the plantation. In her situation, a free white girl could have denounced her harasser to a relative or to another member of her community. But Jacobs was an enslaved girl. Her body legally belonged to her owner, as he told her. Even though many of her enslaved fellows knew about Norcom's abuse, denouncing it was useless. Desperate to escape her owner's threats,

Jacobs entered a liaison with a lawyer and future US congressman Samuel Treadwell Sawyer. He impregnated her with two children, who remained Norcom's property, because of Jacobs's slave legal status, until they were later purchased by Sawyer.

Jacobs was not alone. In Brazil, many other enslaved girls were sexually harassed and forced into coerced sexual intercourse with their male owners. Consider the example of Rosa (alias Rosa Egipcíaca), an African enslaved girl of approximately six years of age transported from the Bight of Benin to Brazil in 1724.[56] We know her story because when she was forty-four years old, the Holy Office of the Catholic Church's Inquisition accused her of heresy because of her unusual religious activities. After being denounced and investigated by the church's officials, she was sent to the Inquisition prison in Lisbon. The several pages of her interrogation reveal information about her life and religious activities. Among other things, she told the inquisitor that when she disembarked in Rio de Janeiro, she was purchased by a man named José de Souza Azevedo, who had her baptized in the Candelária Catholic Church.[57] Unlike Jacobs, who managed to resist her owner's harassment, Rosa was raped by Azevedo, who "had deflowered her and treated her awkwardly" until the age of fourteen, when he sold her to the province of Minas Gerais. But her story of sexual abuse did not end in Rio de Janeiro. Once in Minas Gerais, her new female owner, Anna Gracês de Moraez, and her partner forced Rosa into prostitution, a practice that was not uncommon for enslaved women who worked in urban areas.[58] Abused by her owners and prosecuted by the church, Rosa eventually died of "natural causes" in the Inquisition prison in Lisbon in October 1774.[59]

At the end of the eighteenth century, enslaved women who since their childhood had been sexually exploited by their owners were able to use the courts to demand their freedom, while at the same time denouncing these abuses. Well-known in Brazil is the case of the young Brazilian-born enslaved woman Liberata, who also experienced sexual violence and psychological abuse. In 1790, at ten years old, she was sold to José Vieira Rebello, a man who resided near the city of

Desterro, in present-day Florianópolis in the Brazilian southern state of Santa Catarina. Rebello sexually abused Liberata and manipulated her with the promise of manumission. Within a few years he impregnated her with two children who remained his property. Rebello recognized the paternity of the first female child, baptizing her as Anna Vieira. Yet, as his wife and children condemned the extramarital relations, he refused to baptize the second baby. As late as 1812, Liberata remained enslaved. She began a relationship with Francisco José, a mixed-race free man, who attempted to purchase her freedom to marry her. But her owner rejected the offer, leading her lover to petition the municipal judge in order to obtain his bride-to-be's emancipation. Although Liberata's case made it to the court and she was eventually freed, many other enslaved women in the Americas whose owners promised their freedom in exchange for sex were not able to enjoy the same outcome.[60]

In other parts of the Americas, enslaved women and girls went to court to denounce sexual abuse perpetrated by their male owners, who would often even be supported by their own wives. Although not all testimonies were sustained by detailed evidence, some enslaved women explicitly denounced sexual violations. Cecilie was enslaved in Saint Croix, an island of the Danish West Indies, in the present-day Virgin Islands. In 1829, she testified to the police judge of the Christiansted Police Court that her owner, the overseer of the Boetzberg plantation where she was enslaved, coerced her to have sexual relations with him. Although she resisted, the man eventually raped her, but the manager's wife interrupted the violation. However, instead of blaming her husband, she violently flogged the enslaved girl instead.[61] The case never made it to the lower court, but Christiansted's authorities fined the couple and ordered that Cecilie would no longer work for them.

Similar cases occurred in Brazil. As mentioned at the beginning of this chapter, Henriques Ferreira Ponte raped the enslaved girl Honorata in Olinda, Brazil, immediately after purchasing her on August 3, 1882. Following the violation, Pontes raped Honorata two more times.

After denouncing her owner, medical doctors submitted the enslaved girl to an examination that corroborated her words and those of the witnesses who testified in her favor. As in Cecilie's case, the judge convicted the owner of rape. But Pontes appealed the court decision. The judge considered the rape of an enslaved girl by her owner immoral, revolting, and punishable. Still, he argued that such a violation was not a crime in the Brazilian criminal code, and Pontes was acquitted one year later.[62] A few years before the end of slavery in Brazil, slave owners continued to have the right to rape their enslaved property.

Rape of Enslaved Men

Same-sex sexual relations were legally prohibited in the Americas during the period of slavery, but these interdictions were not enforced. Until the end of the eighteenth century in Latin America, the Inquisition persecuted enslaved men who were denounced for sodomy practices, even when they were raped by their owners. In 1689, Luiz Delgado, a Portuguese guitarist and tobacco merchant, was arrested by the Inquisition and sent into penal exile to Bahia in Brazil for having committed the sin of sodomy. One day before being arrested again by the Inquisition, he raped a fugitive African-born enslaved man who had recently disembarked from Africa. In his testimony, translated into Portuguese for the inquisitors, the bondsman said Delgado was a "bad white man, because on that night he wanted to make [me] a woman."[63] Historian Mariana Candido found the case of José Benguela, an enslaved man who lived and worked Salvador, Brazil, and was accused of sodomy by the Portuguese Inquisition in 1703.[64] During his interrogation, the twenty-year-old bondsman, whose owner was João Carvalho de Barros, declared he was born in Benguela in West Central Africa. He told the Inquisition officers that his owner touched his member and made him touch his own, ejaculating in his hands, an event that happened again two or three more times. He also told the officers that his owner forced him to have sex with an enslaved woman called Domingas and then submitted him to anal penetration. According to José, his owner raped him three or four times.[65]

In 1741, the slave owner João Durão de Oliveira of Sabará, Minas Gerais, in Brazil was also denounced for the "abominable sin of sodomy."[66] During the first phase of Durão's investigation, the parish priest heard eight male witnesses. In the second phase, sixteen witnesses were heard, including one enslaved woman, one freedwoman, and several of his victims. All witnesses reported stories about Durão harassing enslaved men, women, and boys, sodomizing them in exchange for gifts. Whereas some of the enslaved individuals resisted his threats, Durão raped dozens of enslaved men and boys. But the inquisitors were not seeking to avenge the enslaved victims of rape; they were seeking to punish sodomy, which, for the Catholic Church was an abominable, nefarious act.[67] Yet, Catholic priests who were slave owners were also accused of sodomizing bondspeople, including enslaved children. Take the case of the priest José Ribeiro Dias, who owned twenty-seven enslaved men, women, and children. In 1743, Felipe de Santiago, a bondsman owned by him, denounced the priest for "having forced him to perform acts of malice and sodomy." According to Santiago, Dias "raped him with the power and commandeering respect of a master," whereas he "obeyed him out of fear because of his condition as of a slave."[68] Unlike in other cases of rape perpetrated by slave owners, Dias was arrested by the Inquisition and spent ten years in the galleys.

During the same period, many other cases of enslaved men raped by their owners are documented in the Inquisition records. Take the example of Luiz da Costa, an African-born enslaved domestic servant, who worked in Vila da Boa Vista, in the captaincy of Pernambuco, Brazil. In 1743, he accompanied his owner, Manoel Alves Cabral, in a hunting excursion. Threatening him with a musket, Cabral raped Luiz, who described the act as "penetration and ejaculation in his posterior orifice."[69] In 1761, Francisco Serrão de Castro also raped the African-born enslaved man Joaquim Antonio, with anal penetration. According to Joaquim, like him, several other enslaved men were also sexually abused by Castro.[70] These cases bring to light how slave owners coerced enslaved men to have sex with them and how they violated their bodies through rape.

In colonial North America and the antebellum South, sexual encounters between white women of various statuses and enslaved men posed serious challenges. During most of the seventeenth century, the children of a white woman with an enslaved man would carry the legal slave status of the father. Starting in the eighteenth century, sexual relations between a Black man and a white woman were prohibited. And at any time, these liaisons could be denounced as alleged rapes.[71] Similar liaisons obviously existed in Latin America and the West Indies, but there was never any legislation preventing interracial sex and marriage. The Catholic Church punished women who had sexual relations out of wedlock, regardless of whether the sexual partner was enslaved or free, or white. But although unmarried white women who engaged in premarital sex were morally reproached, they were not legally prevented from having sex with whomever they chose.

In a famous passage of an early twentieth-century book, historian and sociologist Manoel Bomfim describes the tragic outcomes of such forbidden sexual liaisons in Brazil: "It is not uncommon for the 'little missy' who was raised touching young black boys, to deliver herself to them, when the degenerate nerves wake up in irrepressible desires; then paternal morality comes: the black or mulatto is castrated with a badly sharped knife, the wound is salted, and he is buried alive afterwards. The girl, with a reinforced dowry, marries a poor cousin."[72] Although castration is perhaps an exaggeration, this description suggests that despite the absence of legislation preventing interracial sex, Brazilian society violently punished enslaved men who engaged in sexual relations with young white elite women.

Other factors also impacted sexual relations among the enslaved population. On plantations and in urban areas, the absence of private spaces where bondspeople could engage in intimate exchanges was an obstacle to sexual activity.[73] Depending on the period and region, fewer enslaved women were available to become sexual partners of enslaved men. In Brazil, the overall gender imbalance of the enslaved population was clear, with two-thirds of the bondspeople in plantation areas being male. In Cuba, there were similar problems. In 1839, for example, bondsmen on the Cuban coffee plantation La Suerte complained to the local authorities about the lack of enslaved women. The complaint generated results, as the authorities "sent them back to the plantation with the promise that the slaveholder would buy women slaves before Christmas."[74]

Regardless of gender imbalance, some bondsmen also chose to engage in sexual relations with other enslaved men. In his account to journalist Domingo Del Monte, former enslaved man Esteban Montejo emphasized that some male slaves preferred to have sex between themselves and did not want to have anything to do with women: "This was their life: sodomy. They washed clothes and if they had a husband they also cooked. They were good workers and were busy cultivating their plots. They gave the harvest to their husbands so that they would sell it to the peasants."[75] However, we can presume that Cuban Catholic society likely rejected and disapproved of same-sex enslaved couples.

Intimacy with and without Manumission

Violence was intrinsic to sexual relations during the era of slavery. But despite abundant evidence, until recent years, many historians tended to romanticize sexual liaisons between slave owners and enslaved women. In countries such as Brazil, these views emerged in part because a number of enslaved women performed work in urban areas, especially in mining towns, and thus could more easily purchase their own freedom. This context led scholars to pay attention to the cases of bondswomen who experienced social mobility in Brazilian slave society and also contributed to the emergence of the myth of the lustful enslaved woman who managed to use her beauty and sex appeal to seduce her owner and take advantage of this kind of intimate relationship.

In some contexts, enslaved women could definitely receive material advantages from having sexual relations with their owners and therefore could have strategically engaged these relations with the hope of being emancipated. Consider the example of the eighteenth-century captaincy of Minas Gerais, a gold and diamond mining region in southeast Brazil. Most of the population in this area was composed of males, including enslaved men, but most freed individuals were women. In this very specific context where a large white and mixed male population predominated, enslaved women had more access to manumission by engaging in sexual relationships with their male owners. As a result, these male slave owners made provisions in their wills to emancipate the women upon their deaths. Despite these opportunities, most freedwomen purchased their own freedom, and very few of them were granted manumission without providing their owners any compensation. Even fewer bondswomen were emancipated by their owners when the owners were still alive.[76]

Consider the case of Francisca da Silva de Oliveira, known as Chica da Silva. Born in the village of Milho Verde in the Brazilian gold and diamond mining region of Minas Gerais between 1731 and 1735, Chica was the daughter of an African-born enslaved woman and a Brazilian-born white man. Sources from the period describe Chica as a light-skinned woman. When she was still a young girl, her owner sold her to Manuel Pires Sardinha, a prosperous Portuguese physician and bachelor who lived in the town of Tejuco, today's Diamantina. In 1750, when Inquisition officers visited Tejuco, an individual accused Sardinha of living in concubinage with two enslaved women, one of whom was Chica. The accusation was apparently genuine, as one year later Chica was pregnant with her first son. Although Sardinha did not recognize the boy's paternity, he freed him immediately after his Catholic baptism. In Sardinha's will, he also made the child one of his heirs.[77]

But Sardinha's sexual exchanges with Chica were again disturbed in 1753, when the representatives of the Portuguese Inquisition returned to Tejuco one more time. As now Chica was a mother of a newborn, the crime of concubinage was established. For the Inquisition officer, there was no doubt that Sardinha purchased Chica with the goal of having sex with her.[78] Thus, after signing an agreement committing to break ties with the enslaved women who lived under his roof, Sardinha sold Chica to João Fernandes de Oliveira, a Portuguese businessman and owner of a gold mine. Oliveira had arrived in Tejuco a few months earlier to represent his father, a diamond contractor who succeeded in obtaining the fourth monopoly contract of diamond extraction in the region. But weeks after purchasing Chica, on Christmas Day, December 25, 1753, Oliveira officially freed her. This unusual, quick, and unconditional manumission suggests that like Chica's previous owner, Oliveira had selected his new enslaved property based on her sexual attractiveness. But here, the situation was different. Oliveira could have engaged in sexual relations with Chica without freeing her.[79] Therefore, this early manumission indicates that bonds of affection connected Chica and Oliveira. After her emancipation, Chica continued to share her life with her former owner for seventeen years, until he returned to Portugal to fight for his father's inheritance. Although never legally married, the couple had thirteen children. Chica lived a very comfortable life. After Oliveira's return to Portugal, she remained living in the couple's large residence, administrating his properties, including dozens of enslaved individuals. Their children inherited property, and the males received university education in Portugal. Chica's story was later adapted into a movie and soap operas and became the theme of Carnaval parades and songs in Brazil.

Stories comparable to that of Chica and Oliveira happened in other parts of Latin America and the West Indies during the era of slavery as well.[80] Similar cases also occurred in Louisiana but were rare elsewhere in the United States. Admittedly, there were periods in which manumission laws restricted the ability of slave owners to free enslaved women. But even when manumission was possible, unlike Brazil, the United States did not witness a trend of slave owners emancipating the enslaved women with whom they had had sexual liaisons. Take the example of Elizabeth Hemings, born in Virginia in

1735, nearly the same year as Chica da Silva. Like Chica, she was the daughter of an African woman and a white man, in this case a certain Captain Hemings, after whom she received her last name. Elizabeth's owner John Wayles was the father of Martha Wayles Skelton, the future first lady Martha Jefferson. After the death of his wife, Wayles had six children with Hemings. But unlike Chica, Elizabeth was never emancipated by her owner. After Wayles's death in 1773, Martha Jefferson inherited Elizabeth and her ten children, six of whom were her half-siblings. None of these children was freed. None of these children received college education. None of these children inherited property. The most famous of them, Sally Hemings, was impregnated by her owner, the US President Thomas Jefferson. Like her mother, Sally also had six children fathered by her owner, all of whom became his property.[81] Jefferson was not the only politician to have ever maintained a long-lasting relationship with a bondswoman. Richard Mentor Johnson, who served as the US vice president from 1837 to 1841, owned an enslaved woman, Julia Ann Chinn, who is referred to as his enslaved common-law wife and with whom he had two children.[82] But in contrast with Brazil's Chica da Silva, the US enslaved women Elizabeth Hemings, Sally Hemings, and Julia Chinn were never freed by their eminent owners.

Sex, Violence, and Human Ownership

Human bodies fueled the Atlantic slave trade and slavery. For more than three centuries slavers captured African men, women, and children who were sold and transported to the Americas by slave traders. Slave owners purchased these captives and held their descendants in bondage. This process entirely relied on the physicality of bodies, transformed into the exemplary locus where human ownership triumphed. Africans and their descendants performed coerced work in rural and urban areas. But being the master of their bodies also meant their owners could use them to gain physical pleasure. Thus, sexuality was a significant part of the institution of slavery, marked by a persisting tension between slavers and enslaved. Slave traders, ship captains, and crewmen sexually assaulted enslaved men, women, boys, and girls while they were confined in trading structures along the African coasts and in the holds of slave ships. In all parts of the Americas, enslaved men and women, no matter their sexual orientation, engaged in sexual encounters with other bondspeople.

Bondspeople had sex with their owners, and these exchanges were coercive by nature because enslaved people were legally conceived as movable property and rarely had the ability to refuse these their owners' advances.[83] As we have seen in this chapter, a great amount of evidence produced by enslavers and enslaved people confirms that sexual violence against enslaved women, men, and children predominated in the Americas. Although not all sexual exchanges between slave owners and enslaved women were based on explicit violence and some liaisons may have been based on mutual agreement, the power imbalance between enslavers and bondspeople was too huge to assume that sexual relations that may have looked consensual were based on mutual agreement—unless, as in rare instances, slave owners decided to free their sexual partners.

CHAPTER II

Creating and Re-creating Families

Oluale Kossola (alias Cudjo Lewis) planned to marry. In 1860, he was still a young man living in a Yoruba village northwest of Abomey, in the Kingdom of Dahomey in today's Republic of Benin. He remembered how he loved to go to the market to see the beautiful girls wearing elaborate bracelets that made a pleasant jangle when they walked. One day he saw a girl whom he liked so much that he wanted to marry her. Although he was still too young to marry, he told his family how much he liked the girl. His parents took it seriously. They reached out to her to ask her to marry their son when he was of age. We do not know what happened with the girl, but we know that this wedding never happened because not long afterward, the Dahomean army captured Kossola. He was brought to the coast, sold into slavery, and transported to Alabama on the infamous schooner *Clotilda* on the eve of the US Civil War. Despite the horrors of the Middle Passage, many years later, when Kossola was a freedman, he still remembered the beautiful girl he wanted to marry when he was a young man.

All stages of the Atlantic slave trade and life under slavery in the Americas disrupted families and led to the separation of loved ones. But despite all the horrors they experienced, enslaved Africans and their descendants created families and re-created kin ties. In coastal slave depots, in the holds of slave vessels, on plantations, and in mines, cities, and towns, enslaved women gave birth to children and fulfilled the role of mother for their own children and the children of their fellow bondspeople. This chapter discusses the multiple dimensions of marriage and family formation under slavery. I show how enslaved men and women resisted family separation by reconstructing and building families under the most varied and often tragic circumstances. To better grasp how bondspeople created, reinvented, and preserved kinship ties, we must expand the common Western idea of the nuclear family and embrace the notion of an extended family. Consideration of enslaved people's wider networks of relatives allows us to examine a variety of associations that do not fit the typical definition of a family but were instead often indebted to traditions prevailing in West African and West Central African societies.[1] Enslaved men and women also refashioned spiritual families with shipmates during the Middle Passage and, once in the Americas, they continued to develop these connections during work hours in the fields, marketplaces, slave quarters, kitchens, and churches. In Roman Catholic societies of the Americas especially, bondspeople and freedpeople could formally marry, and by doing so they were able to re-create family ties, which they also did by diligently selecting godparents when they baptized their children.[2]

Family Formation in West Africa and West Central Africa

Before being captured and sold into slavery, West Africans and West Central Africans had their own conceptions of family. Prior to the rise of the Atlantic slave trade, Africans already practiced polygyny, a system in which men have more than one wife. Some scholars have shown that the deportation of more men than women during the Atlantic slave provoked sex imbalance, exacerbating the relatively higher number of women. This disparity contributed to make polygyny much more widespread, at least in West Africa.[3]

Some slave narratives offer us glimpses of family formation in African societies during the era of the Atlantic slave trade. Let's take again Equiano's case, which we explored in earlier chapters of this book. When he moved from his Igboland hometown to the coast, he narrated his stay with a "chieftain, in a very pleasant country," where people spoke the same language as he did. According to Equiano's account, the head of the family that he identified as his first master was a smith, who "had two wives and some children, and they all used me extremely well, and did all they could to comfort me; particularly the first wife, who was something like my mother."[4] Very early as an enslaved boy, he established bonds of affection with a woman who temporarily fulfilled a maternal role for him. Many other African men, women, and children of various ages developed similar ties with fellow enslaved persons, freedpeople, and even in exceptional cases with their own owners during their harrowing journeys through the Atlantic Ocean and into slavery.

Religion also shaped family formation. In regions where Islam predominated, it was not uncommon for men to have more than one wife with whom they had children. To a certain extent, African societies were not different from other rural societies in Europe and the Americas, where until the late nineteenth century, having many children secured families many hands to cultivate the fields. In addition, as we already explored in the first chapters, during the rise of the Atlantic slave trade, Europeans encountered West African and West Central African societies in which the numerous dependents were regarded as wealth that families could dispose of in times of drought and food shortage. Likewise, in nineteenth-century West Africa, as pointed out by historian Walter Hawthorne, people "represented wealth and power" within lineages. Not only did they provide agricultural work, but they also produced "manufactured goods, carried out trade and fought in wars," which is why for lineages, producing children was crucial.[5]

Mahommah Gardo Baquaqua, who was a Muslim, also explained in his published narrative how marriage and family formation operated in his homeland of Djougou, in the present-day Republic of Benin. According to him, young men who wished to marry selected the bride by having his sister offer the woman kola nuts.[6] Following this initial gesture, courtship started with the groom paying multiple visits to the bride until the day of the marriage. During the ceremony, the wedding guests gave some kind of currency to the couple, musicians, children, and other attendants. Baquaqua emphasizes not only that polygyny was "practiced to a great extent, and sanctioned by law" but that a man's wealth was "sometimes estimated by the number of wives he has," even though he admits that "occasionally a poor man has a number of wives, and then they have to support."[7]

The unrest caused by the Atlantic slave trade also led family members to sell their children into slavery, as discussed in chapter 2. But most of the time, African men, women, and children were captured by outsiders and separated from their families. In 1821 Samuel Ajayi Crowther was captured in Osogun, today's Nigeria, where he lived with his parents, brothers, and sisters, as discussed in chapter 3. His narrative depicted the drama of family separation when Fulani warriors entered his town: "Women, some with three, four, or six children clinging to their arms, with the infants on their backs . . . [were] running as fast as they could. . . . While they found it impossible to go along with their loads, they endeavoured only to save themselves and their children." Whereas his father was left behind, Crowther was captured along "with his mother, two sisters (one an infant about ten months old), and a cousin." During his journey to the coast, he was separated from his mother and sisters. He met several other captives who, exactly like him, left their relatives behind.[8] Nearly two decades after he was released in Sierra Leone, Crowther was able to reunite with his mother. Unfortunately, most enslaved Africans who were transported to the Americas never had the opportunity to experience these rare reunions.[9]

Shipmates as Family Members

The slave ship was often the site where family separation was eventually completed. Still, during several weeks of their dreadful journey to the Americas, when enslaved men, women, and children were forced to share the crowded, asphyxiating, and filthy holds of slave ships, they created bonds with their shipmates. In his narrative, Equiano underscores his encounter and exchanges with other countrymen during the Middle Passage.[10] Although these men were not members of his family, they spoke either the same or related languages, which allowed them to communicate.[11] Language, in addition to other shared experiences, provides clues to understanding how captive Africans re-created links of camaraderie during the extreme traumatic conditions to which they were submitted. Therefore, historians have emphasized the existence of several terms, such as *malungo* (Brazil), *batiment* (Saint-Domingue), *malongue* (Trinidad), and *sippi* and *máti* (Surinam), to describe shipmates.[12]

These bonds help explain the connections that began in the holds of slave ships and survived long after disembarkation in the Americas, depending on where the shipmates were sold.[13] Shipmate bonds are also related to the notion of groups of provenance. This concept, introduced in chapter 6 and developed by historian Mariza de Carvalho Soares, highlights how Africans who were embarked in the same region and over a given period tended to belong to groups sharing the same or similar languages, cultures, and religions.[14] The emphasis on these slave ship families is also a response to erroneous assumptions that the human cargoes on board slave ships were composed of heterogeneous groups of random and unrelated enslaved individuals, which some scholars argue is why their connections only emerged during the Middle Passage.[15] Yet regardless of whether these bonds emerged during the journeys to the coast, inside the coastal trading structures, or aboard slave vessels, the traumatic experiences of enslavement and deportation created special ties among African captives that were maintained during the period they lived under slavery in the Americas.[16]

During the era of slavery, the Portuguese, Spanish, and French crowns controlled the Roman Catholic Church in their specific territories, and the church was in charge of recording births, deaths, and marriages. In 1563 the Council of Trent, an ecumenic council of the

Roman Catholic Church that first convened in 1545 to respond to the Protestant Reformation, established that marriage was a holy sacrament. For the church, marriage was a lawful and formally recognized union between a man and woman. It was an institution that encouraged avoidance of sinful behavior and control of the social order. Therefore, for most of the colonial period, all individuals who wished to marry in Latin America had to obtain permission from the Catholic Church. Future grooms (or their owners, if they were enslaved) would submit an application that provided the ecclesiastical notary with various information, including the names of two witnesses who knew the bride and groom and who could testify that both members of the future couple were single in order to prevent polygamy, a practice condemned by the church.[17]

Although tracing connections among African captives that predated the deportation to the Americas or which emerged on board the slave ships proves to be difficult, marriage records in the Spanish Americas allow us to track these early links among African shipmates.[18] Historian Herman Bennett shows that as early as 1584, Francisco, an enslaved man, went by himself to Mexico City's cathedral to petition to marry Catalina, an enslaved woman who shared with him the same owner. In the petition Francisco and Catalina, as well as Victoria, one of their witnesses, identified themselves as "from the land of Biafara."[19] The use of this term, which in Iberian societies of the time referred to the West African region inhabited by the Biafada peoples in today's Guinea-Bissau, suggests that the three African-born enslaved individuals valued ethnic links that in one way or another predated their forced transportation to the Spanish Americas.[20] Other enslaved men and women born in West Central Africa maintained similar long-lasting connections even though living in different households and neighborhoods of Mexico City during the sixteenth and seventeenth centuries.[21]

Another scholar, historian Alex Borucki, has explored dozens of marriage petitions of enslaved people transported to Montevideo, in present-day Uruguay, showing that African-born and American-born shipmates continued to stay connected many years after being transported to the Americas. For example, in a marriage application of 1778, an enslaved man from Angola testified in favor of another enslaved man from Benguela, by stating that they had known each other for several years, since their time in Africa, then in the ports of Rio de Janeiro, Colonia, and Montevideo.[22] Despite not being linked by blood ties, the connections they acquired because of the Atlantic slave trade sustained their attachment for many years, even across continents.

Formerly enslaved men and women shipmates also married each other. Take the example of the Africans transported to Brazil on board the schooner *Emilia*. In 1820, the vessel left Bahia to trade in Malembo, a West Central African port located south of the equator, on the Loango coast. But instead the vessel sailed to Lagos, in today's Nigeria, north of the equator, a region where since 1815 an international treaty had made the Portuguese slave trade illegal. When the *Emilia* left Lagos transporting 392 men, women, and children, the British naval frigate *Morgiana* intercepted the vessel and established that the Africans on board were acquired illegally. Probably many of these captives had never met one another before boarding the *Emilia*, but some of them may have been relatives, whereas others certainly shared previous experiences in Yorubaland. After several stops and changes in trajectory, the *Morgiana* and *Emilia* arrived in Rio de Janeiro, where the 354 surviving Africans were kept for months in a warehouse.

According to Brazilian legislation, captives who were illegally introduced in the country after 1831 had to be freed and assigned the special status of "liberated Africans" (*africanos livres*), which will be discussed in chapter 16. But despite their emancipation, these Africans still had to serve as so-called apprentices for fourteen years, often under dreadful conditions. Existing records show that a few individuals transported on board the *Emilia* not only nurtured connections acquired during the Atlantic crossing but also married each other during the weeks they spent in a Rio de Janeiro's warehouse waiting to be liberated.[23] Moreover, despite having been separated during the apprenticeship years, these Africans kept bonds of friendship and affection, and together they petitioned the state to be freed earlier. At the end of the apprenticeship years, approximately sixty of the liberated Africans from the *Emilia* returned together to Lagos. One of these individuals was actually able to amass wealth during the apprenticeship years and paid the way back of his comrades' to West Africa.[24]

Marrying and the Catholic Church in the Americas

In colonies such as Jamaica, official marriages were uncommon even among white people. Present in small numbers in the colony, white male settlers, among whom mortality was also high, rarely married white women. Instead they engaged in unofficial unions with Black women or women of color, with whom they had children who sometimes survived until adulthood.[25] But as ideas of purity of blood appeared in English legal codes as early as the seventeenth century, only in rare occurrences did Englishmen officially recognized mixed-race children.[26]

Beginning in 1663, Bermuda prohibited English colonists from marrying people of African descent regardless of their legal status.[27] Likewise, the General Assembly of Maryland in 1664 passed an act imposing lifetime service sentences on white women who married Black enslaved men.[28] Marriages among enslaved people existed in English colonies of West Indies, but these unions were not officially recognized. As we already discussed in previous chapters, it was not unusual for couples and their children to be sold separately. But despite these obstacles and the unfavorable demography for the formation of enslaved couples, in which bondsmen outnumbered bondswomen, during the first three decades of the nineteenth century, a large set of records shows the active role of some enslaved men as fathers and husbands in Berbice (in present-day Guyana), a Dutch colony until 1815, after which it was ceded to the United Kingdom and in 1831 became part of British Guiana.[29]

In the French colonies of the Americas, there were early attempts to prevent slave owners from having children with enslaved women.

Article IX of the French *Code noir* (*Black Code*) of 1685 established that a married freeman who had one child or several children resulting from "concubinage" with a bondswoman had to pay a fine of two thousand pounds of sugar, and if he was the owner of the enslaved woman and the children he fathered, both the mother and the offspring would be confiscated. However, the code also determined that an unmarried freeman who had children with a bondswoman had not only to legally marry her but also to emancipate her and her enslaved children.[30] As one could expect, these measures were not fully enforced and never discouraged slave owners from impregnating enslaved women.

These legal provisions are related to the predominance of Catholicism in the French, Spanish, and Portuguese colonies of the Americas, in contrast to the prevalence of Protestantism in the English colonies of the West Indies and North America.[31] Roman law and the Catholic Church shaped the *Siete partidas* (1251–65), a Castilian code that inspired slavery legislation in the Spanish Americas, as well as the *Code noir* (1685) in force in the French colonies in the West Indies and the Louisiana *Code noir* (1724) that specifically regulated slavery.[32] Roman law and the Catholic Church also shaped Portuguese and Brazilian laws that normalized slavery. Despite the absence of codes specifically regulating the work and daily lives of its enslaved population, as had occurred in the French colonies, volumes 4 and 5 of the Portuguese *Ordenações filipinas* (1603) and later the *Constituições Primeiras do Arcebispado da Bahia* (1707) contained articles addressing slavery.[33]

Notwithstanding these varying legal regimes, all colonies of the Americas immediately or gradually embraced the *partus sequitur ventrem* doctrine, which established that the legal slave's status was inherited through the mother. The Spanish Americas through the *Siete partidas* and Brazil through the *Ordenações filipinas* also adhered to this principle even though these two compilations of laws remained extremely vague regarding *partus sequitur ventrem*. The French *Code noir* of 1685 and the Louisiana *Code noir* of 1724 also incorporated the doctrine, according to which if the mother was enslaved, regardless of the father's status, the newborn would bear the mother's legal status.[34] In the early period of colonization of the Americas, English common law established that the slave's status was transmitted through the father (*partus sequitur partem*), but starting in 1662 the civil law principle of *partus sequitur ventrem* was also adopted in Virginia and therefore in other English colonies.[35] In Latin America, as the institution in charge of performing marriages, the Catholic Church condemned the separation of enslaved married couples. Gradually, written legislation incorporated this principle as well. But the same norm was not applicable to children, who even in Latin America could be sold out away from their mothers by slave owners. Overall, as was the case elsewhere in the Americas, laws theoretically protecting enslaved people were not constantly enforced in practice.

Therefore, although not always encouraged, marriage among enslaved persons was allowed in Brazil and in the French and Spanish colonies of the Americas. In most of these regions, enslaved people also could marry freed and free individuals. The application of the law in the diverse regions of the Americas varied and changed over time. Slave owners were told to baptize and instruct enslaved people in the faith of the Roman Catholic Church, but they did not always follow these recommendations. Slave owners also often refused to respect other measures favoring enslaved people.[36] Moreover, priests were scarce in several regions of Latin America, especially in the rural areas. In colonial Colombia, for example, priests visited some large estates and mines only once a year or even less often.[37]

Despite the power of the Catholic Church in a colony such as Brazil, many free men and women shared the same roof and had children without having received the sacrament of marriage. With the enslaved population, things were often no different. As early as 1619, two Jesuit priests who visited farms and plantations in Bahia reported that because slave owners created numerous obstacles, most of the existing enslaved couples were not formally married. Their findings were certainly accurate.[38] Italian Jesuit priest Giorgio Benci arrived in Brazil in 1683. After his return to Europe in 1700, four of his sermons given in Bahia were published as a book in 1705. Like any other Jesuit of his time, Benci defended slavery. But he also criticized the treatment slave owners imposed on enslaved people. Among other criticisms, he denounced slave owners' failure to ensure that enslaved persons who were nearing death received the last sacrament (Viaticum) mandated by the Roman Catholic Church. Such neglect, however, was not at all unexpected given that, as discussed in chapter 5, slave owners often failed to provide proper Catholic funeral rites to deceased enslaved persons. Benci also condemned slave owners who disobeyed the Catholic Church's orientation in defense of enslaved people's right to marriage, as well as slave owners who prevented enslaved people from marrying and who sold apart enslaved couples.[39]

The priest likewise denounced slave owners who distributed additional rations of food to the enslaved women who provided them with sexual services and condemned slaveholders who lived in concubinage with bondswomen as the most abominable scandal. He also attacked the slave owners who coerced enslaved women "to consent in this sin" and then penalized them "when[,] disgusted," the women rejected "this offense to god." Benci went as far as to defend the judicial punishment of slave owners who raped enslaved women: "Shall we say that in addition to the eternal penalty, with which the masters who thus violate and force their slaves to sin deserve to be punished in the afterlife, they still deserve temporal death, which is imposed by common law and special laws of Portugal upon all those who violently or otherwise coerce and force women of whatever quality to sin . . . [?]"[40] Despite the Jesuit priest's compelling defense of Catholic marriage among enslaved people and his condemnation of extramarital sex between slave owners and enslaved people, until the last decades of the eighteenth century, as already discussed in chapter 10, some Catholic priests themselves engaged in sexual relations with enslaved women and men, going against the church's doctrine. In the late seventeenth century, Bahian residents denounced the behavior of João Calmon, the diocese's vicar general and son of a powerful sugar estate owner. The priest was accused of living in concubinage with a woman, in addition to have an illicit relationship with a nun, and with Brígida, one his enslaved women.[41] Despite this scandalous misconduct, Calmon became the officer of the Bahia's Inquisition three years later.

Still, in both Angola and Brazil, regions under Portugal's jurisdiction in the seventeenth century, male and female slave owners imposed spouses on their enslaved property. Bondspeople who attempted to resist these pressures could face serious consequences. Consider the example of the seventeenth-century enslaved woman Páscoa, whose story was recorded by the Portuguese Inquisition.[42] Páscoa was born in Massangano, a West Central African village nearly 100 miles southeast of Luanda, in today's Angola, in approximately 1660.[43] Before being conquered and colonized by the Portuguese, Massangano was part of the Kingdom of Ndongo (also known as the Kingdom of Angola or Ngola). Páscoa's parents and her maternal grandparents were enslaved in the same estate and owned by the same family as she was. Páscoa's first owner was the Portuguese-born widow Domingas Carvalho, a member of a family of Luso-Africans, a category of mixed-race individuals discussed in chapter 3. As Massangano was not on the coast and priests were not always available, as in Brazilian remote rural areas, slave owners took advantage of a priest's visit to organize collective ceremonies to baptize and marry bondspeople of neighboring estates.

In a ceremony gathering enslaved persons from various plantations of Massangano's surrounding areas, Páscoa, then sixteen or seventeen years old, married Aleixo, an enslaved shoemaker also owned by Carvalho. As slave owners played a decisive role in the selection of spouses for their enslaved property, we can assume that Páscoa and Aleixo were not given much choice in the matter. Performed by a Italian capuchin priest, the ceremony of the arranged marriage essentially consisted of exchanging wedding rings. The ritual may have also been performed in Latin, Italian, or Portuguese, languages that most bondspeople did not understand.[44] From this first marriage, Páscoa conceived two children, who did not survive their childhood. A few years later, Carvalho passed away and bequeathed both Páscoa and her husband to her locally born niece Andreza da Cunha. At this point, Páscoa was no longer very fond of her husband. According to the witnesses who provided testimonies to the Inquisition, she started running away and exerting her natural right of having sexual encounters with other men, therefore transgressing the Catholic Church doctrine, in which adultery was a sin, especially if the sinners were women. Moreover, by running away to meet other partners, she failed to perform her daily duties. As both behaviors were unacceptable in a Catholic slave society, Páscoa's owner decided to sell her overseas. Despite being married, Páscoa was transported alone to Luanda, where she boarded a slave ship sailing to Brazil.

Páscoa landed in Salvador, Bahia, in 1687. Unlike many newly arrived African captives, she was already baptized, spoke Portuguese, and belonged to the third generation of her family living in slavery.[45] Once in Bahia, she became the property of the notary Francisco Álvares Távora and his wife Domingas Vieira, from whom she took the last name Vieira.[46] According to Páscoa's own testimony, upon her arrival, she started having sexual encounters with her owner's son and with another African-born enslaved man named Pedro Arda, an ethnonym referring to the Kingdom of Ardra or Allada, in the Bight of Benin, as previously noted in chapter 6. She then quickly added that she had one child with Pedro, and because they were having sex, she decided to marry him.[47] The marriage was celebrated on May 2, 1688. Later in her testimony, we learn that she had two children with Pedro, including the one born before their marriage.

We will never know Páscoa's motivations to accept this second marriage less than one year after her arrival in Bahia. The wedding may have been her owner's attempt to discourage the contact between Páscoa and his son. The hypothesis that her owner's son was the father of her first Brazilian-born child is not to be discarded either. Moreover, it would not be surprising if Páscoa's owner had put pressure on her and Pedro to formalize their union, as they were already in a relationship and living under the same roof. Perhaps the couple genuinely liked each other, and the marriage was their choice. More likely, more than one of these considerations influenced their decision to marry.[48]

Whatever the motivations of the various interested parties, bigamy was a crime in the eyes of the Catholic Church, hence Páscoa's second marriage put her on the Inquisition's radar.[49] Africans and Brazilians constantly traveled back and forth between Bahia and West Central Africa while trading goods and human beings. The news about the marriage reached Massangano. In 1692, a cousin of Páscoa's owner arrived in Bahia from Angola, bringing the news that the enslaved woman was already married in Massangano, information that had escaped the Catholic Church's investigation which authorized the marriage. In an attempt to separate the couple, Páscoa's owner reacted to the news by selling her husband Pedro to another owner. In 1693, the owner denounced Páscoa to the Portuguese Inquisition, a move that ignited the usual long investigation. Páscoa and Pedro objected to the accusations and took all possible measures to avoid being separated, including calling witnesses on both sides of the Atlantic Ocean who curiously testified that the enslaved woman was never married. Although initially successful in maintaining their marriage, the enslaved couple's efforts were eventually defeated. Upon her arrest by the Inquisition authorities in 1700, Páscoa was emancipated by her owner. She was transported to Lisbon as a freedwoman to face trial for the crime of bigamy and was eventually sentenced to three years of penal exile in a town in southern Portugal. Very ill, she petitioned to reduce her sentence to a few months and was successful. She then demanded to return to her former owner in Brazil, probably in an attempt to see her husband and perhaps reunite with her children. Ultimately, Páscoa's tragic story reveals that enslaved Africans resisted or adhered to the Catholic Church's ideas of marriage, depending on the circumstances.

Impediments to marriage among enslaved people continued during the eighteenth century because in 1707, the *Constituições Primeiras do Arcebispado da Bahia* (1707), a compilation of norms intended to be Brazil's first clerical legislation, reaffirmed bondspeople's right to marry enslaved and free individuals in Brazil. This ecclesiastical code also reiterated that slave owners could neither prevent bondspeople from marrying nor sell an enslaved woman or an enslaved man in order to separate members of married enslaved couples.[50] Undoubtedly, slave owners were still preventing enslaved men and women from marrying at the time of the code's promulgation.

In 1708, Antonio de Brandolini, another Italian Jesuit priest, sent to the pope a letter along with a memorial written by the enslaved members of a Bahia Black Catholic brotherhood in which they complained that slave owners constantly attempted to prevent them from marrying.[51] In his treatise published in 1711, Jesuit missionary Antonil noted that slave owners prohibited bondspeople from marrying each other in Brazil. He underscored that when they allowed enslaved people to marry, slave owners selected the spouses, as had happened with Páscoa in Massangano in the seventeenth century. Moreover, he added that when slaveholders judged it convenient, they did not hesitate in separating these couples.[52] Decades later, obstructions certainly persisted because again, in a treatise published in 1758, the Portuguese priest Manoel Ribeiro Rocha, who spent most of his life in Bahia, repeated the words of the *Constituições Primeiras do Arcebispado da Bahia* (1707) by emphasizing that enslaved people had the right to marry and slave owners could not prevent them from marrying.[53]

When enslaved people were baptized in the Catholic Church in Latin America, priests recorded the names of the parents, regardless their marital statuses. Of course, there were instances when the name of the father was recorded as unknown, including when the father was the enslaved mother's owner, who did not legally recognize the newborn.[54] Although bondsmen and bondswomen could marry in Brazil, the number of enslaved couples varied depending on the region and period. Based on more than three thousand baptism records from three parishes in Bahia, one historian concludes that during the seventeenth century nearly 90 percent of the parents of baptized enslaved children were not formally married because their names were not even listed in these parish documents.[55] Likewise, a large sample of eighteenth-century Rio de Janeiro's baptism records suggests that less than 10 percent of the parents of newborns were formally married.[56]

In Rio de Janeiro, as in Mexico City during the sixteenth and seventeenth centuries, and Bahia during the eighteenth century, African-born enslaved persons tended to marry within the same provenance group. Although most enslaved couples in Brazil did not have a formal Catholic marriage between the end of the eighteenth century and during the nineteenth century, parish records reveal higher numbers of enslaved children whose parents were legally married than in previous centuries. Yet, regardless of growing rates, in most regions of Brazil, groom and bride still needed to request the Catholic Church's permission to marry for most of the colonial period.[57] For example, in 1811, Alexandre Francisco, a Brazilian-born freedman who resided at the Jacuipe do Brito sugar mill in Bahia, petitioned the church to marry Joaquina Maria do Sacramento, a Brazilian-born enslaved woman who resided and worked in the same mill. Despite opposition from the bride's mother, who wanted her daughter to marry an enslaved man who like her was African-born and a Yoruba speaker, Francisco's request to the church received a positive answer.[58] Overall, during the nineteenth century alone, historians estimate that nearly one-third of the enslaved population in Brazilian sugar and coffee plantations was married, especially in the estates with large slaveholdings.[59]

Travelers who sojourned in Brazil during the nineteenth century documented enslaved people's Catholic weddings. In his famous illustrated travelogue, French artist Jean-Baptiste Debret included a lithograph (figure 11.1) based on his watercolor representing the wedding ceremony of three enslaved couples owned by a rich family in Rio de Janeiro. The setting is a Catholic church building's interior. The lithograph features a wooden floor covered with numbered graves where prestigious members of Catholic lay brotherhoods were buried, a practice discussed in chapter 5. The image features a priest in the center of the composition blessing the first couple of enslaved persons,

FIGURE II.1. *Mariage de nègres d'une maison riche* (*Marriage of Slaves of a Rich Household*), in Jean-Baptiste Debret, *Voyage pittoresque et historique au Brésil*, 3 vols. (Paris: Firmin Didot Frères, 1834–39), vol. 3, plate 15.

whereas in the background, between the priest and the bride, the head of the altar boy is also visible. In addition, two other enslaved couples are featured in the midground and the foreground. The brides are wearing sophisticated long white and pastel petticoat dresses, delicate shoes, huge earrings, necklaces, and bracelets. They also wear elaborate braided hairstyles decorated with tiaras, ribbons, and laces. Likewise, the grooms are elegantly dressed, wearing shoes, striped pants, white jabot shirts, and pastel striped smoking jackets, and are also holding bowler hats, confirming their respectable ranks. On the right side, happily watching the sacrament, stands the godfather. A coachman elegantly dressed in bright blue, he holds an elaborate hat and wears shoes with attached spurs. However, Debret's explanation of the engraving emphasizes that brides and grooms were not ordinary couples but belonged to a rich household. Although Debret's visual representations were usually more accurate than his words, he made some interesting observations about marriage among enslaved people in Brazil. He emphasized that in rich households it was a matter of "decency and good tone" to have enslaved women marry, "without opposing too much their inclination in the choice of a husband." Although Debret lived in Rio de Janeiro between 1816 and 1832, far after the first observations by Jesuit priests who denounced Brazilian slave owners for preventing enslaved people from marrying in the late seventeenth century, he subtly suggests that, in the nineteenth century, slave owners still influenced enslaved women's choice of husbands. He also added that usually the bride and groom were part of the same household and that allowing bondswomen to select their spouses was not a benevolent act but rather a custom intended to "attach them more to the home." But in the text explaining the lithograph, Debret also subtly suggested that despite being married, enslaved women continued to provide sexual favors to their owners: "a remarkable fact is that the negress, gifted to an extraordinary extent with the ardor of the senses, although faithful and chaste in the bond of marriage, does not resist the desire to conquer the love of her master through careful care and the gracious expression of her touching affections, which she carefully veils under the appearance of humility; and this maneuver, it must be said, succeeded in all conditions." In other words, as part of a paternalistic set of attitudes, slave owners also used Catholic marriage to control enslaved people, contain insurgent behavior, and yet still sexually exploit enslaved women.[60]

But despite Debret's example, several other cases show how slave owners clearly imposed spouses on enslaved women. Caetana, a seventeen-year-old enslaved woman, lived and worked in a Paraíba Valley coffee plantation in São Paulo, Brazil. Her owner imposed on her an enslaved husband named Custódio, also owned by him. The couple married in October 1835. There were multiple reasons that led Caetana's owner to force her to marry. Yet it is not difficult to infer that with the rise of the coffee production, marriage would lead her to give birth to new enslaved children, therefore increasing her owner's enslaved property. Moreover, as in Rio de Janeiro's rich household, marriage and children would deepen the links of Caetana and Custódio to the plantation.

Still, this story had an alternate ending. After the wedding ceremony, Caetana refused to have sex with her husband, escaped back to her owner's house, and eventually was successful in convincing him to petition the church to nullify her forced marriage.[61]

In Latin America, urban areas could offer more opportunities to enslaved couples to cohabitate. When both members of the couple were enslaved, marriage provided some level of protection, as legal codes in the various colonies of the region included provisions preventing the separation of enslaved couples, as already noted. In the Spanish Americas, enslaved people wishing to marry had to obtain authorization from their owners, who in theory, as in Brazil, could not deny their right to marry. But in plantation settings, when the two members of the couple had different owners and lived and worked in a distinct estate, slave owners often created obstacles preventing marriages. Still, when this rule was not respected, bondspeople living in urban areas could use the courts to contest their owners' refusal to allow them to marry. But in rural areas, challenging the will of slave owners through legal means was rarely an option. During the eighteenth and nineteenth centuries, in several regions of Brazil, slave owners prohibited formal marriages of enslaved men and women belonging to different owners and between bondspeople and free people.[62]

Michelle A. McKinley shows that in Lima's largest parish, enslaved people "married at higher rates than Spaniards" during the seventeenth century.[63] Moreover, nearly one thousand couples in which one of the spouses was enslaved petitioned to marry as well. But despite these formal unions among enslaved men and women, there were circumstances in which slave owners attempted to sell or effectively separate husband and wife. In urban areas such as Lima, in contrast with plantation and rural areas, enslaved people had much more access to the courts. Dozens of enslaved spouses petitioned the ecclesiastical court to avoid being temporarily separated or sold apart during the seventeenth century. Although many bondspeople may have not objected to separation, the large number of marriages among enslaved persons in seventeenth-century Lima suggest that most slave owners respected these unions.[64]

In various parts of the Americas, African-born and locally born enslaved people married and created families, even though the development of these blood or virtual ties was more common in plantation settings with larger slaveholdings than in urban areas, and also depended on the specific demographic elements of each region. In Brazilian mining regions and cattle ranching areas, enslaved women were present in very small numbers in comparison to large contingents of enslaved men, making the formation of enslaved family unities harder.[65] In large sugar estates with sizable slaveholdings, sex imbalance and the dreadful working conditions along with low life expectancy were barriers that prevented bondswomen from having children and consequently hindered the formation of families among bondspeople. During the first half of the nineteenth century, enslaved men continued to greatly outnumber bondswomen in Brazilian coffee plantations with large slaveholdings.[66] Working conditions in these coffee plantations were better than in sugar estates. Moreover, properties with larger slaveholdings provided more opportunities to enslaved women to choose their partners, therefore increasing the number of marriages sanctioned by the Catholic Church and favoring family formation.

Married Except by Word of Mouth

The terms of marriage among enslaved people in present-day North America varied across regions. During the British colonial era, most of the thirteen colonies did not legally recognize marriage of bondspeople. But existing sanctions did not mean that enslaved people never married. In 1681, Eleanor Butler, a white servant known as Irish Nell, married "Negro" Charles, an enslaved man, in a wedding ceremony performed by a Catholic priest on a Maryland plantation.[67] In Puritan Massachusetts, the quite small enslaved Black population could legally marry. However, as historian Wendy Warren underscores, in New England "even a recognized marriage might not protect an enslaved person from the cruelty of separation from his or her partner."[68] Ultimately, Puritans were seeking profit. When necessary, they did not hesitate to sell members of the few existing enslaved couples. In regions of the present-day United States such as Florida, which remained under Spanish jurisdiction until 1821, the Catholic Church recognized marriage among enslaved people. A comparable context existed in French Louisiana, where the *Code noir* of 1724 established that enslaved persons of African descent could marry among themselves, even though it prohibited Black persons, regardless of their legal status, to marry people of European descent.[69] Not surprisingly, marriage between white persons and Black individuals, regardless of enslaved or free legal status, was prohibited throughout the US South during the nineteenth century.

Overall, enslaved people who wanted to marry in colonies where Catholicism prevailed faced similar obstacles. In the Spanish Americas and Brazil, enslaved Black people could marry Black or white free individuals, but as already noted, slave owners established restrictions. Still, the Portuguese and Spanish crowns, and consequently the Catholic Church, discouraged marriages between Black persons and Iberian-born men and women or their white descendants, even though such unions were not prohibited.[70] In Brazil, for example, white upper-class males who defied the social order by marrying Black freedwomen faced public hostility and met obstacles preventing them from occupying public office and other positions in several other institutions during the colonial period.[71] Obviously, local populations contested these written legal prescriptions in the courts and on the ground, especially in the regions where Black people and persons of color outnumbered white people. Thus, despite the seventeenth-century North American example of Butler and Charles, it is accurate to state that all over the Americas, when marriages between enslaved and free people occurred, grooms were usually free or freed, whereas brides were enslaved. Much more rare were the cases in which free white women married enslaved and freed men.

Marriages between freemen and enslaved women posed one major problem for the couple: their children remained enslaved. Often free spouses made attempts to purchase the freedom of their enslaved partners and their children. Historian Tera Hunter, who extensively researched marriage among enslaved people in nineteenth-century United States, uncovered the case of her own ancestor Sally Hunter, who was enslaved and transported from Africa to Jamaica and then to South Carolina. She gave birth to two children, fathered by her owner, but eventually married Dublin Hunter, a freed Black mechanic, who purchased her freedom along with her children. But for many bondspeople, including other members of the Hunter clan, marriage was not a freedom pass.[72] Purchasing the freedom of a spouse required resources that took a very long time to obtain.

Because marriage among enslaved people was not legally sanctioned in most of the thirteen British colonies in North America and the later independent United States, formerly enslaved people referred to these unions as "married except by word of mouth."[73] Marriage arrangements varied from region to region, in urban areas and plantation settings, and also over time. For example, in some regions of colonial Virginia, it was common for couples to live on separate plantations, which is why slave households were either composed of a mother and her enslaved children or of all-male members.[74] The legal prohibition of the international slave trade to the United States in 1808 and the resultant intensification of the domestic slave trade created growing threats of separation among enslaved families, whose members could be sold to the Deep South where cotton production was flourishing.[75] Moreover, as we already explored in chapter 6, when slave owners died or went into debt, enslaved families were often separated.

Marriage among enslaved people did not protect the couple against sexual violence, either, because a slave owner could also directly replace the enslaved husband in the couple's bed.[76] As in other parts of the Western Hemisphere, slave owners often arranged marital unions among bondspeople in colonial North America and the antebellum United States. Moreover, US slave owners who encouraged enslaved couples to have children did so to increase the enslaved population on their plantations in the context of the second slavery. In some cases, forced breeding was not excluded. Some freedpeople narrated how their owners "mated [men and women] indiscriminately and without any regard for family unions." According to one enslaved couple who survived the atrocities of slavery in Virginia, "if their master thought that a certain man and woman might have strong, healthy offspring, he forced them to have sexual relation even though they were married to other slaves."[77] Moreover, if the bondspeople resisted his commands, this owner forced them to have sex in front of him. During the nineteenth century, with or without the benediction of Black ministers of various denominations, wedding ceremonies could include rituals such as "jumping the broom" and were often occasions for drinking, dancing, and eating. Yet wedding rites could also be spaces of sexual violence against bondspeople. In one extreme case, a Virginia slave owner declared a bride and groom married after forcing them to have sexual intercourse in front of him.[78]

Attempting to draw broad trends for more than three centuries in an entire continent is a risky enterprise, but it is safe to state that marital unions were more common on plantations where slaveholdings were bigger than on smaller estates with fewer enslaved people. Marriages were also more frequent when the number of enslaved men and women was more balanced. Most marriages tended to occur among men and women living and working on the same estate and owned by the same slaveholder. Yet, many enslaved persons married men and women who lived and worked on neighboring plantations in the United States. Enslaved partners frequently walked several miles to visit their spouses and children on other estates every weekend. When denied the right to these visits, many other enslaved men decided to temporarily escape to stay close to their families.[79]

Despite all obstacles, marital unions among enslaved men and women took many forms in the Americas. Enslaved families existed in greater numbers in colonial North America and the independent United States than in Latin America and the West Indies. These discrepancies are in part because of the greater gender balance. Moreover, during the nineteenth century, slave owners in the US South made clear efforts to increase the enslaved population on their plantations.

Working conditions on cotton plantations were better than in the sugar estates. Especially starting in the nineteenth century, after the importation of enslaved Africans to the United States was prohibited in 1808, US planters provided bondspeople living conditions that favored birth rate growth, pressuring enslaved women to get pregnant. As we have seen, in some cases, forced sexual intercourse was not excluded. But despite these similarities and contrasts, both in the United States and in Brazil, slave marriages were also an instrument of accommodation and control used by slave owners to prevent the enslaved populations from resisting slavery by escaping and planning revolts.

Temporary Security

Sanctioned or unsanctioned marriages offered enslaved men and women temporary security and stability. Even in regions where the Catholic Church recognized and encouraged marriages among bondspeople, marital unions often depended on obtaining permission from slave owners. Archival records provide an abundance of examples that show how slave owners created all sorts of obstacles that ultimately either hindered or fully prevented enslaved people from marrying. Still, bondspeople fought back and challenged these prohibitions. Also counteracting these obstacles, in Brazil and the West Indies, enslaved people created blood and virtual families.

As explored in this chapter, in some instances, bondsmen and bondswomen had opportunities to select partners of their choice. But in many cases, their owners selected their spouses. Families and marriages among enslaved people were never a given, and even after many years of marital union, husbands and wives could be sold separately. Even in countries where Catholicism predominated, enslaved children were never protected from being sold apart from their parents, an ordeal that we will discuss in further detail in chapter 12.

CHAPTER 12

Mothers in Shackles

Before being captured, forced into slavery, and transported to the Americas, many bondswomen experienced motherhood. Some women and their children were captured and separated during wars and raids when they were still on African shores. Others were caught and transported together to the African coasts, only to be separated at various stages of the Atlantic slave trade, as discussed in chapter 3. Yet we know that some enslaved women did manage to cross the Atlantic Ocean with their offspring. Journals by slave ship captains recorded the deaths of enslaved children who made the crossing with their mothers. African women gave birth to children during the Middle Passage as well. French captain Joseph Crassous de Médeuil even recorded the name of a stillborn baby birthed aboard the La Rochelle slave vessel *Roy Dahomet* during the crossing from Ouidah to Cap Français in Saint-Domingue, the richest French colony in the West Indies in the eighteenth century.[1]

The permanent exhibition of the Nantes History Museum housed in the Château des Ducs de Bretagne in Nantes, France's largest slave-trading port, features an astonishing watercolor including four diagrams representing the French slave ship *La Marie-Séraphique*. The watercolor (figure 12.1), probably executed by the ship captain Jean-Baptiste Fautrel-Gaugy and the officer Jean-René L'Hermite, offers detailed views of the slave vessel that sailed first from Nantes to the Loango coast in West Central Africa and then transported

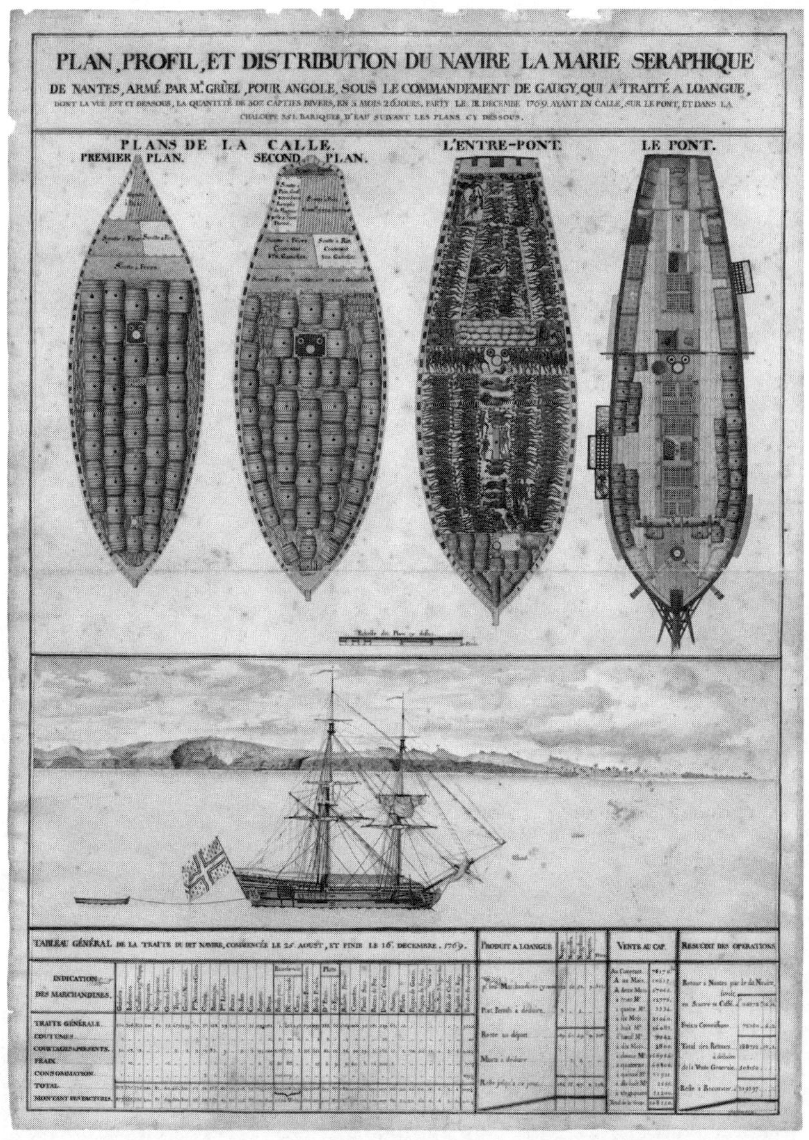

FIGURE 12.1. Diagram of *La Marie-Séraphique*. Photograph by René Lhermitte. Courtesy of Musée d'histoire de Nantes (Nantes History Museum), Nantes, France.

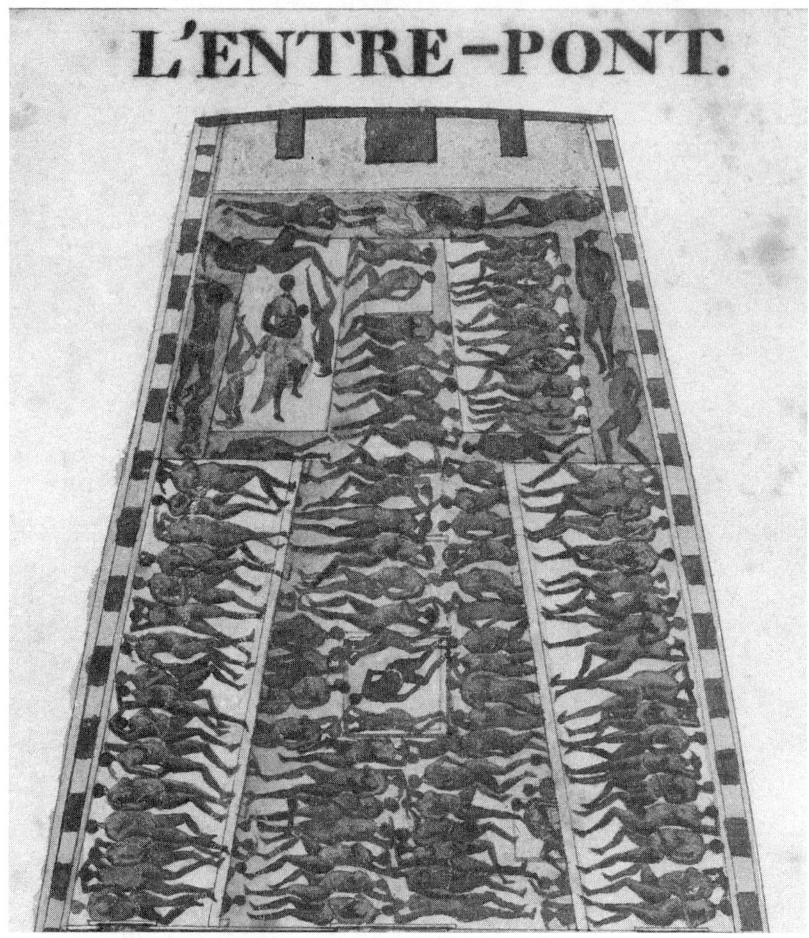

FIGURE 12.2. Detail of the diagram of *La Marie-Séraphique*. Photograph by René Lhermitte. Courtesy of Musée d'histoire de Nantes (Nantes History Museum), Nantes, France.

307 enslaved Africans to Cap Français in 1769.[2] But a close-up view on the upper left side of the representation of the overcrowded lower deck (figure 12.2) reveals the image of one enslaved woman suckling her baby.[3]

We do not know if this is a depiction of an enslaved mother who was actually on board *La Marie-Séraphique*, as the image could also have been created to make a general reference to the occasional presence of breastfeeding mothers among the human cargo of slave ships. Eighteenth-century agents in West African trading posts such as Pierre Simon Gourg, one of the directors of the French fort in Ouidah in the late eighteenth century, reported that European traders avoided purchasing pregnant women or women who had just given birth "on the grounds that they are in the way and make a mess on board." According to Gourg, African agents who knew they could "sell women who have just given birth if they present the child always take it away and threaten the mother with killing her if she says she has any and as soon as the mother is sold, if the child is not weaned or if they have no nurse to give the baby they throw him in the fields" to become "food for tigers, wolves and snakes." The French officer still insisted that "this is not a fiction, it is a known fact to all who come to the coast."[4] But *La Marie-Séraphique*'s detailed rendering suggests that this breastfeeding mother might have been more than just a product of its creators' imagination. There are no words to describe the ordeal of enslaved mothers on board slave ships. The Atlantic crossing from the Loango coast to Saint-Domingue lasted approximately sixty days. More than two days of dehydration compromised the mother's ability to nurse a baby, which also explains the higher levels of mortality among infants during the Middle Passage.

The image of a bondswoman nursing a baby in a floating tomb is one that juxtaposes the certainty of death with the strength of life. Drawing from this powerful representation of African women's resilience during the era of the Atlantic slave trade, this chapter shows that giving birth and raising enslaved children added further layers of violence to the lives of bondswomen. Motherhood under slavery was one of the most challenging and tragic experiences faced by enslaved women.[5] The legal doctrine of *partus sequitur ventrem*, stemming from Roman law and adopted in the Americas, established that newborns inherited the legal status of their mothers. In other words, upon birth, newborns automatically became the property of the enslaved mother's owner. As stated by Jennifer Morgan, for enslaved women in the

Americas, "reproduction almost immediately took on an entirely new and violent significance."[6]

In response, bondswomen in Brazil, the United States, and the West Indies resisted reproduction as much as they could by using plants to induce abortions and by practicing infanticide.[7] Throughout their lives, captive mothers faced the tragic and enduring dilemma of reconciling the love for their sons and daughters with the fact that these same children were the property of the men and women who kept them in bondage. Throughout the Americas, but especially in Brazil, slave owners purchased enslaved mothers to breastfeed their newborns, forcing them to neglect their own progeny. Only with the rise of the abolitionist movement and the enactment of legislation gradually abolishing slavery in the Americas was the conundrum created by the principle of *partus sequitur ventrem* slowly dismantled. Drawing from these themes, this chapter examines how enslaved women responded to the challenges of motherhood.

Mothering Enslaved Children

All over the Americas, male slave owners fathered children with enslaved women who were their property. They also fathered children with bondswomen with whom they had informal unions or with enslaved women owned by other individuals. As part of the sexual economy that emerged with Atlantic slavery, bondswomen impregnated by their own owners who brought to term their pregnancies gave birth to enslaved children, who ultimately contributed to the increase in size of their owner's slaveholdings.[8]

In some cases, enslaved mothers may have considered engaging in sexual relations with their owners and giving birth to their enslaved children as a possible path to emancipation. For example, despite its small numbers, in the British colony of Jamaica, some slave owners used their wills to manumit the offspring they produced with bondswomen, opening the path of social mobility to these freed children.[9] Similarly in Latin America, where Catholicism shaped slavery systems, it was not uncommon for slave owners to use their wills to free the children they had fathered with enslaved women. Take the example of the slave ship captain Jacinto Gomes, who owned the enslaved woman Antonia, with whom he also cohabitated. Together the couple had two male children, Domingos and Manoel. In his will of 1752, Gomes declared that he had already freed Antonia and his two sons. Although born into slavery, because these two men and their mother were emancipated by their white owner and father, they ended up having access to considerable social mobility in eighteenth-century Bahia.[10]

The nineteenth century offers other similar examples. Consider the case of Luzia Jeje, an enslaved woman likely transported from the Bight of Benin to Brazil, who was sold into slavery in Salvador, Bahia, during the second half of the eighteenth century. Luzia became the property of Captain Manoel de Oliveira Barrozo, who impregnated her six times. In his will of 1807, he emancipated Luzia and all six of their children and made them his heirs.[11] Like Gomes's children, and Chica da Silva's children discussed in chapter 10, not only were Luzia's offspring freed, but because they were mixed-race individuals, they could distance themselves and their descendants from a past associated with slavery.[12]

Likewise, Pedro Corrêa e Castro, known as Baron of Tinguá, was a rich owner of coffee plantations and enslaved people in Vassouras, a town in the Paraíba Valley in today's state of Rio de Janeiro. Corrêa e Castro remained a bachelor all his life, but he had six children with his African-born enslaved woman Laura Congo. Corrêa e Castro freed upon baptism his first four enslaved daughters, but like many Brazilian slave owners, Corrêa e Castro failed to publicly recognize the girls as his offspring while he was alive. Still in 1849, he freed Laura Congo as well, therefore her younger daughter and son were born when she was already a freedwoman. In 1865, when Corrêa e Castro wrote his will, four of his daughters were adult and married. In his will, opened after his death, he freed twenty-six of his enslaved people, donated money to his bondspeople, recognized being the father of

Laura's six children, made them his heirs, and bequeathed to Laura and her children a significant amount of money and several enslaved persons.[13] Although Laura was never legally married to her owner, eventually her children not only were recognized but also inherited property. In Córdoba (in present-day Argentina) and other parts of Latin America, men of European descent as well as Black men who married enslaved women owned by other people sought to purchase the freedom of their children, who had inherited their mother's slave legal status. Some enslaved women even sought to pay for their offspring's manumission before their birth.[14]

Mothering enslaved children may have been less difficult when bondswomen were engaged in more stable unions with free and enslaved men, and when they performed less strenuous tasks in domestic environments of urban areas. Whereas slaveholding families delegated childcare to enslaved women, bondswomen faced enormous challenges to provide care for their own babies and young children. Starting at a young age, enslaved mothers worked extremely long hours in the fields, in towns, and in their owners' households. Illustrations of European travel accounts published in the eighteenth and nineteenth centuries (see, for example, figure 8.3) as well as staged photographs featuring Black women who toiled in the cities reveal how bondswomen reconciled motherhood with their daily work activities.

Although it remains hard to determine whether these visual images portray enslaved, freed, or free women, they show us women street vendors transporting food on the tops of their heads, while also transporting their babies in slings. Regardless of the environment, bondswomen had very few hours of rest and sleep. In eighteenth-century urban Brazil, some enslaved women were left with no other choice than anonymously abandoning their babies to charity institutions, which also rented the services of enslaved wet nurses to breastfeed abandoned children.[15] Giving away a newborn allowed these women to get rid of the burden of motherhood under slavery. It was also a possible path to freeing a child whose legal status was often unknown to the religious institutions that received the abandoned babies.[16]

Motherhood was even more challenging where women labored in the fields of large plantations. Take the example of Jamaica. Enslaved women performed field labor while carrying their babies in a sling for several hours under the hot sun in humid weather. When these little ones began to walk, they accompanied their mothers to the field, therefore dividing their attention between childcare and the daily, often heavy tasks of the fields. Starting in the second half of the eighteenth century, plantation managers assigned older enslaved women whose poor health made them less suitable to work in the fields as child caregivers. This innovation not only increased the productivity of enslaved mothers but also introduced the older children to the field work they would perform in the future.[17] Because the abolitionist movement denounced the negative impact of field work on enslaved women's fertility, some planters started exempting enslaved mothers of six or more children from laboring in the fields in the early nineteenth century.[18] But these were not humanitarian gestures. During a new era when planters had to increasingly rely on bondswomen to produce new slaves, these initiatives were rather intended to preserve the lives of future enslaved children.[19] Indeed, on some plantations, slave owners even provided financial and material rewards to pregnant enslaved women.[20]

Breastfeeding Their Own Children, and the Children of Their Owners

Enslaved mothers all over the Americas breastfed their own children and occasionally the babies of other enslaved women. Slave owners also employed nursing bondswomen to breastfeed their newborns. On plantations in the southern colonies of British North America, white women were more likely to nurse their own babies during the eighteenth century.[21] In the nineteenth-century US South, however, observers at that time reported that white mistresses also used their bondswomen to suckle their newborns.[22] In any event, the presence of enslaved nannies in Southern households is well documented in

FIGURE 12.3. Thomas Martin Easterly, *Father, Daughters, and Nurse*, c. 1850. Daguerreotype, hand-colored, 2 13/16 × 3½ inches, 84.XT.1569.1. Courtesy of Jean Paul Getty Museum, Los Angeles, CA, United States.

written records and existing visual images such as daguerreotypes (figures 12.3 and 12.4) featuring these bondswomen, whose ages and names we do not know, posing with their owners and the owners' children. In Jamaica, white elite women used white wet nurses to suckle their babies in the early nineteenth century. But white mothers of lower and middle classes either nursed their own children or employed enslaved women as wet nurses.[23] In Brazil and the United States, several justifications motivated white women to delegate breastfeeding to enslaved women, including the widespread belief that elite white women produced weak milk, the white women's weak health, and even the simple fact that nursing was an exhausting and boring task.[24]

Slave owners also used bondswomen as wet nurses in the Spanish Americas and later in independent countries of Latin America. Michelle McKinley explains that the use of Black enslaved wet nurses to suckle white children in colonial Peru "illustrates the split logic of property most sharply, since legally the mother's milk belonged to her owner and not to her child."[25] In Brazil and in the United States, slaveholding families sought to use their own enslaved women to breastfeed their infants. But when no bondswoman was available to perform this demanding task in the household, slaveholding families either purchased or rented the services of an enslaved wet nurse. Between 1800 and 1865, thousands of advertisements sought wet nurses in dozens of newspapers in several regions of the United

FIGURE 12.4. Unknown maker, *Portrait of a Nurse and a Child*, c. 1850. Daguerreotype, hand-colored, 2 7/16 × 1 7/8 inches. 84.XT.172.4. Courtesy of Jean Paul Getty Museum, Los Angeles, CA, United States.

States, whereas many other ads also announced enslaved wet nurses for sale. Moreover, when the internal slave trade intensified in the decades preceding the Civil War, the market for enslaved wet nurses increased. White women actively sought to purchase enslaved wet nurses and clearly valued their work.[26] But whereas enslaved mothers were forced to breastfeed their owners' newborns, they had to use a bottle to nurse their own babies.[27]

As in the United States (and as discussed in chapter 8), Brazilian newspapers regularly displayed advertisements either offering or seeking enslaved wet nurses for rent or purchase. Many enslaved wet nurses were young mothers, between eighteen and twenty years of age, who were sold with their babies.[28] But some ads described enslaved wet nurses as childless and of "first pregnancy," suggesting that although their babies did not survive, they could still breastfeed.[29] Ads offering for sale and rent grieving mothers who lost a newborn and whose breasts were still full of milk shows how slave owners subjected bondswomen to extreme physical and psychological exploitation in a society in which infant mortality was particularly high, especially among enslaved children.[30]

French traveler Charles Expilly, who sojourned in Brazil during the nineteenth century, observed that owning a wet nurse was also a marker of social status in Brazilian slaveholding families. Because wet nurses were in constant contact with slave owners, they were usually offered better working and living conditions than other enslaved women who performed domestic service. Their social status is confirmed by the existence of early photographic portraits of enslaved wet nurses and nannies holding the babies of their owners in their arms. One of these portraits (figure 12.5) features a young enslaved nanny. Sitting on a chair, and seen from profile, she is holding a white baby. As the daguerreotype is blurred and scratched, both sitters seem to be a ghost of the past. As for many enslaved sitters, her name remains unknown to this day. But we do know she was associated with the family of a British merchant, Alfred Phillips Youle, who lived in Recife, Pernambuco, Brazil, in the middle of the nineteenth century

FIGURE 12.5. Charles DeForest Fredricks, *Black Woman Shown Seated in 3/4 View*. Daguerreotype, 7 × 9 inches. Collection Portraits of a British Merchant Family in Brazil, D2. Courtesy of Getty Research Institute Special Collections, Los Angeles, CA, United States.

and whose wife, Annie Stewart Schwind, belonged to a Liverpool family deeply involved in the trade of enslaved Africans. What was the sitter's name? How old was she? Was Youle her owner? Was she ever manumitted? These answers are unknown, but because her image was captured in a daguerreotype, we can assume she was well regarded. Even though we do not know who she was, she was immortalized in this intimate portrait that feature her large eyes calmly looking at the camera while taking care of the white baby.

Slave owners held enslaved wet nurses in high regard for their potential utility, which is why they were usually provided better clothes and a healthier diet. But by the middle of the nineteenth century, the increasing influence of pseudoscientific racist theories in Brazil led physicians to condemn the use of Black wet nurses to breastfeed white newborns. Using the derogatory term "mercenary nursing," they claimed Black wet nurses transmitted through their milk a variety of diseases and contributed to physically and morally degenerate Brazilian families.[31] One physician criticized mothers of Rio de Janeiro's high society who refused to breastfeed their own children and instead delivered their babies to enslaved wet nurses who were forced to neglect and even abandon their own children.[32]

Although wet nurses did not provide heavy manual labor in the fields, breastfeeding their own babies and their owners' newborns was a very painful and arduous job. Such imposed choices could lead to tragedy. Consider the case of the Brazilian-born enslaved woman Ambrosina, explored by historian Maria Helena Machado. Ambrosina lived and worked in the house of a municipal judge in the town of Mogi Mirim in the Paraíba Valley coffee plantation region. In 1886, two years before the abolition of slavery in Brazil, she gave birth to a baby boy, who according to the Rio Branco Law (Free Womb) of 1871 was a free womb captive who could be totally emancipated once he reached twenty-one years of age. That same year, Ambrosina's owners also welcomed a newborn. Both the Black and the white newborns were named Benedito. As expected, the new enslaved mother became the white baby's wet nurse. But because Ambrosina's mistress was ill, her husband decided to move to Taubaté, nearly 140 miles away, to temporarily live with his mother and brother. He brought with him his newborn, an enslaved nanny, Ambrosina, and her own baby.

This relocation removed the wet nurse from her environment and distanced her from her parents. Yet her owner agreed that he would soon find another wet nurse to replace her, allowing her to return to Mogi Mirim, where her family lived. But he failed to fulfill the agreement. Weeks later, Ambrosina was still in Taubaté, lodged in a small room shared with a nanny and her owner's baby, where she slept on the floor with her own son. Exhausted from being far from her family while breastfeeding two babies day and night, one night Ambrosina used a ragdoll to make the white Benedito stop crying. The newborn suffocated and died. Accused of killing the baby, Ambrosina was arrested. But the jury eventually acquitted her for lack of evidence. Existing records do not allow us to know if the Black Benedito survived his enslaved mother's ordeal.[33] Ambrosina's story ultimately shows how enslaved mothers who were forced to nurse the children of their owners had to neglect their own children, while also risking their own lives if something went wrong when taking care of white people's offspring.

Haunted by Tragedy

Bondswomen were obviously aware that their children were enslaved upon birth. As mothers, they were also conscious that they could be separated from their children at any time. Before their offspring reached adulthood, many enslaved women were likely to face tragic moments that led them to make the extremely difficult choice to unwillingly engage their children in the daily atrocities of slavery. As a drastic measure, some enslaved mothers attempted and sometimes succeeded in killing their children and taking their own lives. Such tragedies occurred throughout the entire era of Atlantic slavery in various regions of the Americas. Although bondswomen's specific motives for infanticide are rarely clear in surviving written sources, one can infer that either one specific traumatic event or the long sequence of atrocities endured by these women led them to commit extreme acts of violence against their own kin. In most cases, enslaved women seemed to have impulsively murdered their own children rather than subject them to the horrors of slavery. But a closer look at their actions may reveal that to some extent these murders were planned. Their stories show how motherhood represented a deadlock for many bondswomen.

The combination of motherhood and slavery was haunted by tragedy. Although the Roman Catholic Church ruled that slave owners should not separate enslaved mothers from their children, especially young children who were still feeding on mother's milk, the principle was not always respected, especially when financial matters were in play.[34] Moreover, even when enslaved parents purchased the freedom of their children, such agreements were not always fulfilled.[35] In the Viceroyalty of New Granada, which corresponds to the present-day region of today's Colombia, Ecuador, Panama, and Venezuela, one historian uncovered the case of Phelipa, a forty-year-old married enslaved woman who lived with her husband and two children in the region of Tolima, in modern-day Colombia. All the family was owned by the same man, Don Pedro de Sarachaga, with whom they went to a rodeo, an event during which cattle were branded and counted, in January 1768. While the owner handled the cattle with other men, the news came that Phelipa had stabbed herself as well as her sixteen-year-old son Joseph Victor and her five-year-old daughter Catharina. Whereas Phelipa and her son survived, the young Catharina died the day after. According to one witness, when asked why she killed her child, Phelipa responded that her owner would separate them. Yet, to another witness she said she stabbed her children for the love she had for them, love that refused to accept the violence of slavery that separated a mother and her children.[36] Phelipa's case was not unique. In the 1780s, in response to the mistreatment inflicted on them by her owner, a case of an enslaved mother who committed infanticide in a gold mine of the province of Barbacoas in Colombia was uncovered as well.[37]

Similar cases of enslaved mothers who took the lives of their enslaved children also occurred in Brazil. In some regions, these cases were documented in detail. Take the example of Maria, an enslaved woman who lived and worked in the then-captaincy of São Pedro do Rio Grande do Sul in Brazil.[38] In 1819, when Maria was around twenty-four years old, she killed her two children by slitting their throats. As with many enslaved women living in remote regions of

Brazil, we do not know much about Maria, but the records of the criminal proceedings and trial that followed this tragedy allow us to draw a broader picture of what her life may have looked like.

Maria was born in the late eighteenth century in Rio Grande, a coastal town in the south of present-day Rio Grande do Sul, not far from the boarder with Uruguay, and lived in slavery in a rural area north of the then municipality of Porto Alegre. With a total population of 52,226, of which nearly 30 percent were enslaved in 1810, the captaincy of Rio Grande do Sul was scarcely populated in comparison to other Brazilian captaincies such as Rio de Janeiro.[39] Unlike other plantation and mining regions in the Americas, cattle ranching and jerk beef factories were the most important economic activities employing the work of enslaved men and women in this region.[40] In addition to the cold and humid weather, the working and living conditions for the enslaved population were extremely hard in Rio Grande do Sul.[41]

Maria's owners, José Bittencourt Cidade and Angélica Velosa da Fontoura Azambuja, owned other human property as well. In 1825, just six years after the tragic death of Maria's children, twenty-eight Brazilian-born and African-born enslaved men, women, and children of various ages were listed in Cidade's postmortem inventory. Like other enslaved women working in rural households, Maria probably performed domestic tasks such as cooking, cleaning, and sewing. We do not know exactly what she looked like, but at age twenty-four, after at least two pregnancies brought to term, her body reportedly was robust. Her face was round, her eyes black, her hair curly, and her lips thick. Identified as single, she had two children, Manoel and Manoela, but surviving records do not reveal their exact ages. Manoel was probably older than five, as he already performed some tasks in the household. Younger, Manoela was likely a toddler.

Existing records do not allow us to understand how Maria became a mother. But a portrait of the enslaved population living in the estate where she was enslaved provides us with some clues. In 1825, Maria's owner held twenty-eight enslaved persons, a high number for a remote region like Rio Grande do Sul. Most of these slaves were born in Africa and were identified as belonging to Hausa, Cabinda, Mina, Mozambique, Benguela, and Congo groups of provenance. Among these enslaved persons, there were twenty-one males, including one enslaved boy and two other enslaved young men fourteen years old. But among the twenty-eight slaves there were only seven enslaved women. Moreover, only four of them, aged between twenty and twenty-eight, were of reproductive age. We do not know who among these enslaved persons already lived and worked in Cidade's estate when Maria killed her two children, and the records do not allow us to conclude that any of these enslaved persons were married. But the large number of men for the small number of women suggests they had more than one male partner. Therefore, Maria's children Manoel and Manoela could have been the offspring of any of the enslaved adult males who lived in the estate, including two enslaved men who were also named Manoel, which, like Maria, was a very common name in Brazil. As with other bondswomen living in the domestic spaces, Maria was also exposed to physical and psychological abuse and was at the mercy of her master and his male children's sexual advances. Consequently, it would not be surprising if her owner or his male children had sex with Maria and impregnated her.[42]

The days that led to the horrible night of March 15 must have been particularly traumatizing to Maria. She worked in the domestic space and so knew where her owner kept his razor. Maria was in her bedroom on March 15, 1819, at dawn after what must have been a warm night in rural Rio Grande do Sul. Like the quarters of other enslaved people living in Brazil during the nineteenth century, the bedroom where she slept with her two children was more likely a narrow filthy dungeon. The room was located near the kitchen, allowing Maria to be available both day and night to respond to her owners' calls. She may have seen him shaving several times before she decided that the razor was the best weapon to end her miserable life and that of her children. On March 14, Maria took her owner's razor and brought it to her room. She needed determination to act fast as she would not be able to keep the razor in her room without her owner noticing the blade was gone. We do not know the horrible thoughts that preceded Maria's fatal actions, but early that morning, about seven o'clock, she slit Manoel's and Manoela's throats and then tried to slit her own.

After being arrested and during her interrogation, Maria did not narrate her tragedy in detail. Even though they did not witness the moment when Maria carried out the infanticide and attempted to end her own life, the various witnesses who provided testimonies during the criminal proceedings repeated the same story, based on what Angélica, Maria's mistress, told them. According to Angélica, she was awake by 7:00 a.m. and noticed that Manoel had failed to show up to perform his early morning tasks. Assuming Maria and her two children had run away, Angélica began to search for the trio but curiously failed to look in the enslaved woman's bedroom near the kitchen. At some point she heard Manoel screaming that his mother was trying to kill him. Angélica asked for help to break the room's door open and found Maria and her two children inside with their throats slit. Manoela was dead, but Manoel and Maria were still alive. When asked what happened to him, by showing his fingers cut by the razor, the enslaved boy indicated that his mother attacked him while he was trying to defend himself. Manoel did not survive, but Maria did.

After being arrested, during her interrogatory, Maria stated that she had no intent to murder her children but only to kill herself. According to her answers, she had been accused of wrongs committed by other enslaved persons on the estate. As argued by Maria's legal representative in his passionate defense, the only plausible explanation she had for attacking her children was the psychological and physical abuse her mistress inflicted on her.[43] His conclusions were not surprising. White women purchased and sold enslaved people. They were not only slave owners, however. They also reinforced the violence their husbands perpetrated on bondspeople. Even sociologist Gilberto Freyre—who wrongly claimed that slave owners and enslaved people entertained harmonious relations in Brazil—has provided numerous examples of how female slave owners inflicted physical punishments on bondswomen. These stories include young mistresses who had the eyes of beautiful enslaved maids "gouged out and then served to their husbands for dessert in a jelly dish, floating in blood that was still fresh," and "young adult baronesses who out of jealousy or spite had fifteen-year-old mulatto girls sold off to old libertines."[44]

Similar accounts also existed in the United States, where enslaved women were likewise victimized by their mistresses.[45] Curiously, Maria's criminal proceedings do not mention the testimonies of Maria's owners, which suggests that they did not testify. As enslaved people could not testify under oath before a judge at the time of these tragic events, we will never know their point of view on the tragedy. But even more disturbing is the fact that Maria's body was not examined for any signs of physical mistreatment. Here, the violence of slavery overpowered the abstract notion of maternal love. Maria knew that as a mother in bondage, the only power she had to keep her children out of slavery was to kill them. Only such a desperate act could free them from a future of extreme physical and psychological abuse.

Maria's tragic story is one of many involving enslaved mothers who killed their children after being constantly abused by male and female slave owners in the Americas. Just a few years after Maria's tragedy, on October 29, 1824, another bondswoman also named Maria killed her son Adão. An African-born enslaved woman in her early forties, this second Maria lived in Rio Pardo, Rio Grande do Sul, in the household of her owners, Captain Manuel Baptista de Mello and his wife Bernardina, who lived off of the income generated by their bondspeople who hired themselves out in the city. Adão's age is not revealed in the criminal proceedings, but he was young enough to live in the same room with his mother, and yet old enough to escape. Therefore, Maria's owners held her responsible for keeping her son locked in her room to prevent him from fleeing at night. Maria knew that if her son escaped, she would be blamed and beaten.

One night, Adão used a nail to pry open the locked door and then escaped. Holding Maria responsible for not properly locking the door, her owners severely punished her. When Adão came back home late at night, Maria had been physically abused. Desperate, she grabbed a knife from the kitchen table and then stabbed her son in the neck, hitting his jugular vein and killing him instantly. The same legal representative who represented the first Maria ardently defended this second Maria as well, by stating that "maternal love, the duty of nature, is only capable of producing in the mother the defense of her child, and it is never cold-blooded to intend, and less, to cause her death." He insisted that a "violent motive, invincible circumstances, and despair certainly guided the defendant."[46] Ultimately, he emphasized that Maria's desperate act was motivated by the physical punishment and psychological abuse inflicted by her owners.

Yet another enslaved woman named Maria killed her one-year-old toddler Ricardo and her five-year old daughter Cecília in Rio Grande do Sul as well. Born in West Central Africa, this third Maria was single, and the records from her interrogation identified her group of provenance as Monjolo. Maria lived in the household of her owner, Sebastião José Bernardes, in Viamão, by then part of the municipality of Porto Alegre. On the night of March 27, 1828, Bernardes started looking for Maria and found two of her three children with their throats slit nearly three hundred feet from his house. Based on Maria's responses to the interrogatory and the defense by her legal representative, she was overcome by rage after her owner repeatedly forced her to provide "services superior to her forces" and inflicted on her and her children excessive physical punishments. As he constantly got enraged and irritated, Maria begged him to be sold, without any success.[47] We do not know what exactly these physical punishments were, but Maria's requests to be sold suggest that she was raped, and no one would be surprised if her three children had been the result of impregnation by Bernardes. Although Maria's defense defined her fatal gesture as a sudden rage, killing her children was her only way out of her owner's abuse and so could have been premeditated. The criminal justice system in place in the colonial era and after 1822 in independent Brazil imposed harsh sentences on enslaved women who killed their infants. But to some extent, the sentences imposed on the three Marias recognized their desperate acts in response to the extreme violence of slavery. The first Maria, who killed her two young children in 1819, was brutally sentenced to five hundred lashes and penal exile in Benguela in West Central Africa, therefore showing how deep the links were between Portuguese colonies on both sides of the South Atlantic Ocean. The second Maria, who killed her son in 1824, was also sentenced to five hundred lashes. By then Brazil was independent from Portugal, and instead of being sent into penal exile in West Central Africa, she was sent into perpetual exile to work in a Brazilian hospital for lepers. The third Maria, who killed two of her three children in 1828, however, received a milder sentence of ten years in prison. In general, these sentences were less harsh than those imposed on enslaved women who committed capital crimes in the United States. Although they can be explained by the influence of Roman Catholicism and the Roman law in the Portuguese Empire and Brazil, keeping alive enslaved women who committed infanticide was also a way to keep exploiting their workforce in the harshest possible conditions in colonies that used penal exile to populate inhospitable regions in the Southern Hemisphere.

Enslaved women were also driven to kill their enslaved children in the United States. Nine years before the abolition of slavery, the enslaved woman Margaret Garner was in her twenties and worked on a plantation in Boone County, Kentucky. She married Robert Garner, a bondsman who worked on a neighboring estate. In 1856, along with other enslaved people, Margaret, her husband, and their four children escaped. The group crossed the Ohio River to arrive in Cincinnati, from where they hoped to reach Canada. But once in Cincinnati, their owner, Archibald Gaines, along with several US officers, besieged the cabin where the family was hiding. Refusing to return to slavery, Margaret slit the throat of her two-year-old daughter. She also unsuccessfully attempted to take the lives of her other three children and her own.[48] Garner's dreadful story inspired the award-winning novel *Beloved* by Toni Morrison, a motion picture and an opera that also resembles in many ways the cases of the three Maria bondswomen who had killed their enslaved children in the deep south of Brazil three decades earlier.[49] Garner's tragedy again brings to light the dilemma faced by enslaved women who gave birth to children who not only were property of their owners but who in a number of cases also were the owners' offspring as well.

Undermining *Partus Sequitur Ventrem*

The American War of Independence helped sow the seeds of doubt that undermined the doctrine of *partus sequitur ventrem*. The first debates on abolishing slavery in the thirteen British colonies started before the war, but most of the legislation aimed at gradually ending slavery in the North of the region that became the United States of America was progressively enacted only after the end of the conflict. In the Northern states where the enslaved population was rather small, enslaved babies born to enslaved women after the enactment of gradual abolition legislation were to be emancipated upon reaching adulthood. For example, in 1777, the constitution of the new state of Vermont declared that enslaved male and female newborns would be declared free, respectively, at twenty-one years and eighteen years of age.[50] The fourth section of Pennsylvania's Act for the Gradual Abolition of Slavery of 1780 included several measures to gradually abolish slavery, including the prohibition of the importation of new enslaved persons and the creation of a slave register. However, the act also established that newly born enslaved children would remain enslaved for twenty-eight years.[51] Although this was still a very long period, slave owners took measures to bypass the legislation. In addition to continuing to import enslaved people to Pennsylvania, they transported pregnant bondswomen to give birth to their children in states where *partus sequitur ventrem* remained in force.

Enslaved mothers in other Northern states of the newly independent United States could also foresee a ray of hope for their enslaved children. Rhode Island adopted legislation stating that the children of enslaved women born after March 1784 were to be freed upon reaching twenty-one years of age if they were male or eighteen years of age if they were female.[52] Likewise, in March 1784, Connecticut passed the "Act Concerning Indian, Mulatto, and Negro Servants and Slaves," which emancipated the offspring of enslaved mothers born after the date of its passing and upon reaching twenty-five years of age.[53] An act adopted in May 1797 reduced the emancipation age to twenty-one. In the decades that followed, Northern states with larger enslaved populations also passed legislation freeing newborns. On July 4, 1799, New York, the US Northern state with the largest number of bondspeople, passed legislation establishing that males born to enslaved women were to be freed at age twenty-eight and females at age twenty-five. On July 4, 1804, New Jersey eventually adopted similar legislation freeing newly born children to enslaved mothers. But there were always age restrictions. Enslaved women would be fully emancipated at twenty-one years and enslaved men at twenty-five years of age.[54] Ultimately, in all these Northern states, enslaved mothers may have been relieved to know that their infants would not spend their entire lives in bondage even though that had no immediate impact on them.

During the nineteenth century, as Spanish colonies in the Americas acquired independence and gradually separated themselves to become sovereign countries, they enacted free womb laws that unsettled the principle according to which children of enslaved women inherited the slave status of their mothers. In 1811, Chile enacted legislation freeing newborns right away. Yet all the other regions made these infants "Free Womb captives," a term coined by historian Yesenia Barragan to underscore that these "children were free yet captive."[55] For example, Buenos Aires, a part of the region of the United Provinces of Río de La Plata, in 1813 ratified a law gradually emancipating newly born children to enslaved mothers. Yet, these freed children had to provide unpaid work to their owners until the age of fifteen, when they started receiving a remuneration of one peso per month. Full emancipation only occurred after they married or when they reached majority age, twenty years old for men and sixteen years old for women. Moreover, slave owners could sell, buy, and bequeath these freed young individuals until they came of age.[56]

Enslaved mothers became acquainted with the new legislation limiting the time that their newly born children would live in bondage in various regions of the Americas. In the Northern colonies of the United States, these mothers had very limited resources to fight slave owners who denied their infants' freedom even after the passage of free womb laws. Moreover, many children born to bondswomen after the enactment of free womb laws did not know their place of birth and exact age. Therefore, they could hardly claim their freedom even once they reached adulthood and were eligible to be fully emancipated. Despite these major obstacles, some enslaved women used this legislation to fight for their children's emancipation. When slave owners circumvented the new laws in Latin America, bondswomen went to the courts to claim the rights of their children.

One particular case, uncovered by historian Magdalena Candioti, illustrates the ways the free womb legislation affected enslaved mothers in what is now Argentina. In 1823, Ana Monterroso, a woman from Buenos Aires, purchased Petrona, an enslaved woman in her early twenties who lived and worked in the small town of Santa Fé. After the purchase was concluded, Petrona was sent to join her new owner in Buenos Aires, 300 miles south east of Santa Fé. Upon Petrona's arrival, Monterroso started arranging her relocation to Montevideo, the capital of present-day Uruguay, a region that remained under Portuguese control from 1816 to 1828. Although this kind of move was not uncommon in the region, after the enactment of legislation prohibiting the slave trade to Buenos Aires and freeing newborns, relocation became a widespread strategy among slave owners seeking to avoid the restrictions imposed by gradual abolition of slavery. Petrona had reason to protest her owner's relocation because she was pregnant. Whereas in Buenos Aires the free womb law had been in force since 1813, in then Portuguese-controlled Montevideo, newborns were to remain enslaved.[57] Petrona's owner gave her a letter manumitting the unborn child, but the enslaved woman continued to resist relocation.

In response, her owner put her up for sale, which led Petrona to go to court to contest her relocation because it would directly affect the legal status of her child. The case generated a rich legal debate regarding the status of the unborn child as free or freed.[58] As the legal case evolved, Petrona's boy was born, baptized, and registered as a freed person. Through her fight, she avoided giving birth in Montevideo, where her baby would have had the legal status of a slave. Yet like all enslaved women's children born after the adoption of free womb laws, the boy remained under the control of Petrona's owner until reaching twenty years of age.

As other parts of South America became independent, they also passed free womb legislation. On July 21, 1821, Gran Colombia (a region corresponding to today's Ecuador, Colombia, Venezuela, and Panama) passed legislation freeing newborns after they reached eighteen years old.[59] As an independent country, Uruguay enacted free womb legislation in 1825; whereas both Bolivia and Paraguay passed laws freeing newly born infants in 1831 and 1842, respectively. In all these countries, as in the North of the United States, slave owners resisted the new legislation. In several newly independent nations, when free womb captives approached the age to be fully emancipated, slave owners managed to delay the age of majority. For example, independent Peru increased the emancipation age to fifty years old in 1839. In 1839 and 1843, respectively, Venezuela and Ecuador delayed the age of full emancipation to twenty-five years.[60] Moreover, Colombia passed new legislation in 1842 imposing on free womb captives who were once expected to be fully emancipated in 1839 an apprenticeship system until the age of twenty-five. In societies where life expectancy was approximately twenty-five years, these new restrictions virtually imposed lifetime bondage on free womb captives.[61]

On July 4, 1870, the Spanish Parliament passed the Moret Law that started the process of gradual abolition of slavery in Puerto Rico and Cuba. Two articles of the law concerned children of bondswomen.[62] The first article declared freed all newborns to enslaved mothers after the law's adoption, and the second article emancipated all slaves born after September 17, 1868. But this new legislation also created a *patronato* (patronage) system determining that *libertos* (freedpeople) were to remain working for the enslaved mother's owner for twenty-two years.[63] Brazil also enacted the Rio Branco Law or Free Womb Law (Law no. 20140) on September 28, 1871.[64] Similarly to legislation emancipating newly born infants of enslaved mothers enacted in other parts of the Americas, the first article of the law established that the child would remain in the custody of the enslaved mother's owner until age eight, when the owner could decide either to free the child and receive financial compensation from the Brazilian state or to continue using the child's services for free until they were twenty-one.[65] In this context, free womb captives remained under the tutelage of their mothers' owners and were even listed as their property in postmortem inventories.[66] In Cuba, the Moret Law prevented the separation of enslaved mothers from their free womb children. But if bondswomen managed to purchase their own freedom within the period of twenty-one years but were not able to amass the necessary amount to pay for the freedom of their offspring, they could be separated from their children.[67] As all these cases show, all over the Americas, even if gradual abolition slowly evolved starting in the late eighteenth century, enslaved mothers kept fighting for the freedom of their children.

In the Womb of Slavery

Slavery and the Atlantic slave trade commodified the bodies of enslaved women by making their wombs the site of production of new enslaved persons. Many bondswomen sought to control their own fertility and avoid giving birth to newborns who they knew would be the property of their owners. In a context of intrinsic violence, where physical punishment was an inherent threat, enslaved mothers had to face the constant dilemma of choosing between their own children and their owners' offspring. From time to time, however, there was no choice. In these circumstances, some bondswomen were pushed to take extreme actions, killing their own children and themselves. Despite the tragedies that permeated the daily lives of enslaved mothers, more often than not in addition to raising their own children, they tended to other bondswomen's kids and took care of their owners' little ones. Eventually, the rise of gradual abolition legislation in the Americas, which started in the late eighteenth century but accelerated during the second half of the nineteenth century, brought hope to enslaved mothers, as free womb laws promised to free their newborns once they reached adulthood. But once again, bondswomen had to fight. They resisted relocation to other regions where free womb legislation was not in force, and they attempted to purchase the freedom of their children before the end of the established terms. When their efforts failed, some bondswomen living in urban areas used the courts to achieve their goals. As we will see in subsequent chapters, enslaved women, including mothers, continued to struggle in all possible ways.

CHAPTER 13

Resisting Bondage

Monica woke up dizzy in the middle of that cold night of July 1820 in the deep south of Brazil. She still could feel the bitter taste of *cachaça* in her dry mouth. Her body was aching from the beating her owner had once again inflicted on her. Drunk, the man had practically passed out and was still sleeping beside her. She spotted an axe that she used to chop wood to cook and heat the house during the infamously cold and humid winters in the then-captaincy of Rio Grande de São Pedro do Sul, today the state of Rio Grande do Sul. She gathered her strength and struck her owner with the axe, killing him.[1]

We do not know if these events occurred exactly in this order. But it is probably accurate to assume that Monica killed her owner while he was sleeping; otherwise, she risked being killed herself during the attack. Also, Monica never confessed to having killed her master, with whom she lived in a remote, rural area, working in the fields and providing him sexual services. But in her testimony during the criminal investigation, she explained that her owner got drunk every weekend, and when he did so, he hit her. That night, she decided that he would never beat her again. Monica was not alone. Despite facing harsh consequences, all over the Americas other enslaved men and women were successful in putting an end to their captivity by killing their owners.

At every stage of the Atlantic slave trade, from their capture and transportation to their life in bondage in the Americas, bondspeople resisted the control and violence imposed by their enslavers.

Sometimes a combination of internal and external factors allowed enslaved men and women to collectively resist slavery—for instance, by running away in groups and forming runaway slave communities. In exceptional situations, enslaved people organized rebellions. In typical plantation settings, enslaved men and women engaged in passive forms of resistance. They reduced the pace of production and damaged equipment and tools. They also petitioned their owners to obtain better working and living conditions.

Take the well-known example of a group of enslaved men at the Santana *engenho* (sugar plantation and mill), in Bahia, Brazil. In 1789, the year of the French Revolution, a group of slaves killed the *engenho*'s overseer and escaped to a nearby settlement of runaway slaves (*mocambo*), bringing with them tools that rendered the mill they had left behind inactive. Public authorities sent an expedition of slave hunters and Native Brazilians to take down the *mocambo*. But the enterprise partly failed, and the fugitives eventually brokered a treaty with their enslavers that included several conditions that would improve their daily lives and give them control over their work.[2] In urban areas, enslaved people who worked in the domestic space daily resisted slavery using strategies such as stealing food to sell in the marketplace, feigning illness to avoid work, and simply undermining the accomplishment of daily tasks.[3]

Under certain circumstances, however, enslaved men and women took specific action to harm their owners. Bondswomen performing domestic work knew every detail concerning the intimate lives of their masters and mistresses. In this regard, kitchens were a crucial site of daily resistance. Gathered around the oven, enslaved women gossiped and plotted at dawn and during the late-night hours. Across the Americas, criminal records reveal stories of enslaved women who poisoned the food they served to their owners' families.[4] British and French planters feared being poisoned by bondspeople to the extent that from the seventeenth century onward, Jamaica's slave code stipulated a death penalty for the use of poison by enslaved people.[5] But enslaved men and women also opted for more extreme solutions to escape bondage, killing their masters and mistresses along with their children.

Enslaved women killed their owners as a response to rape and other forms of physical violence. Similar to the infanticide cases examined in chapter 12, acts of resistance also included self-harm, sometimes even to the point of choosing to die by suicide rather than continue their lives of slavery. By killing themselves, enslaved people halted the persistent cycle of physical and psychological abuse inflicted on them by their enslavers. As human property, their deaths also negatively affected the economic interests of their slave owners. This chapter shows how bondspeople individually and collectively resisted slavery in the Americas, especially in Brazil but also in colonial North America and the independent United States, as well as in the West Indies. In particular, I pay special attention to enslaved women's resistance and compare their insurgent acts with similar rebellious gestures performed by enslaved people in various slave societies throughout the Americas. Looking at acts of violent and passive resistance allows us to see how these contrasting kinds of actions contributed to undermine the institution of slavery, even when it was not possible to destroy it.

Escaping Bondage

Captive Africans attempted to escape their perpetrators during their marches from the interior to the coasts of Africa; they attempted to flee during the period they were kept confined in coastal structures such as fortresses, castles, and barracoons, along the African shores; and they led insurrections even once they were on board slave ships. As we will see, individually or in groups, bondspeople made continuous attempts to escape from bondage. Quite often, surviving records are silent about the details and circumstances that led enslaved men and women to escape from plantations, mines, and urban areas. Yet slave owners and slave merchants were always concerned about fugitive slaves. During the rise of the Atlantic slave trade, slave vessels were equipped with heavy iron chains and shackles, as discussed in chapter 4. Inspired by devices that had been used in ancient societies such as Greece and Rome, slave owners re-created slave collars not only to restrain enslaved individuals who attempted to escape but also to make these insurgent men and women visible in the communities in which they circulated.

Consider the example of Portugal, one of the kingdoms that initiated the Atlantic slave trade to the Iberian Peninsula and the Americas in the fifteenth century, as discussed in previous chapters. Enslaved Africans and their descendants toiled in Portuguese cities and surrounding rural areas. As in all regions where slavery existed, even prior to the massive enslavement of Black Africans, enslaved people resisted, which is why Portuguese compilations of laws, the *Ordenações afonsinas* (1446) and *Ordenações manuelinas* (1521), were created to address the issue of fugitive slaves, while the *Ordenações filipinas* (1603) included sentences to be imposed on people who helped fugitives from slavery.[6] In addition to these laws that coincided with the early days of the Atlantic slave trade, the National Museum of Archaeology in Lisbon recovered two eighteenth-century slave collars from the regions of Óbidos and Benavente that had been forgotten, or perhaps intentionally hidden, in its collections for several decades.[7] The collars illustrate how Portuguese slave owners feared and therefore attempted to prevent their human property from escaping. The two delicate copper-iron alloy necklaces bore large and visible engraved inscriptions that identify their owners and regions of residence. One inscription reads, "This *preto* [slave] belongs to Agostinho de Lafetá Carvalhais of Óbidos," and the other one, "This slave belongs to Luiz Cardozo de Mello resident of Benavente."[8] Both restraints are similar to ancient Roman devices dating back to the fourth and fifth centuries, such as the Zoninus collar that bears an analogous inscription, "I have run away; hold me. When you have brought me back to my master Zoninus you will receive a gold coin."[9]

Portugal was not the only country with museum exhibits that featured early artifacts intended to identify enslaved persons who might have tried to escape. The groundbreaking temporary exhibition *Slavery*

FIGURE 13.1. Collar with the Nassau crest, 1689. Brass, h. 2.8 cm, diam. 12 cm. Inv. no. BK-NM-5144; gift of Preuyt, Terheyden. Courtesy of Rijksmuseum, Amsterdam, Netherlands.

(*Slavernij*), on view at the Rijksmuseum from May 18 to August 29, 2021, included a more sophisticated version of a similar seventeenth-century brass neck restraint bearing the Nassau coat of arms and the year 1689. Whereas there was no doubt that the Portuguese collars were intended to be worn by two enslaved men, the Dutch artifact (figure 13.1) was initially mistakenly described as a dog collar. Any reference to the name of the person who wore it is absent, yet the combination of signs engraved on the collar did identify the likely owner of the human property as Anna Isabella van Beieren van Schagen, the Catholic wife of Maurits, the Count of Nassau La Lecq. Existing records indicate that the couple owned at least one servant named Paulus Maurus, whose name is certainly a reference to his African ancestry and possible slave legal status.[10]

European neck restraints and other instruments of torture became symbols of enslaved people's dehumanization. Secured by a lock, they

FIGURE 13.2. *Le collier de fer, Châtiment des fugitifs* (*Iron collar, Punishment of fugitives*), in Jean-Baptiste Debret, *Voyage pittoresque et historique au Brésil*, 3 vols. (Paris: Firmin Didot Frères, 1834–39), vol. 2, plate 42.

were difficult to remove. Yet in this context, their main purpose was not to physically punish these bondsmen. The neck restraints were instead designed to publicly identify the two enslaved men, thus making attempted escapes in their small communities very difficult. As slavery became a consolidated institution in the Americas, slave owners and their associates created huge and heavy iron slave collars of all sizes and shapes. These artifacts and their visual representations that illustrated many nineteenth-century European travelogues (figure 13.2) are today exhibited in various museums in Europe, Africa, and the Americas. Along with other restraint devices designed to punish enslaved people who attempted to run away, these instruments of torture were also intended to control, intimidate, and dissuade other bondspeople from trying to escape their bondage. Some runaway slave ads published in eighteenth-century newspapers in England and Scotland featured images of some fugitives, including enslaved men and women who fled in slave-trading ports such as Bristol and

Liverpool, wearing iron, steel, copper, and silver collars exactly like those found in Portugal and the Netherlands that bore the names of their owners.[11]

In societies where slavery played a central role such as the West Indies, Brazil, and the South of the United States, slave owners, plantation managers, and overseers instilled fear among enslaved people by publicly displaying their power through employing a variety of instruments of torture. In large sugar and coffee plantations, slaveholders also used other devices to inflict physical abuse, such as wooden bed stocks and whipping posts where recaptured fugitives were punished. Enslaved men and women who attempted to escape were often forced to wear heavy iron collars to deter further attempts. Nevertheless, existing fugitive slave ads indicate that the iron collars did not prevent enslaved people from escaping. In early January 1822, Maria, an African-born enslaved woman twenty-five years of age who worked as a market vendor in Rio de Janeiro, fled her owner while wearing an iron collar. One month later, her owner was still chasing her.[12]

Enslaved people who took the risk to escape either alone or in groups, for longer or shorter periods of time, did so for a variety of reasons. Broadly speaking, bondspeople were of course seeking freedom. But enslaved fugitives were also responding to more specific contexts. Some of them had been recently sold and separated from their families or old comrades, and thus attempted escape to stay close to their family members and loved ones. Others were being sexually and physically abused. Men, women, and children who escaped bondage also ran away during periods of social unrest, especially during wartime. During the nineteenth century, as various regions of the Americas abolished slavery, enslaved people escaped on foot, riding horses, on boats, and by train. They crossed rivers, forests, swamps, and sea pathways in their attempts to reach regions where slavery was outlawed. They joined other runaways in settlements in remote rural areas and the middle of cities.

Since antiquity, enslaved people's flights from bondage have been publicly advertised.[13] During the era of Atlantic slavery, slave owners publicized these escapes through posters and fugitive ads published in local newspapers. Although the contexts of the escapes varied from one region to another, printed advertising announcing the escape of enslaved individuals carried numerous similarities across periods, languages, and regions of the Americas. Intended to be short, they usually included just a few sentences describing the fugitive's physical features, and if the fugitive was born in Africa, ads tended to include descriptions of facial scarifications and mention the runaway's group of provenance.[14] Ads also included information on clothing, personality, and the circumstances of the escape. Sometimes these ads also promised a financial reward to whomever caught the fugitive. Interestingly, the same limited repertory of visual images illustrated these advertisements across the Americas. The vignettes usually represented the full-body profile of a Black man or woman in motion, often carrying a bundle of goods on a stick or on top of their head. The fact that the same images representing fugitive bondspeople illustrated newspaper ads across the Americas shows not only that the institution of slavery shared the same characteristics throughout the Western Hemisphere but also that the slave owners shared the same visual codes to chase their runaway human property.

Fugitive slave ads in the United States, Brazil, and the West Indies reveal that as long as they could face long journeys filled with walking and hiding, either in plantation areas or urban settings, enslaved men and women of various ages escaped as often as they could. As slavery developed in the West Indies, English colonies created legislation responding to slave resistance. In Barbados, the Slave Act of 1661, the first code regulating slavery in English colonies in the Americas, established several provisions to control and prevent enslaved people from escaping, including requiring slave owners and overseers to provide tickets for each bondsperson who left a plantation. Jamaica adopted nearly the same decree in 1664, which was later revised in 1684, and then adopted by South Carolina in 1691.[15]

In the French West Indies, the *Code Noir* of 1685 also determined provisions against insurgent slaves. For example, Articles XV and

XVI not only prohibited enslaved people from carrying weapons and gathering in groups but also prescribed physical punishments for those who broke these rules. Article XXXIII also established that an enslaved person who inflicted bruises on a master, mistress, or their children would be sentenced to death. Enslaved people who escaped were severely punished as well. Article XXXVIII established that bondspeople who ran away and did not return within one month after the owner officially reported the escape "shall have their ears cut off and shall be branded with a *fleur de lys* (lily flower)," which represented the French Bourbon dynasty, on one shoulder. An additional escape would result in similar punishments, but enslaved people who escaped a third time would be sentenced to death. Moreover, the code's Article XXXIX imposed a fine on freedpeople who gave shelter to enslaved fugitives.[16]

Most fugitives in the Americas were men, but depending on the period and region, enslaved women could represent as much as 30 percent of fugitives. Statistics from existing databases of slave ads suggest that in the French West Indies nearly 25 percent of these advertisements included enslaved women, and in Jamaica, the percentage is higher than 27 percent.[17] In the United States, the proportion of enslaved women who ran away was at least 15 percent, and these numbers increased during the American War of Independence to almost 30 percent and then grew again during the Civil War.[18]

Although, all over the Americas, male slave owners signed most of these ads, there were also ads published by female slave owners in colonies such as Jamaica in the early eighteenth century.[19] Moreover, various fugitive slave ads show that enslaved women managed to escape for several weeks without being caught. For example, a newspaper fugitive ad published at Cap Français in the French colony of Saint-Domingue in 1766 sought an enslaved woman named Agathe, who had run away three months prior after being sold to another owner.[20] Although slave owners used all available means to prevent their human property from escaping, enslaved women persisted. On May 28, 1766, another ad published in the newspaper *Affiches américaines* in Saint-Domingue announced that despite being chained together, two enslaved women owned by Mr. Laborde had been on the run for almost four weeks.[21] Such epic escapes show that runaway bondspeople could count on other men and women to help them by breaking their chains and providing them with shelter.[22]

Solidarity among enslaved women was also visible in runaway slave ads. Two years after the pair of enchained women escaped, two other enslaved women stole a dinghy and escaped from Cayes in Saint-Domingue, one of them carrying her two-month-old baby.[23] Two decades before the so-called "age of revolutions," these flights in the French West Indies also support historian Karen Cook Bell's argument about colonial North America and the newly independent United States that "motherhood, freedom, love, and family" did not prevent but rather "propelled women to escape bondage."[24] These escapes naturally carried much greater risks, and existing sources do not always allow us to know whether slave owners were successful in recapturing these enslaved women fugitives. However, we do know that if they had been caught, they would have been severely punished. Nevertheless, punishment did not deter them from escaping again.

Enslaved men and women, owned by powerful slave owners, also escaped during the eighteenth century. Take the famous example of the enslaved woman Ona Judge, the daughter of one of Martha Washington's "dower slaves," who was part of the estate of her deceased first husband. Judge was a seamstress and later became the personal maid of the first lady of the United States. She took the opportunity to escape from bondage while the presidential couple was in Philadelphia in 1796. Historian Erica Dunbar brought attention to this story by showing how during the many months that followed Judge's escape, the Washingtons persistently searched for her but were never able to bring her back to bondage.[25]

Washington was not the only US founding father to chase his fugitive human property. In an ad posted in the *Virginia Gazette* on September 14, 1769, the founding father Thomas Jefferson announced that his bondsman Sandy had escaped. The ad described Sandy as "a Mulatto . . . about 35 years of age, [whose] stature is rather low, inclining to corpulence, and his complexion light." Jefferson also highlighted Sandy's skills: "a shoemaker by trade, in which he uses his left hand principally, can do coarse carpenters work." Running away may not have been very difficult for Sandy because according to the ad, he was "something of a horse jockey" and took with him a white horse. But the ad also emphasized his intelligence and rebellious behavior as a man "greatly addicted to drink, and when drunk he is insolent and disorderly, in his conversation he swears much, and his behavior is artful and knavish; he also carried his shoemaker tools, and he will probably endeavour to get employment that way."[26]

Existing records show that Sandy was recaptured, and Jefferson sold him three years later.[27] But Sandy was not alone. Also owned by Jefferson, James Hubbard worked at the Mulberry nailery. He carried the same name as his father, another enslaved man owned by Jefferson. Hubbard first ran away from Monticello in 1805. Then in late 1810 or early 1811 he escaped again. But Jefferson was sly. While Hubbard was on the run, he sold him in absentia to a hired carpenter, but the sale contract stated that the slave's price would be higher if the enslaved man were captured; therefore Jefferson made additional efforts to recapture Hubbard to get more money for his sale. One year later, the bondsman was caught and brought back to Monticello. Jefferson was vicious, making sure that the fugitive was brutally whipped, then advising the new owner to sell him out of the state. Fortunately, this sale never occurred because Hubbard was intelligent and managed to escape again a few months later.[28]

Enslaved people also escaped temporarily to visit relatives and lovers in nearby estates.[29] But many others who fled from plantations, farms, and households had no intention to come back. Rachel, an enslaved woman of "twenty years of age, no perceptible mark . . . stout made," ran away from her owner Francis Clark in Washington, DC, in 1804. As Rachel was "apparently far advanced in pregnancy," her escape meant that her owners lost not only one bondswoman of reproductive age but also her enslaved offspring. Being pregnant did not prevent Rachel from running away. Moreover, her escape was obviously planned because, as the ad reveals, "she took with her several articles belonging to her mistress."[30]

As elsewhere, fugitive slave ads featuring enslaved women who escaped bondage in Washington, DC, show how they "altered physical appearances and dress, [took] different names," and carried with them "stolen goods."[31] Like Rachel, other pregnant enslaved women escaped slavery as well. On February 11, 1828, an ad published in the North Carolina newspaper *Western Carolinian* offered a five-dollar reward to whoever was able to catch Easter, an enslaved woman twenty-six years of age, "very black, with thick lips . . . and tolerable bold in her looks," who was pregnant.[32] Many others showed great courage when persisting in escaping slavery several times. The *New-Orleans Argus* published an ad on March 24, 1828, offering fifteen dollars in reward for Lucinda, an enslaved woman about twenty-six years old. Described as "of midling stature, American born," who spoke French, and who had "a pleasant appearance [and was] plausible in her manners," the ad informs that she had been on the run already for three weeks and had "runaway frequently before, for a short period."[33]

Brazil did not have newspapers until 1808, when the Portuguese court fled Lisbon and settled in Rio de Janeiro, which then became the capital of the Kingdom of Portugal, Brazil, and Algarve. During the nineteenth century, the main newspapers of Salvador in Bahia and Rio de Janeiro published several fugitive slave ads on a weekly basis. Slave owners would chase their fugitive human property for years, therefore confirming that larger Brazilian cities with significant Black populations offered better opportunities to escape bondage. Female slave owners regularly published ads searching for fugitive enslaved people. For example, on July 23, 1821, Marianna Jozefa Victorina published a curious ad in the *Diário do Rio de Janeiro* seeking two African-born bondswomen who had the same name, Catherina. The first Catherina, identified as belonging to the Ganguela "nation," and the second Catherina, classified as Benguela, had fled together four years earlier, on July 1, 1817.[34]

Catholic priests also published ads searching for their human property who escaped bondage in Rio de Janeiro. On June 25, 1821, the priest Antonio Penteado, who lived in a two-story house at the corner of Ajuda Street and Manuel de Carvalho Alley, published two ads in *Diário do Rio de Janeiro* searching for an enslaved man of the Ganguela "nation" who had escaped a few days earlier, as well as two other enslaved men, one Brazilian born and another one of the Ganguela "nation," who both had escaped one year earlier. It is likely that Penteado never recovered his human property, because five months later, the priest published another ad searching for the same three enslaved men, this time specifying that the two bondsmen of the Ganguela "nation" were named Antonio and Manuel.[35]

Numerous fugitive slave ads published in nineteenth-century Rio de Janeiro newspapers also featured Brazilian-born and African-born bondswomen who ran away bringing their young children with them. On October 29, 1821, a seventeen-year-old African-born enslaved woman named Maria, of "Congo nation," escaped, bringing with her Candida, her four-month daughter, described as light-skinned.[36] On November 4, 1821, another African-born enslaved mother named Maria, of Benguela "nation," who had recently been sold in auction by her owner's widow, escaped from her new master, carrying her sixteen-month-old daughter.[37] On October 5, 1851, two decades before Brazil passed legislation freeing newborns, a Brazilian-born enslaved woman in her forties, and also named Maria, escaped, bringing along her daughter, Amelia, and all their clothes, and took from her owner clothes, several objects, money, and silver.[38] Likewise, in other Brazilian regions, motherhood encouraged bondswomen to flee and join runaway slave communities.[39]

Despite receiving better food and clothing, and their alleged better position in Brazilian households, enslaved wet nurses also escaped bondage and were featured in several runaway slave ads. For example, an ad in the newspaper *Gazeta do Rio de Janeiro* announced that Felicia, an enslaved wet nurse identified as *cabra* (mixed-race Indigenous and African), tall, with big and weak eyes, had escaped on March 4,

1813. Additionally, young men and even enslaved children also escaped in significant numbers. Newspaper ads suggest that many of them were never caught. On June 3, 1821, an ad in the *Diário do Rio de Janeiro* announced that Domingos, of the Monjolo "nation," whose "face is slashed with signs," had disappeared for several weeks. In another ad of June 9, 1821, the slave owner José Antonio de Freiras Amaral sought Francisco, a Brazilian-born enslaved youth, who had run away more than three years earlier, and another enslaved youth, sixteen years of age, identified as of the Kasange "nation," who had escaped more than two years before.[40] Young enslaved girls also escaped bondage in Rio de Janeiro. On June 10, 1821, an ad described a twelve-year-old enslaved girl who had escaped a few days before.[41] In general, enslaved people of all backgrounds, including a significant number of bondswomen and enslaved mothers, escaped bondage whenever they could in a city like Rio de Janeiro, where they could easily blend with the overwhelmingly Black population.

In the United States as well, bondswomen ran away with their children. On March 26, 1845, a New Orleans newspaper ad offered a ten-dollar reward for Eliza, a bondswoman about thirty years of age, who escaped with her four-year-old enslaved daughter Victoria.[42] On April 27, 1847, an ad announced a fifteen-dollar reward offered for Hannah, an enslaved woman approximately thirty-five years old, who had escaped her owner John D. Pipkin in North Carolina. The ad noted that Hannah had taken her three children with her: David, a ten-year-old enslaved boy; Pleasant, a seven-year-old enslaved girl; and Joanna, an enslaved baby aged eighteen months.[43] Once again, the presence of several of runaway slave ads featuring enslaved mothers who escaped bondage carrying their children with them suggests that in urban areas, motherhood was not a great obstacle preventing bondswomen from seeking freedom by running away.

As slavery continued through the middle of the nineteenth century, when photography was becoming widespread, a small number of rare slave fugitive ads featured photographic portraits of enslaved people in the United States. One of these unusual ads features the brave Dolly, an enslaved woman owned by Louis Manigault in Augusta, Georgia, who fled in April 1863, during the American Civil War. To reclaim his human property, Manigault wrote an ad displaying Dolly's photograph, cropped from a carte de visite.[44] Gaining prominence in the middle of the nineteenth century, these small photographic portraits, mounted on cards and whose format corresponded to that of a visiting card, could be reproduced multiples times. Offering a fifty-dollar reward, the ad emphasizes that Dolly's "likeness is here seen," adding that she was "thirty years of age, [with] light complexion—hesitates somewhat when spoken to, and is not a very healthy woman, but rather good looking, with a fine set of teeth. Never changed her owner and has been a house servant always." Marked by a paternalistic tone that made readers believed that the owner cared about the fugitive enslaved woman, the ad also explained that "it is thought that she has been enticed off by some White Man, being herself a stranger to this City, and belonging to a Charleston [*sic*] family." In other words, Manigault wanted the community to believe that Dolly's escape was not her own decision but that she was rather negatively influenced by a white male. But the reality was different. Manigault's private correspondence shows that Dolly's escape was not a last-minute decision but rather that she left during "his absence to the plantation and took with her an ample wardrobe of her own clothes."[45] Dolly was single, good looking, and probably childless, and it is likely that Manigault sexually abused her. In other words, whatever her motives were, like other enslaved women, she ran away to never come back.

All over the Americas, at least in rural areas, slave owners hired slave catchers to hunt enslaved fugitives. Riding horses and followed by dogs, these men could chase fugitives for several weeks.[46] In 1793, the Congress of the newly independent United States passed the Fugitive Slave Act, a federal law that introduced the fugitive clause in the Constitution, which authorized local governments to capture, arrest, and return enslaved fugitives. Acknowledging that fugitives received outside support, the legislation also instated a $500 fine against anyone who assisted escaped slaves. As historian Manisha Sinha has written, in addition to addressing the capture and return of fugitives from beyond the borders of Southern states, the act also "facilitated the kidnapping of free Blacks into slavery."[47] But despite the 1793 Fugitive Slave Act, bondspeople, free Black communities, and abolitionists resisted and continued to challenge the law in multiple ways, especially by assisting in the escape and protection of enslaved fugitives.

During the first half of the nineteenth century, as discussed in chapter 12, US Northern states introduced free womb legislation that gradually abolished slavery. Hence, men, women, and children continued to escape and seek refuge in states that had enacted legislation to progressively eradicate slavery.[48] Supported by Black and white allies, enslaved people created a fugitive corridor through which they sought to reach freedom havens in the Northern states of the United States and also in Canada, where slavery had been formally abolished in 1834. Among the most distinguished fugitives who fled to the North was orator, writer, abolitionist, and statesman Frederick Douglass. Helped by a freeborn Black woman named Anna Murray, he managed to flee from Baltimore on September 3, 1838, and "succeeded in reaching New York without the slightest interruption of any kind."[49] More than a decade later, Harriet Tubman successfully escaped from Maryland and reached Philadelphia.[50] In subsequent years, Tubman helped not only her brothers to escape but also many other enslaved people.

Along with Tubman, this network of freedom seekers, known as the Underground Railroad, has been memorialized in the United States through the protection of historical sites along its route, museum exhibitions, novels, children's books, plays, motion pictures, and television series.[51] But despite the emphasis on this northward fugitive corridor, enslaved people also escaped across borders southward, earlier before the rise of the Underground Railroad.[52] Starting in the late sixteenth century, bondspeople fled the Carolinas and Georgia to find refuge in Spanish Florida, where Spanish colonizers sought to counter English influence. Despite British occupation between 1763 and 1783, this influx of enslaved fugitives continued until the region's acquisition by the United States in 1821.[53] During the nineteenth century, bondspeople from the United States also escaped to Mexico, especially after Vicente Guerrero abolished slavery in 1829.[54] As the domestic slave trade flourished with the second slavery, a group of slaves on board the brig *Creole* that left Richmond to New Orleans transporting 137 enslaved persons led a revolt in 1841. After taking control of the vessel, the insurgents were successful in redirecting the *Creole* to the Bahamas in the British West Indies, where slavery was then abolished, and where they were eventually freed.[55]

Meanwhile, as cotton production increased, slavery persisted and expanded in the US South. During this period, both the federal and state governments led initiatives to apprehend enslaved fugitives. By the middle of the nineteenth century, a clear division was established between Southern slave states and Northern states where slavery had been abolished and to where enslaved people seeking to emancipate themselves attempted to escape. As the number of enslaved fugitives increased, slave states were concerned about the financial losses incurred from these escapes.[56] In 1850, a new Fugitive Slave Act expanded the provisions of the 1793 legislation, making it easier for slave owners to claim, recapture, and recover their escaped human property from beyond state borders.[57] As the Civil War started in the United States in 1861, similarly to what happened decades earlier during the American War of Independence, enslaved people collectively escaped from plantations to join the ranks of the Union Army.[58] In Brazil, a few months before the final abolition of slavery (as we will see in chapter 16), bondspeople also organized collective escapes. In Jeffrey Needell's words, the flights were massive "to the point of threatening the harvests in western São Paulo, Brazil's economic frontier."[59]

Runaway Slave Communities

In Brazil, as well as in the rest of Latin America and the Caribbean, bondspeople who emancipated themselves by running away formed settlements of various sizes in rural and urban areas. Fugitive communities called *cumbes* and *palenques* in the Spanish Americas; *mocambos*, *ladeiras*, *magotes*, and *quilombos* in Brazil; and *maroon communities* in the British West Indies existed during the entire duration of slavery.[60] In the French West Indies, where the French term *villages marrons* (maroon villages) referred to these runaway settlements, there was also a distinction between *petit marronage*, when enslaved people temporarily escaped, and *grand marronage*, when fugitives established more permanent settlements.[61] Beyond the French West Indies, historians have embraced these two terms to frame fugitive activity in other rural and urban areas of the Americas, including the region encompassing today's United States.[62]

With few exceptions, there is no way to know whether enslaved men, women, and children featured in the thousands of existing fugitive slave ads were recaptured by their owners. But many bondspeople who escaped slavery in urban and rural areas of Brazil and the West Indies may have had the opportunity to join runaway settlements. The traditional definition of a *quilombo* or *maroon community* denoted settlements in mountainous regions that were difficult to access. However, in Brazil, for example, as slavery expanded, runaway slave communities became widespread in urban areas and near urban centers, hidden in plain sight. There are countless stories of these settlements, especially the largest and long-lasting ones. African-born fugitives made up most of the early runaway slave communities. Since the 1940s, archaeologists and historians have uncovered documents and artifacts associated with these settlements, therefore illuminating their histories, which also survived in popular memory.[63]

One of the first documented settlements of fugitive enslaved men, women, and children in the Americas emerged in the region of present-day Mexico. In 1609, enslaved fugitives formed a *palenque* in a mountain close to the banks of the Rio Blanco, in Veracruz. In 1631, the Maroons won the conflict against the Spaniards. They not only obtained freedom; they were also granted land to establish San Lorenzo de los Negros, an independent territory considered the first settlement of freedmen and freedwomen in the Americas.[64] In 1932, the village was renamed after its founder, Yanga, whose memory remains alive in the local population's collective memory because of his role in fighting the Spanish and liberating his people.[65] Like many other Maroons in the Americas, Yanga was perceived as an enslaved man who fought against slavery and as a hero who organized resistance against the Spanish colonizers.[66]

A similar settlement emerged in New Granada, in the Spanish Viceroyalty of Peru, part of present-day Colombia. Known as *palenque* San Basilio, this settlement was formed at the end of the sixteenth century. Domingos Bioho (also known as Benkos Bioho, Dionísio Biohó, Rey Benkos, Rey de la Matuna, and Biohó Rey) was one of the leaders of this *palenque*. The few sources that survive describe Bioho as an African-born man who escaped bondage with his family in approximately 1599. By the early seventeenth century, he may have been one of the founders of the *palenque* San Basilio. His name, Bioho, connects him to the Upper Guinea, in today's Guinea-Bissau, where he was probably captured and sold into slavery in the region of New Granada.[67] The Maroons fought the Spanish for several years. Then following a treaty, they succeeded in preserving the *palenque*'s autonomy between 1605 and 1619. But eventually, the Spanish defeated the Maroons. They captured, hanged, and quartered Bioho in 1621. In popular memory, however, Bioho became San Basilio's legendary founder and was transformed into a symbol of Black resistance. Today, tourists who visit San Basilio de Palenque, thirty-five miles from Cartagena, can see a statue honoring the seventeenth-century Maroon. His bust is also displayed in the Apolo Park in Cartagena, along with other white and Native historical actors today portrayed as national heroes.[68]

Powerful Maroon communities based in remote areas surrounding sugar plantations also emerged in Jamaica during the seventeenth century, especially after a series of slave revolts between 1673 and 1694 that followed the English occupation of the island.[69] Many Jamaican Maroons were Akan speakers born in West Africa who brought to the Americas their previous warfare experience. The British military repeatedly fought the Maroons without any success. Starting in 1720 these armed conflicts intensified in what became known as the First Maroon War, which ended with the signature of two treaties in 1739, one with the Leeward Maroons based in the Cockpit Country and one with the Windward Maroons established on the eastern part of the island. By containing the Maroons through these agreements, the British obtained their support to recover enslaved fugitives and suppress slave rebellions; in exchange, the Maroons obtained land. Yet, as the Maroon population dramatically increased in the decades that followed the treaties, their territory became too small. British planters were also concerned about the rise of the slave revolt in the neighboring French colony of Saint-Domingue in 1791. The combination of these factors was exacerbated by the judicial whipping of two Maroons of Trelawny Town in 1795. When the Maroons protested the punishment that violated their sovereignty, the British forces imposed martial law. As the Maroons resisted, the Second Maroon War broke out.[70] Only in 1796 did the British succeed in defeating the Maroons, who were deported to Nova Scotia and then to Sierra Leone, as will be discussed in chapter 17.[71]

Despite the experiences in present-day Mexico and Colombia, as well as in Jamaica, Brazil was the colony and later the independent nation that hosted the greatest number of runaway slave communities in urban and rural areas. In the early seventeenth century, sugar production based on an enslaved African workforce increased in northeast Brazil, especially in the captaincies of Bahia and Pernambuco. As we already explored in chapter 7, living and working conditions in Brazilian sugarcane estates were extremely harsh. Hence, it was not surprising that enslaved people fled these plantations, seeking refuge in forests and mountainous areas. As Stuart Schwartz has emphasized, Portuguese colonial authorities took measures to repress and contain these escapes. In each parish of the captaincy of Pernambuco, and later also in Bahia, they made official the position of slave catcher or bush captain (*capitão do campo* or *capitão do mato*), who would be assisted by Native Brazilians as well. Slave hunters sought not only to destroy runaway slave communities but also to kill or reenslave the members of these communities.[72] Still, these measures never altogether kept enslaved people from escaping to areas of difficult access to slave catchers. Moreover, this strategy never prevented the formation of alliances between African-descended enslaved peoples and Native populations.[73]

The largest and longest-lasting Brazilian Maroon settlement was Palmares, the seventeenth-century *quilombo* in Brazil's northeast region in the present-day state of Alagoas, then the captaincy of Pernambuco. The term *quilombo* and its organization have been connected to West Central African structures. Some historians explained that the Palmares *quilombo* was inspired by the West Central African *kilombo*, a male initiation-based warrior society and military organization created by the Imbangala.[74] Yet this thesis was rejected by historian John K. Thornton, who insisted that West Central Africans from Angola predominated in Palmares. According to him, the Imbangala would not have offered an attractive social model for Africans who had recently arrived in Brazil in the seventeenth century.[75] More recently, by embracing the idea that Brazilian *quilombos* drew from the Imbangala *kilombo*, Toby Green has defined *kilombo* simply as a West Central African group of warriors that gathered "people from different lineages speaking different languages."[76] In the most comprehensive study about Palmares, historian Silvia Hunold Lara puts forth a compromise among these contrasting views. She states that the West Central African *kilombo* was not an institution directly transferred from Africa to Brazil. Instead, it resulted from a broader political process that structured the bonds among fugitives. As these links changed over time, they allowed the formation of a state that followed West Central African models.[77] Yet, Lara also admits that in addition to referring to a specific institution among the Imbangala, the term *kilombo* had several other meanings, such as a permanent or temporary camp of commercial caravans or a military camp, and could also simply refer to a gathering of people.[78] But ultimately, as noted by historian Luiz Felipe de Alencastro, the men who fought against Palmares also participated in the wars waged by the Portuguese in Angola in the late seventeenth century.[79] Therefore, although having emerged in Brazil to designate Palmares, the term *quilombo* was shaped by these long-lasting Southern Atlantic interactions.

The *mocambos* that gave birth to Palmares were scattered refuges located in a mountainous forest area located between forty-five and seventy-five miles from the coast and covering a region of one hundred miles parallel to the coastline.[80] In the 1640s, Palmares was already composed of nine villages. Organized as an independent state and ruled by a monarchy, its population was estimated between twenty thousand and thirty thousand individuals in 1670.[81] Surrounded by palisades, the villages included hundreds of dwellings connected to each other. Residents cultivated gardens and widely used palm trees to build houses and beds. In addition to tapping these trees to produce palm wine, dwellers also consumed the hearts of palms and palm kernels, from which they extracted oil and produced butter.[82] Historians and archaeologists still debate the exact composition of Palmares's population, but most of its residents were enslaved West Central Africans and Brazilian-born fugitives who had escaped sugarcane plantations. Evidence suggests that these men, women, and children spoke a common "Angola" language, probably based on Kimbundu.[83] But archaeological excavations have also revealed material traces suggesting the presence of freed persons, mixed-race persons, and even Jews of Portuguese heritage escaping religious persecution.[84]

The Portuguese attempted to destroy Palmares for the first time in 1612. Years later, during the Dutch occupation of Pernambuco from 1630 to 1654, the *quilombo* had increased in size, and despite a few expeditions, the Dutch failed to destroy it. After the Dutch's expulsion, the Portuguese organized several expeditions against Palmares but were also unsuccessful in suppressing the *quilombo*. In 1677, the Portuguese led an incursion during which they destroyed many *mocambos* and took hundreds of prisoners. In 1678, Gana Zumba, the *quilombo*'s king, eventually signed an agreement with the government of Pernambuco in which the king promised to deliver fugitives and the Portuguese promised to liberate Maroons born in Palmares and grant them a territory in the region of Cucaú, where nearly three hundred people were to be relocated.[85] But Zumbi, one of the leaders of Palmares and purportedly the king's nephew, refused to deliver fugitives born outside Palmares to the Portuguese. Thus, along with his followers, he moved his *mocambo* to the woods, where they continued to resist the Portuguese attacks.[86]

In the following months, Gana Zumba was poisoned and killed by his opponents. As Zumbi and his warriors continued to fight, men and women who had relocated to Cucaú broke the agreement and started plotting to escape to join Zumbi. In response, the Portuguese destroyed Cucaú and reenslaved its tenants in 1680. In the following years, the war against Palmares continued and intensified, badly affecting sugar production in the region. After the destruction of Cucaú, Palmares recentered around the Serra do Barriga mountain range. Portuguese officers reported the settlement's increasing number of members, dwellings, farming animals, and rich plantations, in addition to a greater military organization.[87] After many incursions, and following a long siege, the Portuguese-led forces dismantled Serra do Barriga's settlement in 1694. But the war was not over. Several fighters managed to escape, including Zumbi, who was killed on November 20, 1695. After being beheaded, his head was brought to Recife to be publicly displayed.[88] Despite this defeat, official reports from the period reveal that remnants of Palmares remained, and new fugitive communities continued in surrounding regions.[89]

Scholars and writers have spread the idea that before being captured by the Portuguese, Zumbi killed himself, contributing to the construction of Zumbi's myth, which survived in Afro-Brazilian collective and public memory in the centuries following his death.[90] Long considered by official history to be a bloodthirsty warrior, Zumbi began to emerge around the 1970s as a symbol of resistance for the Brazilian Black movement, and this new image began also to appear in the Brazilian press.[91] The myth of Zumbi is still alive in Brazil and the Atlantic world, where he appears in a large array of cultural productions such as poetry, music, theater, motion pictures, Carnaval parades, and the visual arts. He is also honored in several monuments around the country.[92]

Although Zumbi was killed by Portuguese forces and did not die by suicide, as was widespread in popular culture, especially in the famous movie *Quilombo* (1984), by filmmaker Cacá Diegues, many enslaved men and women did take their own lives to escape the horrors of slavery. One historian has argued that bondspeople who killed themselves in the southern colonies of British North America and antebellum United States had numerous motivations to end their lives, and therefore when doing so, they were not necessarily resisting the evil institution.[93] A similar argument can be made regarding enslaved women who carried out infanticide, as many reasons may have motivated them to take the lives of their own children.

Despite which motivations were foremost in the minds of bondspeople who carried out infanticide or suicide, their extreme actions allowed them to exert their limited agency. In the second half of the nineteenth century, in the final two decades of slavery in Brazil, a significant number of enslaved women died by hanging themselves in the country's deep south. On November 2, 1872, the enslaved woman Selestina hanged herself from a peach tree in the estate of her owner Rosalina Pacheco de Sampaio. On September 7, 1874, the enslaved woman Fortunata, along with her two-year-old son Antônio, owned by Leonardo Paulino de Araújo, were found hanging from a tree on his property. Josefa, an enslaved woman owned by Captain Felício Nunes Garcia, also hanged herself, on December 26, 1875.[94] We will never know exactly why all these women took their own lives because surviving documents reporting their deaths were not intended to underscore their owners' daily physical and mental abuses but precisely to conceal these brutalities.

Nonetheless, there are exceptions. In the final two decades of slavery in Brazil, the courts were increasingly concerned about how slave owners treated bondspeople. Consider the case of Bemvinda, an enslaved woman owned by Francisco Máximo da Silveira, also in Rio Grande do Sul, who hanged herself from a quince tree. Although surviving records do not reveal Bemvinda's age when she took her own life, we can assume she was a young woman. During the quick investigation, her owner was asked how he could explain the bondswoman's suicide. He responded that her mistress (*senhora*) reprimanded her because she was asked to move away from her mother, and he believed that this was "the motive that led her to hang herself because she had very serious judgement."[95]

It is hard to draw definitive conclusions from only this sentence, but it is implausible that a single reproach would lead someone to suicide. Bemvinda was separated from her mother and wanted to live with her. For how long had mother and daughter been living apart and why? The documents do not answer these questions. But entire books could be filled with the cases of women slave owners who abused enslaved women.[96] We can only assume that her mistress's admonition was just one in a long series of abuses, and as in other similar cases such as Maria's story examined in chapter 12, the judicial authorities were not interested in uncovering more details. As noted by Michael Gomez, suicide could be considered the "ultimate form of resistance" because in practical terms, when bondspeople killed themselves, they were directly hurting the interests of slave owners who in losing a life lost their human property.[97]

Individual and Collective Self-Emancipation

Africans had resisted enslavement since the rise of the Atlantic slave trade. Once in the Americas, enslaved men, women, and children always defied slavery. Individually or collectively, through minor actions or through more organized plots, they found ways to oppose their enslavers by escaping, organizing runaway slave communities, taking their own lives, and even in some instances killing their owners, as Monica did in Brazil's deep south in the early nineteenth century, described at the beginning of this chapter.

None of the actions led by individuals and groups examined in this chapter were effective in ending the institution of slavery altogether.

But in some cases, bondspeople were successful in their attempts to emancipate themselves temporarily or permanently. As we will see in chapters 14 and 15, men, women, and children who continued to live in bondage found other ways to resist slavery. By preserving their languages, music, dance, martial arts, and religious traditions, they survived slavery and expanded the possibilities of resistance. Most important, they made African cultures a central and influential component of the cultures of the Americas. Doing so was also a form of resistance.

CHAPTER 14

Ways of Congregating

"It was deemed a disgrace not to get drunk at Christmas," wrote Frederick Douglass in one of his narratives revisiting his life as an enslaved man.[1]

Douglass reminds readers that even the most inhuman slave owner in the United States allowed bondspeople to not work between Christmas and the New Year's Day except for feeding and taking care of the livestock. For enslaved people, the holidays were an opportunity to rest, eat, drink, and socialize. Even more important, these festivities were also a great occasion to run away. Douglass understood, perhaps more than anyone, how paternalism operated in slave societies. Slave owners abused and punished enslaved people all year long. But they represented themselves as knowing what was in the best interests of bondspeople. Therefore, according to Douglass, "a slave who would work during the holidays was considered by our masters as scarcely deserving them."[2]

The reason for this assumption was simple. Access to leisure, food, and drink were, as Douglass put it, "effective means in the hands of the slaveholder in keeping down the spirit of insurrection."[3] The great abolitionist was certainly right in noting how these measures could soften insurgent behaviors among enslaved men and women who worked from dawn to dusk under strict surveillance. This chapter shows that holidays and other festivals were not only spaces of accommodation; they also offered opportunities for resistance. In the next pages, I explore how enslaved people created both formal and informal associations through existing religious institutions that allowed them to appropriate spiritual practices and develop festivals, processions, dances, martial arts, and musical traditions to help survive the horrors of bondage, especially in Brazil but also in other parts of Latin America, the West Indies, and the United States. I especially emphasize the fact that many of these activities carried with them crucial cultural and religious components brought by Africans from their homelands, while also incorporating features from European and Native American societies. In several cases, dialogues between Christianity, Islam, and other African religions were embedded in these cultural events. Despite the nuances across time and regions in the Americas, many bondspeople used cultural and religious practices as resistance tools to build a world of their own. These cultural and religious manifestations emerged during the era of the Atlantic slave trade, but as we will see, many have survived into the present and are tools of cultural assertion and resistance still used by Black populations who continue to experience and fight against racism on a daily basis.

Catholicism, Black Saints, and Brotherhoods

As previously noted, Portuguese colonizers introduced Roman Catholicism in West Central Africa during their first exchanges with the rulers of the Kingdom of Kongo in the fifteenth century. As these sovereigns accepted conversion, they instructed their subjects in the Catholic faith. Some historians interpreted the introduction and incorporation of Christian symbols, rituals, patron saints, and festivals in Kongo as *syncretism*, an approach that privileges the combination of different cultures and religions.[4] To study African cultures and religions in the Americas and to understand these interactions in the broader context of the African diaspora, I embrace here the notion of "spaces of correlation." This is a phrase proposed by the art historian Cécile Fromont, who has emphasized how Kongo rulers and elites did not simply combine African and Christian religious "disparate elements" but rather "transformed and redefined them . . . into a new system of religious thought, artistic expression, and political organization."[5]

It is known that many captives transported from the Iberian Peninsula and West Central Africa to the Americas had already been converted to Catholicism. During the sixteenth and seventeenth centuries, other European powers, such as France and the Kingdoms of Castile and Aragón, also forced Catholic baptism and conversion on bondspeople transported to their colonies in the Americas, as we have seen. Likewise, the English and the Dutch imposed Protestant Christianity on bondspeople transported to their colonies in mainland North America and the West Indies. The rulers of the Kingdom of Kongo could embrace Catholicism on their own terms, but enslaved Africans transported to the Americas did not have the same choice. Despite this imposition, it is nonetheless true that the Roman Catholic Church, with its lay brotherhoods, festivals, and processions; Protestant denominations, with their multiple organizations; and traditional Black churches all offered spaces of autonomy to enslaved individuals in the Americas. Ultimately, the interactions between Christianity and African religions in Europe, Africa, and the Americas gave rise to new ways to display faith in the public space, a process in which enslaved Africans and their descendants played a crucial role.

Black devotional images emerged before the rise of the Atlantic slave trade. In European regions where Romance languages predominated (today's Italy, France, Portugal, Spain, and Romania), these images appeared between the ninth and thirteenth centuries, when the Muslims were occupying a significant part of the Iberian Peninsula. Initially, most of these representations depicted the Virgin Mary as Black. The Virgin being Black carried a variety of meanings and was not an automatic indication of Black African origins. For instance, images of Black Saint Maurice and of the Black magus (Balthasar) emerged in the following centuries as well.[6] Starting in the fifteenth century, exchanges between European and Black Africa led to the adoption of ancient Ethiopian Black saints and of enslaved Black saints. As the Atlantic slave trade evolved in the late fifteenth century, the devotion of these saints first emerged in the Iberian Peninsula and was then transplanted to the Spanish Americas and Brazil, where enslaved and freed Black populations created brotherhoods and confraternities to worship them.

Among the most important of these saints was Saint Elesbán (or Elesbão in Portuguese), who was initially worshipped in the Ethiopian and Coptic churches. Elesbán was an actual historical figure, originally named Kaleb, who ruled the kingdom of Aksum, in present-day Ethiopia and Eritrea, during the sixth century CE. Also from Ethiopia was Efigenia, a legendary beautiful princess, whose story emerged in the first century CE.[7] As early as 1475, Seville had a chapel honoring Saints Elesbán and Efigenia.[8] In addition, two enslaved Black saints, Benedict of Palermo and Saint Anthony of Noto (or Saint Anthony of Categeró), who emerged in Sicily, acquired fame in the Iberian Peninsula during the sixteenth century.

In the Iberian Peninsula, West Central Africa, and the Americas, the devotion to these saints was organized through lay brotherhoods of the Catholic Church. For example, among the seven Black sodalities that existed in Mexico City in the late sixteenth century, there was one Black confraternity of Saint Efigenia located at the Mercedarian monastery. There was also another brotherhood dedicated to Saint Benedict and Coronation Christ housed at the Franciscan monastery.[9] The same way West Central Africans embraced Christianity, African-born enslaved men and women and their descendants who were converted to Catholicism did not simply abandon their African religions. The devotion to a Catholic saint was not necessarily exclusive and did not prevent enslaved people from continuing to worship African deities.

Catholic lay brotherhoods were not sites of insurrection, but they did provide enslaved Africans with some degree of agency, which in some cases offered them pathways to freedom. Because these associations required membership fees, they may have offered loans to their members to allow them to purchase their freedom.[10] But above all, by joining these organizations, these men and women re-created kin ties and new networks that associated them with other freed and free Black individuals who helped them navigate Brazilian slave society and eventually find the means to purchase their freedom. Likewise, as we already discussed, these organizations ensured that their members could have a dignified burial service.

Starting in the early colonial period, Portuguese colonizers through their religious orders transplanted Catholic lay brotherhoods to Brazil. Spanish settlers did the same in their colonies in the Americas. These lay brotherhoods (*irmandades* in Brazil, *cofradías* in the Spanish Americas) and *cabildos de nación* in Cuba congregated devotees of a particular patron saint. In Brazil, Catholic lay brotherhoods included Black members who were either enslaved or descendants of enslaved individuals. Some Black brotherhoods brought together enslaved and freed African-born persons belonging to the same "nation" or "provenience group."[11] As noted in previous chapters, these "nations" often corresponded to the regions on the African coasts where enslaved people were embarked. But sometimes these labels conferred on African-born bondspeople could also be associated with specific ethnic groups. For example, "nations" such as Angola, Jeje, and Nagô rarely corresponded to a specific ethnic group. But by embracing a particular "nation," enslaved Africans reconsidered who they were, based on their existing ties with the African continent and on their needs for physical and cultural survival. Hence, the idea of "nation" referred at the same time to peoples, ethnolinguistic groups, religions, and other forms of association that arose during the period during which they lived under slavery in the Americas.[12]

Undoubtedly the most popular brotherhood among Black men and women was the brotherhood of Our Lady of the Rosary. The rosary devotion was associated with a circlet of beads used for prayer that became known as a *rosarium*. As the Atlantic slave trade gradually intensified, on both sides of the South Atlantic brotherhoods of the rosary attracted a significant number of enslaved Africans and their descendants, who joined them in great part because of the central role rosary prayer beads played during their evangelization.[13]

As early as 1495, Portuguese settlers built a church to host the Black brotherhood of Our Lady of the Rosary on Santiago, an island of Cape Verde's archipelago. A brotherhood of Our Lady of the Rosary of the Black Men was also established on São Tomé in 1526.[14] Starting in the late fifteenth century, Black persons were members of the lay brotherhood of Our Lady of the Rosary in Lisbon. Black members, who were visible in the public activities of the confraternity, even performed a play during the festivities to welcome King Manuel and Queen Leonor in Lisbon in 1521.[15]

Although initially these brotherhoods were not exclusively intended for Black persons, this context gradually changed.[16] In 1565, the brotherhood of Our Lady of the Rosary of the Black Men was officially established in the Monastery of São Domingos in Lisbon. Its bylaws indicated that one of the main goals of the association was to organize the patron saint's feast including a procession held in July on an annual basis. Moreover, the brotherhood also included several elected positions such as kings, princes, and *mordomos* (managing directors) who organized the processions, in addition to dukes, earls, marquises, and cardinals.[17] Lisbon's tangible traces of Black devotion to Our Lady of the Rosary also remain alive in other temples. In the sacristy of the Catholic Church of Santa Catarina, a painted retable produced between the late sixteenth and early seventeenth centuries portrays a Black man and a Black woman revering the Virgin of the Rosary and the baby Jesus, who are framed by the rosary (figure 14.1).[18]

Enslaved Africans and their descendants who joined Catholic brotherhoods shared the same African gods and rituals, and in many cases, they also shared the same language and culture. In the Iberian Peninsula, Africa, and the Americas, members of Black brotherhoods participated in festivals to honor Black saints. These festivals and processions were spaces to celebrate their African origins and their public Catholic identity through dance and music. Many textual and visual records documented their activities in the Iberian Peninsula, West Central Africa,

FIGURE 14.1. Anonymous, *Retable of Our Lady of the Rosary*, Church of Santa Catarina, Lisbon, Portugal. Photograph by Ana Lucia Araujo, 2022.

and the Spanish and Portuguese Americas throughout the era of slavery and the Atlantic slave trade. In 1619, King Filipe III, who ruled Portugal and Spain between 1598 and 1621, during the Iberian Union (1580–1640), attended a sumptuous multiday festival in Lisbon in which members of Black confraternities carried a Saint Benedict's flag, suggesting that the saint's devotion was well established in Lisbon.[19]

In the early seventeenth century, white brotherhoods, such as the Holy House of Mercy in Bahia, Brazil, attracted several rich slave traders. Similarly, the third orders, which were also lay associations subordinated to religious orders (usually the Franciscans, Jesuits, Dominicans, and Carmelites), including the devotees of a specific saint, accepted only white people as members.[20] Consequently, as slavery expanded in Brazil and the Spanish Americas, African-born and locally born enslaved people created new Catholic lay brotherhoods and joined the existing ones that accepted nonwhite members. In Peru, for instance, Black confraternities emerged as early as the years immediately following the Spanish conquest in the sixteenth century.[21] Because colonial authorities recognized that Black confraternities offered autonomy to Black subjects, these authorities attempted to oppose the confraternities' existence in colonial Mexico. Likewise, in Cartagena, public officials in the late seventeenth century also feared that these brotherhoods would serve as spaces of resistance that could offer enslaved people many opportunities to organize rebellions.[22] But despite occasional hostilities, Black brotherhoods and Black saints continued to exist throughout the entire era of Atlantic slavery and exist to this day in many Latin American countries.

During the seventeenth century, brotherhoods dedicated to Our Lady of the Rosary and their churches became quite popular among Africans and their descendants in colonial Brazil, and still today their buildings and brotherhoods can be found in various parts of the country. It would not be an exaggeration to state that wherever there is a church dedicated to Our Lady of the Rosary, there is also a Black community linked to it. During the eighteenth century, the city of Salvador in Bahia hosted fifteen Black brotherhoods, including seven dedicated to Our Lady of the Rosary, three dedicated to Saint Benedict, one to Saint Efigenia, and one to Saint Anthony of Categeró. Few Black brotherhoods had their own churches, and some churches hosted more than one brotherhood by dedicating a chapel inside to venerate their patron saints.[23]

This was the case of the brotherhood of Our Lady of the Rosary of Black Men in Salvador, Bahia, which was founded in 1604. The brotherhood accepted any members, regardless of sex or legal status.

Among its founders were probably African-born individuals identified as "Angolas," whose origins are linked to Bantu-speaking regions in West Central Africa, though over the years most of the members were their Brazilian-born descendants. By the end of the eighteenth century, other African groups also became members of the brotherhood, including individuals from the Bight of Benin associated with the Jeje "nation," a label comprising enslaved Africans from the Gbe-speaking area such as the Ewe from southwest region of present-day Togo, the Fon from Abomey, the Gun from Porto-Novo, the Hueda from Ouidah, the Gen from Little Popo (present-day Aného), and the Mahi from Savalou.[24]

Between 1703 and 1704, the members of the brotherhood of Our Lady of the Rosary of the Black Men amassed funds to construct their own church, designed by a white carpenter called Gabriel Ribeiro.[25] Although the original building was a modest chapel, the foreman Caetano José da Costa created a more elaborated facade and added to the construction two towers and two lateral naves in 1780.[26] Today, the church Our Lady of the Rosary of the Black Men continues to preserve its long-lasting ties with the history of slavery in Bahia. Attracting Black devotees and tourists who attend the masses and visit the church, the building also features a rich material heritage of slavery that tells the story of how Black men and women venerated Catholic Black saints. The church's nave, altar, and sacristy display various statues of Black saints such as Elesbão (figure 14.2) and Saint Anthony of Categeró. Also, as we noted in chapter 5, the flagstones covering the building's floors are the tombstones of the brotherhood's deceased members who, until the early twentieth century, were buried inside the church. Among the prominent Bahia Black citizens interred in the building is the intellectual and artist Manuel Raimundo Querino.[27] Likewise, Rodolfo Manoel Martins de Andrade (Bamboxê Obtikô), one of the founders of Casa Branca, the oldest temple of Candomblé in Bahia, and probably in Brazil as well, is also buried in the building.[28]

These markers highlight the multiple links between the members of Black brotherhoods and the leaders of Candomblé, an Afro-Brazilian

FIGURE 14.2. Anonymous, Saint Elesbão, Church of Our Lady of the Rosary of the Black Men, Salvador, Bahia, Brazil. Photograph by Ana Lucia Araujo, 2009.

religion based on multiple deities, divination, music, dance, and spirit possession.[29] As we will see later, from the era of slavery to this day, Catholicism and African-based religions were not mutually exclusive. Indeed, enslaved people and their descendants often associated Catholic saints with Orisha, Vodun, and West Central African deities brought to Brazil and the Spanish Americas.[30] But in the case of Cuba, for example, John K. Thornton has argued that the worship of Catholic saints by enslaved West Central Africans transported to

Cuba was more likely related to the long history of Christianity in the Kingdom of Kongo.[31] In other words, the long-lasting exchanges between Africans and Europeans were what allowed African religions and Catholicism to remain alive among Black populations in Brazil and Cuba.

Rio de Janeiro's brotherhood of Our Lady of the Rosary and Saint Benedict of the Black Men opened its own very modest church building in 1737. Travelers such as the British scientist Thomas Ewbank, who visited the church in 1846, recorded the presence of a statue depicting the Black Saint Benedict, "Black as jet, and rather low in stature, the baby in his arms, being any thing but a white one." Yet, he also noted the building's state of decay: "Every thing looked old, mean, and worn out, for want of soap and paint."[32] The church is also likely to be the place where the devotion of the enslaved saint Anastácia emerged in the twentieth century.

Although not officially recognized by the Catholic Church, Anastácia became a popular saint not only among Black Catholics but also among devotees of Umbanda, an Afro-Brazilian religion in which several deities represent enslaved people.[33] According to one legend explaining the saint's origin, Anastácia's mother was raped by her white owner. Born as a racially mixed woman, despite her Black skin, she had beautiful blue eyes, which in the Brazilian context is still today a marker of European ancestry. Her mistress was jealous, so she forced Anastácia to wear a mask hiding her face. However, popular culture emphasizes that she was able to communicate with other enslaved people just using her eyes.

Despite these stories, the legend only partly explains why Anastácia is depicted as a bondswoman muzzled by a face mask that during the period of slavery was used to prevent slaves from eating dirt.[34] It is likely that this image emerged through the intervention of Yolando Guerra. One of the members of the brotherhood of Our Lady of the Rosary and Saint Benedict of the Black Men, Guerra was also the director of the Black's Museum (Museu do Negro), a small and modest institution maintained by the brotherhood since 1938, at the back

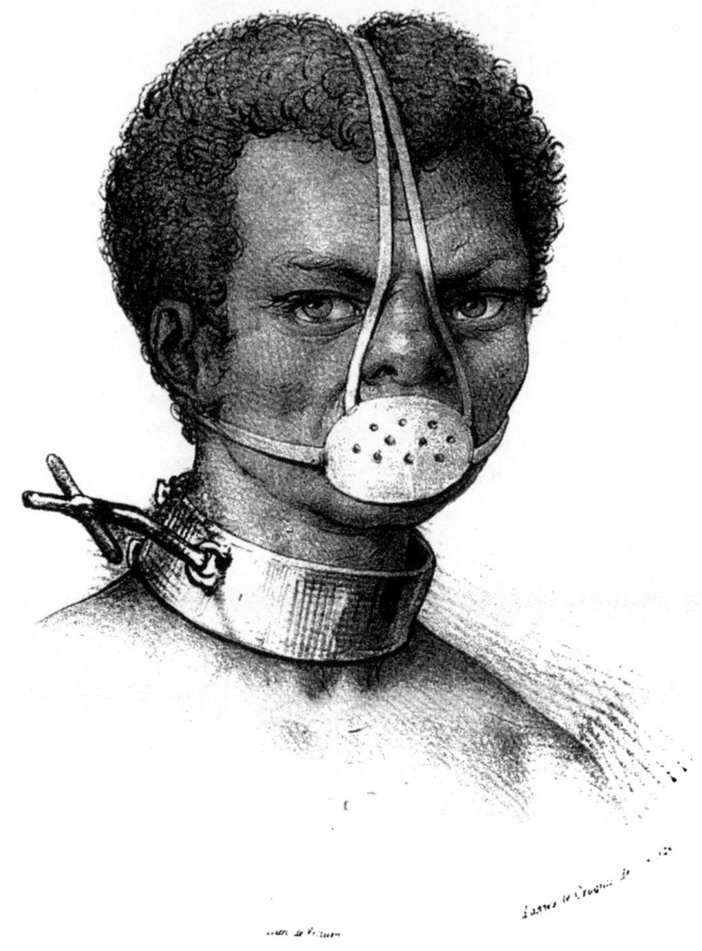

FIGURE 14.3. *Châtiments des esclaves (Brésil)* (*Punishment of Slaves [Brazil]*), in Jacques Arago, *Souvenirs d'un aveugle: Voyage autour du monde*, vol. 1 (Paris: H. Lebrun, 1842), 119.

of the church's building.[35] Guerra curated an exhibition to commemorate the eightieth anniversary of the abolition of slavery in Brazil in 1968.[36] On that occasion, he displayed on one of the museum's walls an engraving depicting an enslaved man that illustrated the nineteenth-century travelogue *Souvenirs d'un aveugle: Voyage autour du monde* (figure 14.3) by French traveler Jacques Étienne Victor Arago.[37] Although legendary Anastácia was a woman, Guerra started lecturing about her using the image of the muzzled enslaved man taken from Arago's travel account, hence circulating her picture as she is currently known in Brazil. Anastácia gained many new followers during the second half of the twentieth century, and through existing brotherhoods of the Rosary, her devotion was disseminated to other Brazilian states. Rio de Janeiro's Black's Museum displays many images of Anastácia. Likewise, the sacristy and an altar of a slave cemetery in Salvador's Church of Our Lady of the Rosary of the Black Men also feature numerous images depicting Anastácia. Moreover, to this day, the brotherhood's members celebrate a Catholic mass paying homage to the enslaved saint on May 13, the date of the abolition of slavery in Brazil.

Black Kings and Queens

Despite the central role of Catholicism in disseminating the devotion to Black saints and creating brotherhoods, the election and processions featuring Black kings were not always associated with the presence of Catholicism. All over the Americas, enslaved Africans and their descendants organized public festivals and coronation of kings held especially during holidays associated with Black saints such as Saint Efigenia, Saint Benedict, and Saint Elesbão, as well as Our Lady of the Rosary, Corpus Christi, Epiphany, Easter, Pentecost, All Saints' Day, All Souls' Day, Saint George's Day, Saint João's Day, and Saint James's Day.[38]

Take the example of New England, where from the middle of the eighteenth century until the middle of the nineteenth century, Africans and their descendants elected their kings or "governors."[39] As in Latin America, bondspeople commemorated these coronations with processions that included music and dance. During the Dutch rule in what was then New Amsterdam (in today's Manhattan), enslaved Africans and their descendants started commemorating Pinkster, a Pentecost holiday celebrated seven weeks after Easter Sunday.

Throughout Pinkster festivities, which lasted a few days, enslaved people also crowned their kings and paraded the streets. As late as in the nineteenth century, enslaved people and white people took the streets of cities such as Albany and Kingston in New York.[40] Albeit in a different context than that of colonial North America and the northern United States, enslaved people in Latin America also commemorated the Brazilian Pentecost holiday by participating in the Catholic feast of *Divino Espírito Santo* (Divine Holy Ghost). Although the festival was not led by a Black brotherhood and did not honor a Black saint, enslaved people appropriated the commemoration by participating in its parades, dancing, drumming, and collecting alms.[41]

In Brazil and the rest of Latin America, the coronation of kings of Congo was associated with the activities of the brotherhood of Our Lady of the Rosary, whose members were usually connected to West Central Africa. Since the seventeenth century, the various chapters of the brotherhood of the Church of Our Lady of the Rosary in Rio de Janeiro and in the gold-producing Minas Gerais had preserved the tradition of choosing Black kings. These kings could belong to any "nation," but their coronation was gradually associated with the election of a king belonging to the "Congo nation," a label that we have already seen referred to enslaved Africans who were embarked in the main ports of West Central Africa.

In a travelogue published in the early nineteenth century, British planter and traveler Henry Koster (who spent most of his short life in Brazil) reported the election of the king and queen of Congo during the festival of Our Lady of the Rosary in the church of Amparo in Olinda, which was at the time the capital of the then-captaincy of Pernambuco in northeast Brazil. He described the members of the court entering the church wearing "cotton dresses of colours and of white, with flags flying and drums beating," whereas the king, the queen, and the secretary of state each "wore upon their heads a crown, which was partly covered with gilt paper, and painted in various colours." Also according to Koster, the "king was dressed in an old fashioned suit of divers tints, green, red, and yellow; coat, waistcoat, and breeches" and holding a wooden scepter; the queen "was in a blue silk gown, also of ancient make"; and the secretary "had to boast of as many colours as his master" even though apparently portions of his costume were "borrowed from a different quarter, for some parts were too tight and others too wide for him."[42] As enslaved people and freedpeople appropriated these festivals, they incorporated, blended, and re-created Christian and African traditions such as songs and dances, and material culture items such as musical instruments and clothing.

Although Black kings and queens along with their courts paraded the streets of various Latin American regions several times during the year, their presence was usually visible when enslaved men, women, and children took to the streets to celebrate *folia de reis* (folly of kings), a festival held between Christmas and the Epiphany (January 6), commemorating the visit of the three Magi to Jesus after his birth. The three kings had a particular significance among Black populations in Latin America because, as we noted earlier, King Balthasar had been depicted as a Black person prior to the rise of the Atlantic slave trade. For instance, when Ewbank visited the Church of Our Lady of Lampadosa in Rio de Janeiro, he observed an image of "Balthazar, King of Congo" standing on the main altar just next to the image of the church's virgin patron saint.[43] But despite the emphasis on kings of Congo, enslaved West Africans from various regions also elected kings. Take the example of the brotherhood of Saint Elesbão and Saint Efigenia and the Mahi congregation housed in the church of Saint Elesbão and Saint Efigenia in Rio de Janeiro. Both associations included enslaved people identified as Mina and Mahi from the Bight of Benin, and they elected not only kings and queens but also other dignitaries and officers such as dukes, counts, marquises, and generals during the eighteenth century.[44]

All over Brazil, these popular festivals became alternative sites of power for both the enslaved and freed populations. These kings and their courts took to the streets to collect donations for the organization of the various festivals of the Catholic Church honoring patron saints. Dressed in full regalia, the king and the members of the court were followed by parades, in which white, Native, and mixed-race individuals also participated. Although tolerated by the public authorities, as noted by French artist Jean-Baptiste Debret, this kind of public Black commemoration of "their homeland" was prohibited in 1808, when the Portuguese royal court moved to Rio de Janeiro, because of the noise and disturbance it caused, therefore confirming the subversive potential of Black festivals.[45]

Historians and anthropologists have attempted to explain the election of Black kings and the rise of Black festivals and other Black cultural manifestations in the Americas in a number of ways. One model relying on the idea that African cultures were transferred and survived in the Americas sought to understand how these celebrations manifested the endurance of practices brought from West Africa and West Central Africa. But this view, which was largely promoted by the early twentieth-century anthropologist Melville J. Herskovits, evoked an idea of Africa as a timeless and therefore ahistorical continent, not taking into consideration that the continent and its populations kept changing during the more than three hundred years of the Atlantic slave trade.[46]

A second line of interpretation contends that these manifestations are not African survivals but rather result from cultural mixture. Defined as *creolization*, this approach explains Black cultures in the Americas as an amalgamation of various African, European, and Indigenous traditions in response to the dehumanization imposed by slavery.[47]

A third framework to understand Black populations and their cultures in the Americas focuses on the forced migration of enslaved people from West Africa and West Central Africa during the era of the Atlantic slave trade. Defined as an *Atlantic model*, this approach has been challenged because of its excessive focus on Europe and the Americas that not only pays little attention to Africa but also excludes the Indian Ocean connections and places an excessive emphasis on the United States.[48]

Finally, a fourth model, which is the one adopted in this book, draws from the idea of the existence of a worldwide African diaspora.

This framework does not emphasize that Africa is part of a distant past but rather highlights that globally dispersed African populations share a common identity and a connection with the homeland. However, even in the context of the Atlantic world, these connections are not fixed. As put by historian Joseph E. Harris, they assume "the character of a dynamic, continuous, and complex phenomenon stretching across time, geography, class, and gender."[49]

In the context of these debates, some Brazilian historians argued that Black Brazilian Catholicism was different from what they refer to as a generic "African" Catholicism. Marina de Mello e Souza, for example, underscored that Black festivals reflected European power while maintaining connections with their African origins and creating their own institutions. According to this perspective, these manifestations were at the same time acts of resistance and accommodation that reinforced the insertion of enslaved Africans in European colonial societies while evoking a mythologized Africa.[50] In the twenty-first century, other scholars have also contested the early views based on a general and vague idea of an Africa frozen in time, among other reasons because they failed to explain how particular African cultures shaped the construction of specific Black cultural manifestations in various parts of Brazil. For example, Elizabeth Kiddy has shown how the coronation of kings of Congo and the parades commemorating these kings in Minas Gerais did not reject a West Central African past but rather embraced it while also incorporating European practices.[51] Mariza de Carvalho Soares relied not only on written documents but also on visual images produced by European artists and travelers in Brazil during the eighteenth and nineteenth centuries to explain how Black brotherhoods and their festivals and elections of kings allowed West Africans from the Bight of Benin, and not only West Central Africa, to keep solid ethnic connections in Rio de Janeiro.[52] More recently, drawing from a rich array of visual images, Cécile Fromont has brought to light the links between Black Brazilian parades and *sangamento*, a "ritual performance from the early modern central African kingdom of Kongo," by explaining how the elections and processions of Black kings and queens in Brazil drew from existing West Central African practices as a response to bondage in the Americas.[53]

In the United States and the West Indies, as in Brazil and the rest of Latin America, bondspeople celebrated Christmas. In the United States, enslaved people described how Christmas was the only period during the entire year when they were allowed to take a break from work. Solomon Northup, who was kidnapped and sold into slavery in 1841, explained that whereas his owner allowed three days off, other slave owners gave their enslaved property between four and six days of rest during the holidays. According to him, this period of "feasting, frolicking, and fiddling" was the "carnival season with the children of bondage."[54]

Northup also reported that every year one slave owner in central Louisiana's Bayou Boeuf offered a Christmas supper to the enslaved people of neighboring plantations, an occasion that could attract as many as five hundred men, women, and children who came "on foot, in carts, on horseback, on mules, riding double and triple" to attend the open-air banquet. Northup noted, "Only the slave who has lived all the years on his scantly allowance of meal and bacon can appreciate such suppers" that included several kinds of meat, vegetables, bacon, cornmeal, and biscuits, as well as peaches, preserves, pies, and tarts.[55] Once the supper ended, bondspeople danced and sang. Northup, who would be the one playing violin during these gatherings, observed how "the African race is a music-loving one" and how his fellow "bondsmen whose organs of tune were strikingly developed . . . could thumb the banjo with dexterity."[56] Music certainly allowed Northup to endure his twelve years living as a slave; as he writes, "Alas! had it not been for my beloved violin, I scarcely can conceive how I could have endured the long years of bondage."[57] The ability to play violin not only allowed him to express himself, but it also occasionally relieved him from working longer hours and gave him access to extra rations of food, tobacco, and even shoes.

Abolitionist Harriet Jacobs, who like Douglass escaped bondage, similarly described how enslaved people enjoyed Christmas festivities in her narrative published about a decade after Northup's account. She reported that "every child rises early on Christmas morning to see the Johnkannaus. Without them, Christmas would be shorn of its greatest attraction."[58] Jacobs is among the very few authors of slave narratives in the United States, if not the only, to mention Johnkannaus (also known as Jonkonu, Johnkonnu, John Conner, and John Canoe). In her own words, the festivity consisted of groups of enslaved people in which "two athletic men, in calico wrappers, have a net thrown over them, covered with all manner of bright-colored stripes. Cows' tails are fastened to their backs, and their heads are decorated with horns."[59] These troupes, which might include up to one hundred enslaved men, started parading early in the morning. Singing and dancing, a dozen members of the group played drums made of boxes covered with sheepskin. Other revelers played triangles and jawbones (idiophone percussion instruments made from the jawbone of a horse, mule, or donkey) and went from door to door asking for contributions.

A similar Christmas masquerade named Jonkonnu was first documented in Jamaica in the late seventeenth century. More than one century later, artist Isaac Mendes Belisario described the performance by illustrating his description in a series of lithographs showing that enslaved revelers played the same musical instruments described by Harriet Jacobs in her narrative (figure 14.4). Scholars have linked Johnkonnu festivals to West African secret societies in the Bight of Biafra by also underscoring how these masquerades changed across the Atlantic Ocean and during the long period of the Atlantic slave trade.[60]

Because nearly 750,000 men, women, and children from Igboland were sent into slavery in the Americas, especially from 1750 to 1830, one historian more specifically associated the rise of Jonkonnu with the presence of Igbo-speaking peoples in North America and the West Indies. Following this interpretation, the term *jonkonu* would

FIGURE 14.4. Isaac Mendes Belisario (1795–1849), *Sketches of character: In illustration of the habits, occupation, and costume of the Negro population, in the island of Jamaica* (Kingston, Jamaica: Published by the artist, at his residence, no. 21 King-Street . . . , 1837[–38]). Courtesy of Yale British Art Center, Yale University, New Haven, CT, United States.

be related to *njokku* (*ifejioku*), the cult of the Yam spirit and the secret male society *Okonko* (also related to yams). Therefore, white settlers and slave owners called the performance John Konu because the male performers, who prepared their Christmas presentations throughout the year, shouted the word *njokku* during the parades.[61] But no matter how these parades were connected to specific ethnic groups and regions and how they changed over time, enslaved people who performed Jonkonnu used it to reclaim their personhood in a society in which slaveholders daily attempted to deny their humanity. As we will see later, in other parts of the Americas, enslaved people participated in several other festivals and processions that incorporated costumes, masks, musical instruments, songs, and dance similar to Jonkonnu, and despite being transformed over time, they are still today largely celebrated by Black populations in the Americas.

During the era of slavery, bondspeople in the United States took advantage of the fact that slave owners and overseers were often distracted during the holidays by planning their escapes to coincide with the festivities. John Andrew Jackson, for example, was owned by a Quaker family of planters in South Carolina. After being separated from his wife and his child, he decided to run away during the three-day Christmas holiday of 1846. His escape was successful. After reaching Charleston, he was able to flee to the North and eventually reached New Brunswick in Canada.[62] Like Jackson, Harriet Tubman also successfully escaped from the plantation where she was enslaved in Maryland in 1849, later returning to rescue her three brothers Ben, Henry, and Robert from slavery on Christmas Day of 1854. These cases remind us that congregating and reveling were also opportunities to *resist* slavery across the Americas, not just seek momentary reprieve from its tragic realities.

Carnivals, Dance, Music, and Martial Arts

Black festivities were not limited to Christmas. Several other festivals carried elements in common with the processions of *folia de reis*. Brazilian Carnaval is one of these festivals. Enslaved, freed, and free Black populations were the main participants in Brazilian *carnaval*, a festival that, like New Orleans's Mardi Gras, is celebrated still today everywhere in the country from Saturday until Tuesday, the last day before the beginning of Lent. *Carnaval* derives from the Portuguese *entrudo*, a popular festivity held three days before the beginning of Lent, brought to Brazil by the Portuguese from the islands of Madeira, Azores, and Cape Verde in the seventeenth century. But unlike the *folias de reis*, the *entrudo* was not an organized and hierarchical celebration. During the *entrudo*, people took to the streets and participated in mock battles with buckets of water and *limões de cheiro*, scent-filled wax balls. In his travel account *Voyage pittoresque et historique au Brésil*, Jean-Baptiste Debret explained that "the only preparations for the Brazilian carnaval consist of manufacturing limões de cheiro, an activity performed by everybody, including the family of the small capitalist, the poor widower, the free Black women who brought two or three friends, and finally the Black female slaves of the rich households who, two months prior to the festival, amass money to buy wax provisions."[63]

According to the same author, during *carnaval*, Black men would gather early in the morning around the market and the fountains and start throwing water and tapioca on Black women. However, he also mentions that these activities created disorder. As more aggressive confrontations took place, public authorities exerted greater control over the festivities. Slowly, this once spontaneous festival, originally celebrated mainly by Black people, became an organized festival that would also attract people of higher classes all over the country.

During the nineteenth century, enslaved people developed other forms of gathering, celebrating, and resisting in Brazil. One of these manifestations is *jongo* (or *caxambu*), an Afro-Brazilian dance and music style associated with enslaved West Central Africans and their descendants who toiled in the coffee plantations of southeast Brazil during the nineteenth century. Men and women gathered in a circle (*roda*) usually around a bonfire, dancing, drumming, and clapping their hands, while a couple dances in the center of the circle, following the rhythm of the music. *Jongo* survived after the end of slavery, but it was largely neglected among the younger Black generations during most of the twentieth century. Nonetheless, since the 1990s, several communities of descendants of enslaved people in the Paraíba Valley have recovered the tradition and today organize festivals promoting the ancestral dance in urban and rural areas in Rio de Janeiro.[64]

Like *jongo*, the first documented references to *capoeira* date back to the early nineteenth century. Evolving from various combat games introduced in Brazil by enslaved West Central Africans and their descendants, capoeira emerged in urban areas where, during the nineteenth century, it was practiced by enslaved, freed, and free Black and mixed-race men.[65] Because capoeira was initially a Black martial art used for self-defense and in street fights, Brazilian authorities considered it a dangerous activity that should be repressed.

Over the years, capoeira gradually incorporated music as well as body movements from other dances and Asian martial arts introduced in Brazil in the early twentieth century. In the twenty-first century, capoeira has been increasingly accepted and embraced by white Brazilians, and today it is practiced in several contexts, even by women. Ultimately, capoeira gained great popularity in Brazil as well as internationally, including in several African countries. It is especially notable in that capoeira's trajectory shows that cultural transfers from Africa to the Americas did not follow a linear direction but rather a circular model.[66]

Gathering to drink, eat, dance, sing, and celebrate saints helped bondspeople survive the ordeals of slavery in the Americas. In Cuba, the Catholic mutual aid societies and *cabildos de nación* (societies that, like Catholic lay brotherhoods, allowed Africans to gather along ethnic lines), also elected kings of Congo.[67] These organizations allowed for the emergence of Santería (also known as Regla de Ocha, Regla de Ifá, or Lucumí) and Palo Mayombe (also Palo Monte or Reglas de Congo), Afro-Cuban religions incorporating elements of Yoruba and

Kongo religious systems.[68] In Brazil, Black brotherhoods that very often preserved the connections among men and women sharing the same languages and ethnic backgrounds favored the development of the first temples of Candomblé in Bahia during the second half of the nineteenth century. Embracing elements of West African religions such as Vodun and Orisa and incorporating elements of Native American cosmologies and Catholicism, enslaved Africans and their descendants formed Candomblé shrines that were organized according to deities (*orixás*) and "nations" associated with their region of provenance on the African continent. After the abolition of slavery, the need to reestablish bonds disrupted by the slave trade encouraged a recuperation and reinvention of African bonds as well. Hence, several leaders of these temples, such as the aforementioned freedman Bamboxê Obitikô (who is buried in the Church of Our Lady of the Rosary of the Black Men), traveled back and forth from Brazil to the Bight of Benin.[69] Likewise, under similar contexts, Africans and Afro-Brazilians created other shrines associated with West African and West Central African religious systems in Rio de Janeiro, Pernambuco, Maranhão, and Rio Grande do Sul, giving birth to Candomblé temples and other Afro-Brazilian religions such as Batuque and Umbanda.

Catholic lay Black brotherhoods (with their saints, church buildings, and masses) and Candomblé temples shape the ways slavery is still remembered and commemorated in Brazil's public space today. Let us take again the example of the brotherhood of Our Lady of the Rosary of the Black Men that also became a popular tourist landmark and an important place of Black cultural assertion in Brazil at the end of the 1980s. The church celebrates Black masses on Sundays and Tuesdays. The service includes dance, food offerings, and music performed by brotherhood members who play drums, tambourines, and *agogôs* (from the Yoruba word *agogo*), an idiophone consisting of a single or double bell.

All these elements associated with Black festivals were not part of the traditional masses but rather related to a broader movement of

Black culture assertion, which was initiated among Catholic youth groups that emerged during the final years of the long civil-military dictatorship that ruled Brazil between 1964 and 1985. During this period, through the activity of other Black organizations, including Carnaval groups such as the renowned *Ilê Aiyê* and *Olodum*, new members associated with local Candomblé temples and whose parents and grandparents had not been historically affiliated started joining the brotherhood. Recognizing how Catholic Black confraternities contributed to the survival of their ancestors, today's members of the brotherhood of Our Lady of the Rosary of the Black Men do not conceive Catholicism and Candomblé as mutually exclusive. Therefore, the church's Black masses are part of a broader set of initiatives that during the 1990s aimed at revitalizing Salvador's historic center. One of these events is the celebration of Blessing Tuesday (*Terça-Feira da Benção*), organized by the famous carnival and musical group *Olodum*, which led the brotherhood to celebrate every Tuesday a Black mass honoring the Black Saint Anthony of Categeró. Although this mass is quite similar to Sunday mass, on Tuesdays the members of the brotherhood share dozens of loaves of bread with a crowd of excited attendants, including tourists, who sing and dance to songs commemorating the slavery past, celebrating Black culture, denouncing the persistence of racism in Brazilian society but also conveying a message of self-esteem.[70]

Reveling as Resistance

On plantations and in cities, enslaved people found time and spaces to revel, with or without the permission of their owners. Bondspeople participated in religious feasts and pagan festivals associated with the Christian calendar and African traditions. Whether celebrating a patron saint or Christmas, enslaved people created and re-created dance and musical traditions brought from Africa. Combining these practices with European and Native American dance and music styles, they passed down these traditions during the era of the Atlantic slave trade, even though some of these festivities were gradually dissociated from their initial religious dimension. Drumming, dancing, and singing were integral parts of festivities and were also present in other informal gatherings held in slave quarters, as well as streets and squares of various cities in the Americas. Knowing about the subversive potential of these meetings, slave owners and overseers carefully watched these meetings and on several occasions unsuccessfully attempted to prohibit them. But despite any attempts to repress these gatherings, as we will see in chapters 15 and 16, formal and informal Black organizations persisted during the nineteenth century and were crucial tools in the fight for emancipation.

CHAPTER 15

Rebellions across Borders

On a warm summer Saturday, January 24, 1835, rumors that Africans, especially of the Nagô "nation," were organizing an insurgence for early the next morning started circulating in the commercial area of Salvador's lower city in Brazil. The news quickly spread among enslaved people and freedpeople, ultimately reaching the ears of white residents. Informed about the plot, the president of the province moved fast and alerted the police chief, who deployed contingents of officers to inspect the houses of suspected African individuals. As these events unfolded, news emerged that several Africans had attacked parts of the city: "In few minutes, they appeared in numbers of 50 to 60, armed with swords, some spears, and even pistols and other weapons."[1] The battle continued for several hours. Led by Muslim Africans, the insurrection became known as the Malê Revolt, the largest urban slave uprising in the Americas.

Whether on plantations or in the dark and stinking streets of urban areas, bondspeople plotted rebellions. On the sugarcane plantations on the island of Hispaniola, as early as 1521, enslaved Africans organized the first slave uprising in the Western Hemisphere. As slavery expanded in the Americas, bondspeople planned a slave rebellion in New York City in 1712, and then again in 1741. Several other revolts followed during the eighteenth century. The Stono Rebellion in South Carolina in 1739 was the largest insurrection led by enslaved men and women in colonial North America. In 1791, in the context of the

French Revolution, a great slave revolt broke out in Saint-Domingue. The insurgence led to the decree of 1794 that abolished slavery in the French colonies in the West Indies and the Indian Ocean. But when slavery was reinstated in 1802, insurrection intensified. The insurgents eventually defeated the French army in Saint-Domingue and cut their ties with France, creating the first Black independent nation in the Americas.

The political transformations brought by the French Revolution contributed to the rise of the Saint-Domingue slave rebellion. But European revolutions were not the only ones to influence rebellions in the colonies. Ongoing transformations on the African continent also impacted the events unfolding in the Americas. Starting at the end of the eighteenth century, several wars broke out in large areas of Yorubaland in West Africa, eventually leading to the fall of the Oyo Empire and the emergence of new urban centers such as Ilorin, Ibadan, and Abeokuta. As we noted earlier in the book, West African social actors involved in these conflicts became war captives and were sold into slavery in the Americas. On the other side of the Atlantic Ocean, the echoes of these conflicts continued to resonate in the rise of slave rebellions in Cuba and Bahia, regions with large concentrations of enslaved individuals born on the African continent. After exploring the multiple ways through which enslaved men and women resisted against slavery throughout the era of the Atlantic slave trade, this chapter considers the larger context of Atlantic revolutions to explore the rise of slave revolts in the Americas.

While considering several slave rebellions in North America, South America, and the West Indies, as well as on slave ships, I will pay particular attention to the broader impact of the Malê Revolt of 1835 in Bahia. Whereas a combination of internal and external factors led to the emergence of this revolt, the repression that evolved in the aftermath of the uprising seriously affected the daily life of enslaved people and freedpeople in Bahia and other parts of Brazil. As newspaper articles show, Brazilian slave owners and government authorities in various regions of the country closely followed the rebellion's aftermath. Several European and US newspapers also paid attention to the news about the insurrection. Moreover, the rebellion also contributed to the first large movement of former enslaved individuals back to West Africa.

African Linkages

Enslaved people resisted slavery in many ways, but in exceptional contexts they were able to organize revolts that brought together dozens and even hundreds of bondspeople. The motivations that led slaves to take the risky route to form a collective rebellion depended on several elements such as local and international revolutions and religion.

Concrete problems such as working conditions also certainly prompted revolts to erupt in a specific moment, and larger uprisings often occurred in places where Black people and enslaved people outnumbered the white population. Several revolts also occurred in regions where the number of African-born enslaved persons was more significant. Most of these Africans were born free in their homelands. Several were religious leaders. Many others who were captured during wars had previous knowledge of warfare. These skills and experiences drove them to join other countrymen and to resist the violence of the legal slave status imposed on them.

Some revolts were either led by or involved freedpeople born either in Africa or the Americas. Existing records associated with most insurrections identify male leaders and participants and rarely reveal the participation of women in these rebellions. But despite this invisibility, bondswomen and freedwomen played all sorts of roles in the preparation of these insurgencies by providing information, shelter, food, and tools to rebels. On the eve of these rebellions, bondswomen individually killed slave owners through various means, including poison.[2] Several slave rebellions were repressed at their inception, but others lasted for several days or weeks until slaveholders eventually successfully defeated the rebels. Not all these revolts clearly sought to end slavery, but all these insurrections destabilized the power of slaveholders. Ultimately, the Saint-Domingue slave revolt succeeded in ending slavery on the western portion of Hispaniola, creating the new Black nation of Haiti in 1804. Ironically, the very same island had been also the site of the first slave rebellion in the Americas nearly three centuries earlier.

Just a few years after disembarking on the island Hispaniola (in what is the present-day Dominican Republic and Haiti), enslaved Africans led the first rebellion in the Americas. As noted in chapter 14, enslaved people took advantage of the end-of-year holiday season to plan escapes, since their owners and overseers were distracted by the festivities. During the first three decades of their presence on Hispaniola, enslaved Africans resisted bondage in various ways, running away individually and in groups. But in 1521, they organized the first slave rebellion. On December 21, they took over the sugar estate owned by Diego Colón (the son of Christopher Columbus), the island's governor and viceroy of the Indies. From the banks of the Nigua River, where the plantation was located, the rebels armed themselves with all the "weapons they could find and made others out of sharpened poles," then walked westward for more than sixty miles, reaching the Nigua village.[3] The insurgents reportedly stole gold from travelers they met along the roads, as well as jewelry and clothes from the properties they attacked.

We can assume most of these rebels were born on the African continent and had been forced to convert to Roman Catholicism. Therefore, their goal was to "kill all the Christians they could and to free themselves and take over the land."[4] Spanish colonists put down the insurrection using their weapons and cavalry to repress the rebels. A few months after the rebellion, they imposed a set of new laws to control the enslaved population, including physical punishments, to prevent new insurrections.[5] Although there were previous regulations to repress slave fugitives, this legislation became the oldest legal code mandating restrictions precisely against enslaved persons in the Americas.

Slave rebellions were not circumscribed to zones where plantation slavery predominated; they also occurred in urban areas. In 1712, the colony of New York witnessed its first slave revolt on the night of April 6, made up of twenty-four slaves, among whom were several West African-born enslaved men and at least two bondswomen, one of whom was pregnant.[6] Armed with axes, knives, firearms, and other weapons, they started an insurrection in New York City by setting fire to the outhouse of Peter Vantilborough, a baker who owned two of the enslaved rebels. As white residents tried to extinguish the fire, the insurgents ambushed them, killing nine white individuals and wounding at least seven others. When the colonial militia and soldiers intervened to stop the insurrection, six enslaved people killed themselves before being captured, including one bondswoman. Colonizers arrested seventy Black persons in the rebellion. Twenty-six enslaved persons were convicted and tried, among whom four were women—Amba and Lilly were acquitted, whereas Sarah and Abigail were convicted. It remains unclear which of the convicted bondswomen was pregnant.[7] In total, twenty-one slaves were sentenced to death.[8]

Beyond the obvious brutality of being held in bondage, what could have led these men and women to organize this uprising? Walter Rucker has noted that nearly half of the convicted rebels in New York City were West African–born, Akan-speaking men identified in the primary documents as Coromantee, a term referring "to two Fante-speaking towns, Upper and Lower Kormantse and a nearby trading factory" on the Gold Coast, in present-day Ghana. Moreover, their names corresponded to days of the week, following the existing tradition among Akan speakers.[9] Hence, a male child born on Monday would be called Kwado on the Gold Coast, but in the Americas this name became Cudjo, whereas a female child born the same day would be called Adwowa on the Gold Coast, which in the Americas became Juba. Likewise, a baby born on Friday on the Gold Coast would be called Kwefi, Cuffy, Cuffee, or Kofi in the Americas.[10]

Among the insurgents was an Akan-speaking conjurer known as "Peter the Doctor." According to his testimony collected by the British colonial authorities, he "administered a powder, which being rubbed on their bodies, was to make them invulnerable."[11] Similarly to the slave rebellion in Hispaniola, contemporaneous accounts reported that New York City's rebels "conspired to murder all the Christians" and "destroy all the White [people] in order to obtain their freedom."[12] As in further revolts, not all rebels were necessarily African-born enslaved people, but Akan speakers had a leading role in the movement. As in the Black Catholic brotherhoods examined in chapter 14, ethnic links certainly played an important role in bringing bondspeople together to organize an insurrection and collectively attempt to free themselves.

The aftermath of the 1712 rebellion was marked by increasingly repressive measures imposed on the enslaved, freed, and free Black population, and also on white people who allegedly helped Black people. The colony's governor, fearing further uprisings, proposed that the colonial legislature pass laws regulating the activity of slaves and recommended increasing the number of white indentured servants in the colony. Knowing that bondspeople plotted and started uprisings during the night, the newly enacted legislation imposed a curfew that limited their movement. But the new laws also affected freeborn and freed Black individuals by preventing the growth of the free Black community and limiting the social mobility of existing free Black people. The new law made it much more difficult for slave owners to emancipate their human property, as to do so they had to pay a security amount between four and six times the price of an adult enslaved person. Furthermore, enslaved people manumitted after 1712 were prohibited from owning real estate.[13]

Almost three decades later, enslaved Africans organized a plot in New York City. On March 18, 1741, a bondsman named Quaco (or Kweku, meaning Wednesday in Akan) burned down Fort George, the headquarters of the British royal government and the governor's residence in New York City. Also, an enslaved man called Cuffee (suggesting he was an Akan speaker) was arrested when fleeing his owner's burning storehouse. In the weeks that followed, other fires broke out around the city. The investigation that followed showed that the fires were part of a plot. Participants comprised enslaved men and women, including Akan speakers, and also slaves seized from a Spanish ship who had been transported to New York City, where they were sold and became locally identified as "Spanish negroes." But English and Irish workers also joined the conspiracy, which led to the series of fires that became known as the New York Conspiracy of 1741 (also called the Negro Plot or Slave Insurrection).[14]

Despite the involvement of African-born individuals in the plot, in contrast with the New York City slave revolt of 1712 and the Hispaniola slave rebellion of 1521, the goal of the plotters of 1741 was not to kill Christians or white people but rather, as historian Leslie M. Harris put it, to "achieve greater economic and political equality."[15] Still, colonial authorities largely targeted enslaved conspirators. Most of the two hundred alleged plotters arrested during the investigation were bondspeople. Thirty enslaved men were sentenced to execution, whereas seventy other bondsmen and bondswomen were deported from the colony. As in the aftermath of other slave insurrections, the control over the enslaved population in New York City increased in the years that followed the conspiracy. But resistance against slavery continued. In the next decades of the eighteenth century, at least three other major rebellions erupted in the Americas.

On September 9, 1739, just two years before the New York Conspiracy of 1741, enslaved people started a major revolt in the Southern colony of South Carolina, where rice cultivation predominated.[16] The insurrection that became known as the Stono Rebellion emerged in a context in which Black and enslaved people had outnumbered the colony's white population for nearly three decades. In 1740, one year after the rebellion, there were 39,200 enslaved Black people for 25,000 white people.[17] Gathered along the banks of the Stono River approximately twenty miles southwest of Charleston, a group of enslaved men armed with stolen firearms and other weapons, flying flags and playing drums, started marching with the goal of reaching St. Augustine in Spanish Florida. The insurrection was likely a response to a call from Spanish colonizers who promised freedom to South Carolina's rebels willing to join Spanish forces. As they passed through other plantations, the rebels attracted nearly one hundred enslaved persons. Eventually the militia stopped the insurgents by killing some men, but a few rebels continued to resist in the following days.

The fact that, in this context, Black people largely outnumbered the white population allowed enslaved people to feel sufficiently empowered to take the risky path of rebellion. The invitation to join the Spanish colony may have been particularly attractive to a number of insurgents who were likely born in the Kingdom of Kongo, in West Central Africa. As previously explained, Kongo rulers and their subjects had embraced Christianity since the late fifteenth century. Moreover, the presence of enslaved rebels born in Kongo could also explain the rebels' familiarity with firearms, as the kingdom was involved in a series of wars that led to the capture of prisoners trained as soldiers who were sold into slavery to North America during the eighteenth century.[18] As the rebellion was suppressed, twenty white persons and approximately forty enslaved rebels were killed. Fear of new rebellions remained, haunting British colonists and slave owners. To prevent new revolts, legislation that stopped, at least temporarily, the introduction of new Africans into the colony passed in April 1740, and one month later, a new act established several other measures to limit the mobility of the enslaved population.[19]

Race Wars in Jamaica and Saint-Domingue

Still during the eighteenth century, two other major slave rebellions broke out in the British colony of Jamaica and in the Dutch colony of Berbice, both colonies where slaves largely outnumbered white settlers. In 1760, enslaved men and women started in Jamaica the largest slave revolt in the eighteenth-century British Empire. The rebellion broke out in the context of the Seven Years' War, a global conflict that lasted from 1756 to 1763, involving all major European powers, and which in the context of the Americas, opposed Great Britain and France. The insurrection became known as Tacky's Revolt, as one of its leaders was a West African–born man named Tacky. The rebels declared a race war against British colonizers, slave owners, and overseers in Jamaica. Once again, enslaved West African Akan speakers from the Gold Coast were prominent participants in the revolt. As Vincent Brown has argued, insurgents drew from their previous experience in West African warfare in their war against white colonists.[20]

In contrast with the previous rebellions in colonial North America involving dozens of bondspeople, Tacky's Revolt gathered more than 1,000 enslaved persons and continued for nearly eighteen months. During the rebellion, whereas the insurgents killed 60 white people, British forces killed 500 Black men and women. On February 27, 1763, just three years after Tacky's Revolt started, a slave revolt broke out in Berbice, a Dutch colony on South America's Caribbean coast in the region of today's Guyana. Burning plantations and scaring away white settlers, the insurgents gathered nearly all the colony's enslaved population, at the time composed of between 4,000 to 5,000 individuals, who controlled Berbice for more than one year. The rebellion's leader, Coffij van Lelienburg, as suggested by his first name, was once again a West African–born Akan speaker. As historian Marjoleine Kars has shown, Coffij and his countrymen embarked in slave ships that left from the Gold Coast and were certainly well versed in military affairs, much like the African-born rebels who led Tacky's Revolt in Jamaica.[21] Whereas the rebels killed dozens of white people, as the Dutch army retook control of the colony, it executed 125 bondsmen and 3 bondswomen.

This long series of slave revolts in societies where many enslaved people were born in Africa and outnumbered European and locally born white settlers eventually culminated with a major slave rebellion in Saint-Domingue in 1791. A French colony located on the western part of the island of Hispaniola, Saint-Domingue was the richest European colony in the Americas by the time of the uprising, which is inseparable from the larger Atlantic repercussions of the French Revolution that broke out in 1789 and led to a decade of political and social change. Taking down the rigid structure of the ancien régime that maintained the majority of the population as members of the third estate (all those below the aristocracy), the revolution propelled ideas of freedom and equality. More important, the Saint-Domingue slave revolt is also part of the long history of slave resistance and rebellions in the Americas during the eighteenth century.

Like Jamaica, Saint-Domingue had a huge Black population that clearly outnumbered the white population at the end of the eighteenth century. On the eve of the French Revolution, about two-thirds of Saint-Domingue's enslaved population, estimated at half a million individuals, were born in Africa.[22] Although smaller than in the Spanish colony of Cuba, Saint-Domingue also had its own population of freed and freeborn people of color (*gens de couleur*). Among the *gens de couleur* who were formerly enslaved, some had been emancipated by their owners. However, more likely, most of them were able to purchase their own freedom with their own resources at some point in their lives. Many *gens de couleur* were of modest means, but some of them became planters and slave owners. Still, their freed or free status combined with their African ancestry placed these men and women in an intermediary position between the enslaved population and white planters. Regardless of these nuances, white planters were fully aware that depending on the circumstances, free people of color could support enslaved Black populations. Therefore, the presence and free circulation of *gens de couleur* in the urban areas provoked concern among the authorities in the 1770s.[23] These administrators knew that slavery could only survive by restricting the political rights of free nonwhite populations. Hence, insisting on preserving racial distinctions, French colonists and planters had already supported legal barriers to restrict the rights of the colony's populations of color with measures that clearly established that a free legal status could not erase the deep mark of African ancestry.[24]

When the members of the third estate in France formed the National Assembly in 1789, the colonial delegates, planters, and merchants obviously opposed the end of slavery simply because the institution generated immense profits. These groups feared the end of slavery and took measures aimed at preventing news about the French Revolution from reaching the colonies in the Americas. For example, as the revolution unfolded in 1789, enslaved people from Saint-Domingue were prohibited to disembark in continental France because they could bring back to the colony ideas promoting insurrection and emancipation.[25] But obviously, the goals of these colonial measures were unsuccessful.

The "common wind" of rebellion, as the historian Julius S. Scott called it, quickly reached Saint-Domingue.[26] As the revolution progressed, the political disparities between the white and free population of color became even more explicit. Despite France's National Constituent Assembly in August 1789 having adopted of the Declaration of the Rights of Man, affirming the equality of rights among all men, the populations of color were not given the same rights as white people. Most white planters feared that granting rights to the *gens de couleur* would lead them to become the ruling class in the colonies. Once in power, they could emancipate their own enslaved property and the slaves owned by the white planters.

In March 1790, the National Assembly approved the creation of a Colonial Committee that established that French colonies would be ruled by their own legislation, therefore protecting slavery and the planters' interests. The committee also determined that only individuals who owned property could vote in the colonial elections, but it failed to explicitly mention the *gens de couleur*, giving them the ability to demand voting rights. As the legal routes closed, the populations of color decided to take up arms to fight for their rights in an anticolonial rebellion. In 1791, a decree by the National Assembly eventually gave voting rights only to *gens de couleur* who owned property and were born from free parents. But by that point, the enslaved people of Saint-Domingue had already been greatly affected by the news of rapid changes brought by the French Revolution. In August 1791, a slave revolt broke out in Saint-Domingue. Thousands of insurgents marched through Saint-Domingue's northern plain. Burning down plantations, big houses, and slave quarters, and killing slave owners, managers, and overseers, they gradually attracted even more insurgents. The rebellion continued for several months and progressively spread over the rest of the colony. At first, the population of color was willing to fight the slave rebels. But as their demands for political rights to the French National Assembly were denied, they decided to fight the white planters and took the slave rebels as their allies.[27]

On September 3, 1791, France adopted a new constitution that ended the ancien régime and established a constitutional monarchy. Despite providing amnesty for revolutionary acts, there was no consensus as to whether insurgent actions by *gens de couleur* and enslaved peoples in the colonies should be pardoned. In these circumstances, bondspeople who were already engaged in destroying slavery by emancipating themselves and killing their owners had nothing to lose.[28] The slave rebellion continued and became more violent. Slave rebels acquired great military experience, as both free persons of color and white people enlisted enslaved people to fight on their side. On April 4, 1792, the National Assembly attempted to neutralize the slave rebellion by giving the free people of color the same political rights as the white people. But bondspeople who had contributed to the victory of free people of color refused to return to the plantations. Ultimately, despite French efforts in gathering soldiers to fight the rebels, the revolt continued and expanded.

After the suspension of the National Assembly and the establishment of a National Convention in France, King Louis XVI was executed in January 1793. The end of the monarchy led Spain and Britain to declare war against France, complicating Saint-Domingue's position in the international arena. The Spanish offered Saint-Domingue's insurgents the option to join their troops in exchange for freedom. Meanwhile, the British obtained support from white planters. Later on, they also recruited African-born soldiers to join their ranks.[29] To counteract the British and the Spanish interventions, the French offered freedom and land to slave rebels who would join the French army. Two freedmen, Toussaint Louverture and André Rigaud, joined the forces that fought against the British invaders until their defeat in

1798.[30] French commissioners who had been in Saint-Domingue since 1792 to oversee the application of the decree giving political rights to the populations of color started freeing the enslaved persons in 1793 by gradually abolishing slavery in the colony. Eventually, on February 4, 1794, the National Convention finally approved the abolition of slavery in the French colonies, even though it was only implemented in Saint-Domingue, Guadeloupe, and Guiana, leaving out the colonies of Senegal, Île de France (Mauritius), Reunion Island, French India, and Martinique, which by that time was under British control. But the newly freed population faced many restrictions, as the threat of war and slavery continued to haunt Saint-Domingue.

As the revolution continued in Saint-Domingue, in 1799, Napoléon Bonaparte led a coup d'état that overthrew the Directory of France and replaced it with the Consulate (the revolutionary governing council), which he headed as first consul. In March 1801, seven years after the abolition of slavery by the National Convention, Louverture called a Constituent Assembly to draft Saint-Domingue's constitution. Promulgated in July 1801, the new constitution affirmed that the entire island of Hispaniola was part of the French empire, including Santo Domingo, the eastern portion formerly under Spanish control but by then controlled by Louverture. Moreover, the constitution also determined that henceforth the island would be ruled by its own legislation. Even more important, the new constitution affirmed the prohibition of slavery in Saint-Domingue.

Relying on the military forces under his command, Louverture named himself governor for life. But his rule did not last long. Napoléon Bonaparte rejected Saint-Domingue's autonomy. In February 1802, he sent an expedition of twenty-two thousand soldiers to the insurgent colony to fight Louverture. In May 1802, Bonaparte issued a decree reestablishing slavery in the French colonies. But the measure had no effect on Saint-Domingue, where insurrection persisted. French troops captured Louverture, imprisoning him and then deporting him to France, where he died one year later. But the rebels continued to fight. As thousands of soldiers of Bonaparte's men succumbed to an epidemic of yellow fever, the slave rebels eventually defeated the French army. On January 1, 1804, Jean-Jacques Dessalines declared Saint-Domingue an independent nation.

Saint-Domingue was the first colony in the Americas to abolish slavery altogether, while simultaneously breaking its colonial ties with France. The new nation was renamed Haiti, and Dessalines appointed himself first as "governor for life" and then emperor.[31] Although the victory of Saint-Domingue's slave rebellion can be explained by specific internal factors and the international context propelled by the French Revolution, the revolt was marked by three elements previously found in other revolts. First, Black, enslaved, freed, and free people greatly outnumbered the white population. Second, a significant number of Saint-Domingue's Black population was born in Africa and had recently arrived in the colony. Several of these newly arrived Africans had previous experience in warfare in their homelands. Third, despite their diverse origins and legal statuses, Black people joined ranks to fight the French colonizer. In the decades that followed the birth of Haiti, slavery would never be the same in the Americas.

New Winds of Freedom

The Saint-Domingue slave rebellion reverberated throughout the Americas, and other revolts soon followed. One insurrection broke out in the mountainous region of the Province of Coro, an area nearly thirty miles from the Caribbean coast, in what is today's northern Venezuela, by then part of the Spanish Viceroyalty of New Granada. By the end of the eighteenth century, Coro's plantations produced mainly cacao and sugar. The region was also commercially connected to the Caribbean, especially the Dutch island of Curaçao. Enslaved people often fled from Curaçao to settle in Coro, where they were emancipated by the Spanish crown.[32] The Coro Rebellion, as the revolt became known, was led by José Leonardo Chirino, identified in sources from the period as a man of mixed Black and Native ancestry. Some accounts mention another leader named José Caridad

González, who was labeled as *luango* (a term used to refer to former slaves from Curaçao, who probably originated on the Loango coast in West Central Africa), but his participation in the rebellion remains uncertain.[33] Regardless of his role, we know that González traveled to Saint-Domingue before the revolt broke out on the then French colony.[34] There is also no doubt that both men and their followers heard stories about the slave rebellion in the French colony that circulated across the Caribbean basin.[35]

On May 10, 1795, the Coro Rebellion started. Driven by local motivations and the news about the Saint-Domingue slave revolt, the rebels gathered more than two hundred enslaved, freed, and free Black individuals and to some extent Native peoples as well. The insurgents had several motivations. Enslaved people may have joined the rebels in response to a rumor about a royal decree emancipating the slaves. But they also gathered to oppose the imposition of new taxes on the goods they locally produced for sale and to protest the tributes imposed on the Native populations. Moreover, some accounts suggest that the insurgents wanted the abolition of slavery and the creation of a republic based on the "Law of the French," likely a reference to the 1794 abolition of slavery in the French colonies.[36] As in other insurrections, rebels marched, killing planters and burning their estates. In a few days, Spanish forces harshly repressed the insurrection. Chirino managed to escape but was found three months later. He was hanged, his body was quartered and salted, and his head and hands publicly displayed. His enslaved wife and children were sold separately to other cities. Dozens of rebels were tortured and killed. Several others, including Indigenous people, were sentenced to perform forced labor and deported to other regions of Venezuela.

Slave insurrections continued to erupt all over the Americas in the early decades of the nineteenth century. In the forty years that followed the end of slavery in Saint-Domingue, several revolts broke out in Cuba, where sugar production was fueling the rise of the second slavery. The birth of Haiti consolidated the Spanish colony as the larger sugar producer in the Americas. Whereas Cuba became a site of refuge for French planters who escaped Saint-Domingue, for the island's slaveholders the new Black nation was a constant reminder of the danger of further insurrections.[37] As in Venezuela, the Saint-Domingue Revolution encouraged enslaved people in Cuba to fight for freedom, and enslaved rebels were motivated by rumors that either an unnamed king or the kings of Britain, Spain, Haiti, or Kongo had issued a decree emancipating the slaves but that Cuban planters had not followed suit.[38]

As with many of the escapes and rebellions examined previously, the first battle of what became known as the Aponte Rebellion was planned and organized toward the end of the year, during Christmas Day 1811 and later on the Day of the Kings on January 6, 1812. José Antonio Aponte, one of the alleged leaders of the insurrection, was a free Black carpenter and appointed captain of Havana's militia in 1812.[39] It remains uncertain whether this series of revolts that erupted on several plantations to "fight against the rich whites" stemmed from a coordinated effort.[40] Nevertheless, the militia gathered enslaved, freed, and free people of color who used *cabildos de nación* to attempt to overthrow slavery. Whereas colonial forces stopped dozens of rebels, more than fifty insurgents were arrested and sent to trial. The alleged leaders of the rebellion, including Aponte, were ultimately sentenced to death.

But slave rebellions inspired by the Haitian example persisted in Cuba. In 1825, another slave revolt started in Matanzas, in the western part of the island, where the quick growth of sugar production led planters to import many new West African–born enslaved men, particularly Yoruba speakers, known as Lucumí in Cuba. Carrying with them significant warfare experience acquired in their homelands, a group of enslaved West Africans started a "war" that gathered nearly two hundred enslaved insurgents, who over twelve hours spread out through twenty-five plantations, killing fifteen white people. As the rebellion was repressed, Cuban authorities imposed a new code of rules in Matanzas. The code included measures to prevent rebellions by limiting enslaved people's mobility and creating *barracones* (barracoons) to accommodate bondspeople on the plantations. Planters knew that in order to avoid future revolts they had to make concessions, which is why the code also instructed slave owners to possibly improve the treatment of the enslaved population.[41]

Similar revolts erupted in the United States. Nat Turner's Rebellion, one of the bloodiest slave insurrections in the history of country, took place in Southampton in 1831. A county relatively isolated, Southampton is located nearly seventy miles south of Richmond in Virginia. The state had had the largest enslaved population in the United States since the late eighteenth century and maintained this position until 1860.[42] Southampton relied on varied agricultural production, including corn, cotton, potatoes, and peas, and locals raised cattle, hogs, and chickens, mostly intended for the local market. Although two-thirds of the county's residents owned human property, most slave owners held fewer than ten enslaved persons, only 13 percent possessed more than twenty bondspeople, and few people owned more than one hundred.[43]

Despite the small size of slaveholdings, Southampton's enslaved population was proportionally large. By 1800, enslaved and free Black people outnumbered the white population in the county, making it one of the places with the largest Black majority in Virginia. In 1830, one year before the rebellion, there were 6,573 white persons, 7,756 enslaved persons, and 1,745 free Black persons, former bondspersons, and their descendants manumitted by Quaker, Methodist, and Baptist slave owners.[44] For bondspeople, this context was not less brutal than in regions with larger slaveholdings.

The rebellion in Southampton was led by Nat Turner, an enslaved man and self-taught preacher, so the revolt is said to have resulted from his possible mystic visions. Unlike many enslaved people, Turner knew how to read and write. But these abilities did not exempt him from the cruelties of bondage. When the rebellion started, he was thirty-one years old and had already changed owners several times. After his first owner Benjamin Turner died, Nat was bequeathed to Benjamin's brother Samuel Turner. When Samuel died, Nat was sold to Thomas Moore. But following Moore's death, Nat Turner was passed down to

Thomas's son Putnam Moore. In 1830, Thomas Moore's widow and Putnam's mother married a carriage maker named Joseph Travis, who at the time of the insurrection was Turner's actual master, even though Putnam Moore was his legal owner.[45]

Nat Turner's Rebellion started in the early hours of August 22, 1831, when six enslaved men entered Travis's farmhouse and killed all members of the family while they were still sleeping. Promising to murder all white people, the rebels gathered as many as fifty participants, including adult men as well as male youths and children.[46] Although all insurgents were described as male, as historian Vanessa M. Holden argues, enslaved women of the local community supported their actions by either preparing food or attempting to murder their owners.[47] As the rebels moved, they attacked fifteen houses and killed fifty-five white men, women, and children. The next day, the local militia managed to stop the rebellion.

As the repression of the insurrection evolved, Turner disappeared for nearly six weeks. Meanwhile, his wife was publicly beaten.[48] All the captured coconspirators were tried and sentenced to death. Lucy, an enslaved woman owned by John T. Barrow, was the only woman tried for participating in the rebellion.[49] Sentenced to death, she was hanged on September 26. In late October, Nat Turner was captured. After a trial on November 5, he was sentenced to death and hanged in Jerusalem (today Courtland), Virginia, on November 11, 1831. As in the aftermath of other rebellions, the months that followed the uprising once again set the stage for brutal repressive measures against the enslaved and free Black populations not only in Southampton and Virginia but also across the US South. For example, on March 5, 1832, Virginia's General Assembly passed legislation prohibiting enslaved and free Black people from preaching, attending religious meetings without white supervision, carrying weapons, purchasing slaves except their own children, and several other restrictions.[50]

Samuel Sharpe, another religious enslaved man, led a rebellion in Jamaica also in 1831. Like Turner, Sharpe learned how to read and write when he was young. An enslaved domestic worker, he became a Baptist lay deacon in his early adulthood. Hence, he used religious meetings to preach his values to enslaved people. Unlike other bondspeople, he could read British newspapers and pamphlets that by that time had been spreading abolitionist ideas for several years. As noted earlier, the Christmas holiday was the only long holiday during which enslaved people could rest as well as gather to eat, drink, dance, and celebrate with their loved ones, but the holiday season also offered an opportunity to resist slavery. Sharpe called a general strike for Christmas Day 1831. The strike aimed to demand wages and better working conditions for the enslaved population. Although the movement was intended to be peaceful, the insurgents knew there was no peace under the brutality of bondage. On the night of December 27, a group of slaves set fire to a trash house in the Kensington estate in Montego Bay. The wooden structure used to store the leaves of old sugarcanes that served as fuel for sugar boilers burned down. As the fire expanded, what was intended to be a strike became a powerful insurrection. In the following days, thousands of enslaved individuals armed with guns and knives marched from plantation to plantation setting fire to sugar fields and factories.[51]

Gathering thousands of enslaved individuals who resisted British forces for nearly two months, the Christmas Rebellion or Baptist War, as it became known, was the largest slave revolt in Jamaica's history.[52] As in previous revolts, the insurgents were violently repressed. At least 540 participants either died in battle or were executed by the British forces.[53] On April 19, 1832, Sharpe was tried and sentenced to death, and on May 23, 1832, he was hanged in Charles Square across from the courthouse in Montego Bay. The carnage of hundreds of enslaved men and women that followed the slave rebellion had great repercussions in Britain. Ultimately, the rebellion added more pressure for the passage of the abolition of slavery in the British Empire in 1833.[54]

Bahia's Malê Revolt

The Brazilian province of Bahia also witnessed a wave of insurrections during the first three decades of the nineteenth century. The country became independent from Portugal in 1822. Unlike elites in the colonies of the Spanish Americas, Brazilian and Portuguese elites negotiated the process of independence that secured the continuation of the monarchy. Yet, this period was marked by great political instability that exposed the difficulties involved in unifying the new nation. An economic crisis caused by severe droughts that provoked food shortages also affected the region.[55] Moreover, the price of enslaved persons increased after 1808, when the Portuguese court moved to Brazil to escape Napoléon Bonaparte. In the following years, Brazil and Britain signed various treaties with the aim of gradually stopping the slave trade, which culminated with the enactment of the law prohibiting imports of enslaved Africans to Brazil in 1831.[56] However, after a few years of steep decline, the illegal slave trade reestablished the volume of slave imports. The demand for slaves in the growing coffee industry increased the internal trade in enslaved people from Bahia and other northeast provinces to the coffee-producing southeast region of São Paulo and Rio de Janeiro. Despite all these obstacles and the competition with the then-blooming Cuban sugar production, the Bahia sugar economy continued to grow between 1827 and 1860. This growth, combined with the decreasing number of available bondspeople, led slave owners to increase enslaved people's workload, thereby worsening their working conditions. Resisting against these difficult conditions, enslaved people escaped, joined runaway slave communities, and organized several revolts.[57]

The Malê Revolt broke out in the city of Salvador. Bahia's African Muslims, enslaved and freed, were known as *malês*. The word *malê* did not refer to a specific ethnic group but was rather derived from the Yoruba word *imale*, meaning "Muslim." Therefore, in Brazil, the term *malê* referred to African-born individuals who were both Yoruba speakers and followers of Islam. As a group of enslaved and freed Yoruba-speaking Muslim men led the revolt of 1835, the insurrection became known as the Malê Revolt. The largest urban slave insurrection in the Americas, this revolt shares several elements in common with previous slave insurrections that erupted in the Americas during the eighteenth and nineteenth centuries, including the large concentration of African-born enslaved people in Bahia, as well as its religious component. But the revolt can be better understood by considering the wars that led to the disintegration of the Oyo Empire, examined in chapter 2.

Approximately 187,700 enslaved men, women, and children who had disembarked in Bahia between 1801 and 1830 were boarded at ports on the Bight of Benin. In the fifteen years preceding the 1835 rebellion, nearly 60 percent of Bahia's African-born population was composed by individuals identified as Nagôs (Yoruba speakers) and Haussás (Hausa speakers), in addition to Jejes (speakers of Gbe languages) and Tapas (Nupe speakers).[58] A number of these enslaved Africans were captured during the wars opposing the Muslim Fulani and the states subjugated by Oyo, as discussed in chapter 2. Others were made prisoners by the Kingdom of Dahomey army that waged war against its Yoruba-speaking neighbors, including Oyo. The concentration of Yoruba speakers in Bahia was central for organizing the uprising of 1835. Several of these Africans were warriors, war prisoners, or captured as byproducts of warfare. Therefore, scholars have argued that the Malê Revolt was the continuation of the African jihad begun on the other side of the Atlantic Ocean.[59]

Since the sixteenth century, as explained in chapter 7, the humid soils of the Recôncavo region, which surrounds the Bay of All of Saints, favored the development of vast sugarcane plantations in Bahia. This slave society was composed of a wealthy upper class whose main group was made of owners of large sugar estates, followed by other slave owners and slave merchants. But most of Bahia's population was formed by enslaved, freed, and free Black people. As historian João José Reis pointed out, according to the census of 1808, the Bahian population comprised 249,314 inhabitants. White people composed nearly 20 percent of the population, while freedpeople, including men and women born in Africa, made up nearly 40 percent. Enslaved people, born either in Africa or in Brazil, made up the other 40 percent of Bahia's inhabitants.[60] In the 1830s, the profile of the province's population remained similar, even though the white population may have been even smaller because of the increasing imports of enslaved Africans during the period.

The Malê Rebellion of 1835 can be understood as the culmination of several previous slave conspiracies that stormed through Salvador and its surrounding areas between 1807 and 1830.[61] By 1835, 63 percent of Salvador's enslaved population consisted of people born in West Africa, and among them were Yoruba, Gbe, Hausa, Nupe, and Borno speakers. Moreover, more than 7 percent of the city's total population was composed of African-born freedmen and freedwomen. All these nuances considered, the city had a total of nearly twenty-two thousand enslaved and freed African-born residents. Most Yoruba speakers adopted the Orisha religion. Whereas some were already Muslims in West Africa, others may have converted to Islam after reaching Brazilian soil. However, we can assume that most of these West African–born individuals of various ethnic groups, especially those living in Salvador, had been baptized in the Roman Catholic Church and therefore received Catholic names.

When these enslaved Africans were able to purchase their freedom, their social position remained very fragile. The Brazilian Constitution of 1824 had established that only Brazilian-born freedpeople became Brazilian citizens after manumission. Hence, emancipated Africans were considered aliens, and the difficult procedure to acquire Brazilian citizenship made it basically impossible.[62] Moreover, freed Africans were subjected to strict control. A decree of 1830, responding to the series of rebellions since the early years of the nineteenth century, restricted the mobility of Africans, even in their own cities, where they had to carry a passport issued by Brazilian authorities confirming their good conduct.[63] In this context of a great concentration of African-born enslaved and freedpeople under increasingly repressive measures, Islam became an umbrella that offered them a tool to resist against slavery and anti-African discrimination.[64] Ultimately, through the leadership of a small number of Muslim Yoruba speakers, many dozens of non-Muslim Yoruba-speaking enslaved men and freedmen joined the Malê Revolt.

The Malê Revolt was planned to start at dawn on Sunday, January 25, 1835, during a festival day commemorating a Catholic saint. As discussed in chapter 14, days of festivity were opportune times for organized resistance, as both enslaved people and slave owners were distracted. More important, in the Arabic or Hijari calendar, January 25 was the date 25-Ramadan-1250 AH, a few days before the end of Muslims' fasting for the holy month of Ramadan. On Saturday, January 24, the enslaved and freed population were circulating rumors about the insurrection planned for the next day. Despite its being a rebellion initiated in the city, the rebels planned to be joined by bondspeople from the plantations surrounding the Bay of All Saints. Their goal was to wage war against the white people or, according to some rebels, against all people in the white man's land, including mixed-race and Black Brazilian-born enslaved, freed, and free individuals.[65] The news about the impending rebellion reached white residents, however. As the Bahian authorities were alerted and took action to dismantle the conspiracy on Saturday night, they found a leading group of enslaved and freed African Muslim insurgents gathered in one residence. Armed mostly with big knives, the rebels still took to the streets and resisted for several hours. But the insurrection was eventually defeated on Sunday. Existing estimates suggest that nearly six hundred individuals participated in the Malê Revolt.[66] Whereas the insurgents killed only nine people, fifty rebels died in battle, and others were wounded and died later.

Bahian authorities interrogated and arrested hundreds of suspects. As the Malê Revolt was dismantled, a report by Bahia's chief police officer narrating in detail the events of the night of January 24–25 was reproduced in one of the main Brazilian newspapers in Rio de Janeiro, the capital of the Brazilian Empire. This report estimated that a total of fifty insurgents were killed in various parts of the city, some hiding in the bushes, and some even drowned in the sea while trying to escape, while many others were wounded and transported to the hospital. As the records produced by the investigation show, and as noted in the report, the African insurgents were Muslims familiar with the Koran, who could read and write in Arabic.[67] The day of the revolt, many rebels took to the streets wearing white gowns (*abadás*) that only the adepts of Islam wore in private spaces in Bahia. Moreover, when the police put down the rebellion, they found insurgents carrying amulets, prayers, devotional manuscripts, and other items written in Arabic, and whose words were even reproduced in one of Rio de Janeiro's newspapers.[68]

For several months, slave owners and government authorities publicly expressed their fear that other rebellions would follow in Bahia. Newspaper articles in Rio de Janeiro complained about Brazil's large population of enslaved Africans and the fact that the illegal slave trade from Africa persisted, and they urged authorities to deport existing free Africans introduced in the country after the legal ban of the slave trade in 1831 back to the African continent.[69] Additional pieces called for increasing surveillance of Africans as a measure to avoid a new rebellion.[70] Some newspaper articles reported rumors of new African conspiracies.[71] One of these plots was reported as being planned in the towns of Cachoeira and Arraial de São Félix in Bahia, where the police arrested suspected African individuals. According to the article, after searching their houses, police officers discovered a great number of "books and leaflets written in Arabic, lose papers with scriptures, rings, bamboo pens, and some packages containing poison" whereas in the second day "were found on the beach, a tablet . . . written on both sides with Arabic letters."[72] Some newspaper articles even warned about the influence of "Haitian doctrines preached with impunity," even though to this day historians have not found evidence of such a direct connection.[73]

Likewise, drawing on the report by Bahia's chief police officer released just after the Malê Revolt, starting in mid-March until at least end of August 1835, numerous newspapers in several cities of Britain, France, Spain, the United States, and even Germany disseminated the news about the slave rebellion in Brazil.[74] One British newspaper reported that "on some of the prisoners were found little Arabic books and folded papers, inscribed with verses from the

Alcoran, which African Mahometans are accustomed to wear about the person as charms." Moreover, because the original Brazilian report stated that some rebels were owned by British nationals residing in Salvador, British newspapers also misleadingly emphasized that "the insurgents consisted almost entirely of negroes who were the favourites of their masters, and had always been particularly well-treated."[75] As the British had already abolished slavery in their colonies by 1835, these articles gave an opportunity not only to present the rebellion as a warning against the horrors of slavery and to denounce the persisting illegal imports of enslaved Africans to Brazil but also to showcase British residents of Brazil as benevolent slave owners. Months later, on May 15 and May 31, 1835, the French newspaper *Le Spectateur* and the Spanish newspaper *El Guerrero y el compilador* reported a story published in the Brazilian newspaper *Jornal do Commercio* back on March 21, in which Brazilian authorities warned that "the same revolutionary symptoms reproduce in the province of Rio de Janeiro." According to the article, an enslaved man arrested in the town of Campos had confessed that "the order had been received from Bahia to act, and that each slave should start by getting rid of his master."[76]

Existing records establish that in the aftermath of the Malê Revolt, 231 people were sent to trial, though only 135 sentences are known. Twenty-eight enslaved people were acquitted, and 4 Africans (1 freedman and 3 enslaved men) were executed, whereas 12 people initially sentenced to death had their sentences commuted to prison and whippings. Sixteen freedpeople were sentenced to prison, and 8 bondspeople and freedpeople were sentenced to forced labor. Whereas 40 enslaved persons were sentenced to floggings, 34 freedmen were sentenced to deportation. But later, more than 150 other freed Africans were added to a list of people to be deported.

Ultimately, the Malê Revolt was the most important slave rebellion staged in Brazil. The uprising confirmed the high degree of organization of African-born enslaved and freedpeople and their distinction from the Brazilian-born enslaved and freed population. Brazilian-born enslaved people and freedpeople were more adapted to the

Brazilian society. Enslaved since their birth, they spoke Portuguese, were Catholics while practicing African-based religions such as Candomblé, and had created bonds with their owners, with whom they shared a language, a religion, and several cultural elements. In contrast, African-born enslaved men and women had not been born in slavery. They remained connected to their homeland, and they preserved their religions, memories, languages, music, and even their names. It comes as no surprise that they resisted enslavement.

After the end of the Malê Revolt, more than ever, freed Africans were considered a serious menace to Brazilian society. As we will see in chapter 17, the revolt launched the deportation and the voluntary migration of hundreds of Africans from Brazil to the Bight of Benin. Yet, Bahia's Muslim insurrection was not the last of its kind. As the second slavery remained in full swing and Cuba became the world's largest producer of sugar, enslaved men and women led two revolts on the island in 1843. In the second of these revolts, known as the Triunvirato Rebellion, Carlota and Fermina, two West African–born enslaved women identified as Lucumí (Yoruba speakers) became famous for attacking plantations in Matanzas.[77] But in 1844, a new larger conspiracy gathered hundreds of free, freed, and enslaved persons, including once again African-born individuals, from urban areas and plantations. Poor white Cubans, unhappy with the Spanish administration, also joined the conspiracy. The insurgents wanted to end the Spanish colonial rule on the island and to abolish slavery. According to an article in a Spanish newspaper of March 1844, the rebellion took over the entire Matanzas territory and there was "not a single mill in which there were no conspirators. . . . Many free blacks from Matanzas were accomplices and it seems that they expected aid, especially weapons, from English abolitionists. . . . Blacks who provided domestic service were part of the plan of those in the fields, to whom they had to open the doors of the houses when they showed up."[78]

As Cuban authorities dismantled the rebellion, they interrogated the alleged participants and witnesses, who were tied face down to a ladder (*escalera*) and beaten. Because of this method of torture, the revolt became known as *La Escalera*. During the interrogations, Black insurgents emphasized the sacred dimension of their participation in the rebellion, and how a large array of objects of power and amulets prepared by specialists of West Central African and Afro-Cuban Palo Monte (or Palo Mayombe) religions offered them protection in the battles waged during the revolt.[79] As in the first slave uprising in New York City in 1712, in which West African conjurer "Peter the Doctor" armored enslaved rebels with a protective powder, and similar to the Malê Revolt, in which Muslim spiritual leaders guided the insurgents, during *La Escalera* enslaved insurgents drew upon African rituals to acquire strength to fight for freedom.

Continuous Warfare

Enslaved people organized insurrections from the early sixteenth century through the nineteenth century. Although these rebellions became the most visible form of resistance against slavery, not all enslaved persons elected collective revolts as the main method to fight for better working conditions and freedom. Most enslaved people actually fought to survive slavery by using the means available to them.[80] Local and international contexts that could either contribute to or prevent insurgencies also varied across time and regions. But in the areas of the Americas where Black people and African-born enslaved people outnumbered the white population, there were often favorable conditions for insurrection. The leading roles played by freed Africans and African-born bondspeople in rebellions demonstrates the connections between their previous experiences in the homeland and their participation in slave rebellions in the Americas, evidence of their determination in joining other countrymen to fight for freedom. The study of several rebellions in which African-born bondsmen were involved suggests that these men brought with them to the Americas previous knowledge of warfare from West Central Africa and West Africa. There was also a sacred dimension attached to wartime, which is why drumming and the guidance of religious specialists were important in periods of rebellion. Bondswomen also actively participated in slave rebellions in a variety of roles, but their presence remained less visible than that of enslaved men. One hopes that further studies will shed greater light on the participation of enslaved women in these insurrections.

As discussed in this chapter, slave rebellions started two centuries before the Saint-Domingue slave rebellion and persisted long after the birth of Haiti. Even though no other slave revolt was successful in dismantling slavery, in its way each insurrection destabilized the societies where they emerged. This persistence eventually paid off. As we will see in chapter 16, during the second half of the nineteenth century, the three largest and last slave societies in the Americas eventually abolished slavery.

CHAPTER 16

Fighting for Freedom

In 1848, an African man of Congo "nation" was transported from West Central Africa to Rio de Janeiro and then transferred to Minas Gerais in 1849. After his owner died, he was sold in an auction to another slaveholder. Likewise, an African woman of Cabinda "nation" was brought from Africa to Rio de Janeiro in 1850 and then also transported to Minas Gerais. Baptized in the Roman Catholic Church, the man was renamed Jacyntho and the woman Anna, and they got married. But despite being baptized in Minas Gerais, there were no baptism records, "surely to avoid knowledge of the fraud, with which the aforementioned priest proceeded, baptizing free African[s] as slaves."[1] This case was denounced in a letter signed by Brazilian Black abolitionist Luiz Gama. His complaint about fraud was a reference to the first law banning the African slave trade to Brazil in 1831, which gave the legal status of "free African" to any African person illegally introduced in the country as a slave after the law's enactment.

Despite their importance, daily resistance and rebellion often failed to liberate bondspeople, which is why during the entire era of the Atlantic slave trade and slavery in the Americas, enslaved men, women, and even children had to find (and create) other paths to gain liberty. As noted in chapter 8, enslaved people could be successful in purchasing their freedom, especially in urban areas, even though manumission by purchase was much more common in Latin America than in the British West Indies, colonial North America, and the

United States. Starting in the late eighteenth century with the end of the American War of Independence and after the rise of Haiti in 1804, the Northern states of the United States and newly independent countries in Latin America began to enact legislation establishing gradual emancipation and banning the slave trade from Africa. Meanwhile, through insurrections and massive flights, bondspeople, along with abolitionists, joined antislavery organizations.

As recent works show, as early as the late seventeenth century, West Central Africans such as Lourenço da Silva Mendonça appealed in court for the end of the slave trade.[2] Historians have also demonstrated that Africans and their descendants were protagonists in this very long fight for the legal prohibition of the slave trade and slavery, which eventually culminated with the final abolition of slavery during the nineteenth century in the Americas.[3] European powers used the end of the Atlantic slave trade and the consequent abolition of slavery in the Americas to justify the scramble for Africa that divided the continent. As European colonization evolved, slavery was banned in various parts of Africa as well. Nonetheless, in other parts of the continent, colonial powers introduced slavery-like labor regimes, which included not only forced labor for long hours under strict surveillance but also physical punishments.

A long fight that combined various forms of collective slave resistance and rebellions led to the gradual and then final legal abolition of slavery in the Americas. From an individual point of view, however, many men, women, and children in many countries were already freed when emancipation finally occurred. In several instances, these freedmen and freedwomen contributed to the organization of slave rebellions (as we saw in chapter 15), and many of them, such as Brazilian formerly enslaved Luiz Gama, also joined the abolitionist movement. While some enslaved women and men individually acquired their freedom, either through self-purchase or when their owners decided to emancipate them for a variety of reasons, a large majority remained in bondage as slavery started gradually being outlawed at the end of the eighteenth century. Despite these varied trajectories, in many ways, the paths of enslaved, freed, and free Africans and their descendants intertwined during the long age of emancipation.

Many Paths to Manumission

Throughout this book so far, we have seen examples of slave owners who freed their enslaved property for many reasons. Recall the story of Chica da Silva presented in chapter 10. In eighteenth-century Brazil, the first owner of Chica da Silva freed her son of whom he was the father and also made him one of his heirs. But later on, Chica was sold to another owner, who was sexually and romantically attracted to her. Given that attraction, weeks after acquiring her, he manumitted her, and together the couple had several children, who were fully recognized by Chica's former slave owner and became his heirs. In other cases, slave owners manumitted enslaved people, especially in their wills, as a way to express gratitude, even though they sometimes only made this gesture when they were infirm. Some manumissions also involved conditions, such as to continue providing services until their owners' deaths.

Enslaved people in Brazil and Latin American regions such as Peru, Colombia, and Cuba could also obtain manumission through self-purchase, which consisted of paying the owner their own market value. But regardless of specific motives and conditions, as explained earlier, manumissions were widespread in these regions. Based on Roman law, Portuguese legal codes and later the Brazilian legislation did not establish clear regulations either allowing or forbidding slave owners to free their enslaved property. Ultimately, emancipating a bondsperson was a private decision taken by the slave owner in agreement with the enslaved person and regulated by custom, in which the state and the Catholic Church rarely interfered. Slave owners granted manumission to reward good service and to express affection in recognition of family ties. Some owners, however, promised manumission in exchange for sexual favors, only to fail to fulfill their promises. By 1834, Ramón Saíz, a slave owner from Havana, Cuba, promised

Florencia, a fourteen-year-old enslaved girl, that he would manumit her if she had sex with him. But after they had sex, not only did he not free her, but he also put her to work in a blacksmith's shop and attempted to torture her by inserting "silver rings in the most secret parts of her nature."[4]

In urban areas, enslaved men and women who had permission to work outside the households of their owners could keep a small part of their income. More autonomous than other enslaved individuals who worked on plantations and farms, they could gradually amass money to purchase their own freedom. The frequency with which self-purchase happened was higher than the occurrence of manumissions and varied according to sex, color, place of birth, region, and period. Manumission by grace and self-purchase existed in other parts of the Americas as well, but the conditions changed over time. In the thirteen British colonies of North America, legal codes imposed restrictions on manumissions several times. For example, in 1691, Virginia prohibited newly freed people from remaining in its territory. Thus, any owner who emancipated an enslaved individual had to transport the newly freed person outside the colony. South Carolina legislature passed a similar restriction in 1735.[5] Following the independence of the thirteen colonies, the "Act to Authorize the Manumission of Slaves" passed in the Virginia General Assembly in 1782, thereby permitting slave owners to manumit their slaves in their wills or any other written document presented before a court. Moreover, the new act also eliminated the previous restriction mandating the transportation of newly freed individuals outside the colony.[6] Similar laws allowing manumissions passed in Maryland and Delaware in the years that followed the birth of the independent United States as well.

Brazilian-born and mixed-race enslaved persons, especially women, had greater access to self-purchase, as noted in chapter 8. In Brazil and the Spanish-speaking Americas, enslaved men and women also purchased their own freedom via *coartación* (in Spanish) and *coartação* (in Portuguese), a system of self-purchase that resulted from an agreement in which the bondsperson paid the owner the amount of their freedom in several installments. In Brazil, *coartação* was not regulated by legislation, but mostly both parties involved in the agreement usually respected its conventions. In addition, as explained in chapter 14, becoming a member of a Catholic lay brotherhood or of societies of mutual assistance was a convenient way to acquire the means to purchase freedom, even though amassing funds could take several years. These paths to freedom, in addition to the free womb laws, altered the profile of enslaved populations in the Americas during the nineteenth century.

In the Northern states of the United States, when final emancipation occurred, the enslaved population was relatively small in most regions. The end of slavery in Saint-Domingue through a revolution, however, liberated many thousands of enslaved people, but even on the independent portion of the island, there was already a visible freed and free Black population, including African-born men and women. In Cuba, both gradual abolition and manumissions by grace or self-purchase contributed to the decrease of the number of enslaved people by the time slavery was finally abolished in the 1886. When slavery finally ended in Brazil in 1888, the country also had a huge freed and free Black population. On the eve of emancipation, enslaved men and women led massive manumission campaigns. Fearing revolts, slave owners started freeing thousands of slaves as well.

Gradual Abolition of Slavery and the Prohibition of the Slave Trade

The abolition of the international slave trade to the Americas was the first of the many steps that led to emancipation in the Western Hemisphere. The first measures to prohibit the importation of enslaved Africans to the thirteen British colonies in North America started in the first half of the eighteenth century, motivated by fear of slave insurrections led by newly arrived enslaved Africans. After the Stono Rebellion of 1739, the largest slave revolt in colonial North America (discussed in chapter 15), South Carolina twice banned the importation of enslaved Africans, and when the international slave trade restarted, colonial authorities created special tariffs to discourage slave imports. The thirteen colonies that became the United States broke ground on the gradual abolition of slavery in the United States. However, independence movements led by creole elites, whether in North America, the Spanish Americas, or Brazil, did not include emancipation of the enslaved population, especially in the regions where the institution of slavery was central to the economy.

Even in the areas where bondage was not dominant, slave owners opposed emancipation, imposing on the enslaved population the long path of gradual abolition. Still, the American War of Independence fueled antislavery discourses and the early abolitionist movement. Enslaved men and women actively participated in this process by petitioning their owners to obtain freedom and in some cases rewards for past services.[7] After the end of the war and with the rise of the French Revolution in 1789, antislavery activity spread in Europe and the United States. As discussed in chapter 12, this new context cleared the way for the passing of gradual emancipation legislation liberating newborns of enslaved mothers in the Northern states of the newly independent country.

The birth of Haiti in 1804 inspired rebellions and the abolitionist movement in Europe and the Americas. In 1807, Napoléon Bonaparte crossed Spain to invade Portugal. In that same year the British Parliament abolished the international slave trade to the British colonies. Also in 1807, following the mandate of the Constitution of 1787, the United States Congress passed an act (made effective in 1808) prohibiting the international slave trade to its territory. Moreover, in 1808, the French and Spanish alliance was dismantled. To resist French occupation, a series of *juntas* (councils) were created all over Spain, which eventually led to the establishment of the Cortes of Cádiz in 1810. Spain's first national assembly with representatives from its various colonies, the Cortes of Cádiz started discussing the abolition of the slave trade and slavery in the Spanish Empire. Between 1814 and 1820, the end of the Napoleonic Wars led to the legal ban of the slave trade in France, Portugal, and Spain, even though the illegal slave trade persisted for several years.[8]

The abolition of the British slave trade in 1807 was the first achievement of a powerful social movement gathering thousands of men and women who for moral and religious reasons condemned the continuation of the evil trade in enslaved Africans even though it still generated significant profits to British planters and slave owners. In the first two decades of the nineteenth century, the movement to abolish slavery in the British West Indies increased as well, fueled by the emergence of slave rebellions in Barbados, Guyana, and Jamaica, and also impacted by the activities of the Anti-Slavery Society that gathered hundreds of thousands of signatures demanding better conditions for the enslaved populations, gradual emancipation, and the total abolition of slavery. After months of intense debates, the Slavery Abolition Act of August 28, 1833, declared the end of slavery in the British colonies starting on August 1, 1834. The act formally freed nearly 800,000 enslaved persons. But except for Antigua, in all other British colonies of the West Indies, bondspeople older than six were submitted to a period of so-called apprenticeship, consisting of four years if they worked as domestic servants and six years if they were agricultural workers.[9] Moreover, the Abolition Act included a provision to compensate 46,000 slave owners with £20 million. Intended to control the former enslaved population, the apprenticeship system preserved most components of the old relations between slave owners and bondspeople.[10]

By the time slavery was outlawed in the British Empire, the industries of tobacco, rice, and especially cotton had quickly expanded in the South of the United States, where the second slavery was flourishing. Meanwhile, the process of legal abolition of slavery in the United States remained gradual, varying from state to state. New York abolished slavery in 1827, Rhode Island in 1842, Pennsylvania in 1847, and Connecticut in 1848. Although New Jersey legally abolished slavery in 1846, freedpeople became apprentices for life. Consequently, the apprentices in New Jersey only obtained free status when slavery was abolished in the United States two decades later.[11]

Similar processes occurred in the Spanish Americas. The early rebellion that gave rise to the Mexican War of Independence in 1810 was a popular movement. Its leaders called attention to the problem of racial and social inequalities that separated white creole elites from the great majority of the poor population of color.[12] Two years after Mexico's independence, on September 26, 1823, the Constituent Assembly passed a decree that prohibited the transatlantic slave trade to Mexico. Even though the Mexican Constitution of 1824 did not address the issue of slavery, constitutions of various Mexican states, enacted between 1824 and 1827, either abolished slavery or determined that newborns should be manumitted.[13] Eventually, President Vicente Guerrero issued a decree on September 15, 1829, ending slavery in Mexico, but the Congress overturned it less than two years later. Only in 1837 did the Congress of Mexico prohibit slavery across the country.[14]

Between 1811 and 1842, the Atlantic slave trade to the various colonies and former Spanish colonies in Central America and South America was legally abolished. Yet from 1843 to 1847 the trade in enslaved Africans reopened in Peru, as well as in Argentina and Uruguay between the 1820s and the early 1830s.[15] In Santo Domingo (today's Dominican Republic), the external slave trade and slavery were abolished in 1822. But other Spanish colonies and former colonies adopted gradual abolition by first enacting free womb legislation and only later abolishing slavery. Chile and the Río de La Plata (in today's Argentina) enacted free womb laws in 1811 and 1813, respectively.[16] The regions of present-day Ecuador, Colombia, Peru, Venezuela, and Panama passed legislation freeing newborns in 1821, Uruguay in 1825, Bolivia in 1831, and finally Paraguay in 1842.

Legal Abolition of Slavery

Following gradual abolition, the actual demise of slavery was a lengthy process in the Spanish Americas. Chile was the first country in South

America to legally abolish slavery. But only a few days after the initial decree of July 24, 1823, another decree restricted the free legal status of freedpeople. Eventually the Chilean Constitution enacted on December 29, 1823, permanently ended slavery. On December 12, 1842, during its civil war, Uruguay also enacted a law abolishing slavery. But a system of apprenticeship was established for women and children, which was reversed only with the end of the war in 1853.[17]

During the next two decades, except for Brazil, Puerto Rico, and Cuba, slavery was abolished all over the Americas. In 1847, Sweden ended slavery in its American colony, Saint Barthélemy. On April 27, 1848, France ended slavery in all of its colonies, including Martinique, Guadeloupe, and French Guiana as well as Reunion Island and Senegal, and one year later it enacted a law awarding financial compensation to the former slave owners. The Danish West Indies also abolished slavery in 1848.[18] The regions of present-day Ecuador, Colombia, and Panama passed legislation prohibiting slavery in 1851 (effective on January 1, 1852), most of Argentina in 1853, Peru and Venezuela in 1854, Bolivia in 1861, and Paraguay in 1869.[19] The Netherlands abolished slavery in its colonies in the Americas in 1863 and, like France, compensated former slave owners.

The gradual abolition of slavery and the end of the Atlantic slave trade to the Americas impacted various regions that largely relied on an enslaved workforce. In the decades that preceded the start of the Civil War in the United States, professional gangs of kidnappers abducted free and freed men, women, and children in cities such as Cincinnati, Philadelphia, New York City, and Washington, DC, and sold them into slavery on plantations in the South of the United States.[20] River ports such as New Orleans, Richmond, and Alexandria were among the busiest slave hubs in the United States during the period of the internal slave trade. Some of the notorious slave pens in these cities remained active until the period of the Civil War. One nineteenth-century photograph shows the slave pen at 1315 Duke Street (figure 16.1), where today is housed the Freedom House

FIGURE 16.1. Mathew B. Brady, *Slave Pens*, Alexandria, VA, United States, 1862. Albumen silver print, 7 × 9 1/16 inches. Courtesy of Jean Paul Getty Museum, Los Angeles, CA, United States.

Museum in Alexandria, Virginia. Successively used by various slave-trading companies, the structure was conceived as a prison with cells to hold enslaved people for several days before their transportation to the sugar and cotton plantations in the Deep South.

Contrasting with the United States, where between the end of the eighteenth century and the first half of the nineteenth century slavery was gradually abolished in the Northern states, slavery existed in the entire Brazilian territory. Without a similar division between north and south, except for the communities of self-emancipated slaves, there was no region within the country where slavery no longer existed and to where enslaved people could escape. But in southern Brazil, enslaved men and women escaped to the present-day region of Uruguay and Argentina, where in the 1850s, slavery had been definitively abolished. Because the enslaved workforce became scarce with the second ban of the Atlantic slave trade to Brazil in 1850, professional kidnappers crossed Brazilian borders to reach Uruguay and Argentina to capture free and freed men, women, and children who had settled in the two neighboring countries and transported them back to Brazil, where slavery remained legal.[21] Although Brazilian legislation punished the illegal enslavement of free people and the reenslavement of freedpeople, as in the United States, most of these criminals were not sentenced to prison time.

By 1850, slavery had been abolished in most of Spanish-speaking Latin America. Meanwhile in the United States, the division between free and slave states became clearer. Slaveholding states were ready to fight to keep slavery in place and to further expand the slavery frontier. This crisis intensified when Abraham Lincoln was elected president of the United States in November 1860, because despite his moderate positions regarding slavery, he was not a representative of the Southern planters and slave owners. By the time of Lincoln's election, nineteen US states had abolished both the slave trade and slavery, outnumbering the fifteen slave states, where the slave trade and slavery still existed. In December 1860, the South Carolina General Assembly announced its secession from the United States, an action it justified by the growing hostility to the institution of slavery by the free states.

During the four months after South Carolina's secession, Alabama, Florida, Georgia, Louisiana, Mississippi, and Texas announced their separation from the Union and formed the Confederate States of America. In his first inaugural address on March 4, 1861, President Lincoln had sought to appease the Southerners by promising not to interfere in the states where slavery existed. But the country was too divided to be soothed. In April 1861, five weeks after Lincoln's inauguration, the Civil War broke out. Between May and June, Virginia, Arkansas, North Carolina, and Tennessee joined the Confederacy.

On April 16, 1862, one year after the beginning of the Civil War, President Lincoln abolished slavery in Washington, DC, by offering financial compensation to former slave owners. As the Civil War continued, many enslaved people escaped bondage by all available means, including crossing rivers on horseback (figure 16.2), whereas the federal government freed bondsmen who agreed to fight alongside the Union Army.[22] On July 17, 1862, the United States Congress passed a second Confiscation Act freeing all slaves owned by Confederates. This measure paved the way for the Emancipation Proclamation of the Confederate States of the South issued by Lincoln on September 22, 1862 (effective January 1, 1863). The initiative was part of a wartime strategy to fight the Confederate states by gaining the support of freedpeople. The proclamation freed more than three million enslaved men, women, and children (figure 16.3), some of whom then enlisted as soldiers in the Union Army.[23] Eventually, after four years of a bloody Civil War, the Union defeated the Confederacy, and slavery was eventually legally abolished in the United States in December 1865 through the Thirteenth Amendment to the US Constitution. The abolition of slavery that followed the end of the Civil

FIGURE 16.2. Timothy H. O'Sullivan and Mathew B. Brady, *Escaping Slaves Crossing Rappahannock River*, United States, August 1862. Albumen silver print, 2 15/16 × 4 1/8 inches. Courtesy of Jean Paul Getty Museum, Los Angeles, CA, United States.

FIGURE 16.3. Timothy H. O'Sullivan, *Slaves, J. J. Smith's Plantation, near Beaufort, South Carolina*, 1862. Albumen silver print, 8 7/16 × 10¾ inches. Courtesy of Jean Paul Getty Museum, Los Angeles, CA, United States.

War in the United States freed a much larger number of enslaved men, women, and children (approximately four million) than previous emancipations. Also, except for Washington, DC, slave owners were not indemnified for their freed bondspeople.[24]

Brazil and Cuba

Brazil was the last country to abolish slavery in the Americas. Contrasting with the United States, where the gradual end of slavery started at the end of the eighteenth century, the first laws gradually extinguishing slavery in Brazil were enacted only in the 1870s, when the abolitionist movement emerged.[25] When the Portuguese royal family moved to Rio de Janeiro in 1808 to escape the invasion of Napoléon Bonaparte, Portugal opened the Brazilian market to the importation of British manufactured products. Britain increasingly pressured Portugal to end the slave trade to Brazil. In 1810, Portugal and Britain signed two treaties that gave Britain a gainful tariff on British goods imported to Brazil and started the gradual end of the slave trade to Brazil, measures that favored Brazilian independence. In 1815, a treaty signed between Portugal and Britain banned the slave trade north of the equator, making illegal the slave trade from West Africa to Brazil. Nonetheless, its requirements were never fully enforced. British pressures on Brazil continued after its independence from Portugal in 1822. Brazil became an empire and the only independent nation in Latin America to maintain a long-term monarchical system. In this new context, neither slavery nor the slave trade were abolished.

In the decade that followed Brazilian independence, nearly half a million enslaved Africans disembarked on the country's shores. In November 1826, a new treaty between Brazil and Britain established that the trade in enslaved Africans from any African region to Brazil was to end within three years. But when the deadline to stop the slave trade as established in the treaty arrived in 1830, the slave trade instead continued as usual. In 1831, the Brazilian parliament finally took a first step to stop the inhumane trade by passing the Feijó Law, which prohibited the import of enslaved Africans to Brazil. Although the law was never effectively enforced, it included several measures to inhibit the trade. Among them, the law stated that Africans who were illegally introduced into the country would be emancipated and reexported. In practice, this provision created a new category of "liberated Africans" (*Africanos livres*, briefly discussed in chapter 11), similar to that of Africans liberated by the British squadrons in other parts of the Atlantic world. But once these Africans had their status confirmed, they were not simply allowed to go. Forced to toil under very harsh conditions, they were employed by the Brazilian state to perform public works or by private individuals whom they should work for as servants or free workers for a period of fourteen years.[26] Despite this legislation, as we have seen in Luiz Gama's letter that opened this chapter, the illegal slave trade to Brazil continued until 1850, when the Eusébio de Queirós Law banned slave imports from Africa to Brazil for a second time.

Between 1831 and 1856, nearly 786,00 enslaved men, women, and children were illegally introduced into Brazil, of which only 11,000 were emancipated by Brazilian authorities. Brazilian abolitionists denounced the illegal enslavement of these Africans and their descendants. As noted in chapter 12, however, only in September 1871 was the Free Womb Law (or Rio Branco Law, no. 20140) enacted, liberating newborns of enslaved mothers, albeit with certain conditions. As in other parts of the Americas, the law established that free newborns would remain the property of the enslaved mother's master until the age of eight. Then, the owner could choose either to continue using the child's labor for free until the child turned twenty-one, the age of maturity, or to free the child and receive a financial compensation of 600 *mil-réis* (literally 1,000 *réis*) from the Brazilian government. Prices of enslaved people in the Brazilian domestic slave market varied according to several factors, especially age and sex. In 1871, this amount would probably not be enough to purchase a new adult enslaved person in the southeastern coffee plantation areas. Existing studies show that in Campinas, São Paulo, the average price of a bondsman in 1870 between fifteen and forty years of age was more than 2 *contos* (1 *conto* corresponded to 1,000 *mil-réis* or 1 million *réis*), whereas the average price of an enslaved woman was 1.1 *conto*.[27] Following the Free Womb Law, São Paulo's province slave owners alone obtained approximately 414 *contos* and 882 *mil-réis* in financial compensation.[28] Although the new legislation did not emancipate any living enslaved persons, it mandated the creation of a register that became a tool to identify Africans introduced illegally in Brazil after 1831.

Likewise, in 1885, the Sexagenarian Law (or Law Saraiva-Cotegipe) emancipated enslaved individuals older than sixty years of age.[29] Unsurprisingly, the new legislation again established financial compensation for slave owners and further declared that the newly freed individuals should work three additional years at no cost or until the age of sixty-five. Despite the pitfalls of this legislation gradually abolishing slavery in Brazil, the growth of the abolitionist movement became evident. Starting in the 1870s, and especially during the 1880s, enslaved people and abolitionists intensified their campaigns to abolish slavery. Bondspeople also engaged in massive flights in both urban and rural areas.[30] Social unrest along with widespread calls to end slavery contributed to the intensification of the crisis of the Brazilian slave system.[31] Fearing revolts, slave owners freed thousands of enslaved men, women, and children, and hundreds of others ran away in the coffee zones of Brazil's southeast. Still, slaveholders counted on their representatives in the Chamber of Deputies to obtain financial compensation, or at least some kind of measure allowing them to maintain a position of dominance over the future freed population.[32] On May 13, 1888, Princess Isabel, the regent, eventually signed the Golden Law, which emancipated nearly 700,000 enslaved men and women.[33] Although the law did not include any provisions to pay indemnities to slave owners, after the abolition they continued to put pressure on the government to be compensated for the loss of their enslaved property, but they were unsuccessful.[34]

Meanwhile, notwithstanding legal prohibitions, the slave trade from Africa to Cuba continued in the first six decades of the nineteenth century. Whereas in Spain the debates about gradual emancipation intensified after the deposition of Queen Isabella II in 1868, in Cuba, the colonists from the eastern part of the island embraced the idea of independence in an uprising that gave origin to the Ten Years War (1868–78).[35] Bondspeople and free people of color, who were also discriminated against by colonial policies, supported the elites in the fight for the abolition of slavery and independence from Spain.[36] As the upper classes feared the movement for independence on July 4, 1870, the Spanish Parliament passed the Moret Law, which in addition to freeing children born to enslaved women after September 17, 1868, also emancipated enslaved people who served under the Spanish flag during the Ten Years War. Moreover, the Moret Law also liberated enslaved people older than sixty. But as pointed out in chapter 12, like the free womb legislation in other regions of Latin America, the law contained several restrictions, through the creation of a *patronato* system, similar to the British apprenticeship. In this framework, Cuban slave owners who remained loyal to the Spanish crown received financial compensation and could use for free the labor of the children newly emancipated from slavery until the age of eighteen, who would become free at age twenty-two.[37] Although the size of Cuba's enslaved population decreased from nearly 300,000 to 200,000 in the decade that followed the enactment of the Moret Law, few of the newly emancipated people were individuals of working age.[38]

The 1870s and 1880s witnessed the last years of slavery in the Spanish Empire. Following popular demonstrations in several Spanish cities, on March 22, 1873, the Spanish Parliament passed a law ending slavery in Puerto Rico. The law freed around 29,335 enslaved individuals, who still had to keep working under three-year labor contracts held by their former owners.[39] Cuba maintained slavery for seven more years. Eventually, on February 13, 1880, the Patronato Law passed in the Spanish Parliament to end slavery in Cuba. In theory, the new law abolished slavery. In practice, it also established an eight-year period of apprenticeship. Ultimately, the *patronato* ended on October 7, 1886, two years prior to the established date of 1888. As many enslaved people freed under the Patronato Law (known as *patrocinados*) obtained their freedom in the five years that followed the creation of *patronato*, upon the final demise of this system, Cuban registers included approximately 99,566 *patrocinados*.[40]

Paths to Colonization in Africa

The trade relations developed during the era of the Atlantic slave trade had opened the path for European conquest of Africa. At the end of the nineteenth century, Britain, France, Portugal, and other European states gradually imposed their presence on the African continent, fueling a process that became known as the "scramble for Africa." The new rule by European colonial powers led to the gradual legal prohibition of slavery on African soil. However, emancipation was a lengthy and complex process that varied over time and from region to region.

Slavery had existed in Africa prior to the arrival of Europeans. Likewise, Muslim slave trade (mainly to North Africa and the Middle East) and the African internal slave trade, which provided captives to the continent's internal market, emerged before the Atlantic slave trade and persisted throughout the nineteenth and the twentieth centuries. Although bondage in Africa differed from the racialized chattel slavery that prevailed in the Americas, the development of the transatlantic slave trade altered the nature of slavery in Africa. During the second half of the nineteenth century, the end of the Atlantic slave trade led many African societies to develop an export-oriented agricultural economy that largely relied on slavery as a mode of production.[41] But in regions such as West Central Africa, slavery continued to expand over the course of the nineteenth century.[42]

Measures to legally prohibit the slave trade and slavery on African soil justified European conquest and colonization. Starting in the second half of the nineteenth century, Britain signed several treaties with African states, including Egypt, Zanzibar, and Madagascar, to legally ban the slave trade.[43] Despite these agreements, during this first phase, Britain tolerated the existence of what many British officials defined as "domestic" slavery, perceived as a more benign and acceptable kind of bondage.[44] In some West African regions such as the Sokoto Caliphate in what is now Nigeria, not only did a plantation economy expand, but the institution of slavery continued to develop under new contours that carried many similarities to chattel slavery in the Americas.[45] In regions controlled by the Portuguese, such as Angola, slavery was abolished in 1869. But in the three years that followed, Portugal imposed an apprenticeship system on former slaves. As a result, slavery remained viable in Angola far beyond the date of its legal abolition.[46] Whereas local rulers, slave traders, and slave owners met the prohibition of slavery with resistance, enslaved men and women took these opportunities to assert their freedom by running away from their masters, returning to their former villages, and creating new communities, very often far from their region of origin.[47] As happened in the Americas, slaves themselves were protagonists of their emancipation.[48]

The consolidation of colonial rule at the turn of the twentieth century contributed to the legal end of slavery in Africa. In 1900, Britain legally abolished slavery in its occupied zones in Nigeria. In 1905, France legally prohibited slavery in its West African colonies.[49] Despite these transformations, European colonial rule in zones controlled by France, Portugal, and Belgium imposed on populations atrocious coercive labor regimes, which in practice were similar to slavery. In most African regions, slavery had disappeared by the time of the Second World War (1939–45). Although illegal, depending on the period and region, slave labor resurfaced several times. A striking example is Mauritania, where slavery was first legally banned during French colonial rule in 1905, yet an actual law abolishing slavery in the country was not enacted until 1981.[50] Even today, the populations of various African countries, such as Angola remember the slavery-like working conditions of forced labor systems imposed by Europeans.[51] Therefore, on both sides of the Atlantic Ocean, the legacy of slavery and the Atlantic slave trade lives on.

Protagonists of Their Own Emancipation

The end of the slave trade and slavery in the Americas and Africa entailed a long and complex process involving several social, economic, and legal dimensions. But despite these various layers, both gradual and final abolitions of slavery were possible through the actions of enslaved men and women who challenged their legal status by petitioning courts. Moreover, as discussed in chapter 15, legislation was shaped by the activities of bondspeople who along with other social actors took their destiny into their own hands by organizing rebellions and undertaking massive flights. These movements were also supported by campaigns including petitions, the publication of manifestos in newspapers, and the organization of public gatherings for the passing of antislavery legislation. In other words, beyond the legal prohibition of slavery, either in the Americas or in Africa, bondspeople were protagonists of their own emancipation. Still, in most regions of the Americas, former slave owners obtained financial compensation to cover the loss of their enslaved property. However, former enslaved persons never obtained financial or material reparations for slavery.[52] In the period that followed the abolition of slavery in the Americas, freedpeople continued to experience economic and social exclusion.

Likewise, during European colonial rule in Africa, freedpeople were submitted to inhumane forms of labor exploitation that, although not being slavery, carried many slavery-like features. In the Americas, many freedmen and freedwomen were subjected to difficult living and working conditions in the period that immediately followed the end of slavery. In the United States, following the quick period of radical Reconstruction between 1863 and 1877, segregation and open racial hatred prevailed in the final decades of the nineteenth century, preventing freedpeople and their descendants from having access to civil rights. In Brazil and the rest of Latin America, freedpeople were denied the same economic opportunities as their white counterparts during slavery and after the end of slavery. These difficult conditions, which varied among regions and periods, led many freedpeople to migrate to West Africa, where they continued to bear the stigma associated with their former lives of bondage. As we will see in chapter 17, however, once on the continent, whereas most former slaves faced frequent hardships, some of the freedmen and freedwomen who survived the ordeal of migrating to Africa became slave traders and later collaborated with European colonial regimes.

CHAPTER 17

Africa's Homecomings

The slogan "Back to Africa" usually evokes the mass movement led by Marcus Garvey, who called upon Black people in the Americas to relocate to Africa in the early twentieth century. But even before Garvey, thousands of formerly enslaved African men, women, and children and their descendants had already been emigrating from the present-day United States to the African continent. Emigration to Africa started as early as the late eighteenth century, continued after emancipation, and persisted during the entire nineteenth century. However, existing narratives of the movement of freedpeople relocating to Africa overlook the fact that thousands of freed Africans and their descendants also migrated from Brazil and Cuba to West Africa and West Central Africa during the eighteenth and nineteenth centuries. Despite specific motivations in each region and period, relocation to Africa was a response to anti-Black racism in the Americas. Individually or in groups, freed Africans and their descendants left the United States, Jamaica, Canada, Brazil, and Cuba to settle on the coastal areas of West Africa and West Central Africa over more than a century.

Following the journeys of these free and freed men, women, and children, this chapter illuminates the shared and individual contexts that led them to leave the Americas and settle in various parts of West Africa and West Central Africa. African ancestry remained a problematic marker connecting Black men and women to slavery in the Americas; having a past associated with slavery followed Black migrants to the other side of the Atlantic Ocean. Returnees who settled on the Bight of Benin joined other freedmen and slave merchants established in the region, and some freedmen who settled in West Africa during the first half of the nineteenth century, as discussed in previous chapters, became slave traders themselves. Although to several African-born settlers the emigration to Africa was a return to the motherland, many of these free and freed men and women were born in the Americas and were therefore setting foot on the continent of their ancestors for the first time. Regardless of their birthplaces, conflict often marked the contact between these new Black immigrants and the various local populations.

Back to Africa's First Wave in the Age of Revolutions

During the Atlantic revolutions, enslaved people emancipated themselves by organizing rebellions and escaping bondage. These actions fueled the abolitionist movement. As discussed in chapter 15, bondspeople led several revolts in the thirteen British colonies of North America during the eighteenth century. The combination of the fight for independence from Britain and slave owners' fear of slave insurrections propelled the long, incremental movement toward the legal abolition of slavery in the Americas. In 1775, nearly 20 percent of the population of 2.5 million people in the thirteen British colonies lived in bondage, whereas only approximately 50,000 Black persons were free.[1] The British promised to emancipate men and women who escaped their owners, recruiting them as soldiers, cooks, tailors, carpenters, boatmen, foragers, nurses, and in several other auxiliary roles.[2] Most enslaved people remained in bondage during the war, but nearly 20,000 slaves from all thirteen colonies joined the British lines to become Black loyalists.[3]

Following the end of the American War of Independence, the British organized the exodus of approximately 75,000 men, women, and children to several regions of the British Empire, including Britain, the West Indies, Australia, India, and British North America (mainly to Nova Scotia but also to New Brunswick and to Quebec, which in 1763 had become a British colony). Most exiles were white people, but among them were Black loyalists who were either already free or freed after joining the British lines. In addition, 15,000 enslaved men, women, and children were also evacuated with their owners, most of them from the Southern colonies, who headed to Jamaica and the Bahamas.[4] Already in 1782, when the armed conflict ended, the provisional articles of the peace treaty had established that the British were prohibited from transporting property, including enslaved people who ran away, outside the newly emancipated territory, a provision confirmed by the Treaty of Paris of 1783, which stated that the British must return runaway Black loyalists to their owners. Despite this interdiction, the British started relocating Black refugees and their families by mostly fulfilling their original agreement with them. Not only did the British pay for the transportation of Black exiles to other territories within the vast British Empire, they also refused to return fugitives from slavery to American slave owners or to pay them any compensation for their loss of human property.[5]

Among these Black exiles were loyalists who fought alongside the British Crown and who received freedom certificates before their departure, as well as enslaved men, women, and children owned by white loyalists. However, bondspeople who were owned by loyalists before the war remained in bondage after the end of the war.[6] In some cases, enslaved children and wives of Black loyalists who did not join British lines within a period of twelve months were returned to their owners and were not allowed to leave the United States.[7]

Approximately 30,000 refugees migrated from the newly independent United States to Nova Scotia, including white loyalists who fled the United States between 1782 and 1783 and transported with them hundreds of enslaved persons. British officers compiled the names of nearly 3,000 Black men, women, and children, most of them freed and free people, who were assigned to board ships that left from New York bound for Nova Scotia.[8] The poignant story of these emigrants is recorded in a ledger titled the *Book of Negroes*, today housed at the National Archives in Britain.[9] The story inspired the award-winning novel *The Book of Negroes* (2007) by Canadian writer Lawrence Hill, published in the United States under the title *Someone Knows My Name* (2008) and adapted as a television miniseries that aired in Canada and the United States in 2015.[10]

The British promised to provide land to Nova Scotia's settlers. But after waiting for five years, only 28 percent of Black emigrants received their lots. Black settlers remained largely segregated from white immigrants in Nova Scotia, where they continued to experience racist treatment in addition to other hardships, including hunger. The burden was so heavy that several freed Black refugees had no choice but to accept indenture contracts, a risky decision that in some cases led them to be sold back into slavery. After moving to Nova Scotia, Black refugees were also sometimes forced to change professions or become sharecroppers for white settlers.[11] Against these odds, Black exiles fought to obtain land and the same rights as white colonizers.[12]

Despite the rising abolitionist movement, the Atlantic slave trade was in full swing in the last decades of the eighteenth century. Freedmen born in Africa and British North America created several mutual aid organizations in New England and the mid-Atlantic that promoted emigration to Africa and elected Sierra Leone as the preferred territory in which to relocate.[13] In 1787, Anthony Taylor, then the president of the Free African Union Society, a mutual relief society of free Black people in Newport, Rhode Island, supported emigration to Africa with hopes that emigrants would obtain land.[14] Also in 1787, British merchants, politicians, and lawyers created the Committee for the Relief of the Black Poor. The group led the creation of the St. George's Bay Company, which aimed to relocate to London's underprivileged Black persons to West Africa. The potential migrants were freedpeople from British colonies and nearly 1,000 loyalists who emigrated to London during and after the end of the American War of Independence.

Efforts like these, however, were not always motivated by goodwill. On the one hand, for British and US white people, relocation of Black residents to the Province of Freedom in Sierra Leone was a way to get rid of them. On the other hand, such an initiative was also part of a larger plan to "civilize" Africa through Christianization and European colonization. In addition, through the creation of a colony in West Africa, Britain sought to exploit that region's natural resources and develop new markets for its manufactured goods.[15] In exchange for a payment of fourteen pounds, the committee promised Black migrants transportation as well as land, clothing, supplies, and tools for a period of four months. But already before their departure as they waited to sail to West Africa, the conditions in which these migrants were held were deplorable. When their departure was delayed, more than fifty of them died while waiting in the ship.[16]

In 1787, more than four hundred British settlers, a group mostly composed of poor Black persons, left London for West Africa. Once in Sierra Leone, the British made an agreement by paying tribute to the local ruler, King Tom, in order to establish Granville Town. But as in previous European and African agreements during the era of the Atlantic slave trade, in an area controlled by a West African state, the contours of this transaction remained ambiguous. Black settlers were foreigners and faced numerous obstacles, including rain, poor housing, lack of food, and hostility from the local populations. Seven months later, nearly one-third of the members of the immigrant group had perished. One year later, another group of thirty-nine additional Black settlers were sent to West Africa. But as the living conditions remained precarious, almost all of them died. In addition to the lack of resources and the climate challenges, these first efforts largely failed because this early settlement was based on an unclear arrangement with local rulers that to some extent reminds us of the early exchanges between Portuguese explorers and African rulers in the fifteenth century, as discussed in chapter 1. Ultimately, King Jimmy, who succeeded King Tom, violated the prior agreements. His men invaded the settlement, seized settlers, sold them into slavery, and eventually burned down Granville Town.[17]

Despite this dramatic initial failure, a few years later the British created the Sierra Leone Company, which replaced the earlier initiative. The directors of the Sierra Leone Company promised land to Black migrants. Black exiles in Nova Scotia demanded relocation in Sierra Leone to escape the inequalities imposed on them by white settlers.[18] Eventually, the new venture was successful in transferring more than 1,196 Black men, women, and children from Nova Scotia to Sierra Leone in 1792.[19] But upon arrival in West Africa, these immigrants from Canada again faced disease, hunger, extremely precarious housing, and much worse. Even before providing any lots of land, the company taxed Black settlers. In the months that followed their relocation, Black immigrants often clashed with the Sierra Leone Company's white directors. As living conditions remained difficult, Black settlers demanded participation in the government, land, and access to credit to purchase items in the company's store. In 1800, settlers organized a rebellion to protest the persisting arduous conditions. The British repressed the revolt using against them another group of Black migrants, the Maroons.

Following the Second Maroon War in Jamaica, as briefly discussed in chapter 13, the British Crown passed an act in 1796 to deport Trelawny Town's Maroons off the island.[20] Although their first destination was Halifax in Nova Scotia, the region's inhospitable climate led the Jamaican Maroons to petition to relocate again, this time to Sierra Leone.[21] Eventually, their demands were heard. In 1800, the British transported nearly six hundred Maroons from Jamaica to Sierra Leone. Unlike other Black migrants, they were not Christians, practiced polygyny, and could neither read nor write English.[22] But this new relocation was not only aimed at fulfilling the Maroons' demands to leave Nova Scotia. It was rather intended to employ them as soldiers to repress the rebellions of Black settlers transported to the region as part of the initiative led by the Sierra Leone Company. After the rebels were defeated, two were executed, and nearly thirty insurgents were relocated from Freetown to Bullom Shore and Gorée Island, in present-day Senegal, which by that time was under British control. In addition to the conflicts with the company's white directors, who relied on the support of deported Jamaican Maroons, the newcomers' contact with Sierra Leone's Koya Temne residents remained fraught with conflict. They often clashed with local populations, as many Black settlers were born in the Americas, spoke English, and had been Christians since a young age, making them very different from the people they now lived among.

The British slave trade was abolished in 1807, just seven years after the suppression of the revolt of Sierra Leone's Black settlers. In the years that followed, other Black migrants reached Sierra Leone as well. For example, Paul Cuffee, a freeborn Black man, Quaker, shipowner, and abolitionist from Massachusetts, was one of the earliest advocates of settling freedpeople in West Africa. After creating two organizations to promote the settlement of freedpeople in Sierra Leone, he successfully transported 38 Black men, women, and children from the United States to Freetown in 1816.[23] Britain signed treaties with Portugal, Brazil, the Netherlands, and Spain between 1815 and 1818 to prohibit the slave trade north of the equator. As the British Royal Navy patrolled the coasts of West Africa to suppress the illegal trade, at least 85,000 out of a total of 175,000 Africans liberated between 1808 and 1862 were brought to Freetown.

During the first half of the nineteenth century, politicians and white elite groups also debated the conditions under which slavery would be abolished in the United States. Fearing insurrection and relying on the assumption that Black people and white people should remain separated, they considered the possible relocation of freedpeople to other parts of the Americas and to West Africa. These discussions took on a more urgent tone following the unsuccessful slave rebellion led by bondsman Gabriel Prosser in Richmond, Virginia, in 1800. White clergyman and educator Robert Finley also promoted the relocation of freedpeople to the western coast of Africa.[24] In 1816, he created the Society for the Colonization of Free People of Color of America, later renamed the American Colonization Society. Led by slave owners and abolitionists, both endeavors relied on racist conceptions that following emancipation, Black people and white populations could not live in the same territory, and to rid the country of free and freed Black individuals, they should be relocated to West Africa. With this goal, the American Colonization Society sent delegates to present-day Liberia in 1821, where the society founded Christopolis (later renamed Monrovia after US President James Monroe) in 1822.

As in Sierra Leone, the creation of this new American colony on African soil generated conflicts with the local populations, who occasionally attacked the new settlement. Moreover, reports about diseases and difficult living conditions also discouraged Black Americans from embracing Liberia as a viable option for migration. But after Liberia became independent from the American Colonization Society in 1847 and received diplomatic recognition from the United States in 1862, Liberian representatives came to Washington, DC, to recruit Black American settlers.[25]

In the years that followed, individually or in groups, African Americans ventured to cross the Atlantic Ocean to settle in Liberia. Historian Lisa A. Lindsay has elucidated the story of one of these men, who left the United States before the rise of the Civil War to relocate in West Africa. James Churchwill Vaughan was born in South Carolina. As his father, a formerly enslaved man, lay on his deathbed, Vaughan promised to migrate to Africa. For his father, as for many freedpeople, the continent of his ancestors' land continued to be promise of redemption for Black people who remained excluded in the United States after emancipation. In 1852, under the auspices of the American Colonization Society, Vaughan sailed to Liberia on board the *Joseph Maxwell*, along with 149 other settlers. Upon arriving in Liberia in 1853, Vaughan was disappointed with the working and living conditions, and so he continued his journey eastward to settle in Lagos, in present-day Nigeria. There he was an active witness to the tumultuous period that marked the end of the Atlantic slave trade and the rise of British colonialism.[26] As we will see in the sections that follow, Vaughan was not alone. Like him, other descendants of enslaved people took similar Atlantic routes, expecting to start a better life on the African continent.

Exodus from Brazil

Movements of emigration back to Africa occurred in Brazil and to a lesser extent in Cuba as well.[27] As discussed in chapter 15, a series of slave insurrections in Brazil occurred in Bahia in the early nineteenth century and culminated with the Malê Revolt in January 1835. Bahia's authorities quickly repressed the rebellion by arresting dozens of individuals suspected of participating in the uprising. Despite the lack of evidence against many of these suspects, the province's government took measures to deport dozens of prisoners a few months later. Hundreds of freed men, women, and children followed the same path.[28]

After the dismantling of the Malê Revolt, Brazilian slave owners and public authorities considered freed Africans a serious menace to Brazilian society. As a result of the rebellion, the Law Number 9 of May 13, 1835, imposed numerous restrictions on freed Africans residing in Brazil. Among these measures, Africans were no longer allowed to acquire real estate in their own names; owners could not rent their houses to freed or enslaved Africans, who now had to pay an annual tax, otherwise they were sent to prison.[29] African-born residents were also required to obtain a proof of residence that had to be annually renewed. As these measures evolved, the government of Bahia started deporting the prisoners who were sentenced for participation or suspected of involvement in the Malê Revolt. In September 1835, the vessel *Maria Damiana* sailed to Ouidah with two hundred passengers on board. Other remaining suspects were deported in smaller groups.[30]

Although Bahia's government should have disbursed the travel costs of deportation, many exiles had no other choice than to pay their own transportation expenses.[31] At least six hundred other men, women, and children decided to follow these deportees.[32] Other individuals traveled back to Africa as well. Considering the climate of persecution established in Salvador, it was not surprising that even freedmen and freedwomen without any connection to the 1835 rebellion were willing to travel to the Bight of Benin, despite this voyage being a very risky journey during a period when the illegal slave trade was still operating in the region.[33] As Lisa Earl Castillo has noted, freed African migrants often left Brazil with several members of their households, including children, and other dependents, such as recently freed enslaved people. Moreover, several former bondspeople traveled back to Africa with their former owners.[34]

Most of the first exiles who arrived in West Africa settled in Ouidah. But once in the region, they moved to other coastal towns such as Little Popo (today's Aného in Togo), Agoué, Porto-Novo, Badagry, Lagos, and even Accra (in today's Ghana).[35] Although some freedmen and freedwomen who left from Salvador resettled in West Central Africa, the greatest majority of the exiles who established themselves in Luanda, Benguela, and Moçâmedes left Brazil from Rio de Janeiro.[36] In many of these regions, formerly enslaved individuals joined existing communities composed of Portuguese and Brazilian slave merchants and their descendants. Over time, as some families increased in size, their members could be found in various coastal towns from Accra to Lagos. Unlike freedpeople who migrated from the United States, British North America, and the West Indies to Sierra Leone and Liberia, most formerly enslaved men and women who traveled from Brazil to West Africa and West Central Africa were born in Africa. But like their exile counterparts who left from other parts of the Americas to Africa, the travel conditions during the Atlantic crossing were also difficult.

Migration patterns from Brazil back to Africa followed the same routes in operation during the era of the Atlantic slave trade. Therefore, most returnees established themselves close to seaports where they could maintain trading connections with Brazil. Many African-born freedpeople preferred to settle in areas far from the places where they had been originally captured. As the illegal slave trade to the Americas was still active until the 1860s, once these African returnees arrived at the motherland, not only could they face hostilities from local communities for whom they were foreigners, but they also risked being captured and sold into slavery again. One dreadful episode took place when the vessel *General Rego* sailed to Lagos transporting a group of forty freedmen and freedwomen from Rio de Janeiro and Bahia in 1856. On its way to Lagos, the ship stopped at Ouidah, the slave-trading port controlled by the Kingdom of Dahomey. Under the excuse that the passengers were Egba people from Abeokuta, a Yoruba state rival to Dahomey, Dahomean agents confiscated the passengers' belongings and sent them to the Dahomean king, who killed the adults and enslaved the children.[37]

Observers at that time reported that freedpeople from Brazil, the West Indies, and the island of Saint Helena (then a British Crown colony) in the South Atlantic Ocean continued to relocate on the Bight of Benin in the 1870s. The exodus to West Africa, including departures from Rio de Janeiro, continued even after the abolition of Brazilian slavery in 1888, until the early twentieth century. Even in these late voyages, some exiles suffered great tragedies. In 1899, the vessel *Aliança* sailed from Bahia to Lagos with sixty passengers on board, almost all of them elder individuals born in the Bight of Benin. But during the Atlantic crossing, an outbreak of diphtheria killed at least twelve passengers, who were thrown into the sea, and upon arrival in Lagos, the survivors had to spend time in quarantine.[38] As many as eight thousand men, women, and children may have migrated from Brazil back to Africa.[39] However, estimates can vary because scholars often counted these migrants only until the 1860s. Moreover, many travelers voyaged back and forth between Brazil and West Africa.

Even the African-born freedpeople who decided by their own initiative to return to the Bight of Benin could experience the Atlantic crossing as a second deportation, as Milton Guran reminds us. As we have seen in previous chapters, although enslaved men and women were baptized and forced to adopt Roman Catholicism, African-born men and women and their descendants managed to keep their own religions, cultures, and languages. Even in bondage, while in Brazil enslaved Africans started new families, created new networks, learned to speak Portuguese, and acquired a variety of skills. Like their counterparts who migrated from the United States and Nova Scotia to Sierra Leone and Liberia, African-born freedmen and freedwomen who left Brazil to resettle in the Bight of Benin had Christian names. Their customs, manners, foodways, new professions, and even the Portuguese language they spoke (although known to many people in the coastal areas) contrasted with those of the locally born population. Decades of Atlantic slave trade had transformed West Africa into a place that no longer resembled the homeland of their childhood recollections. As many avoided inland incursions, few returnees were able to find their relatives or past acquaintances.[40]

An Afro-Luso-Brazilian Community in the Bight of Benin

African freedmen and freedwomen who migrated from Bahia and Rio de Janeiro to the Bight of Benin joined a long-established community of Portuguese and Brazilian slave merchants who had been based in the region's coastal towns since the eighteenth century. These formerly enslaved returnees attempted to keep their Brazilian lifestyle. Preserving their Brazilian way of life was not only an issue of customs and culture. Several freed African-born returnees owned enslaved people in Brazil, and several of them actually became slave merchants after reaching West Africa. Surely, many of these slave traders were not able to amass great fortunes, as other slave merchants of the region did, but some of them prospered. This Afro-Luso-Brazilian community is still today known as "Aguda." This term, originally associated with the Portuguese settlers and also a synonym for "Brazilian" and "Catholic," was gradually applied to all Brazilian returnees living in the Bight of Benin, though among them were also individuals who embraced Islam.

Upon their arrival in Ouidah, freedpeople were assisted by the Brazilian slave merchant Francisco Félix de Souza, one of the most important dignitaries in the region. We do not know much about Souza's early life. Born in Salvador in 1754, he first came to the region in 1792 and may have stayed for approximately three years. In 1800, he returned to the Bight of Benin and settled in Ouidah to work in the Portuguese fort São João Batista da Ajuda. This Portuguese trade outpost, in operation in the area since 1721, was administered directly from Bahia, which until 1763 was the capital of the Viceroyalty of Brazil, then a Portuguese colony. After this initial position, Souza became the fort's director.

Souza's earliest activities in Ouidah coincided with the reign of the infamous King Adandozan, who ruled Dahomey from 1797 to 1818, as already discussed in chapter 3. Adandozan acquired a bad reputation because after taking power he may have sold locally born individuals into slavery. These victims included members of the Dahomean royal family who were allegedly involved in the plot that led to the assassination of his father, King Agonglo, including one of his wives Na Agontimé, as mentioned in chapter 2. Adandozan's selling of noblemen and noblewomen into slavery was considered a transgression, even though previous kings had sold their political enemies into slavery as well. More likely the king's bad reputation was a consequence of the economic and political crisis that marked his reign. Ouidah was in great decline because of the dramatic drop in the French slave trade that followed the victory of the Saint-Domingue Revolution. Further contributing to Ouidah's decline were the final ban of the British slave trade in 1807 and Britain's increasing efforts to prohibit the slave trade from Africa to Brazil, where most Africans who had been embarked in Ouidah were sent into slavery. The growing importance of Lagos threatened Ouidah's position as the largest West African slave-trading port, creating quarrels among the Dahomean king and slave merchants from various European nations and Brazil.[41] Following one of these quarrels, Adandozan sent Souza to prison. While incarcerated, Souza met Prince Gakpé, the king's half brother and future King Gezo, who helped him to escape from prison. After this memorable flight, Souza probably settled in Little Popo, whence he supported Gakpé with goods and weapons to prepare for the putsch against Adandozan.

When King Gezo had successfully deposed Adandozan, he repaid Souza for his support. The new king invited Souza to settle in Ouidah, granted him land, and awarded him with financial advantages and political power. Souza became Gezo's most important agent in Ouidah's slave-trading activities and one of the wealthiest slave merchants of West Africa. His privileged connections with the Dahomean royal family made him the founder of a dynasty of sorts. His nickname "Chacha" became a title, and he was commonly referred to as the viceroy of Dahomey, even though this title did not exist.[42]

The story of Souza, Adandozan, and Gezo is well known and was depicted in the novel *The Viceroy of Ouidah* by British writer Bruce Chatwin, which was later adapted to the big screen as the movie *Cobra Verde* by German filmmaker Werner Herzog.[43] More recently, Gezo was also portrayed in the movie *The Woman King*, though inaccurately represented as a supporter of the slave trade abolition.[44] During the nineteenth century, Souza became the main supporter and benefactor of the community of freedmen and freedwomen returnees in Ouidah. In this powerful capacity, he also distributed favors and, in exchange, obtained political support. Among the members of the Aguda community, however, there was an invisible line that separated and still today keeps apart the descendants of enslaved people who returned from Brazil to settle in the Bight of Benin and the descendants of slave merchants. Members of the community who are descendants of enslaved people could feel uncomfortable highlighting that their ancestors were enslaved people, whereas descendants of slave merchants were often proud of their ancestors, who are perceived by them as wealthy and prosperous men. But despite these divisions within the community, many Aguda families include descendants of both freedpeople and slave traders.[45]

Souza was not the only rich Brazilian slave merchant established in the Bight of Benin with connections with the Aguda community. Take the example of Domingos José Martins (also known as

"Dominguinhos da Costa" and Domingos Martinez). Like Souza, he was one of the most important Brazilian slave traders in the region. Born in Salvador in Bahia, his activities in the Bight of Benin greatly contributed to the trade connections between Bahia, Ouidah, and Lagos. In 1834, after the slave trade to Brazil was outlawed, Martins traveled from Bahia to the Bight of Benin as part of the crew of a slave ship sent to Francisco Félix de Souza, but the British Royal Navy captured the slave vessel, and the crew members had to disembark in Ouidah, where Martins settled and started trading in enslaved Africans under Souza's protection. By 1838, Martins had moved to Lagos. Taking advantage of his Brazilian network, he imported gold and other goods, with which he purchased African captives to be illegally transported and sold in Brazil. In just a few years, he became the most important slave merchant in Lagos.[46] Ten years later, for example, on June 7 1843, the slave ship *Furia*, which sailed from Lagos to Bahia illegally transporting 529 enslaved men, women, and children consigned to Domigos José Martins, was intercepted by the British Royal Navy.[47]

By 1844, Martins went to Bahia, but in 1845 he sailed again from Brazil to the Bight of Benin.[48] By this time, *Oba* Kosoko had overthrown *Oba* Akitoye, Martins's former supporter in Lagos, which is probably why Martins decided to relocate in Porto-Novo (today's Sèmè near today's Porto-Novo, the capital of the Republic of Benin). This slave-trading port was controlled by the Kingdom of Porto-Novo, in competition and often in conflict with the Kingdom of Dahomey. From there, he established another outpost in Ape Vista (today's Cotonou).[49] But Martins was versatile and also maintained a trading post in Ouidah, where his old benefactor Souza still controlled the slave trade.

In Ouidah, Lagos, or Porto-Novo, Martins joined the Aguda community's second generation but kept traveling back and forth to Bahia, where he had family and owned real estate.[50] He became so influential in the region that, following Souza's death, King Gezo considered appointing Martins as Souza's successor. But as Martins was not willing to relocate to Ouidah, he declined the offer. With the rise of the new legitimate trade in palm oil, Martins supported it as complementary to the illegal slave trade. His stance paid off. In 1849, the British identified him as the most important trader of the Bight of Benin. For example, in February 1850, the British Royal Navy apprehended his slave-trading brigantine *Serpente* off Porto-Novo, and in April 1850, it captured the brigantine *Dois Amigos* that departed from Bahia to the coasts of Africa.[51] Over time, Martins increasingly clashed with the king of Porto-Novo as the rival kingdom, Dahomey, continued to be his main supplier of enslaved Africans.

In 1851, the conflicts with the king of Porto-Novo led Martins to move back to Ouidah, where he was appointed as a *caboceer* (local chief). At this point British pressures to abolish the slave trade in the region were becoming successful. In January 1852, King Gezo signed a treaty with the British abolishing the slave trade in Dahomey, but Martins certainly continued trading in enslaved Africans as the British often accused him of not respecting the slave trade prohibition. Although he may have considered returning to Bahia, the slave trade to Brazil was outlawed for the second time in 1850, and he may have feared being prosecuted for his illegal trading activities. Bankrupted in 1859, he avowed that he had given up the slave trade only in 1863. Martins died in Ouidah in 1864. He had married one of Souza's daughters, with whom he had at least one child. Like other Brazilian and Portuguese slave merchants, Martins certainly left descendants in Ouidah, even though he was probably not able to pass down many assets.

By 1850, several former slave returnees were also actively involved in the slave trade in Ouidah, Agoué, Porto-Novo, and Lagos.[52] Among these freedmen was Joaquim de Almeida, to whom we were introduced in chapter 8. In 1835, when the Malê Revolt broke out, he was already freed and became a prosperous slave trader, leading his activities between Bahia and the Bight of Benin. According to his family's oral tradition, disseminated by several scholars, he married Mino, a freedwoman he met in Brazil. Mino was said to have been a wife or a descendant of the infamous King Adandozan.[53] Thus, Almeida and his spouse settled in Agoué, even though he pursued his slave-trading activities eastward in Ouidah (see map 1 at the front of the book), where his activities contributed to breaking Souza's monopoly of the slave trade in the region.[54] According to the British officer Frederick Forbes, who sojourned in the region, Almeida was the most affluent slave merchant established in Ouidah in the 1840s.[55] His reputation as one of the "three most active slave agents on the coast of Africa" along with Domingos José Martins remained intact until as late as 1853.[56] Like the Souza family, the Silva family is among the most prominent Aguda clans of the Republic of Benin. Today, its most famous representative, Urbain-Karim Elisio da Silva, maintains a private museum in Porto-Novo, where he tells the story of the Aguda community and the African diaspora from his personal perspective. However, the trajectory of his first ancestor bearing the name Silva (a very common last name in Brazil and Portugal), is more uncertain than that of other leading members of the Aguda community such as Souza, Martins, and Almeida. According to one version of the oral tradition, the first Silva in the Bight of Benin was José Rodrigues da Silva, a Portuguese slave merchant who started trading enslaved Africans at the port of Jakin (near present-day Godomey) by the middle of the eighteenth century. Silva married a daughter of the *oba* of Benin. The couple sent one of their sons to Bahia, where he married a Brazilian woman. Together they had a son, Firmiano Georges José Rodrigues da Silva, who married Angélica Rosa da Conceição. The couple relocated in Ouidah in the first half of the nineteenth century and had a son baptized Francisco Rodrigues da Silva. But the name Silva had also been transmitted by the patriarch to other children he had with other local African women, including a son named Honório Aruna Georges Rodrigues da Silva.

Despite the oral tradition, historians did not find evidence linking his family to José Rodrigues da Silva. But through his maternal side, Urbain-Karim Elisio da Silva also had connections with Brazilian returnees. His great-grandfather was José Abubakar Paraíso, a Yoruba speaker captured during the wars that led to the fall of the

Oyo Empire and sent into slavery to Bahia in the early nineteenth century. There are several conflicting versions of Paraíso's trajectory as well.[57] What we do know is that once he was emancipated, Paraíso was possibly already converted to Islam and returned from Bahia to the Bight of Benin approximately in 1850. After disembarking at the port of Badagry (in present-day Nigeria) he settled in Porto-Novo, where he became a prominent figure among the community of Yoruba speakers. Like many returnees who settled in the Bight of Benin, Silva's ancestors reinvented themselves, and despite facing numerous hardships, they prospered.

Brazilian Culture in the Bight of Benin

Despite being considered a particular group identifiable by their names, the Aguda community was never a homogeneous group. At the time of its formation, and even today, members of the community were perceived to be Catholics, but among the former returnees there were also Muslims and those who were followers of African-based religions such as Vodun and Orisha.[58] Among them there were African-born former bondspeople who belonged to various ethnic groups and spoke various native languages, mainly Yoruba, but also Gbe languages such as Gen, Aja, and Fon. Over time the community included returnees and their descendants, descendants of Brazilian and Portuguese slave traders, and those who had been bondspeople of these two groups and were then assimilated by their families. These individuals carried the Portuguese names of their former Brazilian owners and shared customs and culture acquired in Brazil and Portugal.[59]

Freedpeople from Brazil brought to the Bight of Benin a particular cuisine that included popular Brazilian dishes such as *feijoada* (beans and pork, similar to the French *cassoulet*), *cozido* (boiled meat and vegetables), and *acará* (deep-fried dough made with white beans) that are still consumed today in Togo, the Republic of Benin, and Nigeria, similar to the Brazilian *acarajé*, very popular in Bahia. Although

Europeans introduced bread to the Bight of Benin, it was the Aguda community who popularized its consumption.[60]

Despite the differences within the Aguda community, the returnees had a common past in which the Atlantic slave trade and slavery played a crucial role. Unlike the local population, the Aguda were Westernized. They were Catholic and baptized with Portuguese and Brazilian names such as Silva, Reis, Assunção, Almeida, Santos, Cruz, Paraíso, Oliveira, Souza, and many others. They also dressed according to the European fashion of the time, wearing Western clothes such as suits, shirts, and ties. Moreover, to preserve their cohesion, the members of the Aguda community often chose to marry within their community. Many Aguda were literate. They also developed in the Bight of Benin new trades they had learned in Brazil. Members of the community were masons, carpenters, tailors, and merchants. Because of their Westernized manners, they were perceived by the local population to be more educated, but they themselves saw their Westernization as European assimilation and denial of their African origins. The professed superiority associated with a Luso-Brazilian culture, imported mainly from Brazil, provoked jealousy among the local residents. Ultimately, being an Aguda meant belonging to a modern bourgeoisie, which is why some families in the Bight of Benin sought to imitate the community's way of living, to the extent of sometimes adopting Portuguese names.

The Aguda community also left its mark in the public space. In coastal towns of the Bight of Benin such as Lagos, Porto-Novo, Ouidah, and Agoué, members of the community built two-story houses with balconies that influenced the local community to emulate the Brazilian architectural style. Adopting some of these formal elements led to the development of a vernacular architecture inspired by the colonial Luso-Brazilian style.[61] Although often in a great state of decay, many of these buildings are still standing in cities such as Agoué, Ouidah, Porto-Novo, and Lagos. For example, the iconic Great Mosque of Porto-Novo (figure 17.1), whose construction started

FIGURE 17.1. Great Mosque of Porto-Novo, Republic of Benin, 2020. Courtesy of Kottiobed, via Creative Commons Attribution-Share Alike 4.0 International license, https://commons.wikimedia.org/wiki/File:Grande_mosquée_de_porto-novo_03.jpg.

in 1912 during French colonial rule, borrowed many elements of colonial Brazilian architecture.

Over several decades, the Aguda community also reproduced, maintained, and re-created on West African soil Brazilian traditions such as Carnaval, samba parades, and the *bouryan*, a popular masquerade in the Brazilian Northeast that is similar to the *bumba-meu-boi*. The Aguda contributed to the development of the Catholic Church in the region, preparing the way for British, French, and German colonizers who took control of the Bight of Benin at the end of the nineteenth century. The Aguda also re-created Catholic brotherhoods such as the Our Lord of the Good End (Nosso Senhor do Bom Fim), an association that, like other Black brotherhoods discussed in chapter 14, contributed to the manumission of numerous enslaved people in Bahia. In 1861, when the French Société des Missions Africaines established a permanent Catholic Church in the Bight of Benin, its main goal was to serve the already existing Aguda Catholic community.

By 1850, when the slave trade to Brazil had again been outlawed, the slave trade in Ouidah had already dramatically declined. Beginning in the 1830s, in reaction to British pressure to put an end to the slave trade, many slave merchants started trading alternative products, but they continued trading in enslaved Africans until the 1860s.[62] The new trade largely relied on the production of palm oil, the demand for which had increased since the eighteenth century. During the nineteenth century, palm oil was sold in the European and North American markets for industrial purposes, such as in the manufacture of lubricants, industrial fuels, candles, and soap, while palm nut oil was used in the production of margarine.[63]

The British fight against the slave trade was not disinterested but already part of Britain's endeavors to establish a permanent presence in the region. In 1851, the British Royal Navy blockaded Ouidah to oppose the refusal by Dahomey to put an end to the slave trade. Years later, in 1876, a quarrel involving the merchant Jacinto da Costa Santos, who was an agent of the British firm of Swanzy, and King Glele, who ruled Dahomey from 1858 to 1889, led to a second British blockade that lasted nearly ten months.[64] But at that point the French conquest of Dahomey and Porto-Novo was already in progress. In 1851, France signed a treaty of commerce and friendship with King Toffa, who reigned Porto-Novo from 1875 to 1908. Britain bombarded Lagos and sent the *Oba* Kosoko into exile to secure control of the region in 1851. On January 13, 1852, Dahomey and Britain eventually signed a treaty to put an end to the Atlantic slave trade, even though the slave trade continued. In 1861, Britain annexed Lagos.[65] One historian estimated that nearly 1,000 residents of Lagos were identified as Brazilians (Aguda) in 1865, in a population of approximately 25,000. This number increased to 5,000 in 1889, when the overall population was assessed at 37,458.[66]

Cotonou became a French protectorate in 1863 and was confirmed as such in 1878, but as French occupation was not yet established at that point, the city remained under Dahomey's control.[67] When the Atlantic slave trade effectively ended in Ouidah in 1865, ten of the eighteen active slave merchants were Brazilians.[68] But despite the end of the trade in enslaved Africans, several returnees who settled at the Bight of Benin continued to travel to Brazil, where slavery remained alive until 1888. These voyages were not only intended to visit relatives left behind but also to continue developing economic, cultural, and religious relationships on both sides of the Atlantic Ocean.[69] Likewise, the most prosperous Aguda families sent their male children to study in Brazil, Portugal, and France. Only the outbreak of the First World War in 1914 slowed down these lively and continuous exchanges.

The movement of freedpeople from Brazil back to Africa continued on the eve of the Brazilian abolition of slavery. After the Berlin Conference of 1884, the Atlantic slave trade was replaced by European conquest and colonization. In 1882, Porto-Novo and France confirmed Porto-Novo's status as French protectorate. Likewise, Little Popo became part of German Togoland in 1885, and in the same year, Grand-Popo and Agoué became French territories. In early 1889, France proposed establishing a trade customhouse in Cotonou. Because King Glele refused to negotiate, France declared war against Dahomey.

During the first French military campaign of 1890, France occupied Ouidah. In October 1890, a treaty establishing peace between Dahomey and France confirmed the loss of Cotonou but gave Dahomey control of Ouidah. However, in March 1892, French troops advanced from Porto-Novo to Abomey. Dahomey's capital was occupied in November 1892 and Ouidah in December 1892. A French decree established Dahomey as a French protectorate that also included Porto-Novo, Ouidah, Savi, Godomey, and Abomey-Calavi. In 1893, King Behanzin, who succeeded his father in December 1889, was defeated, and in 1894 he was forced to abdicate the throne and was sent into exile in Martinique. On January 15, 1894, his brother was made king by the French under the name Agoli-Agbo, but he had no actual powers. During his reign, French colonial rule in Dahomey preserved local sovereigns, but finally as French colonizers imposed a major tax increase, they also replaced local rulers with their own administrators.[70] In 1900, Agoli-Agbo was also sent into exile, to Gabon. Several dynasties continued to exist in Dahomey, but their role was only symbolic because the French regime did not recognize them.

Not all members of the Aguda community supported the French conquest, but some members joined the new French colonial administration in a variety of positions in which they were intermediaries between the local populations and the European colonizers. For example, several Aguda individuals served as interpreters in the treaty negotiations between the French and the local chiefs. Indeed, their Brazilian and African experiences facilitated their mobility in the new colonial context, and many saw the French presence as an opportunity to become prosperous.[71] In general, the end of the Atlantic slave trade diminished the economic and political power of the Aguda community, but those who were economically successful continued to nourish economic and cultural ties with Brazil. Moreover, French colonization allowed the already prosperous Aguda families to forge a distinct place in colonial society. With the new colonial configuration, many Aguda continued to perform the professional activities that they had performed in Brazil (carpenters, tailors, masons), and others occupied administrative positions (clerks, interpreters, traders).[72] They collaborated with the French regime, and they received favors in exchange for their assistance, thus consolidating their privileged position in colonial society. Thus, during French colonial rule, the Aguda became important elite members of the Colony of Dahomey and Dependencies (Colonie du Dahomey et dépendances).[73] To a great extent, the formation of this Afro-Luso-Brazilian community in the Bight of Benin, before the first calls of "back to Africa" in the United States, shows us how the Atlantic exchanges that emerged during the era of the Atlantic slave trade persevered after the end of the inhuman commerce in the 1860s. It also reminds us of the continuous ties of African-descended communities with their homelands and their contribution to the development of an African diaspora that includes descendants of enslaved people and also descendants of individuals who traded in human beings.

The Exodus from the United States

Meanwhile, as the final years of slavery in the United States approached, debates about relocating the future freed populations outside the United States persisted. In December 1861, during the Civil War, when Abraham Lincoln presented his first annual message as the sixteenth president of the United States to the US Senate and House of Representatives, he again evoked the possible acquisition of foreign territory to relocate the future freed population of the United States. As it envisioned the end of slavery, the US government considered relocating free and freed Black populations, including enslaved people who had escaped from their Confederate owners to join the Union Army, in Ecuador, Nicaragua, Costa Rica, Honduras, Mexico, El Salvador, present-day Panama, Haiti, and Liberia. In their plans, US authorities even included Brazil.[74] Confederate supporters such as Matthew Fontaine Maury promoted the project of creating a slaveholding colony in Amazonia, an enterprise that would allow slave owners to transport their human property to Brazil, while at the same time contributing to a decrease in the US Black population.[75] Except for Haiti and Liberia, freedpeople from the United States never emigrated to most of these destinations. Only about 150 Black people based in Washington, DC, left from Alexandria, Virginia, to relocate in Haiti in June 1862.

After the end of the Civil War and the abolition of slavery in the United States in 1865, other waves of formerly enslaved people migrated to Liberia and other regions of West Africa as well. As freedpeople's expectations to have access to land ownership and full citizenship in the United States gradually disappeared with the end of Reconstruction at the end of the nineteenth century, new projects to settle African Americans in exclusively Black territories within the

United States and emigration to Africa reemerged. Existing estimates suggest that between 1820 and 1867, the American Colonization Society relocated ten thousand to twelve thousand Black men, women, and children from the United States in Liberia.[76]

After the closure of the Freedmen's Bureau in 1872 and the unfulfilled promise of land redistribution to freedpeople, Benjamin Singleton, a freedman from Tennessee, founded a company to acquire public land in Kansas, where he relocated thousands of African Americans between 1873 and 1881. But as racial hatred and suppression of civil rights continued to grow in the country in the following years, Singleton shifted to support the emigration of African Americans to Canada and Liberia. Echoing the ideals of such leaders as Henry McNeal Turner, bishop of the African Methodist Episcopal Church who advocated for relocation to Africa as the only solution for African Americans to escape racism and racial hatred, Singleton and his followers founded the United Transatlantic Society in 1885, with the goal of relocating African Americans to Africa. Yet, this initiative was not successful.[77]

The persisting hostility against Black Americans and segregation in the United States propelled the revival of new movements back to Africa in the first decades of the twentieth century through the leadership of Jamaican-born Marcus Mosiah Garvey.[78] Although Garvey's father was born during the apprenticeship period in Jamaica, his grandfather was an enslaved man.[79] Garvey was already invested in becoming a political leader and orator in his twenties. By 1910, he moved to Costa Rica, where he worked for a small newspaper. During this period abroad, he also spent time in Belize, Honduras, and Panama before moving to Britain. Upon his return to Jamaica in 1914, Garvey cofounded the Universal Negro Improvement Association (UNIA) along with Amy Ashwood, who also served as the organization's first secretary and later became his first wife.[80]

By that time of UNIA's creation, Garvey had been in contact with Booker T. Washington, with whom he discussed the possible creation of an industrial and agricultural school in Jamaica based on the model of the Tuskegee Institute in Alabama. In 1916, Garvey moved to the United States. He incorporated UNIA in New York City in 1918. But he quickly understood that his plans of uplifting Black people through professionalization as promoted by Washington would face great obstacles. Garvey arrived in the United States during the First World War and in an era of European colonial rule on most of the African continent. During the war, African American soldiers who had served in segregated units migrated to urban centers. But despite their role in the war, Black Americans continued to experience political and economic exclusion. Whether in the North or the South, anti-Black racism, segregation, and disenfranchisement not only persisted but continued to increase. In the United States, African Americans were denied the same civil rights and economic opportunities available to white Americans, and Black integration into white American society continued to be illusory.

As Black and white integration remained out of reach, Garvey became the foremost advocate of Black nationalism. Promoting a program focusing on the empowerment of populations of African descent in the United States and in the African diaspora, Garvey advanced the Back to Africa movement as the response to the exclusion and racial violence faced by Black populations in the Americas. Most of UNIA's chapters were in the United States, but there were also dozens of chapters in Canada, Central America, the West Indies, and English-speaking colonies in Africa. According to Garvey, at its peak UNIA attracted eleven million members worldwide, and even according to his own enemies, membership grew into the hundreds of thousands.[81]

Through UNIA's auspices, Garvey led several initiatives, including the newspaper *Negro World* and the Universal Printing House. Moreover, he created the Black Star Line, a steamship company that facilitated commercial exchanges between Black populations in the United States, the West Indies, and Africa. Unlike previous organizations that promoted emigration to Africa, UNIA's scope was transnational. Garvey called the sons of Africa to return to the motherland, where he hoped that through UNIA's initiative it would be possible to establish a Black territory in West Africa. His words also resonated among Africans who sought to liberate themselves from European rule.[82] Consequently, because his ideas basically challenged colonialism, Garvey himself was never able to set foot in Africa.[83] In the United States, he faced enormous opposition, was sent to prison over charges of fraud, and was eventually deported to Jamaica in 1927. Ultimately, despite being the largest Black mass movement of the early twentieth century, UNIA's project to resettle its members in an African territory was unsuccessful.

The Atlantic slave trade tragically intensified the connections among the shores of Europe, Africa, and the Americas. Through this horrendous trade, enslaved Africans were forcibly transported from Africa to the Americas. Still, since the inception of this hideous trade, and regardless of their status as enslaved, freed, or free, Africans and their descendants traveled back and forth between the Americas and Africa. In the second half of the eighteenth century, the Atlantic revolutions led to the long process of gradual emancipation. But white slaveholding elites could not envision a society in which Black and white populations lived together and thus planned the relocation of future freed populations outside the territories of British colonies in the Americas. But those plans were also never fully achieved.

Searching for the Promised Land

Many Black men and women embraced emigration to Africa as the most promising path to follow. As the American War of Independence ended and slavery remained alive in the newly created United States, enslaved, freed, and free Black persons who had fought alongside the British relocated in other parts of the British Empire and Sierra Leone. Later efforts in the independent United States led thousands of emigrants to resettle in Liberia as well. In Brazil, many dozens of freedpeople were deported to West Africa after Brazilian authorities dismantled the Malê Revolt of 1835. But thousands of other Black men, women, and children took the same difficult path back to Africa. Most of them settled in coastal towns of the Bight of Benin.

The journey back to Africa was a difficult one. Many of these exiles died not long after reaching African shores. Still, many Black men, women, and children chose to undertake this risky relocation journey rather than continue to experience the rampant racism that prevented freed African-born peoples and their descendants from owning land and having access to education and full citizenship. Although the exodus to Africa did not deliver the promised land to freedpeople, as we will see in the following epilogue, the great majority of Black men, women, and children who decided to stay in the Americas also encountered huge challenges as they continued to be confronted with segregation and economic exclusion.

EPILOGUE

Afterlives of Slavery

After all other societies in the Americas had abolished slavery, Brazil was the last country in the Western Hemisphere to make human bondage illegal, in 1888. Slavery continued to exist in Africa throughout the twentieth century, however. Mauritania, to cite one example, legally abolished slavery only in 1981. The end of the Atlantic slave trade and the abolition of slavery in several regions of Africa did not end exploitative forms of labor. Ultimately, the path opened by the Atlantic slave trade set the stage for the rise of European colonization of the African continent, blurring and blending the history of these two human atrocities.[1]

Despite the similarities and differences between the institution of slavery in various areas examined in this book, the inhuman bondage of Black Africans and their descendants shaped to varying degrees the economies, the societies, and the cultures of Western Europe, West Africa, West Central Africa, Southeastern Africa, and the Americas, which were all involved in these atrocities to some extent. After the legal end of the Atlantic slave trade, European colonization introduced in Africa new modalities of forced labor that are remembered today by local populations as similar to slavery.[2] What were the legacies of more than four centuries of Atlantic slave trade and slavery? Discussing the possible answers to this question allows us to explore the developments that followed emancipation in the Americas and to return our thoughts to the introduction of this book, in which I emphasized the enduring presence of slavery in present-day public debates in the continents that participated in the trade of enslaved Africans and Atlantic slavery.

The first Portuguese raids on the coasts of West Africa occurred in the fifteenth century, and by the middle of the sixteenth century, slavery in the Americas and the Iberian Peninsula had become a racialized institution. As West Africans and West Central Africans were captured and transported to the Iberian Peninsula, being Black and being a slave gradually became synonymous. In the Americas, slavery ignited a process of racialization that was more than just an idea. Africans transported to the Americas as captives were assigned the legal status of slave for life. Children of enslaved women inherited this legal status until the rise of gradual abolition that in several parts of the Americas emancipated newborns. But even after acquiring their freedom and following the legal abolition of slavery in the Americas, freedpeople and their descendants continued to be stigmatized. Ultimately, slavery and the Atlantic slave trade engendered the political idea of race.[3] In other words, race is not natural but rather a social construction according to which people subjectively classify other human beings through perceived physical features.

Labor structures changed during the period that followed the end of slavery in the Americas. In rural areas, planters put pressure on freedpeople to keep them working for low wages. In countries such as Brazil, formerly enslaved people sometimes could provide work only in exchange for food, clothing, and shelter. These not-so-new exploitative systems also restricted the ability of newly emancipated men and women to acquire land. Despite a few exceptions particular to each region in the years that followed emancipation, access to civil rights was limited even in Latin America, a region where land ownership was also hard to achieve.

Deep and Old Scars

The reverberations of the early violent encounters between Portuguese sailors and West Africans in the fifteenth century could still be felt four hundred years later, when the slave trade to the Americas ended. The inhuman commerce of Africans to the Iberian Peninsula and the Americas drew on long-lasting commercial routes that already existed on the African continent, not only transforming the coastal regions of West Africa, West Central Africa, and Southeastern Africa but also inflicting deep impacts in the interior of the continent, where men, women, and children were killed and families were separated over the course of several decades.

Although slavery and the trade in slaves had existed in various parts of the world for many centuries, with the rise of the Atlantic trade in enslaved Africans, for the first time the trade in human beings specifically targeted Black African men, women, and children. The Atlantic slave trade and chattel slavery in the Americas created the idea of race while giving birth to global merchant capitalism and fueling the rise to industrial capitalism during the nineteenth century.[4] The rise of this inhumane trade became the largest transoceanic forced migration in history and also accentuated divisions among African communities who spoke different languages and adhered to different religions.

In some areas, such as the Kingdom of Kongo in West Central Africa, the first encounters with Portuguese explorers and colonizers even led local kings to adopt Roman Catholicism as a religion of state. Over time, the presence of Portuguese and then Brazilian merchants in West Central Africa, in the Bight of Benin, and in Upper Guinea also propelled the emergence of communities who spoke Portuguese or idioms resulting from the mixture of Portuguese and local languages. These mixed communities of intermediaries were central to the rise and development of the Atlantic slave trade. African-born men and women, sometimes with the active assistance of European agents, penetrated far into the continent's interior, captured people, and transported these captives to the coastal areas to be sold and sent into slavery to the Americas.

Beyond the losses occasioned by the division and killing of members of local communities during raids and wars, many of these captives perished in these journeys to the coast and during the dreadful period during which they were kept in captivity in the coastal areas. Forced into ships sailing to the Americas, the tragic trajectories imposed on these men, women, and children was just starting. Along the paths of the Atlantic slave trade, African women were separated from their children and kinfolk. Stories of captive African women who were physically abused and raped by ship captains and crewmen in the hold of slave ships have been well documented. Distressed, traumatized, dehydrated, and malnourished, women who carried their babies or who gave birth during the Atlantic crossing often witnessed the death of their newborns. African men, women, and children who did not survive the Middle Passage had their bodies thrown into the sea, deprived not only of their lives but also of the traditional funeral rites that linked them to their communities of origin.

Family separation followed by forced displacement and long periods spent in warehouses in African coastal areas as well as the long and horrific Atlantic crossings all were part of the broader picture of the inhumane trade in Africans and its catastrophic impacts on local communities in Africa. Despite extreme individual and collective suffering, during the entire period of the Atlantic slave trade, most men, women, and children managed not only to survive the horrors of forced migration and enslavement but also to accomplish unimaginable things. Women gave birth to babies in the hold of slave vessels. African men and women led revolts on board slave ships as well. Resilience and resistance marked these forced Atlantic crossings.

The rise of sugar plantations in the Americas fueled the Atlantic slave trade. Planters purchased most enslaved Africans disembarked on American shores to cultivate cash crops on large, medium, and small estates. But soon other crops such as rice, tobacco, coffee, and cotton also became extremely profitable, leading the trade in enslaved Africans to the Americas to reach its peak in the eighteenth century.

Approximately half of the nearly 12.5 million African captives transported to the Americas between 1501 and 1866 were embarked in West Central African ports. In general, it is safe to state that the ratio of African men to women transported to the Americas was two to one. Approximately 4.8 million enslaved Africans came ashore in Brazil, a number representing nearly half of the 10.7 million African captives who survived the Middle Passage and were disembarked alive in the Americas.[5] Numbers convey very little about the experience of the victims of this inhumane trade, but here statistics call our attention to the crucial role of Portugal as well as colonial and independent Brazil in the trade of enslaved Africans.

The emphasis on Brazil is important because most general histories of the Atlantic slave trade, academic books, conferences, television documentaries, and even motion pictures tend to emphasize the trade in enslaved Africans in the North Atlantic, with a special focus on Britain and the United States. Challenging this view, this book has shown that we can only fully grasp the magnitude of this inhumane trade by recognizing and understanding the central role Brazil and West Central Africa played in this long, tragic history. Yet, centering the role of Brazil and Africa in the history of the Atlantic slave trade and slavery does not mean erasing the importance of other regions of the Americas, as well as the North Atlantic world, the Spanish-speaking Americas, and the British and French West Indies. On the contrary, it is the best way to show how slavery and the trade in enslaved Africans were interconnected during a period of more than three hundred years. As this book covered the history of the slave trade and slavery in these regions, despite the numerous contrasting elements, it has also been possible to identify many similarities. Working and living conditions on rice plantations in South Carolina, sugar estates in Saint-Domingue (today's Haiti), and coffee plantations in the Paraíba Valley in Brazil surely differed in many ways, and in a single region and even in one single estate they have varied over time. But in all these areas, enslaved people faced several similar hardships. They were overworked, poorly fed, and physically punished. In some contexts, they were able to form families, and it was common that they were sold apart from their loved ones. And still, alone or collectively, they resisted these atrocities in the most incredible ways.

Plantation slavery was central to the development of slavery, but slavery also existed to a lesser or greater extent in urban areas. In these spaces, enslaved women occupied important roles by preparing and selling food and performing domestic labor, which in many cases included cooking and taking care of the children of slave owners. Working in urban areas certainly offered bondspeople greater mobility. Circulating in the city allowed enslaved men and women to create networks to run away or organize revolts. In Brazil and the rest of Latin America, the city was also the space where bondspeople could join Catholic brotherhoods to obtain assistance of all kinds. More important, in urban environments, enslaved people could perform a variety of tasks that permitted them to amass funds to purchase their freedom. However, manumission by grace or through self-purchase was much more widespread in Brazil than in any other region of the Americas. Even though both types of manumission existed in British North America and later in the independent United States, few slave owners freed their enslaved property through any of these means in comparison with Brazil and other regions of Latin America, such as Cuba and Peru.

Still, opportunities for manumission must not be understood as deriving from the benevolent nature of slavery in Latin America. When slave owners freed enslaved people in Brazil, they were also making an economic decision that was profitable for them. Therefore, most manumissions were not acts of generosity or gratitude but were provided in exchange for payment and occurred in urban areas. Because the price of enslaved women was usually inferior to that of bondsmen, in urban areas such as Rio de Janeiro and Salvador or small towns in mining regions, bondswomen were also much more successful than bondsmen in purchasing their own freedom as well. But despite these various paths to freedom, most bondspeople who toiled in Brazil—and the same can be said for the United States—died in bondage during the many long decades before the final abolition of slavery in these countries.

Fighting Back

But there were obstacles. Most opportunities for self-purchase or joining mutual aid societies were not available in large and distant plantation settings, the environment where most of the enslaved population lived and worked in Cuba, Brazil, and the rest of Latin America. Whether in Havana, Salvador, or New York City, urban slavery also imposed challenges on enslaved people, and especially on bondswomen. Sexual violence was a constant threat to women working in the streets and providing domestic work, which is why whether in colonial North America, Saint-Domingue, or Brazil, runaway slave ads often searched for enslaved women who escaped bondage. Some of these women fled their owners in the riskiest conditions, even carrying their babies and young children with them. When escaping was not an option, some bondswomen killed their owners and even their own children to spare them the ordeal of slavery.

In colonial North America and the independent United States, despite being forced to adhere to Christianity, enslaved people kept alive religions, ritual practices, and deities from their homelands. Catholicism, Protestantism, Vodun, Orisha, and Islam became instruments to channel slave resistance in the Americas, evident in burial ceremonies, night gatherings, and annual holidays, during which enslaved Africans and their descendants maintained a large array of musical, dance, and martial arts practices. These cultural traditions brought from their African communities were preserved and transformed in the context of bondage in the Americas. These practices also remained dynamic because even after the end of the Atlantic slave trade, freedpeople and their descendants continued to cross the Atlantic Ocean. This movement was particularly visible between Brazil and the region of present-day Angola and the Bight of Benin. Even today, religions such as Candomblé and martial arts such as capoeira express this long history of cultural resistance against the violence of slavery and racism that continued following the abolition era.

As early as the sixteenth century, enslaved Africans and their descendants organized rebellions and created runaway slave communities in the West Indies. As the legal abolition of slavery gradually evolved in the late eighteenth century in North America, enslaved people also managed to find their own paths to freedom, either by escaping, forming Maroon communities, or organizing rebellions. Enslaved people escaped individually or in groups literally everywhere in the Americas. Communities of escaped bondspeople also existed in various regions of the Americas such as today's Mexico and Jamaica. But the largest and longest-lasting community of runaway enslaved people was the *quilombo* of Palmares in seventeenth-century northeast Brazil. Yet forming such communities was not always the preferred method of resisting against slavery. Bondspeople also organized plots, conspiracies, and rebellions. Each slave revolt was shaped by regional contexts, but most of them occurred in regions where plantation slavery predominated, even though enslaved people also carried out revolts in eighteenth-century New York City in the then British colony of New York and in nineteenth-century Salvador in independent Brazil. As we have seen, a spiritual dimension often oriented the leaders of several rebellions who were inspired by the principles of Christianity, Islam, and African-based religions. More important, these rebellions often occurred in regions where Black people—enslaved, freed, and free—predominated, and particularly in areas with large contingents of African-born enslaved and freed populations.

As legal abolition of slavery gradually evolved in the Americas during the nineteenth century, freedpeople migrated to West Africa, and in some cases to West Central Africa. Most of these men, women, and children traveled voluntarily, although others were forced to relocate on the African continent. Several returnees who left from Brazil were born in Africa, but many others who left from the United States were setting foot on the African continent for the first time, with hopes of building a new life of economic prosperity far from segregation and racial hatred. We know, however, that this African exodus also posed numerous challenges for those who survived the first years after relocation. The coastal areas and the hinterlands of the African continent remained deeply divided during the entire nineteenth century when these movements occurred. Several returnees to the Bight of Benin became slave merchants. Perceived as foreigners, African Americans established in Sierra Leone and Liberia often clashed with local peoples.

Workforce and Land

The legacies of slavery in the Americas were shaped not only by how slavery was once structured but also by how the end of slavery evolved and the paths taken by these societies following emancipation. As abolitionist debates had already made clear starting in the eighteenth century, the most important problem faced by former slave societies and societies where slavery existed was how to replace the enslaved workforce for the lowest possible cost. For example, the end of slavery in the British West Indies posed a central problem to planters who needed to find workers willing to perform underpaid labor under harsh conditions.

Sugar and coffee production not only declined but also encountered competition from the Brazilian and Cuban sugar industries that continued to rely on slaves until the last two decades of the nineteenth century. Meanwhile, the freed population pursued better wages and working conditions and rejected toiling for meager salaries. In Antigua, for example, freedpersons who managed to acquire land invested their time working on their own new plots.[6] In Jamaica, freedpeople refused to work for the large landowners, who in turn promoted old stereotypes of Black populations as lazy and unfit to work.[7] Unable to force newly emancipated men and women to work for their old owners, British officials made unsuccessful attempts to attract white laborers from England and Ireland. The eventual solution was to introduce indentured workers from China, India, and Africa into the British West Indies.

There were similar developments in the French West Indies. In Martinique, Guadeloupe, and French Guiana, which also remained

French colonies, former bondspeople left the plantations after 1848. But as no official measures to redistribute land to them were implemented, few peasants succeeded in acquiring their own plots.[8] Moreover, using the excuse of preventing vagrancy, the French colonial government set repressive measures to restrain the mobility of newly emancipated people. As in the British West Indies, planters attempted to coerce former bondspeople to stay working on the plantations.[9] Eventually, France also took the path of indentured servitude. Between 1854 and 1862, France introduced more than eighteen thousand African indentured laborers as well as eighty-two thousand workers from India, China, and the Madeira Islands in Martinique, Guadeloupe, and French Guiana.[10]

Foreseeing the end of slavery and the need to gradually replace the enslaved workforce, Spain also introduced Chinese indentured laborers in Cuba from 1840 to 1878.[11] After the end of slavery, the Cuban context presented some elements in common with the French and British colonies in the West Indies. The island remained under Spanish control until the end of the nineteenth century, and overall, few freedpeople became landowners. Because the sugarcane industry had expanded on the island and was oriented toward the North American market, land became increasingly concentrated in the hands of large landowners.

In the United States, attempts to address the problem of workforce shortage that resulted from the end of slavery and from the trail of death caused by four years of the Civil War included coercive measures, such as the passage of Black Codes in Southern states from 1865 to 1866. Drawing on older slave codes, these laws were designed to restrict Black people's mobility by using criminal charges of vagrancy. This legislation also contributed to the expansion of the existing system of convict leasing. Therefore, the imposition of penal labor on any Black or white individuals serving time in prison expanded in Southern states such as Georgia, Mississippi, Florida, and North Carolina to make up for the slave labor shortage. Vagrancy laws and convict leasing supported the incarceration of freedmen and freedwomen, who hence provided unpaid labor in farms, factories, railroads, and construction projects, especially in the South but also in the North.[12] African Americans fought these measures, just as they had resisted the atrocities of the period of slavery.

Land ownership was also a central topic of abolitionist debates in the United States and remained an issue in the years that followed emancipation. Already during the first two years of the Civil War, the Union had taken official action to confiscate property from the Confederates, including land. All these measures were doomed to failure. In 1865, by the end of the Civil War, General William T. Sherman issued an order that appropriated nearly 400,000 acres of land belonging to Confederate planters along the Atlantic coast from South Carolina to Florida to be redistributed among the freed population. In addition, before the final abolition of slavery in 1865, the fourth section of the "Act to establish a Bureau for the Relief of Freedmen and Refugees" created the Bureau of Refugees, Freedmen and Abandoned Lands, later known simply as the Freedmen's Bureau, and projected the distribution of abandoned lands to freedpeople.[13] As part of this process, the government allocated land that could be rented during a three-year period. Following the measure, nearly forty thousand freedpeople settled on this territory and started growing crops.

Sadly, not only was this policy not expanded, but in 1865 President Andrew Johnson, who succeeded President Lincoln after Lincoln's assassination, pardoned the Confederate landowners and revoked the Freedmen's Bureau's order redistributing land confiscated during the war to former slaves.[14] Despite resistance, former slaveholders succeeded in expelling thousands of families of freedpeople from the previously confiscated estates. Next, the Southern Homestead Act of 1866 made available approximately forty-seven million acres of public land in Alabama, Arkansas, Florida, Louisiana, and Mississippi to be sold in lots of eighty acres to freedpeople and loyal white people. Here again, white people acquired most of the land. In the following years, many newly emancipated men and women lost the lands they had originally been able to purchase.[15]

Racial Disharmony

A decade of unprecedented civil rights to the freed population of the United States opened with the passage of the Reconstruction Act of March 2, 1867, which gave African American men the right to vote and to run for office.[16] Three years later constitutional amendments reinforced these victories. The Fourteenth Amendment to the United States Constitution, ratified on July 9, 1868, established birthright citizenship and equal legal protection, whereas the Fifteenth Amendment, ratified in 1870, ended disenfranchisement based on "race, color, or previous condition of servitude."[17] The Reconstruction era also made possible the creation of historically Black institutions such as Howard University in Washington, DC, which gave African Americans access to higher education.

During this progressive period, freedpeople used their newly acquired civil rights to change local and state governance. But Southern white people and Northern conservatives aggressively fought against their new rights. Therefore, administrations used explicit violence, fraud, poll taxes, and literacy tests to prevent African Americans from registering and voting. In 1883, the US Supreme Court invalidated the Civil Rights Act of 1875, which prohibited racial discrimination by private parties. In 1896, the Supreme Court's *Plessy v. Ferguson* decision affirmed the constitutionality of racial segregation in public spaces, schools, transportation, and the military. In the South, African Americans also faced continuous racial animosity through lynching and other brutal forms of violence. White supremacy and racism prevailed in various spheres in the North as well. To escape this hostile environment, as discussed in chapter 17, some African Americans decided to relocate to West Africa. Other groups took a different path. For example, during this period, thousands of former bondspeople organized themselves to demand pensions from the federal government as reparations for slavery. This movement, as I discussed elsewhere, became the largest organized movement requesting demands of reparations for slavery in the Americas.[18]

In contrast with the United States, legal segregation was neither codified nor implemented in Latin American countries and Brazil, where racism was not (and is not) based on the idea of the "one-drop rule" (i.e., a person with even one Black ancestor, or "one drop" of "Black blood," is considered Black) but instead on a combination of colorism and classism. Ultimately, despite the lack of legal segregation, in practice racial hierarchies and racism continued to operate in Latin America, and especially in Brazil, where the population of African descent was and still is bigger than anywhere else in the Western Hemisphere. As a military coup established a new Republican government in Brazil in November 1889, the state refused to integrate the newly freed population. As elsewhere in the Americas, the idea that Black people would disturb the social order prevailed.[19]

Regardless of regional differences, in Brazil probably more than anywhere else in the Americas, few freedpeople had access to land ownership. Moreover, the Republican military government continued to deny full citizenship to the freed population. A few years before emancipation, Brazil passed legislation preventing illiterate people from voting in a country where 80 percent of the population, including its large Black population, could not read and write.[20] Moreover, the new Constitution of 1891 established that only male individuals older than twenty-one years of age with certain income levels had the right to vote. Both the previous legislation and the new constitution disenfranchised Black Brazilians, most of whom were illiterate and remained living in poor conditions, especially the recently emancipated men and women.

Brazil also faced the question of how to replace its enslaved workforce. As soon as the pressures to ban the Atlantic slave trade started in the early decades of the nineteenth century, and during its final five decades of slavery, the Brazilian monarchy subsidized the arrival of new European immigrants, especially to work on the coffee plantations in the Paraíba Valley. As the abolition of slavery approached and eugenics emerged in Europe, local elites began to embrace views promoting the pseudoscientific idea that it was possible to "whiten" and therefore improve the population's profile by eliminating brown and Black populations considered unsuitable and inferior to white people. Proponents of whitening policies believed that new white European immigrants would mix with the local Black population, gradually leading to its disappearance.[21]

At the turn of the twentieth century, nearly one million European immigrants entered Brazil. European immigration certainly increased Brazil's white and mixed-race population, but whitening was not the only motivation to encourage subsidized European immigration. There was an actual immediate need for skilled workers in São Paulo, a region that was not so attractive by that time. Unlike the British, French, and Spanish colonies in the West Indies, Brazil passed a decree in 1890 banning altogether the immigration of people from Africa and Asia to avoid increasing its population of color.[22] In 1892, a new law permitted Brazil to receive immigrants from China and Japan.[23] Yet, the new law's approval was not extended to immigrants from the African continent.[24] But despite these efforts, the whitening project was much less effective in Brazil than it was in a country such as Argentina, where the Black population was smaller and where a larger number of European immigrants was much more significant.

In the United States, Brazil, and other Latin American societies where slavery existed, race became the dominant tool to regulate whether individuals or groups were identified as enslavers or enslaved. Persons identified as white, regardless of whether their ancestors owned enslaved people or not, inherited the social and economic advantages historically assigned to white individuals. In contrast, persons racialized as Black have carried the stigma associated with the slave past of their ancestors, even though a minority of persons identified as Black became slave traders and slave owners, especially in Latin America and the Caribbean, such as the freedpeople who relocated from Brazil in West Africa during the nineteenth century. In Brazil, although race and racism present similarities with the rest of Latin America, because slavery was so pervasive, the combination of bodily features and social position has been more important than African ancestry alone to determine whether a person is racialized as Black, white, or in between. In the United States, however, individuals with African ancestors are still today identified as Black or African American, regardless of their social class and no matter how light their skin may be.

If whitening failed as a pseudoscientific measure in Brazil, it succeeded instead as an ideology that erased the differences between poor white, Black, and free mixed-race individuals. This new "silence" around race led all these groups, to certain extent, to lose their color, as historian Hebe Mattos put it, because the terms associated with *Black* automatically evoked the legal status of slave among individuals who were now freedpeople.[25] Moreover, whitening policies contributed to support for the ideology that promoted the idea of Brazil as a society free of racism and where harmonious race relations prevailed, while masking the importance of the Brazilian Black population. This belief drew on the contribution of several nineteenth-century European travel accounts, such as the three-volume travelogue of Jean-Baptiste Debret, whose illustrations were discussed in several chapters of this book. These accounts emphasized the overall configuration of Brazil's paternalist slave society, which included a huge enslaved population that participated in all economic and social activities and was omnipresent in the domestic environment. Enslaved people mingling with their owners in multiple settings and the absence of legal racial segregation, in contrast with the United States, helped nurture the idea that the country was a racially mixed nation in which racism did not exist. This view was supported by the work of Brazilian scholars who claimed that slavery had been milder in Brazil than in the United States; that, drawing on the tolerance of Luso-Brazilian Catholicism, Brazilian society had been hybrid since the beginning and therefore harmonious racial relations prevailed.[26] As many scholars have demonstrated, nothing in this misleading view could be further from the truth.[27]

Multiple Legacies

The legacies of slavery and the Atlantic slave trade remain visible and active today in various parts of the continents involved in the Atlantic slave trade and where slavery existed. On a large scale, the profits generated by slavery built the fortune of all Western European nations and the United States of America by financing the creation of banks and industrialization. Slavery and the inhumane trade also contributed to the wealth of families of planters and large slave owners all over the Americas. It also sustained the Roman Catholic Church and universities. On a smaller and more indirect scale, the racialization associated with slavery continues. Today people identified as white, despite having no direct link with slave ownership, are socially and economically privileged by the simple fact that they are racialized as white.

By telling the history of the Atlantic slave trade and slavery in the Americas, this book aimed to underscore that this tragic history of violence, resistance, and resilience cannot be told accurately without emphasizing the importance of Brazil, West Africa, and West Central Africa, and the central role of enslaved women in this multi-century-long process. The largest contingent of enslaved Africans was transported to the Americas from the ports located in present-day Angola, which is why West Central Africa played a crucial role in the economic and cultural formation of the Americas. Port cities such as Luanda and Benguela became Portuguese colonies along with the rise of the Atlantic slave trade. As a whole, today's Angola was among the very few last African countries to become independent from European rule, in 1975.

The number of enslaved Africans transported to Brazil was the largest in the Americas. Moreover, the contingent of captive Africans who came ashore in Brazil is nearly ten times the number of enslaved Africans introduced in the United States. More than 50 percent of the current Brazilian population is of African descent. Outside the African continent, Brazil is the country with the largest Black population.

Most of its Black citizens remain socially and economically marginalized, however, and are also victims of brutal police violence.

Although African women were sent into slavery to the Americas in smaller numbers than men, their work and reproductive capacities were pivotal pillars for the upholding of slavery in the Americas. The role of enslaved women became even more central especially in the United States during the first six decades of the nineteenth century, a period known as the *second slavery*. Because the acquisition and transportation of enslaved persons from Africa to the Americas had been gradually banned starting in 1807, slave owners started relying on the illegal transportation of captive Africans to Cuba and Brazil, and mainly on the wombs of bondswomen who gave birth to enslaved children in the United States.

During the second slavery, although relying on an enslaved workforce, cotton, sugar, and coffee production increasingly drew on mechanization and technological innovation. Therefore, in this phase, the slavery mode of production proved itself compatible with the development of industrial capitalism. Ultimately, the Atlantic slave trade and slavery in the Americas were designed and shaped to generate profits that benefited slave traders and their multiple intermediaries, as well as slave owners, through the ownership and exploitation of Black Africans and their descendants. The work provided by enslaved people also contributed to build the wealth and propel the industrialization of countries and regions, such as Britain and the North of the United States, even when slavery was no longer a central institution or had already been abolished in these regions.[28] The chapters of this book have also shown that the enslavement of Indigenous peoples and then of Africans and their descendants in the Americas accelerated the creation of racial categories that ostracized these groups, giving rise to anti-Black racism.

Although recognizing that Atlantic slavery was a mode of production based on the ownership of human beings, this book is a new effort to write the history of bondage and the trade of enslaved Africans to the Americas through the lens of memory. This perspective of the study of the past centers the lived experiences of the men, women, and children who were victims of these atrocities. By privileging Africa, Brazil, Black women, and resistance in my analysis, this book also seeks to add to our understanding of the formation of contemporary societies in the Americas, and by doing so, it also recognizes how this very long period of human atrocities in our history continues to haunt our present.

Acknowledgments

Many people contributed directly or indirectly to the completion of this book. I am indebted to my graduate and undergraduate students at Howard University who since 2008 have been my best interlocutors in discussing the history of slavery and the Atlantic slave trade by always challenging me to see the central role of Black men and women in the construction of the various societies of Americas and Europe. I also benefited from the contribution of the participants of the monthly seminar "Slavery, Memory, and African Diasporas," which I have convened at Howard University since 2012. This seminar has created a fruitful dialogue among scholars in the Washington, DC, area, and after the rise of the COVID-19 global pandemic, it expanded its outreach to scholars in other parts of the United States as well as in the United Kingdom, France, Portugal, and Brazil.

I am grateful to then chair of the Department of History, Nikki M. Taylor, who has always supported this project, by officially and unofficially recognizing that I needed extra time to complete it. I wrote most chapters of this book between March 2020 and January 2022, when the pandemic led us to endless months of confinement and online teaching. During this period, along with cohosts Jessica Marie Johnson, Vanessa Holden, and Alex Gil, I created the #Slaveryarchive Book Club to foster debates about newly published books on the history of slavery and the Atlantic world. The readings and the conversations we had during 2020–21 have shaped several chapters of this book, and authors who presented their work in the book club will certainly recognize how their works helped me to rethink this book.

While finishing the last chapters of this manuscript, I was a member of the School of Historical Studies at the Institute for Advanced Study (IAS) in Princeton, New Jersey, funded by the Gladys Krieble Delmas Foundation. While working on another project, my time at IAS gave me the space and time I needed in those very difficult final days to finish the manuscript. At IAS, Karen Downing helped me gain access to books and dissertations that were difficult to obtain otherwise. I am especially grateful to Marcia Tucker, who assisted me in getting books as well as locating and digitizing some of the images examined here. A special thanks go to Tsering Wangyal Shawa, geographic information systems (GIS) and map librarian and head of the Map and Geospatial Information Center at Peter B. Lewis Library at Princeton University, who kindly produced the two maps presented at the beginning of this book. A Franklin Research Grant from the American Philosophical Society that funded research in the French archives for another project gave me the opportunity to fill some gaps to complete this book manuscript.

In 2023, I revised the final manuscript while on sabbatical leave and in a residential fellowship at the Getty Research Institute in Los Angeles, California. I am grateful for the time, resources, structure, and intellectual exchanges at the Getty that allowed me to finish this project in the most beautiful and stimulating setting a scholar can dream of. Several photographs in this book are housed at the Jean Paul Getty Museum and the Getty Research Institute Special Collections. I am grateful for the permission to use them to illustrate the book. I thank Alexa Sekyra, Nancy Ulm, Sabine Schlosser, and Virginia Mokslaveskas for their support during my stay at the Getty. I am particularly grateful to the College of Arts and Sciences at Howard University, especially to Dean Rubin Patterson and Associate Deans Thomas A. Foster and Kim D. Lewis, who made possible a research leave in Spring 2022 and then a sabbatical leave in Spring 2023.

This book could not have been written without the support from librarians, archivists, and museum curators in Brazil, France, Portugal, the United Kingdom, the Netherlands, Canada, the United States, and the Republic of Benin, where most of the archival research and fieldwork for this book was conducted either in person or remotely over the past twenty years. Most of this work was solely supported by Howard University through funds from the Provost Office, the Graduate School, the College of Arts and Sciences, and the Department of History. At Howard University, the role of librarians and archivists was crucial, especially during the pandemic, when access to libraries was limited. My special thanks go to Alliah Humber, Angelique Carson, and Lopez Matthews, who responded to all my demands to obtain articles and books to complete this project. Many other colleagues and friends helped during this journey, providing me with additional sources, suggesting me specific readings, and offering words of support. Among them are Edward Baptist, Alex Borucki, Mariana P. Candido, Lisa Earl Castillo, Mariana Dantas, Daniel Domingues da Silva, Natanya Duncan, Rebecca Goetz, Robin Law, Paul E. Lovejoy, Christina Mobley, J. Cameron Monroe, Anna More, Brooke Newman, Mariana Dias Paes, Nicholas Radburn, Carlos da Silva Jr., Mariza de Carvalho Soares, Nikki M. Taylor, and Jennie Williams. Becky Goetz, Lisa Earl Castillo, and Brooke Newman also supported me when I needed it the most. Suzanne Preston Blier provided me with words of wisdom during several difficult moments. Asking colleagues to read your work became more difficult than usual during the pandemic. João José Reis kindly read chapter 15, "Rebellions across Borders," and if there are any mistakes left behind, they are only mine. Historian Toby Green was a patient interlocutor in the past four years when I was writing and revising the manuscript. He always provided me with generous advice and kind words of support; I am deeply grateful to him, and I hope he knows how much his own scholarly work inspired this book.

Priya Nelson, then senior editor at the University of Chicago Press and now senior editor at Princeton University Press, commissioned this book. I am indebted to her for believing in my work and for helping me shaping the initial book proposal. Without her initiative and support, this book would not exist. I am also thankful to the two anonymous reviewers who generously read the book proposal when we were going into lockdown in March 2020 and offered me constructive criticism in their positive reviews. Their comments pushed me to write a book that I hope is much better than the proposal promised. I also thank the two anonymous reviewers who read the final book manuscript. I made all possible efforts to incorporate and to respond to their criticism and to address all their suggestions and corrections. I thank Alan Thomas, editorial director at University of Chicago Press, for his continuous support during these very long four years. I am lucky for having worked with a wonderful editor on this book. Dylan J. Montanari believed in this project and diligently worked with me to overcome the many obstacles that emerged along the way. He patiently read the entire manuscript and provided me with comments and sharp criticism, therefore helping to make my manuscript a better book. I offer him my deepest gratitude. I also thank Fabiola Enríquez Flores, who assisted me during the process of submitting the final manuscript and securing the numerous images that are part of this book, and Kristen Raddatz, who took care of all dimensions of this book's publicity. I am also grateful to Lori Meek Schuldt for meticulously copyediting this manuscript.

Our beloved cat Aby (2004–22) remained on duty until I finished the first version of this manuscript. For two years he woke me every single day to force me to start working during the early hours. I tried to keep his cat schedule while I was adding the last words to the first draft of this manuscript during my term at the Institute for Advanced Study. My parents have also supported me during my stays in southern Brazil, and they forgave my absences to conduct research in the archives.

But first and foremost, this book would not exist without my husband Alain Bélanger. Not only did he accept seeing me spend the greater part of the day in my office working on this book, but he also supported me with his unconditional love, patience, and care during the entire process, including summers and holidays that I spent in front of my computer. Once again, we did it.

This book is dedicated to Alain, to my students at Howard University, and to the enslaved men, women, and children who crossed the Atlantic Ocean to build the Americas where we are allowed to live. I am grateful to be one among the many historians who attempt to honor their history through our words.

Notes

Except where otherwise indicated, all translations to English are mine.

Introduction

1. For example, Marcelo D'Salete comic books, originally published in Portuguese in Brazil, then translated and published in several languages, including English. See Marcelo D'Salete, *Run For It: Stories of Slaves Who Fought for Their Freedom* (Seattle: Fantagraphics, 2017), and Marcelo D'Salete, *Angola Janga: Kingdom of Runaway Slaves* (Seattle: Fantagraphics, 2017).
2. The book was years in the making and was initially self-published. See Gayl Jones, *Palmares* (New York: Beacon Press, 2021).
3. See Vincent Carretta, *Equiano, the African: Biography of a Self-Made Man* (New York: Penguin, 2005); James H. Sweet, *Domingos Álvares: African Healing and the Intellectual History of the Atlantic World* (Chapel Hill: University of North Carolina Press, 2013); João José Reis, *Divining Slavery and Freedom: The Story of Domingos Sodré, an African Priest in Nineteenth-Century Brazil* (New York: Cambridge University Press, 2015); David Blight, *Frederick Douglass: Prophet of Freedom* (New York: Simon and Schuster, 2018); and João José Reis, Flávio dos Santos Gomes, and Marcus J. M. de Carvalho, *The Story of Rufino: Slavery, Freedom, and Islam in the Black Atlantic* (New York: Oxford University Press, 2020).
4. On the statuses of these first Africans and the birth of slavery in the English colonies of the Americas, and in Virginia, see Michael Guasco, *Slaves and Englishmen: Human Bondage in the Early Modern Atlantic World* (Philadelphia: University of Pennsylvania Press, 2014), 1–79.
5. Nikole Hannah-Jones and Jake Silverstein, eds., "The 1619 Project," *New York Times Magazine*, August 14, 2019, 1–93. A revised version of the project was also released as a book; see Nikole Hannah-Jones, *The 1619 Project: A New*

Origin Story (New York: One World, 2021). In 2023, a 1619 docuseries based on the project was launched on Hulu streaming service as well.

6. On its academic critics, see Sean Wilentz, "A Matter of Facts," *Atlantic*, January 22, 2020. In 2020, Donald Trump's administration created the 1776 Commission along with a report in part as a response to the project; see President's Advisory 1776 Commission, *1776 Report*, January 2021, https://trumpwhitehouse.archives.gov/wp-content/uploads/2021/01/The-Presidents-Advisory-1776-Commission-Final-Report.pdf. A few days later, on January 20, 2021, the commission was terminated by President Joe Biden. See also Annette Gordon-Reed et al., "The 1619 Project Forum," *American Historical Review* 127, no. 4 (2022): 1792–873.

7. See, for example, Ana Lucia Araujo, *Slavery in the Age of Memory: Engaging the Past* (London: Academic Bloomsbury, 2021).

8. See Ana Lucia Araujo, *Reparations for Slavery and the Slave Trade: A Transnational and Comparative History* (London: Bloomsbury Academic, 2023).

9. See Ana Lucia Araujo, *Public Memory of Slavery: Victims and Perpetrators in the South Atlantic* (Amherst, NY: Cambria Press, 2010), and Ana Lucia Araujo, *Shadows of the Slave Past: Memory, Heritage, and Slavery* (New York: Routledge, 2014).

10. See Marcus Rediker, *The Slave Ship: A Human History* (New York: Penguin, 2007), and Jennifer Morgan, *Reckoning with Slavery: Gender, Kinship, and Capitalism in the Early Atlantic* (Durham, NC: Duke University Press, 2021).

11. See Michael A. Gomez, *Reversing Sail: A History of the African Diaspora* (New York: Cambridge University Press, 2020); Herman L. Bennett, *African Kings and Black Slaves: Sovereignty and Dispossession in the Early Modern Atlantic* (Philadelphia: University of Pennsylvania Press, 2019); and Toby Green, *A Fistful of Shells: West Africa from the Rise of the Slave Trade to the Age of Revolution* (Chicago: University of Chicago Press, 2019). More recently, in a very accessible book, another historian makes a similar call; see Christopher Ehret, *Ancient Africa: A Global History, to 300 BCE* (Princeton, NJ: Princeton University Press, 2023).

12. These estimates cover the voyages from Africa to the Americas, and they are based on the number of the enslaved Africans who effectively disembarked in the Americas. See "Trans-Atlantic Slave Trade—Estimates," in *Trans-Atlantic Slave Trade Database*, https://slavevoyages.org/assessment/estimates. These numbers are constantly readjusted and do not include imports from other parts of the Americas. For estimates of enslaved people transported within the Western Hemisphere, which now includes more than 28,000 voyages, see *Intra-American Slave Trade Database*, https://www.slavevoyages.org/american/database.

13. As this book went into production, historian Sean M. Kelley published a new synthesis of the history of the US slave trade. Despite the focus on US slave traders, including those who led voyages to regions other than the

United States in the Americas, Kelley pays some attention to the African continent. See Sean M. Kelley, *American Slavers: Merchants, Mariners, and the Transatlantic Commerce in Captives, 1644–1865* (New Haven, CT: Yale University Press, 2023).

14. Among these books centering on economic dimensions are David Eltis, *The Rise of African Slavery in the Americas* (New York: Cambridge University Press, 1999), and Herbert S. Klein and Ben Vinson III, *African Slavery in Latin America and the Caribbean* (New York: Cambridge University Press, 2007).

15. See, for example, Eugene D. Genovese, *The Political Economy of Slavery: Studies in the Economy and Society of the Slave South* (New York: Vintage Books, 1965); Robert William Fogel and Stanley L. Engerman, *Time on the Cross: The Economics of American Negro Slavery* (New York: Norton, 1974); and Eugene D. Genovese, *Roll, Jordan, Roll: The World the Slaves Made* (New York: Vintage Books, 1976). Later books confirmed the trend centering on the United States. See Ira Berlin, *Generations of Captivity: A History of African-American Slaves* (Cambridge, MA: Belknap Press of Harvard University Press, 2003), and Ira Berlin, *Many Thousands Gone: The First Two Centuries of Slavery in North America* (Cambridge, MA: Belknap Press of Harvard University Press, 2000). More recent ones include Calvin Schermerhorn, *Unrequited Toil: A History of United States Slavery* (New York: Cambridge University Press, 2018). General books about slavery in Brazil are also rare even in Portuguese; see Mauricio Goulart, *A escravidão africana no Brasil: das origens à extinção do tráfico* (São Paulo: Editora Alfa-Omega, 1949), and Jacob Gorender, *O Escravismo colonial* (São Paulo: Editora Ática, 1978). Historian Kátia de Queirós Mattoso published a synthesis in French; see Kátia de Queirós Mattoso, *Être Esclave au Brésil, XVIe–XIXe siècle* (Paris: Harmattan, 1994), first published in 1979 by Hachette. The book was later translated into Portuguese as *Ser Escravo No Brasil* (São Paulo: Brasiliense, 1982) and into English as *To Be a Slave in Brazil, 1550–1888*, translated by Arthur Goldhammer (New Brunswick, NJ: Rutgers University Press, 1986). Yet, these books circulated mainly among academic audiences. The only recent survey of Brazilian slavery is a trade book based on secondary literature written by a journalist. See Laurentino Gomes, *Escravidão*, vol. 1, *Do primeiro leilão de cativos em Portugal até a morte de Zumbi dos Palmares* (Rio de Janeiro: Globo Livros, 2019); Laurentino Gomes, *Escravidão*, vol. 2, *Da corrida do ouro em Minas Gerais até a chegada da corte de dom João ao Brasil* (Rio de Janeiro: Globo Livros, 2021); and Laurentino Gomes, *Escravidão*, vol. 3, *Da Independência do Brasil à Lei Áurea* (Rio de Janeiro: Globo Livros, 2022). Despite a few earlier academic monographs comparing Brazil, Cuba, and the United States, such as Laird W. Bergad, *The Comparative Histories of Slavery in Brazil, Cuba, and the United States* (New York: Cambridge University Press, 2007), books providing an overview of Brazilian slavery in English are rare; the only existing one is an economic history, heavily based on demographic data; see Herbert S. Klein and Francisco Vidal Luna, *Slavery in Brazil* (New York: Cambridge University Press, 2010).

16. Among the exceptions is Sterling Stuckey, *Slave Culture in America: The Foundations of Black America and Nationalist Theory* (New York: Oxford University Press, 1987).

17. See, for example, Melville J. Herskovits, *The Myth of the Negro Past* (New York: Harper, 1941), and Sidney W. Mintz and Richard Price, *The Birth of African-American Culture: An Anthropological Perspective* (Boston: Beacon Press, 1992), originally published as Sidney Wilfred Mintz and Richard Price, *An Anthropological Approach to the Afro-American Past* (Philadelphia: Institute for the Study of Human Issues, 1976).

18. Here I refer to the works of historians such as Eric Foner and David W. Blight. See Eric Foner, *Slavery and Freedom in Nineteenth-Century America* (New York: Oxford University Press, 1994), and David W. Blight, *Race and Reunion: The Civil War in American Memory* (Cambridge, MA: Harvard University Press, 2001).

19. The first book fully dedicated to the history of enslaved women in the United States is Deborah G. White, *Ar'n't I a Woman? Female Slaves in the Plantation South* (New York: W. W. Norton, 1985). Especially since 2010, African American women historians have published many monographs focusing on enslaved women both in the United States and in Brazil, even though there are very few overviews. Most existing syntheses also encompass the postemancipation period, including the twentieth century, and sometimes explore individual biographies. See, for example, Darlene Clark Hine and Kathleen Thompson, *A Shining Thread of Hope: The History of Black Women in America* (New York: Broadway Books, 1998), and Daina Ramey Berry and Kali N Gross, *A Black Women's History of the United States: Revisioning American History* (Boston: Beacon Press, 2019). Never translated into English, the first book examining the history of enslaved women in Brazil is a very short study focusing on the second half of the nineteenth century and published by anthropologist Sonia Maria Giacomini; see Sonia Maria Giacomini, *Mulher e escrava: Uma introdução histórica ao estudo da mulher negra no Brasil* (São Paulo: Vozes, 1988).

20. Claude Meillassoux, introduction, to *L'esclavage en Afrique précoloniale: Dix-sept études présentées par Claude Meillassoux* (Paris: François Mapero, 1975), 21.

21. See Moses I. Finley, *Ancient Slavery and Modern Ideology* (New York: Viking, 1980), 77.

22. Orlando Patterson, *Slavery and Social Death: A Comparative Study; With a New Preface* (Cambridge, MA: Harvard University Press, 2018), 13. Patterson's study was originally published in 1982.

23. Paul E. Lovejoy, *Transformations in Slavery: A History of Slavery in Africa* (New York: Cambridge University Press, 2012), 2–3. Lovejoy's volume was first published in 1983.

24. Claude Meillassoux, *Anthropologie de l'esclavage: Le Ventre de fer et d'argent* (Paris: Presses universitaires de France, 1986), 68. For the English translation, see Claude Meillassoux, *The Anthropology of Slavery: The Womb of Iron and Gold* (Chicago: University of Chicago Press, 1991), 67.

25. See Finley, *Ancient Slavery*, 9, 67–92.

26. See Noel Lenski, "Framing the Question: What Is a Slave Society?" in *What Is a Slave Society? The Practice of Slavery in Global Perspective*, ed. Noel Lenski and Catherine M. Cameron (New York: Cambridge University Press, 2018), 15–57.

27. There are few books focusing either on each of these slave trades or comparing them, and most existing studies are articles. For a brief and accessible overview, see Gomez, *Reversing Sail*, 36. See also Patrick Manning, *Slavery and African Life: Occidental, Oriental, and African Slave Trades* (Cambridge: Cambridge University Press, 1990). Among the earliest book-length studies about the African presence in Asia, see Joseph E. Harris, *The African Presence in Asia: Consequences of the East African Slave Trade* (Evanston, IL: Northwestern University Press, 1971). Other overviews include Olivier Pétré-Grenouilleau, *Les traites négrières: Essai d'histoire globale* (Paris: Gallimard, 2004), and Paulin Ismard, Benedetta Rossi, and Cécile Vidal, eds., *Les mondes de l'esclavage: Une histoire comparée* (Paris: Seuil, 2021).

28. See Christina Snyder, "Native American Slavery in Global Context," in Lenski and Cameron, *What Is a Slave Society?* 169–90.

29. On this call to include Indigenous slavery in the analysis of African slavery in the Americas, see Rebecca Anne Goetz, "'Unthinking Decision': Old Questions and New Problems in the History of Slavery and Race in the Colonial South," *Journal of Southern History* 75, no. 3 (2009): 599–612; and Nancy E. van Deusen, "In the Tethered Shadow: Native American Slavery, African Slavery, and the Disappearance of the Past," *William and Mary Quarterly* 80, no. 2 (2023): 355–88. On the persistent enslavement of Indigenous peoples in the United States, see Andrés Reséndez, *The Other Slavery* (Boston: Houghton Mifflin Harcourt, 2016), and in São Paulo, Brazil, see John Manuel Monteiro, *Blacks of the Land: Indian Slavery, Settler Society, and the Portuguese Colonial Enterprise in South America*, ed. and trans. James P. Woodard and Barbara Weinstein, Cambridge Latin American Studies 112 (New York: Cambridge University Press, 2018), which was originally published in Portuguese as John Manuel Monteiro, *Negros da terra: Índios e bandeirantes nas origens de São Paulo* (São Paulo: Companhia das letras, 1994).

30. Among these books centering on economic dimensions are Eltis, *Rise of African Slavery in the Americas*, and H. Klein and Vinson, *African Slavery in Latin America and the Caribbean*. Finally, for a new history of the United States focusing on Indigenous populations, see Ned Blackhawk, *The Rediscovery of America: Native Peoples and the Unmaking of U.S. History* (New Haven, CT: Yale University Press, 2023).

31. My work stands on the shoulders of several historians who examined the South Atlantic system, especially Pierre Verger, *Flux et reflux de la traite des nègres entre le Golfe de Bénin et Bahia de Todos os Santos, du XVIIe au XIXe siècle* (Paris: Mouton, 1968); Joseph C. Miller, *Way of Death: Merchant Capitalism and the Angolan Slave Trade, 1740–1830* (Madison: University of Wisconsin Press, 1988); Roquinaldo Ferreira, *Cross-Cultural Exchange in the Atlantic World: Angola and Brazil during the Era of the Slave Trade* (New York: Cambridge University Press, 2012); Mariana P. Candido, *An African Slaving Port and the Atlantic World: Benguela and Its Hinterland* (New York: Cambridge University Press, 2013); and Luiz Felipe de Alencastro, *Trade in the Living: The Formation of Brazil in the South Atlantic, Sixteenth to Seventeenth Centuries* (Albany: State University of New York Press, 2019), originally published as *O trato dos viventes: Formação do Brasil no Atlântico Sul* (São Paulo: Companhia das Letras, 2000).

32. Dale Tomich and Michael Zeuske, "Introduction, the Second Slavery: Mass Slavery, World-Economy, and Comparative Microhistories," *Review (Fernand Braudel Center)* 31, no. 2 (2008): 91–100.

33. See, for example, Hugh Thomas, *The Slave Trade: The History of the Atlantic Slave Trade 1440–1880* (New York: Simon and Schuster, 1997), and the trilogy Robin Blackburn, *The Making of New World Slavery: From the Baroque to the Modern 1492–1800* (London: Verso, 1997), Robin Blackburn, *The Overthrow of Colonial Slavery: 1776–1848* (London: Verso, 2011), and Robin Blackburn, *The American Crucible: Slavery, Emancipation and Human Rights* (London: Verso, 2011). See also David Brion Davis, *Inhuman Bondage: The Rise and Fall of Slavery in the New World* (New York: Oxford University Press, 2006). Davis also authored a trilogy that attempted to address the problem of slavery in transnational terms, even though he never conducted primary research in any language other than English; see David Brion Davis, *The Problem of Slavery in Western Culture* (Ithaca, NY: Cornell University Press, 1966); David Brion Davis, *The Problem of Slavery in the Age of Revolution, 1770–1823* (Ithaca, NY: Cornell University Press, 1975); and David Brion Davis, *The Problem of Slavery in the Age of Emancipation* (New York: Vintage Books, 2015).

34. For the first proponents of this model, see Joseph E. Harris, introduction to *Global Dimensions of the African Diaspora*, ed. Joseph E. Harris (Washington, DC: Howard University Press, 1982), 3–8. See also Colin A. Palmer, "Defining and Studying the Modern African Diaspora," *Journal of Negro History* 85 (2000): 27–32; Kim D. Butler, "Defining Diaspora, Refining a Discourse," *Diaspora: A Journal of Transnational Studies* 10, no. 2 (2001): 189–219; Kristin Mann, "Shifting Paradigms in the Study of the African Diaspora and of Atlantic History and Culture," *Slavery and Abolition* 22, no. 1 (2001): 3–21; and Paul Tiyambe Zeleza, "Diaspora Dialogues: Engagements between Africa and its Diasporas," *African Studies Review* 53, no. 1 (2010): 1–19.

Chapter 1

1. Johannes Leo Africanus [al-Hasan Ibn Muhammad Al-Wazzan], *The Cosmography and Geography of Africa* (Dublin: Penguin Random House, 2023), 375. The author was captured by pirates in 1518 and brought to the Vatican, where he was baptized as Johannes Leo Africanus. He completed the book in Italian in 1526 and published it in 1550.
2. Several recent studies explain how Africa was connected to global exchanges centuries before the rise of the Atlantic slave trade. See François-Xavier Fauvelle, *Le rhinocéros d'or: Histoires du Moyen Âge africain* (Paris: Alma Éditeur, Paris, 2013), translated into English as *The Golden Rhinoceros: Histories of the African Middle Ages* (Princeton, NJ: Princeton University Press, 2018); Michael A. Gomez, *African Dominion: A New History of Empire in Early and Medieval West Africa* (Princeton, NJ: Princeton University Press, 2018); Green, *Fistful of Shells*; and Ehret, *Ancient Africa*.
3. Mary Kingsley, *West African Studies* (New York: Cambridge University Press, 2011), 226.
4. Gomez, *Reversing Sail*, 18.
5. John K. Thornton, *A Cultural History of the Atlantic World, 1250–1820* (New York: Cambridge University Press, 2012), 12.
6. On the diplomatic mission, see J. Thornton, *Cultural History of the Atlantic World*, 17, and John K. Thornton, "The Portuguese in Africa," in *Portuguese Oceanic Expansion, 1400–1800*, ed. Francisco Bethencourt and Diogo Ramada Curto (New York: Cambridge University Press, 2007), 139. Recent research has contested the existence of this embassy. See Verena Krebs, "Re-Examining Foresti's Supplementum Chronicarum and the 'Ethiopian' Embassy to Europe of 1306," *Bulletin of SOAS* 82, no. 3 (2019): 493–515.
7. Verena Krebs, *Medieval Ethiopian Kingship, Craft, and Diplomacy with Latin Europe* (Cham, Switz.: Palgrave Macmillan, 2021), 62–65.
8. Peter P. Garretson, "A Note on Relations between Ethiopia and the Kingdom of Aragon in the Fifteenth Century," *Rassegna di Studi Etiopici* 37 (1993): 41–42.
9. John K. Thornton, *Africa and Africans in the Making of the Atlantic World, 1400–1800* (New York: Cambridge University Press, 2005), 27.
10. J. Thornton, "Portuguese in Africa," 139.
11. Zurara, "Descobrimento do Senegal," in *Monumenta Missionaria Africana: África Ocidental; Segunda série (1342–1499)*, 7 vols., ed. António Brásio (Lisbon: Agência Geral do Ultramar, 1958), 1:28; João de Barros, "Descoberta do Rio Senegal (1445)," in Brásio, *Monumenta Missionaria Africana: Segunda série*, 1:118; and João de Barros, "Descobrimento do Cabo Verde (1445–1446)," in *Monumenta Missionaria Africana: Segunda série*, 1:124.
12. José da Silva Horta and Francisco Freire, "Os primeiros contatos luso-saarianos: Narrativas europeias quatrocentistas e tradições orais biDān (Mauritânia)," in

As lições de Jill Dias: Antropologia, história, África e academia, ed. Maria Candeira da Silva e Clara Saraiva (Lisbon: Etnográfica Press, 2013), 37–38.

13. For example, J. Thornton, *Africa and Africans in the Making of the Atlantic World*, and more recently Randy J. Sparks, *"Where the Negroes Are Masters": An African Port in the Era of the Slave Trade* (Cambridge, MA: Harvard University Press, 2014).

14. Peter Russell, *Prince Henry the Navigator* (New Haven, CT: Yale University Press, 2000), 239–40.

15. Zurara, "Regresso de Lançarote," in Brásio, *Monumenta Missionaria Africana: Segunda série*, 1:16–17.

16. Zurara, "Partilha das presas em Lagos," in *Monumenta Missionaria Africana: Segunda série*, 1:18. For an English translation of Zurara's chronicle, see Gomes Eannes de Azurara, *The Chronicle of the Discovery and Conquest of Guinea*, 2 vols. (London: Hakluyt Society, 1896–1899).

17. Zurara, "Partilha das presas em Lagos," 18–19.

18. João de Barros, "Descobrimento do Cabo Verde," 126–27.

19. J. Thornton, *Cultural History of the Atlantic World*, 213.

20. Alencastro, *Trade in the Living*, 40.

21. J. Thornton, "Portuguese in Africa," 141.

22. J. Thornton, "Portuguese in Africa," 145.

23. Alencastro, *Trade in the Living*, 23.

24. There is a significant literature on *lançados*; see Walter Rodney, *A History of the Upper Guinea Coast, 1545 to 1800* (New York: Monthly Review Press, 1970); Toby Green, *The Rise of the Trans-Atlantic Slave Trade in Western Africa, 1300–1589* (Cambridge: Cambridge University Press, 2011), 115–19; and Peter Mark, "The Central Upper Guinea Coast in the Pre-Contact and Early Portuguese Period, Fifteenth to Seventeenth Century: The Dynamics of Regional Interaction," *Paideuma: Mitteilungen zur Kulturkunde*, no. 67 (2021): 113–44.

25. Green, *Rise of the Trans-Atlantic Slave Trade*, 33–35.

26. J. Thornton, *Cultural History of the Atlantic World*, 84.

27. João de Barros, "Recepção do Príncipe Bemoim (Outubro—1488)," in Brásio, *Monumenta Missionaria Africana: Segunda série*, 1:531.

28. Ousmane Traoré, "State Control and Regulation of Commerce on the Waterways and Coast of Senegambia, ca. 1500–1800," in *Navigating African Maritime History*, ed. Carina E. Ray and Jeremy Rich (Liverpool: Liverpool University Press, 2009), 59.

29. Barros, "Recepção do Príncipe Bemoim," 1:534.

30. Rui de Pina, "Como Bemoim foi feito cristão," in Brásio, *Monumenta Missionaria Africana: Segunda série*, 1:537–41; Garcia de Resende, "Conversão e baptismo de Bemoim," in Brásio, *Monumenta Missionaria Africana: Segunda série*, 1:543–49.

31. João de Barros, "Morte do Príncipe Bemoim," in Brásio, *Monumenta Missionaria Africana: Segunda série*, 1:553–59. See also Green, *Rise of the*

Trans-Atlantic Slave Trade, 85; and Francisco Bethencourt, *Racisms: From the Crusades to the Twentieth Century* (Princeton, NJ: Princeton University Press, 2014), 85.

32. Resende, "Conversão e baptismo de Bemoim," 549. On this episode, see Bethencourt, *Racisms: From the Crusades to the Twentieth Century*, 130–31. Toby Green differs with Bethencourt in thinking that that members of the crew were indeed punished. See Green, *Fistful of Shells*, 79.

33. Bennett, *African Kings and Black Slaves*, 60.

34. Bennett, *African Kings and Black Slaves*, 51–53.

35. Rebecca Shumway, *The Fante and the Transatlantic Slave Trade* (Rochester, NY: Rochester University Press, 2014), 25.

36. Green, *Fistful of Shells*, 108.

37. David Eltis and David Richardson, *Atlas of the Transatlantic Slave Trade* (New Haven, CT: Yale University Press, 2015), 304. Scholars working strictly in earlier periods use the term Mina along with Gold Coast to refer to this region; see, for example, *Africa's Gold Coast through Portuguese Sources, 1469–1680*, ed. Kwasi Konadu (Oxford: Oxford University Press, 2022).

38. See Florence Abena Dolphyne, "The Volta-Comoé Languages," in *The Languages of Ghana*, ed. Mary E. Kropp Dakubu (New York: Routledge, 2015), 50–90.

39. Shumway, *Fante and the Transatlantic Slave Trade*, 28, and Walter C. Rucker, *Gold Coast Diasporas: Identity, Culture, and Power* (Bloomington: Indiana University Press, 2015), 26.

40. Shumway, *Fante and the Transatlantic Slave Trade*, 17–21, and Rucker, *Gold Coast Diasporas*, 12–13.

41. Rucker, *Gold Coast Diasporas*, 25.

42. Rui de Pina, "Fundamento do castelo e cidade de São Jorge na Mina," in *Monumenta Missionaria Africana: África Ocidental*, 15 vols., ed. António Brásio (Lisbon: Agência Geral do Ultramar, 1952), 1:10–11, and João de Barros, "Construção do castelo da Mina (19-1-1482)," in Brásio, *Monumenta Missionaria Africana*, 1:21.

43. Pina, "Fundamento do castelo e cidade de São Jorge na Mina," 11.

44. On Eguafo shrines, see Sam Spiers, "The Eguafo Polity: Between the Traders and Raiders," in *Power and Landscape in Atlantic West Africa: Archaeological Perspectives*, ed. J. Cameron Monroe and Akinwumi Ogundiran (New York: Cambridge University Press, 2012), 115–41. On stones as shrines in Cape Coast, about seven miles from Elmina, see the mid-eighteenth-century account Thomas Thompson, *An Account of Two Missionary Voyages* (London: Society for Promoting Christian Knowledge, 1937), 39–40. On Anomabu's rock shrines, see Sparks, *"Where the Negroes Are Masters,"* 26.

45. Pina, "Fundamento do castelo e cidade de São Jorge na Mina," 12–14; Barros, "Construção do castelo da Mina," 27. For a detailed analysis of this conflict, centering the trade of gold, see Green, *Fistful of Shells*, 114–17.

46. For examples of this weaponry, including spears, axes, and swords, see Thomas Astley, ed. *A New General Collection of Voyages* [. . .], 2 vols. (London: Thomas Astley, 1745), vol. 2, illustration no. 77 on plate 69, p. 693.
47. Duarte Pacheco Pereira, "Descoberta da Mina e edificação do castelo (jan. 1471-1-1-1482)," in Brásio, *Monumenta Missionaria Africana*, 1:4–5.
48. Duarte Pacheco Pereira, "Descoberta da Mina e edificação do castelo (jan. 1471-1-1-1482)," in Brásio, *Monumenta Missionaria Africana*, 1: 6.
49. Shumway, *Fante and the Transatlantic Slave Trade*, 27.
50. J. Thornton, "Portuguese in Africa," 144.
51. John K. Thornton, *A History of West Central Africa to 1850* (New York: Cambridge University Press, 2020), 16–17.
52. Among historians who have supported the thesis of wealth-in-people to explain accumulation of wealth are Jean Vansina, *Paths in the Rainforest: Toward a History of Political Tradition in Equatorial Africa* (Madison: University of Wisconsin Press, 1990), 251, and Miller, *Way of Death*, 43. On the limitations of the wealth-in-people model, see Jane I. Guyer, "Wealth in People and Self-Realization in Equatorial Africa," *Man* 28, no. 2 (1993): 243–65, and Jane I. Guyer and Samuel M. Eno Belinga, "Wealth in People as Wealth in Knowledge: Accumulation and Composition in Equatorial Africa," *Journal of African History* 36 (1995): 91–120. For a recent bold critique of this thesis in West Central Africa, see Mariana P. Candido, *Wealth, Land and Property in Angola: A History of Dispossession, Slavery, and Inequality* (New York: Cambridge University Press, 2022), 49–51.
53. J. Thornton, *History of West Central Africa to 1850*, 35.
54. J. Thornton, *Cultural History of the Atlantic World*, 183; J. Thornton, *History of West Central Africa to 1850*, 42.
55. Cécile Fromont, *The Art of Conversion: Christian Visual Culture in the Kingdom of Kongo* (Chapel Hill: University of North Carolina Press, 2014), 75.
56. James H. Sweet, *Recreating Africa: Culture, Kinship, and Religion in the African-Portuguese World, 1441–1770* (Chapel Hill: University of North Carolina Press, 2003), 113.
57. See J. Thornton, *Cultural History of the Atlantic World*, 43–44, Fromont, *Art of Conversion*, 74.
58. See Miller, *Way of Death*, 42–43.
59. J. Thornton, *History of West Central Africa to 1850*, 53.
60. Miller, *Way of Death*, 105.
61. Candido, *African Slaving Port*, 9.

Chapter 2

1. Florence Hall (Akeiso), "Memoir of the Life of Florence Hall, 1808–1820?" Powel Family Papers, Historical Society of Pennsylvania, transcribed in Randy M. Browne and John Wood Sweet, "Florence Hall's 'Memoirs':

Finding African Women in the Transatlantic Slave Trade," *Slavery and Abolition* 37, no. 1 (2016): 216. Hall's very short unpublished handwritten narrative is among the earliest firsthand accounts about enslavement by African-born women.

2. See Michael A. Gomez, *Exchanging Our Country Marks: The Transformation of African Identities in the Colonial and Antebellum South* (Chapel Hill: University of North Carolina Press, 1998), 199–214, and John K. Thornton, *Warfare in Atlantic Africa, 1500–1800* (London: University College London Press, 1999), 127–28. See also Araujo, *Shadows of the Slave Past*, 15–45.

3. The only existing published biography of an enslaved person brought to Brazil is that of Mahommah Gardo Baquaqua, published in 1854. See Mahommah Gardo Baquaqua, *Biography of Mahommah G. Baquaqua* [. . .] (Detroit: George Pomeroy, 1854), and Paul E. Lovejoy and Robin Law, *The Biography of Mahommah Gardo Baquaqua: His Passage from Slavery to Freedom in African and America* (Princeton, NJ: Markus Wiener Publishers, 2003). See also Paul E. Lovejoy and Nielson R. Bezerra, *Mahommah Gardo Baquaqua: An Enslaved Muslim of the Black Atlantic* (Chapel Hill: University of North Carolina Press, 2025).

4. J. Thornton, *Africa and Africans in the Making of the Atlantic World*, 99. This was also true for the region of Benguela in West Central Africa during the seventeenth century and until the nineteenth century; see Candido, *African Slaving Port*, 199.

5. Philip D. Curtin, "General Introduction," in *Africa Remembered: Narratives by West Africans from the Era of the Slave Trade*, ed. Philip Curtin (Madison: University of Wisconsin Press, 1967), 7.

6. Candido, *African Slaving Port*, 19.

7. Linda M. Heywood, "Slavery and Its Transformation in the Kingdom of Kongo: 1491–1800," *Journal of African History* 50 (2009): 3.

8. John Thornton, "African Political Ethics and the Slave Trade," in *Abolitionism and Imperialism in Britain, Africa, and the Atlantic*, ed. Derek R. Peterson (Athens: Ohio University Press, 2010), 41.

9. See Heywood, "Slavery and Its Transformation in the Kingdom of Kongo," 5–8.

10. Candido, *African Slaving Port*, 147–49.

11. See Mariana P. Candido, "African Freedom Suits and Portuguese Vassal Status: Legal Mechanisms for Fighting Enslavement in Benguela, Angola, 1800–1830," *Slavery and Abolition* 32, no. 3 (2011): 447–59.

12. On Luanda and Benguela, see Ferreira, *Cross-Cultural Exchange*, 52–54, 77. For more cases in Benguela, see Candido, *African Slaving Port*, 191–93.

13. Candido, *Wealth, Land and Property in Angola*, 8–11.

14. Candido, *African Slaving Port*, 201–2.

15. Candido, *African Slaving Port*, 206–9.

16. Ferreira, *Cross-Cultural Exchange*, 20–23.

17. Candido, *African Slaving Port*, 177–82.

18. Walter Hawthorne, *From Africa to Brazil: Culture, Identity, and an Atlantic Slave Trade, 1600–1830* (New York: Cambridge University Press, 2010), 77–80. On the "iron-slave cycle," see Walter Hawthorne, *Planting Rice and Harvesting Slaves: Transformations along the Guinea-Bissau Coast, 1400–1900* (Portsmouth, UK: Heinemann, 2003), 97–98.

19. Shumway, *Fante and the Transatlantic Slave Trade*, 42–47.

20. Shumway, *Fante and the Transatlantic Slave Trade*, 44; Green, *Fistful of Shells*, 117; 124.

21. On the discussion about Akan and Fante as separate languages or Fante as an Akan dialect, see Dolphyne, "Volta-Comoé Languages," 52–54.

22. On the construction of this complex Fante identity, see Shumway, *Fante and the Transatlantic Slave Trade*, 15.

23. Sparks, *"Where the Negroes Are Masters,"* 129.

24. Shumway, *Fante and the Transatlantic Slave Trade*, 8–9; Sparks, *"Where the Negroes Are Masters,"* 123–24.

25. See A. Le Herissé, *Royaume du Dahomey: Moeurs, Religion, Histoire* (Paris: Emile Larose, 1911), 56, and Robin Law, *Ouidah*: *The Social History of a West African Slaving Port (1727–1892)* (Athens: Ohio University Press, 2004), 149.

26. One example is the case of one of the wives of King Agonglo, Na Agontimé. See Ana Lucia Araujo, "History, Memory and Imagination: Na Agontimé, a Dahomean Queen in Brazil," in *Beyond Tradition: African Women and their Cultural Spaces*, ed. Toyin Falola and Sati U. Fwatshak (Trenton, NJ: Africa World Press, 2011), 45–68.

27. Suzanne Preston Blier, *African Vodun: Art, Psychology, and Power* (Chicago: University of Chicago Press, 1995), 4. See also Archibald Dalzel, *The History of Dahomey: An Inland Kingdom of Africa* (London: T. Spilsbury and Son, 1793).

28. J. Cameron Monroe and Anneke Janzen, "The Dahomean Feast: Royal Women, Private Politics, and Culinary Practices in Atlantic West Africa," *African Archaeological Review* 31, no. 2 (2014): 307.

29. Araujo, *Public Memory of Slavery*, 98–99.

30. According to Robin Law, *Ouidah*, 63, Dahomey became tributary of Oyo in 1748. Monroe states that Dahomey started paying tributes to Oyo after 1729. See J. Cameron Monroe, *The Precolonial State in West Africa: Building Power in Dahomey* (New York: Cambridge University Press, 2014), 87.

31. Francesca Piqué and Leslie Rainer, *Palace Sculptures of Abomey: History Told on Walls* (London: J. Paul Getty Trust, Thames and Hudson, 1999), 42. Today the palaces house the collections of the Musée Historique d'Abomey (Historical Museum of Abomey). For an analysis of the bas-reliefs, see Monroe, *Precolonial State in West Africa*, 207–12.

32. Ana Lucia Araujo, "Dahomey, Portugal, and Bahia: King Adandozan and the Atlantic Slave Trade," *Slavery and Abolition* 3, no. 1 (2012): 1–19. The entire correspondence between Dahomean and Portuguese rulers has been transcribed and published in Portuguese. See Luis Nicolau Parés, "Cartas do Daomé," *Afro-Ásia* 47 (2013): 295–395.

33. "Relation de la Guerre de Juda par le S[ieu]r Ringard Capitaine du Navire le Mars de Nantes." The account was fully transcribed and published by Robin Law, "A Neglected Account of the Dahomian Conquest of Whydah (1727): The 'Relation de la Guerre de Juda' of the Sieur Ringard of Nantes," *History in Africa* 5 (1988): 321–38.

34. See Law, "A Neglected Account of the Dahomian Conquest of Whydah (1727)," 326.

35. Sweet, *Domingos Álvares*, 26–27.

36. Belinda's petition is considered the first known individual demand of reparations for slavery in the United States. See Roy E. Finkenbine, "Belinda's Petition: Reparations for Slavery in Revolutionary Massachusetts," *William and Mary Quarterly* 64, no. 1 (2007): 95–104. I examine Belinda's case in Araujo, *Reparations for Slavery*, 49–51.

37. "Petition of Belinda an African, to the Honourable Senate and House of Representatives in General Court Assembled, February 14, 1783," Digital Archive of Massachusetts Anti-Slavery and Anti-Segregation Petitions, Massachusetts Archives, Boston, MA, v. 239–Revolution Resolves, 1783, SCI/series 45X, 239, fl. 12–16.

38. "Petition of Belinda an African," fl. 12.

39. See Robin Law, *The Ọyọ Empire, c. 1600–c. 1836: A West African Imperialism in the Era of the Atlantic Slave Trade* (Oxford: Oxford University Press, 1991).

40. Historians do not always agree about the dates of the beginning and end of this war. Robin Law identifies a war between Owu and Ife starting in 1812 and the fall of Owu in 1822. See Law, *Ọyọ Empire*, 275. These dates are also corroborated by Aribidesi Usman and Toyin Falola, *The Yoruba from Prehistory to the Present* (New York: Cambridge University Press, 2019), 161.

41. Paul E. Lovejoy, *Slavery in the Global Diaspora of Africa* (New York: Routledge, 2019), 28.

42. J. Reis, Gomes, and Carvalho, *Story of Rufino*, 7–8.

43. Francis de Castelnau, *Renseignements sur l'Afrique Centrale* [. . .] (Paris: Chez P. Bertrand, 1851), 22–23. Robin Law and Paul E. Lovejoy, "Borgu in the Atlantic Slave Trade," *African Economic History*, no. 27 (1999): 82.

44. Donald Pierson, *Brancos e pretos na Bahia: Estudo de contato racial* (São Paulo: Companhia Editora Nacional, 1945), 304–5. See also Feliz Ayoh'Omidire and Alcione M. Amos, "O Babalaô fala: A autobiografia de Martiniano Eliseu do Bomfim," *Afro-Ásia* no. 46 (2012): 238.

45. See Kristin Mann, "One Yoruba Man's Transatlantic Passages from Slavery to Freedom," in *The Rise and Demise of Slavery and the Slave Trade in the Atlantic World*, ed. Philip Misevich and Kristin Mann (Rochester, NY: University of Rochester Press, 2016), 220–46, and Kristin Mann, "Gendered

Authority, Gendered Violence: Family, Household and Identity in the Life and Death of a Brazilian Freed Woman in Lagos," in *African Women in the Atlantic World: Property, Vulnerability and Mobility, 1660–1880*, ed. Mariana P. Candido and Adam Jones (Rochester, NY: James Currey, 2019), 148–68.

46. On this story of Otampê Ojaró, see Lisa Earl Castillo, "The Alaketu Temple and its Founders: Portrait of an Afro-Brazilian Dynasty," *Luso-Brazilian Review* 50, no. 1 (2013): 83–112.

47. The account was written in 1594 and published for the first time in 1733. See André Alvares d'Almada, *Tratado breve dos rios de Guiné do Cabo-Verde desde o rio do Sanaga até aos Baixos de Sant'Anna* (Porto: Typographia Comercial Portuense, 1841), 29–34.

48. Hawthorne, *From Africa to Brazil*, 64.

49. John Atkins, *A Voyage to Guinea, Brazil and the West Indies* (London: Ward and Chandler, 1737), 151.

50. Paul E. Lovejoy, "Speculations on the African Origins of Venture Smith," in *The Changing Worlds of Atlantic Africa: Essays in Honor of Robin Law*, ed. Toyin Falola and Matt D. Childs (Durham, NC: Carolina Academic Press, 2009), 374.

51. Venture Smith, *A Narrative of the Life and Adventures of Venture Smith* [. . .] *Related by Himself* (New London, CT: Holt, 1798), 6.

52. Lovejoy, "Speculations on the African Origins of Venture Smith," 377–78.

53. Lovejoy, "Speculations on the African Origins of Venture Smith," 376–77.

54. Vincent Carretta has argued that Equiano's birthplace was South Carolina and not Igboland. See Carretta, *Equiano, the African*. Africanist historians Paul E. Lovejoy and James H. Sweet each have challenged this interpretation by showing that the ways enslaved Africans who had been transported to the Americas, sometimes at very young age, identified themselves could change over time; therefore, when examining written evidence, historians must also consider that identities are not always fixed. Consequently, despite having declared South Carolina as his birthplace years after he had endured the Middle Passage, and earlier before he wrote his autobiography in no way invalidates Equiano's Igboland birthplace. For the main responses by Lovejoy and Sweet, see Paul E. Lovejoy, "Autobiography and Memory: Gustavus Vassa, alias Olaudah Equiano, the African," *Slavery and Abolition* 27, no. 3 (2006): 317–47, and James H. Sweet, "Mistaken Identities? Olaudah Equiano, Domingos Álvares, and the Methodological Challenges of Studying the African Diaspora," *American Historical Review* 114, no. 2: (2009): 279–306.

55. Olaudah Equiano and Vincent Carretta, *The Interesting Narrative and Other Writings* (New York: Penguin Books, 2003), 47.

56. Equiano and Carretta, *Interesting Narrative*, 47.

57. Quobna Ottobah Cugoano, *Thoughts and Sentiments on the Evil of Slavery and Other Writings* (New York: Penguin Books, 1999), 12–13. Page numbers for *Thoughts and Sentiments* in subsequent notes refer to this edition. For the original edition, see Ottobah Cugoano, *Thoughts and Sentiments on the Evil of Slavery* [. . .] (London: Printed by the author, 1791).

58. "The Ijebu kingdom stretched southwestward to the territory of Lagos and eastward across the Sasa River to the Oni River and its largest extent. It was bounded on the west by Egba, on the north by Oyo, on the northeast by Ife and on the east by Ondo." See Toyin Falola and Aribidesi Usman, *The Yoruba from Prehistory to the Present* (New York: Cambridge University Press, 2019), 97.

59. Osifekunde's story was made public by Marie-Armand Pascal de Castera-Macaya d'Avezac in 1845, when he interviewed him in Paris. See M. d'Avezac, *Notice sur le pays et le people des Yébous en Afrique* (Paris: Librairie Orientale de Mme Ve Dondey-Dupré, 1845). For an English translation, see Peter C. Lloyd, "Osifekunde of Ijebu," in Curtin, *Africa Remembered*, 217–88.

60. On the Owu war, see Falola and Usman, *Yoruba from Prehistory to the Present*, 161–65. Historian Aderivaldo Santana connects Osifekunde's abduction with the Owu war; see Aderivaldo Ramos de Santana, "A extraordinário odisseia do comerciante ijebu que foi escravo no Brasil e homem livre na França (1820–1842)," *Afro-Ásia* 57 (2018): 9–53.

61. James Albert Ukawsaw Gronniosaw, *Narrative of the Most Remarkable Particulars in the Life of James Albert Ukawsaw Gronniosaw, an African Prince, as Related by Himself* (Bath: W. Gye, 1770), 4–5. According to Paul E. Lovejoy, he was taken by kola traders who made the route from Borno to the Asante territory on the Gold Coast, see Paul E. Lovejoy, *Jihād in West Africa During the Age of Revolutions* (Athens: Ohio University Press, 2016), 63.

62. Gronniosaw, *Narrative*, 5.

63. Lovejoy and Law, *Biography of Mahommah Gardo Baquaqua*, 41.

64. Baquaqua, *Biography of Mahommah G. Baquaqua*, 24.

65. See Lovejoy and Law, *Biography of Mahommah Gardo Baquaqua*, 137n151.

66. For West Central African cases, see Candido, *African Slaving Port*, 221.

67. Greene first recorded this story in 1998. See Sandra E. Greene, *West African Narratives of Slavery: Texts from Late Nineteenth- and Early Twentieth-Century Ghana* (Bloomington: Indiana University Press, 2011), 187–89.

68. Bailey recorded several versions of this story in interviews she undertook in Ghana between 1992 and 2003. See Anne C. Bailey, *African Voices of the Atlantic Slave Trade: Beyond the Silence and the Shame* (Boston: Beacon Press, 2005), 27–56.

69. Greene, *West African Narratives of Slavery*, 188.

70. Pawnship and panyarring often appear in the literature as blurred categories. See Paul E. Lovejoy, "Pawnship, Debt, and 'Freedom' in Atlantic Africa during the Era of the Slave Trade: A Reassessment," *Journal of African History* 55 (2014): 59.

71. Sparks, *"Where the Negroes Are Masters,"* 28; 37. For a discussion on pawnship and its relationship with credit and trust, see Green, *Fistful of Shells*, 277.

72. See Document 525, Charles Towgood, Allampo Road, 19 Marc 1681/2 in *The English in West Africa 1681–1683: The Local Correspondence of the Royal African Company of England, 1681–1699, Part I*, ed. Robin Law (Oxford: Oxford University Press, 1997), 272.

73. The ship pilot was taken as a pawn. See Lieutenant Durand, "Journal de bord d'un négrier, 1731–1732," Gen Mss, vol. 7, 49, Beinecke Rare Book and Manuscript Library, Yale University (hereafter cited as BLY). See also Robert W. Harms, *The Diligent: A Voyage Through the Words of the Slave Trade* (New York: Basic Books, 2002), 147.

74. Miller, *Way of Death*, 179.

75. Louis-Marie-Joseph Ohier de Grandpré, *Voyage à la côte occidentale d'Afrique* [. . .], vols. 1 and 2 (Paris: Dentu, 1801), 2:63–64.

76. See Robin Law, "The Politics of Commercial Transition: Factional Conflict in Dahomey in the Context of the Ending of the Atlantic Slave Trade," *Journal of African History* 38 (1997): 213–33.

77. On Agontimé's history, see Edna G. Bay, *Wives of the Leopard: Gender, Politics, and Culture in the Kingdom of Dahomey* (Charlottesville: University of Virginia Press, 1998), 178–81. On Agontimé's legend, see Araujo, "History, Memory and Imagination," 45–68. On Agontimé as the woman who introduced Dahomey Vodun in Brazil, see Pierre Verger, "Le culte des vodoun d'Abomey aurait-il été apporté à Saint Louis de Maranhão par la mère du roi Ghèzo?" *Études Dahoméennes* 8 (1952): 19–24. See also Luis Nicolau Parés, "The Jeje in the Tambor de Mina of Maranhão and in the Candomblé of Bahia," *Slavery and Abolition* 22, no. 1 (2001): 91–115.

78. Papa Joãozinho, interview by Milton Guran, in Milton Guran, *Agudás: Os "Brasileiros" do Benim* (Rio de Janeiro: Editora Nova Fronteira, 1999), 78.

79. Jacqueline Abul (born Vieyra) and Renée Sadeler (born Vieyra), interview by Ana Lucia Araujo, Cotonou, Benin, June 25, 2005.

80. See Araujo, *Public Memory of Slavery*, chap. 7.

81. See *SlaveVoyages*, www.slavevoyages.org. See also Eltis and Richardson, *Atlas of the Transatlantic Slave Trade*, 15.

82. See Randy J. Sparks, *The Two Princes of Calabar: An Eighteenth-Century Atlantic Odyssey* (Cambridge, MA: Harvard University Press, 2004), 20–23.

83. Today, the archives of Sierra Leone and the United Kingdom preserve the registers of about 92,230 of these individuals. See Richard Anderson et al., "Using African Names to Identify the Origins of Captives in the Transatlantic Slave Trade: Crowd-Sourcing and the Registers of Liberated Africans, 1808–1862," *History in Africa* (2013): 1–27. A growing number of works focus on the harrowing trajectories and legal statuses of these individuals. See Sharla M. Fett, *Recaptured Africans: Surviving Slave Ships, Detention, and Dislocation in the Final Years of the Slave Trade* (Chapel Hill: University of North Carolina Press, 2016), Beatriz G. Mamigonian, *Africanos livres: A abolição do tráfico de escravos no Brasil* (São Paulo: Companhia das Letras, São

Paulo, 2017), Richard Peter Anderson, *Abolition in Sierra Leone: Re-Building Lives and Identities in Nineteenth-Century West Africa* (New York: Cambridge University Press, 2020), and Richard Anderson and Henry B. Lovejoy, eds. *Liberated Africans and the Abolition of the Slave Trade, 1807–1896* (Rochester, NY: Rochester University Press, 2020).

84. See Sigismund W. Koelle, *Polyglotta Africana or A Comparative Vocabulary of Nearly Three Hundred Words and Phrases in More Than One Hundred African Languages* (London: Church Missionary House, 1854), and Paul E. H. Hair, "The Enslavement of Koelle's Informants," *Journal of African History* 6, no. 2 (1965): 195n5.

85. See Ferreira, *Cross-Cultural Exchange*, 77–81; Daniel Domingues da Silva, *The Atlantic Slave Trade from West Central Africa 1780–1867* (New York: Cambridge University Press, 2017), 2–3.

Chapter 3

1. Zora Neale Hurston, *Barracoon: The Story of the Last "Black Cargo"* (New York: Amistad, 2018), 45.

2. The approximate date based on a British report is given by Sylviane A. Diouf, *The Dreams of Africa in Alabama: The Slave Ship Clotilda and the Story of the Last Africans Brought to America* (New York: Oxford University Press, 2007), 69.

3. Herbert S. Klein, *The Atlantic Slave Trade* (Cambridge: Cambridge University Press, 1999), 130.

4. See Lovejoy, "Autobiography and Memory," 323. Based on an entry in a parish register and the muster book of the ship *Racehorse*, Vincent Carretta has contested Equiano's birthplace, by arguing that he was born in South Carolina; see Carretta, *Equiano, the African*, 17.

5. Equiano and Carretta, *Interesting Narrative*, 47.

6. Equiano and Carretta, *Interesting Narrative*, 37.

7. Equiano and Carretta, *Interesting Narrative*, 37.

8. Ferreira, *Cross-Cultural Exchange*, 32.

9. Candido, *African Slaving Port*, 219.

10. Equiano and Carretta, *Interesting Narrative*, 52.

11. See Colleen E. Kriger, *Making Money: Life, Death, and Early Modern Trade on Africa's Guinea Coast* (Athens: Ohio University Press, 2017), 18–19, and Green, *Fistful of Shells*, 17. On cowrie shells as currency, see Jan Hogendorn and Marion Johnson, *The Shell Money of the Slave Trade* (Cambridge: Cambridge University Press, 1986), and Bin Yang, *Cowrie Shells and Cowrie Money: A Global History* (New York: Routledge, 2018).

12. Atkins, *Voyage to Guinea, Brazil, & the West Indies*, 112. See also Law, *Ouidah*, 136.

13. Alain Yacou, *Journaux de bord et de traite de Joseph Crassous de Médeuil: De La Rochelle à la côte de Guinée et aux Antilles (1772–1776)* (Paris: Karthala, 2001), 173.

14. Lovejoy, *Transformations in Slavery*, 107.
15. Cugoano, *Thoughts and Sentiments*, 13.
16. Cugoano, *Thoughts and Sentiments*, 14.
17. On these fears of being eaten on the Gold Coast, see Sparks, *"Where the Negroes Are Masters,"* 155.
18. Miller, *Way of Death*, 5. See also Green, *Fistful of Shells*, 86, 220.
19. Kriger, *Making Money*, 69.
20. Cugoano, *Thoughts and Sentiments*, 14. See also Rucker, *Gold Coast Diasporas*, 68.
21. Jacob Festus Adeniyi Ajayi, "Samuel Ajayi Crowther of Oyo," in Curtin, *Africa Remembered*, 304; 308. See also Anderson, *Abolition in Sierra Leone*, 72.
22. Ajayi, "Samuel Ajayi Crowther of Oyo," 303.
23. Ajayi, "Samuel Ajayi Crowther of Oyo," 310–11.
24. Philip D. Curtin, "Joseph Wright of the Egba," in Curtin, *Africa Remembered*, 326–27.
25. Curtin, "Joseph Wright of the Egba," 329.
26. Curtin, "Joseph Wright of the Egba," 330.
27. Lovejoy and Law, *Biography of Mahommah Gardo Baquaqua*, 139.
28. Lovejoy and Law, *Biography of Mahommah Gardo Baquaqua*, 140.
29. Lovejoy and Law, *Biography of Mahommah Gardo Baquaqua*, 144.
30. Lovejoy and Law, *Biography of Mahommah Gardo Baquaqua*, 149, 149n201. See also Law, *Ouidah*, 138.
31. Lovejoy and Law, *Biography of Mahommah Gardo Baquaqua*, 150.
32. Diouf, *Dreams of Africa in Alabama*, 48.
33. Hurston, *Barracoon*, 52.
34. See Robin Law, "'My Head Belongs to the King': On the Political and Ritual Significance of Decapitation in Pre-Colonial Dahomey," *Journal of African History* 30, no. 3 (1989): 413. See William Snelgrave, *A New Account of Some Parts of Guinea and the Slave-Trade* (London, 1734), 160–61.
35. Instituto Histórico e Geográfico Brasileiro, Rio de Janeiro, Brazil (hereafter cited as IHGB), Lata 137, Pasta 62, Doc. 1, ff. 6v, 7, n.d. See Araujo, "Dahomey, Portugal, and Bahia," 10.
36. Law, "'My Head Belongs to the King,'" 403–5.
37. Hurston, *Barracoon*, 53.
38. Sparks, *"Where the Negroes Are Masters,"* 123. See also Nicholas Radburn, *Traders in Men: Merchants and the Transformation of the Transatlantic Slave Trade* (New Haven, CT: Yale University Press, 2023), chap. 2.
39. See, for example, entries of Thursday, November 1, 1750, and Friday, January 25, 1751, in John Newton, Bernard Martin, and Mark Spurrell, *The Journal of a Slave Trader (John Newton), 1750–1754; with Newton's "Thoughts Upon the African Slave Trade"* (London: Epworth Press, 1962), 14.
40. On Ouidah, see Law, *Ouidah*, 140–41. On Cape Coast, see Sparks, *"Where the Negroes Are Masters,"* 155.

41. See D. da Silva, *Atlantic Slave Trade*, 100–103. See also Lovejoy, *Slavery in the Global Diaspora of Africa*, 53.
42. Carlos Liberato et al., "Laços entre a África e o mundo atlântico durante a era do comércio de africanos escravizados: Uma introdução," in Laços atlânticos: África e africanos durante a era do comércio transatlântico de escravos, ed. Carlos Liberato et al. (Luanda, Angola: Ministério da Cultura, Museu Nacional da Escravatura, 2016), 14–15.
43. Bruce L. Mouser, ed., *A Slaving Voyage to Africa and Jamaica: The Log of the Sandown, 1793–1794* (Bloomington: Indiana University Press, 2002), 87.
44. Entries of January 11, 1751, and January 20, 1751, in John Newton, Bernard Martin, and Mark Spurrell, *The Journal of a Slave Trader* (London: Epworth Press, 1962), 30, 31.
45. Reported by Samuel Gamble in two separate entries of the ship log in January 1794; see Mouser, *Slaving Voyage to Africa and Jamaica*, 97. Successful escape attempts from forts on the Gold Coast also occurred in the seventeenth century, see Stephanie Smallwood, *Saltwater Slavery: A Middle Passage from Africa to American Diaspora* (Cambridge, MA: Harvard University Press, 2007), 41–42.
46. Pieter van den Broecke and James D. La Fleur, *Pieter Van Den Broecke's Journal of Voyages to Cape Verde, Guinea and Angola: (1605–1612)* (London: Hakluyt Society, 2000), 54–55.
47. Sparks, *"Where the Negroes Are Masters,"* 227.
48. I explore these rivalries in Ana Lucia Araujo, *The Gift: How Objects of Prestige Shaped the Atlantic Slave Trade and Colonialism* (New York: Cambridge University Press, 2024).
49. Phyllis M. Martin, "The Kingdom of Loango," in *Kongo: Power of Majesty*, ed. Alisa Lagamma (New York: Metropolitan Museum of Art, 2015), 75.
50. See Roquinaldo Ferreira, *Dos sertões ao Atlântico: Tráfico ilegal de escravos e comércio lícito em Angola, 1830–1860* (Luanda, Angola: Kilombelombe, 2012), and D. da Silva, *Atlantic Slave Trade*, 29.
51. See Eltis and Richardson, *Atlas of the Transatlantic Slave Trade*, 8, and D. da Silva, *Atlantic Slave Trade*, 38–39; 46.
52. See H. Klein, *Atlantic Slave Trade*, 97.
53. On the *asiento*, see Linda A. Newson and Susie Minchin, *From Capture to Sale: The Portuguese Slave Trade to Spanish South America in Early Seventeenth Century* (Leiden, Neth.: Brill, 2007), 18–21.
54. H. Klein and Vinson, *African Slavery in Latin America*, 42.
55. See Charles R. Boxer, *Salvador de Sá and the Struggle for Brazil and Angola, 1602–1654* (Oxford: Clarendon Press, 1957); Alencastro, *O trato dos viventes*; and Filipa Ribeiro da Silva, *Dutch and the Portuguese in Western Africa: Empires, Merchants and the Atlantic System 1580–1674* (Leiden, Neth.: Brill, 2011).
56. These estimates are based on *SlaveVoyages*, http://www.slavevoyages.org.

57. These gifts had an important role in local exchanges and the custom of exchanging gifts was extended to the transactions associated with the Atlantic slave trade. See Miller, *Way of Death*, 50–51; Kriger, *Making Money*, 31; and Green, *Fistful of Shells*, 133, 223–24.

58. Luiz Felipe de Alencastro, "Continental Drift: The Independence of Brazil (1822), Portugal and Africa," in *From Slave Trade to Empire: Europe and the Colonisation of Black Africa, 1780s–1880s*, ed. Olivier Pétré-Grenouilleau (London: Routledge, 2004), 103, 108n8.

59. On West Central Africa, see Miller, *Way of Death*, 66–67. On the Loango coast, see also Jean-Michel Deveau, *La traite rochelaise* (Paris: Karthala, 1990), 74–75.

60. Samuel Robinson, *A Sailor Boy's Experience Aboard a Slave Ship in the Beginning of the Present Century* (Wigtown, UK: GC Book Publishers, 1996), 13–14.

61. See Green, *Fistful of Shells*, 13. See also Kriger, *Making Money*, 12–14, 23.

62. Johann Peter Oettinger, Craig Koslofsky, and Roberto Zaugg, *A German Barber-Surgeon in the Atlantic Slave Trade: The Seventeenth-Century Journal of Johann Peter Oettinger* (Charlottesville: University of Virginia Press, 2020), 42–43. For cotton locally produced in West Africa, see Colleen E. Kriger, "'Guinea Cloth': Production and Consumption of Cotton Textiles in West Africa before and during the Atlantic Slave Trade," in *The Spinning World: A Global History of Cotton Textiles, 1200–1850*, ed. Giorgio Riello and Prasannan Parthasarathi (Oxford: Oxford University Press, 2009), 105–26.

63. Miller, *Way of Death*, 74.

64. Kriger, *Making Money*, 23.

65. See Lovejoy, *Transformations in Slavery*, 51, and Chris Evans and Louise Miskell, *Swansea Copper: A Global History* (Baltimore: Johns Hopkins University Press, 2020), 227.

66. Green, *A Fistful of Shells*, 237–38.

67. Timothy Insoll and Thurstan Shaw, "Gao and Igbo-Ukwu: Beads, Interregional Trade, and Beyond," *African Archaeological Review* 14, no. 1 (1997): 9–23.

68. Araujo, *Public Memory of Slavery*, 168.

69. To understand the early and long-lasting relations between Brazil and the Bight of Benin, in which the trade in third-rate tobacco and enslaved people was central, see Verger, *Flux et reflux de la traite des nègres*.

70. On Luanda, see José Curto, *Enslaving Spirits: The Portuguese-Brazilian Alcohol Trade at Luanda and Its Hinterland, c. 1550–1830* (Leiden, Neth.: Brill, 2004), 69. On Benguela, see Candido, *African Slaving Port*, 161.

71. Archives Départementales de Charente-Maritime (hereafter cited as ADCM), 41 ETP 217/6659, fl. 1v.

72. IHGB, Lata 137, Pasta 62, Doc.1, ff.3–3v, n.d. This undated letter was probably written in 1804 and sent to Brazil with the Dahomean embassy of 1805. On these grievances, see Araujo, "Dahomey, Portugal, and Bahia."

73. See Ty M. Reese, "'Eating' Luxury: Fante Middlemen, British Goods, and Changing Dependencies on the Gold Coast, 1750–1821," *William and Mary Quarterly* 66, no. 4 (2009): 851–72, and Shumway, *Fante and the Transatlantic Slave Trade*, 41.

74. In West Central Africa, see Grandpré and Ohier, *Voyage à la côte occidentale d'Afrique*, 1:191; Phyllis M. Martin, *The External Trade of the Loango Coast, 1576–1870: The Effects of Changing Commercial Relations on the Vili Kingdom of Loango* (Oxford: Clarendon Press, 1972), 79; Miller, *Way of Death*, 71–72; Christina Frances Mobley, "The Kongolese Atlantic: Central Africa Slavery and Culture from Mayombe to Haiti" (PhD diss., Duke University, 2015), 88; and Stacey Jean Muriel Sommerdyk, "Trade and Merchant Community of the Loango Coast in the Eighteenth Century" (PhD diss., University of Hull, 2012), 102, 168. See also Araujo, *Gift*.

75. David Ross, "The Dahomean Middleman System, 1727–c. 1818," *Journal of African History* 28 (1987): 364–65.

76. Law, *Ouidah*, 61.

77. On Afro-European communities in African ports during the era of the Atlantic slave trade, see Peter Mark, *"Portuguese" Style and Luso-African Identity: Precolonial Senegambia, Sixteenth–Nineteenth Century* (Bloomington: Indiana University Press, 2002) 13–14. See also George E. Brooks, *Eurafricans in Western Africa: Commerce, Social Status, Gender, and Religious Observance from the Sixteenth to the Eighteenth Century* (Oxford: James Currey, 2003), and Green, *Rise of the Trans-Atlantic Slave Trade*. On African women traders on Gorée Island and Saint-Louis, see Hilary Jones, *The Métis of Senegal: Urban Life and Politics in French West Africa* (Bloomington: Indiana University Press, 2013), 19–39; Bronwen Everill, "'All The Baubles That They Needed': 'Industriousness' and Slavery in Saint-Louis and Gorée," *Early American Studies: An Interdisciplinary Journal* 15, no. 15 (2017): 714–39; and Jessica M. Johnson, *Wicked Flesh: Black Women, Intimacy, and Freedom in the Atlantic World* (Philadelphia: University of Pennsylvania Press, 2020), 16–76. On European traders and African women and their children on the Gold Coast, see Harvey M. Feinberg, *Africans and Europeans in West Africa: Elminans and Dutchmen on the Gold Coast during the Eighteenth Century* (Philadelphia: American Philosophical Society, 1989), and Pernille Ipsen, *Daughters of the Trade: Atlantic Slavers and Interracial Marriage on the Gold Coast* (Philadelphia: University of Pennsylvania Press, 2015).

78. See Ipsen, *Daughters of the Trade*, 9.

79. See Ty M. Reese, "Wives, Brokers, and Laborers: Women at Cape Coast, 1750–1807," in *Women in Port: Gendering Communities, Economies, and Social Networks in Atlantic Port Cities, 1500–1800*, ed. Douglas Catterall and Jodi Campbell (Leiden, Neth.: Brill, 2012), 291–314.

80. On African-born women traders and their unions with Portuguese men in Benguela, see Mariana P. Candido, "Aguida Gonçalves da Silva, une *dona* à

Benguela à la fin du XVIIIe siècle," *Brésil(s): Sciences humaines et sociales*, no. 1 (2012): 33–54. For Luanda, see Vanessa Oliveira, *Slave Trade and Abolition: Gender, Commerce, and Economic Transition in Luanda* (Madison: University of Wisconsin Press, 2021).

81. In West Central African slave-trading routes, these agents had a variety of names. See D. da Silva, *Atlantic Slave Trade*, 64.

Chapter 4

1. Lovejoy and Law, *Biography of Mahommah Gardo Baquaqua*, 150–53.

2. The term *tumbeiro* emerged in a seventeenth-century sermon by the Jesuit priest Antônio Vieira and soon was embraced by Brazilian and Portuguese slave traders referring to slave ships. See Charles R. Boxer, *The Golden Age of Brazil, 1695–1750* (Los Angeles: University of California Press, 2022), 5; José Gonçalves Salvador, *Os Magnatas do tráfico negreiro (séculos XVI e XVII)* (São Paulo: Editora da Universidade de São Paulo, 1981), 91; and Miller, *Way of Death*, 314.

3. But there were shorter voyages. The Rhode Island sloop *Hare* departed from Sierra Leone on January 6, 1755, and arrived in Barbados just twenty days later. See Sean M. Kelley, *A Journey into Captivity from Sierra Leone to South Carolina* (Chapel Hill: University of North Carolina Press, 2016), 110. The *Transatlantic Slave Trade Database* features the voyage, Voyage ID 36175.

4. Equiano and Carretta, *Interesting Narrative*, 55.

5. Cugoano, *Thoughts and Sentiments*, 15.

6. According to Robin Law, the port was probably Little Popo; see Law, *Ouidah*, 138.

7. Lovejoy and Law, *Biography of Mahommah Gardo Baquaqua*, 150–51.

8. Lovejoy and Law, *Biography of Mahommah Gardo Baquaqua*, 152.

9. Rediker, *Slave Ship*, 9.

10. Mouser, *A Slaving Voyage to Africa and Jamaica*, 7.

11. Rediker, *Slave Ship*, 65.

12. "Consulta ao Conselho Ultramarino (12-8-1664)," in Brasio, *Monumenta Missionaria Africana*, 7:490–91. See also Arlindo Manuel Caldeira, *Escravos e traficantes no império português: O comércio negreiro no Atlântico durante os séculos XV à XIX* (Lisbon: A Esfera dos Livros, 2013), 123–24.

13. Jaime Rodrigues, "Arquitetura naval: Imagens, textos e possibilidades de descrições dos navios negreiros," in *Tráfico, cativeiro, liberdade: Rio de Janeiro, séculos XVII–XIX*, ed. Manolo Florentino (Rio de Janeiro: Civilização Brasileira, 2005), 105.

14. Historian José Lingna Nafafé suggests that this legislation was a response to a court case presented by Black abolitionist Lourenço da Silva Mendonça before the Vatican denouncing the enslavement of Africans by the Portuguese. For a broader discussion of this case, see José Lingna Nafafé, *Lourenço* *da Silva Mendonça and the Black Atlantic Abolitionist Movement in the Seventeenth Century* (Cambridge: Cambridge University Press, 2022), 43.

15. "Regimento sobre o embarque de negros de Angola (18-3-1684)," in Brasio, *Monumenta Missionaria Africana*, 8:551–58.

16. Caldeira, *Escravos e traficantes no império português*, 125, and Smallwood, *Saltwater Slavery*, 71–72.

17. Herbert S. Klein, "The Portuguese Slave Trade from Angola in the Eighteenth Century," *Journal of Economic History* 32, no. 4 (1972): 898.

18. Kate McMahon, "The Transnational Dimensions of Africans and African Americans in Northern England, 1776–1865" (PhD diss., Howard University, 2017), 89.

19. Rediker, *Slave Ship*, 53, and Reinaldo Funes Monzote, *From Rainforest to Cane Field in Cuba: An Environmental History Since 1492* (Chapel Hill: University of North Carolina Press, 2008), 23. See also the website SlaveVoyages, https://www.slavevoyages.org/. European and American shipbuilders used a variety of light and resistant woods to construct slave vessels, including red cedar, oak, mahogany, and pine, and often relied on timber imported from the Americas.

20. In Brazil, shipbuilders employed an assortment of native woods obtained in various regions of the country such as *sucupira*, *vinhático*, *oiticica*, *tapinhoã*, *jequitibá*, *jenipapo*, *pau d'arco*, *sapucaia*, *angelim*, *maçaranduba*, and *jacaranda*; see Rodrigues, "Arquitetura naval," 87, 115n16.

21. Manolo Florentino, *Em costas negras: Uma história do tráfico de escravos entre a África e o Rio de Janeiro* (São Paulo: Companhia das Letras, 2002), 121.

22. Rediker, *Slave Ship*, 56. For other details, see David Richardson, ed., *Bristol, Africa, and the Eighteenth-Century Slave Trade to America*, vol. 3, *The Years of Decline 1746–1769* (Bristol: Bristol Record Society, 1991), 21.

23. Deveau, *La traite rochelaise*, 150–51.

24. Jaime Rodrigues, *De Costa à Costa: Escravos, marinheiros e intermediários do tráfico negreiro de Angola ao Rio de Janeiro (1780–1860)* (São Paulo: Companhia das Letras, 2005), 189–90.

25. J. Rodrigues, *De costa à costa*, 186–87.

26. Florentino, *Em costas negras*, 152.

27. See Mariana P. Candido, "Different Slave Journeys: Enslaved African Seamen on Board of Portuguese Ships, c. 1760–1820s," *Slavery and Abolition* 31, no. 3 (2010): 398, and Ferreira, *Cross-Cultural Exchange*, 135–37.

28. Candido, "Different Slave Journeys," 402.

29. Walter Hawthorne, "Gorje: An African Seaman and His Flights from 'Freedom' Back to 'Slavery' in the Early Nineteenth Century," *Slavery and Abolition* 31, no. 3 (2010): 411–28. The name was misspelled as Gorje, but the name in Portuguese is Jorge.

30. Their owner had probably rented them to work aboard the slave ship. See Beatriz Gallotti Mamigonian, "José Majojo e Francisco Moçambique, marinheiros das rotas atlânticas: Notas sobre a reconstituição de trajetórias da era da abolição," *Topoi* 11, no. 20 (2010): 79. On this voyage, see *Transatlantic Slave Trade Database: Voyages*, Voyage ID 2105.

31. Mary Hicks, "The Sea and the Shackle: African and Creole Mariners and the Making of a Luso-African Atlantic Commercial Culture, 1721–1835" (PhD diss., University of Virginia, 2015), 117. See also Mary E. Hicks, "Transatlantic Threads of Meaning: West African Textile Entrepreneurship in Salvador da Bahia, 1770–1870," *Slavery and Abolition* 41, no. 4, (2020): 701.

32. See *Idade d'ouro do Brazil*, April 19, 1816, 4; *Idade d'ouro do Brazil*, March 25, 1817, 4; *Idade d'ouro do Brazil*, February 24, 1821, 4; *Idade d'ouro do Brazil*, September 23, 1817, 4.

33. *Diário do Rio de Janeiro*, September 16, 1825, 1.

34. Emma Christopher, *Slave Ship Sailors and Their Captive Cargoes, 1730–1807* (New York: Cambridge University Press, 2006), 57–58.

35. See Lisa Earl Castillo, "O terreiro do Gantois: Redes sociais e etnografia histórica no século XIX," *Revista de História*, no. 176 (2017): 24.

36. Pierre Verger, *Os libertos: Sete caminhos da liberdade* (Salvador, Brazil: Corrupio: 1992), 9–10. On Oliveira, see also Daniele Santos de Souza, "De escravo a cabeceira: A Trajetória do africano João de Oliveira no mundo atlântico setecentista." *Revista da ABPN (Associação Brasileira de Pesquisadores Negros)* 12 (2020): 113–39.

37. Christopher, *Slave Ship Sailors*, 52.

38. See Jean Mettas, *Répertoire des expéditions négrières françaises au XVIIIe siècle*, vol. 2, *Ports autres que Nante*s (Paris: Société française d'histoire d'outre-mer, 1984), 579, and Jessica Marie Johnson, *Wicked* Flesh, 77. On this voyage, see also *Transatlantic Slave Trade Database*, Voyage ID 32905.

39. See Brice Marinetti, *Les négociants de La Rochelle au XVIIIe siècle* (Paris: Presses universitaires de Rennes, 2013), 75.

40. Kelley, *American Slavers*, 284–85.

41. On Florinda Joanes Gaspar, see Mariana P. Candido, "Women, Family, and Landed Property in Nineteenth-Century Benguela," *African Economic History* 43 (2015): 136–61.

42. The four ships were *Boa União*, *Felina*, *Nazareth*, and *Minerva*. See V. Oliveira, *Slave Trade and Abolition*, 34. However, only the ship *Boa União* appears in the *Transatlantic Slave Trade Database* as belonging to Ana Joaquina dos Santos Silva; see Voyage ID 47030.

43. See entries of Monday, October 8; Friday, November 30; and Monday, December 3, 1750, in Newton, Martin, and Spurrell, *Journal of a Slave Trader*, 10, 20, 21; and Rediker, *Slave Ship*, 59.

44. Cândido Eugênio Domingues de Souza, "'Perseguidores da espécie humana': Capitães negreiros da Cidade da Bahia a primeira metade do século XVIII" (MA thesis, Universidade Federal da Bahia, 2011), 141.

45. See Rediker, *Slave Ship*, 390n18.

46. Lieutenant Durand, "Journal de bord d'un négrier, 1731–1732," BLY, Gen Mss, vol. 7, 66. See also Harms, *Diligent*, 263.

47. See Florentino, *Em costas negras*,153; Ferreira, *Cross-Cultural Exchange*, 25; and C. de Souza, "'Perseguidores da espécie humana,'" 161.

48. Verger, *Flux et reflux de la traite des nègres*, 476–78.

49. Rediker, *Slave Ship*, 137.

50. Christopher, *Slave Ship Sailors*, 37, 39.

51. See Newton, Martin, and Spurrell, *Journal of a Slave Trader*, ix–x.

52. Deveau, *La traite rochelaise*, 111–12.

53. See, for example, the case of Jean-Amable Lessenne in Araujo, *Gift*, 49.

54. Rediker, *Slave Ship*, 59.

55. See Bailey, *African Voices of the Slave Trade*, 133.

56. Oettinger, Koslofsky, and Zaugg, *German Barber-Surgeon in the Atlantic Slave Trade*, 39.

57. Oettinger, Koslofsky, and Zaugg, *German Barber-Surgeon in the Atlantic Slave Trade*, xviii–xx.

58. Here I refer to hundreds of crew lists (*rôles d'équipage*) from La Rochelle and Nantes, in Archives de la Marine, Rochefort, France (hereafter cited as AMR) and Archives départementales de la Loire Atlantique, Nantes, France (hereafter cited as ADLA).

59. J. Rodrigues, *De costa à costa*, 272–77; Castillo, "O terreiro do Gantois," 19.

60. Robinson, *A Sailor Boy's Experience*, 54.

61. Rediker, *Slave Ship*, 68; Smallwood, *Saltwater Slavery*, 73–74.

62. Cugoano, *Thoughts and Sentiments*, 15.

63. See entry of Wednesday, December 5, 1750, in Newton, Martin, and Spurrell, *Journal of a Slave Trader*, 21.

64. Jessica Carney and Richard Nicholas Rosomoff, *In the Shadow of Slavery: Africa's Botanical Legacy in the Atlantic World* (Berkeley: University of California Press, 2010), 73.

65. On São Tomé and Príncipe as an island where slave ships stopped to fetch provisions, see Oettinger, Koslofsky, and Zaugg, *German Barber-Surgeon in the Atlantic Slave Trade*, 48. See also Yacou, *Journaux de bord et de traite de Joseph Crassous de Médeuil*, 173. See also Arlindo Caldeira, "Learning the Ropes in the Tropics: Slavery and the Plantation System on the Island of São Tomé," *African Economic History* 39 (2011): 35–71.

66. Oettinger, Koslofsky, and Zaugg, *German Barber-Surgeon in the Atlantic Slave Trade*, 50.

67. Smallwood, *Saltwater Slavery*, 136.

68. Smallwood, *Saltwater Slavery*, 33.

69. Christopher, *Slave Ship Sailors*, 29–32.

70. Robinson, *Sailor Boy's Experience*, 52–53.

71. Jessica Marie Johnson, *Wicked Flesh*, 92–94.

72. See entry of Sunday, May 26, 1751, in Newton, Martin, and Spurrell, *Journal of a Slave Trader*, 54–55.

73. Entry of Monday, December, 11, 1752, in Newton, Martin, and Spurrell, *Journal of a Slave Trader*, 71.

74. Kelley, *Journey into Captivity from Sierra Leone to South Carolina*, 49.

75. On the tragic Atlantic crossing of the *Sally*, see Center for Digital Scholarship, Brown University Library, *Voyage of the Slave Ship Sally, 1764–1765*, https://cds.library.brown.edu/projects/sally/.

76. On the slave trade in Rhode Island and the Browns' involvement in the trade, see Christy Clark-Pujara, *Dark Work: The Business of Slavery in Rhode Island* (New York: New York University Press, 2016), 23.

77. Eltis and Richardson, *Atlas of the Transatlantic Slave Trade*, 161.

78. James Walvin, *The Zong: A Massacre, the Law & the End of Slavery* (New Haven, CT: Yale University Press, 2011), 97–98.

79. Oettinger, Koslofsky, and Zaugg, *German Barber-Surgeon in the Atlantic Slave Trade*, 44.

80. Marcus Rediker, "History from Below the Water Line: Sharks and the Atlantic Slave Trade," *Atlantic Studies* 5, no. 2 (2008): 286.

81. "Auto de inquirição a Gonçalo Roiz (11-12-1511–15-1-1512)," in Brasio, *Monumenta Missionaria Africana*, 1:215–21.

82. See David Richardson, ed. *Bristol, Africa and the Eighteenth-Century Slave Trade to America*, vol. 4, *The Final Years, 1770–1807* (Bristol: Bristol Record Society, 1996), 193. One report suggests that 299 enslaved Africans were embarked at New Calabar, whereas another report refers to 304 African captives. The *Transatlantic Slave Trade Database* that features the voyage (Voyage ID 18161) indicates that 321 enslaved Africans boarded the ship, and 105 perished during the Middle Passage.

83. *The Trial of Captain John Kimber, for the Murder of Two Female Negro Slaves on Board the Recovery, African Slave Ship: Tried at the Admiralty Sessions, held at the Old Baily, the 7th of June, 1792* (London: C. Stalker, 1792), 4.

84. *Trial of Captain John Kimber*, 20–21.

85. Saidiya Hartman masterfully tells this tragic story in her acclaimed *Lose Your Mother: A Journey along the Atlantic Slave Route* (New York: Farrar, Straus and Giroux, 2008), 137–53. Later she explored the case of Venus, the second girl murdered by Kimber; see Saidiya Hartman, "Venus in Two Acts," *Small Axe* 12, no. 2 (2008): 1–14.

86. Sowande Mustakeem, *Slavery at Sea: Terror, Sex, and Sickness in the Middle Passage* (Urbana: University of Illinois Press, 2016), 146.

87. Srivdhya Swaminathan, "Reporting Atrocities: A Comparison of the *Zong* ang the Trial of Captain John Kimber," *Slavery and Abolition* 31, no. 4 (2010): 487–88.

88. On the illegal slave trade and Brazil's resistance to abolishing the trade in enslaved Africans, see Sidney Chalhoub, *A força da escravidão: Ilegalidade e costume no Brasil oitocentista* (São Paulo: Companhia das Letras, 2012).

89. Marcus J. M. de Carvalho, "O patacho Providência, um navio negreiro: Política, justiça e redes depois da lei antitráfico de 1831," *Varia História* 30, no. 54 (2014): 794.
90. J. Rodrigues, "Arquitetura naval," 191.
91. See the website SlaveVoyages, https://slavevoyages.org/, Voyage ID 4315.

Chapter 5

1. See Grandpré, *Voyage à la côte occidentale d'Afrique*, 1:141–53, and Araujo, *Gift*, 99–101.
2. Lovejoy and Law, *Biography of Mahommah Gardo Baquaqua*, 117.
3. For example, see multiple entries of the logbook of British ship captain Samuel Gamble in Mouser, *Slaving Voyage to Africa and Jamaica*, 104–11.
4. Miller, *Way of Death*, 391. On burial conditions in Benguela, see also Candido, *African Slaving Port*, 119, and Kalle Kananoja, *Healing Knowledge in Atlantic Africa: Medical Encounters, 1500–1850* (New York: Cambridge University Press, 2021), 209–10.
5. Miller, *Way of Death*, 391.
6. A "bar" was the currency used to trade in the region, corresponding to the value of an iron bar. Mouser, *Slaving Voyage to Africa and Jamaica*, 56.
7. Mouser, *Slaving Voyage to Africa and Jamaica*, 69.
8. Hugh Crow and John R. Pinfold, *The Memoirs of Captain Hugh Crow: The Life and Times of a Slave Trade Captain* (Oxford: Bodleian Library, 2007), 166.
9. See Alexander Falconbridge, *An Account of the Slave Trade on the Coast of Africa* (London: James Phillips, 1788), 52. See also Rediker, *Slave Ship*, 38.
10. See this expression "buried at sea" in Oettinger, Koslofsky, and Zaugg, *German Barber-Surgeon in the Atlantic Slave Trade*, 45. See also Mouser, *Slaving Voyage to Africa and Jamaica*, 104–11.
11. See, for example, Archives Municipales de La Rochelle (hereafter cited as AMLR), EEARCHANC 48, "Navire Le Roy Dahomet, Journal de navigation, 1772–1774," entries of July 15 to July 16, and July 16 to July 17, 1773. On throwing the dead bodies of enslaved Africans into the sea during the night, see Harms, *Diligent*, 274.
12. Crow and Pinfold, *Memoirs of Captain Hugh Crow*, 152–53.
13. Ludewig Ferdinand Rømer, *A Reliable Account of the Coast of Guinea (1760)* (New York: Diasporic Africa Press, 2013), 183.
14. Rømer, *Reliable Account of the Coast of Guinea*, 184.
15. "Relação da Batalha de Ambuíla (29-10-1665)," in Brasio, *Monumenta Missionaria Africana*, 12:588; See also Antonio de Oliveira Cadornega, *Historia geral das guerras angolanas*, vol. 2 (Lisbon: Typographia da Companhia Nacional Editora, 1902), 136–37. See also Luiz Felipe de Alencastro, "História geral das guerras sul-atlânticas: O episódio de Palmares," in *Mocambos de*

Palmares: História, historiografia e fontes, ed. Flávio Gomes (Rio de Janeiro: 7Letras editora/FAPERJ, 2010), 61–99.

16. Araujo, "Dahomey, Portugal, and Bahia," 5.

17. On the Rio de Janeiro context, see Mary C. Karasch, *Slave Life in Rio de Janeiro, 1808–1850* (Princeton, NJ: Princeton University Press, 1987), 92–93. See also Mariza de Carvalho Soares, *People of Faith: Slavery and African Catholics in Eighteenth-Century Rio de Janeiro* (Durham, NC: Duke University Press, 2011), 133. On Benguela and Luanda, see Miller, *Way of Death*, 391.

18. Maria João Neves, Miguel Almeida, and Maria Teresa Ferreira, "O caso do 'Poço dos Negros' (Lagos)," *Antrope* 2 (2015): 141–60.

19. Maria João Neves, Miguel Almeida, and Maria Teresa Ferreira, "Separados na vida e na morte," *Actas do 7º Encontro de Arqueologia do Algarve, Silves, 22, 23, e 24 de outubro de 2009*, 549.

20. Arlindo Manuel Caldeira, *Escravos em Portugal: Das origens ao século XIX* (Lisbon: A Esfera dos Livros, 2017), 382–83.

21. Arquivo Municipal de Lisboa (hereafter cited as AML), Arquivo Histórico, Provimento da Saúde, Livro 1º do provimento da saúde, "D. Manuel I ordena à camara de Lisboa a abertura de um grande poço," November 13, 1515, f1, PT/AMLSB/CMLSB/ADMG-E/02/1425.

22. Caldeira, *Escravos em Portugal*, 380–81.

23. See, for example, Isabel Castro Henriques, *Os africanos em Portugal: História e memória, séculos XV–XXI* (Lisbon: Comité Português do Projeto UNESCO "A Rota do Escravo," 2011), 17, and Alastair Corston de Custance Maxwell Saunders, *A Social History of Black Slaves and Freedmen in Portugal* (London: Cambridge University Press, 1982), 110.

24. On Portugal, see Saunders, *Social History of Black Slaves*, 110. In Cádiz, Spain, see Arturo Morgado García, "El ciclo vital de los esclavos em el Cádiz de la modernidad," *Revista de historia moderna: Anales de la Universidad de Alicante*, no. 34 (2016): 313.

25. Matt D. Childs, *The 1812 Aponte Rebellion in Cuba and the Struggle against Atlantic Slavery* (Chapel Hill: University of North Carolina Press, 2006), 52.

26. See Pablo F. Gómez, *The Experimental Caribbean: Creating Knowledge and Healing in the Early Modern Atlantic* (Chapel Hill: University of North Carolina Press, 2017), 32, and Vincent Brown, *The Reaper's Garden: Death and Power in the World of Atlantic Slavery* (Cambridge, MA: Harvard University Press, 2008), 70–71.

27. Genovese, *Roll, Jordan, Roll*, 195–201.

28. David R. Watters, "Mortuary Patterns at the Harney Site Slave Cemetery, Montserrat, in Caribbean Perspective," *Historical Archaeology* 28, no. 3 (1994): 66, and Patrice Courtaud, "Le cimetière, comme miroir de l'esclavage: Approche méthodologique; Le cimetière d'Anse Sainte-Marguerite (Guadeloupe)," *In Situ* 20 (2013): 11.

29. Jerome S. Handler, "An African-Type Healer/Diviner and His Grave Goods: A Burial from a Plantation Cemetery in Barbados, West Indies," *International Journal of Historical Archaeology* 1, no. 2 (1997): 91–130.

30. Maria Graham, *Journal of a Voyage to Brazil and Residence There, During Part of the Years 1821, 1822, and 1823* (London: Longman, Hurst, Rees, Orme, Brown, and Green, 1824), 137.

31. See, for example, Luis Nicolau Parés, "Milicianos, barbeiros e traficantes numa irmandade católica de africanos minas e jejes (Bahia, 1770–1830)," *Revista Tempo* 20 (2014): 19.

32. João José Reis, *Death Is a Festival: Funeral Rites and Rebellion in Nineteenth-Century Brazil* (Chapel Hill: University of North Carolina Press, 2003), 185.

33. Lovejoy, "Speculations on the African Origins of Venture Smith," 344–45.

34. Smith, *Narrative of the Life and Adventures of Venture Smith*, 13.

35. Equiano and Carretta, *Interesting Narrative*, 60.

36. This case is discussed in Manuel Barcia, "White Cannibalism in the Illegal Slave Trade: The Peculiar Case of the Portuguese Schooner Arrogante in 1837," *New West Indian Guide* (2021): 1–28.

37. M. Graham, *Journal of a Voyage to Brazil*, 111.

38. M. Graham, *Journal of a Voyage to Brazil*, 111.

39. M. Graham, *Journal of a Voyage to Brazil*, 128.

40. M. Soares, *People of Faith*, 125.

41. M. Soares, *People of Faith*, 125–26.

42. See Maurício Almeida Abreu, *A evolução urbana do Rio de Janeiro* (Rio de Janeiro: Zahar, 1987). See also Júlio César Medeiros da Silva, *À flor da terra: O cemitério dos pretos novos no Rio de Janeiro* (Rio de Janeiro: Garamond, 2007), 32.

43. Henry Chamberlain and Rubens Borba de Moraes, *Vistas e costumes da cidade e arredores do Rio de Janeiro em 1819–1820* (Rio de Janeiro: Livraria Kosmos Editora and Erich Eichner, 1943), 233; for the watercolor, see plate on page 183.

44. Robert Walsh, *Notices of Brazil in 1828 and 1829*, 2 vols. (London: Frederick Westley and A. H. Davis, 1830), 1:395.

45. Joseph François Xavier Sigaud, "Discurso sobre a Statistica Médica no Brasil," in *Relatorio dos trabalhos da Sociedade de Medicina do Rio de Janeiro* [. . .], ed. Luiz Vicente de Simoni (Rio de Janeiro: Seygnot-Plancher, 1832), 13.

46. Luciana Mendes Gandelman, "A Santa Casa da Misericórdia do Rio de Janeiro nos séculos XVI a XIX," *História, ciência, saúde Manguinhos* 8, no. 3 (2001): 619. See also J. da Silva, *À flor da terra*, 37.

47. See J. Rodrigues, *De costa a costa*, 298–99, and Cláudio de Paula Honorato, "O mercado do Valongo e comércio de escravos africanos—RJ (1758–1831)," in *Escravidão africana no Recôncavo da Guanabara*, ed. Mariza de Carvalho Soares and Nielson Rosa Bezerra (Niterói, Brazil: Editora da Universidade Federal Fluminense, 2011), 68–69.

48. These are general estimates for enslaved Africans disembarked in the city of Rio de Janeiro. See the website SlaveVoyages, https://www.slavevoyages.org/.

49. For more on the Valongo Wharf memorialization, see Ana Lucia Araujo, "Sites of Disembarkation and the Public Memory of the Atlantic Slave Trade," in *A Stain on Our Pasts: Slavery and Memory*, ed. Abdoulaye Gueye and Johann Michel (Trenton, NJ: Africa World Press, 2018), 137–69, and Andre Cicalo, "From Public Amnesia to Public Memory: Rediscovering Slavery Heritage in Rio de Janeiro," in *African Heritage and Memories of Slavery in Brazil and the South Atlantic World*, ed. Ana Lucia Araujo (Amherst, NY: Cambria Press, 2015), 171–202.

50. J. Rodrigues, *De costa a costa*, 286.

51. Arquivo Histórico Ultramarino, Lisbon, Portugal (hereafter cited as AHU), Conselho Ultramarino, Rio de Janeiro, Caixa 12, D. 1391.

52. Georg Wilhelm Freyreiss, *Reisen in Brasilien* (Stockholm: Carl Svanberg, 1968), 96.

53. Florentino, *Em costas negras*, 148.

54. J. da Silva, *À flor da terra*, 81–87.

55. On these complaints, see Karasch, *Slave Life in Rio de Janeiro*, 38–39.

56. V. Brown, *Reaper's Garden*, 244.

57. Genovese, *Roll, Jordan, Roll*, 194.

58. Michael L. Blakey, "The New York African Burial Ground Project: An Examination of Enslaved Lives, A Construction of Ancestral Ties," *Transforming Anthropology* 7, no. 1 (1998): 53, https://doi.org/10.1525/tran.1998.7.1.53.

59. Erik R. Seeman, *Across the Waters: Cross-Cultural Encounters, 1492–1800*. Philadelphia: University of Pennsylvania Press, 2010, 207. For the detailed description and analysis of the remains, see Michael L. Blakey and Lesley M. Rankin-Hill, *The Skeletal Biology of the New York African Burial Ground* (Washington, DC: Howard University Press, 2009); Warren R. Perry, Jean Howson, and Barbara A. Bianco, *The Archaeology of the New York African Burial Ground* (Washington, DC: Howard University Press, 2009); and Edna G. Medford, *Historical Perspectives of the African Burial Ground: New York Blacks and the Diaspora* (Washington, DC: Howard University Press, 2009).

60. I have used the #slaveryarchive hashtag on social media to feature this kind of news. A quick search on Google using the terms in English "slave burial ground" and its variations will show recent news on slave burial grounds found around the United States. Yet, similar sites have been recovered in other countries in the Caribbean and South America.

61. Rachel E. Fleskes et al., "Ancestry, Health, and Lived Experiences of Enslaved Africans in 18th-Century Charleston: An Osteobiographical Analysis," *American Journal of Physical Anthropology* 175, no. 1 (2021): 3– 24.

Chapter 6

1. Zurara, "Partilha das presas em Lagos," 19.
2. Equiano and Carretta, *Interesting Narrative*, 60.
3. Equiano and Carretta, *Interesting Narrative*, 60.
4. Trevor Burnard, "Kingston, Jamaica: Crucible of Modernity," in *The Black Urban Atlantic in the Age of the Slave Trade*, ed. Jorge Cañizares-Esguerra, Matt D. Childs, and James Sidbury (Philadelphia: University of Pennsylvania Press, 2013), 131.
5. Equiano and Carretta, *Interesting Narrative*, 60–61.
6. Equiano and Carretta, *Interesting Narrative*, 61.
7. Hurston, *Barracoon*, 56.
8. Jane Landers, "The African Landscape of Seventeenth-Century Cartagena and Its Hinterlands," in Cañizares-Esguerra, Childs, and Sidbury, *Black Urban Atlantic in the Age of the Slave Trade*, 149.
9. Landers, "African Landscape of Seventeenth-Century Cartagena," 149.
10. Alonso de Sandoval and Nicole Von Germeten, *Treatise on Slavery: Selections from "De Instauranda Aethiopum Salute"* (Indianapolis: Hackett, 2008), 58.
11. Ildefonso Gutiérrez Azopardo, "El comercio y mercado de negros esclavos en Cartagena de Indias," *Quinto Centenario* 12 (1987): 199–202.
12. See Burnard, "Kingston, Jamaica," 126–27, 130–31.
13. See Christina Walker, *Jamaica Ladies: Female Slaveholders and the Creation of Britain's Atlantic Empire* (Chapel Hill: University of North Carolina Press, 2020), 98–99.
14. Thomas Lindley, *Narrative of a Voyage to Brazil: Terminating in the Seizure of a British Vessel; with General Sketches of the Country, its Natural Productions, Colonial Inhabitants* (London: J. Johnson, 1805), 176.
15. Lindley, *Narrative of a Voyage to Brazil*, 176–77.
16. M. Graham, *Journal of a Voyage to Brazil*, 155.
17. See M. Graham, *Journal of a Voyage to Brazil*, 137.
18. M. Graham, *Journal of a Voyage to Brazil*, 105.
19. Amédée-François Frézier, *Relation du voyage de la mer du Sud aux côtes du Chili et du Pérou fait pendant les années 1712, 1713, et 1714*, vol. 2, (Paris: J-G. Nyon, E. Ganeau, J. Quillau, 1716), 533.
20. Mary Prince, *The History of Mary Prince* (New York: Penguin Books, 2004), 11.
21. Harriet Jacobs, *Incidents in the Life of a Slave Girl* (New York: Barnes and Noble Classics, 2005), 22.
22. For examples, see Walter Johnson, *Soul by Soul: Life Inside the Antebellum Slave Market* (Cambridge, MA: Harvard University Press, 1999), 41–42.
23. Weeks before this book went into production, graduate student Lauren Davila uncovered a larger auction of 770 enslaved people in Charleston, South Carolina, in February 1835.

24. The sale was believed to be the largest known slave auction in the United States, but in 2023, College of Charleston MA candidate Lauren Davila uncovered an auction of six hundred enslaved individuals that took place in Charleston on February 24, 1835. See Jennifer Berry Hawes, "How a Graduate Student Uncovered the Largest Known Slave Auction in the U.S.," ProPublica, June 16, 2023, https://www.propublica.org/article/how-grad-student-discovered-largest-us-slave-auction.

25. Anne C. Bailey, *The Weeping Time: Memory and the Largest Slave Auction in the American History* (New York: Cambridge University Press, 2017), 132–52.

26. For example, see the case of the descendants of the 272 men, women, and children sold by the Jesuits to save Georgetown University in 1838, in Rachel L. Swarns, *The 272: The Families Who Were Enslaved and Sold to Build the American Catholic Church* (New York: Random House, 2023).

27. David Wheat, *Atlantic Africa and the Spanish Caribbean: 1570–1640* (Chapel Hill: University of North Carolina Press, 2016), 29.

28. For an overview of slave sales in Cartagena, see Azopardo, "El comercio y mercado de negros esclavos," 187–210.

29. Azopardo, "El comercio y mercado de negros esclavos," 188–89.

30. David Geggus, "The Slaves and Free People of Color of Cap Français," in Cañizares-Esguerra, Childs, and Sidbury, *Black Urban Atlantic in the Age of the Slave Trade*, 112.

31. Walsh, *Notices of Brazil in 1828 and 1829*, 2:323.

32. Auguste de Saint-Hilaire, *Voyage dans les provinces de Saint-Paul et de Sainte-Catherine*, vol. 1, (Paris: Arthus Bertrand, 1851), 192; Marco Antonio da Silva Mello et al., "Os ciganos do Catumbi: De 'andores do Rei' e comerciantes de escravos a oficiais de justiça na cidade do Rio de Janeiro," *Cidades, Comunidades e Territórios*, no. 18 (2009): 80.

33. See Jean-Baptiste Debret, *Voyage pittoresque et historique au Brésil*, 3 vols. (Paris: Firmi-Didot Frères, 1834–39), 2:78–79, plate 24. On Roma in Rio de Janeiro, see Karasch, *Slave Life in Rio de Janeiro*, 54.

34. Walsh, *Notices of Brazil in 1828 and 1829*, 2:323.

35. Walsh, *Notices of Brazil in 1828 and 1829*, 2:325.

36. Debret, *Voyage pittoresque et historique au Brésil*, 2 :78, plate 23.

37. Debret, *Voyage pittoresque et historique au Brésil*, 2 :78, plate 23.

38. Maurice Rugendas, *Voyage pittoresque dans le Brésil* (Paris: Engelmann, 1835), 4e division, 1er cahier, 4e livraison, 7. Rugendas's account was likely authored by his friend and scholar Victor-Aimé Huber, who relied on Rugendas's observations.

39. Rugendas, *Voyage dans le Brésil*, 4e division, 1er cahier, 4e livraison, 7.

40. M. Graham, *Journal of a Voyage to Brazil*, 170.

41. On these "nations" in Brazil, see Maria Inês Cortês Oliveira, "La Grande tente Nagô: Rapprochements ethniques chez les Africains de Bahia au XIXe siècle," in *Identifying Enslaved Africans: The "Nigerian" Hinterland and the*

African Diaspora, ed. Paul E. Lovejoy (Toronto: York University, 1997), 286, and J. Lorand Matory, *Black Atlantic Religion: Tradition, Transnationalism and Matriarchy in the Afro-Brazilian Candomblé* (Princeton, NJ: Princeton University Press, 2005), 5–6. On African ethnicities in the Americas, see Gwendolyn Midlo Hall, "African Ethnicities and the Meanings of 'Mina,'" in *Trans-Atlantic Dimensions of Ethnicity in the African Diaspora*, ed. Paul E. Lovejoy and David R. Trotman (London, New York: Continuum, 2003), 65–81, and Robin Law, "Ethnicities of Enslaved Africans in the Diaspora: On the Meanings of 'Mina' (Again)," *History in Africa* 32 (2005): 247–67.

42. See André João Antonil, *Cultura e opulência do Brasil por suas Drogas e minas* (Lisbon: Na Officina Real Deslandesiana, 1711). I use here the nineteenth-century edition, André João Antonil, *Cultura e opulência do Brasil por suas drogas e minas* (Rio de Janeiro: Typ. Imp. E Const. De J. Villeneuve., 1837), 31. On Ardra and Mina ethnicities in the Atlantic slave trade to Bahia, see Carlos da Silva Jr., "Ardras, minas e jejes, ou escravos de 'primeira reputação': Políticas africanas, tráfico negreiro e identidade étnica na Bahia do século XVIII," *Almanack*, no. 12 (2016): 11. On the Congo "nation" and its various meanings to Brazilians, English, Portuguese, and other Europeans, see Joseph C. Miller, "Central Africa during the Era of the Slave Trade, c. 1490s–1850s," in *Central Africans and Cultural Transformations in the American Diaspora*, edited by Linda M. Heywood (New York: Cambridge University Press, 2002), 21–69.

43. Jean-Baptiste Alban Imbert, *Manual do fazendeiro, ou tratado doméstico sobre as enfermidades dos negros, generalisado às necessidades medicas de todas as classes* (Rio de Janeiro: Typographia Nacional, 1839), 2–3.

44. Gomez, *Exchanging Our Country Marks*, 115.

45. Malachy Postlethwayt, *The Universal Dictionary of Trade and Commerce*, vol. 1 (London, 1774), s.v. "Angola."

46. See Darold D. Wax, "Preferences for Slaves in Colonial America," *Journal of Negro History* 58, no. 4 (1973): 371–401.

47. W. Johnson, *Soul by Soul*, 113–14.

48. W. Johnson, *Soul by Soul*, 119.

49. Edward E. Baptist, *The Half Has Never Been Told: Slavery in the Making of American Capitalism* (New York: Basic Books, 2014).

50. David Eltis, Frank D. Lewis, and David Richardson, "Slave Prices, the African Slave Trade, and Productivity in the Caribbean, 1674–1807," *Economic History Review* 58, no. 4 (2005): 677.

51. Eltis, Lewis, and Richardson, "Slave Prices," 677.

52. Azopardo, "El comercio y mercado de negros esclavos," 202.

53. David Eltis and David Richardson, "Prices of African Slaves Newly Arrived in the Americas, 1673–1865: New Evidence on Long-Run Trends and Regional Differentials," in *Slavery in the Development of the Americas*, ed. David Eltis, Frank D. Lewis, and Kenneth L. Sokoloff (Cambridge: Cambridge University Press, 2004), 200.

54. Azopardo, "El comercio y mercado de negros esclavos," 204.
55. Mattoso, *Être esclave au Brésil XVIe-XIXe siècles*, 81–82.
56. Gregory E. O'Malley, "Slavery's Converging Ground: Charleston's Slave Trade as the Black Heart of the Lowcountry," *William and Mary Quarterly* 74, no. 2 (2017): 271–302.
57. The voyage appears in the *Transatlantic Slave Trade Database*, Voyage ID 26031.
58. "Advertisement for Sale of Newly Arrived Africans, Charleston, July 24, 1769," Slavery Images: A Visual Record of the African Slave Trade and Slave Life in the Early African Diaspora, http://slaveryimages.org/s/slaveryimages/item/1971.
59. Archives of Maryland Online, *Maryland Gazette*, *Maryland Gazette* Collection, MSA SC 2731, M 1281, December 26, 1770, 489, image no. 1213.
60. *Diário do Rio de Janeiro*, December 16, 1826, 50.
61. Alcide Marie Dessalines d'Orbigny, *Voyage pittoresque dans les deux Amériques* (Paris: Furne et Cie, 1841), 25.
62. See W. Johnson, *Soul by Soul*, 89. On white women at slave markets, see Stephanie E. Jones-Rogers, *They Were Her Property: White Women as Slave Owners in the American South* (New Haven, CT: Yale University Press, 2019).
63. See Jones-Rogers, *They Were Her Property*, 123–49.
64. Eltis and Richardson, "Prices of African Slaves," 192.
65. W. Johnson, *Soul by Soul*, 6.
66. See Baptist, *Half Has Never Been Told*, 173–74. See also W. Johnson, *Soul by Soul*, 26. For a detailed discussion about the monetary value of enslaved persons in the United States during the nineteenth century, see Daina Ramey Berry, *The Price for Their Pound of Flesh: The Value of the Enslaved, from Womb to Grave, in the Building of a Nation* (Boston: Beacon Press, 2017).
67. W. Johnson, *Soul by Soul*, 141–45.
68. Manuel Moreno Fraginals, Herbert S. Klein, and Stanley L. Engerman, "The Level of Slave Prices on Cuban Plantations in the Mid-Nineteenth Century: Some Comparative Perspectives," *American Historical Review* 88, no. 5 (1983): 1207. Also on slave prices in Cuba in the mid-nineteenth century, see Laird W. Bergad, "Slave Prices in Cuba, 1840–1875," *Hispanic American Historical Review* 67, no. 4 (1987): 631–55.
69. For an overview of the evolution of prices of enslaved people in Bahia, Brazil, see Mattoso, *Être esclave au Brésil XVIe–XIXe siècles*, 100–110.
70. Brazilian currency in the nineteenth century was the *real* (plural *réis*), and this amount was shown as 1:758$118 *réis* in Portuguese. Superunits were *mil réis* (1000 réis) and the *conto de réis* (1,000,000). On these data, see Renato Leite Marcondes and José Flávio Motta, "Duas fontes documentais para o estudo dos preços dos escravos no Vale do Paraíba paulista," *Revista Brasileira de História* 21, no. 42 (2001): 503.

Chapter 7

1. Antonil, *Cultura e opulência do Brasil por suas Drogas e minas*, 31.
2. Solomon Northup and David Wilson, *Twelve Years a Slave; Narrative of Solomon Northup* [. . .] (Albany: Derby and Miller, 1853), 179.
3. Northup and Wilson, *Twelve Years A Slave*, 166.
4. See Joseph E. Inikori, "Atlantic Slavery and the Rise of the Capitalist Global Economy," *Current Anthropology* 61, no 22 (2020): S159–S171.
5. I refer here to the classic work by classical scholar Moses I. Finley; see Finley, *Ancient Slavery and Modern Ideology*.
6. For studies expanding the notion of slave society, see Lenski and Cameron, *What Is a Slave Society?*
7. There is a large body of literature on the extermination and the enslavement of Indigenous populations in the Americas. See, for example Russell Thornton, *American Indian Holocaust and Survival: A Population History since 1492* (Norman: University of Oklahoma Press, 1987); David E. Stannard, *American Holocaust: The Conquest of the New World* (New York: Oxford University Press, 1992); W. George Lovell, "Heavy Shadows and Black Night: Disease and Depopulation in Colonial Spanish America," *Annals of the Association of American Geographers* 82, no. 3 (1992): 426–43; and Ward Churchill, *A Little Matter of Genocide: Holocaust and Denial in the Americas, 1492 to the Present* (San Francisco: City Lights Books, 1997). On how forced labor regimes provoked mortality among Indigenous populations of Peru, see Ward Stavig, "Continuing the Bleeding of These Pueblos Will Shortly Make Them Cadavers: The Potosi *Mita*, Cultural Identity, and Communal Survival in Colonial Peru," *Americas* 56, no. 4 (April 2000): 529–62.
8. See Matthew Restall, "Black Conquistadors: Armed Africans in Early Spanish America," *Americas* 57, no. 2 (2000): 171–205, and Wheat, *Atlantic Africa and the Spanish Caribbean*, 7.
9. Restall, "Black Conquistadors," 177.
10. On *encomienda*, see Kris Lane, "The Transition from Encomienda to Slavery in Seventeenth-Century Barbacoas (Colombia)," *Slavery & Abolition* 21, no. 1 (2000): 73–95. On *repartimiento* (*mita*), see Jeffrey A. Cole, *The Potosí Mita, 1573–1700: Compulsory Indian Labor in the Andes* (Stanford, CA: Stanford University Press, 1985); and Stavig, "Continuing the Bleeding of These Pueblos"; and Toby Green, "Baculamento or Encomienda? Legal Pluralisms and the Contestation of Power in the Pan-Atlantic World of the Sixteenth and Seventeenth Centuries," *Journal of Global Slavery* (2017): 310–36.
11. H. Klein and Vinson, *African Slavery in Latin America*, 29.
12. See the website SlaveVoyages, http://www.slavevoyages.org.
13. On the early sugar industry in Hispaniola, see Genaro Rodríguez Morel, "The Sugar Economy of Española in the Sixteenth Century," in *Tropical*

Babylons: Sugar and the Making of the Atlantic World, 1450–1680, ed. Stuart B. Schwartz (Chapel Hill: University of North Carolina Press, 2004), 85–114.

14. Philippe Hroděj, "Les esclaves à Saint-Domingue aux temps pionniers (1630–1700): La rafle, la traite et l'interlope," in *L'esclave et les plantations: De l'établissement de la servitude à son abolition*, ed. Philippe Hroděj (Rennes, Fr.: Presses Universitaires de Rennes, 2009), 62–63.

15. Stuart B. Schwartz, *Sugar Plantations in the Formation of Brazilian Society: Bahia, 1550–1835* (New York: Cambridge University Press, 1985), 16. Although Schwartz's book focuses on Bahia, his description and analysis of sugar production is applicable to other Brazilian regions and remains the most complete work about Brazilian sugar industry during the era of slavery published in English.

16. On Portugal's migration policies, see Vitorino Magalhães Godinho, "L'émigration portugaise (XVe–XXe Siècles): Une constante structurale et les réponses aux changements du monde," *Revista de história econômica e social* 1 (1978): 5–32.

17. Although focusing on the southeast region, the best work on the early history of enslaved Indigenous populations in Brazil is J. Monteiro, *Negros da terra*, translated as J. Monteiro, *Blacks of the Land.*

18. H. Klein and Luna, *Slavery in Brazil*, 31–32.

19. See Schwartz, *Sugar Plantations*, 51–72, and Bergad, *Comparative Histories of Slavery*, 13.

20. In both Portuguese and Spanish, the term *plantation* was not in use during the era of slavery. See Schwartz, *Sugar Plantations*, xvii, and Stuart B. Schwartz, introduction to Schwartz, *Tropical Babylons*, 2.

21. Schwartz, *Sugar Plantations*, 23.

22. On Jesuit slave ownership in Brazil, see Eunicia Fernandes, ed. *A Companhia de Jesus na América* (Rio de Janeiro: Contra Capa, 2013); in Brazil and Argentina, see Márcia Amantino, Eliane Cristina Deckman Fleck and Carlos Engemann, eds. *Companhia de Jesus na America por seus colégios e fazendas: Aproximações entre Brasil e Argentina (século XVIII)* (Rio de Janeiro: Garamond, 2015); in the state of Maryland, in the United States, see Thomas Murphy, *Jesuit Slaveholding in Maryland, 1717–1838* (New York: Routledge, 2001); in Peru, see Jean-Pierre Tardieu, "Los esclavos de los jesuitas del Perú en la época de la expulsion (1767)," *Caravelle: Cahiers du monde hispanique et luso-brésilien* (2003): 61–109.

23. See Luiz Felipe de Alencastro, "Le versant brésilien de l'Atlantique-Sud: 1550–1850," *Annales: Histoire, Sciences Sociales* 61, no. 2 (2006): 348.

24. Antonil, *Cultura e opulência do Brazil por suas drogas e minas*, 7–8.

25. Antonil, *Cultura e opulência do Brazil por suas drogas e minas*, 53. See also Schwartz, *Sugar Plantations*, 141, 528n56.

26. In Bahia, see Schwartz, *Sugar Plantations*, 370.

27. See Roberto Simonsen, *História econômica do Brasil, 1500–1820* (Brasília: Senado Federal, 2005), 174. See Mattoso, *Être esclave au Brésil XVIe–XIXe* *siècles*, 135; Vera Lúcia Amaral Ferlini, *A civilização do açúcar séculos XVI a XVIII* (São Paulo: Brasiliense, 1994), 60; and Betty Wood, "The Origins of Slavery in the Americas, 1500–1700," in *The Routledge History of Slavery*, ed. Gad Heuman and Trevor Burnard (London: Routledge, 2011), 65.

28. Herbert Klein has challenged the "seven years" as a general rule; see Herbert S. Klein, "Novas interpretações do tráfico de escravos do Atlântico," *Revista História* 120 (1989): 19. Yet, Brazilian historians who presented that average were referring to recently arrived Africans who were put to work on sugarcane plantations. In another work, Klein also loosely discusses life expectancy but never clearly refers to sugar plantations; see H. Klein and Luna, *Slavery in Brazil*, 169–70.

29. Schwartz, *Sugar Plantations*, 100; 146. See Bernard Moitt, *Women and Slavery in the French Antilles, 1635–1848* (Bloomington: Indiana University Press, 2001), 47.

30. Antonil, *Cultura e opulência do Brazil por suas drogas e minas*, 64, and Schwartz, *Sugar Plantations*, 143.

31. Richard S. Dunn, *A Tale of Two Plantations: Slave Life and Labor in Jamaica and Virginia* (Cambridge, MA: Harvard University Press, 2014), 165.

32. Bibliothèque Sainte-Geneviève, Paris, France (hereafter cited as BSG), Louis-François de Tollenare, *Notes dominicales prises pendant un voyage en Portugal et au Brésil en 1816, 1817 et 1818*, f. 315–16.

33. Jean-Baptiste Labat, *Nouveau voyage aux isles de l'Amérique*, vol. 3 (Paris: Chez Guillaume Cavelier, 1722), 202–4.

34. On these accidents, see Labat, *Nouveau voyage aux isles de l'Amérique*, 205–7. See also Moitt, *Women and Slavery in the French Antilles, 1635–1848*, 48–52. See also Laurent Dubois, *Avengers of the New World: The Story of the Haitian Revolution* (Cambridge, MA: Belknap Press of Harvard University Press, 2004), 45.

35. Schwartz, *Sugar Plantations*, 145.

36. See Padre Antônio Veira, "Sermão décimo quarto do Rosário: Pregado na Bahia à Irmandade dos Pretos de um engenho de açúcar na Bahia, em dia de São João Evangelista, no ano de 1633," in *Essencial Padre Antônio Vieira*, ed. Alfredo Bosi (São Paulo: Penguin, Companhia das Letras, 2011), 201–2.

37. Antonil, *Cultura e opulência do Brazil por suas drogas e minas*, 69.

38. James Lockhart and Stuart Schwartz, *Early Latin America: A History of Colonial Spanish America and Brazil* (New York: Cambridge University Press, 1999), 249.

39. Antonio Barros de Castro, "Escravos e senhores nos engenhos do Brasil: um estudo sobre os trabalhos do açúcar e a política econômica dos senhores" (PhD diss., Universidade de Campinas, 1976), 4.

40. On the early industry, see Alejandro de la Fuente, "Sugar and Slavery in Early Colonial Cuba," in Schwartz, *Tropical Babylons*, 115–57.

41. Richard S. Dunn, *Sugar and Slaves: The Rise of the Planter Class in the English West Indies, 1624–1713* (Chapel Hill: University of North Carolina Press, 2000), 15.

42. On the comparison between enslaved Africans and European indentured servants, see Jerome S. Handler and Matthew C. Reilly, "Contesting 'White Slavery' in the Caribbean: Enslaved Africans and European Indentured Servants in Seventeenth-Century Barbados," *New West Indian Guide / Nieuwe West-Indische Gids* 91, no. 1–2 (2017): 30–55.

43. Richard B. Sheridan, *Sugar and Slavery: An Economic History of the British West Indies, 1623–1775* (Kingston, Jamaica: Canoe Press, 1994), 132–33, and Dunn, *Sugar and Slaves*, 26, 46.

44. Hilary M. Beckles, *Natural Rebels: A Social History of Enslaved Black Women in Barbados* (New Brunswick, NJ: Rutgers University Press, 2000), 29–30.

45. Beckles, *Natural Rebels*, 39–40.

46. On British West Indies absentee slave owners, see Nicholas Draper, *The Price of Emancipation: Slave-ownership, Compensation and British Society at the End of Slavery* (Cambridge: Cambridge University Press, 2010), 17–74. See also Thomas C. Holt, *The Problem of Freedom: Race, Labor, and Politics in Jamaica and Britain, 1832–1938* (Baltimore: Johns Hopkins University Press, 1992), 89, and V. Brown, *Reaper's Garden*, 21–22. On attorneys who managed several estates, see Caitlin Rosenthal, *Accounting for Slavery: Masters and Management* (Cambridge, MA: Harvard University Press, 2019), 26–27. On slave owners' absenteeism in the French West Indies, see Antoine Gisler, *L'esclavage aux Antilles françaises (XIIe–XIXe siècle)* (Paris: Karthala, 1981), 87–88.

47. Philip D. Morgan, *Slave Counterpoint: Black Culture in the Eighteenth-Century Chesapeake and Lowcountry* (Chapel Hill: University of North Carolina Press, 1998), 8–9.

48. H. Klein and Vinson, *African Slavery in Latin America*, 54.

49. Holt, *Problem of Freedom*, 87.

50. V. Brown, *Reaper's Garden*, 15.

51. H. Klein and Vinson, *African Slavery in Latin America*, 55.

52. See Rafael de Bivar Marquese, *Feitores do corpo, missionários da mente: Senhores, letrados e o controle dos escravos nas Américas, 1660–1860* (São Paulo: Companhia das Letras, 2004), and Rosenthal, *Accounting for Slavery*.

53. See Carolyn E. Fick, *The Making of Haiti: The Saint Domingue Revolution from Below* (Knoxville: University of Tennessee Press, 1990), 278n14, and Dubois, *Avengers of the New World*, 19–21, 30.

54. Trevor Burnard, *Planters: Plantation Societies in British America, 1650–1820* (Chicago: University of Chicago Press, 2015), 175.

55. V. Brown, *Reaper's Garden*, 56.

56. See Testimony of Dr. Harrison, February 12, 1791, cited in V. Brown, *Reaper's Garden*, 188. See also Bergad, *Comparative Histories of Slavery*, 102. For a comparison of mortality rates in Bahia and Jamaica plantations see Schwartz, *Sugar Plantations*, 373.

57. See Dubois, *Avengers of the New World*, 40.

58. John J. McCusker and Russell R. Menard, *The Economy of British America, 1607–1789* (Chapel Hill: University of North Carolina Press, 1991), 45.
59. Bergad, *Comparative Histories of Slavery*, 23.
60. Berlin, *Many Thousands Gone*, 7–8.
61. See Peter H. Wood, *Black Majority: Negroes in Colonial South Carolina from 1670 through the Stono Rebellion* (New York: Knopf, 1996), 25.
62. Berlin, *Many Thousands Gone*, 65.
63. P. Wood, *Black Majority*, 36.
64. P. Wood, *Black Majority*, 43.
65. See P. Wood, *Black Majority*, 57–62, Judith Carney, "Rice Milling, Gender and Slave Labour in Colonial South Carolina.," *Past & Present*, no. 153 (1996): 108–34, and Judith Carney, *Black Rice: The African Origins of Rice Cultivation in the Americas* (Cambridge, MA. Harvard University Press, 2001). Known as the "black rice thesis," Wood's and Carney's conclusions were challenged in David Eltis, Philip Morgan, and David Richardson, "Agency and Diaspora in Reassessing the African Contribution to Rice Cultivation in the Americas," *American Historical Review* 12, no. 5 (2007): 1329–58. But since 2007, other studies brought new contributions to the rice thesis. See Edda. L. Fields-Black, *Deep Roots: Rice Farmers in West Africa and the African Diaspora* (Bloomington: Indiana University Press, 2008), and Walter Hawthorne, "From 'Black Rice' to 'Brown': Rethinking the History of Risiculture in the Seventeenth- and Eighteenth-Century Atlantic," *American Historical Review* 115, no. 1 (2010): 151–63.
66. See Leslie Schwalm, *A Hard Fight for We: Women's Transition from Slavery to Freedom in South Carolina* (Urbana: University of Illinois Press, 1997), 19, and Carney, *Black Rice*, 107–41.
67. For a specific study on the Allston, Butler, and Manigault rice plantations as capitalistic ventures, see William Dusinberre, *Them Dark Days: Slavery in the American Rice Swamps* (New York: Oxford University Press, 1996).
68. On this transformation, see Allan Kulikoff, *Tobacco and Slaves: The Development of Southern Cultures in the Chesapeake, 1680–1800* (Chapel Hill: University of North Carolina Press, 1986).
69. See Walter Johnson, *River of Dark Dreams: Slavery and Empire in the Cotton Kingdom* (Cambridge, MA: Harvard University Press, 2013), 155–59. For an accessible description of cotton production, see also Dale W. Tomich et al., *Reconstructing the Landscapes of Slavery: A Visual History of the Plantation in the Nineteenth-Century Atlantic World* (Chapel Hill: University of North Carolina Press, 2021), 72–74.
70. Sven Beckert, *Empire of Cotton: A Global History* (New York: Alfred A. Knopf, 2014), 56–57.
71. Northup and Wilson, *Twelve Years a Slave*, 166.
72. Northup and Wilson, *Twelve Years a Slave*, 167–68.
73. Beckert, *Empire of Cotton*, 103.

74. Department of Commerce and Labor Bureau of the Census, *A Century Population Growth from the First Census of the United States: From the First Census of the United States to the Twelfth, 1790–1900* (Washington, DC: Government Printing Office, 1909), 132.

75. See W. Johnson, *River of Dark Dreams*, 153–75, Baptist, *Half Has Never Been Told*, 115, and Tomich et al., *Reconstructing the Landscapes of Slavery*, 78–81.

76. See Eric Williams, *Capitalism and Slavery* (Chapel Hill: University of North Carolina Press, 1944), 126–28. On the new studies addressing the relationship between slavery and capitalism in the Americas, see Beckert, *Empire of Cotton*; Baptist, *Half Has Never Been Told*; Sven Beckert and Seth Rockman, *Slavery's Capitalism: A New History of American Economic Development* (Philadelphia: University of Pennsylvania Press, 2016); D. Berry, *Price for Their Pound of Flesh*; and Rosenthal, *Accounting for Slavery*.

77. See Dale Tomich, *Through the Prism of Slavery: Labor, Capital and World Economy* (Lanham, MD: Rowman & Littlefield, 2004), and Tomich and Zeuske, "Introduction, the Second Slavery," 91–100. See also Baptist, *Half Has Never Been Told*, 153.

78. Some new studies are finally emphasizing the role of Africa in the rise of second slavery and industrial capitalism; see Dale W. Tomich and Paul E. Lovejoy, eds., *The Atlantic and Africa: The Second Slavery and Beyond* (Albany: State University of New York Press, 2021), and Toby Green, "Africa and Capitalism: Repairing a History of Omission," *Capitalism: A Journal of History and Economics* 3, no. 2 (2022): 301–32.

79. Manuel Moreno Fraginals, *El Ingenio: Complejo económico-social cubano del azúcar*, vol. 1 (Havana: Editorial de Ciencias Sociales, 2014), 12.

80. Fraginals, *El Ingenio*, 166.

81. See "Royal Decree and Instructional Circular for the Indies on the Education, Treatment, and Work Regimen of Slaves," May 31, 1789, 49, and "Statement from Havana's Ingenio Owners to the King," Havana, January 19, 1790, in Gloria García Rodríguez, *Voices of the Enslaved in Nineteenth-Century Cuba: A Documentary History* (Chapel Hill: University of North Carolina Press, 2011), 59.

82. On the impacts of the Saint Domingue Revolution in Cuba, see Ada Ferrer, *Freedom's Mirror: Cuba and Haiti in the Age of Revolution* (New York: Cambridge University Press, 2014).

83. Fraginals, *El Ingenio*, 207. See also Tomich et al., *Reconstructing the Landscapes of Slavery*, 98.

84. On this modernization process, see the first four chapters of Daniel B. Rood, *The Reinvention of Atlantic Slavery: Technology, Labor, Race, and Capitalism in the Greater Caribbean* (New York: Oxford University Press, 2017).

85. Justo G. Cantero and Eduardo Laplante, *Los ingenios: Colleción de vistas de los principales ingenios de azúcar de la isla de Cuba* (Havana: Litografía de Luis Marquier, 1847).

86. Bergad, *Comparative Histories of Slavery*, 7.
87. On the impacts of the Saint Domingue Revolution in Brazil, see João José Reis and Flávio dos Santos Gomes, "Repercussions of the Haitian Revolution in Brazil, 1791–1850," in *The World of the Haitian Revolution*, ed. David Patrick Geggus and Norman Fiering (Bloomington: Indiana University Press, 2009), 284–313.
88. M. Graham, *Journal of a Voyage to Brazil*, 277.
89. Auguste de Saint-Hilaire, *Voyages dans l'intérieur du Brésil: Seconde Partie* (Paris: Librairie Gide, 1837), 130, 147–52.
90. Ricardo Salles, *E o Vale era o escravo: Vassouras, século XIX; Senhores e escravos no coração do império* (Rio de Janeiro: Civilização Brasileira, 2008), 141–46.
91. H. Klein and Luna, *Slavery in Brazil*, 142–43.
92. Rafael de Bivar Marquese, "African Diaspora, Slavery, and the Paraíba Valley Coffee Plantation Landscape: Nineteenth-Century Brazil," *Review (Fernand Braudel Center)* 31, no. 2 (2008): 200.
93. For a careful analysis of these images, see Mariana de Aguiar Ferreira Muaze, "Violence Appeased: Slavery and Coffee Raising in the Photography of Marc Ferrez (1882–1885)," *Revista brasileira de história*, 37, no. 74 (2017): 1–30.

Chapter 8

1. Baquaqua, *Biography of Mahommah G. Baquaqua*, 46.
2. Thomas H. Holloway, "Prefácio: Haddock Lobo e o recenseamento do Rio de Janeiro em 1849," in Roberto Hadock Lobo, "Texto introdutório do recenseamento do Rio de Janeiro de 1849," special issue, Boletim de História Demográfica 15, no. 50 (July 2008), http://historia_demografica.tripod.com/bhds/bhd50/thrj.pdf.
3. Davis, *Inhuman Bondage*, 125.
4. Sandra R. Joshel, *Slavery in the Roman World* (New York: Cambridge University Press, 2010), 8. See also Neville Morley, *Metropolis and Hinterland: The City of Rome and the Italian Economy, 200 BC–AD 200* (Cambridge: Cambridge University Press, 1996), 182.
5. Thomas Wiedemann, *Greek and Roman Slavery* (New York: Routledge, 1994), 17. See also Paulin Ismard, *La cité et ses esclaves: Institutions, fictions, expériences* (Paris: Seuil, 2019), 23.
6. Finley, *Ancient Slavery and Modern Ideology*, 69–70.
7. Wiedeman, *Greek and Roman Slavery*, 22–25.
8. Ismard, *La cité et ses esclaves*, 96–97.
9. On enslaved Muslims in Portugal, see Caldeira, *Escravos em Portugal*, 31–32.
10. Aurelia Martín Casares, "Free and Freed Black Africans in Granada in the Time of the Spanish Renaissance," in *Black Africans in Renaissance Europe*, ed. Thomas Foster Earle and Kate J. P. Lowe (Cambridge: Cambridge University Press, 2005), 248.

11. Saunders, *Social History of Black Slaves*, 114.
12. Biblioteca Nacional de Portugal (hereafter cited as BNP), Cristóvão Rodrigues de Oliveira, *Sumario e[m] que brevemente se contem alguas cousas assi eclesiásticas como seculares que ha na cidade de Lisboa* (Lisbon: Em casa de Germão Galharde, 1554), 103.
13. Jorge Fonseca, "Black Africans in Portugal during Cleynaerts's Visit (1533–1538)," in Earle and Lowe, *Black Africans in Renaissance Europe*, 114n5.
14. Saunders, *Social History of Black Slaves and Freedmen in Portugal*, 55. See also Didier Lahon, "Esclavage, confréries noires, sainteté noire et pureté de sang au Portugal (XVIe et XVIIIe siècles)," *Lusitania Sacra* 2, no. 15 (2003): 120, and António de Almeida Mendes, "Les réseaux de la traite ibérique dans l'Atlantique nord (1440–1640)," *Annales: Histoire, Sciences Sociales*, no. 4 (2008): 742.
15. Caldeira, *Escravos em Portugal*, 143.
16. See William D. Phillips Jr., *Slavery in Medieval and Early Modern Iberia* (Philadelphia: University of Pennsylvania Press, 2014), 10. On Valencia, see Debra Blumenthal, *Enemies and Familiars: Slavery and Mastery in Fifteenth-Century Valencia* (Ithaca, NY: Cornell University Press, 2009), 4. On Valencia and Barcelona, see Iván Armenteros Martínez, "Un caso de reestructuración de redes comerciales: El mercado de esclavos de Barcelona entre 1472 y 1516" (paper presented at the eleventh Congrés de Història de la Ciutat de Barcelona, Institut de Cultura, Ajuntament de Barcelona, December 1–3, 2009), 5, 9. On sixteenth-century Seville, see Manuel F. Fernández Chavez and Rafael M. Pérez García, *En los márgenes de la ciudad de Dios: Moriscos en Sevilla* (Valencia: Publicaciones de la Universitat de València; Granada: Editorial Universidad de Granada; Zaragoza: Servicio de Publicaciones de la Universida de Zaragoza, 2009), 86–87.
17. Saunders, *Social History of Black Slaves and Freedmen in Portugal*, 77.
18. Saunders, *Social History of Black Slaves and Freedmen in Portugal*, 27, and Fonseca, "Black Africans in Portugal during Cleynaerts's Visit," 16.
19. Imtiaz Habib, *Black Lives in the English Archives, 1500–1677: Imprints of the Invisible* (London: Routledge, 2007), 64. On Black Tudors, see also Miranda Kaufmann, *Black Tudors: The Untold Story* (London: Oneworld Publications, 2018).
20. Mark Ponte, "'Al de swarten die hier ter stede comen': Een Afro-Atlantische gemeeschap in zeventiended-eeuws Amsterdam," *TSEG* 15, no. 4 (2018): 34.
21. Existing graves of enslaved and free Black Africans attest to this early presence in Amsterdam and its surroundings. See Dienke Hondius, "Access to the Netherlands of Enslaved and Free Black Africans: Exploring Legal and Social Historical Practices in the Sixteenth–Nineteenth Centuries," *Slavery and Abolition* 32, no. 3 (2011): 380–81. For tangible traces of slavery in Amsterdam and Leiden, see Dienke Hondius et al., *Gids Slavernijverleden, Amsterdam Slavery Heritage Guide* (Arnhem, Neth.: LM Publishers, 2018),

Gert Oostindie and Karwan Fatah-Black, *Sporen van de slavernij in Leiden* (Leiden, Neth.: Leiden University Press, 2018), and Olivette Otele, *African Europeans: An Untold History* (New York: Basic Books, 2021), 70–72.

22. Ponte, "'Al de swarten die hier ter stede comen,'" 38.

23. On the Hemingses, see Annette Gordon-Reed, *The Hemingses of Monticello: An American Family* (New York: W. W. Norton, 2008). On the legal debates about slavery in metropolitan eighteenth-century France, see Sue Peabody, *"There Are No Slaves in France": The Political Culture of Race and Slavery in the Ancien Régime* (New York: Oxford University Press, 1996).

24. See, for example, Lorelle Semley, "Beyond the Dark Side of the Port of the Moon: Rethinking the Role of Bordeaux's Slave Trade Past," *Histoire Sociale / Social History* 53, no. 107 (2020): 43–68, and Julie Duprat, *Bordeaux Métisse: Esclaves et affranchis de couleur du XVIII à l'empire* (Bordeaux, Fr.: Mollat, 2021).

25. See Cole, *Potosí Mita*, Kris Lane, *Potosí: The Silver City That Changed the World* (Oakland: University of California Press, 2019), and James Almeida, "Minting Slavery in the Colonial Andes: Labor and Race in Potosi and Lima" (PhD diss., Harvard University, 2022).

26. See, for example, Karen B. Graubart, *With Our Labor and Sweat: Indigenous Women and the Formation of Colonial Society in Peru, 1550–1700* (Stanford, CA: Stanford University Press, 2007), 60–61, 89.

27. See Mieko Nishida, *Slavery and Identity: Ethnicity, Gender, and Race in Salvador, Brazil, 1808–1888* (Bloomington: Indiana University Press, 2003), 19.

28. On enslaved Asians, see Tatiana Seijas, *Asian Slaves in Colonial Mexico: From Chinos to Indians* (New York: Cambridge University Press, 2014).

29. See Pablo Miguel Sierra Silva, *Urban Slavery in Colonial Mexico: Puebla de los Ángeles, 1531–1706* (New York: Cambridge University Press, 2019), and Karen B. Graubart, "As Slaves and Not Vassals: Interethnic Claims of Freedom and Unfreedom in Colonial Peru," *Población & Sociedad* 27, no. 2 (2020): 30–53.

30. See Marisa Fuentes, *Dispossessed Lives: Enslaved Women, Violence, and the Archive* (Philadelphia: University of Pennsylvania Press, 2016), chaps. 2 and 3.

31. According to the first census of Cuba in 1774; see Ramón Sagra, *Historia economico-politica y estadística de la islã de Cuba* (Havana: Printed by the Widows Arazoza and Soler, 1831), 3.

32. Ynaê Lopes dos Santos, "Irmãs do Atlântico: Escravidão e espaço urbano no Rio de Janeiro e Havana (1763–1844)" (PhD diss., University of São Paulo, 2012), 51, 60–64.

33. H. Klein and Vinson, *African Slavery in Latin America*, 41.

34. Ann Twinam, *Purchasing Whiteness: Pardos, Mulattos, and the Quest for Social Mobility in the Spanish Indies* (Stanford, CA: Stanford University Press, 2015).

35. Mariana L. R. Dantas, *Black Townsmen: Urban Slavery and Freedom in the Eighteenth-Century Americas* (New York: Palgrave Macmillan, 2008), 86, 105–6, and H. Klein and Luna, *Slavery in Brazil*, 45.

36. See Eduardo França Paiva, *Escravidão e universo cultural na colônia: Minas Gerais, 1716–1789* (Belo Horizonte, Brazil: Editora da Universidade de Minas Gerais, 2006).

37. Leila Mezan Algranti, *O feitor ausente: Estudo sobre a escravidão urbana no Rio de Janeiro* (Petrópolis. Brazil: Vozes, 1988), 49, and Nishida, *Slavery and Identity*, 20.

38. H. Klein and Luna, *Slavery in Brazil*, 141.

39. Bergad, *Comparative Histories of Slavery*, 196–97.

40. Alejandro de la Fuente and Ariela J. Gross, *Becoming Free, Becoming Black: Race, Freedom, and Law in Cuba, Virginia, and Louisiana* (New York: Cambridge University Press, 2020), 106.

41. James H. Sweet, "Manumission in Rio de Janeiro, 1749–54: An African Perspective," *Slavery and Abolition* 24, no. 1 (2003): 63, 66.

42. See Afua Cooper, *The Hanging of Angélique: The Untold Story of Canadian Slavery and the Burning of Old Montréal* (Athens: University of Georgia Press, 2007), and Frank Mackey, *Done with Slavery: The Black Fact in Montreal, 1760–1840* (Montreal: McGill-Queen's University Press, 2010).

43. On New York City, see Graham Russell Gao Hodges, *Root & Branch: African Americans in New York and East Jersey, 1613–1863* (Chapel Hill: University of North Carolina Press, 1999); Leslie Harris, *In the Shadow of Slavery: African Americans in New York City, 1626–1863* (Chicago: University of Chicago Press, 2003); Jill Lepore, *New York Burning: Liberty, Slavery, and Conspiracy in Eighteenth-Century Manhattan* (New York: Knopf, 2005); and Daniel Nathaniel Gellman, *Emancipating New York: The Politics of Slavery and Freedom, 1777–1827* (Baton Rouge: Louisiana State University Press, 2008).

44. L. Harris, *In the Shadow of Slavery*, 30.

45. Cécile Vidal, *Caribbean New Orleans: Empire, Race, and the Making of a Slave Society* (Chapel Hill: University of North Carolina Press, 2019), 323.

46. On the use of an enslaved workforce to build the capital, see Felicia Bell, "'The Negroes Alone Work': Enslaved Craftsmen, the Building Trades, and the Construction of the United States Capitol, 1790–1800" (PhD diss., Howard University, 2009).

47. See Tamika Y. Nunley, *At the Threshold of Liberty: Women, Slavery, and Shifting Identities in Washington, D.C.* (Chapel Hill: University of North Carolina Press, 2021), 18–20.

48. See Dantas, *Black Townsmen*, 55–58, 72. See also Seth Rockman, S*craping By: Wage Labor, Slavery, and Survival in Early Baltimore* (Baltimore: Johns Hopkins University Press, 2009), 233.

49. Midori Takagi, *Rearing Wolves to Our Own Destruction: Slavery in Richmond, Virginia, 1782–1865* (Charlottesville: University Press of Virginia, 1999), 22–24.

50. Lucia C. Stanton, *"Those Who Labor for My Happiness": Slavery at Thomas Jefferson's Monticello* (Charlottesville: University of Virginia Press, 2012), 21, 116.

51. Justene Hill Edwards, *Unfree Markets: The Slaves' Economy and the Rise of Capitalism in South Carolina* (New York: Columbia University Press, 2021), 52–53.

52. Richard C. Wade, *Slavery in the Cities: The South 1820–1860* (New York: Oxford University Press, 1967), 40.
53. Ethan J. Kytle and Blain Roberts, *Denmark Vesey's Garden: Slavery and Memory in the Cradle of the Confederacy* (New York: New Press, 2018), 23.
54. João José Reis, "African Nations in Nineteenth-Century Salvador, Bahia," in Cañizares-Esguerra, Childs, and Sidbury, *Black Urban Atlantic in the Age of the Slave Trade*, 64.
55. For an overview of what these ethnonyms meant in nineteenth-century Bahia, see J. Reis, "African Nations in Nineteenth-Century Salvador," 65–68.
56. Nishida, *Slavery and Identity*, 39.
57. Daniel Parish Kidder and James Cooley Fletcher, *Brazil and the Brazilians, Portrayed in Historical and Descriptive Sketches* (Philadelphia: Childs and Peterson, 1857), 475.
58. Kidder and Fletcher, *Brazil and the Brazilians*, 476.
59. François-Auguste Biard, *Deux années au Brésil* (Paris: Hachette, 1862), 41.
60. See Stuart B. Schwartz, "Cantos and Quilombos: A Hausa Rebellion in Bahia, 1814," in *Slaves, Subjects, and Subversives: Blacks in Colonial Latin America*, ed. Landers, Jane, and Barry Robinson (Albuquerque: University of New Mexico Press, 2006), 257–59.
61. See João José Reis, *Ganhadores: A greve negra de 1857 na Bahia* (São Paulo: Companhia das Letras, 2019). See also an article in English providing an overview of the movement, João José Reis, "'The Revolution of the Ganhadores': Urban Labour, Ethnicity and the African Strike of 1857 in Bahia, Brazil," *Journal of Latin American Studies* 29, no. 2 (1997): 355–93.
62. On slaves who owned slaves, see Mattoso, *Être Esclave au Brésil XVIe–XIXe siècles*, 150–51; João José Reis, "From Slave to Wealthy African Freedman: The Story of Manoel Joaquim Ricardo," in *Biography and the Black Atlantic*, ed. Lisa A. Lindsay and John Wood Sweet (Philadelphia: University of Pennsylvania Press, 2014), 131–48; and Castillo, "O terreiro do Gantois," 25.
63. J. Reis, "African Nations in Nineteenth-Century Salvador," 70.
64. Several monographs explore cases of former slaves who owned slaves in Brazilian urban areas. In Bahia, see João José Reis, *Slave Rebellion in Brazil: The Muslim Uprising of 1835 in Bahia* (Baltimore: Johns Hopkins University Press, 1993), 3; João José Reis, *Domingos Sodré: Um sacerdote africano; Escravidão, liberdade e candomblé na Bahia do século XIX* (São Paulo: Companhia das Letras, 2008); and J. Reis, Gomes, and Carvalho, *Story of Rufino*, originally published as João José Reis, Flávio dos Santos Gomes, and Marcus J. M. de Carvalho, *O alufá Rufino: tráfico, escravidão e liberdade no Atlântico Negro (c. 1822–c. 1853)* (São Paulo: Companhia das Letras, 2010). On former slaves who owned slaves in Minas Gerais, see Kathleen J. Higgins, *Licentious Liberty in a Brazilian Gold-Mining Region: Slavery, Gender and Social Control in Eighteenth-Century Sabará, Minas Gerais* (University Park, PA: Penn State University Press, 1999), 43–88; in Rio de Janeiro, see Karasch, *Slave Life in*

Rio de Janeiro, and Luiz Carlos Soares, *O 'povo de Cam' na capital do Brasil: A escravidão urbana no Rio de Janeiro do século XIX* (Rio de Janeiro: 7Letras, 2007).

65. See Luis Nicolau Parés, "Afro-Catholic Baptism and the Articulation of a Merchant Community, Agoué, 1840–1860," *History in Africa* 42 (2015): 165–201, and Luis Nicolau Parés, "Entre Bahia e a Costa da Mina, libertos africanos no tráfico ilegal" in *Salvador da Bahia: Interações entre América e África (séculos XVI–XIX)*, ed. Giuseppina Raggi, João Figuerôa-Rego, and Roberta Stumpf (Salvador, Brazil: Editora da Universidade Federal da Bahia, 2017), 19–20.

66. Arquivo Público do Estado da Bahia (hereafter cited as APEB), Seção Judiciária, Maço 1697, document 13, 2v-f3. For a transcription of this will, see Verger, *Os Libertos*, 116–20.

67. Édouard Manet, *Lettres du siège de Paris: Précédées des lettres du voyage à Rio de Janeiro* (Paris: Éditions de l'Amateur, 1996), 23.

68. Manet, *Lettres du siège de Paris*, 24.

69. Karasch, *Slave Life in Rio de Janeiro*, 223.

70. On Salvador and Rio de Janeiro, see Sylvia Hunold Lara, "The Signs of Color: Women's Dress and Racial Relations in Salvador and Rio de Janeiro, ca. 1750–1815," *Colonial Latin American Review* 6, no. 2 (1997): 205–24. On Lima, see Tamara J. Walker, "'He Outfitted His Family in Notable Decency': Slavery, Honour and Dress in Eighteenth-Century Lima, Peru," *Slavery & Abolition* 30, no. 3 (2009): 383–402, and Tamara J. Walker, *Exquisite Slaves: Race, Clothing, and Status in Colonial Lima* (New York: Cambridge University Press, 2017). On Mexico City, see Herman Bennett, *Africans in Colonial Mexico: Absolutism, Christianity, and Afro-Creole Consciousness, 1570–1640* (Bloomington: Indiana University Press, 2005), 30–32. On Mexico City and Santiago de Chile, see Rebecca Earle, '"Two Pairs of Pink Satin Shoes!!': Clothing, Race and Identity in the Americas, 17th–19th Centuries," *History Workshop Journal* 52 (2001): 175–95.

71. ADCM 17, 4J 45 2318, *Mémoires de Jacques Proa dit Proa des îles*, 115.

72. See Maria Odila Silva Dias, *Power and Everyday Life: The Lives of Working Women in Nineteenth-Century Brazil* (New Brunswick, NJ: Rutgers University Press, 1995), 55–56.

73. Lara, "Signs of Color," 205–8.

74. Luís dos Santos Vilhena, *A Bahia no século XVIII*, vol. 1 (Salvador, Brazil: Editora Itapuã, 1969), 54–55.

75. On March 21, 1817, the vessel *Lucrecia* from Porto-Novo anchored in Bahia with a cargo of *panos da costa*; see *Idade d'ouro do Brazil*, March 25, 1817, 4.

76. James Wetherell, *Brazil: Stray Notes from Bahia: Being Extracts from Letters, &c., During a Residence of Fifteen Years* (Liverpool: Webb and Hunt, 1860), 73. On the trade of this cloth, see Hicks, "Transatlantic Threads of Meaning."

77. Biblioteca Nacional, Rio de Janeiro (hereafter cited as BN), Icon 3030647, "Noticia summaria do gentilismo da Asia com dez Riscos iluminados. Ditos

de Figurinhos de Brancos e Negros dos Uzos do Rio de Janeiro e Serro do Frio. Ditos de Vazos e Tecidos Peruvianos," c. 17—, plate XXVI. For more details about the original manuscript with watercolors and its various editions, see Valéria Piccoli Gabriel da Silva, "Figurinhas de brancos e negros: Carlos Julião e o mundo colonial português" (PhD diss., Universidade de São Paulo, 2010).

78. See the example of eighteenth-century Minas Gerais in Paiva, *Escravidão e universo cultural na colônia*, 50, 151.

79. Lucilene Reginaldo, "André do Couto Godinho," in *Oxford Research Encyclopedia of African History*, Oxford University Press, article published May 26, 2021, https://oxfordre.com/africanhistory/view/10.1093/acrefore/9780190277734.001.0001/acrefore-9780190277734-e-962.

80. On this portrait and other nineteenth-century photographs of enslaved people in Brazil, see Margrit Prussat, *Bilder Der Sklaverei: Fotografien Der Afrikanischen Diaspora in Brasilien 1860–1920* (Berlin: Reimer, 2008). See also Margrit Prussat, "Icons of Slavery: Black Brazil in Nineteenth-Century Photography and Image Art," in *Living History: Encountering the Memory of the Heirs of Slavery*, ed. Ana Lucia Araujo (Newcastle upon Tyne: Cambridge Scholars Publishing, 2009), 203–30.

81. Grandpré, *Voyage à la côte occidentale*, 1:75.

82. Mariana P. Candido, "Women's Material World in Nineteenth-Century Benguela," in Candido and Jones, *African Women in the Atlantic World*, 70–85.

83. Debret, *Voyage pittoresque et historique au Brésil*, 2:91.

84. Ferreira, *Cross-Cultural Exchange*, 61.

85. Karasch, *Slave Life in Rio de Janeiro*, 223.

86. See Ana Lucia Araujo, *Brazil through French Eyes: A Nineteenth-Century Artist in the Tropics* (Albuquerque: University of New Mexico Press, 2015), chap. 3.

87. A similar scene, titled *A Brazilian Family*, was also depicted by the British traveler Henry Chamberlain; see Henry Chamberlain and Rubens Borba de Moraes, *Vistas e costumes da cidade e arredores do Rio de Janeiro em 1819–1820* (Rio de Janeiro: Livraria Kosmos editora, 1943), 39. A similar satirical engraving portraying a female slave owner strolling with her slaves also appears in Biard, *Deux années au Brésil*, 85.

88. L. Soares, *O 'povo de Cam' na capital do Brasil*, 363.

89. On white women's seclusion in Brazil, see Dias, *Power and Everyday Life*, 59.

90. Debret, *Voyage pittoresque et historique au Brésil*, 2:31.

91. Debret, *Voyage pittoresque et historique au Brésil*, 2:31–32.

92. See Mattoso, *Être esclave au Brésil, XVIe–XIXe siècles*, 230–31. See also Manuela Carneiro da Cunha, *Negros, Estrangeiros: Os escravos libertos e sua volta à África* (São Paulo: Companhia das Letras, 2012), 99.

93. Biard, *Deux années au Brésil*, 38.

94. Biard, *Deux années au Brésil*, 64.

Chapter 9

1. Biard, *Deux années au Brésil*, 38.
2. L. Soares, *O 'povo de Cam' na capital do Brasil*, 107.
3. Akinwumi Ogundiran, *The Yorùbá: A New History* (Bloomington: Indiana University Press, 2020), 323.
4. Paul Hair, ed., *Barbot in Guinea: The Writings of Jean Barbot on West Africa, 1678–1712*, vol. 1 (London: Hakluyt Society, 1992), 90. See also Klas Rönnbäck, *Labour and Living Standards in Pre-Colonial West Africa: The Case of the Gold Coast* (Oxford: Routledge, 2015), 76–78.
5. See Niara Sudarkasa, *Where Women Work: A Study of Yoruba Women in the Marketplace and in the Home* (Ann Arbor: University of Michigan Press, 1973), 27–35.
6. Carney and Rosomoff, *In the Shadow of Slavery*, 49, 59.
7. Ogundiran, *Yorùbá*, 319.
8. Equiano and Carretta, *Interesting Narrative*, 37.
9. Selma Pantoja, "A Dimensão Atlântica das Quitandeiras," in *Diálogos Oceânicos: Minas Gerais e as Novas Abordagens para uma História do Império Ultramarino Português*, ed. Júnia F. Furtado (Belo Horizonte, Brazil: Editora da Universidade Federal de Minas Gerais, 2001), 45–68.
10. Pantoja, "A Dimensão Atlântica das Quitandeiras," 47; Ferreira, *Cross-Cultural Exchange*, 133; and Vanessa S. Oliveira, "Baskets, Stalls and Shops: Experiences and Strategies of Women in Retail Sales in Nineteenth-Century Luanda," *Canadian Journal of African Studies / Revue canadienne des études africaines* 54, no. 3 (2020): 425.
11. Ferreira, *Cross-Cultural Exchange*, 133–34, and V. Oliveira, *Slave Trade and Abolition*, 45.
12. D. Silva, *Atlantic Slave Trade*, 76, and V. Oliveira, *Slave Trade and Abolition*, 81, 89.
13. Pantoja, "A Dimensão Atlântica das Quitandeiras," 47.
14. Candido, *African Slaving Port*, 105–6.
15. Selma Pantoja, "Women's Work in the Fairs and Markets of Luanda," in *Women in the Portuguese Colonial Empire: The Theatre of Shadows*, ed. Clara Sarmento (Newcastle upon Tyne: Cambridge Scholars Publishing, 2008), 81–93.
16. V. Oliveira, *Slave Trade and Abolition*, 97.
17. Susan Kellogg, *Weaving the Past: A History of Latin America's Indigenous Women from the Prehispanic Period to the Present* (New York: Oxford University Press, 2005), 64–65.
18. Jean-Pierre Tardieu, *El negro em la Real Audiencia de Quito, Siglos XVI–XVIII* (Lima, Peru: Institut français d'études andines, 2015), 144, 151n81.
19. Tadeo Haënke, *Descripción del Perú* (Lima, Peru: Imprenta El Lucero, 1901), 3.

20. Hilary M. Beckles, "An Economic Life of Their Own: Slaves as Commodity Producers and Distributors in Barbados," *Slavery and Abolition: A Journal of Slave and Post-Slave Studies* 12, no. 1 (1991): 40.

21. Beckles, "Economic Life of Their Own," 41; Fuentes, *Dispossessed Lives*, 28, 54.

22. Beckles, "Economic Life of Their Own," 45n2.

23. See *Affiches américaines*, May 21, 1766, and May 21, 1775.

24. Jean-Baptiste Rouvellat de Cussac, *Situation des esclaves dans les colonies françaises; urgence de leur émancipation* (Paris: Pagnerre, 1845), 44.

25. For example, on the case of Cap-Français in Saint-Domingue, see Geggus, "Slaves and Free People of Color of Cap Français," 209. On the French West Indies in general, see Moitt, *Women and Slavery in the French Antilles*, 55.

26. See Beckles, "Economic Life of Their Own," 33–35, and Lucille Mathurin Mair, *A Historical Study of Women in Jamaica, 1655–1844* (Mona: University of the West Indies Press, 2006), 65.

27. See Camillia Cowling, *Conceiving Freedom: Women of Color, Gender, and the Abolition of Slavery in Havana and Rio de Janeiro* (Chapel Hill: University of North Carolina Press, 2013), 230n44.

28. See Crystal Eddins, *Rituals, Runaways, and the Haitian Revolution: Collective Action in the African Diaspora* (New York: Cambridge University Press, 2022).

29. On the word *mondongo* in Spanish, see Laura Álvarez López and Magdalena Coll, "Registers of African-Derived Lexicon in Uruguay: Etymologies, Demography and Semantic Change," *Zeitschrift für romanische Philologie* 135, no. 1 (2019): 223–55. On *mondongo* in Portuguese, see Yeda Passos de Castro, *Falares africanos na Bahia: Um vocabulário afro-brasileiro* (Rio de Janeiro: Academia Brasileira de Letras, 2001), 288. Castro suggests that the word may be related to the Kikongo terms *mungungu* and *mundungu* designating the entrails of animals. But the matter remains unsettled; see Thomas Johnen, "*Bomba*, *kanga*, *makamba* e outros africanismos lexicais no papiamento: Comparações com o português do Brasil e o espanhol uruguaio," in *Una historia sin fronteras: Léxico de origen africano em Brasil y Uruguay*, ed. Laura Álvarez López and Magdalena Coll (Stockholm: Acta Universitattis Stockholmiensis, 2012), 176–78. On the dish, see Marco Polo Hernandéz Cuevas, *African Mexicans and the Discourse on Modern Nation* (Lanham, MD: University Press of America, 2004), 46–47.

30. On *mondongueras* in San Juan, see Félix V. Matos-Rodríguez, "Street Vendors, Pedlars, Shop-Owners and Domestics: Some Aspects of Women's Economic Roles in Nineteenth-Century San Juan, Puerto Rico (1820–1870)," in *Engendering History: Caribbean Women in Historical Perspective*, ed. Verene Shepherd, Bridget Brereton, and Barbara Bailey (New York: Palgrave Macmillan, 1995), 181–83.

31. J. Edwards, *Unfree Markets*, 22.

32. Robert Olwell, "'Loose, Idle and Disorderly': Slave Women in the Eighteenth-Century Charleston Marketplace," in *More Than Chattel: Black

Women and Slavery in the Americas, ed. David Barry Gaspar and Darlene Clark Hine (Bloomington: Indiana University Press, 1996), 98.

33. See J. Edwards, *Unfree Markets*, 30–33.

34. J. Edwards, *Unfree Markets*, 32. On the marketplace as haven for enslaved fugitives in the British colonies of the Americas, see Jennifer Morgan, *Laboring Women: Reproduction and Gender in New World Slavery* (Philadelphia: University of Pennsylvania Press, 2004), 159–61. On Jamaica, see Shauna Sweeney, "Market Marronage: Fugitive Women and the Internal Marketing System in Jamaica, 1781–1834," *William and Mary Quarterly* 76, no. 2 (2019): 197–222.

35. J. Edwards, *Unfree Markets*, 30, 50–53.

36. Sophie White, *Voices of the Enslaved: Love, Labor, and Longing in French Louisiana* (Chapel Hill: University of North Carolina Press, 2019), 209; J. Johnson, *Wicked Flesh*, 183.

37. Vidal, *Caribbean New Orleans*, 361.

38. Rashauna Johnson, *Slavery's Metropolis: Unfree Labor in New Orleans during the Age of Revolutions* (New York: Cambridge University Press, 2016), 65–73.

39. Vilhena, *A Bahia no século XVIII*, 93.

40. Nishida, *Slavery and Identity*, 44–45.

41. See Carney and Rosomoff, *In the Shadow of Slavery*, 183–85.

42. Richard Graham, *Feeding the City: From Street Market to Liberal Reform in Salvador, Brazil, 1780–1860* (Austin: University of Texas Press, 2010), 35.

43. Cecília Moreira Soares, "As ganhadeiras: Mulher e resistência negra em Salvador no século XIX," *Afro-Ásia*, no. 17 (1996): 57.

44. R. Graham, *Feeding the City*, 37–41.

45. Vilhena, *A Bahia no século XVIII*, 130.

46. Wetherell, *Brazil: Stray Notes from Bahia*, 95–96.

47. R. Graham, *Feeding the City*, 44–45.

48. *O Monitor*, September 26, 1877, 3; *Correio Mercantil*, December 12, 1840, 4.

49. See *Correio da Bahia*, July 17, 1877, 1; *Correio da Bahia*, August 9, 1877, 1; *Correio da Bahia*, August 12, 1877, 2; *O Guarany*, May 10, 1878, 3.

50. I explore these issues in Araujo, *Brazil through French Eyes*.

51. Karasch, *Slave Life in Rio de Janeiro*, 206.

52. Cowling, *Conceiving Freedom*, 31.

53. Debret, *Voyage pittoresque et historique au Brésil*, 2:44.

54. Juliana Barreto Farias, *Mercados Minas: Africanos ocidentais na Praça do Mercado do Rio de Janeiro (1830–1890)* (Rio de Janeiro: Arquivo Geral da Cidade do Rio de Janeiro, 2015), 39.

55. Karasch, *Slave Life in Rio de Janeiro*, 58.

56. Karasch, *Slave Life in Rio de Janeiro*, 73.

57. Thomas Ewbank, *Life in Brazil; or, a Journal of a Visit to the Land of Cocoa* (New York: Harper and Brothers, 1856), 92–93.

58. Ewbank, *Life in Brazil*, 54.

59. On Mina women street vendors, see M. Soares, *People of Faith*, 99–100. On Mina women in this specific market, see Farias, *Mercados Minas*, 106.
60. Louis Agassiz and Elizabeth Agassiz, *Journey in Brazil* (Boston: Ticknor and Fields, 1868), 82–85.
61. This case is explored in Juliana Barreto Farias, "De escrava a Dona: A trajetória da africana mina Emília Soares do Patrocínio no Rio de Janeiro do século XIX," *Locus: Revista de História* 18, no. 2 (2012): 13–40.
62. On this case, see Farias, *Mercados Minas*, 103.
63. See Sheila Siqueira de Castro Faria, "Sinhás pretas, damas mercadoras: As pretas minas nas cidades do Rio de Janeiro e de São João del Rey (1700–1850)" (diss. for full professor promotion, Universidade Federal Fluminense, 2004), 200–202.
64. *Diário do Rio de Janeiro*, March 30, 1825, 94.
65. Patricia Acerbi, *Street Occupations: Urban Vending in Rio de Janeiro* (Austin: University of Texas Press, 2017), 60–61.

Chapter 10

1. "Defloramento da escrava pelo senhor: Questões connexas," *O Direito: Revista mensal de legislação, doutrina e jurisprudencia* 35 (1884): 103–18.
2. Gilberto Freyre, *Casa-grande e senzala* (São Paulo: Global, 2003). Published in 1933 in Brazil, this book was translated into English as Gilberto Freyre, *The Masters and the Slaves: A Study in the Development of Brazilian Civilization* (New York: Alfred A. Knopf, 1946).
3. Marc Epprecht, "Sexuality, Africa, History," *American Historical Review* 114, no. 5 (2009): 1259.
4. Oyèrónké Oyěwùmí, *The Invention of Women: Making an African Sense of Western Gender Discourses* (Minneapolis: University of Minnesota Press, 1997), 29, 44.
5. Dapper also reports this tradition in the Kingdom of Jolof, in present-day Senegal, and the Gold Coast. Olfert Dapper, *Description de l'Afrique* [. . .] (Amsterdam: Chez Wolfgang, Waesberge, Bom & van Someren, 1686), 234–35, 299.
6. Oyěwùmí, *Invention of Women*, 53–54.
7. See Kwasi Konadu, "'To Satisfy My Savage Appetite': Slavery, Belief, and Sexual Violence on the Mina (Gold) Coast, 1471–1571," *Journal of African History* (2022): 1–16. For a longer and more detailed study of these cases, see also Kwasi Konadu, *Many Black Women of This Fortress: Graça, Mónica and Adwoa, Three Enslaved Women of Portugal's African Empire* (London: Hurst, 2022).
8. Dapper, *Description de l'Afrique*, 260.
9. Olfert Dapper, *Naukeurige beschrijvinge der Afrikaensche gewesten* [. . .], vol. 2 (Amsterdam: J. van Meurs, 1676), 219, 106. The passage describing these

women is absent from the French edition of 1686; see Dapper, *Description de l'Afrique*, 277. For an English translation of this passage, see Adam Jones, "Prostitution, Polyandry or Rape? On the Ambiguity of European Sources for the West African Coast 1660–1860," in Candido and Jones, *African Women in the Atlantic World*, 90.

10. Emmanuel Akyeampong, "Sexuality and Prostitution among the Akan of the Gold Coast c. 1650–1950," *Past & Present*, no. 156 (1997): 146.
11. A. Jones, "Prostitution, Polyandry or Rape?" 93, 97–105.
12. See Bay, *Wives of the Leopard*.
13. See Lynne Ellsworth Larsen, "Wives and Warriors: The Royal Women of Dahomey as Representatives of the Kingdom," in *The Routledge Companion to Black Women's Cultural Histories*, ed. Janell Hobson (London: Routledge, 2021), 227. See Gina Prince-Bythewood, dir., *The Woman King* (TriStar Pictures, 2022).
14. Melville J. Herskovits, *Dahomey: An Ancient West African Kingdom* (Evanston, IL: Northwestern University Press, 1967), 2:46.
15. Robin Law, "The 'Amazons' of Dahomey," *Paideuma: Mitteilungen zur Kulturkunde* 39 (1993): 256.
16. See Law, " 'Amazons' of Dahomey," 256.
17. Suzanne Preston Blier, "Mort et créativité dans la tradition des amazones du Dahomey," in *Ethnocentrisme et création*, ed. Annie Dupuis (Paris: Éditions de la Maison des sciences de l'homme, 2013), 73.
18. Melville J. Herskovits, "A Note on 'Woman Marriage' in Dahomey," *Africa: Journal of the International African Institute* 10, no. 3 (1937): 335–41.
19. Nwando Achebe, *The Female King of Colonial Nigeria: Ahebi Ugbabe* (Bloomington: Indiana University Press, 2011), 81.
20. Equiano and Carretta, *Interesting Narrative*, 33.
21. On European and African notions of childhood, see Benjamin N. Lawrance, *Amistad's Orphans: An Atlantic Story of Children, Slavery, and Smuggling* (New Haven, CT: Yale University Press, 2014), 20, 29. See also D. da Silva, *Atlantic Slave Trade*, 111–12.
22. "Viagens de Cadamosto e Pedro de Sintra: Primeira viagem de Cadamosto (22-3-1455)" in Brásio, *Monumenta Missionaria Africana: Segunda série*, 1:322.
23. On Senegal, see H. Jones, *Métis of Senegal*, and J. Johnson, *Wicked Flesh*. On the Gold Coast, see Feinberg, *Africans and Europeans in West Africa*, and Ipsen, *Daughters of the Trade*. On Benguela and Luanda, see Candido, "Aguida Gonçalves da Silva," and V. Oliveira, *Slave Trade and Abolition*.
24. Mustakeem, *Slavery at Sea*, 38–41.
25. On sexual violence in these early exchanges on the Gold Coast, see Konadu, " 'To Satisfy My Savage Appetite,' " and Kwasi Konadu, *Many Black Women of This Fortress*.
26. Eustache de la Fosse, *Voyage à la côte occidentale d'Afrique en Portugal et en Espagne (1479–1480)* (Paris: Foulché-Delbosc, 1897), 14–15.

27. Audra A. Diptee, *From Africa to Jamaica: The Making of an Atlantic Slave Society, 1775–1807* (Gainesville: University Press of Florida, 2010), 22–23.
28. Lawrance, *Amistad's Orphans*, 120.
29. Harms, *Diligent*, 312.
30. Harms, *Diligent*, 312, and Deveau, *La traite rochelaise*, 241.
31. Johannes Menne Postma, *The Dutch in the Atlantic Slave Trade 1600–1815* (Cambridge: Cambridge University Press, 1990), 243; Mustakeem, *Slavery at Sea*, 85.
32. ADCM 17, 4J 45 2318, *Mémoires de Jacques Proa dit Proa des îles*, 113–14. On Proa's memoir, see Antoine Régis, "Aventures d'un jeune négrier français d'après un manuscrit inédit du XVIIIe siècle," *Notes africaines*, April 1974 , 51–56. See also J. Johnson, *Wicked Flesh*, 83.
33. Cugoano, *Thoughts and Sentiments*, 15.
34. See Deveau, *La traite rochelaise*, 241. On this specific slave voyage, see Slave-Voyages, Voyage ID 32363, www.slavevoyages.org/voyage/database.
35. ADLA B4596, Rapports des capitaines à l'Amirauté de Nantes, Rapports des capitaines au long cours, August 23, 1777, ff113–14. Part of the document is summarized in Jean Mettas and Serge Daget, *Répertoire des expéditions négrières françaises au XVIIIe siècle*, vol. 1 (Nantes: Société française d'histoire d'outre-mer et Librairie orientaliste Paul Geuthner, 1979), voyage 1048, pp. 600–601. The case is also quoted in Robert Stein, *The French Slave Trade in the Eighteenth Century: An Old Regime Business* (Madison: University of Wisconsin Press, 1979), 101.
36. James Field Stanfield, *The Guinea Voyage, a Poem* [. . .] (Edinburgh: J. Robertson, 1807), 74. See Rediker, *Slave Ship*, 152.
37. Falconbridge, *Account of the Slave Trade*, 23.
38. John Newton, *Upon the African Slave Trade* (London, 1788), 20. See also Harms, *Diligent*, 313.
39. Entry of February 3, 1753, in Newton, Martin, and Spurrell, *Journal of a Slave Trader*, 75. See also Rediker, *Slave Ship*, 179, and Mustakeem, *Slavery at Sea*, 86.
40. House of Commons Parliamentary Papers, United Kingdom (hereafter cited as HCPP), *Correspondence with the British Commissioners Relating to the Slave Trade, 1838–9*, [180.] Class A, Correspondence with the British Commissioners at Sierra Leone, The Havana, Rio de Janeiro, and Surinam, Relating to the Slave Trade from May 1st 1838 to February 2nd 1839, vol. XLVIII, Sess. 1839 (London: Clowes and Sons, 1839), 27.
41. Rapes are mentioned in Manuel Barcia, *The Yellow Demon of Fever: Fighting Disease in the Nineteenth-Century Transatlantic* (New Haven, CT: Yale University Press, 2020), 49. Details about these rapes are in Barcia, "White Cannibalism in the Illegal Slave Trade," 1–28.
42. The National Archives, Kew, UK (hereafter cited as TNA), Foreign Office 84/347, vol. 45, Draft to the H. Ms. Commission, Havana, August 9, 1841, no. 20, 54v. Contemporaneous observers described the case in John Flude

Johnson, *Proceedings of the General Anti-Slavery Convention, and held in London from Tuesday, June 13th, to Tuesday, June 20th, 1843* (London: British and Foreign Anti-Slavery Society, 1843), 228–29. The incident was widely reported in the abolitionist press that employed the term *rape*; see "Tidings from Cuba," *British and Foreign Anti-Slavery Reporter*, May 5, 1841, 85. See also Dale T. Graden, *Disease, Resistance, and Lies: The Demise of the Transatlantic Slave Trade to Brazil and Cuba* (Baton Rouge: Louisiana State University Press, 2014), 50.

43. Edward E. Baptist, "'Cuffy,' 'Fancy Maids,' and 'One-Eyed Men': Rape, Commodification, and the Domestic Slave Trade in the United States," *American Historical Review* 106, no. 5 (2001): 1641–42.

44. For the Iberian Peninsula, see the case of sixteenth-century enslaved breeders in Vila Viçosa, Évora, in Portugal, documented in the travel account by Alessandrino Legato, an Italian emissary sent to Portugal by Pope Pius V. See Biblioteca da Ajuda, Lisbon, Portugal (hereafter cited as BA), "Rerum Lusitanicarum—Symmicta Lusitanica," Viaggio del Cardinale Alessandrino Legato Apostolico Alli Ser Re di Francia, Spanha e Portogallo, 1571, 46-IX-3; and Jorge Fonseca, *Escravos e senhores na Lisboa quinhentista* (Lisbon: Edições Colibri, 2010). For seventeenth-century New England, see John Jesselyn, *An Account of Two Voyages to New England: Made During the Years 1638, 1663* (Boston: W. Veazie, 1865), 26.

45. See Gregory D. Smithers, *Slave Breeding: Sex, Violence, and Memory in African American History* (Gainesville: University Press of Florida, 2012), and Thomas A. Foster, *Rethinking Rufus: Sexual Violations of Enslaved Men* (Athens: University of Georgia Press, 2019), 50.

46. Daina Ramey Berry, *"Swing the Sickle for the Harvest Is Ripe": Gender and Slavery in Antebellum Georgia* (Champaign: University of Illinois Press, 2010), 79. On forced breeding, see also Berry, *Price for Their Pound of Flesh*, 78–80.

47. See Smithers, *Slave Breeding*, 1–2, and Foster, *Rethinking Rufus*, 55.

48. See Marinaldo Fernando de Souza, "Além da escola: Reflexões teórico-metodológicas com base na análise de práticas educativas alternativas descobertas em áreas rurais da região de São Carlos, S.P." (PhD diss., Universidade Estadual Paulista, 2016).

49. Clóvis Moura, *Dicionário da escravidão negra no Brasil* (São Paulo: Editora da Universidade de São Paulo, 2004), 346.

50. Hebe Mattos, "Os Combates da Memória: Escravidão e liberdade nos arquivos orais de descendentes de escravos brasileiros," *Tempo* 3, no. 6 (1998): 10–11.

51. Trevor Burnard, *Mastery, Tyranny, and Desire: Thomas Thistlewood and His Slaves in the Anglo-Jamaican World* (Chapel Hill: University of North Carolina Press, 2004), 82.

52. Vincent Brown, *Tacky's Revolt: The Story of an Atlantic War* (Cambridge, MA: Harvard University Press, 2020), 58.

53. Burnard, *Mastery, Tyranny, and Desire*, 261.
54. Prince, *History of Mary Prince*, 24.
55. Jacobs, *Incidents in the Life of a Slave Girl*, 34.
56. Arquivo Nacional da Torre do Tombo, Lisbon, Portugal (hereafter cited as ANTT), Tribunal do Santo Ofício, Inquisição de Lisboa, Processo 9065. Anthropologist Luiz Mott was the first scholar to bring this case to light. See Luiz Mott, *Rosa Egipcíaca: Uma santa africana no Brasil* (Rio de Janeiro: Bertrand do Brasil, 1993), and Luiz Mott, "Rosa Egipcíaca: De escrava da Costa da Mina à Flor do Rio de Janeiro," in *Rotas atlânticas da diáspora africana: Da Baía do Benim ao Rio de Janeiro*, ed. Mariza de Carvalho Soares (Rio de Janeiro: Editora da Universidade Federal Fluminense, 2007), 135–55.
57. ANTT, Tribunal do Santo Ofício, Inquisição de Lisboa, Processo 9065, fl. 77v.
58. ANTT, Tribunal do Santo Ofício, Inquisição de Lisboa, Processo 9065, fl. 77v–78.
59. ANTT, Tribunal do Santo Ofício, Inquisição de Lisboa, "Minuta da certidão da fé de notários e auto de falecimento da ré Rosa Maria Egicíaca," October 12–13, 1771, 18078, fl. 1–2.
60. See Keila Grinberg, *Liberata: A lei da ambigüidade; As ações de liberdade da corte de apelação do Rio de Janeiro no século XIX* (Rio de Janeiro: Centro Edelstein de Pesquisas Sociais, 2008), and Keila Grinberg, "Manumission, Gender, and the Law in Nineteenth-Century Brazil: Liberata's Legal Suit for Freedom," in *Paths to Freedom: Manumission in the Atlantic World*, ed. Rosemary Brana-Shute and Randy J. Sparks (Columbia: University of South Carolina Press, 2009), 219–34.
61. Gunvor Simonsen, *Slave Stories: Law, Representation, and Gender in the Danish West Indies* (Aarhus, Denmark: Aarhus University Press, 2017), 77, 97.
62. "Defloramento da escrava pelo senhor." See the transcription of this case translated in English in Robert Conrad, *Children of God's Fire: A Documentary History of Black Slavery in Brazil* (Princeton, NJ: Princeton University Press, 1997), 273–80.
63. On this case, see Luiz Mott, *Bahia: Inquisição e sociedade* (Salvador, Brazil: Editora da Universidade da Bahia, 2010), 142–43.
64. Mariana P. Candido, "Transatlantic Links: The Benguela-Bahia Connections, 1700–1850," in *Paths of the Atlantic Slave Trade: Interactions, Identities and Images*, ed. Ana Lucia Araujo (Amherst, NY: Cambria Press, 2011), 247–48.
65. ANTT, Tribunal do Santo Ofício, Inquisição de Lisboa, Process 6478, December 6, 1703, fl. 2–2v.
66. ANTT, Tribunal do Santo Ofício, Inquisição de Lisboa, Process 5708, May 20, 1741, fl. 4.
67. See Ronaldo Vainfas, "Sodomy, Love, and Slavery in Colonial Brazil: A Case Study of Minas Gerais during the Eighteenth Century," in *Sex, Power, and*

Slavery, ed. Gwyn Campbell and Elizabeth Elbourne (Athens: Ohio University Press, 2014), 534.

68. Vainfas, "Sodomy, Love, and Slavery in Colonial Brazil," 535.

69. This trial is transcribed and translated in English in Richard A. Gordon, "Confessing Sodomy, Accusing a Master: The Lisbon Trial of Pernambuco's Luiz da Costa, 1743," in *Afro-Latino Voices: Narratives from the Early Modern Ibero-Atlantic World, 1550–1812*, ed. Kathryn Joy McKnight and Leo J. Garofalo (Indianapolis: Hackett, 2009), 277.

70. Moura, *Dicionário da escravidão negra no Brasil*, 225.

71. See Martha Hodes, *White Women, Black Men: Illicit Sex in the 19th Century* (New Haven, CT: Yale University Press, 1997), and Foster, *Rethinking Rufus*, 33.

72. Manoel Bomfim, *A América Latina: Males de origem* (Rio de Janeiro: H. Garnier, 1905), 153.

73. Ulrike Schmieder, "Sexual Relations between Enslaved and between Slaves and Nonslaves in Nineteenth-Century Cuba," in Campbell and Elbourne, *Sex, Power, and Slavery*, 234–35.

74. On this case, see Schmieder, "Sexual Relations between Enslaved and between Slaves and Nonslaves," 236, 249n35.

75. Miguel Barnet, *Biografía de un cimarrón* (Buenos Aires: Centro Editor de América Latina, 1977), 31. The original edition of this biography is Miguel Barnet, *Biografía de un cimarrón* (Havana: Instituto de Etnología y Folklore, 1966).

76. Júnia Ferreira Furtado, *Chica da Silva: A Brazilian Slave of the Eighteenth Century* (New York: Cambridge University Press, 2009), 15–16.

77. Furtado, *Chica da Silva*, 46–47.

78. Furtado, *Chica da Silva*, 50.

79. Furtado, *Chica da Silva*, 105.

80. See, for example, the cases of Bernabela and Petrona Funes in eighteenth-century Córdoba in present-day Argentina, in Erika Denise Edwards, *Hiding in Plain Sight: Black Women, the Law, and the Making of a White Argentine Republic* (Tuscaloosa: University of Alabama Press, 2020), chap. 3.

81. See Gordon-Reed, *Hemingses of Monticello*. On the history and memory of Sally Hemings, see also Araujo, *Slavery in the Age of Memory*, 24–31.

82. On Chinn, see Amrita Chakrabarti Myers, *The Vice President's Black Wife: The Untold Life of Julia Chinn* (Chapel Hill: University of North Carolina Press, 2023).

83. According to Joshua D. Rothman, in the context of antebellum Virginia, some bondswomen were successful in resisting the sexual advances of slave owners and overseers. See Joshua D. Rothman, *Sex and Families across the Color Line in Virginia, 1787–1861* (Chapel Hill: University of North Carolina Press, 2003), 154–55.

Chapter 11

1. See James H. Sweet, "Defying Social Death: The Multiple Configurations of African Slave Family in the Atlantic World," *William and Mary Quarterly* 70, no. 2 (2013): 251–72.
2. See E. Edwards, *Hiding in Plain Sight*, 21–22.
3. John T. Dalton and Tin Cheuk Leung, "'Why Is Polygyny More Prevalent in Western Africa? An African Slave Trade Perspective," *Economic Development and Cultural Change* 62, no. 4 (2014): 599–632.
4. Equiano and Carretta, *Interesting Narrative*, 48.
5. Walter Hawthorne, "Being Now, as It Were One Family: Shipmate Bonding on the Slave Vessel Emilia, in Rio de Janeiro and throughout the Atlantic World," *Luso-Brazilian Review* 45, no. 1 (2008): 58.
6. Lovejoy and Law, *Biography of Mahommah Gardo Baquaqua*, 115.
7. Lovejoy and Law, *Biography of Mahommah Gardo Baquaqua*, 116.
8. Ajayi, "Samuel Ajayi Crowther of Oyo," 303.
9. Laura Murphy, "Obstacles in the Way of Love: The Enslavement of Intimacy in Samuel Crowther and Ama Ata Aidoo," *Research in African Literatures* 40, no. 4 (2009): 50.
10. Equiano and Carretta, *Interesting Narrative*, 56–59.
11. On the similarities of several Bantu languages that may have created a Bantu lingua franca in Brazil and facilitated exchanges between enslaved Africans transported from West Central Africa to Brazil, see Robert W. Slenes, "'Malungu, ngoma vem!' África coberta e descoberta do Brasil," *Revista USP* 12 (1992): 48–67. For a different perspective of these linguistic connections, see Marcos Abreu Leitão de Almeida, "African Voices from the Congo Coast: Languages and the Politics of Identification in the Slave Ship *Jovem Maria* (1850)," *Journal of African History* 60, no. 2 (2019): 167–89.
12. Hawthorne, "Being Now, as It Were One Family," 55–56, and Fett, *Recaptured Africans*, 9.
13. See Philip D. Curtin, *Two Jamaicas: The Role of Ideas in a Tropical Colony, 1830–1865* (Cambridge, MA: Harvard University Press, 1955), 26. Benjamin Lawrance explores these virtual slave ship families among the children of the slave vessel *Amistad*; see Lawrance, *Amistad's Orphans*, 6–15. For a summary of the shipmate debates, see Hawthorne, "Being Now, as It Were One Family," 55–57; Rosanne Adderley, *"New Negroes from Africa": Slave Trade Abolition and Free African Settlement in the Nineteenth-Century Caribbean* (Bloomington: Indiana University Press, 2006), 67; and Alex Borucki, *From Shipmates to Soldiers: Emerging Black Identities in the Rio de La Plata* (Albuquerque: University of New Mexico Press, 2015), 60–61.
14. See M. Soares, *People of Faith*, 16.
15. See Mintz and Price, *Birth of African-American Culture*.

16. V. Brown, *Reaper's Garden*, 45–46.
17. Susan Migden Socolow, "Permission to Marry: Eighteenth-Century Matrimonial Files (Montevideo, 1786)," in *Colonial Lives: Documents on Latin American History, 1550–1850*, ed. Richard Boyer and Geoffrey Spurling (New York: Oxford University Press, 2000), 236.
18. Borucki, *From Shipmates to Soldiers*, 63.
19. Bennett, *Africans in Colonial Mexico*, 79.
20. On Biafara, Biafada, or Beafada, see Wheat, *Atlantic Africa and the Spanish Caribbean*, 41.
21. See several other cases in Bennett, *Africans in Colonial Mexico*, 87–109.
22. Borucki, *From Shipmates to Soldiers*, 69.
23. Hawthorne, "Being Now, as It Were One Family," 63–64.
24. Hawthorne, "Being Now, as It Were One Family," 67–69.
25. Barbara Bush, "White 'Ladies,' Coloured 'Favourites' and Black 'Wenches'; Some Considerations on Sex, Race and Class Factors in Social Relations in White Creole Society in the British Caribbean," *Slavery and Abolition* 2, no. 3 (1981): 249, and Trevor Burnard, "'Rioting in Goatish Embraces': Marriage and Improvement in Early British Jamaica," *History of the Family* 11 (2006): 185–97.
26. See Brooke Newman, *A Dark Inheritance: Blood, Race, and Sex in Colonial Jamaica* (New Haven, CT: Yale University Press, 2018), 96. See also Daniel Livesay, *Children of Uncertain Fortune: Mixed-Race Jamaicans in Britain and the Atlantic Family, 1733–1833* (Chapel Hill: University of North Carolina Press, 2018), 403. Livesay's analysis of wills left by white men in Jamaica from 1773 to 1815 shows that less than 10 percent of these men acknowledged mixed-race children.
27. Rebecca Anne Goetz, *The Baptism of Early Virginia: How Christianity Created Race* (Baltimore: Johns Hopkins University Press, 2012), 80.
28. See Goetz, *Baptism of Early Virginia*, 80, and an "An act concerning Negroes and other Slaves," Maryland, September 1664, in Proceedings and Acts of the General Assembly of Maryland, January 1637/8–September 1664, ed. William Hand Browne (Baltimore, 1883), I:533–34, cited in Newman, *Dark Inheritance*, 81.
29. See Randy M. Browne and Trevor Burnard, "Husbands and Fathers: The Family Experience of Enslaved Men in Berbice, 1819–1834," *New West Indian Guide* 91 (2017): 193–222.
30. *Le Code Noir* [. . .] (Paris: Chez Claude Girard, 1685), 5.
31. On how Catholicism and the Roman law shaped Latin American legal codes regulating slavery, see the classic, although controversial, Frank Tannenbaum, *Slave and Citizen* (Boston: Beacon Press, 1992). For a more complete and updated view of the various legal systems inspired by Roman law, see Michelle McKinley, "Fractional Freedoms: Slavery, Legal Activism, and Ecclesiastical Courts in Colonial Lima, 1593–1689," *Law and History Review* 28, no. 3 (2010): 749–90, and Michelle A. McKinley, *Fractional Freedoms:*

Slavery, Intimacy, and Legal Mobilization in Colonial Lima, 1600–1700 (New York: Cambridge University Press, 2016), 10–11.

32. See Robert I. Burns and Samuel Parsons Scott, *Las Siete Partidas*, vol. 4, *Family, Commerce, and the Sea: The Worlds of Women and Merchants* (Philadelphia: University of Pittsburgh Press, 2000). For the *Code noir* of 1685 and the Louisiana *Code noir* of 1724, see *Recueil d'édits, déclarations et arrests de sa majesté, Concernant l'Administration de la Justice la Police des Colonies françaises de l'Amérique, & les Engagés* (Paris: Chez les Libraires Associez, 1744), 81–101 and 135–64.

33. See Cândido Mendes de Almeida, *Codigo philippino, ou, Ordenações e leis do reino de Portugal* (Rio de Janeiro: Typographia do Instituto Philomathico, 1870), vols. 1–5. For a commented version of volume 5, see Silvia Hunold Lara, ed. *Ordenações filipinas*, vol. 5 (São Paulo: Companhia das Letras, 1999). The *Ordenações filipinas* were complemented by uncodified laws (*leis extravagantes*). For later legislation, see *Constituições primeiras do* Sebastião Monteiro da Vide [. . .] (São Paulo: Typographia 2 de Dezembro, 1853).

34. Burns and Scott, *Family, Commerce, and the Sea*, Title XXI, Law II, 977. On the *Code noir* of 1685 and the Louisiana *Code noir* of 1724, see *Recueil d'édits*, Article XIII, 86, and Article IX, 139. Jurists commented on the notion of *partus sequitur ventrem* in late nineteenth-century editions of the *Ordenações filipinas*; see Almeida, *Codigo philippino*, Title XCVII, 4:970.

35. William Waller Hening, *The statutes at large: being a collection of all the laws of Virginia* [. . .], vol. 2 (Richmond: Samuel Pleasants, Junior, Printer to the Commonwealth, 1810), Act XII, 170. On the principle of *partus sequitur ventrem* in the English colonies of the Americas, see Jennifer L. Morgan, "Partus sequitur ventrem: Law, Race, and Reproduction in Colonial Slavery," *Small Axe* 22, no. 1 (2018): 1–17, and B. Newman, *Dark Inheritance*, 81–82.

36. Alejandro de La Fuente and Ariela J. Gross, "Comparative Studies of Law, Slavery, and Race in the Americas," *Annual Review of Law and Social Science* 6 (2010): 469–85.

37. David L. Chandler, "Family Bonds and the Bondsman: The Slave Family in Colonial Colombia," *Latin American Research Review* 16, no. 2 (1981): 109.

38. Schwartz, *Sugar Plantations*, 385.

39. Jorge Benci de Arimino, *Economia Christã dos senhores no governo dos escravos deduzida a das palavras do capitulo trinta e três do Ecclesiastico* [. . .] (Rome: Officina de Antonio de Rossi, 1705), 85–91.

40. Arimino, *Economia Christã dos senhores*, 117–18.

41. Mott, *Bahia: Inquisição e sociedade*, 47. See Coleção Luísa da Fonseca, AHU, ACL, CU 005, Cx. 32, docs. 4131 and 4132, February 12, 1698.

42. ANTT, Tribunal do Santo Ofício, Inquisição de Lisboa, Processo 10026.

43. For a detailed analysis of Páscoa's trajectory in Angola and Brazil, see Rita de Cássia Santos Silva, "A vida desinquieta de Páscoa Vieira: Uma escrava nas malhas do Santo Ofício" (MA thesis, Universidade do Estado da Bahia, 2018).

44. ANTT, Tribunal do Santo Ofício, Inquisição de Lisboa, Processo 10026, fl. 68. R. Silva, "A vida desinquieta de Páscoa Vieira," 85–87.
45. For a more general overview of Páscoa's story with a focus on marriage and the Catholic Church, see Charlotte Castelnau-L'Estoile, *Páscoa et ses deux maris: Une esclave entre Angola, Brésil et Portugal au XVIIe siècle* (Paris: Presses Universitaires de France, 2019).
46. Castelnau-L'Estoile, *Páscoa et ses deux maris*, 70.
47. The terms employed in the case to refer to sexual relations outside marriage are "estar em mau estado" and "andar em mau estado," which literally mean "to be" or "to go" "in a bad state." ANTT, Tribunal do Santo Ofício, Inquisição de Lisboa, Processo 10026, fl. 68–69v.
48. R. Silva, "A vida desinquieta de Páscoa Vieira," 57–58.
49. Bigamy was also criminalized in the Portuguese compiled laws. See Cândido Mendes de Almeida, *Codigo philippino*, Title XIX, 5:1170.
50. *Constituições primeiras do Sebastião Monteiro da Vide*, vol. 1, Title LXXI, paragraph 303, p. 125.
51. See Charlotte de Castelnau-L'Estoile, "La liberté du sacrement: Droit canonique et mariage des esclaves dans le Brésil colonial," *Annales: Histoire, Sciences sociales* 65 (2010) 1349–83.
52. Antonil, *Cultura e opulência do Brasil por suas drogas e minas*, 33.
53. Manoel Ribeiro Rocha, *Ethiope resgatado, empenhado, sustentado, corregido, instruído, e liberado* [. . .] (Lisbon: Officina Patriarcal de Francisco Luiz Ameno: 1758), 272–73.
54. McKinley, *Fractional Freedoms*, 164.
55. Thiago Krause, "Compadrio e escravidão na Bahia seiscentista," *Afro-Ásia* 50 (2014): 199–228.
56. M. Soares, *People of Faith*, 95.
57. There were exceptions. For example, in 1791, lay authorities determined that the church could not request these permissions to marry to free and enslaved people born in the parish of São Paulo, Brazil.
58. Kenneth Mills, William B. Taylor, and Sandra Lauderdale Graham, ed. *Colonial Latin America: A Documentary History* (Lanham, MD: SR Books, 2004), 373.
59. H. Klein and Luna, *Slavery in Brazil*, 223–24, and Castelnau-L'Estoile, "La liberté du sacrement," 1357.
60. Debret, *Voyage pittoresque et historique au Brasil*, 3:149, plate 15.
61. On Caetana's story, see Sandra Lauderdale Graham, *Caetana Says No: Women's Stories from a Brazilian Slave Society* (New York: Cambridge University Press, 2002).
62. Historian Robert Slenes studied Campinas, in São Paulo, in the second half of the nineteenth century, but this prohibition was also recorded by other historians working in regions such as Bahia and Rio de Janeiro. Robert Slenes, *Na Senzala, uma flor: Esperanças e recordações na formação da família escrava* (Campinas, Brazil: Editora da Universidade Estadual de Campinas, 1999), 83–84, 127 n23.

63. McKinley, *Fractional Freedoms*, 79.
64. McKinley, *Fractional Freedoms*, 79–81.
65. Laird W. Bergad, *Slavery and the Demographic and Economic History of Minas Gerais, Brazil, 1720–1888* (New York: Cambridge University Press, 1999), 104.
66. Manolo Florentino and José Roberto Góes, *A paz nas senzalas: Famílias escravas e tráfico atlântico, Rio de Janeiro, c. 1790–c. 1850* (Rio de Janeiro: Civilização Brasileira: 1997), 61–64, and Slenes, *Na Senzala, uma flor*, 84.
67. See Hodes, *White Women, Black Men*, chap. 2.
68. Wendy Warren, *New England Bound: Slavery and Colonization in Early America* (New York: Liveright, 2016), 159.
69. *Recueil d'édits*, Article VI, p. 138.
70. The Spanish crown issued legislation (Real Pragmatica of 1776–78) seeking to prohibit marriage between individuals of different social ranks. See McKinley, *Fractional Freedoms*, 116–17.
71. Ronaldo Vainfas, *Trópico dos pecados: Moral, Sexualidade e inquisição no Brasil* (Rio de Janeiro: Civilização Brasileira, 2010), 114.
72. See Tera Hunter, *Bound in Wedlock: Slave and Free Black Marriage in the Nineteenth Century* (Cambridge, MA: Belknap Press of Harvard University Press, 2017), 1.
73. H. B. Holloway, interview, Federal Writers' Project of the Works Progress Administration for the State of Arkansas, *Slave Narratives: A Folk History of Slavery in the United States with Interviews with Former Slaves* (Washington, DC: Library of Congress, 1941), vol. 2, pt. 3, p. 288.
74. Brenda E. Stevenson, *Life in Black and White: Family and Community in the Slave South* (New York: Oxford University Press, 1996), 209.
75. See Hunter, *Bound in Wedlock*, 26, and Tyler D. Parry, *Jumping the Broom: The Surprising Multicultural Origins of a Black Wedding Ritual* (Chapel Hill: University of North Carolina Press, 2020), 43.
76. Hunter, *Bound in Wedlock*, 51.
77. Sam and Louisa Everett, interview, October 8, 1936, Federal Writers' Project, *Slave Narratives*, vol. 3, p. 126.
78. Sam and Louisa Everett, interview, p. 128. See also Parry, *Jumping the Broom*, 46.
79. Stephanie M. H. Camp, *Closer to Freedom: Enslaved Women and Everyday Resistance in the Plantation South* (Chapel Hill: University of North Carolina Press, 2004), 45.

Chapter 12

1. AMLR, EEARCHANC "Journal de navigation à l'usage de J. Crassous-Médeuil," "Du Jeudy 26 au Vendredy 27 août 1773," 46. This birth can also be found in the commented edition of this journal; see Yacou, *Journaux de bord et de traite de Joseph Crassous de Médeuil*, 193.

2. For details on the vessel *La Marie-Séraphique*, see Bertrand Guillet, *La Marie-Séraphique: Navire négrier* (Nantes, Fr.: MeMo, 2010).
3. The watercolor also shows a representation of an additional enslaved woman with a child at her feet, who could be her child, see Nicholas Radburn and David Eltis, "Visualizing the Middle Passage: The *Brooks* and the Reality of Ship Crowding in the Transatlantic Slave Trade," *Journal of Interdisciplinary History* 99, no. 4 (2019): 548.
4. Archives Nationales d'outre-mer, Aix-en-Provence, France (FR ANOM), COL E 209TER 1774/1793, Pierre Simon Gourg, écrivain principal des colonies, faisant fonction de commissaire ordonnateur au comptoir de Juda, "Mémoire du Sieur Gourg," no. 54, 68.
5. Sasha Turner, "The Nameless and the Forgotten: Maternal Grief, Sacred Protection, and the Archive of Slavery," *Slavery and Abolition* 30, no. 2 (2017): 233.
6. J. Morgan, *Laboring Women*, 68.
7. See Sharla M. Fett, *Working Cures: Healing, Health, and Power on Southern Slave Plantations* (Chapel Hill: University of North Carolina Press, 2002), 195; Katherine Paugh, *The Politics of Reproduction: Race, Medicine, and Fertility in the Age of Abolition* (Oxford: Oxford University Press, 2017), 97; Cassia Roth, "From Free Womb to Criminalized Woman: Fertility Control in Brazilian Slavery and Freedom," *Slavery and Abolition* 38, no. 2 (2017): 273; and Deirdre Cooper-Owens, *Medical Bondage: Race, Gender, and the Origins of American Gynecology* (Athens: University of Georgia Press, 2017), 87.
8. On Jamaica's "racialized sexual economy," see B. Newman, *Dark Inheritance*, esp. chap. 4.
9. See the case of Susanna Augier, in B. Newman, *Dark Inheritance*, 95–96.
10. See C. de Souza, "'Perseguidores da espécie humana,'" 82–83, 93.
11. See Adriana Dantas Reis Alves, "As mulheres negras por cima: O caso de Luzia Jeje; Escravidão família e mobilidade social-Bahia, c. 1780–c. 1830" (PhD diss., Universidade Federal Fluminense, 2010).
12. For more on Luzia Jeje, see Adriana Dantas Reis, "Mulheres 'Afro-descendentes' na Bahia Gênero, cor e mobilidade social (1780–1830)," in *Mulheres negras no Brasil escravista e do pós emancipação*, ed. Giovana Xavier, Juliana Barreto Farias, and Flavio Gomes (Rio de Janeiro: Selo Negro, 2012), 30.
13. See Olívia Dulce Lobo, "Laura Congo e a família escrava do Barão de Tinguá: Reflexões sobre a família no Vale do Paraíba fluminense (1830–1888)" (MA thesis, Universidade Federal do Estado do Rio de Janeiro, 2017), 64, 86.
14. On Brazil, see Mariana Dantas, "Child Abandonment and Foster Care in Colonial Brazil: Expostos and the Free Population of African Descent in Eighteenth-Century Minas Gerais," in Brana-Shute and Sparks, *Paths to Freedom: Manumission in the Atlantic World*, 199. On Córdoba, see E. Edwards, *Hiding in Plain Sight*, 24–25.

15. Maria Elizabeth Ribeiro Carneiro, "Procura-se 'preta,' com muito bom leite, prendada e carinhosa: Uma cartografia das amas-de-leite na sociedade carioca (1850–1888)" (PhD diss., Universidade de Brasília, 2006), 48–50.
16. See Dantas, "Child Abandonment and Foster Care in Colonial Brazil," 204.
17. See Diana Paton, "The Driveress and the Nurse: Childcare, Working Children and Other Work under Caribbean Slavery," *Past & Present* 246, no. 15 (2020): 27–28.
18. Sasha Turner, *Contested Bodies: Pregnancy, Childrearing, and Slavery in Jamaica* (Philadelphia: University of Pennsylvania Press, 2017), 106.
19. Also on Jamaica's nurseries in the early nineteenth century, see Richard B. Sheridan, *Doctors and Slaves: A Medical and Demographic History of Slavery in the British West Indies, 1680–1834* (New York: Cambridge University Press, 1985), 281–82.
20. S. Turner, *Contested Bodies*, 108.
21. Catherine Clinton, *The Plantation Mistress: Woman's World in the Old South* (New York: Pantheon Books, 1982), 155.
22. Emily West and R. J. Knight, "Mother's Milk: Slavery, Wet-Nursing, and Black and White Women in the Antebellum South," *Journal of Southern History* 133, no. 1 (2017): 55.
23. S. Turner, *Contested Bodies*, 121–23.
24. Maria Helena Pereira Toledo Machado, "Between Two Beneditos: Enslaved Wet-Nurses Amid Slavery's Decline in Southeast Brazil," *Slavery and Abolition* 38, no. 2 (2017): 320–21, and West and Knight, "Mother's Milk," 54, 58.
25. McKinley, *Fractional Freedoms*, 91.
26. Stephanie E. Jones-Rogers, "'[S]he Could . . . Spare One Ample Breast for the Profit of her Owner': White Mothers and Enslaved Wet Nurses' Invisible Labor in American Slave Markets," *Slavery and Abolition* 38, no. 2 (2017): 337–55.
27. West and Knight, "Mother's Milk," 41.
28. *Gazeta do Rio de Janeiro*, June 25, 1814, 4.
29. *Gazeta do Rio de Janeiro*, July 10, 1813, 4; *Gazeta do Rio de Janeiro*, January 5, 1820, 4.
30. Enslaved infants' mortality in nineteenth-century Rio de Janeiro was higher than 50 percent; see Karasch, *Slave Life in Rio de Janeiro*, 100–101.
31. The use of the pejorative term "mercenary nursing" to refer to "nursing by a stranger" was already in use in French (*allaitement mercenaire*) in the early nineteenth century; see Jacques-Pierre Maygrier, *Nouvelles démonstrations d'accouchemens* (Paris: Béchet, 1822), 78. See also Carneiro, "Procura-se 'preta,'" 148–61, Sandra Sofia Machado Koutsoukos, "'Amas mercenárias': O discurso dos doutores em medicina e os retratos de amas–Brasil, segunda metade do século XIX," *História, Ciências, Saúde–Manguinhos* 16, no. 2 (2009): 307; Okezi T. Otovo, *Progressive Mothers: Better Babies: Race, Public Health, and the State in Brazil, 1850–1945* (Austin: University of Texas Press, 2016), 39; and M. Machado, "Between Two Beneditos," 322.

32. Francisco José Coelho de Moura, "Do aleitamento natural, artificial e mixto em geral e em particular do mercenario attentas às condições da cidade do Rio de Janeiro: These apresentada à Faculdade de Medicina do Rio de Janeiro" (Rio de Janeiro: Typographia Carioca, 1874), 25–26.
33. For the full story, see M. Machado, "Between Two Beneditos."
34. See Renée Soulodre-La France, "'Por El Amor!' Child Killing in Colonial Nueva Granada," *Slavery and Abolition* 23, no. 1 (2002): 90.
35. See, for example, the case of the Viceroyalty of Peru, in McKinley, *Fractional Freedoms*, 91.
36. This case is explored in Soulodre-La France, "'Por El Amor!'" 87–100.
37. See Marcela Echeverri, "'Enraged to the Limit of Despair': Infanticide and Slave Judicial Strategies in Barbacoas, 1788–98," *Slavery and Abolition* 30, no. 3 (2009): 403–26.
38. I explored this case in more detail, but from the point of view of slave resistance, in Ana Lucia Araujo, "Black Purgatory: Enslaved Women's Resistance in Nineteenth-Century Rio Grande do Sul, Brazil," *Slavery and Abolition* 36 no. 4 (2015): 568–85.
39. Dario Scott, "A população do Rio Grande de São Pedro pelos mapas populacionais de 1780 a 1810," *Revista brasileira de estudos populacionais* 34, no. 3 (2017): 624.
40. H. Klein and Luna, *Slavery in Brazil*, 62–63.
41. Classic early studies on slavery in Rio Grande do Sul include Fernando Henrique Cardoso, *Capitalismo e escravidão no Brasil meridional* (São Paulo: Difusão Europeia do Livro, 1962), 54–66; Mário Maestri Filho, *O escravo no Rio Grande do Sul: A charqueada e a gênese do escravismo gaúcho* (Caxias do Sul, Brazil: Editora da Universidade de Caxias do Sul, 1984); and Jacob Gorender, *A escravidão reabilitada* (São Paulo: Ática, 1990), 422.
42. Arquivo Público do Estado do Rio Grande do Sul (hereafter cited as APERS), 874, 26, 31, March 5, 1825.
43. APERS, 003, 117, 01, 33, January 7, 1822, 9v.
44. Freyre, *Casa-grande e senzala*, 421. Mary C. Karasch also observes that "women often had the reputation for cruelty and brutality." See Karasch, *Slave Life in Rio de Janeiro*, 113–15.
45. Camp, *Closer to Freedom*, 43.
46. APERS, 223, 09, 33, March 21, 1826, f11.
47. APERS, 272, 11, 10, 1828, 8v.
48. The best and only history monograph about Garner's case is Nikki M. Taylor, *Driven toward Madness: The Fugitive Slave Margaret Garner and Tragedy on the Ohio* (Athens: Ohio University Press, 2016).
49. See Toni Morrison, *Beloved: A Novel* (New York: Knopf, 1987). On the motion picture, see Jonathan Demme, dir., *Beloved* (Buena Vista Pictures, 1998). On the opera, see Richard Danielpour, Toni Morrison, and Mary Lou

Humphrey, *Margaret Garner: An Opera in Two Acts* (New York: Associated Music Publishers, 2005).

50. The Avalon Project: Documents in Law, History, and Diplomacy, Yale Law School, Lillian Goldman Law Library, "Constitution of Vermont, July 8, 1777," http://avalon.law.yale.edu/18th_century/vt01.asp. On Vermont, see also Harvey Amani Whitfield, *The Problem of Slavery in Early Vermont, 1777–1810: Essays and Primary Sources* (Barre: Vermont Historical Society, 2014), 16, 19.

51. Avalon Project, "Pennsylvania: An Act for the Gradual Abolition of Slavery, 1780," http://avalon.law.yale.edu/18th_century/pennst01.asp.

52. Rhode Island State Archives (hereafter cited as RISA), Rhode Island General Assembly, "An Act Authorizing the Manumission of Negroes, Mallattoes, & Others, and for the Gradual Abolition of Slavery," 1784, in Virtual Exhibits, Item #71, http://sos.ri.gov/virtualarchives/items/show/71.

53. "Title CL. Slaves, Chap. I, An Act Concerning Indian, Mulatto, and Negro Servants and Slaves," in *Acts and Laws Passed by the General Assembly of the State of Connecticut, The Public Laws of the State of Connecticut*, Book 1 (Hartford, CT: Hudson and Goodwin, 1808), 625. See also David Menschel, "Abolition without Deliverance: The Law of Connecticut Slavery 1784–1848." *Yale Law Journal* 111, no. 1 (2001): 187–88.

54. Library of Congress, Washington, DC, United States (hereafter cited as LOC), "An Act for the Gradual Abolition of Slavery . . . Passed at Trenton Feb. 15, 1804" (Burlington, S. C. Ustick, printer [1804]). See also James J. Gigantino II, *The Ragged Road to Abolition: Slavery and Freedom in New Jersey, 1775–1865* (Philadelphia: University of Pennsylvania Press, 2015), 117.

55. On the term "free womb captives," see Yesenia Barragan, *Freedom's Captives: Slavery and Gradual Emancipation on the Colombia Pacific* (New York: Cambridge University Press, 2021), 5–6.

56. On Chile, see Guillermo Feliú Cruz, *La abolición de la esclavitud en Chile* (Santiago de Chile: Editorial Universitaria, 1973), 39–40. On Argentina, see George Reid Andrews, *Los afroargentinos de Buenos Aires* (Buenos Aires: Ediciones de la Flor, 1989), 59.

57. See Magdalena Candioti, "Free Womb Law, Legal Asynchronies, and Migrations: Suing for an Enslaved Woman's Child in Nineteenth-Century Río de La Plata," *Americas* 77, no. 1 (2020): 73–99. Petrona's case is also explored in Magdalena Candioti, *Una historia de la emancipación negra* (Buenos Aires: Siglo Veintiuno Editores, 2021), chap. 2.

58. Candioti, "Free Womb Law, Legal Asynchronies, and Migrations," 90.

59. Barragan, *Freedom's Captives*, 109.

60. See George Reid Andrews, *Afro-Latin America, 1800–2000* (New York: Oxford University Press, 2004), 64, and Barragan, *Freedom's Captives*, 188.

61. Barragan, *Freedom's Captives*, 186.

62. For a comparison between Cuba's Moret Law of 1870 and Brazil's Free Womb Law of 1871, see Cowling, *Conceiving Freedom*, 56–57.

63. *Ley de Cuatro de Julio de 1870 Sobre Abolición de la Esclavitud y Reglamento para su ejecución en las islas de Cuba y Puerto Rico* (Havana: Gobierno y Capitania general por S. M., 1872).
64. Biblioteca Digital do Senado Federal, Brasília, Brazil, Lei no. 2040 de 28 de setembro de 1871 [Lei do Ventre Livre], manuscript document.
65. Angela Alonso, *Flores, votos e balas: O movimento abolicionista brasileiro (1868–1888)* (São Paulo: Companhia das Letras, 2015), 78, 80.
66. Maíra Chinelatto Alves, "Crimes de escravos e os caminhos da autônima, Campinas, 1876," in *Tornando-se livre: Agentes históricos e lutas sociais no processo de abolição*, ed. Helena P. T. Machado and Celso Thomas Castilho (São Paulo: Editora da Universidade de São Paulo, 2014), 43.
67. Cowling, *Conceiving Freedom*, 88.

Chapter 13

1. APERS, 139, 06, 123, October 6, 1820. On this case, see Araujo, "Black Purgatory."
2. The story of Santana's *engenho* treaty, brought to light by historian Stuart B. Schwartz, is reproduced in Stuart B. Schwartz, "Resistance and Accommodation in Eighteenth-Century Brazil: The Slaves' View of Slavery," *Hispanic American Historical Review* 57, no. 1 (1977): 69–81.
3. For an introduction on everyday resistance, see Gomez, *Reversing Sail*, 136.
4. On enslaved women poisoning their owners in eighteenth-century Massachusetts, see Nikki M. Taylor, *Brooding over Bloody Revenge: Enslaved Women's Lethal Resistance* (New York: Cambridge University Press, 2023), chap. 1, and in nineteenth-century Virginia, see Tamika Y. Nunley, *The Demands of Justice: Enslaved Women, Capital Crime, and Clemency in Early Virginia* (Chapel Hill: University of North Carolina Press, 2023), chap. 2.
5. Diana Paton, "Witchcraft, Poison, Law, and Atlantic Slavery," *William and Mary Quarterly* 69, no. 2 (2012) 235–64.
6. See Almeida, *Codigo philippino*, title LXIII, 5:1212, and Caldeira, *Escravos em Portugal*, 253.
7. Anabela Natário, Christiana Martins, and José Carlos Carvalho, "Coleiras de escravos foram encontradas," *Expresso*, March 27, 2017. The collars were displayed in the temporary exhibition *Um Museu, tantas coleções! Testemunho da Escravatura. Memória Africana* at the National Museum of Archaeology in Lisbon from April 22 to July 8, 2018.
8. See also Isabel Castro Henriques, *A presença africana em Portugal: Uma história secular; Preconceito, integração, reconhecimento (séculos XV–XX)* (Lisbon: Alto Comissariado para as Imigrações, 2019), 14–15.
9. For an analysis of this collar, see Jennifer Trimble, "The Zoninus Collar and the Archaeology of Roman Slavery," *American Journal of Archaeology* 120, no. 3 (2016): 447–72.

10. Valika Smeulders and Lisa Lambrechts, "Paulus: A 'Moor' in the Dutch Republic," in *Slavery: The Story of João, Wally, Oopjen, Paulus, Van Bengalen, Surapati, Sapali, Tula, Drik, Lohkay*, ed. Eveline Sint Nicolaas and Valika Smeulders (Amsterdam: Rijksmuseum, Atlas Contact, 2021), 128.
11. Simon P. Newman, "Freedom-Seeking Slaves in England and Scotland, 1700–1780," *English Historical Review* 134, no. 570 (2019): 1161–68.
12. *Diário do Rio de Janeiro*, February 11, 1822, 32.
13. Paulin Ismard, "Identification," in Ismard, Rossi, and Vidal, *Les mondes de l'esclavage*, 544.
14. On these African identities as they appear in fugitive slave ads, see Gomez, *Exchanging our Country Marks*, 38–40, 103, 137–40. Fugitive slave ads in nineteenth-century Brazilian newspapers constantly featured African-born fugitives. Some ads described their facial marks; see Gilberto Freyre, *O escravo nos anúncios de jornais brasileiros do século XIX* (São Paulo: Editora Nacional, 1979). On Rio de Janeiro, see Raphael Neves, "Experiências capturadas: A fuga de escravos no Rio de Janeiro," (Rio de Janeiro: Fundação Biblioteca Nacional, 2009).
15. Edward B. Rugemer, *Slave Law and the Politics of Resistance in the Early Atlantic World* (Cambridge, MA: Harvard University Press, 2018), 29–30, 35–36. See also Fuente and Gross, *Becoming Free, Becoming Black*, 19–20.
16. *Le Code Noir*, 5–8.
17. For the French West Indies, see the database *Le Marronage dans le monde atlantique: Sources et trajectoires de vie*, Université de Sherbrooke, http://www.marronnage.info/fr/index.html. See also Léon Robichaud, "Behind the Marronage Project. Balancing Resources, Methodology and Access in an Online Archive," *Esclavages & Post~Esclavages / Slaveries and Post~Slaveries*, no. 3 (2020), https://doi.org/10.4000/slaveries.3112. On Louisiana, Jamaica, and South Carolina, see Jean-Pierre Le Glaunec, *Esclaves mais résistants: Dans le monde des annonces pour esclaves en fuite, Louisiane, Jamaïque, Caroline du Sud (1801–1815)* (Paris: Karthala, 2021).
18. Gary Nash and Karen Cook Bell each provide similar rates of enslaved women fugitives during the American War of Independence; see Gary B. Nash, *The Forgotten Fifth: African-Americans and the Age of Revolution* (Cambridge, MA: Harvard University Press, 2006), 27–28, and Karen Cook Bell, *Running from Bondage: Enslaved Women and Their Remarkable Fight for Freedom in Revolutionary Era America* (New York: Cambridge University Press, 2021), 9. Edward Baptist's preliminary analysis of the data from the database *Freedom on the Move* (https://freedomonthemove.org/) reveals that at least 15 percent of the fugitives before the US Civil War were women. Based on a sample of 11,112 US slave ads from her personal database, historian Jennie Williams concluded that slave ads between the 1740s and the 1860s included nearly 17 percent of enslaved fugitives who were women.
19. C. Walker, *Jamaica Ladies*, 102.

20. *Affiches américaines*, October 8, 1766, 352.

21. *Affiches américaines*, May 28, 1766, 196.

22. Eddins, *Rituals, Runaways, and the Haitian Revolution*, 175.

23. *Affiches américaines*, February 10, 1768, 52.

24. K. Bell, *Running from Bondage*, 3.

25. See Erica Dunbar, *Never Caught: The Washingtons' Relentless Pursuit of Their Runaway Slave, Ona Judge* (New York: Atria/37 INK, 2017).

26. "Advertisement for a Runaway Slave, 7 September 1769," *Founders Online*, National Archives, https://founders.archives.gov/documents/Jefferson/01-01-02-0021. Original source: Thomas Jefferson, *The Papers of Thomas Jefferson*, vol. 1, *1760–1776*, ed. Julian P. Boyd (Princeton, NJ: Princeton University Press, 1950), 33.

27. Lucia C. Stanton, *"Those Who Labor for My Happiness": Slavery at Thomas Jefferson's Monticello* (Charlottesville: University of Virginia Press, 2012), 151.

28. Stanton, *"Those Who Labor for My Happiness,"* 150–52.

29. Camp, *Closer to Freedom*, 44–45.

30. *Washington DC National Intelligencer*, August 30, 1804, retrieved in the database *Freedom on the Move*, https://freedomonthemove.org/. On Rachel, see Nunley, *At the Threshold of Liberty*, 45–46.

31. Nunley, *At the Threshold of Liberty*, 43.

32. *Western Carolinian*, February 11, 1828, retrieved in the database *Freedom on the Move*, https://freedomonthemove.org/.

33. *New-Orleans Argus*, March 24, 1828, retrieved in the database *Freedom on the Move*, https://freedomonthemove.org/.

34. *Diário do Rio de Janeiro*, July 23, 1821, 150–51.

35. *Diário do Rio de Janeiro*, June 25, 1821, 160, and *Diário do Rio de Janeiro*, November 5, 1821, 23.

36. *Diário do Rio de Janeiro*, November 5, 1821, 24.

37. *Diário do Rio de Janeiro*, November 12, 1821, 72.

38. *Diário do Rio de Janeiro*, October 6, 1851, 3.

39. See Yuko Miki, *Frontiers of Citizenship: A Black and Indigenous History of Postcolonial Brazil* (New York: Cambridge University Press, 2018), 196–97.

40. *Gazeta do Rio de Janeiro*, March 17, 1813, 4, *Diário do Rio de Janeiro*, June 3, 1821, 11, and *Diário do Rio de Janeiro*, June 9, 1821, 47.

41. *Diário do Rio de Janeiro*, June 10, 1821, 55.

42. *Daily Picayune*, March 26, 1845, retrieved in the database *Freedom on the Move*, https://freedomonthemove.org/.

43. *East Carolina Republican*, June 8, 1847, retrieved in the database *Freedom on the Move*, https://freedomonthemove.org/.

44. For two recent monographs discussing this ad and this photograph, see Deborah Willis and Barbara Krauthamer, *Envisioning Emancipation: Black Americans and the End of Slavery* (Philadelphia: Temple University Press, 2017), 11–14, and Matthew Fox-Amato, *Exposing Slavery: Photography,*

Human Bondage, and the Birth of Modern Visual Politics in America (New York: Oxford University Press, 2019), 64–67.

45. Fox-Amato, *Exposing Slavery*, 65.

46. On dogs used to hunt enslaved fugitives in the Americas, see Tyler D. Parry and Charlton W. Yingling, "Slave Hounds and Abolition in the Americas," *Past & Present* 246, no. 1 (2020): 69–108.

47. Manisha Sinha, *The Slave's Cause: A History of Abolition* (New Haven, CT: Yale University Press, 2016), 382.

48. On slave escapes in cities and rural areas during the nineteenth century in the United States, see Damian Pargas, *Freedom Seekers: Fugitive Slaves in North America, 1800–1860* (New York: Cambridge University Press, 2022).

49. John Stauffer and Henry Louis Gates Jr., *Portable Frederick Douglass* (New York: Penguin, 2016), 87. On Douglass's escape, see Blight, *Frederick Douglass*, 79–86. On the Underground Railroad in New York City, see Eric Foner, *Gateway to Freedom: The Hidden History of the Underground Railroad* (New York: W.W. Norton, 2015).

50. On Tubman's escape, see Milton C. Sernett, *Harriet Tubman: Myth, Memory, and History* (Durham: Duke University Press, 2007), 19–21.

51. Among the countless examples, see Colston Whitehead, *The Underground Railroad: A Novel* (New York: Knopf Doubleday, 2016), adapted as a miniseries available for streaming: Barry Jenkins, dir., *The Underground Railroad* (Amazon Studios, 2021). See also the motion picture Kasi Lemmons, dir., *Harriet* (Martin Chase Productions, 2019).

52. See Jeffrey Kerr-Ritchie, *Freedom's Seekers: Essays on Comparative Emancipation* (Baton Rouge: Louisiana State University Press, 2014), 21–40.

53. See Jane Landers, *Black Society in Spanish Florida* (Urbana: University of Illinois Press, 1999).

54. On enslaved fugitives who escaped to Mexico in the nineteenth century, see Alice L. Baumgartner, *South to Freedom: Runaway Slaves to Mexico and the Road to the Civil War* (New York: Basic Books, 2020).

55. See Jeffrey R. Kerr-Ritchie, *Rebellious Passage: The Creole Revolt and America's Coastal Slave Trade* (New York: Cambridge University Press, 2019).

56. Richard J. M. Blackett, *The Captive's Quest For Freedom: Fugitive Slaves, the 1850 Fugitive Slave Law, and the Politics of Slavery* (New York: Cambridge University Press, 2018), 5.

57. On the law, see Blackett, *Captive's Quest for Freedom*, 3–41, and Matthew Pinsker, "After 1850: Reassessing the Impact of the Fugitive Slave Law," in *Fugitive Slaves and Spaces of Freedom in North America*, ed. Damian Pargas (Gainesville: University Press of Florida, 2018), 93–115.

58. The scholarship on enslaved people who escaped slavery during the Civil War era is far too vast to be included here. I will highlight a few recent excellent studies addressing enslaved men and women who escaped bondage during this period. On enslaved women, see Camp, *Closer to Freedom*, chap. 5, and Thavolia Glymph, *The Women's Fight: The Civil War's Battles for Home, Freedom, and Nation* (Chapel Hill: University of North Carolina Press, 2020), chaps. 3 and 7. On enslaved men and women, see Amy Murrell Taylor, *Embattled Freedom: Journeys through the Civil War's Slave Refugee Camps* (Chapel Hill: University of North Carolina Press, 2018).

59. Jeffrey D. Needell, *The Sacred Cause: The Abolitionist Movement, Afro-Brazilian Mobilization, and Imperial Politics in Rio de Janeiro* (Stanford, CA: Stanford University Press, 2020), 182.

60. Today the remnants of these communities in Brazil are referred to as *quilombos*. On the use of the term *quilombo* to refer to maroon communities in Brazil starting in the seventeenth century, see Silvia Hunold Lara, *Palmares e Cucaú: O aprendizado da dominação* (São Paulo: Editora da Universidade de São Paulo, 2021), 362–63, 367. On this variety of terms, see Stuart Schwartz, *Slaves, Peasants, and Rebels: Reconsidering Brazilian Slavery* (Urbana: University of Illinois Press, 1996), 103.

61. See Gabriel Debien, "Le marronage aux Antilles françaises au XVIIIe siècle," *Caribbean Studies* 6, no. 3 (1966): 3–43.

62. See Sylviane A. Diouf, *Slavery's Exiles: The Story of American Maroons* (New York: New York University Press, 2014). For the region of southeastern Virginia and northeastern North Carolina, see Marcus P. Nevius, *City of Refuge: Slavery and Petit Marronage in the Great Dismal Swamp, 1763–1856* (Athens: University of Georgia Press, 2020). On *petit marronage* in Brazil, see Flávio Gomes, "Africans and *Petit Marronage* in Rio de Janeiro, ca. 1800–1840," *Luso-Brazilian Review* 47, no. 2 (2010): 74–99.

63. There are many published studies and unpublished PhD dissertations and MA theses on specific communities; for an overview, see João José Reis and Flávio dos Santos Gomes, ed. *Liberdade por um Fio: História dos quilombos no Brasil* (São Paulo: Companhia das Letras, 1996), translated in English as João José Reis and Flávio dos Santos Gomes, ed. *Freedom by a Thread: The History of Quilombos in Brazil* (New York: Diasporic Africa Press, 2016).

64. See Jane Landers, "Transforming Bondsmen into Vassals: Arming Slaves in Colonial Spanish America," in *Arming Slaves: From Classical Times to the Modern Age*, ed. Christopher Leslie Brown and Philip D. Morgan (New Haven, CT: Yale University Press, 2006), 124.

65. See Christina A. Sue, *Land of the Cosmic Race: Race Mixture, Racism, and Blackness in Mexico* (New York: Oxford University Press, 2013), 118, and William D. Phillips Jr., "Slavery in the Atlantic Islands and the Early Modern Spanish Atlantic World," in *The Cambridge World History of Slavery*, vol. 3, *AD 1420–AD 1804*, ed. David Eltis, Keith R. Bradley, Stanley L. Engerman, and Paul Cartledge (New York: Cambridge University Press, 2011), 345.

66. Sagrario Cruz Carretero, Alfredo Martínez Maranto, and Angélica Santiago Silva, *El Carnaval en Yanga: Notas y comentarios sobre una fiesta de la negritud* (San Angel, Mexico: Consejo Nacional para la Cultura y las Artes, Dirección

General de Culturas Populares, Unidad Regional Centro de Veracruz, 1990), 27–28.

67. Chapters 6 and 11 note the presence of enslaved people from Upper Guinea disembarking in the port of Cartagena in the early period of the Atlantic slave trade. On the term "Bioho," see Wheat, *Atlantic Africa and the Spanish Caribbean*, 25–26. See also Margaret M. Olsen, "African Reinscription of Body and Space in New Granada," in *Mapping Colonial Spanish America Places and Commonplaces of Identity, Culture, and Experience*, ed. Santa Arias and Mariselle Meléndez (Lewisburg, PA: Bucknell University Press; London: Associated University Press, 2002), 61; Aquiles Escalante, "Palenques in Colombia," in *Maroon Societies: Rebel Slave Communities in the Americas*, ed. Richard Price (Baltimore: Johns Hopkins University Press, 1996), 77–79; Leslie B. Rout, *The African Experience in Spanish America, 1502 to the Present Day* (Cambridge: Cambridge University Press, 1976), 110; Clara Inés Guerrero García, "Memorias palenqueras de la libertad," in *Afro-reparaciones: Memoria de la esclavitud y justicia reparativa para negros, afrocolombianos y raizales*, ed. Claudia Mosquera Rosero-Labbé and Luís Claudio y Barcelos (Bogotá: Universidad Nacional de Colombia, 2007), 368.

68. I discuss Bioho's bust and the monument in Araujo, *Shadows of the Slave Past*, 195–96.

69. Dunn, *Sugar and Slaves*, 259.

70. "The Second Maroon War," in *The Jamaica Reader: History, Culture, Politics*, ed. Diana Paton and Matthew J. Smith (Durham, NC: Duke University Press, 2021), 132–33.

71. On these conflicts and consecutive deportations, see Ruma Chopra, *Almost Home: Maroons between Slavery and Freedom in Jamaica, Nova Scotia, and Sierra Leone* (New Haven, CT: Yale University Press, 2018).

72. Schwartz, *Slaves, Peasants, and Rebels*, 109–11.

73. See, for example, Miki, *Frontiers of Citizenship*, esp. chap. 5.

74. See Schwartz, *Slaves, Peasants, and Rebels*, 126–27; Joseph C. Miller, *Kings and Kinsmen: Early Mbundu States* (Oxford: Clarendon Press, 1976), 151, 161–62.

75. John K. Thornton, "Les États de l'Angola et la formation de Palmares (Brésil)," *Annales: Histoire, Sciences Sociales* 63, no. 4 (2008): 789.

76. For an accessible discussion on *quilombo/kilombo* as a military organization, see Green, *Fistful of Shells*, xxxiv, 189.

77. Lara, *Palmares e Cucaú*, 148, 219.

78. Lara, *Palmares e Cucaú*, 364–67.

79. Luiz Felipe de Alencastro, "South Atlantic Wars: The Episode of Palmares," *Portuguese Studies Review* 19, no. 1–2 (2011): 47.

80. Pedro Paulo A. Funari, "Conflict and the Interpretation of Palmares, a Brazilian Runaway Polity," *Historical Archaeology* 27, no. 3 (2003): 83.

81. J. Thornton, "Les États de l'Angola et la formation de Palmares," 775.

82. Lara, *Palmares e Cucaú*, 170, 248.
83. Lara, *Palmares e Cucaú*, 194.
84. Funari, "Conflict and the Interpretation of Palmares," 84–85. See also Pedro Paulo de Abreu Funari, "A arqueologia de Palmares: Sua contribuição para o conhecimento da história da cultura afro-americana," in Reis and Gomes, *Liberdade por um fio*, 26–51.
85. Lara, *Palmares e Cucaú*, 250–51.
86. Lara, *Palmares e Cucaú*, 253.
87. Lara, *Palmares e Cucaú*, 322–23.
88. Lara, *Palmares e Cucaú*, 341–42.
89. Lara, *Palmares e Cucaú*, 352.
90. See Marc Hertzman, "Fatal Differences: Suicide, Race, and Forced Labor in the Americas," *American Historical Review* 122, no. 2 (2017): 333–35.
91. Mariza de Carvalho Soares, "Nos atalhos da memória: Monumento a Zumbi," in *Cidade Vaidosa: Imagens Urbanas do Rio de Janeiro*, ed. Paulo Knauss (Rio de Janeiro: 7Letras, 1999), 119.
92. See Francine Saillant and Ana Lucia Araujo, "*Zumbi*: Mort, mémoire et résistance," *Frontières* 19, no. 1 (2006): 37–42.
93. Terri L. Snyder, *The Power to Die: Slavery and Suicide in British North America* (Chicago: University of Chicago Press, 2015), 66.
94. APERS 1208, 42, 95, December 17, 1872; APERS 1580, 44, 143, September 12, 1874; APERS 1583, 44, 143, 1875, December 28, 1875.
95. APERS 2542, 84, 123, December 9, 1883.
96. In Rio de Janeiro during this same period, see Sidney Chalhoub, *Visões da liberdade: Uma história das últimas décadas da escravidão na Corte* (São Paulo: Companhia de Bolso, 2011), 201–10.
97. Gomez, *Exchanging Our Country Marks*, 120. See also V. Brown, *Reaper's Garden*, 132.

Chapter 14

1. Frederick Douglass, *Narrative of the Life of Frederick Douglass: An American Slave Written by Himself* (Boston: Anti-Slavery Office, 1845), 74.
2. Douglass, *Narrative of the Life of Frederick Douglass*, 74.
3. Douglass, *Narrative of the Life of Frederick Douglass*, 74.
4. See John K. Thornton, "Afro-Christian Syncretism in the Kingdom of Kongo," *Journal of African History* 54, no. 1 (2013): 53–77; Fromont, *Art of Conversion*; and Green, *Fistful of Shells*, 205–13.
5. Fromont, *Art of Conversion*, 1–2.
6. Erin Kathleen Rowe, *Black Saints in Early Modern Global Catholicism* (New York: Cambridge University Press, 2019), 15–24.
7. Erin Kathleen Rowe, "Visualizing Black Sanctity in Early Modern Spanish Polychrome Sculpture," in *Envisioning Others: Race, Color, and the Visual in*

Iberia and Latin America, ed. Pamela A. Patton (Leiden, Neth.: Brill, 2016), 67–68.

8. Jeremy Lawrance, "Black Africans in Renaissance Spanish Literature," in Earle and Lowe, *Black Africans in Renaissance Europe*, 70.

9. Miguel A. Valerio, "'That There Be No Black Brotherhood': The Failed Suppression of Afro-Mexican Confraternities, 1568–1612." *Slavery and Abolition* 42, no. 2 (2021): 297.

10. Anthony John R. Russell-Wood, *Slavery and Freedom in Colonial Brazil* (Oxford: One World, 2002).

11. See M. Soares, *People of Faith*, chap. 3.

12. These nations were not fixed entities; they changed over time and space. For example, an African labeled as "Jeje" in Bahia would probably be identified as "Mina" in Rio de Janeiro. For a detailed discussion on these denotations, see Luis Nicolau Parés, *The Formation of Candomblé: Vodun History and Ritual in Brazil* (Chapel Hill: University of North Carolina Press, 2013), 1–34.

13. See Elizabeth W. Kiddy, *Blacks of the Rosary: Memory and History in Minas Gerais Brazil* (University Park: Pennsylvania State University Press, 2005), 32; Sweet, *Recreating Africa*, 207; and Lucilene Reginaldo, "Os Rosários dos Angolas: Irmandades Negras, Experiências Escravas e Identidades Africanas na Bahia Setecentista" (PhD diss., Universidade Estadual de Campinas, 2005), 38.

14. Green, *Rise of the Trans-Atlantic Slave Trade*, 105, 114.

15. Eduardo Freire de Oliveira, *Elementos para a história do município de Lisboa*, vol. 1 (Lisbon: Typhographia Universal, 1882), 516, and Saunders, *Social History of Black Slaves*, 105.

16. See Marina de Mello e Souza, *Reis negros no Brasil escravista: História da festa de coroação de Rei Congo* (Belo Horizonte, Brazil: Editora da Universidade Federal de Minas Gerais, 2014), 164–65.

17. BNP, IL 151, Compromisso da Irmandade de Nossa Senhora do Rosário dos Homens Pretos, Lisbon, December 2, 1565, chap. 16, 6v, and chap. 26, 9v.

18. For the identification of this painting, see Isabel Castro Henriques, *Historical Guide to an African Lisbon: 15th to 21st Century* (Lisbon: Colibri, 2021), 53.

19. Rowe, *Black Saints in Early Modern Global Catholicism*, 16.

20. Russell-Wood, *Slavery and Freedom in Colonial Brazil*, 138.

21. Karen B. Graubart, "'So color de una cofradía': Catholic Confraternities and the Development of Afro-Peruvian Ethnicities in Early Colonial Peru," *Slavery and Abolition* 23, no. 1 (2011): 43–65.

22. J. Thornton, *Africa and Africans in the Making of the Atlantic World*, 203.

23. Miguel A. Valerio, "Architects of Their Own Humanity: Race, Devotion, and Artistic Agency in Afro-Brazilian Confraternal Churches in Eighteenth-Century Salvador and Ouro Preto," *Colonial Latin American Review* 30, no. 2 (2021): 247.

24. See João José Reis, "Identidade e Diversidade Étnicas nas Irmandades Negras no Tempo da Escravidão," *Tempo* 2, no. 3 (1996): 6.

25. Carlos Ott, "A Irmandade de Nossa Senhora do Rosário dos Pretos do Pelourinho." *Afro-Ásia* no. 6/7 (1968): 121.
26. Ott, "A Irmandade de Nossa Senhora do Rosário dos Pretos do Pelourinho," 123.
27. See Maria das Graças de Andrade Leal, *Manuel Querino: Entre Letras e Lutas Bahia 1851–1923* (São Paulo: Annablume, 2009), and Sabrina Gledhill, ed., *Manuel Querino (1851–1923): An Afro-Brazilian Pioneer in the Age of Scientific Racism* (Crediton, UK: Funmilayo Publishing, 2021).
28. On Bamboxê Obitikô, see Lisa Earl Castillo, "Bamboxê Obitikô and the Nineteenth-Century Expansion of Orisha Worship in Brazil," *Tempo* 22, no. 30 (2016): 126–53.
29. Early manifestations during the colonial period were rather referred to as *calundus*, labeled as witchcraft by the Catholic Church; see Laura de Mello e Souza, *The Devil and the Land of the Holy Cross: Witchcraft, Slavery, and Popular Religion in Colonial Brazil* (Austin: University of Texas Press, 2010).
30. For example, Marina de Mello e Souza associates Black saints with *minkisi* (plural of *nkisi*), power figures that when activated, like the saints, could intervene on behalf of a person making a plea. See Marina de Mello e Souza, "The Construction of a Black Catholic Identity in Brazil: Saints and Minkisi; A Reflection of Cultural Miscegenation," in *Africa, Brazil, and the Construction of Black Atlantic Identities*, ed. Livio Sansone, Elisée Soumonni, and Boubacar Barry (Trenton, NJ: Africa World Press, 2008), 261–62. On these connections, see also Fromont, *Art of Conversion*, 70, and Valerio, "Architects of Their Own Humanity," 246.
31. John K. Thornton, "The Kingdom of Kongo and Palo Mayombe: Reflections on an African-American Religion," *Slavery and Abolition* 37, no. 1 (2016): 1–22.
32. Ewbank, *Life in Brazil*, 290.
33. On popular Christianity in Brazil, see John Burdick, *Blessed Anastacia: Women, Race and Popular Christianity in Brazil* (New York: Routledge, 1998). Regarding Afro-Brazilian deities embodying enslaved individuals, see Lindsay Lauren Hale, "Preto Velho: Resistance, Redemption, and Engendered Representations of Slavery in a Brazilian Possession-Trance Religion," *American Ethnologist* 24, no. 2 (1997): 392–414.
34. On the rise of Anastácia's representation and also on her mask, see Jerome Handler and K. Hayes, "Escrava Anastácia: The Iconographic History of a Brazilian Popular Saint," *African Diaspora: Journal of Transnational Africa in a Global World* 2 (2009): 1–27.
35. On Anastácia in Rio de Janeiro's Black's Museum, see Ana Lucia Araujo, *Museums and Atlantic Slavery* (Oxford: Routledge, 2021), chap. 2. See also Marcus Wood, "The Museu do Negro in Rio and the Cult of Anastácia as a New Model for the Memory of Slavery," *Representations*, no. 113 (2011): 111–49.

36. Mônica Dias de Souza, "Escrava Anastácia e pretos-velhos: A rebelião silenciosa da memória popular," in *Memória afro-brasileira: Imaginário, cotidiano e poder*, ed. Vagner Gonçalves da Silva (São Paulo: Selo Negro, 2007), 18–20, and M. Wood, "Museu do Negro in Rio and the Cult of Anastácia," 125.
37. Jacques Arago, *Souvenirs d'un aveugle: Voyage autour du monde*, vol. 1 (Paris: H. Lebrun, 1842), 119. About the use of this image to represent Anastácia, see Jerome Handler and Annis Steiner, "Identifying Pictorial Images of Atlantic Slavery: Three Case Studies," *Slavery and Abolition* 27 (2006): 56–62, and Handler and Hayes, "Escrava Anastácia."
38. For a recent rich overview of these festivals, especially in Brazil, Mexico, the United States, and Trinidad, see the various chapters in Cécile Fromont, ed., *Afro-Catholic Festivals in the Americas: Performance, Representation, and the Making of Black Atlantic Tradition* (University Park: Pennsylvania State University Press, 2019).
39. Jeroen Dewulf, "Black Brotherhoods in North America: Afro-Iberian and West Central African Influences," *African Studies Quarterly* 15, no. 3 (2015): 25–28.
40. On Pinkster, see Jeroen Dewulf, *The Pinkster and the King of Kongo: The Forgotten History of America's Dutch-Owned Slaves* (Jackson: University of Mississippi Press, 2019).
41. On the Divine Holy Ghost festival, see Martha Abreu, *O império do divino: Festas religiosas e cultura popular no Rio de Janeiro, 1830–1900* (Rio de Janeiro: Nova Fronteira, 1999).
42. Henry Koster, *Travels in Brazil by Henry Koster in the Years from 1809 to 1815* (Philadelphia: M. Carey & Son, 1817), 274.
43. Ewbank, *Life in Brazil*, 398. On Balthasar as king of Congo and on the coronation of African kings and queens at Lampadosa's church in Rio de Janeiro, see also Karasch, *Slave Life in Rio de Janeiro*, 19, 58.
44. For more details on this brotherhood and its Mahi congregation, see M. Soares, *People of Faith*, and Mariza de Carvalho Soares, ed., *Diálogos Makii de Francisco Alves de Souza: Manuscrito de uma congregação de africanos Mina, 1786* (Rio de Janeiro: Chão Editora, 2019).
45. Debret, *Voyage pittoresque et historique*, 3:283. See Lisa Voigt, *Spectacular Wealth: The Festivals of Colonial South American Mining Towns* (Austin: University of Texas Press, 2016), 135–36.
46. Herskovits, *Myth of the Negro Past*, 14.
47. On this approach, see Mintz and Price, *Birth of African-American Culture*.
48. See Ira Berlin, "From Creole to African: Atlantic Creoles and the Origins of African-American Society in Mainland North America," *William and Mary Quarterly* 53, no. 2 (1996): 251–88; Berlin, *Many Thousands Gone*; and Linda M. Heywood and John K. Thornton, *Central Africans, Atlantic Creoles, and the Foundation of the Americas, 1585–1660* (New York: Cambridge University Press, 2007).

49. J. Harris, *Global Dimensions of the African Diaspora*, 3–8. See also Palmer, "Defining and Studying the Modern African Diaspora," 27–32; Butler, "Defining Diaspora, Refining a Discourse," 189–219; Mann, "Shifting Paradigms," 3–21; and Zeleza, "Diaspora Dialogues," 1–19.
50. See Marina de Mello e Souza, *Reis negros no Brasil escravista*, 340–50.
51. Elizabeth W. Kiddy, "Who Is the King of Congo? A New Look at African and Afro-Brazilian Kings in Brazil," in Heywood, *Central Africans and Cultural Transformations in the American Diaspora*, 181–82.
52. See Mariza de Carvalho Soares, "Art and the History of African Slave Folias in Brazil," in *Crossing Memories: Slavery and African Diaspora*, ed. Ana Lucia Araujo, Mariana P. Candido, and Paul E. Lovejoy (Trenton, NJ: Africa World Press, 2011), 224.
53. Cécile Fromont, "Dancing for the King of Congo from Early Modern Central Africa to Slavery-Era Brazil," *Colonial Latin America Review* 22, no. 2 (2013): 184–208, and Cécile Fromont, "Envisioning Brazil's Afro-Christian Congados: The Black King and Queen Festival Lithographs of Johann Moritz Rugendas," in Fromont, *Afro-Catholic Festivals in the Americas*, 117–39.
54. Northup and Wilson, *Twelve Years a Slave*, 213.
55. Northup and Wilson, *Twelve Years a Slave*, 214.
56. Northup and Wilson, *Twelve Years a Slave*, 216.
57. Northup and Wilson, *Twelve Years a Slave*, 217.
58. Jacobs, *Incidents in the Life of a Slave Girl*, 131.
59. Jacobs, *Incidents in the Life of a Slave Girl*, 131–32.
60. On Belisario's representations of Jonkonnu, see Laura M. Smalligan, "An Effigy for the Enslaved: Jonkonnu in Jamaica and Belisario's Sketches of Character," *Slavery and Abolition* 32, no. 4 (2011): 561–81.
61. Douglas B. Chambers, "'My Own Nation': Igbo Exiles in the Diaspora," in *Routes to Slavery: Direction, Ethnicity and Mortality in the Atlantic Slave* Trade, ed. David Eltis and David Richardson (London: Frank Cass, 1997), 83, 87.
62. John Andrew Jackson, *The Experience of a Slave in South Carolina* (London: Passmore & Alabaster, 1862).
63. See Debret, *Voyage pittoresque et historique*, 2:103, plate 33.
64. See Pedro Meira Monteiro and Michael Stone, eds., *Cangoma Calling Spirits and Rhythms of Freedom in Brazilian Jongo Slavery Songs* (Dartmouth: University of Massachusetts, 2013), and Hebe Mattos and Martha Abreu, "Memories of Captivity and Freedom in São José's Jongo Festivals," in Araujo, *African Heritage and Memories of Slavery in Brazil and the South Atlantic World*, 149–77.
65. On capoeira in Rio de Janeiro, see Carlos Eugênio Líbano Soares, *A negregada instituição: Os capoeiras na corte imperial (1850–1890)* (Rio de Janeiro: Access, 1999), and Carlos Eugênio Líbano Soares, *A capoeira escrava e outras tradições rebeldes no Rio de Janeiro, 1808–1850* (Campinas, Brazil: Editora da Universidade do Estado de São Paulo, 2004). See also Matthias Röhrig

Assunção, "Stanzas and Sticks: Poetics and Physical Challenges in the Afro-Brazilian Culture of the Paraíba Valley, Rio de Janeiro," *History Workshop Journal* 77, no. 1 (2014): 103–36.

66. On capoeira from an Atlantic perspective, see Matthias Röhrig Assunção, *Capoeira A History of the Afro-Brazilian Martial Art* (New York: Routledge, 2004). On the West Central African "origins" of capoeira, see Matthias Röhrig Assunção, "Engolo e capoeira: Jogos de combate étnico e diaspóricos no Atlântico Sul," *Tempo* 26, no. 3 (2020): 522–56, and for its various styles, see Matthias Röhrig Assunção, "Capoeira Circle or Sports Academy? The Emergence of Modern Styles of Capoeira and Their Global Context," *História, Ciências, Saúde–Manguinhos* (2014): 135–50.

67. Childs, *1812 Aponte Rebellion*, 111.

68. The literature on *cabildos de nación* is extensive; for a useful overview, see Matt D. Childs, "Re-Creating African Ethnic Identities in Cuba," in Cañizares-Esguerra, Childs, and Sidbury, *Black Urban Atlantic in the Age of the Slave Trade*, 85–100. On the relations between cabildos de nación and Afro-Cuban religions, see María del Carmen Barcia, Andrés Rodríguez Reyes, and Milagros Niebla Delgado, *Del cabildo de "nación" a la casa de santo* (Havana: Fundación Fernando Ortiz, 2012).

69. See Castillo, "Bamboxê Obitikô."

70. Interview by Ana Lucia Araujo with Júlio César Soares da Silva, then a member of the board of directors of the brotherhood of Our Lady of the Rosary of the Black Men, May 13, 2009, and author's interview with Antônio Carlos dos Santos (Vovô), founder of the *Ilê Aiyê*, June 2, 2009. I also had the opportunity to attend several Catholic masses on Sunday and Tuesday between May and June 2009, while conducting fieldwork in Salvador, Bahia.

Chapter 15

1. "Bahia: Policia," *Jornal do Commercio* (Rio de Janeiro), February 10, 1835, 1.

2. Marjoleine Kars, "Dodging Rebellion: Politics and Gender in the Berbice Slave Uprising of 1763," *American Historical Review* 121, no. 1 (2016): 39–69, and J. Morgan, *Reckoning with Slavery*, 207–28.

3. Anthony Stevens-Acevedo, *The Santo Domingo Slave Revolt of 1521 and the Slave Laws of 1522: Black Slavery and Black Resistance in the Early Colonial Americas* (New York: CUNY Dominican Studies Institute, 2019), 11.

4. Stevens-Acevedo, *The Santo Domingo Slave Revolt of 1521*, 11.

5. "Decree by Viceroy Diego Colón Including Ordinances on Blacks and Slaves of La Española and Puerto Rico, January 6, 1522," in Stevens-Acevedo, *Santo Domingo Slave Revolt of 1521*, 23–29.

6. See also Rebecca Hall, "Not Killing Me Softly: African American Women, Slave Revolts, and Historical Constructions of Racialized Gender," *Freedom Center Journal* 2, no. 1 (2007): 1–47.

7. R. Hall, "Not Killing Me Softly," 29.
8. L. Harris, *In the Shadow of Slavery*, 37–38.
9. Along with the Akan-speaking individuals were "Spanish Indians" as well as Africans identified as "Pappa" (which probably corresponded to Popo, in the Bight of Benin); see Rucker, *Gold Coast Diasporas*, 158.
10. Walter Rucker, "Conjure, Magic, and Power: The Influence of Afro-Atlantic Religious Practices on Slave Resistance and Rebellion," *Journal of Black Studies* 32, no. 1 (2001): 87–88.
11. Rucker, "Conjure, Magic, and Power," 87. On African and African-derived names of enslaved people in the US South, see also Genovese, *Roll, Jordan, Roll*, 440–50.
12. Rucker, "Conjure, Magic, and Power," 87.
13. L. Harris, *In the Shadow of Slavery*, 32, 39–40.
14. For an accessible account of this rebellion, see Lepore, *New York Burning*.
15. L. Harris, *In the Shadow of Slavery*, 43.
16. See Daniel C. Littlefield, *Rice and Slaves: Ethnicity and the Slave Trade in Colonial South Carolina* (Urbana: University of Illinois Press, 1991).
17. P. Wood, *Black Majority*, 116, and Russell R. Menard, "Slave Demography in the Lowcountry, 1670–1740: From Frontier Society to Plantation Regime," *South Carolina Historical Magazine* 101, no. 3 (2000): 192–93.
18. See John K. Thornton, "African Dimensions of the Stono Rebellion," *American Historical Review* 96, no. 4 (1991): 1101–13.
19. "Act for the Better Ordering and Governing of Negroes and Other Slaves in this Province," May 1740, in *The Statutes at Large of South Carolina*, vol. 7, ed. Thomas Cooper and David James McCord (Columbia, SC: Johnston, 1840), 397–417.
20. V. Brown, *Tacky's Revolt*.
21. Marjoleine Kars, *Blood in the River: A Chronicle of Mutiny and Freedom on the Wild Coast* (New York: New Press, 2020), 78.
22. Fick, *Making of Haiti*, 25.
23. Julius Scott, *The Common Wind: Afro-American Currents in the Age of the Haitian Revolution* (London: Verso, 2018), 25–26.
24. Dubois, *Avengers of the New World*, 68.
25. Dubois, *Avengers of the New World*, 77.
26. See Scott, *Common Wind*.
27. Cyril Lionel Robert James, *The Black Jacobins: Toussaint L'Ouverture and the San Domingo Revolution* (New York: Vintage Books, 1963), 89.
28. Dubois, *Avengers of the New World*, 126. On enslaved people emancipating themselves prior to the Saint Domingue Revolution, see Eddins, *Rituals, Runaways, and the Haitian Revolution*.
29. Dubois, *Avengers of the New World*, 216.
30. There are two recent biographies of Toussaint Louverture in English; see Philippe R. Girard, *Toussaint Louverture: A Revolutionary Life* (New York:

Basic Books, 2016), and Sudhir Hazareesingh, *Black Spartacus: The Epic Life of Toussaint Louverture* (New York: Farrar Straus and Giroux, 2020).

31. Dubois, *Avengers of the New World*, 300. See also TNA, "Haitian Declaration of Independence," January 1, 1804, 7v.
32. Cristina Soriano, *Tides of Revolution: Information, Insurgencies, and the Crisis of Colonial Rule in Venezuela* (Albuquerque: University of New Mexico Press, 2018), 124.
33. Soriano, *Tides of Revolution*, 132.
34. See Alejandro E. Gómez, *Le spectre de la révolution noire: L'impact de la révolution haïtienne dans le monde atlantique, 1790–1886* (Rennes, Fr.: Presses universitaires de Rennes, 2013), 127. Geggus states that both men went to Saint Domingue before the revolt; see David Patrick Geggus, "Slavery, War, and Revolution in the Greater Caribbean, 1789–1815," in *A Turbulent Time: The French Revolution and the Greater Caribbean*, ed. David Barry Gaspar and David Patrick Geggus (Bloomington: Indiana University Press, 1997), 42n115.
35. Soriano, *Tides of Revolution*, 143.
36. Soriano, *Tides of Revolution*, 118–19.
37. On the impacts of the Saint Domingue revolution in Cuba, see Ferrer, *Freedom's Mirror*.
38. See Childs, *1812 Aponte Rebellion*, 157–58.
39. For more information on Aponte, including primary sources, see the website Digital Aponte, https://aponte.hosting.nyu.edu/.
40. See Childs, *1812 Aponte Rebellion*, 124.
41. See Manuel Barcia, *The Great African Slave Revolt of 1825: Cuba and the Fight for Freedom in Matanzas* (Baton Rouge: Louisiana State University Press, 2012), 162–63.
42. Charles Manfred Thompson, *History of the United States: Political, Industrial, Social* (Chicago: Benj. H. Sanborn, 1917), 293.
43. Kenneth S. Greenberg, ed., *"The Confessions of Nat Turner" and Related Documents* (Boston: Bedford Books of St. Martin's Press, 1996), 6–7.
44. Greenberg, *"Confessions of Nat Turner" and Related Documents*, 6–7.
45. Greenberg, *"Confessions of Nat Turner" and Related Documents*, 2.
46. On the many dimensions of the rebellion, see Kenneth S. Greenberg, ed., *Nat Turner: A Slave Rebellion in History and Memory* (New York: Oxford University Press, 2003).
47. Vanessa M. Holden, *Surviving Southampton: African American Women and Resistance in Nat Turner's Community* (Urbana: University of Illinois Press, 2021), 28–29.
48. Holden, *Surviving Southampton*, 107.
49. Greenberg, *"Confessions of Nat Turner" and Related Documents*, 13.
50. Chapter XXII, "An act to amend an act entitled, 'an act reducing into one the several acts concerning slaves, free negroes and mulattoes, and for other

purposes,'" in *Acts Passed at a General Assembly of the Commonwealth of Virginia* (Richmond: Thomas Ritchie, 1832), 20–22.

51. V. Brown, *Reaper's Garden*, 232.

52. Gad Heuman, *Between Black and White: Race, Politics, and the Free Coloreds in Jamaica, 1792–1865* (Westport, CT: Greenwood Press, 1981), 86. For a recent accessible history of the rebellion, see Tom Zoellner, *Island on Fire: The Revolt that Ended Slavery in the British Empire* (Cambridge, MA: Harvard University Press, 2020).

53. See Michael Craton, *Testing the Chains: Resistance to Slavery in the British West Indies* (Ithaca, NY: Cornell University Press, 1982), 313–15, and V. Brown, *Reaper's Garden*, 233.

54. Jean Besson, "Missionaries, Planters, and Slaves in the Age of Abolition," in *The Caribbean: A History of the Region and Its Peoples*, ed. Stephan Palmié and Francisco A. Scarano (Chicago: University of Chicago Press, 2011), 324.

55. Reis, *Slave Rebellion in Brazil*, 15.

56. The Law of November 7, 1831. See also Nishida, *Slavery and Identity*, 17.

57. There were revolts in 1814 and 1816, and others between 1827 and 1831. See Reis, *Slave Rebellion in Brazil*, 45–68. For an updated and expanded analysis of the rebellion, see the newest Portuguese edition, João José Reis, *Rebelião escrava no Brasil: A história do levante dos malês em 1835* (São Paulo: Companhia das letras, 2003).

58. Reis, *Slave Rebellion in Brazil*, 139. See also Reis, *Rebelião escrava no Brasil*, 161–63.

59. To know more, see Reis, *Rebelião escrava no Brasil*, 272–73. Two more recent books support this view of the Malê Revolt; see Manuel Barcia, *West African Warfare in Bahia and Cuba: Soldier Slaves in the Atlantic World, 1807–1844* (Oxford: Oxford University Press, 2014) and Lovejoy, *Jihād in West Africa During the Ages of Revolutions*.

60. Reis, *Slave Rebellion in Brazil*, 5. See also Reis, *Rebelião escrava no Brasil*, 24.

61. On the early Hausa rebellions in 1807, see João José Reis, "La révolte haoussa de Bahia en 1807: Résistance et contrôle des esclaves au Brésil," *Annales: Histoire, Sciences Sociales* no. 2 (2006): 383–418. On the revolt of 1809, see João José Reis, "A revolta haussá de 1809 na Bahia," in *Revoltas escravas no Brasil*, ed. João José Reis and Flávio dos Santos Gomes (São Paulo: Companhia das Letras, 2021), 177–226. On the rebellion of 1814, the most serious one, see Schwartz, "Cantos and Quilombos," 247–72, and João José Reis, "Há duzentos anos: A revolta escrava de 1814 na Bahia," *Topoi* 15, no. 28 (2014): 68–115.

62. Mattoso, *Être esclave au Brésil XVIe–XIXe siècles*, 230.

63. On the repressive measures, see Cunha, *Negros, Estrangeiros*, 99.

64. Reis, *Slave Rebellion in Brazil*, 127.

65. Reis, *Slave Rebellion in Brazil*, 121.

66. Reis, *Slave Rebellion in Brazil*, 91.

67. "Bahia: Policia," *Jornal do Commercio*, February 10, 1835, 1.

68. *Jornal do Commercio*, February 27, 1835, 2. On how Brazilian press reported on the rebellion, see José Antônio Teófilo Cairus, "*Jihad*, cativeiro e redenção: Escravidão, resistência e irmandade, Sudão Central e Bahia (1835)" (MA thesis, Universidade Federal do Rio de Janeiro, 2002), chap. 1. On the material, visual, and spiritual dimensions of these amulets, see Matthew Francis Rarey, *Insignificant Things: Amulets and the Art of Survival in the Early Black Atlantic* (Durham, NC: Duke University Press, 2023), chap. 4.
69. *Jornal do Commercio*, February 17, 1835, 3.
70. *Jornal do Commercio*, March 21, 1835, 1.
71. *Jornal do Commercio*, April 8, 1835, 4.
72. *Jornal do Commercio*, April 8, 1835, 1.
73. *Jornal do Commercio*, April 1, 1835, 2.
74. Among the several British newspapers were the *Caledonian Mercury*, the *Dorset County Chronicle*, and the *Liverpool Albion*. French newspapers included the *Journal du commerce*, *La Quotidienne*, *La Tribune des départemens*, and several others. Spanish newspapers included the *Anales administrativos*, June 3, 1835, 1. US newspapers included the *Herald of the Times*, the *Martinsburg Gazette*, and the *South Branch Intelligencer*. German newspapers included the *Schwäbischer Merkur*, March 26, 1835, 508, and *Karlsruher Zeitung*, November 17, 1835, 2856.
75. *Dorset County Chronicle* (Dorchester, UK), March 26, 1835, 2.
76. *Le Spectateur* (Dijon, France), May 15, 1835, 4, and *El Guerrero y el compilador*, May 31, 1835, 208. The original story was published in the *Jornal do Commercio*, March 21, 1835, 1.
77. On the role of Carlota and Fermina in *La Escalera*, see Aisha K. Finch, *Rethinking Slave Rebellion in Cuba: La Escalera and Insurgencies of 1841–1844* (Chapel Hill: University of North Carolina Press, 2015), 169–77.
78. "Revista de las Provincias," *El Catolico*, April 10, 1844, 80.
79. Finch, *Rethinking Slave Rebellion in Cuba*, chap. 7.
80. See, for example, the case of the West Indies colony of Berbice during British rule in Randy Browne, *Surviving Slavery in the British Caribbean* (Philadelphia: University of Pennsylvania Press, 2017).

Chapter 16

1. *Radical Paulistano*, November 13, 1869, 1.
2. See Nafafé, *Lourenço da Silva Mendonça.*
3. See Sinha, *Slave's Cause.*
4. Digna Castañeda, "The Female Slave in Cuba During the First Half of the Nineteenth Century," in Shepherd, Brereton, and Bailey, *Engendering History*, 145. On Cuba and also for a broader discussion on Latin America, see Adriana Chira, "Freedom with Local Bonds: Custom and Manumission in the Age of Emancipation," *American Historical Review* 126, no. 3 (2021):

949–77. See also Adriana Chira, *Patchwork Freedoms: Law, Slavery and Race Beyond Cuba's Plantations* (New York: Cambridge University Press, 2022), chap. 4.

5. See "Acts relating to Slaves" (1735), in Cooper and McCord, *Statutes at Large of South Carolina*, 396.

6. "An Act to Authorize the Manumission of Slaves" (May 1782 of Commonwealth), in William Waller Hening, ed., *The Statutes at Large; Being a Collection of All the Laws of Virginia from the First Session of the Legislature, in the Year 1619*, vol. 11 (Richmond: J. & G. Cochran, 1821), 39.

7. Sinha, *Slave's Cause*, 41–44, and Araujo, *Reparations for Slavery*, 49.

8. Joel Quirk, *The Anti-Slavery Project: From the Slave Trade to Human Trafficking* (Philadelphia: University of Pennsylvania Press, 2014), 61.

9. On Antigua, see Lightfoot, *Troubling Freedom: Antigua and the Aftermath of British Emancipation* (Durham, NC: Duke University Press, 2015).

10. Simon Drescher, *Abolition: A History of Slavery and Antislavery* (Cambridge: Cambridge University Press, 2009), 212.

11. Gigantino, *Ragged Road to Abolition*, 214–15.

12. Andrews, *Afro-Latin America, 1800–2000*, 87.

13. Jaime Olveda Legaspi, "La abolición de la esclavitud en México, 1810–1917," *Signos Históricos*, no. 29 (2013): 22–26.

14. Baumgartner, *South to Freedom*, 67, 117–18.

15. Borucki, *From Shipmates to Soldiers*, 50–51.

16. On Chile, see Cruz, *La abolición de la esclavitud en Chile*, 39–40. On Argentina, see Andrews, *Los afroargentinos de Buenos Aires*, 59, and E. Edwards, *Hiding in Plain Sight*, 2020, 4.

17. Borucki, *From Shipmates to Soldiers*, 136.

18. Lawrence C. Jennings, *French Anti-Slavery: The Movement for the Abolition of Slavery in France, 1802–1848* (Cambridge: Cambridge University Press, 2000).

19. Jason McGraw, *The Work of Recognition: Caribbean Colombia and the Postemancipation Struggle for Citizenship* (Chapel Hill: University of North Carolina Press, 2014), 28–29, and Andrews, *Los afroargentinos de Buenos Aires*, 57.

20. Among the several new recent studies on the illegal slave trade in the United States, see W. Caleb McDaniel, *Sweet Taste of Liberty: A True Story of Slavery and Restitution in America* (New York: Oxford University Press, 2019); Richard Bell, *Stolen: Five Free Boys Kidnapped into Slavery and Their Astonishing Odyssey Home* (New York: 37 Ink, 2019); Jeff Forret, *Williams' Gang: A Notorious Slave Trader and His Cargo of Black Convicts* (New York: Cambridge University Press, 2020); Jonathan Daniel Wells, *The Kidnapping Club: Wall Street, Slavery, and Resistance on the Eve of the Civil War* (New York: Bold Type, 2020); and Joshua D. Rothman, *The Ledger and the Chain: How Domestic Slave Traders Shaped America* (New York: Basic Books, 2021).

21. Keila Grinberg, "Illegal Enslavement, International Relations, and International Law on the Southern Border of Brazil," *Law and History Review* 35, no. 1 (2017): 31–52.
22. Ira Berlin, *The Long Emancipation: The Demise of Slavery in the United States* (Cambridge, MA: Harvard University Press, 2015), 15.
23. Eric Foner, *Reconstruction: America's Unfinished Revolution, 1863–1877* (New York: HarperCollins, 2014), 7.
24. Araujo, *Reparations for Slavery*, 65–66.
25. See Celso Thomas Castilho, *Slave Emancipation and Transformations in Brazilian Political Citizenship* (Pittsburgh, PA: University of Pittsburgh Press, 2016); Needell, *Sacred Cause*; and Alonso, *Flores, votos e balas*, translated into English as Angela Alonso, *The Last Abolition: The Brazilian Antislavery Movement, 1868–1888* (New York: Cambridge University Press, 2021).
26. For more, see Mamigonian, *Africanos livres*.
27. Maria Alice Rosa Ribeiro, "Preços de escravos em Campinas no século XIX," *História econômica & história de empresas* 20, no. 1 (2017): 111–12.
28. Kim D. Butler, *Freedoms Given, Freedoms Won: Afro-Brazilians in Post-Abolition São Paulo and Salvador* (New Brunswick, NJ: Rutgers University Press, 2000), 28.
29. See L. Soares, *O 'povo de Cam' na capital do Brasil*, 299, and Cowling, *Conceiving Freedom*, 42.
30. Flávio dos Santos Gomes, "Slavery, Black Peasants and Post-Emancipation Society in Brazil (Nineteenth-Century Rio de Janeiro)," *Social Identities* 10, no. 6 (2004): 742, and Castilho, *Slave Emancipation*, 88.
31. Maria Helena Machado, *O plano e o pânico: Os movimentos sociais na década da abolição* (São Paulo: Editora da Universidade de São Paulo, 1994), 76, 82.
32. Wlamyra Albuquerque, *O jogo da dissimulação: Abolição e cidadania negra no Brasil* (São Paulo: Companhia das Letras, 2009), 105.
33. Emília Viotti da Costa, *A Abolição* (São Paulo: Editora da Universidade Estadual de São Paulo, 2008), 10.
34. Ana Flávia Magalhães Pinto, *Escritos da liberdade: Literatos negros, racismo e cidadania no Brasil oitocentista* (Campinas Brazil: Editora da Universidade Estadual de Campinas, 2019), 263–64.
35. Ada Ferrer, *Insurgent Cuba: Race, Nation, and Revolution, 1868–1898* (Chapel Hill: University of North Carolina Press, 1999), 39.
36. Ferrer, *Insurgent Cuba*, 27.
37. Araujo, *Reparations for Slavery*, 74–75.
38. Rebecca J. Scott, *Slave Emancipation in Cuba: The Transition to Free Labor, 1860–1899* (Pittsburgh: University of Pittsburgh Press, 2000), 73.
39. Christopher Schmidt-Nowara, *Empire and Antislavery: Spain, Cuba, and Puerto Rico, 1833–1874* (Pittsburgh, PA: Pittsburgh University Press, 1999), 153, and Luis A. Figueroa, *Sugar, Slavery, and Freedom in Nineteenth-Century Puerto Rico* (Chapel Hill: University of North Carolina Press, 2005), 126.

40. R. Scott, *Slave Emancipation in Cuba*, 140.
41. Manning, *Slavery and African Life*, 106.
42. Mariana P. Candido, "The Expansion of Slavery in Benguela during the Nineteenth Century," *International Review of Social History* 65, S28 (2020): 70–71.
43. Quirk, *Anti-Slavery Project*, 73.
44. Quirk, *Anti-Slavery Project*, 95.
45. See the classic Lovejoy, *Transformations in Slavery*; Mohammed Bashir Salau, *The West African Slave Plantation: A Case Study* (Basingstoke, UK: Palgrave Macmillan, 2011); and Mohammed Bashir Salau, *Plantation Slavery in the Sokoto Caliphate: A Historical and Comparative Study* (Suffolk, UK: University of Rochester Press, 2018).
46. Marcia C. Schenk and Mariana P. Candido, "Uncomfortable Pasts: Talking About Slavery in Angola" in Araujo, *African Heritage and Memories of Slavery in Brazil and the South Atlantic World*, 218, and Candido, "Expansion of Slavery in Benguela," 71. See also Candido, *Wealth, Land and Property in Angola*, chap. 5.
47. Lovejoy, *Transformations in Slavery*, 253; Martin Klein, *Slavery and Colonial Rule in French West Africa* (Cambridge: Cambridge University Press, 1998), 159; and Marie Rodet, "Escaping Slavery and Building Diasporic Communities in French Soudan and Senegal, ca. 1880–1940," *International Journal of African Historical Studies* 48, no. 2 (2015): 363–86.
48. Lovejoy, *Transformations in Slavery*, 261.
49. Rodet, "Escaping Slavery and Building Diasporic Communities," 363.
50. Drescher, *Abolition*, 454.
51. On how residents of Angola associate and sometimes conflate the past of slavery and the forced labor system imposed by the Portuguese in the nineteenth century, see Schenck and Candido, "Uncomfortable Pasts," 216. On the international debates about the persistence of forced labor regimes in Portuguese colonies, see José Pedro Monteiro, *The Internationalization of the 'Native Labour' Question in Portuguese Late Colonialism 1945–1965* (Cham, Switz.: Palgrave Macmillan, 2023).
52. I explore these dimensions in Araujo, *Reparations for Slavery*.

Chapter 17

1. Alain Gilbert, *Black Patriots and Loyalists: Fighting for Emancipation in the War for Independence* (Chicago: University of Chicago Press, 2012), 95.
2. See Cassandra Pybus, *Epic Journey of Freedom: Runaway Slaves of the American Revolution and Their Global Quest for Liberty* (Boston: Beacon Press, 2006), 41–42; Gilbert, *Black Patriots and Loyalists*, 191; and Sinha, *Slave's Cause*, 50.
3. See Maya Jasanoff, *Liberty's Exiles: American Loyalists in the Revolutionary World* (New York: HarperCollins, 2011), 46, 48.
4. Jasanoff, *Liberty's Exiles*, 9.

5. Christopher Leslie Brown, *Moral Capital: Foundations of British Abolitionism* (Chapel Hill: University of North Carolina Press, 2006), 298–301.
6. C. Brown, *Moral Capital*, 301.
7. Pybus, *Epic Journey of Freedom*, 70.
8. See Alex Byrd, *Captives and Voyagers: Black Migrants across the Eighteenth-Century British Atlantic World* (Baton Rouge: Louisiana State University Press, 2008), 155. On age and sex breakdown, see Gilbert, *Black Patriots and Loyalists*, 200–201.
9. TNA, Public Records Office, Guy Carleton, 1st Baron Dorchester, Papers, 30/55/100, Subseries C. Folios 10427. An online searchable version of *The Book of Negroes* is also at the Nova Scotia National Archives https://archives.novascotia.ca/africanns/book-of-negroes/.
10. Lawrence Hill, *The Book of Negroes* (Toronto: HarperCollins, 2007), and Lawrence Hill, *Someone Knows My Name* (New York: W.W. Norton, 2007). Lawrence Hill and Clement Virgo's miniseries *The Book of Negroes* aired on CBC Television (Canada) on January 7, 2015, and BET (United States) on February 16, 2015.
11. Gilbert, *Black Patriots and Loyalists*, 209–14.
12. Brandon Mills, *The World Colonization Made: The Racial Geography of Early American Empire* (Philadelphia: University of Pennsylvania Press, 2020), 39.
13. See Samantha Seeley, *Race, Removal, and the Right to Remain: Migration and the Making of the United States* (Chapel Hill: University of North Carolina Press, 2021), 179–85.
14. See the letter from Anthony Taylor to William Thornton, the architect of the US Capitol in Washington, DC, dated January 24, 1787, in Dorothy Sterling, ed., *Speak Out in Thunder Tones: Letters and Other Writings by Black Northerners, 1787–1865* (New York: Da Capo Press, 1998), 4–6.
15. Ruma Chopra, "'Wayward Humours' and 'Perverse Disputings': Exiled Blacks and the Foundation of Sierra Leone, 1787–1800," in *Africans in Exile: Mobility, Law, and Identity*, ed. Nathan Riley Carpenter and Benjamin N. Lawrance (Bloomington: Indiana University Press, 2018), 38–39.
16. Byrd, *Captives and Voyagers*, 142.
17. See Byrd, *Captives and Voyagers*, 224–33, and Simon Schama, *Rough Crossings: The Slaves, the British and the American Revolution* (New York: HarperCollins, 2007), 201–2, 216.
18. C. Brown, *Moral Capital*, 283.
19. Chopra, "'Wayward Humours' and 'Perverse Disputings,'" 42.
20. Jeffrey A. Fortin, "'An Act of Deportation': The Jamaican Maroons' Journey from Freedom to Slavery and Back Again, 1796–1836," in Araujo, *Paths of the Atlantic Slave Trade*, 82. See also Chopra, *Almost Home*.
21. See James D. Lockett, "The Deportation of the Maroons of Trelawny Town to Nova Scotia, then Back to Africa," *Journal of Black Studies* 30, no. 1 (1999): 5–14.

22. Chopra, "'Wayward Humours' and 'Perverse Disputings,'" 46–47.

23. Nemata Amelia Ibitayo Blyden, *African Americans and Africa: A New History* (New Haven, CT: Yale University Press, 2019), 89.

24. On Finley's plans to relocate US Black populations in Africa, see Isaac V. Brown, *Memoirs of the Rev. Robert Finley* [. . .] (New-Brunswick, NJ: Terhune & Letson, 1819).

25. Kate Masur, "The African American Delegation to Abraham Lincoln: A Reappraisal," *Civil War History* 56, no. 2 (2010): 117–44, 121.

26. On Vaughan's and his family's story, see Lisa A. Lindsay, *Atlantic Bonds: A Nineteenth-Century Odyssey from America to Africa* (Chapel Hill: University of North Carolina Press, 2017).

27. On Cuba, see Rodolfo Sarracino, *Los que volvieron a África* (Havana: Editorial de Ciencias Sociales, 1988), and Solimar Otero, *Afro-Cuban Diasporas in the Atlantic World* (Rochester, NY: University of Rochester Press, 2010).

28. On the various waves of exiles from Bahia to the Bight of Benin, see Lisa Earl Castillo, "Mapping the Nineteenth-Century Brazilian Returnee Movement: Demographics, Life Stories and the Question of Slavery," *Atlantic Studies: Global Currents* 13, no. 1 (2016): 25–52.

29. Cunha, *Negros, Estrangeiros*, 77. Also regarding these repressive measures, see Ricardo Figueiredo Pirola, *Escravos e rebeldes nos tribunais do Império: Uma história social da lei de 10 de junho de 1835* (Rio de Janeiro: Arquivo Nacional, 2015); Luciana da Cruz Brito, *Temores da África: Segurança, Legislação e População Africana* (Salvador, Brazil: Editora da Universidade da Bahia, 2016); and Castillo, "Mapping the Nineteenth-Century Brazilian Returnee Movement," 26.

30. Castillo, "Mapping the Nineteenth-Century Brazilian Returnee Movement," 28.

31. Reis, *Slave Rebellion in Brazil*, 220.

32. Lisa Earl Castillo, "The Exodus of 1835: Agudá Life Stories and Social Networks," in *The Vile Trade: Slavery and the Slave Trade in Africa*, ed. Abi Alabo Derefaka et al. (Durham, NC: Carolina Academic Press, 2015), 211.

33. See Lisa Earl Castillo and Luis Nicolau Parés, "Marcelina da Silva: A Nineteenth-Century *Candomblé* Priestess in Bahia," *Slavery and Abolition* 31, no. 1 (2010): 1–27.

34. Castillo, "Mapping the Nineteenth-Century Brazilian Returnee Movement," 29.

35. On returnees to the region of present-day Togo, see Alcione M. Amos, "Afro-Brazilians in Togo: The Case of the Olympio Family, 1882–1945," *Cahier d'études africaines* 41, no. 162 (2001): 293–314, and especially Silke Strickrodt, *Afro-European Trade in the Atlantic World: The Western Slave Coast, c. 1550–1885* (Woodbridge, UK: James Currey, 2015). In present-day Nigeria, see Cunha, *Negros, Estrangeiros*, and Alcione M. Amos, "The Amaros and Agudás: The Afro-Brazilian Returnee Community in Nigeria in the

Nineteenth Century," in *Yoruba in Brazil, Brazilians in Yorubaland: Cultural Encounter, Resilience, and Hybridity in the Atlantic World*, ed. Niyi Afolabi and Toyin Falola (Durham, NC: Carolina Academic Press, 2017), 65–110. In today's Ghana, see Alcione Meira Amos, *Os que voltaram: A história dos retornados afro-brasileiros na África Ocidental no século XIX* (Belo Horizonte, Brazil: Tradição Planalto, 2007), 69–89; Kwame Essien, *Brazilian-African Diaspora in Ghana: The Tabom, Slavery, Dissonance of Memory, Identity, and Locating Home* (East Lansing: Michigan State University Press, 2016).

36. For the movement of return from Rio de Janeiro, see Mônica Lima e Souza, "Entre margens: O retorno à África de libertos no Brasil, 1830–1870" (PhD diss., Universidade Federal Fluminense, 2008), 122–23.

37. Verger, *Fluxo et refluxo*, 646.

38. Nina Rodrigues, *Os Africanos no Brasil* (São Paulo: Companhia Editora Nacional, 1976), 108.

39. Pierre Verger estimated 3,000 returnees; see Verger, *Flux et reflux de la traite des nègres*, 633. Jerry Michael Turner estimated 4,000 returnees; see Jerry Michael Turner, "Les Brésiliens: The Impact of Former Slaves Upon Dahomey" (PhD diss., Boston University, 1975), 85. Manuela Carneiro da Cunha estimated 7,000 to 8,000 returnees; see Manuela Carneiro da Cunha, *Da Senzala ao Sobrado* (São Paulo: Nobel, Editora da Universidade de São Paulo, 1985), 17.

40. Guran, *Agudás*, 73.

41. See Araujo, "Dahomey, Portugal, and Bahia," 7.

42. On Souza, see Alberto da Costa e Silva, *Francisco Félix de Souza, mercador de escravos* (Rio de Janeiro: Nova Fronteira, 2004), and Ana Lucia Araujo, "Forgetting and Remembering the Atlantic Slave Trade: The Legacy of Brazilian Slave Merchant Francisco Felix de Souza," in *Crossing Memories: Slavery and African Diaspora*, ed. Ana Lucia Araujo, Mariana P. Candido, and Paul Lovejoy (Trenton, NJ: Africa World Press, 2011), 79–103.

43. Bruce Chatwin, *The Viceroy of Ouidah* (London: Jonathan Cape, 1980), and Werner Herzog, dir., *Cobra Verde* (1987; Beverly Hills, CA: Anchor Bay Entertainment, 2002), DVD.

44. Prince-Bythewood, *The Woman King*.

45. I extensively discussed these issues in Araujo, *Public Memory of Slavery*.

46. Law, *Ouidah*, 201.

47. HCPP, *Correspondence with the British Commissioners Relating to the Slave Trade, 1844*. Class A, Correspondence with the British Commissioners at Sierra Leone, Havana, Rio de Janeiro, Surinam, Cape of Good Hope, Jamaica, Loanda, and Boa Vista, Relating to the Slave Trade from January 1 to December 31, 1844, inclusive, Enclosure in No. 18, *Abstract of the Proceedings in the British and Brazilian Court of Mixed Commission established in Sierra Leone, for the Repression of the Slave Trade, during the year 1843* (London: William Clowes and Sons, 1845), 21. See also HCPP, *Correspondence* *with the British Commissioners Relating to the Slave Trade, 1844*. Class A, Correspondence with the British Commissioners at Sierra Leone, Havana, Rio de Janeiro, Surinam, Cape of Good Hope, Jamaica, Loanda, and Boa Vista, Relating to the Slave Trade from January 1 to December 31, 1845, inclusive, Class A, 1845, letter from Cuban slave trader Rafael de Toca to Don Thomas da Costa Ramos, March 15, 1844 (London: William Clowes and Sons, 1846), 313.

48. HCPP, *Correspondence on the Slave Trade with Foreign Powers, Parties to Treaties under which Captured Vessels Are to Be Tried by Mixed Tribunals, from January 1 to December 21, 1846, inclusive*, Class B. 1846, Brazil, Enclosure 7 in no. 152 (London: T. R. Harrison, 1847), 244.

49. Olatunji Ojo, "Document 2: Letters Found in the House of Kosoko, King of Lagos (1851)," *African Economic History* 40 (2012): 41.

50. APEB, Tribunal da Relação, Salvador. "Testamento dc Domingos José Martins." No. 52904. E5, CX 2190, M2659, N5, 1864, fol. 6.

51. HCPP, Correspondence with the British Commissioners at Sierra Leone, Havana, The Cape of Good Hope, Jamaica, Loanda, and the Cape Verd Islands; and Reports from British Vice-Admiralty Courts, and from British Naval Officers, Relating to the Slave Trade. From April 1, 1850, to March 31, 1851, Class A, Enclosure 1 in No. 134 and Enclosure 7 in no. 140 (London: Harrison and Son, 1851), 147, 168–69.

52. See Cunha, *Negros, Estrangeiros*, 109.

53. See Fio Agbanon II, *Histoire de Petit-Popo et du Royaume Guin* (Paris: Karthala; Lomé, Togo: Haho, 1991), 87; Verger, *Os libertos*, 43–48; Alberto da Costa e Silva, *Um rio chamado Atlântico: A África no Brasil e o Brasil na África* (Rio de Janeiro: Nova Fronteira, 2003), 169; and Alberto da Costa e Silva, "Portraits of African Royalty in Brazil," in *Identity in the Shadow of Slavery*, ed. Paul E. Lovejoy (London: Continuum, 2000), 130. This version was also found in Verger's research notes; see Fundação Pierre Verger, Salvador, Brazil (hereafter cited as FPV), Verger's Research Documents, Caixa "Dahomey" I, handwritten note.

54. See Robin Law, "A carreira de Francisco Félix de Souza na África Ocidental (1800–1849)," *Topoi* (2001): 5, and Robin Law, "A comunidade brasileira de Uidá e os últimos anos do tráfico atlântico de escravos, 1850–66," *Afro-Ásia* 27 (2002): 46. See also Costa e Silva, *Francisco Félix de Souza*, 12, and Parés, "Afro-Catholic Baptism," 170–72.

55. "Enclosure 9: Lieutenant Forbes to Commodore Fanshawe 'Bonetta,' at sea, November 5, 1849," in Tim Coates, ed., *King Gezo of Dahomey, 1850–52: The Abolition of Slave Trade on the West Coast of Africa, 1850–52*, Uncovered Editions (London: Stationery Office, 2001), 37.

56. HCPP, Correspondence with British Ministers and Agents in Foreign Countries, and with Foreign Ministers in England Relating to the Slave Trade. From April 1, 1853 to March 31, 1854, Brazil (Consular) Bahia, no. 169,

Letter from Consul Morgan to Lord John Russell, Bahia, March 18, 1853 (London: Harrison and Sons, 1854), 245.

57. I conducted several interviews with Silva in Porto-Novo in 2005. I explore the different versions of Paraíso's possible trajectories in Araujo, *Public Memory of Slavery*, 363–65.

58. Júlio Santana Braga, "Notas sobre o 'Quartier Brésil' no Daomé," *Afro-Ásia*, no. 6–7 (1968): 189; Guran, *Agudás*, 15; and Cunha, *Negros, Estrangeiros*, 189.

59. Guran, *Agudás*, 88.

60. Sylvain Coovi Anignikin, Bellarmin Coffi Codo, and Léopold Dossou, "Le Dahomey (Bénin)," in *L'Afrique occidentale au temps des Français*, ed. Catherine Coquery-Vidrovitch, in collaboration with Odile Goerg (Paris: La Découverte, 1992), 392.

61. Alain Sinou, "La valorisation du patrimoine architectural et urbain: L'exemple de la ville de Ouidah au Bénin," *Cahiers des Sciences Humaines* 29, no. 1 (1993): 36.

62. See Law, "A comunidade brasileira de Uidá," 52; Law, *Ouidah*, 203; Kristin Mann, *Slavery and the Birth of an African City: Lagos, 1760–1900* (Bloomington: Indiana University Press, 2007), 85.

63. Cunha, *Negros, Estrangeiros*, 109.

64. See Bay, *Wives of the Leopard*, 276.

65. Mann, *Slavery and the Birth of Lagos*, 84.

66. Lisa A. Lindsay, "'To Return to the Bosom of Their Fatherland': Brazilian Immigrants in Nineteenth-Century Lagos," *Slavery and Abolition* 15, no. 1 (1994): 27.

67. Catherine Coquery-Vidrovitch, *L'Afrique et les Africains au XIXe siècle: Mutations, révolutions, crises* (Paris: Armand Colin 1999), 166, and Law, *Ouidah*, 263.

68. Cunha, *Negros, Estrangeiros*, 109.

69. See Castillo and Parés, "Marcelina da Silva," 1–27.

70. Patrick Manning, *Slavery, Colonialism and Economic Growth in Dahomey, 1640–1960* (Cambridge: Cambridge University Press, 1982), 163.

71. Anignikin, Codo, and Dossou, "Le Dahomey (Bénin)," 373.

72. Nassirou Bako-Arifari, "La Mémoire de la traite négrière dans le débat politique au Bénin dans les années 1990," *Journal des Africanistes* 70, nos. 1–2 (2000): 222, and Amos, *Os que voltaram*, 53–55.

73. Dov Ronen, "The Colonial Elite in Dahomey," *African Studies Review* 17, no. 1 (1974): 58, and Araujo, *Public Memory of Slavery*, 112–13.

74. On these projects of relocating US black populations in Liberia, Haiti, and Central America, see Masur, "African American Delegation to Abraham Lincoln," 117–44. On Brazil and Central America, see Maria Clara Sales Carneiro Sampaio, "Negros sonhos: Os projetos de colonização de afroamericanos no Brasil e na América Central durante a Guerra de Secessão," in H. Machado and Castilho, *Tornando-se Livre*, 399–421.

75. On Amazonia, see Gerald Horne, *The Deepest South: The United States, Brazil,*

and the African Slave Trade (New York: New York University Press, 2007), 116–17, and Matthew Karp, *This Vast Southern Empire: Slaveholders at the Helm of American Foreign Policy* (Cambridge, MA: Harvard University Press, 2016), 145–46.

76. Blyden, *African Americans and Africa*, 89.

77. See Henry McNeal Turner, "Justice or Emigration Should Be Our Watch-Word," in *African American Political Thought*, vol. 5, *Integration vs. Separatism: The Colonial Period to 1945*, ed. Marcus D. Pohlmann (New York: Routledge, 2003), 92–93, and Nell Irvin Painter, *Exodusters: Black Migration to Kansas after Reconstruction* (New York: Knopf, 1976), 126–27.

78. See "Speech by Marcus Garvey," Liberty Hall, January 1, 1922 in Marcus Garvey, *The Marcus Garvey and Universal Negro Improvement Association Papers*, 12 vols., ed. Robert A. Hill (Berkeley: University of California Press, 1983), 4:323.

79. Garvey, *Marcus Garvey and Universal Negro Improvement Association Papers*, 1:13, and Colin Grant, *Negro with a Hat: The Rise and Fall of Marcus* Garvey (New York: Oxford University Press, 2008), 8.

80. Keisha N. Blain, *Set the World on Fire: Black Nationalist Women and the Global Struggle for Freedom* (Philadelphia: Pennsylvania University Press, 2018), 14.

81. See Emory Tolbert, "Outpost Garveyism and the UNIA Rank and File," *Journal of Black Studies* 5, no. 3 (1975): 233–53.

82. Blyden, *African Americans and Africa*, 132.

83. Ula Yvette Taylor, *The Veiled Garvey: The Life and Times of Amy Jacques Garvey* (Chapel Hill: University of North Carolina Press, 2002), 214.

Epilogue

1. See Walter Rodney, *How Europe Underdeveloped Africa* (Washington, DC: Howard University Press, 1981), and Green, *Fistful of Shells*.

2. See Schenck and Candido, "Uncomfortable Pasts."

3. On the political idea of race, see Charles Mills, *The Racial Contract* (Ithaca, NY: Cornell University Press, 1997); Jemima Pierre, *The Predicament of Blackness: Postcolonial Ghana and the Politics of Race* (Chicago: University of Chicago Press, 2012); Achille Mbembe and Laurent Dubois, *Critique of Black Reason* (Durham, NC: Duke University Press, 2017); and Crystal Fleming, *Resurrecting Slavery: Racial Legacies and White Supremacy in France* (Philadelphia: Temple University Press, 2017).

4. On race, see C. Mills, *Racial Contract*. On capitalism, or the creation of the West and modernity, see the very accessible book by Howard French, *Born in Blackness: Africa, Africans, and the Making of the Modern World, 1471 to the Second World War* (New York: Liveright, 2021).

5. See SlaveVoyages, https://www.slavevoyages.org/assessment/estimates.

6. Lightfoot, *Troubling Freedom*, 84–85.

7. Diana Paton, *No Bound but the Law: Punishment, Race, and Gender in Jamaican State Formation, 1780–1870* (Durham, NC: Duke University Press, 2004), 146.
8. Ulrike Schmieder, "Martinique and Cuba Grande: Commonalities and Differences during the Periods of Slavery, Abolition, and Post-Emancipation," *Review (Fernand Braudel Center)* 36, no. 1 (2013): 95.
9. See Christine Chivallon, *L'esclavage, du souvenir à la mémoire: Contribution à une anthropologie de la Caraïbe* (Paris: Karthala, 2012), 205–6, 211, and Schmieder, "Martinique and Cuba Grande," 97.
10. See Céline Flory, *De l'esclavage à la liberté forcée: Histoire des travailleurs africains engagés dans la Caraïbe française au XIXe siècle* (Paris: Karthala, 2015), 19–21, and Céline Flory, "New Africans in the Post-Slavery French West Indies and Guiana: Close Encounters? (1857–1889)," in Araujo, *Paths of the Atlantic Slave Trade*, 109–30.
11. Schmieder, "Martinique and Cuba Grande," 89. On Indian immigration to the British West Indies and other Caribbean islands, see Lomarsh Roopharnine, *The Indian Caribbean: Migration and Identity in the Diaspora* (Jackson: University of Mississippi Press, 2018).
12. See Alex Lichtenstein, *Twice the Work of Free Labor: The Political Economy of Convict Labor in the New South* (London: Verso, 1996), and Kim Gilmore, "Slavery and Prison: Understanding the Connections," *Social Justice* 27, no. 3 (1981): 198.
13. *Statutes at Large, Treaties, and Proclamations of the United States of America, from December 1863 to December 1865*, vol. 13 (Boston: Little, Brown, 1866), 508.
14. See Rebecca J. Scott, *Degrees of Freedom: Louisiana and Cuba after Slavery* (Cambridge, MA: Belknap Press of Harvard University Press, 2005), 38.
15. Foner, *Reconstruction*, 246; R. Scott, *Degrees of Freedom*, 38.
16. Mary Frances Berry, *My Face Is Black Is True: Callie House and the Struggle for Ex-Slave Reparations* (New York: Alfred A. Knopf, 2005), 24.
17. Cornell University Law School, Legal Information Institute, U.S. Constitution, 15th Amendment, Section 1, https://www.law.cornell.edu/constitution/amendmentxv.
18. See Araujo, *Reparations for Slavery*, chap. 3, and more specifically M. Berry, *My Face Is Black Is True*.
19. See Hebe Mattos, *Das cores do silêncio: Os significados da liberdade no sudeste escravista, Brasil século XIX* (Campinas, Brazil: Editora da Universidade Estadual de Campinas, 2013), 282–86. See also Petrônio Domingues, *A nova abolição* (São Paulo: Selo Negro Edições, 2008), 48–50.
20. According to the Census of 1872. See Alceu Ravanello Ferraro and Michele de Leão, "Lei Saraiva (1881): Dos argumentos invocados pelos liberais para a exclusão dos analfabetos do direito de voto," *Educação Unisinos* 16, no. 3 (2012): 241–50. See also Araujo, *Reparations for Slavery*, 123.
21. There is a huge body of literature in Portuguese and English about whitening

in Brazil. For a clear overview, see Edward E. Telles, *Race in Another America: The Significance of Skin Color in Brazil* (Princeton, NJ: Princeton University Press, 2014).

22. Decree no. 528, June 28, 1890.

23. Law no. 97, October 5, 1892.

24. For an overview of the history of immigration in Brazil, see Jeffrey Lesser, *Immigration, Ethnicity, and National Identity in Brazil, 1808 to the Present* (New York: Cambridge University Press, 2013).

25. Mattos, *Das cores do silêncio* 106–7.

26. The leading scholar to promote these ideas was sociologist Gilberto Freyre; see Freyre, *Casa-grande e senzala*, and its English translation, Freyre, *Masters and Slaves*.

27. See Telles, *Race in Another America*, and Ynaê Lopes dos Santos, *Racismo Brasileiro: Uma história da formação do país* (São Paulo: Todavia, 2022).

28. See, for example, Williams, *Capitalism and Slavery*; Beckert, *Empire of Cotton*; Beckert and Rockman, *Slavery's Capitalism*; and Marika Sherwood, *After Abolition: Britain and the Slave Trade Since 1897* (London: I. B. Tauris, 2007).

Bibliography

Archives and Libraries

Archives de la Marine, Rochefort, France (AMR)

Archives Départementales de Charente-Maritime, La Rochelle, France (ADCM)

Archives Départementales de Loire-Atlantique, Nantes, France (ADLA)

Archives Municipales de La Rochelle, La Rochelle, France (AMLR)

Archives Nationales d'outre-mer, Aix-en-Provence, France (FR ANOM)

Arquivo Histórico Ultramarino, Lisbon, Portugal (AHU)

Arquivo Municipal de Lisboa, Lisbon, Portugal (AML)

Arquivo Nacional da Torre do Tombo, Lisbon, Portugal (ANTT)

Arquivo Público do Estado da Bahia, Salvador, Brazil (APEB)

Arquivo Publico do Estado do Rio Grande do Sul (APERS)

Beinecke Rare Book and Manuscript Library, Yale University, United States (BLY)

Biblioteca da Ajuda, Lisbon, Portugal (BA)

Biblioteca Nacional, Rio de Janeiro, Brazil (BN)

Biblioteca Nacional de Portugal, Lisbon, Portugal (BNP)

Bibliothèque Nationale de France, Paris, France (BNF)

Bibliothèque Sainte-Geneviève, Paris, France (BSG)

Fundação Pierre Verger, Salvador, Brazil (FPV)

House of Commons Parliamentary Papers, United Kingdom (HCPP)

Instituto Histórico e Geográfico Brasileiro, Rio de Janeiro, Brazil (IHGB)

Library of Congress, Washington, DC, United States (LOC)

Massachusetts Archives, Boston, MA, United States (MA)

Rhode Island State Archives, Providence, RI, United States (RISA)

The National Archives, Kew, United Kingdom (TNA)

Newspapers

Affiches américaines, Port-au-Prince and Cap Français, Saint-Domingue, France

Anales administrativos, Madrid, Spain

British and Foreign Anti-Slavery Reporter, London, United Kingdom

Caledonian Mercury, Edinburgh, Scotland, United Kingdom

Correio da Bahia, Salvador, Brazil

Correio Mercantil, Rio de Janeiro, Brazil

Daily Picayune, New Orleans, LA, United States

Diário do Rio de Janeiro, Rio de Janeiro, Brazil

Dorset County Chronicle, Dorchester, England, United Kingdom

East Carolina Republican, Goldsboro, NC, United States

El Guerrero y el compilador, Madrid, Spain

Expresso, Lisbon, Portugal

Gazeta do Rio de Janeiro, Rio de Janeiro, Brazil

Herald of the Times, Newport, RI, United States

Idade d'ouro do Brazil, Salvador, Brazil

Jornal do Commercio, Rio de Janeiro, Brazil

Journal du commerce, Paris, France

Karlsruher Zeitung, Karlsruhe, Germany

La Quotidienne, Paris, France

La Tribune des départemens, Paris, France

Le Spectateur, Dijon, France

Liverpool Albion, Liverpool, England, United Kingdom

Martinsburg Gazette, Martinsburg, VA [present-day WV], United States
Maryland Gazette, Annapolis, MD, United States
New-Orleans Argus, New Orleans, LA, United States
O Guarany, Salvador, Brazil
O Monitor, Salvador, Brazil
Radical Paulistano, São Paulo, Brazil
Schwäbischer Merkur, Stuttgart, Germany
South Branch Intelligencer, VA [present-day WV], United States
Washington DC National Intelligencer, Washington, DC, United States
Western Carolinian, Salisbury, NC, United States

Published Primary Sources

Acts and Laws Passed by the General Assembly of the State of Connecticut, The Public Laws of the State of Connecticut. Book 1. Hartford, CT: Hudson and Goodwin, 1808.

Acts Passed at a General Assembly of the Commonwealth of Virginia. Richmond: Thomas Ritchie, 1832.

Agassiz, Louis, and Elizabeth Agassiz. *Journey in Brazil*. Boston: Ticknor and Fields, 1868.

Ajayi, Jacob Festus Adeniyi. "Samuel Ajayi Crowther of Oyo." In Curtin, *Africa Remembered*, 289–316.

Almada, André Alvares d'. *Tratado breve dos rios de Guiné do Cabo-Verde desde o rio do Sanaga até aos Baixos de Sant'Anna*. Porto: Typographia Comercial Portuense, 1841.

Almeida, Cândido Mendes de. *Codigo philippino, ou, Ordenações e leis do reino de Portugal*. Vols. 1–5. Rio de Janeiro: Typographia do Instituto Philomathico, 1870.

Antonil, André João. *Cultura e opulência do Brasil por suas drogas e minas*. Rio de Janeiro: Typ. Imp. E Const. De J. Villeneuve, 1837.

Arago, Jacques. *Souvenirs d'un aveugle: Voyage autour du monde*. Vol. 1. Paris: H. Lebrun, 1842.

Arimino, Jorge Benci de. *Economia Christã dos senhores no governo dos escravos deduzida a das palavras do capitulo trinta e três do Ecclesiastico:*

Panis, & disciplina & opus servo; Reduzida a quatro discursos morais. Rome: Officina de Antonio de Rossi, 1705.

Astley, Thomas, ed. *A New General Collection of Voyages and Travels Consisting of the Most Esteemed Relations, which have been hitherto published in any language: Comprehending every Thing remarkable in its Kind, in Europe, Asia, Africa, and America.* Vol. 2. London: Thomas Astley, 1745.

Atkins, John. *A Voyage to Guinea, Brazil, & the West Indies: In his Majesty's Ships, the Swallow and Weymouth.* London: Ward and Chandler, 1737.

Avezac, Marie-Armand Pascal de Castera-Macaya d'. *Notice sur le pays et le people des Yébous en Afrique.* Paris: Librairie Orientale de Mme Ve Dondey-Dupré, 1845.

Azurara, Gomes Eannes de. *The Chronicle of the Discovery and Conquest of Guinea.* 2 vols. London: Hakluyt Society, 1896–99.

Barnet, Miguel. *Biografía de un cimarrón.* Buenos Aires: Centro Editor de América Latina, 1977.

Barnet, Miguel. *Biografía de un cimarron.* Havana: Instituto de Etnología y Folklore, 1966.

Baquaqua, Mahommah Gardo. *Biography of Mahommah G. Baquaqua. A Native of Zoogoo, in the Interior of Africa (A Convert to Christianity,) with a Description of that Part of the World; including the Manners and Customs of the Inhabitants.* Detroit: George Pomeroy, 1854.

Biard, François-Auguste. *Deux années au Brésil.* Paris: Hachette, 1862.

Bosi, Alfredo, ed. *Essencial Padre Antônio Vieira.* São Paulo: Penguin, Companhia das Letras, 2011.

Brásio, António, ed. *Monumenta Missionaria Africana: África Ocidental.* 15 vols. Lisbon: Agência Geral do Ultramar, 1952–88.

Brásio, António, ed. *Monumenta Missionaria Africana: África Ocidental; Segunda série (1342–1499).* 7 vols. Lisbon: Agência Geral do Ultramar, 1958–2004.

Broecke, Pieter van den, and James D. La Fleur. *Pieter Van Den Broecke's Journal of Voyages to Cape Verde, Guinea and Angola: (1605–1612).* London: Hakluyt Society, 2000.

Brown, Isaac V. *Memoirs of the Rev. Robert Finley, D. D. Late Pastor of the Presbyterian Congregation at Bank Ridge New-Jersey and President of Franklin College Located in the State of Georgia with Brief Skecthes of Some of His Contemporaries and Numerous Notes*. New-Brunswick: Terhune & Letson, 1819.

Burns, Robert I., and Samuel Parsons Scott. *Las Siete Partidas*. Vol. 4, *Family, Commerce, and the Sea: The Worlds of Women and Merchants*. Philadelphia: University of Pittsburgh Press, 2000.

Cadornega, Antonio de Oliveira. *Historia geral das guerras angolanas*. Vol. 2. Lisbon: Typographia da Companhia Nacional Editora, 1902.

Cantero, Justo G., and Eduardo Laplante. *Los ingenios: Colleción de vistas de los principales ingenios de azúcar de la isla de Cuba*. Havana: Litografía de Luis Marquier, 1847.

Castelnau, Francis de. *Renseignements sur l'Afrique centrale et sur une nation d'hommes à queue qui s'y trouverait, d'après le rapport des nègres du Soudan, esclaves à Bahia*. Paris: Chez P. Bertrand, 1851.

Chamberlain, Henry, and Rubens Borba de Moraes. *Vistas e costumes da cidade e arredores do Rio de Janeiro em 1819–1820*. Rio de Janeiro: Livraria Kosmos Editora and Erich Eichner, 1943.

Coates, Tim, ed. *King Gezo of Dahomey, 1850–52: The Abolition of Slave Trade on the West Coast of Africa, 1850–52*. Uncovered Editions. London: Stationery Office, 2001.

Conrad, Robert. *Children of God's Fire: A Documentary History of Black Slavery in Brazil*. Princeton, NJ: Princeton University Press, 1997.

Constituições primeiras do Sebastião Monteiro da Vide, *Constituições primeiras do Arcebispado da Bahia feitas, e ordenadas pelo illustrissimo, e reverendissimo Senhor D. Sebastião Monteiro da Vide, 5º Arcebispo do dito Arcebispado, e do Conselho de Sua Magestade: propostas e aceitads em o Synodo Diocesano, que o dito Senhor celebrou em 12 de junho do anno de 1707*. São Paulo: Typographia 2 de Dezembro, 1853.

Crow, Hugh, and John R. Pinfold. *The Memoirs of Captain Hugh Crow: The Life and Times of a Slave Trade Captain*. Oxford: Bodleian Library, 2007.

Cugoano, Ottobah. *Thoughts and Sentiments on the Evil of Slavery, or, The Nature of Servitude As Admitted by the Law of God, Compared to the Modern Slavery of the Africans in the West Indies In an Answer to the Advocates for Slavery and Oppression: Addressed to the Sons of Africa.* London: Printed by the author, 1791.

Cugoano, Quobna Ottobah. *Thoughts and Sentiments on the Evil of Slavery and Other Writings.* New York: Penguin Books, 1999.

Curtin, Philip D., ed. *Africa Remembered: Narratives by West Africans from the Era of the Slave Trade.* Madison: University of Wisconsin Press, 1967.

Cussac, Jean-Baptiste Rouvellat de. *Situation des esclaves dans les colonies françaises; urgence de leur émancipation.* Paris: Pagnerre, 1845.

Dapper, Olfert. *Description de l'Afrique, contenant les noms, la situation et les confins de toutes les parties, leur rivières, leurs villes et leurs habitations, leurs plantes et leurs animaux; les mœurs, les coûtumes, la langue, les richesses, la religion et le gouvernement de ses peuples.* Amsterdam: Chez Wolfgang, Waesberge, Bom & van Someren, 1686.

Dapper, Olfert. *Naukeurige beschrijvinge der Afrikaensche gewesten van Egypten, Barbaryen, Lybien, Biledulgerid, Negroslant, Guinea, Ethiopiën, Abyssinie.* Vol. 2. Amsterdam: J. van Meurs, 1676.

Dalzel, Archibald. *The History of Dahomey: An Inland Kingdom of Africa.* London: T. Spilsbury and Son, 1793.

Debret, Jean-Baptiste. *Voyage pittoresque et historique au Brésil.* 3 vols. Paris: Firmi-Didot Frères, 1834–39.

"Defloramento da escrava pelo senhor: Questões conexas." *O Direito: Revista mensal de legislação, doutrina e jurisprudencia* 35 (1884): 103–18.

Department of Commerce and Labor Bureau of the Census. *A Century Population Growth from the First Census of the United States: From the First Census of the United States to the Twelfth, 1790–1900.* Washington, DC: Government Printing Office, 1909.

Douglass, Frederick. *Narrative of the Life of Frederick Douglass: An American Slave Written by Himself.* Boston: Anti-Slavery Office, 1845.

Equiano, Olaudah, and Vincent Carretta. *The Interesting Narrative and Other Writings.* New York: Penguin Books, 2003.

Ewbank, Thomas. *Life in Brazil; or, a Journal of a Visit to the Land of Cocoa.* New York: Harper and Brothers, 1856.

Falconbridge, Alexander. *An Account of the Slave Trade on the Coast of Africa*. London: James Phillips, 1788.

Federal Writers' Project of the Works Progress Administration for the State of Arkansas. *Slave Narratives: A Folk History of Slavery in the United States with Interviews with Former Slaves*. Washington, DC: Library of Congress, 1941.

Fosse, Eustache de la. *Voyage à la côte occidentale d'Afrique en Portugal et en Espagne (1479–1480)*. Paris: Foulché-Delbosc, 1897.

Freyreiss, Georg Wilhelm. *Reisen in Brasilien*. Stockholm: Carl Svanberg, 1968.

Frézier, Amédée-François. *Relation du voyage de la mer du Sud aux côtes du Chili et du Pérou fait pendant les années 1712, 1713, et 1714*. Vol. 2. Paris: J-G. Nyon, E. Ganeau, J. Quillau, 1716.

Graham, Maria. *Journal of a Voyage to Brazil and Residence There, During Part of the Years 1821, 1822, and 1823*. London: Longman, Hurst, Rees, Orme, Brown, and Green, 1824.

Grandpré, Louis-Marie-Joseph Ohier de. *Voyage à la côte occidentale d'Afrique: fait dans les années 1786 et 1787, contenant la description des mœurs, usages, lois, gouvernement et commerce des états du Congo; suivi d'un voyage au cap de Bonne-Espérance: contenant la description militaire de cette colonie*. Vols. 1 and 2. Paris: Dentu, 1801.

Gronniosaw, James Albert Ukawsaw. *Narrative of the Most Remarkable Particulars in the Life of James Albert Ukawsaw Gronniosaw, an African Prince, as Related by Himself*. Bath, UK: W. Gye, 1770.

Hair, Paul, ed. *Barbot in Guinea: The Writings of Jean Barbot on West Africa, 1678–1712*. Vol. 1. London: Hakluyt Society, 1992.

Hening, William Waller. *The statutes at large: being a collection of all the laws of Virginia, from the first session of the legislature, in the year 1619: published pursuant to an act of the General Assembly of Virginia, passed on the fifth day of February one thousand eight hundred and eight*. Vol. 2. Richmond: Samuel Pleasants, Junior, Printer to the Commonwealth, 1810.

Hening, William Waller, ed. *The Statutes at Large; Being a Collection of All the Laws of Virginia from the First Session of the Legislature, in the Year 1619*. Vol. 11. Richmond: J. & G. Cochran, 1821.

Holloway, Thomas H. "Prefácio: Haddock Lobo e o recenseamento do Rio de Janeiro em 1849." In Roberto Hadock Lobo, "Texto introdutório do recenseamento do Rio de Janeiro de 1849," *Boletim de História Demográfica* 15, no. 50 (2008), http://historia_demografica.tripod.com/bhds/bhd50/thrj.pdf.

Hurston, Zora Neale. *Barracoon: The Story of the Last "Black Cargo."* New York: Amistad, 2018.

Imbert, Jean-Baptiste Alban. *Manual do fazendeiro, oủ tratado doméstico sobre as enfermidades dos negros, generalisado às necessidades medicas de todas as classes*. Rio de Janeiro: Typographia Nacional, 1839.

Jackson, John Andrew. *The Experience of a Slave in South Carolina*. London: Passmore & Alabaster, 1862.

Jacobs, Harriet. *Incidents in the Life of a Slave Girl*. New York: Barnes and Noble Classics, 2005.

Jefferson, Thomas. *The Papers of Thomas Jefferson*. Vol. 1, *1760–1776*. Edited by Julian P. Boyd. Princeton, NJ: Princeton University Press, 1950.

Jesselyn, John. *An Account of Two Voyages to New England: Made During the Years 1638, 1663*. Boston: W. Veazie, 1865.

Johannes Leo Africanus [al-Hasan Ibn Muhammad Al-Wazzan]. *The Cosmography and Geography of Africa*. Dublin: Penguin Random House, 2023.

Johnson, John Flude. *Proceedings of the General Anti-Slavery Convention, and held in London from Tuesday, June 13th, to Tuesday, June 20th, 1843*. London: British and Foreign Anti-Slavery Society, 1843.

Kidder, Daniel Parish, and James Cooley Fletcher. *Brazil and the Brazilians, Portrayed in Historical and Descriptive Sketches*. Philadelphia: Childs and Peterson, 1857.

Koelle, Sigismund W. *Polyglotta Africana or A Comparative Vocabulary of Nearly Three Hundred Words and Phrases in More Than One Hundred African Languages*. London: Church Missionary House, 1854.

Konadu, Kwasi, ed. *Africa's Gold Coast through Portuguese Sources, 1469–1680*. Oxford: Oxford University Press, 2022.

Koster, Henry. *Travels in Brazil by Henry Koster in the Years from 1809 to 1815*. Philadelphia: M. Carey & Son, 1817.

Labat, Jean-Baptiste. *Nouveau voyage aux isles de l'Amérique*. Vol. 3. Paris: Chez Guillaume Cavelier, 1722.

Lara, Silvia Hunold, ed. *Ordenações filipinas*. Vol. 5. São Paulo: Companhia das Letras, 1999.

Law, Robin, ed. *The English in West Africa 1681–1683: The Local Correspondence of the Royal African Company of England, 1681–1699, Part I*. Oxford: Oxford University Press, 1997.

Le Code Noir ou Edit dur Roy servant de reglement pour le Gouvernement & l'Administration de Justice & la Police des Isles Françoises de l'Amerique, & pour la Discipline & le Commerce des Negres & Esclaves dans ledit Pays. Paris: Chez Claude Girard, 1685.

Ley de Cuatro de Julio de 1870 Sobre Abolición de la Esclavitud y Reglamento para su ejecución en las islas de Cuba y Puerto Rico. Havana: Gobierno y Capitania general por S. M., 1872.

Lindley, Thomas. *Narrative of a Voyage to Brazil: Terminating in the Seizure of a British Vessel; with General Sketches of the Country, its Natural Productions, Colonial Inhabitants*. London: J. Johnson, 1805.

Lloyd, Peter C. "Osifekunde of Ijebu." In Curtin, *Africa Remembered*, 217–88.

Lovejoy, Paul E., and Robin Law. *The Biography of Mahommah Gardo Baquaqua: His Passage from Slavery to Freedom in Africa and America*. Princeton, NJ: Markus Wiener, 2003.

Manet, Édouard. *Lettres du siège de Paris: Précédées des lettres du voyage à Rio de Janeiro*. Paris: Éditions de l'Amateur, 1996.

Maygrier, Jacques-Pierre. *Nouvelles demonstrations d'accouchemens*. Paris: Béchet, 1822.

McCord, David J., ed. *The Statutes at Large of South Carolina, containing the acts relating to Charleston, Courts, Slaves, and Rivers*. Vol. 7, *Acts Relating to Slaves, 1735*. Columbia, SC: A. S. Johnson, 1840.

Mettas, Jean. *Répertoire des expéditions négrières françaises au XVIIIe siècle*. Vol. 2, Ports autres que Nantes. Paris: Société française d'histoire d'outre-mer, 1984.

Mettas, Jean, and Serge Daget. *Répertoire des expéditions négrières françaises au XVIIIe siècle*. Vol. 1. Nantes: Société française d'histoire d'outre-mer et Librairie orientaliste Paul Geuthner, 1979.

Mills, Kenneth, William B. Taylor, and Sandra Lauderdale Graham, eds. *Colonial Latin America: A Documentary History*. Lanham, MD: SR Books, 2004.

Moura, Francisco José Coelho de. "Do aleitamento natural, artificial e mixto em geral e em particular do mercenario attentas às condições da cidade do Rio de Janeiro: These apresentada à Faculdade de Medicina do Rio de Janeiro." Rio de Janeiro: Typographia Carioca, 1874.

Mouser, Bruce L., ed. *A Slaving Voyage to Africa and Jamaica: The Log of the Sandown, 1793–1794*. Bloomington: Indiana University Press, 2002.

Newton, John. *Upon the African Slave Trade*. London: Buckland & Johnson, 1788.

Newton, John, Bernard Martin, and Mark Spurrell. *The Journal of a Slave Trader (John Newton), 1750–1754; with Newton's "Thoughts Upon the African Slave Trade."* London: Epworth Press, 1962.

Northup, Solomon, and David Wilson. *Twelve Years a Slave; Narrative of Solomon Northup, Citizen of New-York, Kidnapped in Washington City in 1841, and Rescued in 1853, From a Cotton Plantation Near the Red River, in Louisiana*. Albany, NY: Derby and Miller, 1853.

Oettinger, Johann Peter, Craig Koslofsky, and Roberto Zaugg. *A German Barber-Surgeon in the Atlantic Slave Trade: The Seventeenth-Century Journal of Johann Peter Oettinger*. Charlottesville: University of Virginia Press, 2020.

Oliveira, Cristóvão Rodrigues de. *Sumario e[m] que brevemente se contem alguas cousas assi eclesiásticas como seculares que ha na cidade de Lisboa*. Lisbon: Germão Galharde, 1554.

Orbigny, Alcide Marie Dessalines d'. *Voyage pittoresque dans les deux Amériques*. Paris: Furne, 1841.

Postlethwayt, Malachy. *The Universal Dictionary of Trade and Commerce: With Large Additions and Improvements, Adapting the same to the*

Present State of British Affairs in America, since the last Treaty of Peace made in the Year 1763. Vol. 1. London, 1774.

President's Advisory 1776 Commission. *1776 Report*. January 2021. https://trumpwhitehouse.archives.gov/wp-content/uploads/2021/01/The-Presidents-Advisory-1776-Commission-Final-Report.pdf.

Prince, Mary. *The History of Mary Prince*. New York: Penguin Books, 2004.

Recueil d'édits, déclarations et arrests de sa majesté, Concernant l'Administration de la Justice la Police des Colonies françaises de l'Amérique, & les Engagés. Paris: Chez les Libraires Associez, 1744.

Robinson, Samuel. *A Sailor Boy's Experience Aboard a Slave Ship in the Beginning of the Present Century*. Wigtown, UK: GC Book Publishers, 1996.

Rocha, Manoel Ribeiro. *Ethiope resgatado, empenhado, sustentado, corregido, instruído, e liberado: Discurso theologico-juridico, em que se propõem o modo de comerciar, haver, e possuir validamente, quanto a hum, e outro foro, os Pretos cativos Africanos, e as principaes obrigações, que correm a quem deles se servir*. Lisbon: Officina Patriarcal de Francisco Luiz Ameno, 1758.

Rodríguez, Gloria García. *Voices of the Enslaved in Nineteenth-Century Cuba: A Documentary History*. Chapel Hill: University of North Carolina Press, 2011.

Rømer, Ludewig Ferdinand. *A Reliable Account of the Coast of Guinea (1760)*. New York: Diasporic Africa Press, 2013.

Rugendas, Maurice. *Voyage pittoresque dans le Brésil*. Paris: Engelmann, 1835.

Sagra, Ramón. *Historia economico-politica y estadística de la islã de Cuba*. Havana: Printed by the Widows Arazoza and Soler, 1831.

Saint-Hilaire, Auguste de. *Voyages dans l'intérieur du Brésil: Seconde Partie*. Paris: Librairie Gide, 1837.

Saint-Hilaire, Auguste de. *Voyage dans les provinces de Saint-Paul et de Sainte-Catherine*. Vol. 1. Paris: Arthus Bertrand, 1851.

Sandoval, Alonso de, and Nicole Von Germeten. *Treatise on Slavery: Selections from De Instauranda Aethiopum Salute*. Indianapolis: Hackett, 2008.

Sigaud, Joseph François Xavier. "Discurso sobre a Statistica Medica no Brasil." In *Relatorio dos trabalhos da Sociedade de Medicina do Rio de Janeiro, desde 24 de abril de 1831 até 30 de junho de 1832, lido na sessão pública de 30 de junho de 1832, anniversario da fundação da sociedade, pelo Dr. Luiz Vicente De-Simoni, Secretario Perpetuo da mesma Sociedade, etc.*, edited by Luiz Vicente de Simoni, 3–21. Rio de Janeiro: Seygnot-Plancher, 1832.

Smith, Venture. *A Narrative of the Life and Adventures of Venture Smith, A Native of Africa: but Resident about Sixty Years in the United States of America; Related by Himself.* New London, CT: Holt, 1798.

Snelgrave, William. *A New Account of Some Parts of Guinea and the Slave-Trade*. London, 1734.

Stanfield, James Field. *The Guinea Voyage, a Poem, in Three Books to Which Are Added, Observations on a Voyage to the Coast of Africa, in a Series of Letters to Thomas Clarkson*. Edinburgh: J. Robertson, 1807.

Statutes at Large, Treaties, and Proclamations of the United States of America, from December 1863 to December 1865. Vol. 13. Boston: Little, Brown, 1866.

Stevens-Acevedo, Anthony. *The Santo Domingo Slave Revolt of 1521 and the Slave Laws of 1522: Black Slavery and Black Resistance in the Early Colonial Americas*. New York: CUNY Dominican Studies Institute, 2019.

The Trial of Captain John Kimber, for the Murder of Two Female Negro Slaves on Board the Recovery, African Slave Ship: Tried at the Admiralty Sessions, held at the Old Baily, the 7th of June, 1792. London: C. Stalker, 1792.

Vilhena, Luís dos Santos. *A Bahia no século XVIII*. Vol. 1. Salvador, Brazil: Editora Itapuã, 1969.

Walsh, Robert. *Notices of Brazil in 1828 and 1829*. 2 vols. London: Frederick Westley and A. H. Davis, 1830.

Wetherell, James. *Brazil: Stray Notes from Bahia: Being Extracts from Letters, &c., During a Residence of Fifteen Years*. Liverpool: Webb and Hunt, 1860.

Whitfield, Harvey Amani. *The Problem of Slavery in Early Vermont, 1777–1810: Essays and Primary Sources*. Barre: Vermont Historical Society, 2014.

Secondary Sources

Abreu, Martha. *O império do divino: Festas religiosas e cultura popular no Rio de Janeiro, 1830–1900*. Rio de Janeiro: Nova Fronteira, 1999.

Abreu, Maurício Almeida. *A evolução urbana do Rio de Janeiro*. Rio de Janeiro: Zahar, 1987.

Acerbi, Patricia. *Street Occupations: Urban Vending in Rio de Janeiro*. Austin: University of Texas Press, 2017.

Achebe, Nwando. *The Female King of Colonial Nigeria: Ahebi Ugbabe*. Bloomington: Indiana University Press, 2011.

Adderley, Rosanne. *"New Negroes from Africa": Slave Trade Abolition and Free African Settlement in the Nineteenth-Century Caribbean*. Bloomington: Indiana University Press, 2006.

Agbanon, Fio, II. *Histoire de Petit-Popo et du Royaume Guin*. Paris: Karthala; Lomé, Togo: Haho, 1991.

Akyeampong, Emmanuel. "Sexuality and Prostitution among the Akan of the Gold Coast c. 1650–1950." *Past & Present*, no. 156 (1997): 144–73.

Albuquerque, Wlamyra. *O jogo da dissimulação: Abolição e cidadania negra no Brasil*. São Paulo: Companhia das Letras, 2009.

Alencastro, Luiz Felipe de. "Continental Drift: The Independence of Brazil (1822), Portugal and Africa." In *From Slave Trade to Empire: Europe and the Colonisation of Black Africa, 1780s–1880s*, edited by Olivier Pétré-Grenouilleau, 98–109. London: Routledge, 2004.

Alencastro, Luiz Felipe de. "História geral das guerras sul-atlânticas: O episódio de Palmares." In *Mocambos de Palmares: História, historiografia e fontes*, edited by Flávio Gomes, 61–99. Rio de Janeiro: 7Letras editora / FAPERJ, 2010.

Alencastro, Luiz Felipe de. "Le versant brésilien de l'Atlantique-Sud: 1550–1850." *Annales: Histoire, Sciences Sociales* 61, no. 2 (2006): 339–82.

Alencastro, Luiz Felipe de. *O trato dos viventes: Formação do Brasil no Atlântico Sul, séculos XVI e XVII*. São Paulo: Companhia das Letras, 2000.

Alencastro, Luiz Felipe de. "South Atlantic Wars: The Episode of Palmares." *Portuguese Studies Review* 19, no. 1–2 (2011): 35–58.

Alencastro, Luiz Felipe de. *Trade in the Living: The Formation of Brazil in the South Atlantic, Sixteenth to Seventeenth Centuries*. Albany: State University of New York Press, 2019.

Algranti, Leila Mezan. *O feitor ausente: Estudo sobre a escravidão urbana no Rio de Janeiro*. Petrópolis, Brazil: Vozes, 1988.

Almeida, James. "Minting Slavery in the Colonial Andes: Labor and Race in Potosi and Lima." PhD diss., Harvard University, 2022.

Almeida, Marcos Abreu Leitão de. "African Voices from the Congo Coast: Languages and the Politics of Identification in the Slave Ship *Jovem Maria* (1850)." *Journal of African History* 60, no. 2 (2019): 167–89.

Alonso, Angela. *Flores, votos e balas: O movimento abolicionista brasileiro (1868–1888)*. São Paulo: Companhia das Letras, 2015.

Alonso, Angela. *The Last Abolition: The Brazilian Antislavery Movement, 1868–1888*. New York: Cambridge University Press, 2021.

Álvarez López, Laura, and Magdalena Coll. "Registers of African-Derived Lexicon in Uruguay: Etymologies, Demography and Semantic Change." *Zeitschrift für romanische Philologie* 135, no. 1 (2019): 223–55.

Alves, Adriana Dantas Reis. "As mulheres negras por cima: O caso de Luzia Jeje; Escravidão família e mobilidade social-Bahia, c. 1780–c. 1830." PhD diss., Universidade Federal Fluminense, 2010.

Alves, Maíra Chinelatto. "Crimes de escravos e os caminhos da autônima, Campinas, 1876." In Machado and Castilho, *Tornando-se livre*, 37–57.

Amantino, Márcia, Eliane Cristina Deckman Fleck, and Carlos Engemann. *Companhia de Jesus na America por seus colégios e fazendas: Aproximações entre Brasil e Argentina (século XVIII)*. Rio de Janeiro: Garamond, 2015.

Amos, Alcione M. "Afro-Brazilians in Togo: The Case of the Olympio Family, 1882–1945." *Cahier d'études africaines* 41, no. 162 (2001): 293–314.

Amos, Alcione M. "The Amaros and Agudás: The Afro-Brazilian Returnee Community in Nigeria in the Nineteenth Century." In *Yoruba in Brazil, Brazilians in Yorubaland: Cultural Encounter,*

Resilience, and Hybridity in the Atlantic World, edited by Niyi Afolabi and Toyin Falola, 65–110. Durham, NC: Carolina Academic Press, 2017.

Amos, Alcione Meira. *Os que voltaram: A história dos retornados afro-brasileiros na África Ocidental no século XIX*. Belo Horizonte, Brazil: Tradição Planalto, 2007.

Anderson, Richard Peter. *Abolition in Sierra Leone: Re-Building Lives and Identities in Nineteenth-Century West Africa*. New York: Cambridge University Press, 2020.

Anderson, Richard, Alex Borucki, Daniel Domingues da Silva, David Eltis, Paul Lachance, Philip Misevich, and Olatunji Ojo. "Using African Names to Identify the Origins of Captives in the Transatlantic Slave Trade: Crowd-Sourcing and the Registers of Liberated Africans, 1808–1862." *History in Africa* (2013): 1–27.

Anderson, Richard, and Henry B. Lovejoy, eds. *Liberated Africans and the Abolition of the Slave Trade, 1807–1896*. Rochester: Rochester University Press, 2020.

Andrews, George Reid. *Afro-Latin America, 1800–2000*. New York: Oxford University Press, 2004.

Andrews, George Reid. *Los afroargentinos de Buenos Aires*. Buenos Aires: Ediciones de la Flor, 1989.

Anignikin, Sylvain Coovi, Bellarmin Coffi Codo, and Léopold Dossou. "Le Dahomey (Bénin)." In *L'Afrique occidentale au temps des Français*, edited by Catherine Coquery-Vidrovitch, in collaboration with Odile Goerg, 371–405. Paris: La Découverte, 1992.

Araujo, Ana Lucia, ed. *African Heritage and Memories of Slavery in Brazil and the South Atlantic World*. Amherst, NY: Cambria Press, 2015.

Araujo, Ana Lucia. "Black Purgatory: Enslaved Women's Resistance in Nineteenth-Century Rio Grande do Sul, Brazil." *Slavery and Abolition* 36, no. 4 (2015): 568–85.

Araujo, Ana Lucia. *Brazil through French Eyes: A Nineteenth-Century Artist in the Tropics*. Albuquerque: University of New Mexico Press, 2015.

Araujo, Ana Lucia. "Dahomey, Portugal, and Bahia: King Adandozan and the Atlantic Slave Trade." *Slavery and Abolition* 3, no. 1 (2012): 1–19.

Araujo, Ana Lucia. "Forgetting and Remembering the Atlantic Slave Trade: The Legacy of Brazilian Slave Merchant Francisco Felix de Souza." In *Crossing Memories: Slavery and African Diaspora*, edited by Ana Lucia Araujo, Mariana P. Candido, and Paul Lovejoy, 79–103. Trenton, NJ: Africa World Press, 2011.

Araujo, Ana Lucia. *The Gift: How Objects of Prestige Shaped the Atlantic Slave Trade and Colonialism*. New York: Cambridge University Press, 2024.

Araujo, Ana Lucia. "History, Memory and Imagination: Na Agontimé, a Dahomean Queen in Brazil." In *Beyond Tradition: African Women and their Cultural Spaces*, edited by Toyin Falola and Sati U. Fwatshak, 45–68. Trenton, NJ: Africa World Press, 2011.

Araujo, Ana Lucia. *Museums and Atlantic Slavery*. Oxford: Routledge, 2021.

Araujo, Ana Lucia, ed. *Paths of the Atlantic Slave Trade: Interactions, Identities, and Images*. Amherst, NY: Cambria Press, 2011.

Araujo, Ana Lucia. *Public Memory of Slavery: Victims and Perpetrators in the South Atlantic*. Amherst, NY: Cambria Press, 2010.

Araujo, Ana Lucia. *Reparations for Slavery and the Slave Trade: A Transnational and Comparative History*. London: Bloomsbury Academic, 2023.

Araujo, Ana Lucia. *Shadows of the Slave Past: Memory, Heritage, and Slavery*. New York: Routledge, 2014.

Araujo, Ana Lucia. "Sites of Disembarkation and the Public Memory of the Atlantic Slave Trade." In *A Stain on Our Pasts: Slavery and Memory*, edited by Abdoulaye Gueye and Johann Michel, 137–69. Trenton, NJ: Africa World Press, 2018.

Araujo, Ana Lucia. *Slavery in the Age of Memory: Engaging the Past*. London: Bloomsbury Academic, 2021.

Assunção, Matthias Röhrig. *Capoeira: A History of the Afro-Brazilian Martial Art*. New York: Routledge, 2004.

Assunção, Matthias Röhrig. "Capoeira Circle or Sports Academy? The Emergence of Modern Styles of Capoeira and Their Global Context." *História, Ciências, Saúde–Manguinhos* (2014): 135–50.

Assunção, Matthias Röhrig. "Engolo e capoeira: Jogos de combate étnico e diaspóricos no Atlântico Sul." *Tempo* 26, no. 3 (2020): 522–56.

Assunção, Matthias Röhrig. "Stanzas and Sticks: Poetics and Physical Challenges in the Afro-Brazilian Culture of the Paraíba Valley, Rio de Janeiro." *History Workshop Journal* 77, no. 1 (2014): 103–36.

Ayoh'Omidire, Feliz, and Alcione M. Amos. "O Babalaô fala: A autobiografia de Martiniano Eliseu do Bomfim." *Afro-Ásia*, no. 46 (2012): 229–61.

Azopardo, Ildefonso Gutiérrez. "El comercio y mercado de negros esclavos en Cartagena de Indias (1533–1850)." *Quinto Centenario* 12 (1987): 187–210.

Bailey, Anne C. *African Voices of the Atlantic Slave Trade: Beyond the Silence and the Shame*. Boston: Beacon Press, 2005.

Bailey, Anne C. *The Weeping Time: Memory and the Largest Slave Auction in the American History*. New York: Cambridge University Press, 2017.

Bako-Arifari, Nassirou. "La Mémoire de la traite négrière dans le débat politique au Bénin dans les années 1990." *Journal des Africanistes* 70, no. 1–2 (2000): 221–31.

Baptist, Edward E. "'Cuffy,' 'Fancy Maids,' and 'One-Eyed Men': Rape, Commodification, and the Domestic Slave Trade in the United States." *American Historical Review* 106, no. 5 (2001): 1641–42.

Baptist, Edward E. *The Half Has Never Been Told: Slavery in the Making of American Capitalism*. New York: Basic Books, 2014.

Barcia, Manuel. *The Great African Slave Revolt of 1825: Cuba and the Fight for Freedom in Matanzas*. Baton Rouge: Louisiana State University Press, 2012.

Barcia, Manuel. *West African Warfare in Bahia and Cuba: Soldier Slaves in the Atlantic World, 1807–1844*. Oxford: Oxford University Press, 2014.

Barcia, Manuel. "White Cannibalism in the Illegal Slave Trade: The Peculiar Case of the Portuguese Schooner Arrogante in 1837." *New West Indian Guide* (2021): 1–28.

Barcia, Manuel. *The Yellow Demon of Fever: Fighting Disease in the Nineteenth-Century Transatlantic*. New Haven, CT: Yale University Press, 2020.

Barcia, María del Carmen, Andrés Rodríguez Reyes, and Milagros Niebla Delgado. *Del cabildo de "nación" a la casa de santo*. Havana: Fundación Fernando Ortiz, 2012.

Barragan, Yesenia. *Freedom's Captives: Slavery and Gradual Emancipation on the Colombia Pacific*. New York: Cambridge University Press, 2021.

Baumgartner, Alice L. *South to Freedom: Runaway Slaves to Mexico and the Road to the Civil War*. New York: Basic Books, 2020.

Bay, Edna. *Wives of the Leopard: Gender, Politics, and Culture in the Kingdom of Dahomey*. Charlottesville: University of Virginia Press, 1998.

Beckert, Sven. *Empire of Cotton: A Global History*. New York: Alfred A. Knopf, 2014.

Beckert, Sven, and Seth Rockman. *Slavery's Capitalism: A New History of American Economic Development*. Philadelphia: University of Pennsylvania Press, 2016.

Beckles, Hilary M. "An Economic Life of Their Own: Slaves as Commodity Producers and Distributors in Barbados." *Slavery and Abolition: A Journal of Slave and Post-Slave Studies* 12, no. 1 (1991): 31–47.

Beckles, Hilary M. *Natural Rebels: A Social History of Enslaved Black Women in Barbados*. New Brunswick, NJ: Rutgers University Press, 2000.

Bell, Felicia. "'The Negroes Alone Work': Enslaved Craftsmen, the Building Trades, and the Construction of the United States Capitol, 1790–1800." PhD diss., Howard University, 2009.

Bell, Karen Cook. *Running from Bondage: Enslaved Women and Their Remarkable Fight for Freedom in Revolutionary America*. New York: Cambridge University Press, 2021.

Bell, Richard. *Stolen: Five Free Boys Kidnapped into Slavery and Their Astonishing Odyssey Home*. New York: 37 Ink, 2019.

Bennett, Herman L. *African Kings and Black Slaves: Sovereignty and Dispossession in the Early Modern Atlantic*. Philadelphia: University of Pennsylvania Press, 2019.

Bennett, Herman L. *Africans in Colonial Mexico: Absolutism, Christianity, and Afro-Creole Consciousness, 1570–1640*. Bloomington: Indiana University Press, 2005.

Bergad, Laird W. *The Comparative Histories of Slavery in Brazil, Cuba, and the United States*. New York: Cambridge University Press, 2007.

Bergad, Laird W. "Slave Prices in Cuba, 1840–1875." *Hispanic American Historical Review* 67, no. 4 (1987): 631–55.

Bergad, Laird W. *Slavery and the Demographic and Economic History of Minas Gerais, Brazil, 1720–1888*. New York: Cambridge University Press, 1999.

Berlin, Ira. "From Creole to African: Atlantic Creoles and the Origins of African-American Society in Mainland North America." *William and Mary Quarterly* 53, no. 2 (1996): 251–88.

Berlin, Ira. *Generations of Captivity: A History of African-American Slaves*. Cambridge, MA: Belknap Press of Harvard University Press, 2003.

Berlin, Ira. *The Long Emancipation: The Demise of Slavery In the United States*. Cambridge, MA: Harvard University Press, 2015.

Berlin, Ira. *Many Thousands Gone: The First Two Centuries of Slavery in North America*. Cambridge, MA: Belknap Press of Harvard University Press, 1998.

Berry, Daina Ramey. *The Price for Their Pound of Flesh: The Value of the Enslaved, from Womb to Grave, in the Building of a Nation*. Boston: Beacon Press, 2017.

Berry, Daina Ramey. *"Swing the Sickle for the Harvest Is Ripe": Gender and Slavery in Antebellum Georgia*. Champaign: University of Illinois Press, 2007.

Berry, Daina Ramey, and Kali N Gross. *A Black Women's History of the United States*. Boston: Beacon Press, 2019.

Berry, Mary Frances. *My Face Is Black Is True: Callie House and the Struggle for Ex-Slave Reparations*. New York: Alfred A. Knopf, 2005.

Besson, Jean. "Missionaries, Planters, and Slaves in the Age of Abolition." In *The Caribbean: A History of the Region and Its Peoples*, edited by Stephan Palmié and Francisco A. Scarano, 317–29. Chicago: University of Chicago Press, 2011.

Bethencourt, Francisco. *Racisms: From the Crusades to the Twentieth Century*. Princeton, NJ: Princeton University Press, 2014.

Blackburn, Robin. *The American Crucible: Slavery, Emancipation and Human Rights*. London: Verso, 2011.

Blackburn, Robin. *The Making of New World Slavery: From the Baroque to the Modern 1492–1800*. London: Verso, 1997.

Blackburn, Robin. *The Overthrow of Colonial Slavery: 1776–1848*. London: Verso, 2011.

Blackett, Richard J. M. *The Captive's Quest for Freedom: Fugitive Slaves, the 1850 Fugitive Slave Law, and the Politics of Slavery*. New York: Cambridge University Press, 2018.

Blackhawk, Ned. *The Rediscovery of America: Native Peoples and the Unmaking of U.S. History*. New Haven, CT: Yale University Press, 2023.

Blain, Keisha N. *Set the World on Fire: Black Nationalist Women and the Global Struggle for Freedom*. Philadelphia: Pennsylvania University Press, 2018.

Blakey, Michael L. "The New York African Burial Ground Project: An Examination of Enslaved Lives, A Construction of Ancestral Ties." *Transforming Anthropology* 7, no. 1 (1998): 53–58. https://doi.org/10.1525/tran.1998.7.1.53.

Blakey, Michael L., and Lesley M. Rankin-Hill. *The Skeletal Biology of the New York African Burial Ground*. Washington, DC: Howard University Press, 2009.

Blier, Suzanne Preston. *African Vodun: Art, Psychology, and Power*. Chicago: University of Chicago Press, 1995.

Blier, Suzanne Preston. "Mort et créativité dans la tradition des amazones du Dahomey." In *Ethnocentrisme et création*, edited by Annie Dupuis, 64–80. Paris: Éditions de la Maison des sciences de l'homme, 2013.

Blight, David. *Frederick Douglass: Prophet of Freedom*. New York: Simon and Schuster, 2018.

Blight, David W. *Race and Reunion: The Civil War in American Memory*. Cambridge, MA: Harvard University Press, 2001.

Blumenthal, Debra. *Enemies and Familiars: Slavery and Mastery in Fifteenth-Century Valencia*. Ithaca, NY: Cornell University Press, 2009.

Blyden, Nemata Amelia Ibitayo. *African Americans and Africa: A New History*. New Haven, CT: Yale University Press, 2019.

Bomfim, Manoel. *A América Latina: Males de origem*. Rio de Janeiro: H. Garnier, 1905.

Borucki, Alex. *From Shipmates to Soldiers: Emerging Black Identities in the Rio de La Plata*. Albuquerque: University of New Mexico Press, 2015.

Boxer, Charles R. *The Golden Age of Brazil, 1695–1750*. Los Angeles: University of California Press, 2022.

Boxer, Charles R. *Salvador de Sá and the Struggle for Brazil and Angola, 1602–1654*. Oxford: Clarendon Press, 1957.

Braga, Júlio Santana. "Notas sobre o 'Quartier Brésil' no Daomé." *Afro-Ásia*, no. 6–7 (1968): 55–62.

Brana-Shute, Rosemary, and Randy J. Sparks. *Paths to Freedom: Manumission in the Atlantic World*. Columbia: University of South Carolina Press, 2009.

Brito, Luciana da Cruz. *Temores da África: Segurança, Legislação e População Africana*. Salvador, Brazil: Editora da Universidade da Bahia, 2016.

Brooks, George E. *Eurafricans in Western Africa: Commerce, Social Status, Gender, and Religious Observance from the Sixteenth to the Eighteenth Century*. Oxford: James Currey, 2003.

Brown, Christopher Leslie. *Moral Capital: Foundations of British Abolitionism*. Chapel Hill: University of North Carolina Press, 2006.

Brown, Vincent. *The Reaper's Garden: Death and Power in the World of Atlantic Slavery*. Cambridge, MA: Harvard University Press, 2008.

Brown, Vincent. *Tacky's Revolt: The Story of an Atlantic War*. Cambridge, MA: Harvard University Press, 2020.

Browne, Randy. *Surviving Slavery in the British Caribbean*. Philadelphia: University of Pennsylvania Press, 2017.

Browne, Randy M., and Trevor Burnard. "Husbands and Fathers: The Family Experience of Enslaved Men in Berbice, 1819–1834." *New West Indian Guide* 91 (2017): 193–222.

Browne, Randy M., and John Wood Sweet. "Florence Hall's 'Memoirs': Finding African Women in the Transatlantic Slave Trade." *Slavery and Abolition* 37, no. 1 (2016): 206–21.

Burdick, John. *Blessed Anastacia: Women, Race and Popular Christianity in Brazil*. New York: Routledge, 1998.

Burnard, Trevor. "Kingston, Jamaica: Crucible of Modernity." In Cañizares-Esguerra, Childs, and Sidbury, *Black Urban Atlantic in the Age of the Slave Trade*, 122–44, 296–300.

Burnard, Trevor. *Mastery, Tyranny, and Desire: Thomas Thistlewood and His Slaves in the Anglo-Jamaican World*. Chapel Hill: University of North Carolina Press, 2004.

Burnard, Trevor. *Planters: Plantation Societies in British America, 1650–1820*. Chicago: University of Chicago Press, 2015.

Burnard, Trevor. "'Rioting in Goatish Embraces': Marriage and Improvement in Early British Jamaica." *The History of the Family* 11 (2006): 185–97.

Bush, Barbara. "White 'Ladies,' Coloured 'Favourites' and Black 'Wenches': Some Considerations on Sex, Race and Class Factors in Social Relations in White Creole Society in the British Caribbean." *Slavery and Abolition* 2, no. 3 (1981): 245–62.

Butler, Kim D. "Defining Diaspora, Refining a Discourse." *Diaspora: A Journal of Transnational Studies* 10, no. 2 (2001): 189–219.

Butler, Kim D. *Freedoms Given, Freedoms Won: Afro-Brazilians in Post-Abolition São Paulo and Salvador*. New Brunswick, NJ: Rutgers University Press, 2000.

Byrd, Alex. *Captives and Voyagers: Black Migrants across the Eighteenth-Century British Atlantic World*. Baton Rouge: Louisiana State University Press, 2008.

Cairus, José Antônio Teófilo. "*Jihad*, cativeiro e redenção: Escravidão, resistência e irmandade, Sudão Central e Bahia (1835)." MA thesis, Universidade Federal do Rio de Janeiro, 2002.

Caldeira, Arlindo Manuel. *Escravos em Portugal: Das origens ao século XIX*. Lisbon: A Esfera dos Livros, 2017.

Caldeira, Arlindo Manuel. *Escravos e traficantes no império português: O comércio negreiro no Atlântico durante os séculos XV à XIX*. Lisbon: A Esfera dos Livros, 2013.

Caldeira, Arlindo Manuel. "Learning the Ropes in the Tropics: Slavery and the Plantation System on the Island of São Tomé." *African Economic History* 39 (2011): 35–71.

Camp, Stephanie M. H. *Closer to Freedom: Enslaved Women and Everyday Resistance in the Plantation South*. Chapel Hill: University of North Carolina Press, 2004.

Campbell, Gwyn, and Elizabeth Elbourne, eds. *Sex, Power, and Slavery*. Athens: Ohio University Press, 2014.

Candido, Mariana P. "African Freedom Suits and Portuguese Vassal Status: Legal Mechanisms for Fighting Enslavement in Benguela, Angola, 1800–1830." *Slavery and Abolition* 32, no. 3 (2011): 447–59.

Candido, Mariana P. *An African Slaving Port and the Atlantic World: Benguela and Its Hinterland*. New York: Cambridge University Press, 2013.

Candido, Mariana P. "Aguida Gonçalves da Silva, une *dona* à Benguela à la fin du XVIIIe siècle." *Brésil(s): Sciences humaines et sociales*, no. 1 (2012): 33–54.

Candido, Mariana P. "Different Slave Journeys: Enslaved African Seamen on Board of Portuguese Ships, c. 1760–1820s." *Slavery and Abolition* 31, no. 3 (2010): 395–409.

Candido, Mariana P. "The Expansion of Slavery in Benguela during the Nineteenth Century." *International Review of Social History* 65, S28 (2020): 67–92.

Candido, Mariana P. "Transatlantic Links: The Benguela-Bahia Connections, 1700–1850." In Araujo, *Paths of the Atlantic Slave Trade*, 239–72.

Candido, Mariana P. *Wealth, Land and Property in Angola: A History of Dispossession, Slavery, and Inequality*. New York: Cambridge University Press, 2022.

Candido, Mariana P. "Women, Family, and Landed Property in Nineteenth-Century Benguela." *African Economic History* 43 (2015): 136–61.

Candido, Mariana P. "Women's Material World in Nineteenth-Century Benguela." In Candido and Jones, *African Women in the Atlantic World*, 70–85.

Candido, Mariana P., and Adam Jones. *African Women in the Atlantic World: Property, Vulnerability and Mobility, 1660–1880*. Rochester, NY: James Currey, 2019.

Candioti, Magdalena. "Free Womb Law, Legal Asynchronies, and Migrations: Suing for an Enslaved Woman's Child in Nineteenth-Century Río de La Plata." *Americas* 77, no. 1 (2020): 73–99.

Candioti, Magdalena. *Una historia de la emancipación negra*. Buenos Aires: Siglo Veintiuno Editores, 2021.

Cañizares-Esguerra, Jorge, Matt D. Childs, and James Sidbury. *The Black Urban Atlantic in the Age of the Slave Trade*. Philadelphia: University of Pennsylvania Press, 2013.

Cardoso, Fernando Henrique. *Capitalismo e escravidão no Brasil meridional*. São Paulo: Difusão Europeia do Livro, 1962.

Carneiro, Maria Elizabeth Ribeiro. "Procura-se 'preta,' com muito bom leite, prendada e carinhosa: Uma cartografia das amas-de-leite na sociedade carioca (1850–1888)." PhD diss., Universidade de Brasília, 2006.

Carney, Judith. *Black Rice: The African Origins of Rice Cultivation in the Americas*. Cambridge, MA: Harvard University Press, 2001.

Carney, Judith. "Rice Milling, Gender and Slave Labour in Colonial South Carolina." *Past & Present*, no. 153 (1996): 108–34.

Carney, Judith, and Richard Nicholas Rosomoff. *In the Shadow of Slavery: Africa's Botanical Legacy in the Atlantic World*. Berkeley: University of California Press, 2010.

Carretero, Sagrario Cruz, Alfredo Martínez Maranto, and Angélica Santiago Silva. *El Carnaval en Yanga: Notas y comentarios sobre una fiesta de la negritud*. San Angel, Mexico: Consejo Nacional para la Cultura y las Artes, Dirección General de Culturas Populares, Unidad Regional Centro de Veracruz, 1990.

Carretta, Vincent. *Equiano, the African: Biography of a Self-Made Man*. New York: Penguin, 2005.

Carvalho, Marcus J. M. de. "O patacho Providência, um navio negreiro: Política, justiça e redes depois da lei antitráfico de 1831." *Varia História* 30, no. 54 (2014): 777–806.

Casares, Aurelia Martín. "Free and Freed Black Africans in Granada in the Time of the Spanish Renaissance." In Earle and Lowe, *Black Africans in Renaissance Europe*, 247–60.

Castañeda, Digna. "The Female Slave in Cuba During the First Half of the Nineteenth Century." In Shepherd, Brereton, and Bailey, *Engendering History*, 141–54.

Castelnau-L'Estoile, Charlotte de. "La liberté du sacrement: Droit canonique et mariage des esclaves dans le Brésil colonial." *Annales: Histoire, Sciences sociales* 65 (2010) 1349–83.

Castelnau-L'Estoile, Charlotte de. *Páscoa et ses deux maris: Une esclave entre Angola, Brésil et Portugal au XVIIe siècle*. Paris: Presses Universitaires de France, 2019.

Castilho, Celso Thomas. *Slave Emancipation and Transformations in Brazilian Political Citizenship*. Pittsburgh, PA: University of Pittsburgh Press, 2016.

Castillo, Lisa Earl. "The Alaketu Temple and Its Founders: Portrait of an Afro-Brazilian Dynasty." *Luso-Brazilian Review* 50, no. 1 (2013): 83–112.

Castillo, Lisa Earl. "Bamboxê Obitikô and the Nineteenth-Century Expansion of Orisha Worship in Brazil." *Tempo* 22, no. 30 (2016): 126–53.

Castillo, Lisa Earl. "The Exodus of 1835: Agudá Life Stories and Social Networks." In *The Vile Trade: Slavery and the Slave Trade in Africa*, edited by Abi Alabo Derefaka, Wole Ogundele, Akin Alao, and Augustus Babajide Ajibola, 211–23. Durham, NC: Carolina Academic Press, 2015.

Castillo, Lisa Earl. "Mapping the Nineteenth-Century Brazilian Returnee Movement: Demographics, Life Stories and the Question of Slavery." *Atlantic Studies: Global Currents* 13, no. 1 (2016): 25–52.

Castillo, Lisa Earl. "O terreiro do Gantois: Redes sociais e etnografia histórica no século XIX." *Revista de História*, no. 176 (2017): 1–57.

Castillo, Lisa Earl, and Luis Nicolau Parés. "Marcelina da Silva: A Nineteenth-Century *Candomblé* Priestess in Bahia." *Slavery and Abolition* 31, no. 1 (2010): 1–27.

Castro, Antonio Barros de. "Escravos e senhores nos engenhos do Brasil: Um estudo sobre os trabalhos do açúcar e a política econômica dos senhores." PhD diss., Universidade de Campinas, 1976.

Castro, Yeda Passos de. *Falares africanos na Bahia: Um vocabulário afro-brasileiro*. Rio de Janeiro: Academia Brasileira de Letras, 2001.

Chalhoub, Sidney. *A força da escravidão: Ilegalidade e costume no Brasil oitocentista*. São Paulo: Companhia das Letras, 2012.

Chalhoub, Sidney. *Visões da liberdade: Uma história das últimas décadas da escravidão na Corte*. São Paulo: Companhia de Bolso, 2011.

Chamberlain, Henry, and Rubens Borba de Moraes. *Vistas e costumes da cidade e arredores do Rio de Janeiro em 1819–1820*. Rio de Janeiro: Livraria Kosmos editora, 1943.

Chambers, Douglas B. "'My Own Nation': Igbo Exiles in the Diaspora." In *Routes to Slavery: Direction, Ethnicity and Mortality in the Atlantic Slave Trade*, edited by David Eltis and David Richardson, 72–97. London: Frank Cass, 1997.

Chandler, David L. "Family Bonds and the Bondsman: The Slave Family in Colonial Colombia." *Latin American Research Review* 16, no. 2 (1981): 107–31.

Chatwin, Bruce. *The Viceroy of Ouidah*. London: Jonathan Cape, 1980.

Chavez, Manuel F. Fernández, and Rafael M. Pérez García. *En los márgenes de la ciudad de Dios: Moriscos en Sevilla*. Valencia: Publicaciones de la Universitat de València; Granada: Editorial Universidad de Granada; Zaragoza: Servicio de Publicaciones de la Universidade Zaragoza, 2009.

Childs, Matt D. *The 1812 Aponte Rebellion in Cuba and the Struggle against Atlantic Slavery*. Chapel Hill: University of North Carolina Press, 2006.

Childs, Matt D. "Re-Creating African Ethnic Identities in Cuba." In Cañizares-Esguerra, Childs, and Sidbury, *Black Urban Atlantic in the Age of the Slave Trade*, 85–100.

Chira, Adriana. "Freedom with Local Bonds: Custom and Manumission in the Age of Emancipation." *American Historical Review* 126, no. 3 (2021): 949–77.

Chira, Adriana. *Patchwork Freedoms: Law, Slavery and Race Beyond Cuba's Plantations*. New York: Cambridge University Press, 2022.

Chivallon, Christine. *L'esclavage, du souvenir à la mémoire: Contribution à une anthropologie de la Caraïbe*. Paris: Karthala, 2012.

Chopra, Ruma. *Almost Home: Maroons between Slavery and Freedom in Jamaica, Nova Scotia, and Sierra Leone*. New Haven, CT: Yale University Press, 2018.

Chopra, Ruma. "'Wayward Humours' and 'Perverse Disputings': Exiled Blacks and the Foundation of Sierra Leone, 1787–1800." In *Africans in Exile: Mobility, Law, and Identity*, edited by Nathan Riley Carpenter and Benjamin N. Lawrance, 37–53. Bloomington: Indiana University Press, 2018.

Christopher, Emma. *Slave Ship Sailors and Their Captive Cargoes, 1730–1807*. New York: Cambridge University Press, 2006.

Churchill, Ward. *A Little Matter of Genocide: Holocaust and Denial in the Americas, 1492 to the Present*. San Francisco: City Lights Books, 1997.

Cicalo, Andre. "From Public Amnesia to Public Memory: Rediscovering Slavery Heritage in Rio de Janeiro." In Araujo, *African Heritage and Memories of Slavery in Brazil and the South Atlantic World*, 171–202.

Clark-Pujara, Christy. *Dark Work: The Business of Slavery in Rhode Island*. New York: New York University Press, 2016.

Clinton, Catherine. *The Plantation Mistress: Woman's World in the Old South*. New York: Pantheon Books, 1982.

Cole, Jeffrey A. *The Potosí Mita, 1573–1700: Compulsory Indian Labor in the Andes*. Stanford, CA: Stanford University Press, 1985.

Cooper, Afua. *The Hanging of Angélique: The Untold Story of Canadian Slavery and the Burning of Old Montréal*. Athens: University of Georgia Press, 2007.

Cooper-Owens, Deirdre. *Medical Bondage: Race, Gender, and the Origins of American Gynecology*. Athens: University of Georgia Press, 2017.

Coquery-Vidrovitch, Catherine. *L'Afrique et les Africains au XIXe siècle: Mutations, révolutions, crises.* Paris: Armand Colin, 1999.

Costa, Emília Viotti da. *A Abolição.* São Paulo: Editora da Universidade Estadual de São Paulo, 2008.

Costa e Silva, Alberto da. *Francisco Félix de Souza, mercador de escravos.* Rio de Janeiro: Nova Fronteira, 2004.

Costa e Silva, Alberto da. "Portraits of African Royalty in Brazil." In *Identity in the Shadow of Slavery*, edited by Paul E. Lovejoy, 129–36. London: Continuum, 2000.

Costa e Silva, Alberto da. *Um rio chamado Atlântico: A África no Brasil e o Brasil na África.* Rio de Janeiro: Nova Fronteira, 2003.

Courtaud, Patrice. "Le cimetière, comme miroir de l'esclavage: Approche méthodologique; Le cimetière d'Anse Sainte-Marguerite (Guadeloupe)." *In Situ* 20 (2013): 1–21.

Cowling, Camillia. *Conceiving Freedom: Women of Color, Gender, and the Abolition of Slavery in Havana and Rio de Janeiro.* Chapel Hill: University of North Carolina Press, 2013.

Craton, Michael. *Testing the Chains: Resistance to Slavery in the British West Indies.* Ithaca, NY: Cornell University Press, 1982.

Cruz, Guillermo Feliú. *La abolición de la esclavitud en Chile.* Santiago de Chile: Editorial Universitaria, 1973.

Cuevas, Marco Polo Hernandéz. *African Mexicans and the Discourse on Modern Nation.* Lanham, MD: University Press of America, 2004.

Cunha, Manuela Carneiro da. *Da Senzala ao Sobrado.* São Paulo: Nobel, Editora da Universidade de São Paulo, 1985.

Cunha, Manuela Carneiro da. *Negros, Estrangeiros: Os escravos libertos e sua volta à África.* São Paulo: Companhia das Letras, 2012.

Curtin, Philip D. *Two Jamaicas: The Role of Ideas in a Tropical Colony, 1830–1865.* Cambridge, MA: Harvard University Press, 1955.

Curto, José. *Enslaving Spirits: The Portuguese-Brazilian Alcohol Trade at Luanda and Its Hinterland, c. 1550–1830.* Leiden, Neth.: Brill, 2004.

Dalton, John T., and Tin Cheuk Leung. "Why Is Polygyny More Prevalent in Western Africa? An African Slave Trade Perspective." *Economic Development and Cultural Change* 62, no. 4 (2014): 599–632.

Danielpour, Richard, Toni Morrison, and Mary Lou Humphrey. *Margaret Garner: An Opera in Two Acts*. New York: Associated Music Publishers, 2005.

Dantas, Mariana L. R. *Black Townsmen: Urban Slavery and Freedom in the Eighteenth-Century Americas*. New York: Palgrave Macmillan, 2008.

Dantas, Mariana L. R. "Child Abandonment and Foster Care in Colonial Brazil: Expostos and the Free Population of African Descent in Eighteenth-Century Minas Gerais." In Brana-Shute and Sparks, *Paths to Freedom: Manumission in the Atlantic World*, 197–208.

Davis, David Brion. *Inhuman Bondage: The Rise and Fall of Slavery in the New World*. New York: Oxford University Press, 2006.

Davis, David Brion. *The Problem of Slavery in the Age of Emancipation*. New York: Vintage Books, 2015.

Davis, David Brion. *The Problem of Slavery in the Age of Revolution, 1770–1823*. Ithaca, NY: Cornell University Press, 1975.

Davis, David Brion. *The Problem of Slavery in Western Culture*. Ithaca, NY: Cornell University Press, 1966.

Debien, Gabriel. "Le marronage aux Antilles françaises au XVIIIe siècle." *Caribbean Studies* 6, no. 3 (1966): 3–43.

Deusen, Nancy E. van. "In the Tethered Shadow: Native American Slavery, African Slavery, and the Disappearance of the Past." *William and Mary Quarterly* 80, no. 2 (2023): 355–88.

Deveau, Jean-Michel. *La traite rochelaise*. Paris: Karthala, 1990.

Dewulf, Jeroen. "Black Brotherhoods in North America: Afro-Iberian and West Central African Influences." *African Studies Quarterly* 15, no. 3 (2015): 19–38.

Dewulf, Jeroen. *The Pinkster and the King of Kongo: The Forgotten History of America's Dutch-Owned Slaves*. Jackson: University of Mississippi Press, 2019.

Dias, Maria Odila Silva. *Power and Everyday Life: The Lives of Working Women in Nineteenth-Century Brazil*. New Brunswick, NJ: Rutgers University Press, 1995.

Diouf, Sylviane A. *The Dreams of Africa in Alabama: The Slave Ship Clotilda and the Story of the Last Africans Brought to America.* New York: Oxford University Press, 2007.

Diouf, Sylviane A. *Slavery's Exiles: The Story of American Maroons.* New York: New York University Press, 2014.

Diptee, Audra A. *From Africa to Jamaica: The Making of an Atlantic Slave Society, 1775–1807.* Gainesville: University Press of Florida, 2010.

Dolphyne, Florence Abena. "The Volta-Comoé Languages." In *The Languages of Ghana*, edited by Mary E. Kropp Dakubu, 50–90. New York: Routledge, 2015.

Domingues, Petrônio. *A nova abolição.* São Paulo: Selo Negro Edições, 2008.

Draper, Nicholas. *The Price of Emancipation: Slave-Ownership, Compensation and British Society at the End of Slavery.* Cambridge: Cambridge University Press, 2010.

Drescher, Simon. *Abolition: A History of Slavery and Antislavery.* Cambridge: Cambridge University Press, 2009.

Dubois, Laurent. *Avengers of the New World: The Story of the Haitian Revolution.* Cambridge, MA: Belknap Press of Harvard University Press, 2004.

Dunbar, Erica. *Never Caught: The Washingtons' Relentless Pursuit of Their Runaway Slave, Ona Judge.* New York: Atria/37 INK, 2017.

Dunn, Richard S. *Sugar and Slaves: The Rise of the Planter Class in the English West Indies, 1624–1713.* Chapel Hill: University of North Carolina Press, 2000.

Dunn, Richard S. *A Tale of Two Plantations: Slave Life and Labor in Jamaica and Virginia.* Cambridge, MA: Harvard University Press, 2014.

Duprat, Julie. *Bordeaux Métisse: Esclaves et affranchis de couleur du XVIII à l'empire.* Bordeaux, Fr.: Mollat, 2021.

Dusinberre, William. *Them Dark Days: Slavery in the American Rice Swamps.* New York: Oxford University Press, 1996.

Earle, Rebecca. '"Two Pairs of Pink Satin Shoes!!': Clothing, Race and Identity in the Americas, 17th–19th Centuries." *History Workshop Journal* 52 (2001): 175–95.

Earle, Thomas Foster, and Kate J. P. Lowe. *Black Africans in Renaissance Europe*. Cambridge: Cambridge University Press, 2005.

Echeverri, Marcela. "'Enraged to the Limit of Despair': Infanticide and Slave Judicial Strategies in Barbacoas, 1788–98." *Slavery and Abolition* 30, no. 3 (2009): 403–26.

Eddins, Crystal. *Rituals, Runaways, and the Haitian Revolution: Collective Action in the African Diaspora*. New York: Cambridge University Press, 2022.

Edwards, Erika Denise. *Hiding in Plain Sight: Black Women, the Law, and the Making of a White Argentine Republic*. Tuscaloosa: University of Alabama Press, 2020.

Edwards, Justene Hill. *Unfree Markets: The Slaves' Economy and the Rise of Capitalism in South Carolina*. New York: Columbia University Press, 2021.

Ehret, Christopher. *Ancient Africa: A Global History, to 300 BCE*. Princeton, NJ: Princeton University Press, 2023.

Eltis, David. *The Rise of African Slavery in the Americas*. New York: Cambridge University Press, 1999.

Eltis, David, Frank D. Lewis, and David Richardson, "Slave Prices, the African Slave Trade, and Productivity in the Caribbean, 1674–1807." *Economic History Review* 58, no. 4 (2005): 673–700.

Eltis, David, Philip Morgan, and David Richardson. "Agency and Diaspora in Reassessing the African Contribution to Rice Cultivation in the Americas." *American Historical Review* 12, no. 5 (2007): 1329–58.

Eltis, David, and David Richardson. *Atlas of the Transatlantic Slave Trade*. New Haven, CT: Yale University Press, 2015.

Eltis, David, and David Richardson. "Prices of African Slaves Newly Arrived in the Americas, 1673–1865: New Evidence on Long-Run Trends and Regional Differentials." In *Slavery in the Development of the Americas*, edited by David Eltis, Frank D. Lewis, and Kenneth L. Sokoloff, 181–218. Cambridge: Cambridge University Press, 2004.

Epprecht, Marc. "Sexuality, Africa, History." *American Historical Review* 114, no. 5 (2009): 1258–72.

Escalante, Aquiles. "Palenques in Colombia." In *Maroon Societies: Rebel Slave Communities in the Americas*, edited by Richard Price, 74–81. Baltimore: Johns Hopkins University Press, 1996.

Essien, Kwame. *Brazilian-African Diaspora in Ghana: The Tabom, Slavery, Dissonance of Memory, Identity, and Locating Home*. East Lansing: Michigan State University Press, 2016.

Evans, Chris, and Louise Miskell. *Swansea Copper: A Global History*. Baltimore: Johns Hopkins University Press, 2020.

Everill, Bronwen. "'All The Baubles That They Needed': 'Industriousness' and Slavery in Saint-Louis and Gorée." *Early American Studies: An Interdisciplinary Journal* 15, no. 15 (2017): 714–39.

Falola, Toyin, and Aribidesi Usman. *The Yoruba from Prehistory to the Present*. New York: Cambridge University Press, 2019.

Faria, Sheila Siqueira de Castro. "Sinhás pretas, damas mercadoras: As pretas minas nas cidades do Rio de Janeiro e de São João del Rey (1700–1850)." Dissertation for full professor promotion, Universidade Federal Fluminense, 2004.

Farias, Juliana Barreto. "De escrava a Dona: A trajetória da africana mina Emília Soares do Patrocínio no Rio de Janeiro do século XIX." *Locus: Revista de História* 18, no. 2 (2012): 13–40.

Farias, Juliana Barreto. *Mercados Minas: Africanos ocidentais na Praça do Mercado do Rio de Janeiro (1830–1890)*. Rio de Janeiro: Arquivo Geral da Cidade do Rio de Janeiro, 2015.

Fauvelle, François-Xavier. *The Golden Rhinoceros: Histories of the African Middle Ages*. Princeton, NJ: Princeton University Press, 2018.

Fauvelle, François-Xavier. *Le rhinocéros d'or: Histoires du Moyen Âge africain*. Paris: Alma Éditeur, Paris, 2013.

Feinberg, Harvey M. *Africans and Europeans in West Africa: Elminans and Dutchmen on the Gold Coast during the Eighteenth Century*. Philadelphia: American Philosophical Society, 1989.

Ferlini, Vera Lúcia Amaral. *A civilização do açúcar séculos XVI a XVIII*. São Paulo: Brasiliense, 1994.

Fernandes, Eunicia, ed. *A Companhia de Jesus na América*. Rio de Janeiro: Contra Capa, 2013.

Ferraro, Alceu Ravanello, and Michele de Leão. "Lei Saraiva (1881): Dos argumentos invocados pelos liberais para a exclusão dos analfabetos do direito de voto." *Educação Unisinos* 16, no. 3 (2012): 241–50.

Ferreira, Roquinaldo. *Cross-Cultural Exchange in the Atlantic World: Angola and Brazil during the Era of the Slave Trade.* New York: Cambridge University Press, 2012.

Ferreira, Roquinaldo. *Dos sertões ao Atlântico: Tráfico ilegal de escravos e comércio lícito em Angola, 1830–1860.* Luanda, Angola: Kilombelombe, 2012.

Ferrer, Ada. *Freedom's Mirror: Cuba and Haiti in the Age of Revolution.* New York: Cambridge University Press, 2014.

Ferrer, Ada. *Insurgent Cuba: Race, Nation, and Revolution, 1868–1898.* Chapel Hill: University of North Carolina Press, 1999.

Fett, Sharla M. *Recaptured Africans: Surviving Slave Ships, Detention, and Dislocation in the Final Years of the Slave Trade.* Chapel Hill: University of North Carolina Press, 2017.

Fett, Sharla M. *Working Cures: Healing, Health, and Power on Southern Slave Plantations.* Chapel Hill: University of North Carolina Press, 2002.

Fick, Carolyn E. *The Making of Haiti: The Saint Domingue Revolution from Below.* Knoxville: University of Tennessee Press, 1990.

Fields-Black, Edda L. *Deep Roots: Rice Farmers in West Africa and the African Diaspora.* Bloomington: Indiana University Press, 2008.

Figueroa, Luis A. *Sugar, Slavery, and Freedom in Nineteenth-Century Puerto Rico.* Chapel Hill: University of North Carolina Press, 2005.

Filho, Mário Maestri. *O escravo no Rio Grande do Sul: A charqueada e a gênese do escravismo gaúcho.* Caxias do Sul, Brazil: Editora da Universidade de Caxias do Sul, 1984.

Finch, Aisha K. *Rethinking Slave Rebellion in Cuba: La Escalera and Insurgencies of 1841–1844.* Chapel Hill: University of North Carolina Press, 2015.

Finkenbine, Roy E. "Belinda's Petition: Reparations for Slavery in Revolutionary Massachusetts." *William and Mary Quarterly* 64, no. 1 (2007): 95–104.

Finley, Moses I. *Ancient Slavery and Modern Ideology*. New York: Viking, 1980.

Fleming, Crystal. *Resurrecting Slavery: Racial Legacies and White Supremacy in France*. Philadelphia: Temple University Press, 2017.

Fleskes, Rachel E, Ade A. Ofunniyin, Joanna J. Gilmore, Eric Poplin, Suzanne M. Abel, Wolf D. Bueschgen, Chelsey Juarez, Nic Butler, Grant Mishoe, La'Sheia Oubré, Graciela S. Cabana, and Theodore G. Schurr. "Ancestry, Health, and Lived Experiences of Enslaved Africans in 18th-Century Charleston: An Osteobiographical Analysis." *American Journal of Physical Anthropology* 175, no. 1 (2021): 3–24.

Florentino, Manolo. *Em costas negras: Uma história do tráfico de escravos entre a África e o Rio de Janeiro*. São Paulo: Companhia das Letras, 2002.

Florentino, Manolo, and José Roberto Góes. *A paz nas senzalas: Famílias escravas e tráfico atlântico, Rio de Janeiro, c. 1790–c. 1850*. Rio de Janeiro: Civilização Brasileira, 1997.

Flory, Céline. *De l'esclavage à la liberté forcée: Histoire des travailleurs africains engagés dans la Caraïbe française au XIXe siècle*. Paris: Karthala, 2015.

Flory, Céline. "New Africans in the Post-Slavery French West Indies and Guiana: Close Encounters? (1857–1889)." In Araujo, *Paths of the Atlantic Slave Trade*, 109–30.

Fogel, Robert William, and Stanley L. Engerman. *Time on the Cross: The Economics of American Negro Slavery*. New York: Norton, 1974.

Foner, Eric. *Gateway to Freedom: The Hidden History of the Underground Railroad*. New York: W. W. Norton, 2015.

Foner, Eric. *Reconstruction: America's Unfinished Revolution, 1863–1877*. New York: HarperCollins, 2014.

Foner, Eric. *Slavery and Freedom in Nineteenth-Century America*. New York: Oxford University Press. 1994.

Fonseca, Jorge. "Black Africans in Portugal during Cleynaerts's Visit (1533–1538)." In Earle and Lowe, *Black Africans in Renaissance Europe*, 113–24.

Fonseca, Jorge. *Escravos e senhores na Lisboa quinhentista*. Lisbon: Edições Colibri, 2010.

Forret, Jeff. *Williams' Gang: A Notorious Slave Trader and His Cargo of Black Convicts*. New York: Cambridge University Press, 2020.

Fortin, Jeffrey A. "'An Act of Deportation': The Jamaican Maroons' Journey from Freedom to Slavery and Back Again, 1796–1836." In Araujo, *Paths of the Atlantic Slave Trade*, 71–106.

Foster, Thomas A. *Rethinking Rufus: Sexual Violations of Enslaved Men*. Athens: University of Georgia Press, 2019.

Fox-Amato, Matthew. *Exposing Slavery: Photography, Human Bondage, and the Birth of Modern Visual Politics in America*. New York: Oxford University Press, 2019.

Fraginals, Manuel Moreno. *El Ingenio: Complejo económico-social cubano del azúcar*. Vol. 1.Havana: Editorial de Ciencias Sociales, 2014.

Fraginals, Manuel Moreno, Herbert S. Klein, and Stanley L. Engerman. "The Level of Slave Prices on Cuban Plantations in the Mid-Nineteenth Century: Some Comparative Perspectives." *American Historical Review* 88, no. 5 (1983): 1201–18.

French, Howard. *Born in Blackness: Africa, Africans, and the Making of the Modern World, 1471 to the Second World War*. New York: Liveright, 2021.

Freyre, Gilberto. *Casa-grande e senzala*. Rio de Janeiro: Global, 2003.

Freyre, Gilberto. *The Masters and the Slaves: A Study in the Development of Brazilian Civilization*. New York: Alfred A. Knopf, 1946.

Freyre, Gilberto. *O escravo nos anúncios de jornais brasileiros do século XIX*. São Paulo: Editora Nacional, 1979.

Fromont, Cécile, ed. *Afro-Catholic Festivals in the Americas: Performance, Representation, and the Making of Black Atlantic Tradition*. University Park: Pennsylvania State University Press, 2019.

Fromont, Cécile. *The Art of Conversion: Christian Visual Culture in the Kingdom of Kongo*. Chapel Hill: University of North Carolina Press, 2014.

Fromont, Cécile. "Dancing for the King of Congo from Early Modern Central Africa to Slavery-Era Brazil." *Colonial Latin America Review* 22, no. 2 (2013): 184–208.

Fromont, Cécile. "Envisioning Brazil's Afro-Christian Congados: The Black King and Queen Festival Lithographs of Johann Moritz

Rugendas." In Fromont, *Afro-Catholic Festivals in the Americas*, 117–39.

Fuente, Alejandro de la. "Sugar and Slavery in Early Colonial Cuba." In Schwartz, *Tropical Babylons*, 115–57.

Fuente, Alejandro de la, and Ariela J. Gross. *Becoming Free, Becoming Black: Race, Freedom, and Law in Cuba, Virginia, and Louisiana*. New York: Cambridge University Press, 2020.

Fuente, Alejandro de la, and Ariela J. Gross. "Comparative Studies of Law, Slavery, and Race in the Americas." *Annual Review of Law and Social Science* 6 (2010): 469–85.

Fuentes, Marisa. *Dispossessed Lives: Enslaved Women, Violence, and the Archive*. Philadelphia: University of Pennsylvania Press, 2016.

Funari, Pedro Paulo A. "Conflict and the Interpretation of Palmares, a Brazilian Runaway Polity." *Historical Archaeology* 27, no. 3 (2003): 81–92.

Funari, Pedro Paulo de Abreu. "A arqueologia de Palmares: Sua contribuição para o conhecimento da história da cultura afro-americana." In Reis and Gomes, *Liberdade por um Fio*, 26–51. São Paulo: Companhia das Letras, 2005.

Furtado, Júnia Ferreira. *Chica da Silva: A Brazilian Slave of the Eighteenth Century*. New York: Cambridge: Cambridge University Press, 2009.

Gandelman, Luciana Mendes. "A Santa Casa da Misericórdia do Rio de Janeiro nos séculos XVI a XIX." *História, Ciência, Saúde–Manguinhos* 8, no. 3 (2001): 613–30.

García, Arturo Morgado. "El ciclo vital de los esclavos em el Cádiz de la modernidade." *Revista de historia moderna: Anales de la Universidad de Alicante*, no. 34 (2016): 297–315.

García, Clara Inés Guerrero. "Memorias palenqueras de la libertad." In *Afro-reparaciones: Memoria de la esclavitud y justicia reparativa para negros, afrocolombianos y raizales*, edited by Claudia Mosquera Rosero-Labbé and Luís Claudio y Barcelos, 363–68. Bogotá: Universidad Nacional de Colombia, Facultad de Ciencias Humanas, Departamento de Trabajo Social y Centro de Estudios Sociales, Grupo de Estudios Afrocolombianos, 2007.

Garretson, Peter P. "A Note on Relations between Ethiopia and the Kingdom of Aragon in the Fifteenth Century." *Rassegna di Studi Etiopici* 37 (1993): 37–44.

Garvey, Marcus. *The Marcus Garvey and Universal Negro Improvement Association Papers*. 12 vols. Edited by Robert A. Hill. Berkeley: University of California Press, 1983.

Geggus, David Patrick. "Slavery, War, and Revolution in the Greater Caribbean, 1789–1815." In *A Turbulent Time: The French Revolution and the Greater Caribbean*, edited by David Barry Gaspar and David Patrick Geggus, 1–54. Bloomington: Indiana University Press, 1997.

Geggus, David. "The Slaves and Free People of Color of Cap Français." In Cañizares-Esguerra, Childs, and Sidbury, *Black Urban Atlantic in the Age of the Slave Trade*, 101–21.

Gellman, Daniel Nathaniel. *Emancipating New York: The Politics of Slavery and Freedom, 1777–1827*. Baton Rouge: Louisiana State University Press, 2008.

Genovese, Eugene D. *The Political Economy of Slavery: Studies in the Economy and Society of the Slave South*. New York: Vintage Books, 1965.

Genovese, Eugene D. *Roll, Jordan, Roll: The World the Slaves Made*. New York: Vintage Books, 1976.

Giacomini, Sonia Maria. *Mulher e escrava: Uma introdução histórica ao estudo da mulher negra no Brasil*. São Paulo: Vozes, 1988.

Gigantino, James J., II. *The Ragged Road to Abolition: Slavery and Freedom in New Jersey, 1775–1865*. Philadelphia: University of Pennsylvania Press, 2015.

Gilbert, Alain. *Black Patriots and Loyalists: Fighting for Emancipation in the War for Independence*. Chicago: University of Chicago Press, 2012.

Gilmore, Kim. "Slavery and Prison: Understanding the Connections." *Social Justice* 27, no. 3 (1981): 195–205.

Girard, Philippe R. *Toussaint Louverture: A Revolutionary Life*. New York: Basic Books, 2016.

Gisler, Antoine. *L'esclavage aux Antilles françaises (XIIe–XIXe siècle)*. Paris: Karthala, 1981.

Gledhill, Sabrina, ed. *Manuel Querino (1851–1923): An Afro-Brazilian Pioneer in the Age of Scientific Racism*. Crediton, UK: Funmilayo Publishing, 2021.

Glymph, Thavolia. *The Women's Fight: The Civil War's Battles for Home, Freedom, and Nation*. Chapel Hill: University of North Carolina Press, 2020.

Godinho, Vitorino Magalhães. "L'émigration portugaise (XVe–XXe Siècles): Une constante structural et les réponses aux changements du monde." *Revista de História Econômica e Social* 1 (1978): 5–32.

Goetz, Rebecca Anne. *The Baptism of Early Virginia: How Christianity Created Race*. Baltimore: Johns Hopkins University Press, 2012.

Goetz, Rebecca Anne. "'Unthinking Decision': Old Questions and New Problems in the History of Slavery and Race in the Colonial South." *Journal of Southern History* 75, no. 3 (2009): 599–612.

Gomes, Flávio dos Santos. "Africans and *Petit Marronage* in Rio de Janeiro, ca. 1800–1840." *Luso-Brazilian Review* 47, no. 2 (2010): 74–99.

Gomes, Flávio dos Santos. "Slavery, Black Peasants and Post-Emancipation Society in Brazil (Nineteenth-Century Rio de Janeiro)." *Social Identities* 10, no. 6 (2004): 735–56.

Gomes, Laurentino. *Escravidão*. Vol. 1, *Do primeiro leilão de cativos em Portugal até a morte de Zumbi dos Palmares*. Rio de Janeiro: Globo Livros, 2019.

Gomes, Laurentino. *Escravidão*. Vol. 2, *Da corrida do ouro em Minas Gerais até a chegada da corte de dom João ao Brasil*. Rio de Janeiro: Globo Livros, 2021.

Gomes, Laurentino. *Escravidão*. Vol. 3, *Da Independência do Brasil à Lei Áurea*. Rio de Janeiro: Globo Livros, 2022.

Gómez, Alejandro E. *Le spectre de la révolution noire: L'impact de la révolution haïtienne dans le monde atlantique, 1790–1886*. Rennes, Fr.: Presses universitaires de Rennes, 2013.

Gomez, Michael A. *African Dominion: A New History of Empire in Early and Medieval West Africa*. Princeton, NJ: Princeton University Press, 2018.

Gomez, Michael A. *Exchanging Our Country Marks: The Transformation of African Identities in the Colonial and Antebellum South*. Chapel Hill: University of North Carolina Press, 1998.

Gomez, Michael A. *Reversing Sail: A History of the African Diaspora*. New York: Cambridge University Press, 2020.

Gómez, Pablo F. *The Experimental Caribbean: Creating Knowledge and Healing in the Early Modern Atlantic*. Chapel Hill: University of North Carolina Press, 2017.

Gordon, Richard A. "Confessing Sodomy, Accusing a Master: The Lisbon Trial of Pernambuco's Luiz da Costa, 1743." In *Afro-Latino Voices: Narratives from the Early Modern Ibero-Atlantic World, 1550–1812*, edited by Kathryn Joy McKnight and Leo J. Garofalo, 269–83. Indianapolis: Hackett, 2009.

Gordon-Reed, Annette. *The Hemingses of Monticello: An American Family*. New York: W. W. Norton, 2008.

Gordon-Reed, Annette, Rose Stremlau, Malinda Lowery, Julie L. Reed, Joanne Barker, Daniel Sharfstein, Daryl Michael Scott, Karin Wulf, Sandra E. Greene, James H. Sweet, Eve M. Troutt Powell, Rachel Schine, Alan Mikhail, Erika Denise Edwards, Danielle Terrazas Williams, Indrani Chatterjee, Jeannette Eileen Jones, Crystal Moten, Faithe J. Day, and Jake Silverstein. "The 1619 Project Forum." *American Historical Review* 127, no. 4 (2022): 1792–1873.

Gorender, Jacob. *A escravidão reabilitada*. São Paulo: Ática, 1990.

Gorender, Jacob. *O Escravismo colonial*. São Paulo: Ática, 1978.

Goulart, Mauricio. *A escravidão africana no Brasil: Das origens à extinção do tráfico*. São Paulo: Alfa-Omega, 1949.

Graden, Dale T. *Disease, Resistance, and Lies: The Demise of the Transatlantic Slave Trade to Brazil and Cuba*. Baton Rouge: Louisiana State University Press, 2014.

Graham, Richard. *Feeding the City: From Street Market to Liberal Reform in Salvador, Brazil, 1780–1860*. Austin: University of Texas Press, 2010.

Graham, Sandra Lauderdale. *Caetana Says No: Women's Stories from a Brazilian Slave Society*. New York: Cambridge University Press, 2002.

Grant, Colin. *Negro with a Hat: The Rise and Fall of Marcus Garvey*. New York: Oxford University Press, 2008.

Graubart, Karen B. "As Slaves and Not Vassals: Interethnic Claims of Freedom and Unfreedom in Colonial Peru." *Población & Sociedad* 27, no. 2 (2020): 30–53.

Graubart, Karen B. "'So color de una cofradía': Catholic Confraternities and the Development of Afro-Peruvian Ethnicities in Early Colonial Peru." *Slavery and Abolition* 23, no. 1 (2011): 43–65.

Graubart, Karen B. *With Our Labor and Sweat: Indigenous Women and the Formation of Colonial Society in Peru, 1550–1700*. Stanford, CA: Stanford University Press, 2007.

Green, Toby. "Africa and Capitalism: Repairing a History of Omission." *Capitalism: A Journal of History and Economics* 3, no. 2 (2022): 301–32.

Green, Toby. "Baculamento or Encomienda? Legal Pluralisms and the Contestation of Power in the Pan-Atlantic World of the Sixteenth and Seventeenth Centuries." *Journal of Global Slavery* (2017): 310–36.

Green, Toby. *A Fistful of Shells: West Africa from the Rise of the Slave Trade to the Age of Revolution*. Chicago: University of Chicago Press, 2019.

Green, Toby. *The Rise of the Trans-Atlantic Slave Trade in Western Africa, 1300–1589*. Cambridge: Cambridge University Press, 2011.

Greenberg, Kenneth S., ed. *"The Confessions of Nat Turner" and Related Documents*. Boston: Bedford Books of St. Martin's Press, 1996.

Greenberg, Kenneth S., ed. *Nat Turner: A Slave Rebellion in History and Memory*. New York: Oxford University Press, 2003.

Greene, Sandra E. *West African Narratives of Slavery: Texts from Late Nineteenth- and Early Twentieth-Century Ghana*. Bloomington: Indiana University Press, 2011.

Grinberg, Keila. "Illegal Enslavement, International Relations, and International Law on the Southern Border of Brazil." *Law and History Review* 35, no. 1 (2017): 31–52.

Grinberg, Keila. *Liberata: A lei da ambigüidade; As ações de liberdade da corte de apelação do Rio de Janeiro no século XIX*. Rio de Janeiro: Centro Edelstein de Pesquisas Sociais, 2008.

Grinberg, Keila. "Manumission, Gender, and the Law in Nineteenth-Century Brazil: Liberata's Legal Suit for Freedom." In Brana-Shute and Sparks, *Paths to Freedom: Manumission in the Atlantic World*, 219–34.

Guasco, Michael. *Slaves and Englishmen: Human Bondage in the Early Modern Atlantic World*. Philadelphia: University of Pennsylvania Press, 2014.

Guillet, Bertrand. *La Marie-Séraphie: Navire négrier*. Nantes: MeMo, 2010.

Guran, Milton. *Agudás: Os "Brasileiros" do Benim*. Rio de Janeiro: Editora Nova Fronteira, 1999.

Guyer, Jane I. "Wealth in People and Self-Realization in Equatorial Africa." *Man* 28, no. 2 (1993): 243–65.

Guyer, Jane I., and Samuel M. Eno Belinga. "Wealth in People as Wealth in Knowledge: Accumulation and Composition in Equatorial Africa." *Journal of African History* 36 (1995): 91–120.

Habib, Imtiaz. *Black Lives in the English Archives, 1500–1677: Imprints of the Invisible*. London: Routledge, 2007.

Haënke, Tadeo. *Descripción del Perú*. Lima, Peru: Imprenta El Lucero, 1901.

Hair, Paul E. H. "The Enslavement of Koelle's Informants." *Journal of African History* 6, no. 2 (1965): 193–203.

Hale, Lindsay Lauren. "Preto Velho: Resistance, Redemption, and Engendered Representations of Slavery in a Brazilian Possession-Trance Religion." *American Ethnologist* 24, no. 2 (1997): 392–414.

Hall, Gwendolyn Midlo. "African Ethnicities and the Meanings of 'Mina.'" In *Trans-Atlantic Dimensions of Ethnicity in the African Diaspora*, edited by Paul E. Lovejoy and David R. Trotman, 65–81. London, New York, 2003.

Hall, Rebecca. "Not Killing Me Softly: African American Women, Slave Revolts, and Historical Constructions of Racialized Gender." *Freedom Center Journal* 2, no. 1 (2007): 1–47.

Handler, Jerome S. "An African-Type Healer/Diviner and His Grave Goods: A Burial from a Plantation Cemetery in Barbados, West

Indies." *International Journal of Historical Archaeology* 1, no. 2 (1997): 91–130.

Handler, Jerome S., and K. Hayes. "Escrava Anastácia: The Iconographic History of a Brazilian Popular Saint." *African Diaspora: Journal of Transnational Africa in a Global World* 2 (2009): 1–27.

Handler, Jerome S., and Matthew C. Reilly. "Contesting 'White Slavery' in the Caribbean: Enslaved Africans and European Indentured Servants in Seventeenth-Century Barbados." *New West Indian Guide / Nieuwe West-Indische Gids* 91, no. 1–2 (2017): 30–55.

Handler, Jerome S., and Annis Steiner. "Identifying Pictorial Images of Atlantic Slavery: Three Case Studies." *Slavery and Abolition* 27 (2006): 56–62.

Hannah-Jones, Nikole. *The 1619 Project: A New Origin*. New York: One World, 2021.

Hannah-Jones, Nikole, and Jake Silverstein, eds. "The 1619 Project." *New York Times Magazine*, August 14, 2019.

Harms, Robert W. *The Diligent: A Voyage Through the Worlds of the Slave Trade*. New York: Basic Books, 2002.

Harris, Joseph E. *The African Presence in Asia: Consequences of the East African Slave Trade*. Evanston, IL: Northwestern University Press, 1971.

Harris, Joseph E., ed. *Global Dimensions of the African Diaspora*. Washington, DC: Howard University Press, 1982.

Harris, Leslie M. *In the Shadow of Slavery: African Americans in New York City, 1626–1863*. Chicago: University of Chicago Press, 2003.

Hartman, Saidiya. *Lose Your Mother: A Journey Along the Atlantic Slave Route*. New York: Farrar, Straus and Giroux, 2008.

Hartman, Saidiya. "Venus in Two Acts." *Small Axe* 12, no. 2 (2008): 1–14.

Hawes, Jennifer Berry. "How a Graduate Student Uncovered the Largest Known Slave Auction in the U.S." ProPublica, June 16, 2023. https://www.propublica.org/article/how-grad-student-discovered-largest-us-slave-auction.

Hawthorne, Walter. "Being Now, as It Were One Family: Shipmate Bonding on the Slave Vessel Emilia, in Rio de Janeiro and throughout the Atlantic World." *Luso-Brazilian Review* 45, no. 1 (2008): 53–77.

Hawthorne, Walter. *From Africa to Brazil: Culture, Identity, and an Atlantic Slave Trade, 1600–1830*. New York: Cambridge University Press, 2010.

Hawthorne, Walter. "From 'Black Rice' to 'Brown': Rethinking the History of Risiculture in the Seventeenth- and Eighteenth-Century Atlantic." *American Historical Review* 115, no. 1 (2010): 151–63.

Hawthorne, Walter. "Gorje: An African Seaman and His Flights from 'Freedom' Back to 'Slavery' in the Early Nineteenth Century." *Slavery and Abolition* 31, no. 3 (2010): 411–28.

Hawthorne, Walter. *Planting Rice and Harvesting Slaves: Transformations along the Guinea-Bissau Coast, 1400–1900*. Portsmouth, UK: Heinemann, 2003.

Hazareesingh, Sudhir. *Black Spartacus: The Epic Life of Toussaint Louverture*. New York: Farrar, Straus and Giroux, 2020.

Henriques, Isabel Castro. *A presença africana em Portugal: Uma história secular; Preconceito, integração, reconhecimento (séculos XV–XX)*. Lisbon: Alto Comissariado para as Imigrações, 2019.

Henriques, Isabel Castro. *Historical Guide to an African Lisbon: 15th to 21st Century*. Lisbon: Colibri, 2021.

Henriques, Isabel Castro. *Os africanos em Portugal: História e memória, séculos XV–XXI*. Lisbon: Comité Português do Projeto UNESCO "A Rota do Escravo," 2011.

Herissé, A. Le. *Royaume du Dahomey: Moeurs, Religion, Histoire*. Paris: Emile Larose, 1911.

Herskovits, Melville J. *Dahomey: An Ancient West African Kingdom*. 2 vols. Evanston, IL: Northwestern University Press, 1967.

Herskovits, Melville J. *The Myth of the Negro Past*. New York: Harper, 1941.

Herskovits, Melville J. "A Note on 'Woman Marriage' in Dahomey." *Africa: Journal of the International African Institute* 10, no. 3 (1937): 335–41.

Hertzman, Marc. "Fatal Differences: Suicide, Race, and Forced Labor in the Americas." *American Historical Review* 122, no. 2 (2017): 317–45.

Heuman, Gad. *Between Black and White: Race, Politics, and the Free Coloreds in Jamaica, 1792–1865*. Westport, CT: Greenwood Press, 1981.

Heywood, Linda M., ed. *Central Africans and Cultural Transformations in the American Diaspora*. Cambridge: Cambridge University Press, 2002.

Heywood, Linda M. "Slavery and Its Transformation in the Kingdom of Kongo: 1491–1800." *Journal of African History* 50 (2009): 1–22.

Heywood, Linda M., and John K. Thornton. *Central Africans, Atlantic Creoles, and the Foundation of the Americas, 1585–1660*. New York: Cambridge University Press, 2007.

Hicks, Mary E. "The Sea and the Shackle: African and Creole Mariners and the Making of a Luso-African Atlantic Commercial Culture, 1721–1835." PhD diss., University of Virginia, 2015.

Hicks, Mary E. "Transatlantic Threads of Meaning: West African Textile Entrepreneurship in Salvador da Bahia, 1770–1870." *Slavery and Abolition* 41, no. 4, (2020): 695–722.

Higgins, Kathleen J. *Licentious Liberty in a Brazilian Gold-Mining Region: Slavery, Gender and Social Control in Eighteenth-Century Sabará, Minas Gerais*. University Park: Penn State University Press, 1999.

Hill, Lawrence. *The Book of Negroes*. Toronto: Harper Collins, 2007.

Hill, Lawrence. *Someone Knows My Name*. New York: W. W. Norton, 2007.

Hine, Darlene Clark, and Kathleen Thompson. *A Shining Thread of Hope: The History of Black Women in America*. New York: Broadway Books, 1999.

Hodes, Martha. *White Women, Black Men: Illicit Sex in the 19th-Century South*. New Haven, CT: Yale University Press, 1997.

Hodges, Graham Russell Gao. *Root & Branch: African Americans in New York and East Jersey, 1613–1863*. Chapel Hill: University of North Carolina Press, 1999.

Hogendorn, Jan, and Marion Johnson. *The Shell Money of the Slave Trade*. Cambridge: Cambridge University Press, 1986.

Holden, Vanessa M. *Surviving Southampton: African American Women and Resistance in Nat Turner's Community*. Urbana: University of Illinois Press, 2021.

Holt, Thomas C. *The Problem of Freedom: Race, Labor, and Politics in Jamaica and Britain, 1832–1938*. Baltimore: Johns Hopkins University Press, 1992.

Hondius, Dienke. "Access to the Netherlands of Enslaved and Free Black Africans: Exploring Legal and Social Historical Practices in the Sixteenth–Nineteenth Centuries." *Slavery and Abolition* 32, no. 3 (2011): 377–95.

Hondius, Dienke, Nancy Jowe, Dineke Stam, Jeniffer Tosch, and Annemarie de Wildt. *Gids Slavernijverleden, Amsterdam Slavery Heritage Guide*. Arnhem, Neth.: LM Publishers, 2018.

Honorato, Cláudio de Paula. "O mercado do Valongo e comércio de escravos africanos—RJ (1758–1831)." In *Escravidão africana no Recôncavo da Guanabara*, edited by Mariza de Carvalho Soares and Nielson Rosa Bezerra, 138–65. Niterói, Brazil: Editora da Universidade Federal Fluminense, 2011.

Horne, Gerald. *The Deepest South: The United States, Brazil, and the African Slave Trade*. New York: New York University Press, 2007.

Horta, José da Silva, and Francisco Freire. "Os primeiros contatos luso-saarianos: Narrativas europeias quatrocentistas e tradições orais biDān (Mauritânia)." In *As lições de Jill Dias: Antropologia, história, África e academia*, edited by Maria Candeira da Silva e Clara Saraiva, 37–53. Lisbon: Etnográfica Press, 2013.

Hroděj, Philippe. "Les esclaves à Saint-Domingue aux temps pionniers (1630–1700): La rafle, la traite et l'interlope." In *L'esclave et les plantations: De l'établissement de la servitude à son abolition*, edited by Philippe Hroděj, 59–84. Rennes, Fr.: Presses Universitaires de Rennes, 2009.

Hunter, Tera. *Bound in Wedlock: Slave and Free Black Marriage in the Nineteenth Century*. Cambridge, MA: Belknap Press of Harvard University Press, 2017.

Inikori, Joseph E. "Atlantic Slavery and the Rise of the Capitalist Global Economy." *Current Anthropology* 61, no 22 (2020): S159–S171.

Insoll, Timothy, and Thurstan Shaw. "Gao and Igbo-Ukwu: Beads, Interregional Trade, and Beyond." *African Archaeological Review* 14, no. 1 (1997): 9–23.

Ipsen, Pernille. *Daughters of the Trade: Atlantic Slavers and Interracial Marriage on the Gold Coast*. Philadelphia: University of Pennsylvania Press, 2015.

Ismard, Paulin. "Identification." In Ismard, Rossi, and Vidal, *Les mondes de l'esclavage*, 537–48.

Ismard, Paulin. *La cité et ses esclaves: Institutions, fictions, expériences*. Paris: Seuil, 2019.

Ismard, Paulin, Benedetta Rossi, and Cécile Vidal, eds. *Les mondes de l'esclavage: Une histoire comparée*. Paris: Seuil, 2021.

James, Cyril Lionel Robert. *The Black Jacobins: Toussaint L'Ouverture and the San Domingo Revolution*. New York: Vintage Books, 1963.

Jasanoff, Maya. *Liberty's Exiles: American Loyalists in the Revolutionary World*. New York: HarperCollins, 2011.

Jennings, Lawrence C. *French Anti-Slavery: The Movement for the Abolition of Slavery in France, 1802–1848*. Cambridge: Cambridge University Press, 2000.

Johnen, Thomas. "*Bomba*, *kanga*, *makamba* e outros africanismos lexicais no papiamento: Comparações com o português do Brasil e o espanhol uruguaio." In *Una historia sin fronteras: Léxico de origen africano em Brasil y Uruguay*, edited by Laura Álvarez López and Magdalena Coll, 161–87. Stockholm: Acta Universitattis Stockholmiensis, 2012.

Johnson, Jessica Marie. *Wicked Flesh: Black Women, Intimacy, and Freedom in the Atlantic World*. Philadelphia: University of Pennsylvania Press, 2020.

Johnson, Rashauna. *Slavery's Metropolis: Unfree Labor in New Orleans during the Age of Revolutions*. New York: Cambridge University Press, 2016.

Johnson, Walter. *River of Dark Dreams: Slavery and Empire in the Cotton Kingdom*. Cambridge, MA: Harvard University Press, 2013.

Johnson, Walter. *Soul by Soul: Life Inside the Antebellum Slave Market*. Cambridge, MA: Harvard University Press, 1999.

Jones, Adam. "Prostitution, Polyandry or Rape? On the Ambiguity of European Sources for the West African Coast 1660–1860." In Candido and Jones, *African Women in the Atlantic World*, 89–108.

Jones, Gayl. *Palmares*. New York: Beacon Press, 2021.

Jones, Hilary. *The Métis of Senegal: Urban Life and Politics in French West Africa*. Bloomington: Indiana University Press, 2013.

Jones-Rogers, Stephanie E. "'[S]he Could . . . Spare One Ample Breast for the Profit of Her Owner': White Mothers and Enslaved Wet Nurses' Invisible Labor in American Slave Markets." *Slavery and Abolition* 38, no. 2 (2017): 337–55.

Jones-Rogers, Stephanie E. *They Were Her Property: White Women as Slave Owners in the American South*. New Haven, CT: Yale University Press, 2019.

Joshel, Sandra R. *Slavery in the Roman World*. New York: Cambridge University Press, 2010.

Kananoja, Kalle. *Healing Knowledge in Atlantic Africa: Medical Encounters, 1500–1850*. New York: Cambridge University Press, 2021.

Karasch, Mary C. *Slave Life in Rio de Janeiro, 1808–1850*. Princeton, NJ: Princeton University Press, 1987.

Karp, Matthew. *This Vast Southern Empire: Slaveholders at the Helm of American Foreign Policy*. Cambridge, MA: Harvard University Press, 2016.

Kars, Marjoleine. *Blood in the River: A Chronicle of Mutiny and Freedom on the Wild Coast*. New York: New Press, 2020.

Kars, Marjoleine. "Dodging Rebellion: Politics and Gender in the Berbice Slave Uprising of 1763." *American Historical Review* 121, no. 1 (2016): 39–69.

Kaufmann, Miranda. *Black Tudors: The Untold Story*. London: Oneworld Publications, 2018.

Kelley, Sean M. *A Journey into Captivity from Sierra Leone to South Carolina*. Chapel Hill: University of North Carolina Press, 2016.

Kelley, Sean M. *American Slavers: Merchants, Mariners, and the Transatlantic Commerce in Captives, 1644–1865*. New Haven, CT: Yale University Press, 2023.

Kellogg, Susan. *Weaving the Past: A History of Latin America's Indigenous Women from the Prehispanic Period to the Present*. New York: Oxford University Press, 2005.

Kerr-Ritchie, Jeffrey R. *Freedom's Seekers: Essays on Comparative Emancipation*. Baton Rouge: Louisiana State University Press, 2014.

Kerr-Ritchie, Jeffrey R. *Rebellious Passage: The Creole Revolt and America's Coastal Slave Trade*. New York: Cambridge University Press, 2019.

Kiddy, Elizabeth W. *Blacks of the Rosary: Memory and History in Minas Gerais Brazil*. University Park: Pennsylvania State University Press, 2005.

Kiddy, Elizabeth W. "Who Is the King of Congo? A New Look at African and Afro-Brazilian Kings in Brazil." In Heywood, *Central Africans and Cultural Transformations in the American Diaspora*, 153–82.

Kingsley, Mary. *West African Studies*. New York: Cambridge University Press, 2011.

Klein, Herbert S. *The Atlantic Slave Trade*. Cambridge: Cambridge University Press, 1999.

Klein, Herbert S. "Novas interpretações do tráfico de escravos do Atlântico." *Revista História* 120 (1989): 3–25.

Klein, Herbert S. "The Portuguese Slave Trade from Angola in the Eighteenth Century." *Journal of Economic History* 32, no. 4 (1972): 894–918.

Klein, Herbert S., and Francisco Vida Luna. *Slavery in Brazil*. New York: Cambridge University Press, 2010.

Klein, Herbert S., and Ben Vinson III. *African Slavery in Latin America and the Caribbean*. New York: Cambridge University Press, 2007.

Klein, Martin. *Slavery and Colonial Rule in French West Africa*. Cambridge: Cambridge University Press, 1998.

Konadu, Kwasi. *Many Black Women of This Fortress: Graça, Mónica and Adwoa, Three Enslaved Women of Portugal's African Empire*. London: Hurst, 2022.

Konadu, Kwasi. "'To Satisfy My Savage Appetite': Slavery, Belief, and Sexual Violence on the Mina (Gold) Coast, 1471–1571." *Journal of African History* (2022): 1–16.

Koutsoukos, Sandra Sofia Machado. "'Amas mercenárias': O discurso dos doutores em medicina e os retratos de amas–Brasil, segunda metade do século XIX." *História, Ciências, Saúde–Manguinhos* 16, no. 2 (2009): 305–24.

Krause, Thiago. "Compadrio e escravidão na Bahia seiscentista." *Afro-Ásia* 50 (2014): 199–228.

Krebs, Verena. *Medieval Ethiopian Kingship, Craft, and Diplomacy with Latin Europe*. Cham, Switz.: Palgrave Macmillan, 2021.

Krebs, Verena. "Re-Examining Foresti's Supplementum Chronicarum and the 'Ethiopian' Embassy to Europe of 1306." *Bulletin of SOAS* 82, no. 3 (2019): 493–515.

Kriger, Colleen E. "'Guinea Cloth': Production and Consumption of Cotton Textiles in West Africa before and during the Atlantic Slave Trade." In *The Spinning World: A Global History of Cotton Textiles, 1200–1850*, edited by Giorgio Riello and Prasannan Parthasarathi, 105–26. Oxford: Oxford University Press, 2009.

Kriger, Colleen E. *Making Money: Life, Death, and Early Modern Trade on Africa's Guinea Coast*. Athens: Ohio University Press, 2017.

Kulikoff, Allan. *Tobacco and Slaves: The Development of Southern Cultures in the Chesapeake, 1680–1800*. Chapel Hill: University of North Carolina Press, 1986.

Kytle, Ethan J., and Blain Roberts. *Denmark Vesey's Garden: Slavery and Memory in the Cradle of the Confederacy*. New York: New Press, 2018.

Lahon, Didier. "Esclavage, confréries noires, sainteté noire et pureté de sang au Portugal (XVIe et XVIIIe siècles)." *Lusitania Sacra* 2, no. 15 (2003): 119–62.

Landers, Jane. "The African Landscape of Seventeenth-Century Cartagena and Its Hinterlands." In Cañizares-Esguerra, Childs, and Sidbury, *Black Urban Atlantic in the Age of the Slave Trade*, 149–64.

Landers, Jane. *Black Society in Spanish Florida*. Urbana: University of Illinois Press, 1999.

Landers, Jane. "Transforming Bondsmen into Vassals: Arming Slaves in Colonial Spanish America." In *Arming Slaves: From Classical Times to the Modern Age*, edited by Christopher Leslie Brown and Philip D. Morgan, 120–45. New Haven, CT: Yale University Press, 2006.

Lane, Kris. *Potosí: The Silver City That Changed the World*. Oakland: University of California Press, 2019.

Lane, Kris. "The Transition from Encomienda to Slavery in Seventeenth-Century Barbacoas (Colombia)." *Slavery & Abolition* 21, no. 1 (2000): 73–95.

Lara, Silvia Hunold. *Palmares e Cucaú: O aprendizado da dominação*. São Paulo: Editora da Universidade de São Paulo, 2021.

Lara, Sylvia Hunold. "The Signs of Color: Women's Dress and Racial Relations in Salvador and Rio de Janeiro, ca. 1750–1815." *Colonial Latin American Review* 6, no. 2 (1997): 205–24.

Larsen, Lynne Ellsworth. "Wives and Warriors: The Royal Women of Dahomey as Representatives of the Kingdom." In *The Routledge Companion to Black Women's Cultural Histories*, edited by Janell Hobson, 225–35. London: Routledge, 2021.

Law, Robin. "A carreira de Francisco Félix de Souza na África Ocidental (1800–1849)." *Topoi* (2001): 9–39.

Law, Robin. "A comunidade brasileira de Uidá e os últimos anos do tráfico atlântico de escravos, 1850–66." *Afro-Ásia* 27 (2002): 41–77.

Law, Robin. "The 'Amazons' of Dahomey." *Paideuma: Mitteilungen zur Kulturkunde* 39 (1993): 245–60.

Law, Robin. "Ethnicities of Enslaved Africans in the Diaspora: On the Meanings of 'Mina' (Again)." *History in Africa* 32 (2005): 247–67.

Law, Robin. "'My Head Belongs to the King': On the Political and Ritual Significance of Decapitation in Pre-Colonial Dahomey." *Journal of African History* 30, no. 3 (1989): 399–415.

Law, Robin. "A Neglected Account of the Dahomian Conquest of Whydah (1727): The 'Relation de la Guerre de Juda' of the Sieur Ringard of Nantes." *History in Africa* 5 (1988): 321–38.

Law, Robin. *Ouidah: The Social History of a West African Slaving Port (1727–1892)*. Athens: Ohio University Press, 2004.

Law, Robin. *The Ọyọ Empire, c. 1600–c. 1836: A West African Imperialism in the Era of the Atlantic Slave Trade*. Oxford: Oxford University Press, 1991.

Law, Robin. "The Politics of Commercial Transition: Factional Conflict in Dahomey in the Context of the Ending of the Atlantic Slave Trade." *Journal of African History* 38 (1997): 213–33.

Law, Robin, and Paul E. Lovejoy. "Borgu in the Atlantic Slave Trade." *African Economic History*, no. 27 (1999): 69–92.

Lawrance, Benjamin N. *Amistad's Orphans: An Atlantic Story of Children, Slavery, and Smuggling*. New Haven, CT: Yale University Press, 2014.

Lawrance, Jeremy. "Black Africans in Renaissance Spanish Literature." In Earle and Lowe, *Black Africans in Renaissance Europe*, 70–93.

Leal, Maria das Graças de Andrade. *Manuel Querino: Entre Letras e Lutas Bahia 1851–1923*. São Paulo: Annablume, 2009.

Legaspi, Jaime Olveda. "La abolición de la esclavitud en México, 1810–1917." *Signos Históricos*, no. 29 (2013): 8–34.

Le Glaunec, Jean-Pierre. *Esclaves mais résistants: Dans le monde des annonces pour esclaves en fuite, Louisiane, Jamaïque, Caroline du Sud (1801–1815)*. Paris: Karthala, 2021.

Lenski, Noel. "Framing the Question: What Is a Slave Society?" In Lenski and Cameron, *What Is a Slave Society?* 15–57.

Lenski, Noel, and Catherine M. Cameron, eds. *What Is a Slave Society? The Practice of Slavery in Global Perspective*. New York: Cambridge University Press, 2018.

Lepore, Jill. *New York Burning: Liberty, Slavery, and Conspiracy in Eighteenth-Century Manhattan*. New York: Alfred A. Knopf, 2005.

Lesser, Jeffrey. *Immigration, Ethnicity, and National Identity in Brazil, 1808 to the Present*. New York: Cambridge University Press, 2013.

Liberato, Carlos, Mariana P. Candido, Paul E. Lovejoy, and Renée Soulodre-La France. "Laços entre a África e o mundo atlântico durante a era do comércio de africanos escravizados: Uma introdução." In *Laços atlânticos: África e africanos durante a era do comércio transatlântico de escravos*, edited by Carlos Liberato, Mariana P. Candido, Paul E. Lovejoy, and Renée Soulodre-La France, 1–30. Luanda, Angola: Ministério da Cultura, Museu Nacional da Escravatura, 2016.

Lichtenstein, Alex. *Twice the Work of Free Labor: The Political Economy of Convict Labor in the New South*. London: Verso, 1996.

Lightfoot, Natasha. *Troubling Freedom: Antigua and the Aftermath of British Emancipation*. Durham, NC: Duke University Press, 2015.

Lima e Souza, Mônica. "Entre margens: O retorno à África de libertos no Brasil, 1830–1870." PhD diss., Universidade Federal Fluminense, 2008.

Lindsay, Lisa A. *Atlantic Bonds: A Nineteenth-Century Odyssey from America to Africa*. Chapel Hill: University of North Carolina Press, 2017.

Lindsay, Lisa A. "'To Return to the Bosom of Their Fatherland': Brazilian Immigrants in Nineteenth Century Lagos." *Slavery and Abolition* 15, no. 1 (1994): 22–50.

Littlefield, Daniel C. *Rice and Slaves: Ethnicity and the Slave Trade in Colonial South Carolina*. Urbana: University of Illinois Press, 1991.

Livesay, Daniel. *Children of Uncertain Fortune: Mixed-Race Jamaicans in Britain and the Atlantic Family, 1733–1833*. Chapel Hill: University of North Carolina Press, 2018.

Lobo, Olívia Dulce. "Laura Congo e a família escrava do Barão de Tinguá: Reflexões sobre a família no Vale do Paraíba fluminense (1830–1888)." MA thesis, Universidade Federal do Estado do Rio de Janeiro, 2017.

Lockett, James D. "The Deportation of the Maroons of Trelawny Town to Nova Scotia, then Back to Africa." *Journal of Black Studies* 30, no. 1 (1999): 5–14.

Lockhart, James, and Stuart Schwartz. *Early Latin America: A History of Colonial Spanish America and Brazil*. New York: Cambridge University Press, 1999.

López, Laura Álvarez, and Magdalena Coll. "Registers of African-Derived Lexicon in Uruguay: Etymologies, Demography and Semantic Change." *Zeitschrift für romanische Philologie* 135, no. 1 (2019): 223–55.

Lovejoy, Paul E. "Autobiography and Memory: Gustavus Vassa, alias Olaudah Equiano, the African." *Slavery and Abolition* 27, no. 3 (2006): 317–47.

Lovejoy, Paul E. *Jihād in West Africa During the Ages of Revolution*. Athens: Ohio University Press, 2016.

Lovejoy, Paul E. "Pawnship, Debt, and 'Freedom' in Atlantic Africa during the Era of the Slave Trade: A Reassessment." *Journal of African History* 55 (2014): 55–78.

Lovejoy, Paul E. *Slavery in the Global Diaspora of Africa*. New York: Routledge, 2019.

Lovejoy, Paul E. "Speculations on the African Origins of Venture Smith." In *The Changing Worlds of Atlantic Africa: Essays in Honor of Robin Law*, edited by Toyin Falola and Matt D. Childs, 371–85. Durham, NC: Carolina Academic Press, 2009.

Lovejoy, Paul E. *Transformations in Slavery: A History of Slavery in Africa*. New York: Cambridge University Press, 2012.

Lovejoy Paul E., and Nielson R. Bezerra. *Mahommah Gardo Baquaqua: An Enslaved Muslim of the Black Atlantic*. Chapel Hill: University of North Carolina Press, 2025.

Lovell, William George. "Heavy Shadows and Black Night: Disease and Depopulation in Colonial Spanish America." *Annals of the Association of American Geographers* 82, no. 3 (1992): 426–43.

Machado, Helena P. T., and Celso Thomas Castilho, eds. *Tornando-se livre: Agentes históricos e lutas sociais no processo de abolição*. São Paulo: Editora da Universidade de São Paulo, 2014.

Machado, Maria Helena Pereira Toledo. "Between Two Beneditos: Enslaved Wet-Nurses amid Slavery's Decline in Southeast Brazil." *Slavery and Abolition* 38, no. 2 (2017): 320–36.

Machado, Maria Helena P. T. *O plano e o pânico: Os movimentos sociais na década da abolição*. São Paulo: Editora da Universidade de São Paulo, 1994.

Mackey, Frank. *Done with Slavery: The Black Fact in Montreal, 1760–1840*. Montreal: McGill-Queen's University Press, 2010.

Mair, Lucille Mathurin. *A Historical Study of Women in Jamaica, 1655–1844*. Mona, Jamaica: University of the West Indies Press, 2006.

Mamigonian, Beatriz G. *Africanos livres: A abolição do tráfico de escravos no Brasil.* São Paulo: Companhia das Letras, 2017.

Mamigonian, Beatriz Gallotti. "José Majojo e Francisco Moçambique, marinheiros das rotas atlânticas: Notas sobre a reconstituição de trajetórias da era da abolição." *Topoi* 11, no. 20 (2010): 75–91.

Mann, Kristin. "Gendered Authority, Gendered Violence: Family, Household and Identity in the Life and Death of a Brazilian Freed Woman in Lagos." In Candido and Jones, *African Women in the Atlantic World*, 148–68.

Mann, Kristin. "One Yoruba Man's Transatlantic Passages from Slavery to Freedom." In *The Rise and Demise of Slavery and the Slave Trade in the Atlantic World*, edited by Philip Misevich and Kristin Mann, 220–46. Rochester, NY: University of Rochester Press, 2016.

Mann, Kristin. "Shifting Paradigms in the Study of the African Diaspora and of Atlantic History and Culture." *Slavery and Abolition* 22, no. 1 (2001): 3–21.

Mann, Kristin. *Slavery and the Birth of an African City: Lagos, 1760–1900*. Bloomington: Indiana University Press, 2007.

Manning, Patrick. *Slavery and African Life: Occidental, Oriental, and African Slave Trades*. New York: Cambridge University Press, 1990.

Manning, Patrick. *Slavery, Colonialism and Economic Growth in Dahomey, 1640–1960*. Cambridge: Cambridge University Press, 1982.

Marcondes, Renato Leite, and José Flávio Motta. "Duas fontes documentais para o estudo dos preços dos escravos no Vale do Paraíba paulista." *Revista Brasileira de História* 21, no. 42 (2001): 495–514.

Marinetti, Brice. *Les négociants de La Rochelle au XVIIIe siècle*. Paris: Presses universitaires de Rennes, 2013.

Mark, Peter. "The Central Upper Guinea Coast in the Pre-Contact and Early Portuguese Period, Fifteenth to Seventeenth Century: The Dynamics of Regional Interaction." *Paideuma: Mitteilungen zur Kulturkunde*, no. 67 (2021): 113–44.

Mark, Peter. *"Portuguese" Style and Luso-African Identity: Precolonial Senegambia, Sixteenth–Nineteenth Century*. Bloomington: Indiana University Press, 2002.

Marquese, Rafael de Bivar. "African Diaspora, Slavery, and the Paraíba Valley Coffee Plantation Landscape: Nineteenth-Century Brazil." *Review (Fernand Braudel Center)* 31, no. 2 (2008): 195–216.

Marquese, Rafael de Bivar. *Feitores do corpo, missionários da mente: Senhores, letrados e o controle dos escravos nas Américas, 1660–1860*. São Paulo: Companhia das Letras, 2004.

Martin, Phyllis M. *The External Trade of the Loango Coast, 1576–1870: The Effects of Changing Commercial Relations on the Vili Kingdom of Loango*. Oxford: Clarendon Press, 1972.

Martin, Phyllis M. "The Kingdom of Loango." In *Kongo: Power of Majesty*, edited by Alisa Lagamma, 47–86. New York: Metropolitan Museum of Art, 2015.

Martínez, Iván Armenteros. "Un caso de reestructuración de redes comerciales: El mercado de esclavos de Barcelona entre 1472 y 1516." Paper presented at the eleventh Congrés de Història de la Ciutat de Barcelona, Institut de Cultura, Ajuntament de Barcelona, December 1–3, 2009.

Masur, Kate. "The African American Delegation to Abraham Lincoln: A Reappraisal." *Civil War History* 56, no. 2 (2010): 117–44.

Matory, James Lorand. *Black Atlantic Religion: Tradition, Transnationalism and Matriarchy in the Afro-Brazilian Candomblé*. Princeton, NJ: Princeton University Press, 2005.

Matos-Rodríguez, Félix V. "Street Vendors, Pedlars, Shop-Owners and Domestics: Some Aspects of Women's Economic Roles in Nineteenth-Century San Juan, Puerto Rico (1820–1870)." In Shepherd, Brereton, and Bailey, *Engendering History*, 176–93.

Mattos, Hebe. *Das cores do silêncio: Os significados da liberdade no sudeste escravista, Brasil século XIX*. Campinas, Brazil: Editora da Universidade Estadual de Campinas, 2013.

Mattos, Hebe. "Os Combates da Memória: Escravidão e liberdade nos arquivos orais de descendentes de escravos brasileiros." *Tempo* 3, no. 6 (1998): 1–12.

Mattos, Hebe, and Martha Abreu. "Memories of Captivity and Freedom in São José's Jongo Festivals." In Araujo, *African Heritage and Memories of Slavery in Brazil and the South Atlantic World*, 149–77.

Mattoso, Kátia M. de Queirós. *Être esclave au Brésil XVIe–XIXe siècles*. Paris: L'Harmattan, 1994. First published 1979 by Hachette (Paris).

Mattoso, Kátia M. de Queirós. *Ser Escravo No Brasil*. Translated by Sonia Furhmann. São Paulo: Brasiliense, 1982.

Mattoso, Kátia M. de Queirós. *To Be a Slave in Brazil, 1550–1888*. Translated by Arthur Goldhammer. New Brunswick, NJ: Rutgers University Press, 1986.

Mbembe, Achille, and Laurent Dubois. *Critique of Black Reason*. Durham, NC: Duke University Press, 2017.

McCusker, John J., and Russell R. Menard. *The Economy of British America, 1607–1789*. Chapel Hill: University of North Carolina Press, 1991.

McDaniel, William Caleb. *Sweet Taste of Liberty: A True Story of Slavery and Restitution in America*. New York: Oxford University Press, 2019.

McGraw, Jason. *The Work of Recognition: Caribbean Colombia and the Postemancipation Struggle for Citizenship*. Chapel Hill: University of North Carolina Press, 2014.

McKinley, Michelle A. *Fractional Freedoms: Slavery, Intimacy, and Legal Mobilization in Colonial Lima, 1600–1700*. New York: Cambridge University Press, 2016.

McKinley, Michelle A. "Fractional Freedoms: Slavery, Legal Activism, and Ecclesiastical Courts in Colonial Lima, 1593–1689." *Law and History Review* 28, no.3 (2010): 749–90.

McMahon, Kate. "The Transnational Dimensions of Africans and African Americans in Northern England, 1776–1865." PhD diss., Howard University, 2017.

Medford, Edna G. *Historical Perspectives of the African Burial Ground: New York Blacks and the Diaspora*. Washington, DC: Howard University Press, 2009.

Meillassoux, Claude. *Anthropologie de l'esclavage: Le Ventre de fer et d'argent*. Paris: Presses Universitaires de France, 1986.

Meillassoux, Claude. *The Anthropology of Slavery: The Womb of Iron and Gold*. Chicago: University of Chicago Press, 1991.

Meillassoux, Claude. *L'esclavage en Afrique précoloniale: Dix-sept études présentées par Claude Meillassoux*. Paris: François Mapero, 1975.

Mello, Marco Antonio da Silva, Felipe Berocan Veiga, Patrícia Brandão Couto, and Miran Alves de Souza. "Os ciganos do Catumbi: De 'andores do Rei' e comerciantes de escravos a oficiais de justiça na cidade do Rio de Janeiro." *Cidades: Comunidades e Territórios*, no. 18 (2009): 79–92.

Mello e Souza, Laura de. *The Devil and the Land of the Holy Cross: Witchcraft, Slavery, and Popular Religion in Colonial Brazil*. Austin: University of Texas Press, 2010.

Mello e Souza, Marina de. "The Construction of a Black Catholic Identity in Brazil: Saints and Minkisi; A Reflection of Cultural Miscegenation." In *Africa, Brazil, and the Construction of Black Atlantic Identities*, edited by Livio Sansone, Elisée Soumonni, and Boubacar Barry, 255–68. Trenton, NJ: Africa World Press, 2008.

Menard, Russell R. "Slave Demography in the Lowcountry, 1670–1740: From Frontier Society to Plantation Regime." *South Carolina Historical Magazine* 101, no. 3 (2000): 190–213.

Mendes, António de Almeida. "Les réseaux de la traite ibérique dans l'Atlantique nord (1440–1640)." *Annales: Histoire, Sciences Sociales*, no. 4 (2008): 739–68.

Menschel, David. "Abolition without Deliverance: The Law of Connecticut Slavery 1784–1848." *Yale Law Journal* 111, no. 1 (2001): 187–88.

Mettas, Jean. *Répertoire des expéditions négrières françaises au XVIIIe siècle*. Vol. 2, *Ports autres que Nantes*. Paris: Société française d'histoire d'outre-mer, 1984.

Miki, Yuko. *Frontiers of Citizenship: A Black and Indigenous History of Postcolonial Brazil*. New York: Cambridge University Press, 2018.

Miller, Joseph C. "Central Africa During the Era of the Slave Trade, c. 1490s–1850s." In Heywood, *Central Africans and Cultural Transformations in the American Diaspora*, 21–69.

Miller, Joseph C. *Kings and Kinsmen: Early Mbundu States*. Oxford: Clarendon Press, 1976.

Miller, Joseph C. *Way of Death: Merchant Capitalism and the Angolan Slave Trade, 1740–1830*. Madison: University of Wisconsin Press, 1988.

Mills, Brandon. *The World Colonization Made: The Racial Geography of Early American Empire*. Philadelphia: University of Pennsylvania Press, 2020.

Mills, Charles. *The Racial Contract*. Ithaca, NY: Cornell University Press, 1997.

Mintz, Sidney W., and Richard Price. *An Anthropological Approach to the Afro-American Past*. Philadelphia: Institute for the Study of Human Issues, 1976.

Mintz, Sidney W., and Richard Price. *The Birth of African-American Culture: An Anthropological*. Boston: Beacon Press, 1992.

Mobley, Christina Frances. "The Kongolese Atlantic: Central Africa Slavery and Culture from Mayombe to Haiti." PhD diss., Duke University, 2015.

Moitt, Bernard. *Women and Slavery in the French Antilles, 1635–1848*. Bloomington: Indiana University Press, 2001.

Monroe, J. Cameron. *The Precolonial State in West Africa: Building Power in Dahomey*. New York: Cambridge University Press, 2014.

Monroe, J. Cameron, and Anneke Janzen. "The Dahomean Feast: Royal Women, Private Politics, and Culinary Practices in Atlantic West Africa." *African Archaeological Review* 31, no. 2 (2014): 299–337.

Monteiro, John Manuel. *Blacks of the Land: Indian Slavery, Settler Society, and the Portuguese Colonial Enterprise in South America*. Edited and translated by James P. Woodard and Barbara Weinstein. Cambridge Latin American Studies 112. New York: Cambridge University Press, 2018.

Monteiro, John Manuel. *Negros da terra: Índios e bandeirantes nas origens de São Paulo*. São Paulo: Companhia das Letras, 1994.

Monteiro, José Pedro. *The Internationalisation of the "Native Labour" Question in Portuguese Late Colonialism 1945–1965*. Cham, Switz.: Palgrave Macmillan, 2023.

Monteiro, Pedro Meira, and Michael Stone, eds. *Cangoma Calling Spirits and Rhythms of Freedom in Brazilian Jongo Slavery Songs*. Dartmouth: University of Massachusetts, 2013.

Monzote, Reinaldo Funes. *From Rainforest to Cane Field in Cuba: An Environmental History Since 1492*. Chapel Hill: University of North Carolina Press, 2008.

Morel, Genaro Rodríguez. "The Sugar Economy of Española in the Sixteenth Century." In Schwartz, *Tropical Babylons*, 85–114.

Morgan, Jennifer. *Laboring Women: Reproduction and Gender in New World Slavery*. Philadelphia: University of Pennsylvania Press, 2004.

Morgan, Jennifer. "Partus sequitur ventrem: Law, Race, and Reproduction in Colonial Slavery." *Small Axe* 22, no. 1 (2018): 1–17.

Morgan, Jennifer. *Reckoning with Slavery: Gender, Kinship, and Capitalism in the Early Atlantic*. Durham, NC: Duke University Press, 2021.

Morgan, Philip D. *Slave Counterpoint: Black Culture in the Eighteenth-Century Chesapeake and Lowcountry*. Chapel Hill: University of North Carolina Press, 1998.

Morley, Neville. *Metropolis and Hinterland: The City of Rome and the Italian Economy, 200 BC–AD 200*. Cambridge: Cambridge University Press, 1996.

Morrison, Toni. *Beloved: A Novel*. New York: Knopf, 1987.

Mott, Luiz. *Bahia: Inquisição e sociedade*. Salvador, Brazil: Editora da Universidade da Bahia, 2010.

Mott, Luiz. "Rosa Egipcíaca: De escrava da Costa da Mina à Flor do Rio de Janeiro." In *Rotas atlânticas da diáspora africana: Da Baía do Benim ao Rio de Janeiro*, edited by Mariza de Carvalho Soares, 135–55. Rio de Janeiro: Editora da Universidade Federal Fluminense, 2007.

Mott, Luiz. *Rosa Egipcíaca: Uma santa africana no Brasil*. Rio de Janeiro: Bertrand do Brasil, 1993.

Moura, Clóvis. *Dicionário da escravidão negra no Brasil*. São Paulo: Editora da Universidade de São Paulo, 2004.

Muaze, Mariana de Aguiar Ferreira. "Violence Appeased: Slavery and Coffee Raising in the Photography of Marc Ferrez (1882–1885)." *Revista brasileira de história*, 37, no. 74 (2017): 1–30.

Murphy, Laura. "Obstacles in the Way of Love: The Enslavement of Intimacy in Samuel Crowther and Ama Ata Aidoo." *Research in African Literatures* 40, no. 4 (2009): 47–64.

Murphy, Thomas. *Jesuit Slaveholding in Maryland, 1717–1838*. New York: Routledge, 2001.

Mustakeem, Sowande. *Slavery at Sea: Terror, Sex, and Sickness in the Middle Passage*. Urbana: University of Illinois Press, 2016.

Myers, Amrita Chakrabarti. *The Vice President's Black Wife: The Untold Life of Julia Chinn*. Chapel Hill: University of North Carolina Press, 2023.

Nafafé, José Lingna. *Lourenço da Silva Mendonça and the Black Atlantic Abolitionist Movement in the Seventeenth Century*. Cambridge: Cambridge University Press, 2022.

Nash, Gary B. *The Forgotten Fifth: African-Americans and the Age of Revolution*. Cambridge, MA: Harvard University Press, 2006.

Natário, Anabela, Christiana Martins, and José Carlos Carvalho. "Coleiras de escravos foram encontradas." *Expresso*, March 27, 2017.

Needell, Jeffrey D. *The Sacred Cause: The Abolitionist Movement, Afro-Brazilian Mobilization, and Imperial Politics in Rio de Janeiro*. Stanford, CA: Stanford University Press, 2020.

Neves, Maria João, Miguel Almeida, and Maria Teresa Ferreira. "O caso do 'Poço dos Negros' (Lagos): Da urgência do betão ao conhecimento das práticas funerárias esclavagistas no Portugal Moderno a partir duma escavação de Arqueologia Preventiva." *Antrope* 2 (2015): 141–60.

Neves, Maria João, Miguel Almeida, and Maria Teresa Ferreira. "Separados na vida e na morte: Retrato do tratamento mortuário dados aos escravos africanos na cidade moderna de Lagos." In "Actas do 7º Encontro de Arqueologia do Algarve, Silves, 22, 23, e 24 de outubro de 2009," special issue, *XELB: Revista de arqueologia, arte, etnologia e história* 10 (2009): 547–60.

Neves, Raphael. "Experiências capturadas: A fuga de escravos no Rio de Janeiro." Rio de Janeiro: Fundação Biblioteca Nacional, 2009.

Nevius, Marcus P. *City of Refuge: Slavery and Petit Marronage in the Great Dismal Swamp, 1763–1856*. Athens: University of Georgia Press, 2020.

Newman, Brooke. *A Dark Inheritance: Blood, Race, and Sex in Colonial Jamaica*. New Haven, CT: Yale University Press, 2018.

Newman, Simon P. "Freedom-Seeking Slaves in England and Scotland, 1700–1780." *English Historical Review* 134, no. 570 (2019): 1136–68.

Newson, Linda A., and Susie Minchin. *From Capture to Sale: The Portuguese Slave Trade to Spanish South America in Early Seventeenth Century*. Leiden, Neth.: Brill, 2007.

Nishida, Mieko. *Slavery and Identity: Ethnicity, Gender, and Race in Salvador, Brazil, 1808–1888*. Bloomington: Indiana University Press, 2003.

Nunley, Tamika Y. *At the Threshold of Liberty: Women, Slavery, and Shifting Identities in Washington, D.C.* Chapel Hill: University of North Carolina Press, 2021.

Nunley, Tamika Y. *The Demands of Justice: Enslaved Women, Capital Crime, and Clemency in Early Virginia*. Chapel Hill: University of North Carolina Press, 2023.

Ogundiran, Akinwumi. *The Yorùbá: A New History*. Bloomington: Indiana University Press, 2020.

Ojo, Olatunji. "Document 2: Letters Found in the House of Kosoko, King of Lagos (1851)." *African Economic History* 40 (2012): 37–61.

Oliveira, Eduardo Freire de. *Elementos para a história do município de Lisboa*. Vol. 1. Lisbon: Typhographia Universal, 1882.

Oliveira, Maria Inês Cortês. "La Grande tente Nagô: Rapprochements ethniques chez les Africains de Bahia au XIXe siècle." In *Identifying Enslaved Africans: The "Nigerian" Hinterland and the African Diaspora*, edited by Paul E. Lovejoy, 286–301. Toronto: York University, 1997.

Oliveira, Vanessa. "Baskets, Stalls and Shops: Experiences and Strategies of Women in Retail Sales in Nineteenth-Century Luanda." *Canadian Journal of African Studies / Revue canadienne des études africaines* 54, no. 3 (2020): 419–36.

Oliveira, Vanessa. *Slave Trade and Abolition: Gender, Commerce, and Economic Transition in Luanda*. Madison: University of Wisconsin Press, 2021.

Olsen, Margaret M. "African Reinscription of Body and Space in New Granada." In *Mapping Colonial Spanish America Places and Commonplaces of Identity, Culture, and Experience*, edited by Santa Arias and Mariselle Meléndez, 263–94. Lewisburg, PA: Bucknell University Press; London: Associated University Press, 2002.

Olwell, Robert. "'Loose, Idle and Disorderly': Slave Women in the Eighteenth-Century Charleston Marketplace." In *More Than Chattel: Black Women and Slavery in the Americas*, edited by David Barry Gaspar and Darlene Clark Hine, 97–110. Bloomington: Indiana University Press, 1996.

O'Malley, Gregory E. "Slavery's Converging Ground: Charleston's Slave Trade as the Black Heart of the Lowcountry." *William and Mary Quarterly* 74, no. 2 (2017): 271–302.

Oostindie, Gert, and Karwan Fatah-Black. *Sporen van de slavernij in Leiden*. Leiden, Neth.: Leiden University Press, 2018.

Otele, Olivette. *African Europeans: An Untold History*. New York: Basic Books, 2021.

Otero, Solimar. *Afro-Cuban Diasporas in the Atlantic World*. Rochester, NY: University of Rochester Press, 2010.

Otovo, Okezi T. *Progressive Mothers: Better Babies: Race, Public Health, and the State in Brazil, 1850–1945*. Austin: University of Texas Press, 2016.

Ott, Carlos. "A Irmandade de Nossa Senhora do Rosário dos Pretos do Pelourinho." *Afro-Ásia*, no. 6/7 (1968): 119–26.

Oyěwùmí, Oyèrónké. *The Invention of Women: Making an African Sense of Western Gender Discourse*. Minneapolis: University of Minnesota Press, 1997.

Painter, Nell Irvin. *Exodusters: Black Migration to Kansas after Reconstruction*. New York: Knopf, 1976.

Paiva, Eduardo França. *Escravidão e universo cultural na colônia: Minas Gerais, 1716–1789*. Belo Horizonte, Brazil: Editora da Universidade de Minas Gerais, 2006.

Palmer, Colin A. "Defining and Studying the Modern African Diaspora." *Journal of Negro History* 85 (2000): 27–32.

Pantoja, Selma. "A Dimensão Atlântica das Quitandeiras." In *Diálogos Oceânicos. Minas Gerais e as Novas Abordagens para uma História do Império Ultramarino Português*, edited by Júnia F. Furtado, 45–68.

Belo Horizonte, Brazil: Editora da Universidade Federal de Minas Gerais, 2001.

Pantoja, Selma. "Women's Work in the Fairs and Markets of Luanda." In *Women in the Portuguese Colonial Empire: The Theatre of Shadows*, edited by Clara Sarmento, 81–93. Newcastle upon Tyne: Cambridge Scholars Publishing, 2008.

Parés, Luis Nicolau. "Afro-Catholic Baptism and the Articulation of a Merchant Community, Agoué, 1840–1860." *History in Africa* 42 (2015): 165–201.

Parés, Luis Nicolau. "Cartas do Daomé." *Afro-Ásia* 47 (2013): 295–395.

Parés, Luis Nicolau. "Entre Bahia e a Costa da Mina, libertos africanos no tráfico ilegal." In *Salvador da Bahia: Interações entre América e África (séculos XVI–XIX)*, edited by Giuseppina Raggi, João Figuerôa-Rego, and Roberta Stumpf, 19–20. Salvador, Brazil: Editora da Universidade Federal da Bahia, 2017.

Parés, Luis Nicolau. *The Formation of Candomblé: Vodun History and Ritual in Brazil*. Chapel Hill: University of North Carolina Press, 2013.

Parés, Luis Nicolau. "The Jeje in the Tambor de Mina of Maranhão and in the Candomblé of Bahia." *Slavery and Abolition* 22, no. 1 (2001): 91–115.

Parés, Luis Nicolau. "Milicianos, barbeiros e traficantes numa irmandade católica de africanos minas e jejes (Bahia, 1770–1830)." *Revista Tempo* 20 (2014): 1–32.

Pargas, Damian. *Freedom Seekers: Fugitive Slaves in North America, 1800–1860*. New York: Cambridge University Press, 2022.

Parry, Tyler D. *Jumping the Broom: The Surprising Multicultural Origins of a Black Wedding Ritual*. Chapel Hill: University of North Carolina Press, 2020.

Parry, Tyler D., and Charlton W. Yingling. "Slave Hounds and Abolition in the Americas," *Past & Present* 246, no. 1 (2020): 69–108.

Paton, Diana. "The Driveress and the Nurse: Childcare, Working Children and Other Work under Caribbean Slavery." *Past & Present* 246, no. 15 (2020): 27–53.

Paton, Diana. *No Bound but the Law: Punishment, Race, and Gender in Jamaican State Formation, 1780–1870*. Durham, NC: Duke University Press, 2004.

Paton, Diana. "Witchcraft, Poison, Law, and Atlantic Slavery." *William and Mary Quarterly* 69, no. 2 (2012) 235–64.

Paton, Diana, and Matthew J. Smith, eds. *The Jamaica Reader: History, Culture, Politics*. Durham, NC: Duke University Press, 2021.

Patterson, Orlando. *Slavery and Social Death: A Comparative Study; With a New Preface*. Cambridge, MA: Harvard University Press, 2018.

Paugh, Katherine. *The Politics of Reproduction: Race, Medicine, and Fertility in the Age of Abolition*. Oxford: Oxford University Press, 2017.

Peabody, Sue. *"There Are No Slaves in France": The Political Culture of Race and Slavery in the Ancien Régime*. New York: Oxford University Press, 1996.

Perry, Warren R., Jean Howson, and Barbara A. Bianco. *The Archaeology of the New York African Burial Ground*. Washington, DC: Howard University Press, 2009.

Pétré-Grenouilleau, Olivier. *Les traites négrières: Essai d'histoire globale*. Paris: Gallimard, 2004.

Phillips, William D., Jr. *Slavery in Medieval and Early Modern Iberia*. Philadelphia: University of Pennsylvania Press, 2014.

Phillips, William D., Jr. "Slavery in the Atlantic Islands and the Early Modern Spanish Atlantic World." In *The Cambridge World History of Slavery*, vol. 3, *AD 1420–AD 1804*, edited by David Eltis, Keith R. Bradley, Stanley L. Engerman, and Paul Cartledge, 325–49. New York: Cambridge University Press, 2011.

Pierre, Jemima. *The Predicament of Blackness: Postcolonial Ghana and the Politics of Race*. Chicago: University of Chicago Press, 2012.

Pierson, Donald. *Brancos e pretos na Bahia: Estudo de contato racial*. São Paulo: Companhia Editora Nacional, 1945.

Pinsker, Matthew. "After 1850: Reassessing the Impact of the Fugitive Slave Law." In *Fugitive Slaves and Spaces of Freedom in North*

America, edited by Damian Pargas, 93–115. Gainesville: University Press of Florida, 2018.

Piqué, Francesca, and Leslie Rainer. *Palace Sculptures of Abomey: History Told on Walls*. London: J. Paul Getty Trust, Thames and Hudson, 1999.

Pirola, Ricardo Figueiredo. *Escravos e rebeldes nos tribunais do Império: Uma história social da lei de 10 de junho de 1835*. Rio de Janeiro: Arquivo Nacional, 2015.

Ponte, Mark. "'Al de swarten die hier ter stede comen': Een Afro-Atlantische gemeeschap in zeventiended-eeuws Amsterdam." *TSEG* 15, no. 4 (2018): 33–62.

Postma, Johannes Menne. *The Dutch in the Atlantic Slave Trade 1600–1815*. Cambridge: Cambridge University Press, 1990.

Prussat, Margrit. *Bilder Der Sklaverei: Fotografien Der Afrikanischen Diaspora in Brasilien 1860–1920*. Berlin: Reimer, 2008.

Prussat, Margrit. "Icons of Slavery: Black Brazil in Nineteenth-Century Photography and Image Art." In *Living History: Encountering the Memory of the Heirs of Slavery*, edited by Ana Lucia Araujo, 203–30. Newcastle upon Tyne: Cambridge Scholars Publishing, 2009.

Pybus, Cassandra. *Epic Journey of Freedom: Runaway Slaves of the American Revolution and Their Global Quest for Liberty*. Boston: Beacon Press, 2006.

Quirk, Joel. *The Anti-Slavery Project: From the Slave Trade to Human Trafficking*. Philadelphia: University of Pennsylvania Press, 2014.

Radburn, Nicholas. *Traders in Men: Merchants and the Transformation of the Transatlantic Slave Trade*. New Haven, CT: Yale University Press, 2023.

Radburn, Nicholas, and David Eltis. "Visualizing the Middle Passage: The *Brooks* and the Reality of Ship Crowding in the Transatlantic Slave Trade." *Journal of Interdisciplinary History* 99, no. 4 (2019): 533–65.

Rarey, Matthew Francis. *Insignificant Things: Amulets and the Art of Survival in the Early Black Atlantic*. Durham, NC: Duke University Press, 2023.

Rediker, Marcus. "History from Below the Water Line: Sharks and the Atlantic Slave Trade." *Atlantic Studies* 5, no. 2 (2008): 285–97.

Rediker, Marcus. *The Slave Ship: A Human History*. New York: Penguin, 2007.

Reese, Ty M. "'Eating' Luxury: Fante Middlemen, British Goods, and Changing Dependencies on the Gold Coast, 1750–1821." *William and Mary Quarterly* 66, no. 4 (2009): 851–72.

Reese, Ty M. "Wives, Brokers, and Laborers: Women at Cape Coast, 1750–1807." In *Women in Port: Gendering Communities, Economies, and Social Networks in Atlantic Port Cities, 1500–1800*, edited by Douglas Catterall and Jodi Campbell, 291–314. Leiden: Brill, 2012.

Reginaldo, Lucilene. "André do Couto Godinho." In *Oxford Research Encyclopedia of African History*, Oxford University Press. Article published May 26, 2021. https://oxfordre.com/africanhistory/view/10.1093/acrefore/9780190277734.001.0001/acrefore-9780190277734-e-962.

Reginaldo, Lucilene. "Os Rosários dos Angolas: Irmandades Negras, Experiências Escravas e Identidades Africanas na Bahia Setecentista." PhD diss., Universidade Estadual de Campinas, 2005.

Régis, Antoine. "Aventures d'un jeune négrier français d'après un manuscrit inédit du XVIIIe siècle." *Notes africaines*, April 1974, 51–56.

Reis, Adriana Dantas. "Mulheres 'Afro-descendentes' na Bahia Gênero, cor e mobilidade social (1780–1830)." In *Mulheres negras no Brasil escravista e do pós emancipação*, edited by Giovana Xavier, Juliana Barreto Farias, and Flávio dos Santos Gomes, 24–34. Rio de Janeiro: Selo Negro, 2012.

Reis, João José. "African Nations in Nineteenth-Century Salvador, Bahia." In Cañizares-Esguerra, Childs, and Sidbury, *Black Urban Atlantic in the Age of the Slave Trade*, 63–82.

Reis, João José. "A revolta haussá de 1809 na Bahia." In *Revoltas escravas no Brasil*, edited by João José Reis and Flávio dos Santos Gomes, 177–226. São Paulo: Companhia das Letras, 2021.

Reis, João José. *Death Is a Festival: Funeral Rites and Rebellion in Nineteenth-Century Brazil*. Chapel Hill: University of North Carolina Press, 2003.

Reis, João José. *Divining Slavery and Freedom: The Story of Domingos Sodré, an African Priest in Nineteenth-Century Brazil.* New York: Cambridge University Press, 2015.

Reis, João José. *Domingos Sodré: Um sacerdote africano; Escravidão, liberdade e candomblé na Bahia do século XIX.* São Paulo: Companhia das Letras, 2008.

Reis, João José. "From Slave to Wealthy African Freedman: The Story of Manoel Joaquim Ricardo." In *Biography and the Black Atlantic*, edited by Lisa A. Lindsay and John Wood Sweet, 131–48. Philadelphia: University of Pennsylvania Press, 2014.

Reis, João José. *Ganhadores: A greve negra de 1857 na Bahia.* São Paulo: Companhia das Letras, 2019.

Reis, João José. "Há duzentos anos: A revolta escrava de 1814 na Bahia." *Topoi* 15, no. 28 (2014): 68–115.

Reis, João José. "Identidade e Diversidade Étnicas nas Irmandades Negras no Tempo da Escravidão." *Tempo* 2, no. 3 (1996): 1–33.

Reis, João José. "La révolte haoussa de Bahia en 1807: Résistance et contrôle des esclaves au Brésil." *Annales: Histoire, Sciences Sociales*, no. 2 (2006): 383–418.

Reis, João José. *Rebelião escrava no Brasil: A história do levante dos malês em 1835.* São Paulo: Companhia das letras, 2003.

Reis, João José. "'The Revolution of the Ganhadores': Urban Labour, Ethnicity and the African Strike of 1857 in Bahia, Brazil." *Journal of Latin American Studies* 29, no. 2 (1997): 355–93.

Reis, João José. *Slave Rebellion in Brazil: The Muslim Uprising of 1835 in Bahia.* Baltimore: Johns Hopkins University Press, 1993.

Reis, João José, and Flávio dos Santos Gomes, eds. *Freedom by a Thread: The History of Quilombos in Brazil.* New York: Diasporic Africa Press, 2016.

Reis, João José, and Flávio dos Santos Gomes, eds. *Liberdade por um Fio: História dos quilombos no Brasil.* São Paulo: Companhia das Letras, 1996.

Reis, João José, and Flávio dos Santos Gomes. "Repercussions of the Haitian Revolution in Brazil, 1791–1850." In *The World of the Haitian*

Revolution, edited by David Patrick Geggus and Norman Fiering, 284–313. Bloomington: Indiana University Press, 2009.

Reis, João José, Flávio dos Santos Gomes, and Marcus J. M. de Carvalho. *O alufá Rufino: Tráfico, escravidão e liberdade no Atlântico Negro (c. 1822–c. 1853)*. São Paulo: Companhia das Letras, 2010.

Reis, João José, Flávio dos Santos Gomes, and Marcus J. M. de Carvalho. *The Story of Rufino: Slavery, Freedom, and Islam in the Black Atlantic*. New York: Oxford University Press, 2020.

Reséndez, Andrés. *The Other Slavery*. Boston: Houghton Mifflin Harcourt, 2016.

Restall, Matthew. "Black Conquistadors: Armed Africans in Early Spanish America." *Americas* 57, no. 2 (2000): 171–205.

Ribeiro, Maria Alice Rosa. "Preços de escravos em Campinas no século XIX." *História econômica & história de empresas* 20, no. 1 (2017): 85–123.

Richardson, David, ed. *Bristol, Africa and the Eighteenth-Century Slave Trade to America*. Vol. 3, *The Years of Decline 1746–1769*. Bristol, UK: Bristol Record Society, 1991.

Richardson, David, ed. *Bristol, Africa and the Eighteenth-Century Slave Trade to America*. Vol. 4, *The Final Years, 1770–1807*. Bristol, UK: Bristol Record Society, 1996.

Robichaud, Léon. "Behind the Marronage Project: Balancing Resources, Methodology and Access in an Online Archive." *Esclavages & Post~Esclavages / Slaveries & Post~Slaveries*, no. 3 (2020). https://doi.org/10.4000/slaveries.3112.

Rockman, Seth. *Scraping By: Wage Labor, Slavery, and Survival in Early Baltimore*. Baltimore: Johns Hopkins University Press, 2009.

Rodet, Marie. "Escaping Slavery and Building Diasporic Communities in French Soudan and Senegal, ca. 1880–1940." *International Journal of African Historical Studies* 48, no. 2 (2015): 363–86.

Rodney, Walter. *A History of the Upper Guinea Coast, 1545 to 1800*. New York: Monthly Review Press, 1970.

Rodney, Walter. *How Europe Underdeveloped Africa*. Washington, DC: Howard University Press, 1981.

Rodrigues, Jaime. "Arquitetura naval: Imagens, textos e possibilidades de descrições dos navios negreiros." In *Tráfico, cativeiro, liberdade: Rio de Janeiro, séculos XVII–XIX*, edited by Manolo Florentino, 80–123. Rio de Janeiro: Civilização Brasileira, 2005.

Rodrigues, Jaime. *De costa à costa: Escravos, marinheiros e intermediários do tráfico negreiro de Angola ao Rio de Janeiro (1780–1860)*. São Paulo: Companhia das Letras, 2005.

Rodrigues, Nina. *Os Africanos no Brasil*. São Paulo: Companhia Editora Nacional, 1976.

Ronen, Dov. "The Colonial Elite in Dahomey." *African Studies Review* 17, no. 1 (1974): 55–76.

Rönnbäck, Klas. *Labour and Living Standards in Pre-Colonial West Africa: The Case of the Gold Coast*. Oxford: Routledge, 2015.

Rood, Daniel B. *The Reinvention of Atlantic Slavery: Technology, Labor, Race, and Capitalism in the Greater Caribbean*. New York: Oxford University Press, 2017.

Roopharnine, Lomarsh. *The Indian Caribbean: Migration and Identity in the Diaspora*. Jackson: University of Mississippi Press, 2018.

Rosenthal, Caitlin. *Accounting for Slavery: Masters and Management*. Cambridge, MA: Harvard University Press, 2019.

Ross, David. "The Dahomean Middleman System, 1727–c. 1818." *Journal of African History* 28 (1987): 357–75.

Roth, Cassia. "From Free Womb to Criminalized Woman: Fertility Control in Brazilian Slavery and Freedom." *Slavery and Abolition* 38, no. 2 (2017): 269–86.

Rothman, Joshua D. *The Ledger and the Chain: How Domestic Slave Traders Shaped America*. New York: Basic Books, 2021.

Rothman, Joshua D. *Sex and Families across the Color Line in Virginia, 1787–1861*. Chapel Hill: University of North Carolina Press, 2003.

Rout, Leslie B. *The African Experience in Spanish America, 1502 to the Present Day*. Cambridge: Cambridge University Press, 1976.

Rowe, Erin Kathleen. *Black Saints in Early Modern Global Catholicism*. New York: Cambridge University Press, 2019.

Rowe, Erin Kathleen. "Visualizing Black Sanctity in Early Modern Spanish Polychrome Sculpture." In *Envisioning Others: Race, Color, and the Visual in Iberia and Latin America*, edited by Pamela A. Patton, 51–82. Leiden, Neth.: Brill, 2016.

Rucker, Walter C. "Conjure, Magic, and Power: The Influence of Afro-Atlantic Religious Practices on Slave Resistance and Rebellion." *Journal of Black Studies* 32, no. 1 (2001): 84–103.

Rucker, Walter C. *Gold Coast Diasporas: Identity, Culture, and Power*. Bloomington: Indiana University Press, 2015.

Rugemer, Edward B. *Slave Law and the Politics of Resistance in the Early Atlantic World*. Cambridge, MA: Harvard University Press, 2018.

Russell, Peter. *Prince Henry the Navigator*. New Haven, CT: Yale University Press, 2000.

Russell-Wood, Anthony John R. *Slavery and Freedom in Colonial Brazil*. Oxford: One World, 2002.

Saillant, Francine, and Ana Lucia Araujo. "*Zumbi*: Mort, mémoire et résistance." *Frontières* 19, no. 1 (2006): 37–42.

Salau, Mohammed Bashir. *Plantation Slavery in the Sokoto Caliphate: A Historical and Comparative Study*. Suffolk, UK: University of Rochester Press, 2018.

Salau, Mohammed Bashir. *The West African Slave Plantation: A Case Study*. Basingstoke, UK: Palgrave Macmillan, 2011.

Salles, Ricardo. *E o Vale era o escravo: Vassouras, século XIX; Senhores e escravos no coração do império*. Rio de Janeiro: Civilização Brasileira, 2008.

Salvador, José Gonçalves. *Os Magnatas do tráfico negreiro (séculos XVI e XVII)*. São Paulo: Editora da Universidade de São Paulo, 1981.

Sampaio, Maria Clara Sales Carneiro. "Negros sonhos: Os projetos de colonização de afro-americanos no Brasil e na América Central durante a Guerra de Secessão." In Machado and Castilho, *Tornando-se Livre*, 399–421.

Santana, Aderivaldo Ramos de. "A extraordinário odisseia do comerciante ijebu que foi escravo no Brasil e homem livre na França (1820–1842)." *Afro-Ásia* 57 (2018): 9–53.

Santos, Ynaê Lopes dos. "Irmãs do Atlântico: Escravidão e espaço urbano no Rio de Janeiro e Havana (1763–1844)." PhD diss., Universidade de São Paulo, 2012.

Santos, Ynaê Lopes dos. *Racismo Brasileiro: Uma história da formação do país*. São Paulo: Todavia, 2022.

Sarracino, Rodolfo. *Los que volvieron a África*. Havana: Editorial de Ciencias Sociales, 1988.

Saunders, Alastair Corston de Custance Maxwell. *A Social History of Black Slaves and Freedmen in Portugal*. London: Cambridge University Press, 1982.

Schama, Simon. *Rough Crossings: The Slaves, the British and the American Revolution*. New York: HarperCollins, 2007.

Schenk, Marcia C., and Mariana P. Candido. "Uncomfortable Pasts: Talking about Slavery in Angola." In Araujo, *African Heritage and Memories of Slavery in Brazil and the South Atlantic World*, 213–52.

Schermerhorn, Calvin. *Unrequited Toil: A History of United States Slavery*. New York: Cambridge University Press, 2018.

Schmidt-Nowara, Christopher. *Empire and Antislavery: Spain, Cuba, and Puerto Rico, 1833–1874*. Pittsburgh, PA: Pittsburgh University Press, 1999.

Schmieder, Ulrike. "Martinique and Cuba Grande: Commonalities and Differences during the Periods of Slavery, Abolition, and Post-Emancipation." *Review (Fernand Braudel Center)* 36, no. 1 (2013): 83–112.

Schmieder, Ulrike. "Sexual Relations between Enslaved and between Slaves and Nonslaves in Nineteenth-Century Cuba." In Campbell and Elbourne, *Sex, Power, and Slavery*, 227–52.

Schwalm, Leslie. *A Hard Fight for We: Women's Transition from Slavery to Freedom in South Carolina*. Urbana: University of Illinois Press, 1997.

Schwartz, Stuart B. "Cantos and Quilombos: A Hausa Rebellion in Bahia, 1814." In *Slaves, Subjects, and Subversives: Blacks in Colonial Latin America*, edited by Jane Landers and Barry Robinson, 247–72. Albuquerque: University of New Mexico Press, 2006.

Schwartz, Stuart B. Introduction to Schwartz, *Tropical Babylons*.

Schwartz, Stuart B. "Resistance and Accommodation in Eighteenth-Century Brazil: The Slaves' View of Slavery." *Hispanic American Historical Review* 57, no. 1 (1977): 69–81.

Schwartz, Stuart B. *Slaves, Peasants, and Rebels: Reconsidering Brazilian Slavery*. Urbana: University of Illinois Press, 1996.

Schwartz, Stuart B. *Sugar Plantations in the Formation of Brazilian Society: Bahia, 1550–1835*. New York: Cambridge University Press, 1985.

Schwartz, Stuart B., ed. *Tropical Babylons: Sugar and the Making of the Atlantic World, 1450–1680*. Chapel Hill: University of North Carolina Press, 2004.

Scott, Dario. "A população do Rio Grande de São Pedro pelos mapas populacionais de 1780 a 1810." *Revista brasileira de estudos populacionais* 34, no. 3 (2017): 617–33.

Scott, Julius. *The Common Wind: Afro-American Currents in the Age of the Haitian Revolution*. London: Verso, 2018.

Scott, Rebecca J. *Degrees of Freedom: Louisiana and Cuba after Slavery*. Cambridge, MA: Belknap Press of Harvard University Press, 2005.

Scott, Rebecca J. *Slave Emancipation in Cuba: The Transition to Free Labor, 1860–1899*. Pittsburgh: University of Pittsburgh Press, 2000.

Seeley, Samantha. *Race, Removal, and the Right to Remain: Migration and the Making of the United States*. Chapel Hill: University of North Carolina Press, 2021.

Seeman, Erik R. *Across the Waters: Cross-Cultural Encounters, 1492–1800*. Philadelphia: University of Pennsylvania Press, 2010.

Seijas, Tatiana. *Asian Slaves in Colonial Mexico: From Chinos to Indians*. New York: Cambridge University Press, 2014.

Semley, Lorelle. "Beyond the Dark Side of the Port of the Moon: Rethinking the Role of Bordeaux's Slave Trade Past." *Histoire Sociale / Social History* 53, no. 107 (2020): 43–68.

Sernett, Milton C. *Harriet Tubman: Myth, Memory, and History*. Durham, NC: Duke University Press, 2007.

Sheridan, Richard B. *Doctors and Slaves: A Medical and Demographic History of Slavery in the British West Indies, 1680–1834*. New York: Cambridge University Press, 1985.

Sheridan, Richard B. *Sugar and Slavery: An Economic History of the British West Indies, 1623–1775*. Kingston, Jamaica: Canoe Press, 1994.

Shepherd, Verene, Bridget Brereton, and Barbara Bailey. *Engendering History: Caribbean Women in Historical Perspective*. New York: Palgrave Macmillan, 1995.

Sherwood, Marika. *After Abolition: Britain and the Slave Trade Since 1897*. London: I. B. Tauris, 2007.

Shumway, Rebecca. *The Fante and the Transatlantic Slave Trade*. Rochester, NY: Rochester University Press, 2014.

Silva, Carlos da, Jr. "Ardras, minas e jejes, ou escravos de 'primeira reputação': Políticas africanas, tráfico negreiro e identidade étnica na Bahia do século XVIII." *Almanack*, no. 12 (2016): 6–33.

Silva, Daniel Domingues da. *The Atlantic Slave Trade from West Central Africa 1780–1867*. New York: Cambridge University Press, 2017.

Silva, Filipa Ribeiro da. *Dutch and the Portuguese in Western Africa: Empires, Merchants and the Atlantic System 1580–1674*. Leiden, Neth.: Brill, 2011.

Silva, Júlio César Medeiros da. *À flor da terra: O cemitério dos pretos novos no Rio de Janeiro*. Rio de Janeiro: Garamond, 2007.

Silva, Pablo Miguel Sierra. *Urban Slavery in Colonial Mexico: Puebla de los Ángeles, 1531–1706*. New York: Cambridge University Press, 2019.

Silva, Rita de Cássia Santos. "A vida desinquieta de Páscoa Vieira: Uma escrava nas malhas do Santo Ofício." MA thesis, Universidade do Estado da Bahia, 2018.

Silva, Valéria Piccoli Gabriel da. "Figurinhas de brancos e negros: Carlos Julião e o mundo colonial português." PhD diss., Universidade de São Paulo, 2010.

Simonsen, Gunvor. *Slave Stories: Law, Representation, and Gender in the Danish West Indies*. Aarhus, Denmark: Aarhus University Press, 2017.

Simonsen, Roberto. *História econômica do Brasil, 1500–1820*. Brasília: Senado Federal, 2005.

Sinha, Manisha. *The Slave's Cause: A History of Abolition*. New Haven, CT: Yale University Press, 2016.

Sinou, Alain. "La valorisation du patrimoine architectural et urbain: L'exemple de la ville de Ouidah au Bénin." *Cahiers des Sciences Humaines* 29, no. 1 (1993): 33–51.

Slenes, Robert W. "'Malungu, ngoma vem!': África coberta e descoberta do Brasil." *Revista USP* 12 (1992): 48–67.

Slenes, Robert W. *Na Senzala, uma flor: Esperanças e recordações na formação da família escrava.* Campinas, Brazil: Editora da Universidade Estadual de Campinas, 1999.

Smalligan, Laura M. "An Effigy for the Enslaved: Jonkonnu in Jamaica and Belisario's Sketches of Character." *Slavery and Abolition* 32, no. 4 (2011): 561–81.

Smallwood, Stephanie. *Saltwater Slavery: A Middle Passage from Africa to American Diaspora.* Cambridge, MA: Harvard University Press, 2007.

Smeulders, Valika, and Lisa Lambrechts. "Paulus: A 'Moor' in the Dutch Republic." In *Slavery: The Story of João, Wally, Oopjen, Paulus, Van Bengalen, Surapati, Sapali, Tula, Drik, Lohkay*, edited by Eveline Sint Nicolaas and Valika Smeulders, 122–44. Amsterdam: Rijksmuseum, Atlas Contact, 2021.

Smithers, Gregory D. *Slave Breeding: Sex, Violence, and Memory in African American History.* Gainesville: University Press of Florida, 2012.

Snyder, Christina. "Native American Slavery in Global Context." In *What Is a Slave Society?* 169–90.

Snyder, Terri L. *The Power to Die: Slavery and Suicide in British North America.* Chicago: University of Chicago Press, 2015.

Soares, Carlos Eugênio Líbano. *A capoeira escrava e outras tradições rebeldes no Rio de Janeiro, 1808–1850.* Campinas, Brazil: Editora da Universidade do Estado de São Paulo, 2004.

Soares, Carlos Eugênio Líbano. *A negregada instituição: Os capoeiras na corte imperial (1850–1890).* Rio de Janeiro: Access, 1999.

Soares, Cecília Moreira. "As ganhadeiras: Mulher e resistência negra em Salvador no século XIX." *Afro-Ásia*, no. 17 (1996): 57–71.

Soares, Luiz Carlos. *O 'povo de Cam' na capital do Brasil: A escravidão urbana no Rio de Janeiro do século XIX.* Rio de Janeiro: 7Letras, 2007.

Soares, Mariza de Carvalho. "Art and the History of African Slave Folias in Brazil." In *Crossing Memories: Slavery and African Diaspora*, edited by Ana Lucia Araujo, Mariana P. Candido, and Paul E. Lovejoy, 209–35. Trenton, NJ: Africa World Press, 2011.

Soares, Mariza de Carvalho, ed. *Diálogos Makii de Francisco Alves de Souza: Manuscrito de uma congregação de africanos Mina, 1786*. Rio de Janeiro: Chão Editora, 2019.

Soares, Mariza de Carvalho. "Nos atalhos da memória: Monumento a Zumbi." In *Cidade Vaidosa: Imagens Urbanas do Rio de Janeiro*, edited by Paulo Knauss, 117–35. Rio de Janeiro: 7Letras, 1999.

Soares, Mariza de Carvalho. *People of Faith: Slavery and African Catholics in Eighteenth-Century Rio de Janeiro*. Durham, NC: Duke University Press, 2011.

Socolow, Susan Migden. "Permission to Marry: Eighteenth-Century Matrimonial Files (Montevideo, 1786)." In *Colonial Lives: Documents on Latin American History, 1550–1850*, edited by Richard Boyer and Geoffrey Spurling, 236–48. New York: Oxford University Press, 2000.

Sommerdyk, Stacey Jean Muriel. "Trade and Merchant Community of the Loango Coast in the Eighteenth Century." PhD diss., University of Hull, 2012.

Soriano, Cristina. *Tides of Revolution: Information, Insurgencies, and the Crisis of Colonial Rule in Venezuela*. Albuquerque: University of New Mexico Press, 2018.

Soulodre-La France, Renée. "'Por El Amor!' Child Killing in Colonial Nueva Granada." *Slavery and Abolition* 23, no. 1 (2002): 87–100.

Souza, Cândido Eugênio Domingues de. "'Perseguidores da espécie humana': Capitães negreiros da Cidade da Bahia a primeira metade do século XVIII." MA thesis, Universidade Federal da Bahia, 2011.

Souza, Daniele Santos de. "De escravo a cabeceira: A Trajetória do africano João de Oliveira no mundo atlântico setecentista." *Revista da ABPN (Associação Brasileira de Pesquisadores Negros)* 12 (2020): 113–39.

Souza, Marina de Mello e. *Reis negros no Brasil escravista: História da festa de coroação de Rei Congo*. Belo Horizonte, Brazil: Editora da Universidade Federal de Minas Gerais, 2014.

Souza, Marinaldo Fernando de. "Além da escola: Reflexões teórico-metodológicas com base na análise de práticas educativas alternativas descobertas em áreas rurais da região de São Carlos, S.P." PhD diss., Universidade Estadual Paulista, 2016.

Souza, Mônica Dias de. "Escrava Anastácia e pretos-velhos: A rebelião silenciosa da memória popular." In *Memória afro-brasileira: Imaginário, cotidiano e poder*, edited by Vagner Gonçalves da Silva, 15–42. São Paulo: Selo Negro, 2007.

Sparks, Randy J. *The Two Princes of Calabar: An Eighteenth-Century Atlantic Odyssey*. Cambridge, MA: Harvard University Press, 2004.

Sparks, Randy J. *"Where the Negroes Are Masters": An African Port in the Era of the Slave Trade*. Cambridge, MA: Harvard University Press, 2014.

Spiers, Sam. "The Eguafo Polity: Between the Traders and Raiders." In *Power and Landscape in Atlantic West Africa: Archaeological Perspectives*, edited by J. Cameron Monroe and Akinwumi Ogundiran, 115–41. New York: Cambridge University Press, 2012.

Stannard, David E. *American Holocaust: The Conquest of the New World*. New York: Oxford University Press, 1992.

Stanton, Lucia C. *"Those Who Labor for My Happiness": Slavery at Thomas Jefferson's Monticello*. Charlottesville: University of Virginia Press, 2012.

Stauffer, John, and Henry Louis Gates Jr. *Portable Frederick Douglass*. New York: Penguin, 2016.

Stavig, Ward. "Continuing the Bleeding of These Pueblos Will Shortly Make Them Cadavers: The Potosi Mita, Cultural Identity, and Communal Survival in Colonial Peru." *Americas* 56, no. 4 (2000): 529–62.

Stein, Robert. *The French Slave Trade in the Eighteenth Century: An Old Regime Business*. Madison: University of Wisconsin Press, 1979.

Sterling, Dorothy, ed. *Speak Out in Thunder Tones: Letters and Other Writings by Black Northerners, 1787–1865*. New York: Da Capo Press, 1998.

Stevenson, Brenda E. *Life in Black and White: Family and Community in the Slave South*. New York: Oxford University Press, 1996.

Strickrodt, Silke. *Afro-European Trade in the Atlantic World: The Western Slave Coast, c. 1550–1885*. Woodbridge, UK: James Currey, 2015.

Stuckey, Sterling. *Slave Culture in America: The Foundations of Black America and Nationalist Theory*. New York: Oxford University Press, 1987.

Sudarkasa, Niara. *Where Women Work: A Study of Yoruba Women in the Marketplace and in the Home*. Ann Arbor: University of Michigan Press, 1973.

Sue, Christina A. *Land of the Cosmic Race: Race Mixture, Racism, and Blackness in Mexico*. New York: Oxford University Press, 2013.

Swaminathan, Srivdhya. "Reporting Atrocities: A Comparison of the *Zong* and the Trial of Captain John Kimber." *Slavery and Abolition* 31, no. 4 (2010): 487–88.

Swarns, Rachel L. *The 272: The Families Who Were Enslaved and Sold to Build the American Catholic Church*. New York: Random House, 2023.

Sweeney, Shauna. "Market Marronage: Fugitive Women and the Internal Marketing System in Jamaica, 1781–1834." *William and Mary Quarterly* 76, no. 2 (2019): 197–222.

Sweet, James H. "Defying Social Death: The Multiple Configurations of African Slave Family in the Atlantic World." *William and Mary Quarterly* 70, no. 2 (2013): 251–72.

Sweet, James H. *Domingos Álvares: African Healing and the Intellectual History of the Atlantic World*. Chapel Hill: University of North Carolina Press, 2013.

Sweet, James H. "Manumission in Rio de Janeiro, 1749–54: An African Perspective." *Slavery and Abolition* 24, no. 1 (2003): 54–70.

Sweet, James H. "Mistaken Identities? Olaudah Equiano, Domingos Álvares, and the Methodological Challenges of Studying the African Diaspora." *American Historical Review* 114, no. 2: (2009): 279–306.

Sweet, James H. *Recreating Africa: Culture, Kinship, and Religion in the African-Portuguese World, 1441–1770*. Chapel Hill: University of North Carolina Press, 2003.

Takagi, Midori. *Rearing Wolves to Our Own Destruction: Slavery in Richmond, Virginia, 1782–1865*. Charlottesville: University Press of Virginia, 1999.

Tannenbaum, Frank. *Slave and Citizen*. Boston: Beacon Press, 1992.

Tardieu, Jean-Pierre. *El negro em la Real Audiencia de Quito, Siglos XVI–XVIII*. Lima, Peru: Institut français d'études andines, 2015.

Tardieu, Jean-Pierre. "Los esclavos de los jesuitas del Perú en la época de la expulsion (1767)." *Caravelle: Cahiers du monde hispanique et luso-brésilien* (2003): 61–109.

Taylor, Amy Murrell. *Embattled Freedom: Journeys through the Civil War's Slave Refugee Camps*. Chapel Hill: University of North Carolina Press, 2018.

Taylor, Nikki M. *Brooding over Bloody Revenge: Enslaved Women's Lethal Resistance*. New York: Cambridge University Press, 2023.

Taylor, Nikki M. *Driven toward Madness: The Fugitive Slave Margaret Garner and Tragedy on the Ohio*. Athens: Ohio University Press, 2016.

Taylor, Ula Yvette. *The Veiled Garvey: The Life and Times of Amy Jacques Garvey*. Chapel Hill: University of North Carolina Press, 2002.

Telles, Edward E. *Race in Another America: The Significance of Skin Color in Brazil*. Princeton, NJ: Princeton University Press, 2014.

Thomas, Hugh. *The Slave Trade: The History of the Atlantic Slave Trade 1440–1880*. New York: Simon and Schuster, 1997.

Thompson, Charles Manfred. *History of the United States: Political, Industrial, Social*. Chicago: Benj. H. Sanborn, 1917.

Thompson, Thomas. *An Account of Two Missionary Voyages*. London: Society for Promoting Christian Knowledge, 1937.

Thornton, John K. *Africa and Africans in the Making of the Atlantic World, 1400–1800*. New York: Cambridge University Press, 2005.

Thornton, John K. "African Dimensions of the Stono Rebellion." *American Historical Review* 96, no. 4 (1991): 1101–13.

Thornton, John K. "African Political Ethics and the Slave Trade." In *Abolitionism and Imperialism in Britain, Africa, and the Atlantic*, edited by Derek R. Peterson, 38–62. Athens: Ohio University Press, 2010.

Thornton, John K. "Afro-Christian Syncretism in the Kingdom of Kongo." *Journal of African History* 54, no. 1 (2013): 53–77.

Thornton, John K. *A Cultural History of the Atlantic World, 1250–1820*. New York: Cambridge University Press, 2012.

Thornton, John K. *A History of West Central Africa to 1850*. New York: Cambridge University Press, 2020.

Thornton, John K. "The Kingdom of Kongo and Palo Mayombe: Reflections on an African-American Religion." *Slavery and Abolition* 37, no. 1 (2016): 1–22.

Thornton, John K. "Les États de l'Angola et la formation de Palmares (Brésil)." *Annales: Histoire, Sciences Sociales* 63, no. 4 (2008): 769–97.

Thornton, John K. "The Portuguese in Africa." In *Portuguese Oceanic Expansion, 1400–1800*, edited by Francisco Bethencourt and Diogo Ramada Curto, 138–60. New York: Cambridge University Press, 2007.

Thornton, John K. *Warfare in Atlantic Africa, 1500–1800*. London: University College London Press, 1999.

Thornton, Russell. *American Indian Holocaust and Survival: A Population History since 1492*. Norman: University of Oklahoma Press, 1987.

Tolbert, Emory. "Outpost Garveyism and the UNIA Rank and File." *Journal of Black Studies* 5, no. 3 (1975): 233–53.

Tomich, Dale W. *Through the Prism of Slavery: Labor, Capital and World Economy*. Lanham, MD: Rowman & Littlefield, 2004.

Tomich, Dale W., and Paul Lovejoy, eds. *The Atlantic and Africa: The Second Slavery and Beyond*. Albany: State University of New York Press, 2021.

Tomich, Dale W., Rafael de Bivar Marquese, Reinaldo Funes Monzote, and Carlos Venegas Fornias. *Reconstructing the Landscapes of Slavery: A Visual History of the Plantation in the Nineteenth-Century Atlantic World*. Chapel Hill: University of North Carolina Press, 2021.

Tomich, Dale W., and Michael Zeuske. "Introduction, the Second Slavery: Mass Slavery, World-Economy, and Comparative Microhistories." *Review (Fernand Braudel Center)* 31, no. 2 (2008): 91–100.

Traoré, Ousmane. "State Control and Regulation of Commerce on the Waterways and Coast of Senegambia, ca. 1500–1800." In *Navigating*

African Maritime History, edited by Carina E. Ray and Jeremy Rich, 57–80. Liverpool: Liverpool University Press, 2009.

Trimble, Jennifer. "The Zoninus Collar and the Archaeology of Roman Slavery." *American Journal of Archaeology* 120, no. 3 (2016): 447–72.

Turner, Henry McNeal. "Justice or Emigration Should Be Our Watchword." In *African American Political Thought*, vol. 5, *Integration vs. Separatism: The Colonial Period to 1945*, edited by Marcus D. Pohlmann, 91–100. New York: Routledge, 2003.

Turner, Jerry Michael. "Les Brésiliens: The Impact of Former Slaves upon Dahomey." PhD diss., Boston University, 1975.

Turner, Sasha. *Contested Bodies: Pregnancy, Childrearing, and Slavery in Jamaica*. Philadelphia: University of Pennsylvania Press, 2017.

Turner, Sasha. "The Nameless and the Forgotten: Maternal Grief, Sacred Protection, and the Archive of Slavery." *Slavery and Abolition* 30, no. 2 (2017): 232–50.

Twinam, Ann. *Purchasing Whiteness: Pardos, Mulattos, and the Quest for Social Mobility in the Spanish Indies*. Stanford, CA: Stanford University Press, 2015.

Usman, Aribidesi, and Toyin Falola. *The Yoruba from Prehistory to the Present*. New York: Cambridge University Press, 2019.

Vainfas, Ronaldo. "Sodomy, Love, and Slavery in Colonial Brazil: A Case Study of Minas Gerais during the Eighteenth Century." In Campbell and Elbourne, *Sex, Power, and Slavery*, 526–40.

Vainfas, Ronaldo. *Trópico dos pecados: Moral, Sexualidade e inquisição no Brasil*. Rio de Janeiro: Civilização Brasileira, 2010.

Valerio, Miguel A. "Architects of Their Own Humanity: Race, Devotion, and Artistic Agency in Afro-Brazilian Confraternal Churches in Eighteenth-Century Salvador and Ouro Preto." *Colonial Latin American Review* 30, no. 2 (2021): 238–71.

Valerio, Miguel A. "'That There Be No Black Brotherhood': The Failed Suppression of Afro-Mexican Confraternities, 1568–1612." *Slavery and Abolition* 42, no. 2 (2021): 293–314.

Vansina, Jean. *Paths in the Rainforest: Toward a History of Political Tradition in Equatorial Africa*. Madison: University of Wisconsin Press, 1990.

Verger, Pierre. *Flux et reflux de la traite des nègres entre le Golfe de Bénin et Bahia de Todos os Santos, du XVIIe au XIXe siècle*. Paris: Mouton, 1968.

Verger, Pierre. *Fluxo et refluxo do tráfico de escravos entre o Golfo do Benin e a Bahia de Todos os Santos, dos séculos XVII a XIX*. Salvador, Brazil: Corrupio, 1987.

Verger, Pierre. "Le culte des vodoun d'Abomey aurait-il été apporté à Saint Louis de Maranhão par la mère du roi Ghèzo?" *Études Dahoméennes* 8 (1952): 19–24.

Verger, Pierre. *Os libertos: Sete caminhos da liberdade*. Salvador, Brazil: Corrupio: 1992.

Vidal, Cécile. *Caribbean New Orleans: Empire, Race, and the Making of a Slave Society*. Chapel Hill: University of North Carolina Press, 2019.

Voigt, Lisa. *Spectacular Wealth: The Festivals of Colonial South American Mining Towns*. Austin: University of Texas Press, 2016.

Wade, Richard C. *Slavery in the Cities: The South 1820–1860*. New York: Oxford University Press, 1967.

Walker, Christina. *Jamaica Ladies: Female Slaveholders and the Creation of Britain's Atlantic Empire*. Chapel Hill: University of North Carolina Press, 2020.

Walker, Tamara J. *Exquisite Slaves: Race, Clothing, and Status in Colonial Lima*. New York: Cambridge University Press, 2017.

Walker, Tamara J. "'He Outfitted His Family in Notable Decency': Slavery, Honour and Dress in Eighteenth-Century Lima, Peru." *Slavery & Abolition* 30, no. 3 (2009): 383–402.

Walvin, James. *The Zong: A Massacre, the Law & the End of Slavery*. New Haven, CT: Yale University Press, 2011.

Warren, Wendy. *New England Bound: Slavery and Colonization in Early America*. New York: Liveright, 2016.

Watters, David R. "Mortuary Patterns at the Harney Site Slave Cemetery, Montserrat, in Caribbean Perspective." *Historical Archaeology* 28, no. 3 (1994): 56–73.

Wax, Darold D. "Preferences for Slaves in Colonial America." *Journal of Negro History* 58, no. 4 (1973): 371–401.

Wells, Jonathan Daniel. *The Kidnapping Club: Wall Street, Slavery, and Resistance on the Eve of the Civil War*. New York: Bold Type, 2020.

West, Emily, and R. J. Knight. "Mother's Milk: Slavery, Wet-Nursing, and Black and White Women in the Antebellum South." *Journal of Southern History* 133, no. 1 (2017): 37–68.

Wheat, David. *Atlantic Africa and the Spanish Caribbean 1570–1640*. Chapel Hill: University of North Carolina Press, 2016.

White, Deborah G. *Ar'n't I a Woman? Female Slaves in the Plantation South*. New York: W.W. Norton, 1985.

White, Sophie. *Voices of the Enslaved: Love, Labor, and Longing in French Louisiana*. Chapel Hill: University of North Carolina Press, 2019.

Whitehead, Colston. *The Underground Railroad: A Novel*. New York: Knopf Doubleday, 2016.

Wiedemann, Thomas. *Greek and Roman Slavery*. New York: Routledge, 1994.

Wilentz, Sean. "A Matter of Facts." *Atlantic*, January 22, 2020.

Williams, Eric. *Capitalism and Slavery*. Chapel Hill: University of North Carolina Press, 1944.

Willis, Deborah, and Barbara Krauthamer. *Envisioning Emancipation: Black Americans and the End of Slavery*. Philadelphia: Temple University Press, 2017.

Wood, Betty. "The Origins of Slavery in the Americas, 1500–1700." In *The Routledge History of Slavery*, edited by Gad Heuman and Trevor Burnard, 64–79. London: Routledge, 2011.

Wood, Marcus. "The Museu do Negro in Rio and the Cult of Anastácia as a New Model for the Memory of Slavery." *Representations*, no. 113 (2011): 111–49.

Wood, Peter H. *Black Majority: Negroes in Colonial South Carolina from 1670 through the Stono Rebellion*. New York: Knopf, 1996.

Yacou, Alain. *Journal de bord et de traite de Joseph Crassous de Médeuil, de La Rochelle à la côte de Guinée et aux Antilles (1772–1776)*. Paris: Karthala, 2001.

Yang, Bin. *Cowrie Shells and Cowrie Money: A Global History*. New York: Routledge, 2018.

Zeleza, Paul Tiyambe. "Diaspora Dialogues: Engagements Between Africa and Its Diasporas." *African Studies Review* 53, no. 1 (2010): 1–19.

Zoellner, Tom. *Island on Fire: The Revolt That Ended Slavery in the British Empire*. Cambridge, MA: Harvard University Press, 2020.

Databases, Online Repositories, Digital Sources, and Films

The Avalon Project: Documents in Law, History, and Diplomacy. Yale Law School, Lillian Goldman Law Library. https://avalon.law.yale.edu.

Biblioteca Digital do Senado Federal, Brasília, Brazil. https://www2.senado.leg.br/bdsf/.

Center for Digital Scholarship. Brown University Library. *Voyage of the Slave Ship Sally, 1764–1765*. https://cds.library.brown.edu/projects/sally/.

Cornell University Law School. Legal Information Institute, US Constitution. https://www.law.cornell.edu/constitution/.

Demme, Jonathan, dir. *Beloved*. Buena Vista Pictures, 1998.

Digital Aponte. https://aponte.hosting.nyu.edu/.

Freedom on the Move: Rediscovering the Stories of Self-Liberating People; A Database of Fugitives from American Slavery. https://freedomonthemove.org/.

Herzog, Werner. *Cobra Verde*. Werner Herzog Filmproduktion, , 1987. Beverly Hills, CA: Anchor Bay Entertainment, 2002. DVD.

The Intra-American Slave Trade Database. Compiled by Slave Voyages Consortium, a collaboration of ten universities and organizations. http://www.slavevoyages.org.

Jenkins, Barry, dir. *The Underground Railroad.* Amazon Studios, 2021.
Lemmons, Kasi. *Harriet.* Martin Chase Productions, 2019.
National Archives. *Founders Online.* https://founders.archives.gov/.
Nova Scotia Archives. https://archives.novascotia.ca/.
Prince-Bythewood, Gina, dir. *The Woman King.* TriStar Pictures, 2022.
Slavery Images: A Visual Record of the African Slave Trade and Slave Life in the Early African Diaspora. http://slaveryimages.org.
The Trans-Atlantic Slave Trade Database. Compiled by Slave Voyages Consortium, a collaboration of ten universities and organizations. http://www.slavevoyages.org.
Université de Sherbrooke. *Le Marronage dans le monde atlantique: Sources et trajectoires de vie.* http://www.marronnage.info/fr/index.html.

Index

Page numbers in italics refer to figures.